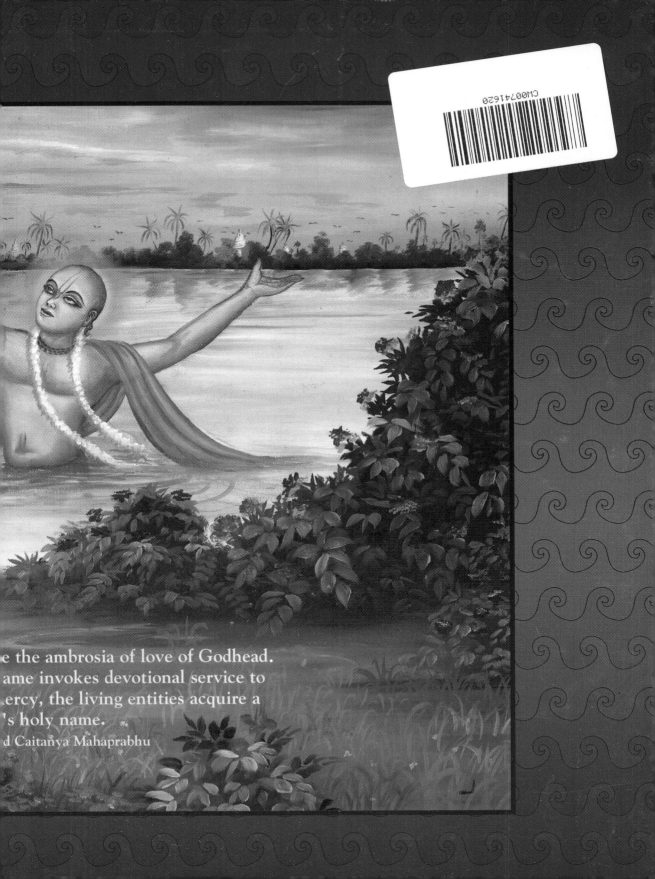

e the ambrosia of love of Godhead.
ame invokes devotional service to
ercy, the living entities acquire a
's holy name.

d Caitañya Mahāprabhu

Our Merciful
Mother Gaṅgā

Jaya Vijaya Dāsa

PadayātrāPress

Readers interested in the subject matter of this book
are invited to correspond with the author:
Jaya Vijaya Dāsa
Padayātrā Press
B-40, Sector 56
Noida 201 301
U.P., India
E-mail: jayavijaya@hotmail.com

First Edition of 2,000 copies

ISBN 81-901132-0-8

Front cover painting of Śrī Gaṅgā-devī by
Yogendra Rastogi
Back cover top photo of the Gaṅgā near Gomukha by
Ashok Dilwali
Back cover middle photo of the sunset over the Gaṅgā
at Māyāpur and bottom photo of the Gaṅgā below Mukhwa by
Jaya Vijaya Dāsa
Inside front cover painting of Śrī Caitanya Mahāprabhu
bathing in the Gaṅgā in Navadvīpa and inside back cover
painting of Śrī Gaura-ārati at Śrīdhāma Māyāpur by Praśanta Dāsa
Design & Layout by Kūrma Rūpa Dāsa

DEDICATION

To my Mother,
who first instructed me with the words
"Traveling is your best education";

To my Father,
who kind-heartedly blessed my travels around the world;

To my Spiritual Master,
His Holiness Śrīla Lokanātha Swami Mahārāja,
who taught me *bhakti-yoga* through the means of Padayātrā India;

And to the Founder-*Ācārya* of ISKCON,
His Divine Grace A.C. Bhaktivedanta Swami Prabhupāda,
who is the embodiment of pure loving devotional service
unto the Supreme Personality of Godhead, Lord Kṛṣṇa,
who is the personified form of all sacred places,
and who is purifying everyone throughout the world.

YOGENDRA
RASTOGI

CONTENTS

CHAPTER THREE

Chapter Six

Chapter Seven

Chapter Eight

Oṁ namo Gaṅgā-devyai

OUR MERCIFUL MOTHER GAṄGĀ

MAṄGALĀCARANA
(Invocation)

oṁ ajñāna-timirāndhasya jñānāñjana-śalākayā
cakṣur unmīlitaṁ yena tasmai śrī-gurave namaḥ

I was born in darkest ignorance, and my spiritual master opened by eyes with the torch of knowledge. I offer my respectful obeisances unto him.

nama oṁ viṣṇu-pādāya kṛṣṇa-preṣṭhāya bhū-tale
śrīmate bhaktivedānta-svāmin iti nāmine
namas te sārasvate deve gaura-vāṇī-pracāriṇe
nirviśeṣa-śūnyavādi-pāścātya-deśa-tāriṇe

I offer my respectful obeisances unto His Divine Grace A.C. Bhaktivedanta Swami Prabhupāda, who is very dear to Lord Kṛṣṇa, having taken shelter at His lotus feet. Our respectable obeisances are unto you, O spiritual master, servant of Sarasvatī Gosvāmī. You are kindly preaching the message of Lord Caitanya Mahāprabhu and delivering the Western countries, which are filled with impersonalism and voidism.

vāñchā-kalpatarubhyaś ca kṛpā-sindhubhya eva ca
patitānāṁ pāvanebhyo vaiṣṇavebhyo namo namaḥ

I offer my respectful obeisances unto all the Vaiṣṇavas. They are just like desire trees who can fulfill the desires of everyone, and they are full of compassion for the fallen souls.

sadyaḥ pātaka-saṁhantrī sadhyo duḥkha-vināśinī
sukhadā mokṣadā gaṅgā gaṅgaiva paramā gatiḥ

O Gaṅgā, you immediately destroy all sins and miseries. You bestow ultimate happiness and the supreme liberation, for you are the ultimate shelter.

gaṅge ca yamune caiva godāvari sarasvatī
narmade sindho kāveri jale 'smin sannidhiṁ kuru

May water from the holy Rivers Gaṅgā, Yamunā, Godāvarī, Sarasvatī, Narmadā, Sindhu, and Kāverī kindly be present.

chalayasi vikramaṇe balim adbhuta-vāmana
pada-nakha-nīra-janita-jana-pāvana
keśava dhṛta-vāmana-rūpa jaya jagadīśa hare

All glories to Lord Keśava, who assumed the form of a dwarf. O Lord of the universe, who takes away everything inauspicious for the devotees. O wonderful Vāmanadeva! You tricked the great demon Bali Mahārāja by Your steps. The water that touched the nails of Your lotus feet when You pierced through the covering of the universe purifies all living entities in the form of the River Gaṅgā.

ketus tri-vikrama-yutas tri-patat-patāko
yas te bhayābhaya-karo 'sura-deva-camvoḥ
svargāya sādhuṣu khaleṣv itarāya bhūman
padaḥ punātu bhagavan bhajatām aghaṁ naḥ

O omnipotent Lord, in Your incarnation as Trivikrama, You raised Your leg like a flagpole to break the shell of the universe, allowing the holy Gaṅgā to flow down, like a banner of victory, in three branches throughout the three planetary systems. By three mighty steps of Your lotus feet, Your Lordship captured Bali Mahārāja, along with his universal kingdom. Your lotus feet inspire fear in the demons by driving them down to hell and fearlessness among Your devotees by elevating them to the perfection of heavenly life. We are sincerely trying to worship You, our Lord; therefore may Your lotus feet kindly free us from all of our sinful reactions.

namo mahā-vadānyāya kṛṣṇa-prema-pradāya te
kṛṣṇāya kṛṣṇa-caitanya-nāmne gaura-tviṣe namaḥ

I offer my respectful obeisances to Śrī Caitanya Mahāprabhu, who is Śrī Kṛṣṇa Himself. He has assumed the golden hue of Śrīmatī Rādhikā, and is munificently distributing *kṛṣṇa-prema*.

śrī-kṛṣṇa-caitanya prabhu nityānanda
śrī-advaita gadādhara śrīvāsādi-gaura-bhakta-vṛnda

All glories to Śrī Kṛṣṇa Caitanya and to His eternal expansions and associates, Śrī Nityānanda Prabhu, Śrī Advaita Ācārya, Śrī Gadādhara Paṇḍita and Śrī Śrīvāsa Ṭhākura. All glories to the devotees of Lord Caitanya Mahāprabhu.

Hare Kṛṣṇa Hare Kṛṣṇa Kṛṣṇa Kṛṣṇa Hare Hare
Hare Rāma Hare Rāma Rāma Rāma Hare Hare

FOREWORD

The holy river Gaṅgā is our most affectionate and merciful mother. If we appreciate this fact we can take advantage of her kind support. With her help we can easily be washed of materialistic contamination and return to our original natural happy life. Like any good mother, Gaṅgā offers herself unconditionally to her children. She is always accessible to anyone who comes to her shores for a purifying bath, or even remembers her glories from far away.

Unlike the common prison inmates of this material world, the Supreme Lord and His pure devotees are free to come and go from this world as they like. Since the Lord and His servants have no interest in selfish enjoyment, they almost always come down to our limited world for one purpose only—to deliver us from the cycle of birth and death. They need nothing from us, because they are eternally established in perfect knowledge and bliss, but we can benefit by their association in whatever form we can obtain it. God Himself descends from time to time in His incarnations to exhibit the same sports He plays in His spiritual kingdom, thus attracting fallen souls to join Him again. The Lord's pure devotees also come down from the spiritual world to assist in this mission. They sometimes act as sages, teaching us how to revive our love of God, and sometimes they assume the forms of rivers, mountains, and other holy places to give everyone—the wise and foolish, the reverent and faithless—easy opportunities for purification. Mother Gaṅgā is one such holy river; and of all the sacred rivers on this earth, she is doubtlessly the most generous. She flows thousands of kilometres from the top of the Himālayas to the Bay of Bengal, and at every point along her course she makes the nectar of her pure waters available to anyone who wants it. Certainly those who consider themselves followers of the ancient religion of the *Vedas* and *Purāṇas* are eager to approach mother Gaṅgā—to at least take bath once in her, and if possible to live nearby her or to find final rest for their ashes within her.

My dear friend Jaya Vijaya Prabhu has done a wonderful job of presenting in this book the story of mother Gaṅgā, including elaborate descriptions of her history and the reasons why she is so great. The author's involvement with the Gaṅgā is more than just theoretical. In the service of his spiritual master, His Holiness Lokanātha Swami, for years he helped lead the ISKCON Padayātrā party walk all over India on pilgrimage, traveling the course of the Gaṅgā from one end to the other several times. Having had the good fortune to join him for bath in mother Gaṅgā once (at Śuka-tāla, where *Śrīmad-Bhāgavatam* was spoken), I can vouch that his devotion to her is very real. Just as mother Gaṅgā has been giving herself selflessly for millions of years, so Jaya Vijaya Prabhu had dedicated the last three years to working hard on this book, not with expectation of much wealth or fame, but just with the desire to glorify our mother Gaṅgā. I am very glad, therefore, to commend this book to its readers; I wish them good luck on their pilgrimage, only asking that while taking their sacred bath of reading these pages, they offer mother Gaṅgā a palmful of her own water with a prayer for their guide Jaya Vijaya Prabhu, and maybe one for me also. In addition, it was a pleasure to contribute to this publication in the area of Sanskrit.

Gopīparāṇadhana Dāsa
Bhaktivedanta Book Trust (BBT)
Sanskrit Editor
Mānasa-gaṅgā, Govardhana

Prelude

I had the great fortune of being able to participate for eleven years (1985-1996) in Śrīla Prabhupāda's Indian Saṅkīrtana Padayātrā, organized by the International Society for Krishna Consciousness (ISKCON). For those who are not familiar with what that means, I will try to explain. In 1976 the Founder-*Ācārya* of ISKCON, His Divine Grace A.C. Bhaktivedanta Swami Prabhupāda, instructed one of his disciples, H.H. Lokanātha Swami, to organize a simple preaching program in the Indian villages using bullock carts. They were to go from village to village and engage the villagers in chanting the Hare Kṛṣṇa *mahā-mantra*: Hare Kṛṣṇa Hare Kṛṣṇa Kṛṣṇa Kṛṣṇa Hare Hare/Hare Rāma Hare Rāma Rāma Rāma Hare Hare, as well as distribute *prasāda* (spiritual food) and Śrīla Prabhupāda's transcendental literatures. This successful program lasted several months, until H.H. Lokanātha Swami was assigned another service.

Later on, in 1984, ISKCON decided to organize a Padayātrā (walking pilgrimage) that was to be accompanied by *saṅkīrtana* (the congregational chanting of the Hare Kṛṣṇa *mahā-mantra*) in honor of the 500th birth anniversary of Śrī Caitanya Mahāprabhu (the devotional incarnation of Lord Śrī Kṛṣṇa for this present age). At that time the ISKCON leaders assigned H.H. Lokanātha Swami to head up the Padayātrā. In the years that followed, H.H. Lokanātha Swami inspired the inauguration of Padayātrā programs in more than one hundred other countries. Padayātrā India's center of attraction was a unique four metre high bullock cart, designed as a temple on wheels, wherein the most beautiful captivating forms of Lord Nityānanda and Lord Caitanya (known as Śrī Śrī Nitāi-Gaurasundara) and Śrīla Prabhupāda resided. To pull this most attractive bullock cart were two of India's most attractive bulls (Kankrej oxen from Gujarat), with their large bodies (nearly seven hundred kilos), sweet faces, great stamina, and towering horns. As a further attraction, an elephant named Lakṣmī walked in front of the chariot bullock cart. The starting point was Dvārakā, Gujarat; on the second day of September in 1984 (Rādhāṣṭamī, Śrīmatī Rādhārāṇī's appearance day), ISKCON's Padayātrā began their first tour on foot around India with more than two hundred devotees from various nations of the world.

Since then, Padayātrā has walked around India four times, covering some 90,000 kilometres and distributing thousands of Śrīla Prabhupāda's books in ten languages. The Padayātrā has successfully introduced or revived the chanting of the Hare Kṛṣṇa *mahā-mantra* in over 6,000 villages throughout twenty of India's twenty-eight states. It has visited all major *tīrthas* (holy places) in India, including four visits to the Indian Char-dhāma (Jagannātha Purī, Rāmeśvaram, Dvārakā, and Badarīnātha) and the Himālayan Char-dhāma (Yamunotrī, Gaṅgotrī, Kedāranātha, and Badarīnātha). Padayātrā has also visited the complete list of 108 Divya Deśams (108 Lord Viṣṇu temples or *tīrthas* of the Śrī-sampradāya) and participated in four major Kumbha-melās (Prayāga '89-'01, Naśika '92, and Ujjain '93). But perhaps the most important contribution of Padayātrā was initiating the ISKCON Vraja-maṇḍala Parikramā (a thirty day walk around the land of Vṛndāvana during the month of Kārtika) and the

Navadvīpa-maṇḍala Parikramā (a nine day walk around the nine islands surrounding Śrīdhāma Māyāpur during the Gaura Pūrṇimā festival). Still today, Padayātrā is going on stronger than ever.

In between all those kilometres, villages, and major *tīrthas* there are unlimited local holy places, temples, sacred rivers, and mountains. Practically speaking, every square millimetre of this country is sacred due to the unlimited pastimes of the Supreme Personality of Godhead Lord Kṛṣṇa, His incarnations, and His associates that have taken place and are still being enacted today. Even though we may see only modern India and its foolish competition with western technology, which simply pollutes the land and the people, still, underneath or beyond all this modern pollution is a rich spiritual heritage that revolves around Lord Kṛṣṇa. Regardless of our birth and upbringing, we have the right and duty to discover our actual spiritual roots—to understand that we are more than just our bodies and to understand that life is more than what we survey from the tip of our nose. We are all parts and parcels of the Supreme Personality of Godhead, and His pastimes are for our benefit—to uplift and inspire our mundane consciousness to spiritual consciousness, by which we will understand our real mission in this material world. And that mission is to realize our eternal constitutional position and act according to our spiritual natures, which ultimately means to love and serve the Supreme Lord.

All these years on Padayātrā, I and the other *padayātris* (walking members of Padayātrā) felt greatly blessed to visit and have *darśana* of the Lord in His numerous earthly abodes where He performs His wonderful pastimes. Each time we returned to a *tīrtha* or temple, the Lord allowed us to enter deeper and deeper into His unlimited pastimes, helping us understand and realize just a bit more of His infinite and omniscient nature. A similar comparison is when one reads the *Bhagavad-gītā* again and again. Each time the reader will have deeper realizations of Lord Kṛṣṇa's instructions to Arjuna and how to apply these teachings in life.

Whenever we would enter a *tīrtha* or temple with a sincere reverential mood, we could understand that these sacred places are not of this material world, but something inconceivable. One should try to understand such places by learning about the pastimes related with them, or at least try to hear and appreciate the pastime with whatever fund of knowledge one possesses. The Lord and His various incarnations, along with Their entourage, decide to appear out Their own sweet will, which is ultimately for our benefit. We should take advantage of Their blessings and become fortunate rather than continue a misfortunate material life. As Śrīla Prabhupāda once said, "The beauty of a pilgrimage site is that automatically one remembers the holy glories of the Lord."

Various problems often arise when visiting the holy places in this Kali-yuga (the age of quarrel and hypocrisy); the *tīrthas* or temples may externally appear dirty and not maintained, the priests may simply demand money, real spiritual authority may be lacking, or the atmosphere may simply be devoid of *bhakti*, or devotional love. In reality, the *tīrthas* are eternally perfect, fully spiritual, and unlimited, but due to our intelligence being tinged with mundane matter, we tend to misunderstand them. Our *guru-paramparā* (disciplic succession of spiritual masters) warns us not to commit offenses while seeing the local residents of a *tīrtha* or temple, thinking they are not qualified or that they are just ordinary people. Also, without searching out the pure-hearted devotee of the Lord and inquiring from him about the pastimes that have occurred there, the only result one obtains is the effort of traveling there, nothing else. Śrīla Prabhupāda further states, "*tīrthī-kurvanti tīrthāni:* a *tīrtha* is a place where there are saintly persons. That is a *tīrtha*. Not that one goes ten thousand miles and simply takes a dip in the water and then comes back." The authorities also recommend that one serve the lotus feet of Lord Govinda (Kṛṣṇa) wherever one may reside, instead of taking the trouble of traveling to the *tīrthas*. In reality, the pure heart is the living holy place. To understand more about how to properly see a *tīrtha*, please see Book One, Chapter Six: THE CONCLUSION, *The Pure Devotees*.

Though the Padayātrā has visited so many holy places and temples, including numerous holy rivers and mountains, it would be incorrect to say that any one *tīrtha* or temple is better than the next, since they all inspired us in one way or another. All the pastimes of the Lord and His associates are most relishable and inspiring, especially for the devotees residing in the holy places where those pastimes took place. Every state in India has its own special flavor and mood, which ultimately reflect the spiritual pastimes that the Lord choose to manifest there. Since we Gauḍīya Vaiṣṇavas (devotees in the line of Śrī Caitanya Mahāprabhu) worship Lord Kṛṣṇa and Lord Caitanya, we are naturally more closely connected and attracted to the holy abodes of Vṛndāvana, Navadvīpa-Māyāpur, Jagannātha Purī, and Dvārakā. Since Śrī Vṛndāvana-dhāma is the original abode of the Supreme Personality of Godhead, Lord Kṛṣṇa, it is considered *svayam-dhāma*, as every single holy abode or *dhāma* originates from Vṛndāvana and resides within Vṛndāvana. And since Śrī Navadvīpa-dhāma (the birthplace of Śrī Caitanya Mahāprabhu) is a direct manifestation of Śrī Vṛndāvana-dhāma, they are both nondifferent, so there is no need to go elsewhere for spiritial advancement. In fact, it stated in the *Śrī Navadvīpa Māhātmya* that if one who resides in Navadvīpa leaves to try for spiritual advancement elsewhere, that person will only go to hell. But if one travels to other holy places first and then resides in Śrī Vṛndāvana-dhāma or Śrī Navadvīpa-dhāma, that is perfection.

Personally, besides the sacred *tīrthas* or *dhāmas* of the Gauḍīya Vaiṣṇavas, my heart has always been absorbed in the heavenly Himālayas. Throughout the Vedic literatures and the religious thoughts of this ancient land, the Himālayas occupy a position of universal respect and adoration. As Lord Kṛṣṇa states in the *Bhagavad-gītā* (10.25): *sthāvarāṇāṁ himālayaḥ*—"Of immovable things I am the Himālayas." The word *himālayaḥ* means "the abode of snow"; these mountains are always covered in order to inspire reverence, and the peaks are considered objects of worship. During our treks in the Himālayas, we were able to preach amongst the inhabitants of the interior regions, have *darśana* of some hidden *tīrthas*, collect 108 sacred waters for Śrīla Prabhupāda's Centennial (1896-1996) Celebrations, associate with *sādhus* (the holy residents), as well as appreciate what mother nature has provided through the creative energy of the Lord. We were fortunate to have the opportunity to understand some of the secret meanings of these powerful mountains, not only once, but on several occasions. After each visit, I would feel very depressed when we would have to return 'down-below' to the maddening rush of modern India. Due to the strong impressions that the Himālayas left, I had a desire to first compile a book pertaining to the Himālayas, particularily regarding the Char Dhāmas.

Over the years on Padayātrā, Śrīla Prabhupāda's books guided us around the sacred places in India. In addition, I was able to find and collect various other books and pamphlets, known as *māhātmyams*, or glorifications of the holy places condensed from the *Purāṇas*. These other books supplemented Śrīla Prabhupāda's books, especially his *Śrīmad-Bhāgavatam* and *Śrī Caitanya-caritāmṛta*, which were the basis for our research and compilation of articles. But my main disadvantage is knowing only one language, especially when it is far from the original Sanskrit of the Vedic scriptures. This hindrance certainly hampered our attempts at making more thorough investigation of any *tīrtha* or pastime that had occurred. Somehow or another, whatever was available in the English language, particularly in Śrīla Prabhupāda's books, was enough to relish a few drops of the sweet nectarean narrations of the Lord's pastimes in His various abodes.

Most of the pastimes of the Himālayas are beautifully described in the various *Purāṇas*, which contain the essence of the important historical incidents occurring on all the planets within this universe. In the *Śrīmad-Bhāgavatam*, or *Bhāgavata Purāṇa*, which is the most important of all the major *Purāṇas* because it describes loving devotion unto the Supreme Personality of Godhead, Lord Śrī Kṛṣṇa, Śrīla Prabhupāda comments on these sacred scriptures as follows: "The *Purāṇas*, or old histories, are sometimes neglected by unintelligent men who consider their descriptions mythological. Actually, the descriptions of the *Purāṇas*, or the old histories of the universe, are factual, although not chronological. The *Purāṇas* record the chief incidents that have occurred over many millions of years, not only on this planet but also on other planets within the universe. Therefore all learned and realized Vedic scholars speak with reference to the incidents in the *Purāṇas*. Śrīla Rūpa Gosvāmī accepted the *Purāṇas* to be as important as the *Vedas* (original scriptures) themselves. Therefore, in *Bhakti-rasāmṛta-sindhu*, Rūpa Gosvāmī quotes the following verse from the *Brahma-yamala*: 'Devotional service of the Lord that ignores the authorized Vedic literatures like the *Upaniṣads*, *Purāṇas* and *Nārada-pañcarātra* is simply an unnecessary disturbance in society.' A devotee of Kṛṣṇa must refer not only to the *Vedas*, but also to the *Purāṇas*. One should not foolishly consider the *Purāṇas* mythological." The *Śrīmad-Bhāgavatam* (1.4.20) also states: "The four divisions of the original sources of knowledge (the *Vedas*) were made separately. But the historical facts and authentic stories mentioned in the *Purāṇas* are called the fifth *Veda*." And in his commentary on the *Śrī Caitanya-caritāmṛta* (*Ādi* 5.14) Śrīla Prabhupāda writes: "Indeed, in reality we can get knowledge only from the Vedic sources. The four *Vedas*, with their supplementary *Purāṇas*, the *Mahābhārata*, the *Rāmāyaṇa* and their corollaries, which are known as *smṛtis*, are all authorized sources of knowledge. If we are at all to gather knowledge, we must gather if from these sources without hesitation."

In March 1996, while Padayātrā was at our ISKCON world headquarters in Śrīdhāma Māyāpur, West Bengal, on the bank of the Bhāgīrathī Gaṅgā, I began researching various *Purāṇas* at our Bhaktivedanta Academy (Gurukula Library) to gather narrations and information on the Himālayas. But while reading the different *Purāṇas*, I repeatedly encountered narrations of the pastimes of mother Gaṅgā; numerous accounts, page after page, relating to our merciful, glorious mother kept my mind absorbed in only, "Gaṅgā! Gaṅgā! Gaṅgā! and more Gaṅgā!" However, I became somewhat confused; although mother Gaṅgā has her earthly beginning in the Himālayas, I found different information giving her origin from places other than the Himālayas.

Thereafter, I continued with additional research in New Delhi and subsequently purchased several volumes of various *Purāṇas* before heading off to Haridvāra at the foothills of the Himālayas for the winter season of 1996-97. By the mercy of the Lord, I was able to locate a small private room in one *āśrama* on the bank of the Gaṅgā in a very auspicious area known as Sapta-sarovara, or Sapta Gaṅgā. Here Gaṅgā forms seven streams due to a pastime associated with the Sapta-ṛṣis (seven great sages). As I continued my research, I had the realization that before pilgrims begin their Himālayan Char-dhāma-yātrā, their first activity is to take a purification bath in the Gaṅgā at Haridvāra. Similarly, before I could properly enter into the pastimes of the Himālayas through the medium of a book, I must first receive the purifying mercy of mother Gaṅgā through a book dedicated to her. Thus, the beginnings of *Our Merciful Mother Gaṅgā* began to manifest.

Now, after residing in the land of Lord Kṛṣṇa, Śrī Vṛndāvana-dhāma, since the winter season of 1997-98, my research continues. After I had conducted more research I discovered the original source of the River Gaṅgā: the divine couple of Goloka, Śrī Śrī Rādhā-Kṛṣṇa, melt Themselves and become Gaṅgā. Moreover, her personified form is that of a leading *mañjarī* (maidservant) assisting the divine couple in Their pastimes in Goloka. All these topics are further elaborated in Book One, Chapters Two and Three.

INTRODUCTION

gaṅgā rāṇī gaṅgā rāṇī gaṅgā rāṇī rakṣa mām
bhāgīrathī bhāgīrathī bhāgīrathī pāhi mām

O Celestial Queen Gaṅgā, please protect us.
O descendant of Mahārāja Bhagīratha, please maintain us.

Our Merciful Mother Gaṅgā is a Purāṇic-līlā-tīrtha guide, a guide to the historical pastimes that have occurred in holy places on or near the banks of Gaṅgā. The contents have been compiled from a variety of scriptures (mostly *Purāṇas*), as well as other references that are listed in the bibliography. Even though some of the literature may not be accepted by some conventional schools of Gauḍīya Vaiṣṇavism, my only desire and goal was to extract glorifications of Śrī Gaṅgā-devī that directly relate to her or to pastimes that have occurred on her banks that are favorable to devotional service, not to dwell on deep philosophical differences, arguments, or conclusions. Since Gaṅgā is dealt with in every *Purāṇa*, she is known as Purāṇa-paṭhitā. She is also described in the *Rāmāyaṇa* and *Mahābhārata* as well as in numerous Bengali classics describing Lord Caitanya's pastimes, all of which glorify her. Is it by mere chance that she is mentioned and glorified so thoroughly throughout Vedic literature?* There is also a branch of knowledge known as *Sthala Purāṇa*, which is the history of a particular holy place that has been passed down from generation to generation by the area's *paṇḍitas* (scholars). Such local stories about Gaṅgā are also numerous.

In addition to the unlimited pastimes that have occurred directly on Gaṅgā's shores, there are numerous other pastimes in which she has manifest in other areas of Bhārata-varṣa (India). For example, when the inhabitants of Vṛndāvana desired to go and bathe in Gaṅgā, Lord Kṛṣṇa explained that there was no need to travel outside Śrī Vraja-maṇḍala (the area surrounding Vṛndāvana) because all the *tīrthas* within the three planetary systems reside therein. He then brought them to Mānasa-gaṅgā at the middle of Govardhana where Gaṅgā-devī personally appeared before Lord Kṛṣṇa. (Please see Book One, Chapter Four, Number 12). Also in Dvārakā, where Lord Kṛṣṇa scratched the earth with His nail and Gaṅgā appeared so that Rukmiṇī could quench her thirst; at Brahmagiri (Tryambaka), where Gaṅgā manifested as the River Godāvarī for the pleasure of Gautama Ṛṣi; at Arbuda (Abu) mountain, where Lord Śiva desired to see Gaṅgā daily, so she appeared in his Śiva-

---

*A special note regarding the variety of narrations that have been compiled. Srila Prabhupāda has given us the cream of all *Purāṇas*, the *Śrīmad-Bhāgavatam*, which is compared to "the ripened fruit of the desire tree of Vedic literature." Srila Prabhupāda states in this regard: "*Śrīmad-Bhāgavatam* is the most complete and authoritative exposition of all Vedic knowledge. It is meant for the ultimate good of all people, and it is all-successful, all-blissful and all-perfect. *Śrīmad-Bhāgavatam* is also a *Purāṇa*, but the special significance of this *Purāṇa* is that the activities of the Lord are central and not just supplementary historical facts." Because of the eternal arrangement of the Lord's creation, when He, His incarnations, and His associates repeatedly appear and disappear in different *kalpas* (ages), some of the narrations may overlap one another and the details may change. This may cause some confusion while comparing one Purāṇic narration with another. As mentioned earlier, my only desire is to extract the glorification of mother Gaṅgā and not to cause any disagreements.

gaṅgā-kuṇḍa; on the Gandhamādana mountain at Rāmeśvaram, where the holy rivers Gaṅgā, Yamunā, and Phalgu appeared for the great sage Raikva, who desired to bathe in them but was unable to travel due to being lame; at the Rivers Narmadā and Śiprā, where Gaṅgā-devī practiced austerities and then bathed in order to purify herself, thus Gaṅgā-vahaka-tīrtha and Nīlagaṅgā manifested; at Kotapetah (Sapta-Godāvarī), where Gaṅgā is continuously flowing from the lotus feet of Lord Viṣṇu known as Śrī Cena-keśava-svāmī; and in Kerala at Pāpa-mocanī-tīrtha, where Lord Brahmā requested Gaṅgā and more than six hundred million other water *tīrthas* to appear, before he collected these waters for Lord Rāmacandra's coronation in Ayodhyā. Gaṅgā is also known as Tripathagā, or one who travels the three worlds, so she is not bound to only one geographical location, such as India. Gaṅgā also appeared in the country of Mauritius, an island located in the Indian Ocean. One hundred years ago a local devotee there had a 'divinely inspired revelation' in a dream that an ancient volcanic crater lake named Grand Bassin was connected to the waters of Gaṅgā and could be used for worship. Then, in 1972, Gaṅgā water was brought from India and poured into this ancient lake. Grand Bassin then became known as Gaṅgā Talab.

Besides the scriptural research, I have visited most of the *tīrthas* glorified in this book several times, sometimes with the Padayātrā and sometimes traveling alone. I had the blessing of being able to visit the Himālayas numerous times and have personally walked with the deity of Śrī Gaṅgā-devī twice on her annual pilgrimage to and from Gaṅgotrī. (Please see Book Two, Chapters One and Two). Although innumerable *tīrthas* are situated along Gaṅgā's sacred shores, using whatever information is readily available, thirty-five *tīrthas* are highlighted herein.

It is mentioned in the *Brahma-vaivarta Purāṇa* that after this degrading age of Kali has progressed 10,000 years (5,000 years of Kali-yuga have already passed) Gaṅgā, other holy rivers, and all *tīrthas* will go underground, as the River Sarasvatī has already done, and wait until the next golden age of Satya-yuga. At that time, the sinful actions and reactions will be too great for Gaṅgā-devī or any other river or *tīrtha* to assimilate and maintain their purity. Even today, Gaṅgā has already changed her course, and of the thirty-five *tīrthas* that are glorified in this book, she has already left ten (Haridvāra/Kanakhala, Suka-tāla, Vidura Kutir, Hastināpura, Garhmukteśvara, Sūkara-kṣetra, Kānyakubja, Sāntipura, Āṭisārā-nagara, and Chatrabhoga). Gaṅgā is still very much present at other *tīrthas* such as Deva-prayāga, Prayāga-rāja, Kāśī, Kānāi-nāṭaśālā, Navadvīpa, and Gaṅgā-sāgara. Also, ISKCON has the great fortune of having eight centers on or near the banks of Gaṅgā: at Haridvāra, Prayāga-rāja/Allahabad, Vārāṇasī/Kāśī, Patna, Kānāi-nāṭaśālā, Rājapura, Māyāpur, and Calcutta. Our ISKCON centers in Kānāi-nāṭaśālā, Rājapura, and Māyāpur have specific historical significance focused directly on the pastimes of Lord Caitanya and His associates.

This book has five main objectives. The main one is simply to glorify our mother Gaṅgā for her unfathomable mercy that she bestows upon all living entites, ultimately liberating us from our material enslavement. Regardless of how long we have neglected her, like our own mother, she is always there with open arms to offer loving comfort to her disobedient children. Śrīla Prabhupāda often said that if we wanted to know who our father was, we must ask our mother. Similarly, Gaṅgā is known as Jagan-mātā and Viśva-mātā (mother of the universe), so she can nourish us and guide us to our real Father. The second purpose is to reveal Gaṅgā-devī's original *svarūpa* (form) as Varā-prema, one of the important *mañjarīs* eternally serving the divine couple, Śrī Śrī Rādhā-Kṛṣṇa, in Goloka Vṛndāvana and to introduce the various accounts of the River Gaṅgā's origin from Lord Kṛṣṇa's spiritual realm. The third objective is intended specifically for all the devotees, members, friends, and well-wishers of ISKCON. Śrīla Vṛndāvana dāsa Ṭhākura (who is the incarnation of Śrīla Vedavyāsa in Lord Caitanya's pastimes) states in the *Śrī Caitanya-bhāgavata* (*Madhya* 21.81) that Lord Kṛṣṇa exists in this world in four forms: the *Śrīmad-Bhāgavatam*, Tulasī, Gaṅgā, and Vaiṣṇavas. The Deity form of the Lord may be worshiped only after performing the *prāṇa-pratiṣṭhā* (installation ceremony). However, the *Vedas* enjoin that these four forms are as good as the Supreme Lord Himself from the moment they appear in this world. In our ISKCON society, three of these four forms take a prominent role in our daily spiritual practices. We conduct daily *Śrīmad-Bhāgavatam* classes, as well as read and discuss the *Śrīmad-Bhāgavatam;* our neck beads and chanting beads are made from *tulasī*, and we perform *tulasī-pūjā* twice daily; most of us have constant association with fellow Godbrothers and sisters, as well as other Vaiṣṇavas/Vaiṣṇavis—and Gaṅgā? How many members of ISKCON remember, glorify, worship, or even pray to Gaṅgā on a daily basis, except for some of the residents of Śrīdhāma Māyāpur or a few *pūjārīs*? Some of us are reminded of Gaṅgā while chanting the evening *Gaura-ārati* song: *jaya jaya gorācānder āratiko śobhā jāhnavī-taṭa-vane jaga-mana-lobhā*—"Lord Caitanya's beautiful evening *ārati* is taking place in a grove on the bank of Jāhnavī (Gaṅgā) and is attracting the minds of all living entities in the universe," or during the *prema-dhvani* prayers: *gaṅgā-mayī-ki jaya*! or when taking *caraṇāmṛta*.** But beyond this? So, I am hoping and praying to bring mother Gaṅgā more into our daily meditations so that everyone will become a little more Gaṅgā-conscious. It is mentioned in the *Nārada Purāṇa:* "One who always remembers Gaṅgā while waking, standing, sleeping, meditating, walking, eating, laughing, or crying (wherever he may be) becomes liberated from material bondage." And in the *Brahma-vaivarta Purāṇa*, Lord Nārāyaṇa tells Nārada Muni that the entire universe worships mother Gaṅgā. So, what are we waiting for?

The fourth objective is to emphasis for the benefit of the Hindu population the important instructions and conclusive words of Śrila Prabhupāda's Bhaktivedanta Purports, particularly those concerning the merciful potency of a pure-hearted devotee of the Lord, who can deliver even Gaṅgā herself. The final aim is to highlight the importance of the most sacred *tīrtha* on the banks of Gaṅgā today: Śrīdhāma

---

**When we accept the nectarean water that has bathed the Lord's feet everyday, we are actually drinking Gaṅgā, as explained by Śrila Prabhupāda in *Conversations with Śrila Prabhupāda* (Vol. 23, Washington D.C. July 8, 1976): "In this country (U.S.A.) or that country, there is no such distinction. This *patraṁ* (leaf) *puṣpaṁ* (flower) *phalaṁ* (fruit) *toyaṁ* (water), any country you can get it. You cannot say in America there is no *patraṁ puṣpaṁ phalaṁ toyaṁ*, in India only. No. Everywhere it is available. Therefore, this general prescription is there. Even Kṛṣṇa does not say Gaṅgā-jala. Because Gaṅgā, if you say Gaṅgā-jala, that is available in India. He says *toyaṁ*, any *jala*, any water. Because any water, as soon as it touches the lotus feet of Kṛṣṇa, it becomes Gaṅgā. Why Gaṅgā is so adorned? Because it is coming from the toes of Kṛṣṇa. So any water touching Kṛṣṇa's toes, that becomes Gaṅgā."

Māyāpur, the birthplace of Śrī Caitanya Mahāprabhu. Most Hindus and foreigners are not currently aware of the spiritual magnitude of Māyāpur or the real identity of Lord Caitanya. Vedic tradition glorifies Haridvāra, Prayāga, Kāśī, and Gaṅgā-sāgara as the major *tīrthas* on the banks of Gaṅgā, but now, through the mercy of the Gauḍīya Vaiṣṇava spiritual masters, especially Śrīla Prabhupāda, Śrīdhāma Māyāpur is slowly beginning to reveal itself to the whole world. Also, one of the many names of Gaṅgā is Tīrtha-tīrtha, which indicates that she is the holiest of all holy places. Thus the combined magnanimity of Śrīdhāma Māyāpur and the River Gaṅgā creates the rarest and most revered of all holy places in the universe.

Regarding the contents of Book One of *Our Merciful Mother Gaṅgā*, the reader is first introduced to the original form of Gaṅgā-devī, who is a maidservant of Śrī Śrī Rādhā-Kṛṣṇa in Goloka Vṛndāvana, known as Vara-prema-mañjarī. It is also descibed how Gaṅgā-devi appears in this material universe riding on her crocodile. Then narrations from various *Purāṇas* describe different versions of Gaṅgā's origins, as well as other pastimes directly related to her. Afterwards, Gaṅgā is glorified by Ādi Śaṅkarācārya, Śrīla Vyāsadeva, and Śrīla Prabhupāda. And to end the first book, we learn how the pure devotees of the Lord can deliver even Gaṅgā herself.

In Book Two, the author takes the reader on a pilgrimage with Gaṅgā-devī from her winter home in Mukhwa to her summer abode in Gaṅgotri and from Gaṅgotri to Mukhwa. Then we travel to thirty-five sacred places along the banks of the Gaṅgā, covering the entire length of the river from Gomukha to Gaṅgā-sāgara. Next, Gaṅgā's final destination in the form of the River Vaitaraṇī is described. Afterwards, we learn how to bathe in Gaṅgā, and finally, several devotees share their personal realizations with Gaṅgā.

The narrations that appear in this book are those that have inspired or attracted me in one way or another. Most of the narrations have been quoted as they appear in a particular reference, while some are in summarized form. Practically speaking, the contents of this book are not something new, since these pastimes have been occurring since time immemorial, but the pastimes in this book have been presented in a unique sequence that follows her descent from her origin in Goloka all the way to Lord Yamarāja's abode. Her glories are insurmountable, and I am sure some readers will know pastimes that I have missed or neglected. Whatever has been collected, I simply wanted to share with those who have similar interest and those who desire to increase their love and devotion towards Lord Kṛṣṇa through our merciful loving mother.

Just as the waters of Gaṅgā on this planet are considered only one drop of the Causal Ocean, these few narrations are comparable to only one grain of sand out of the totality found on her shores. Just as the waters of Gaṅgā are constantly flowing, the pastimes occurring on her holy banks, from the icy Gomukha to the warm waters of the Bay of Bengal, are also constantly flowing. Even though one cannot narrate her entire glories, I have tried to compile a few of them; and in spite of so many personal limitations and inadequacies, which are many, my only hope is that the pastimes of *Our Merciful Mother Gaṅgā* that have entered into my heart, will also enter yours.

"JAI GAṄGĀ-MAYĪ KI JAI"

A note regarding the intentions or meanings behind the different names of Gaṅgā that are used in this book. When Gaṅgā-devī is used, this is referring to her personified form in this universe; Gaṅgā-mayī is the Bengali name for mother Gaṅgā, but I have used this name when referring to her form as a river; and Gaṅgā-mātā is used to mean mother Gaṅgā. The name Ganges is foreign and also refers to Gaṅgā but most Indians know her only as she is mentioned in the scriptures as Gaṅgā. In the past fifteen years I have seldom met anyone who has used the name Ganges, except for foreigners and a few British Raja Indians. For this reason, I only use the name Gaṅgā, which is also her personal name. However, Śrīla Prabhupāda used Ganges most of the time in his Bhaktivedanta translations and purports, since Ganges is exclusively used outside of India and Śrīla Prabhupāda was keeping the foreigners in mind when writing his books. Also, Śrīla Prabhupada was brought up during the rule of the British, who used the name Ganges instead of Gaṅgā. Ganges is used when Śrīla Prabhupāda speaks in his translations and purports.

The Glories of Śrīla Prabhupāda

His Divine Grace A. C. Bhaktivedanta Swami Prabhupāda appeared in this world in 1896 in Calcutta, India. He first met his spiritual master, Śrīla Bhaktisiddhānta Sarasvatī Gosvāmī, in Calcutta in 1922. Bhaktisiddhānta Sarasvatī, a prominent religious scholar and the founder of sixty-four Gauḍīya Maṭhas, liked this educated young man and convinced him to dedicate his life to teaching Vedic knowledge. Śrīla Prabhupāda became his student, and eleven years later in 1933 at Allahabad he became his formally initiated disciple.

At their first meeting in 1922, Śrīla Bhaktisiddhānta Sarasvatī Ṭhākura requested Śrīla Prabhupāda to broadcast Vedic knowledge through the English language. In the years that followed, Śrīla Prabhupāda wrote a commentary on the *Bhagavad-gītā*, assisted the Gauḍīya Maṭha in its work, and, in 1944, started *Back to Godhead*, an English fortnightly magazine. Maintaining the publication was a struggle. Single-handedly, Śrīla Prabhupāda edited, typed the manuscripts, checked the galley proofs, and even distributed the individual copies. Once begun, the magazine never stopped; his disciples now publish it in several languages in the West as well as in India.

Recognizing Śrīla Prabhupāda's philosophical learning and devotion, the Gauḍīya Vaiṣṇava Society honored him in 1947 with the title "Bhaktivedanta." In 1950, at the age of fifty-four, Śrīla Prabhupāda retired from married life and adopted the *vānaprastha* (retired) order to devote more time to his studies and writing. Śrīla Prabhupāda traveled to the holy city of Vṛndāvana, where he lived in very humble circumstances in the historic medieval temple of Rādhā-Dāmodara. For several years there, he engaged in deep study and writing. He accepted *sannyāsa* (renounced life of the fourth spiritual order in Vedic society) in 1959. At Rādhā-Dāmodara, Śrīla Prabhupāda began work on his life's masterpiece: a multivolume translation and commentary on the eighteen-thousand-verse *Śrīmad-Bhāgavatam* (*Bhāgavata Purāṇa*). He also wrote *Easy Journey to Other Planets*.

After publishing three volumes of the *Śrīmad-Bhāgavatam*, Śrīla Prabhupāda went to the United States in September 1965, to fulfill the order of his spiritual master. Subsequently, His Divine Grace wrote more than sixty volumes of authoritative commentated translations and summary studies of the philosophical and religious classics of India.

When he first arrived by freighter in New York City, Śrīla Prabhupāda was practically penniless. Only after almost a year of great difficulty did he establish the International Society for Krishna Consciousness in July of 1966. Before his passing away on November 14, 1977, he guided the Society and saw it grow to a worldwide confederation of more than one hundred *āśramas*, schools, temples, institutes, and farm communities.

In 1968 Śrīla Prabhupāda created New Vṛndāvana, an experimental Vedic community in the hills of West Virginia. Inspired by the success of New Vṛndāvana, which became a thriving farm community of more than two thousand acres, his students founded several similar communities in the United States and abroad.

In 1972 His Divine Grace introduced the Vedic system of primary and secondary education in the West by founding the Gurukula school in Dallas, Texas. Since then, under his supervision, his disciples have established children's schools throughout the United States and the rest of the world, with the principal educational centers now located in Vṛndāvana and Māyāpur, India.

Śrīla Prabhupāda also inspired the construction of several large international cultural centers in India. The center at Śrīdhāma Māyāpur in West Bengal is the site for a planned spiritual city, an ambitious project for which construction will extend over many years to come. In Vṛndāvana, there is a project consisting of a magnificent Kṛṣṇa-Balarāma Temple, an international guesthouse, and Śrīla Prabhupāda's Samādhi Memorial and Museum. There are also major cultural and educational centers in New Delhi, Mumbai (Bombay), Bangalore, Bhubaneśvar, Ahmedabad, and Baroda. Other centers are planned in a dozen important locations on the Indian subcontinent.

Śrīla Prabhupāda's most significant contribution, however, is his books. Highly respected by the academic community for their authority, depth, and clarity, they are used as standard textbooks in numerous college courses worldwide. His writings have been translated into over seventy languages. The Bhaktivedanta Book Trust, established in 1972 to publish the works of His Divine Grace, has thus become the world's largest publisher of books in the field of Indian religion and philosophy.

In just twelve years, in spite of his advanced age, Śrīla Prabhupāda circled the globe fourteen times on lecture tours that took him to six continents. In spite of such a vigorous schedule, Śrīla Prabhupāda continued to write prolifically. His writings constitute a veritable library of Vedic philosophy, religion, literature, and culture.

Moreover, the activities of Śrīla Prabhupāda have been predicted in the ancient scriptures of India. Some references are quoted herein from H. H. Mahānidhi Swami's *Appreciating Navadvipa-dhāma*:

The following is from the *Brahma-vaivarta Purāṇa*: "Speaking on behalf of all the sacred rivers (Yamunā, Godāvarī, Sarasvatī, Narmadā, Sindhu, Kāverī, etc.), Gaṅgā-devī said, 'Lord Kṛṣṇa, we can see that Your pastimes are about to end, and people are becoming more and more materialistic. You have been very merciful to us. After You leave, however, all the sinful people of Kali will take bath in our waters, and we will become overwhelmed with sinful reactions.'

"Lord Kṛṣṇa smiled and replied to Gaṅgā-devī, 'Be patient. After five thousand years My *mantra upāsaka* (worshiper of the holy name) will appear in this world and spread the chanting of the holy names everywhere. Not only in India, but all over the world people will chant: *Hare Kṛṣṇa Hare Kṛṣṇa Kṛṣṇa Kṛṣṇa Hare Hare/Hare Rāma Hare Rāma Rāma Rāma Hare Hare*. By this chanting the whole world will become *eka varṇa* (one class), one designation, namely, *hari-bhaktas*, devotees of the Supreme Lord Viṣṇu (Kṛṣṇa). Because the devotees of Hari are so pure, anyone who contacts them will become purified from sinful reactions. These pure devotees will visit India and purify you of sinful reactions by bathing in your sacred waters. This period of worldwide chanting of Hare Kṛṣṇa will continue for ten thousand years. After that the devotees will see the full force of Kali-yuga overtaking the world. At that time, all of the sacred rivers should hide under the earth like Sarasvatī has already done, and wait for the next Satya-yuga.'

"In the *Śrī Caitanya-maṅgala*, Śrī Caitanya Mahāprabhu has said, 'I want to flood the whole world with the chanting of the holy names. I will personally preach and flood India with *hari-nāma-saṅkīrtana*. My *senapati bhakta* (commander-in-chief) will come, preach in distant countries, and flood the world with the chanting of Hare Kṛṣṇa.'

"Nārada Muni, the great *mahājana* (religious authority), foretold Śrīla Prabhupāda's extraordinary worldwide preaching in the *Padma Purāṇa (Bhāgavata-māhātmyam)*: 'O Bhakti-devī, O beautiful-faced one, there is no other age like Kali-yuga, because you will be established in every house as well as in the heart of every person. Hear my vow. If I do not preach your message, subdue all other religions, and make devotional festivals prominent, then I shall not be considered the servant of Lord Hari. In Kali-yuga, those people who follow you, even if they are sinful, will attain the abode of Lord Kṛṣṇa without doubt.'

"Unlike anyone else, Śrīla Prabhupāda fulfilled the prediction of Lord Caitanya that is mentioned in the *Śrī Caitanya-bhāgavata* (*Antya-khaṇḍa* 4.126): *pṛthivīte āche yata nagarādi grāma sarvatra pracāra haibe mora nāma*—'In every town and village in the world, My name will be heard.'

"In the 1800s, Ṭhākura Bhaktivinoda published an article entitled *Nityānanda Suryodaya* in his magazine *Sajjana-toṣaṇī*, wherein he states: 'Soon there will be a time when the chanting of Kṛṣṇa's name will be heard in England, France, Russia, Germany, and America.'

"From these passages, one can clearly see that Śrī Kṛṣṇa and His empowered devotees have precisely predicted the phenomenal preaching success of Śrīla Prabhupāda. Just as Śrīla Prabhupāda's glorious activities were foretold and practically seen, his appearance and disappearance were also glorious. Śrīla Prabhupāda appeared on Nandotsava, a day happily celebrated by millions of pious Indians every year. Nandotsava means: 'Nanda Mahārāja's birth festival for Kṛṣṇa.' Five thousand years ago, Lord Kṛṣṇa appeared in Vṛndāvana at midnight on Janmāṣṭamī, when all the Vrajavāsīs were sleeping. The next day, which became known as Nandotsava, Nanda Mahārāja dressed in luxuriant garments and held a huge festival to honor the auspicious appearance of his divine son. Overwhelmed with ecstasy, Nanda Mahārāja distributed profuse charity to everyone in his kingdom. He gave away opulent cloth, ornaments, and two million richly decorated cows to the *brāhmaṇas* (intellectual members of the first social division in Vedic society). Nanda Mahārāja satisfied everyone's desires with his abundant gifts.

"The atmosphere of Vrajabhūmi (Vṛndāvana) was alive with the vibration of auspicious Vedic hymns. Everything was lavishly decorated to create happiness. Bursting with bliss, the Vrajavāsīs expressed their joy by throwing butter, yogurt, and ghee all around and on each other. In Vṛndāvana and all over India, Nandotsava is still joyously celebrated. Just over one hundred years ago, on this most auspicious spiritual occasion, His Divine Grace Śrīla Prabhupāda appeared in this world to fulfill the mission of the Supreme Lord.

"Śrīla Prabhupāda appeared amidst an atmosphere surcharged with thoughts of Kṛṣṇa. He grew up as a pure devotee of Lord Kṛṣṇa, and distributed Kṛṣṇa consciousness all over the world. After fulfilling all the divine predictions mentioned above, Prabhupāda came to Vṛndāvana to leave his body during Kārtika (October/November).

"November 14, 1977, 7:20 p.m. At that time in the heavens, the constellations were uniting to form *amṛta-yoga*, which is the most auspicious time to embark on a journey. It also indicates the successful completion of any endeavor. While surrounded by loving disciples singing their hearts out in *kīrtana* (chanting), Śrīla Prabhupāda chanted Hare Kṛṣṇa and entered the pastimes of Śrī Śrī Rādhā-Govinda.

"Śrīla Prabhupāda: a perfect appearance, a perfect life, and a perfect disappearance. Śrīla Prabhupāda said Vṛndāvana was his home and Māyāpur (Śrī Navadvipa-dhāma) was where he worshiped Śrī Caitanya Mahāprabhu. Śrīla Prabhupāda lives forever in his books worshiping Lord Caitanya by teaching everyone to serve Śrī Kṛṣṇa and always chant: Hare Kṛṣṇa Hare Kṛṣṇa Kṛṣṇa Kṛṣṇa Hare Hare/Hare Rāma Hare Rāma Rāma Rāma Hare Hare."

BOOK ONE

Scriptural Stories & References

Abhirāma Ṭhākura, Lord Nityānanda, Śrī Gaṅgā-devī, Vasudhā-devī, and Jāhnavā-devī

1) Śrī Śrī Rādhā-Kṛṣṇa become Gaṅgā

2) Śrī Kṛṣṇa, Śrīmatī Rādhārāṇī, and Śrī Gaṅgā-devī

Syamapriya Devi Dasi

3) Nārada's sweetness melts Śrī Kṛṣṇa

Śyāmapriyā Devī Dāsī

3) The descent of Viṣṇupadī

5) Gautamī Gaṅgā's appearance

8) The origin of Bhāgīrathī Gaṅgā

Book One
Chapter One

Śrī Gaṅgā Stavam
Descriptions of Śrī Gaṅgā-devi
Expansions of Gaṅgā
Gaṅgā's Vehicle, the Crocodile

Śrī Gaṅgā Stavam

by Śrīmat Abhirāma Ṭhākura Gosvāmī

Śrī Rāmadāsa, later known as Abhirāma Ṭhākura, was formerly Śrīdāmā, one of the twelve *gopālas* (cowherd boyfriends in Vṛndāvana) who appeared in Lord Caitanya's pastimes. In the *Śrī Caitanya-caritāmṛta, Ādi* 11.13, Abhirāma Ṭhākura's glories are mentioned as follows: "By the order of Śrī Nityānanda Prabhu, Abhirāma Ṭhākura became a great *ācārya* (spiritual master) and preacher of the Caitanya cult of devotional service. Empowered by Nityānanda Prabhu, he was always in ecstasy and was extremely kind to all fallen souls."

The following hymn was compiled by Abhirāma Ṭhākura in glorification of Śrī Gaṅgā-devī, who also appeared five hundred years ago in Bengal as the daughter of Śrī Nityānanda Prabhu. It is found in the last chapter of *Śrī Śrī Abhirāma-līlāmṛta*, a history of the life of Abhirāma Ṭhākura. Abhirāma Ṭhākura herein reveals Gaṅgā-devī's original name, position, and form in the spiritual world, where she is eternally performing direct, loving devotional service to the divine couple of Goloka Vṛndāvana, Śrī Śrī Rādhā-Kṛṣṇa.

Śrī Nityānanda-nandinyai namaḥ

Residing in Goloka, the divine couple became overwhelmed with feelings of intense love for one another. The inundation that flowed from Them is none other than Śrī Gaṅgā-devī herself. Now that personality has most mercifully appeared as the little emperoress of our day, the daughter of the daughter of Sūryadāsa Sarakhela.

Nityānanda-sute prasīda
varade premno vara-mañjarī

O lovely little girl, daughter of Śrī Nityānanda Prabhu, please propitiously bestow your blessings of divine love.

Dear mother of this earth, you have so mercifully appeared on the day of your own worship (Gaṅgā-dushara). Your glories are celebrated throughout the three worlds. The sins acquired in ten lifetimes are neutralized by worshiping you on the most auspicious occasion of your appearance day, itself endowed with uncommon majestic potency.

The true essence of your nature is inaccesible to all but those endowed with devotion. Your munificence is the expedient for our ultimate destination. There is no limit to your compassion. O lovely little girl, daughter of Śrī Nityānanda Prabhu, please propitiously bestow your blessings of divine love.

Beginning even from the *sūtikā mandira* (maternity room), you exhibited your prowess through your most wonderful pastimes. Though as a newborn infant you were expected to be anxious to drink milk from your mother Vasudhā's breast, you refused to do so. Nityānanda Prabhu, however, could understand your mind, so He requested His other consort, Jāhnavā-devī, to accept you as a disciple. O lovely little girl, daughter of Śrī Nityānanda Prabhu, please propitiously bestow your blessings of divine love.

Thus she did utter in your ear the *mantra* (spiritual sound vibration) for worshiping the divine couple. This engendered ecstatic delight within your mind, and so you happily accepted your mother's breast, to the joy of all who were present, especially your mother and father. O lovely little girl, daughter of Śrī Nityānanda Prabhu, please propitiously bestow your blessings of divine love.

You are worshiped by the demigods and demigoddesses as the ornament adorning Lord Śiva's matted locks. You are also the object of affection of Śrī Murāri (Kṛṣṇa) as the water that washes His feet. Thus you are the deliverer of all the three worlds. Human beings attain all perfection by serving you with fondness and affection. O lovely little girl, daughter of Śrī Nityānanda Prabhu, please propitiously bestow your blessings of divine love.

My name is Śrīdāmā-sakhā. As the eternal companion of my master (Nityānanda Prabhu), I accompany Him wherever He goes, including this earthly planet. I am therefore acquainted with whatever there is to be known, whenever and wherever we wander. Thus I could recognize you after offering my obeisances to you twelve times. Even then, as you smiled at me, the entire earth smiled along with your eyes, and I was certain that you are the direct energy of Lord Viṣṇu. By taking shelter of you, the living entities are imbued with devotion. O lovely little girl, daughter of Śrī Nityānanda Prabhu, please propitiously bestow your blessings of divine love.

O goddess, in your direct manifestation you appear in liquid form, flowing throughout the universe. Subsequently you are to be found in your greatest manifestation, residing on the big toe of the left foot of Kṛṣṇa (Viṣṇu), who is the reservoir of loving mellows, transcendental erotic passion incarnate, in the company of His consort, Śrī Rādhikā, whose disciple you are. O lovely little girl, daughter of Śrī Nityānanda Prabhu, please propitiously bestow your blessings of divine love.

Dear mother! Whoever worships your feet attains the supreme benediction. By your unlimited and gracious favor, even those who are nourished by only a semblance of devotion to you attain their desired destination. Why would you award them only the dry fruit of *jñāna* (knowledge)? You are the form of Śrī Kṛṣṇa Himself. O lovely little girl, daughter of Śrī Nityānanda Prabhu, please propitiously bestow your blessings of divine love.

O Bhagavati-devī! With love as your only purpose, your waters of love wait in loving attendance upon Advaita Ācārya, Gadādhara Paṇḍita, and all of the others, including Śrīvāsa Ṭhākura, Rāma, and Hari. You are the loving servant of Śrī Caitanya Mahāprabhu, Nityānanda Prabhu, Narahari

Sarakāra, Vakreśvara Paṇḍita, and Rāghava Paṇḍita. O lovely little girl, daughter of Śrī Nityānanda Prabhu, please propitiously bestow your blessings of divine love.

You are the dear consort of Śrī Kṛṣṇa. Your bodily complexion is the purest white, tinged with the yellow of a *campaka* flower. Nowadays you, the authoress of your own transcendental pastimes, frolic about the house of Nityānanda Prabhu. O Bhāgīrathī Jāhnavī, imbued with the potency of Śrī Hari, you are the source of unlimited delight for your father. O lovely little girl, daughter of Śrī Nityānanda Prabhu, please propitiously bestow your blessings of divine love.

O you who are now simply like a *mañjarī* (bud of *tulasī*), yet proficient to confer the benediction of divine love! Those who contemplate your service and become your devoted followers in loving attendance will find their intention and purpose in life illuminated by the path of *rāgānuga* devotion (following in the wake of those who have already attained spontaneous love for Kṛṣṇa). They thus attain the service of the lotus feet of Śrī Hari, your divine consort. You are so merciful that you bestow upon them your own position as His mistress and maidservant. O lovely little girl, daughter of Śrī Nityānanda Prabhu, please propitiously bestow your blessings of divine love.

Dear mother! Just as Śrī Kṛṣṇacandra has unlimited forms or separated plenary portions allocated by Him to accomplish various objectives, such as creating and maintaining the universes, establishing the principles of religion, etc., your unlimited forms also eternally pervade the material and spiritual universes. Your pastimes are glorified in prayers and hymns. Yet just as Śrī Govinda is the first manifestation, the original cause of all causes, I have had the great fortune to have had *darsana* of your original and most enchanting form, as you have taken birth here today. O lovely little girl, daughter of Śrī Nityānanda Prabhu, please propitiously bestow your blessings of divine love.

Amongst unlimited *tīrthas* throughout the universes, you are the supreme mother of the universe (Viśva-jananī), the most qualified to be offered prayers, and the most sanctified, since Śrī Hari is always near to you. The *munis* (sages) sing your glories and have offered prayers to you since time immemorial. Aho! Who is in full knowledge of your uncommon magnanimity and greatness? O lovely little girl, daughter of Śrī Nityānanda Prabhu, please propitiously bestow your blessings of divine love.

When the Supreme Personality of Godhead Śrī Hari advented Himself as Śrī Caitanya Mahāprabhu, His secondary expansion and self-same Supreme Personality (Nityānanda) also appeared as the son of Padmāvatī. Your pastime of taking birth in His house has immersed the inhabitants in billowing waves of delight, produced from the ocean of *prema* (love of Godhead). O lovely little girl, daughter of Śrī Nityānanda Prabhu, please propitiously bestow your blessings of divine love.

Here you are seen as a new-born baby girl, and then you are seen as the liquified essence of love, flowing throughout the universes. Next, you are seen as Varā-prema-mañjari amongst the other *mañjaris*, situated by the side of Śrī Mādhava (Kṛṣṇa), within the forest groves of Nidhuvana. Thereafter you are seen situated on the toe of Śrī Hari. By your wonderful and unlimited qualities you bring pleasure to Him. O lovely little girl, daughter of Śrī Nityānanda Prabhu, please propitiously bestow your blessings of divine love.

O goddess! You are a venerable member of the esteemed *mañjarīs*, the most intimate maidservants of Śrī Rādhā, in that you bestow the greatest happiness upon the daughter of Mahārāja Vṛṣabhānu. Thus have you endeared yourself to Her as the embodiment of loving service within this land of Vraja (area encircling Vṛndāvana). By your perspicacious understanding of time, place, and cirsumstances and according to your hints and gestures, the service of your Prāṇanātha (Lord of your life) is effected, as you arrange various favorable situations from His side, all to His supreme satisfaction. O lovely little girl, daughter of Śrī Nityānanda Prabhu, please propitiously bestow your blessings of divine love.

In the pleasure groves of Vṛndāvana, upon the jewelled throne of Cupid's dalliance, the divine couple, like two children conceived from Śrī Rādhā's ecstasy, enjoy Their wanton sports with the assistance of Their maidservants. As the maidservants bandy words about in their gentle speech, you engage in various services according to the instructions of Rūpa Mañjarī. O lovely little girl, daughter of Śrī Nityānanda Prabhu, please propitiously bestow your blessings of divine love.

Your divine form is the original abode of supreme sweetness. This truth I have been able to glimpse only due to the mercy of Śrīmatī Rādhikā. Dear mother, only by your beneficience and compassion might I attain the shelter of your feet, the source of all strength. Please do not neglect me. By your mercy may my heart be purified. Please accept me always as your own servant.

Whoever sings the glories of the daughter of Śrīpāda Nityānanda Prabhu will have lit in their hearts the lamp of the sweetest emotions. Your fame destroys the darkness of ignorance, being the direct and original source of all knowledge. Your praises relieve us from heaps and heaps of sinful reaction and enable us to establish a loving relationship with the Supreme Lord. Whoever recites these prayers with loving devotion will always remain victorious and will, as well, obtain a garland of *prema*.

I, Rāmadāsa, celebrated as an eternal *gopa* (cowherd boy) have composed the nectarean syllables of this hymn, churned from the sound of your ankle bells, which are the essence of the esoteric meaning of the *śāstras* (scriptures). O Devī! I am nothing more than your eternal servant. Since I am an ignorant fool, it is only by your mercy, Bhagavati, that these words of praise could bloom in my heart. I eternally offer at your lotus feet the petals of these words, your *prasāda*, just as your devotees offer drops of your transcendental water back to you.

Descriptions of Śrī Gaṅgā-devī

The form that Śrī Gaṅgā-devī manifests in the upper, middle (earthly), and lower planetary systems of this universe is described in the Vedic literatures as follows.

"The personified form of Śrī Gaṅgā-devi is white in color, sitting on top a *makara* (crocodile), and holding a pot and lotus in her hands." (*Agni Purāṇa* 50.16)

"Dharmasva saw Gaṅgā-devi seated on a *makara*—white like a *kunda* flower, the moon, or a conch—and adorned with all ornaments." (*Padma Purāṇa, Kriyā-yoga-sāra-khaṇḍa* 7.114)

"One should meditate on Gaṅgā-devī as follows: She has four arms and three eyes. All her limbs are splendidly formed. She

holds a jewelled pot and a white lotus, while she displays the gestures of granting boons and fearlessness with her other two hands. She is dressed in white garments, she is bedecked in pearls and jewels, she is pleased, her face is splendid, and her lotus-like heart melts with pity. She has flooded the entire surface of the earth with her nectar, and she is worshiped throughout the three worlds." (*Nārada Purāṇa, Uttara-bhāga* 41.33-35)

"The form of Gaṅgā-devī for a deity as well as a picture is as follows: She has four arms and her eyes are beautiful. She has the luster of ten thousand moons, and she is fanned with *cāmaras* (yak-tail whisk). She is always delighted, and a white umbrella over her head further embellishes her. Her heart melts with pity, and she is ready to grant boons. She is adorned with divine jewels, and she wears garlands and unguents." (*Nārada Purāṇa, Uttara-bhāga* 41.49-51)

"Gaṅgā's complexion is white like a *campaka* flower. She removes everyone's sins. She is decorated in white clothing and adorned with jewelled ornaments. Her effulgence is the shelter of millions of moons. She is always smiling, and her youth is never diminished. She is the beloved of Lord Viṣṇu, and fortune is always with her. She wears a garland of *mālatī* flowers, and her head is decorated with *kuṅkuma* (red powder) and sandlewood paste. Her lips look like the red *bimba* fruit, and her teeth appear like a string of pearls. Her eyes are very enchanting, and her chest is broad. Her feet grant liberation to those who deserve it. She is able to award the lotus feet of Lord Viṣṇu, therefore she is known as Viṣṇupadī." (*Śrī Brahma-vaivarta Purāṇa, Prakṛti-khaṇḍa* 9)

"One should meditate on Gaṅgā-devī as follows: She is very gentle with four arms and three eyes. She is served by Nadīs and Nadas. Her entire physical form radiates loveliness. With her four hands she holds a *pūrṇa-kumbha* (pot) and a white lotus, and she makes the gestures of granting boons and freedom from fear. Her luster is like that of ten thousand moons. She is fanned with *cāmaras* and besmeared with divine scents and unguents. Her feet are adored by all three worlds. She is eulogized by *devas* (demigods) and other divine sages." (*Skanda Purāṇa, Kāśī-khaṇḍa* 27.141-145)

THE EXPANSIONS OF GAṄGĀ

The Supreme Personality of Godhead, Lord Śrī Kṛṣṇa, has innumerable expansions and associates, who appear and disappear throughout the numerous universes during various *kalpas* in order to enact specific pastimes for His own pleasure and for the pleasure of His devotees. As stated in the *Bhagavad-gītā* (4.8): "To deliver the pious and to annihilate the miscreants, as well as to reestablish the principles of religion, I Myself appear, millennium after millennium." The various kinds of *avatāras* (incarnations of the Lord or His associates) all appear on schedule. From the *Nārada Purāṇa* (*Uttara-bhāga* 59.24) we get an understanding of the similarity between different forms or expansions of Śrīmatī Rādhārāṇī: "She who is Rādhārāṇī is also Lakṣmī, Sāvitrī, Sarasvatī, and Gaṅgā. There is no factual difference between these five different forms."

The original position of Gaṅgā-devī is as a *mañjarī* named Varā-prema, assisting in the pastimes of the divine couple, Śrī Śrī Rādhā-Kṛṣṇa, in Goloka Vṛndāvana. She is also considered by Lord Brahmā as the eternal daughter of Śrīmatī Rādhārāṇī. Since she originates from the lotus feet of Lord Kṛṣṇa, who is also know as Govinda, she is also known as Govindāṅghri-samudbhavā. When Kṛṣṇa prepared to descend on earth for His pastimes in Vṛndāvana, Mathurā, and Dvārakā, Gaṅgā-devī appeared as Mitravindā, one of the three children born to the Queen of Avantī. Mitravindā was eventually married with Kṛṣṇa and became one of His dearest wives in Dvārakā. Also, Gaṅgā is one of the three eternal consorts (others being Lakṣmī and Sarasvatī) of Lord Viṣṇu in the spiritual world of Vaikuṇṭhaloka.

Since Gaṅgā-devī carried Lord Śiva's vital seed in her veins, she is called Śarajanma-prasū, and as the mother of Skanda (Kārtikeya), she is called Skandasū. Since Gaṅgā has intimate pastimes with Śiva and resides in his matted locks, Gaṅgā is also considered Lord Śiva's beloved wife, known as Bhava-priyā, Giriśa-priyā, and Hara-priyā. As the daughter of Himavān, the King of the Himālayan mountains, she is the elder sister of Umā (Pārvatī) known as Adri-rāja-sutā. Whenever Gaṅgā-devī appears, Yamunā-devī also appears with her, so she is also considered the sister of Yamunā known as Uṣṇa-raśmi-sutā-priyā, the beloved of Yamunā. She is called Bhāgīrathī, for due to Mahārāja Bhagīratha's austerities and prayers to Lord Viṣṇu, she appeared on this planet and is considerd his eldest daughter. After she disturbed Jahnu Ṛṣi, he swallowed the entire river and later released her; she therefore became known as Jāhnavī, the descendant of Jahnu. As the beautiful beloved wife of King Śāntanu, she is called Kamrā and Śāntanu-vallabhā. In this pastime she was the mother of the eight Vasus; after the first seven were killed, she bore the eighth child, who became the famous devotee warrior, Bhīṣmadeva.

The following narration is from the last chapter of the *Garuḍa Purāṇa* (*Brahma-kāṇḍa* 29), wherein Lord Kṛṣṇa describes some of the historical pastimes of Gaṅgā-devī to Garuḍa, Lord Viṣṇu's carrier: "After Prahlāda came Gaṅgā, who became Samudra-rūpiṇī, the consort of Varuṇa, the lord of the oceans. Gaṅgā is so named because she purifies the world by her waters. The devotees call her Viṣṇupadī out of devotion for her. In the beginning, she broke through the upper part of the cosmic shell. She is the destroyer of people's sins, and she purifies herself by contact with the Lord's lotus feet. By seeing, touching, or bathing in her waters, all one's impurities are destroyed and devotion towards Lord Viṣṇu is awakened. Her complexion is white like the rays of the moon, and her eyes resemble those of fish. She is worthy of worship, and whoever remembers that she emanated from the lotus feet of Hari attains liberation. Knowing that Gaṅgā emanated from the feet of Lord Hari, Śiva, the chief among the devotees of Viṣṇu, was moved by devotion to accept her with reverence upon his head and became auspicious by her touch.

"O lord of birds, Gaṅgā has four forms. As the wife of the chief physician Janendra, she was called Abhiṣecanī. As the wife of the monkey-chief Susena, she was named Susenā. In her third form she became the wife of Mahārāja Śāntanu. And, as the wife of Maṇḍūka, she was called Maṇḍūkinī."

In the *Skanda Purāṇa* (*Kāśī-khaṇḍa* 29), *Gaṅgā-sahasra-nāma*, (Thousand Names of Gaṅgā), is described as the most brilliant of all excellent prayers. This prayer is also called *Gaṅgeya-stava-rāja*, or the king of prayers to Gaṅgā. It is on par with the *Vedas* and *Upaniṣads*. If anyone recites *Gaṅgā-sahasra-nāma* everyday, Gaṅgā-devī will personally serve that person. Amongst these thousand names, several of them describe Gaṅgā-devī as being nondifferent from other personalities: Aupendrī, Padmālayā, and Pratyakṣa-lakṣmī identify her as Lakṣmī; Gaṇanāthāmbikā and Ḍhuṇḍhi-vighneśa-jananī identify her as the mother of Gaṇeśa; Añjanā identify her as Hanumān's mother;

Devamātā identify her as Aditi (the mother of the demigods); Durgā, Pārvatī, and Satī identify her as Durgā, Pārvatī, and Dākṣāyaṇī; Nāgā identifies her as a Nāga (a celestial serpent); Brāhmī, Mādhavī (Nārāyaṇī), and Vaiśvānarī identify her as the *śakti* (energy) of Brahmā, Viṣṇu, and Agni; Brahmeśa-viṣṇu-rūpā identify her as Brahmā, Isa (Śiva), and Viṣṇu; Rati identifies her as Kāmadeva's wife; Yajñeśī identifies her as the presiding goddess of *yajñas*, or sacrifices; Yoga-yoni identifies her as the origin of *yogas*; Mahādevī and Viśveśī identify her as the great goddess of the universe; Prāṇijananī identifies her as the mother of all living beings; Bhikṣumātā identifies her as the mother of all mendicants; and Vaiṣṇavapriyā identifies her as the beloved of the devotees of Lord Viṣṇu.

In the *Śrī Gaura-gaṇoddeśa-dīpikā* (69) we learn of Gaṅgā's most recent advent, around five hundred years ago, when she appeared as the daughter of Lord Nityānanda: "The River Gaṅgā, who was born from the lotus feet of Lord Viṣṇu, appeared in Lord Caitanya's pastimes as Śrīmatī Gaṅgā-devi, the daughter of Lord Nityānanda. Her husband, Śrī Mādhava, was formerly Mahārāja Śāntanu."

Gaṅgā's Vehicle, the Makara (Crocodile)

The following story has been adapted from the bi-monthly publication of *Tattvaloka* (Vol.XIII, No.5), which is compiled under the auspices of the Śaṅkarācārya of Śṛṅgerī-maṭha, Karnataka.

"According to the *Purāṇas*, the crocodile is the carrier of goddess Gaṅgā. Crocodiles, lazing in the shallows and on the banks of Gaṅgā, were a common sight even at the end of the nineteenth century, until their indiscriminate slaughter by game hunters was begun. In the state of Kerala (India), a form of trial by ordeal was enacted in which the accused had to cross a crocodile infested river. Also, crocodiles are maintained in tanks or rivers adjacent to temples at Pommala, Palliport, and Tripayar Madai in Kerala.

"The *makara* is associated with both earth and water. *Yogīs* (transcendentalists, or those practicing *aṣṭāṅga-yoga*, the eightfold path) with internal vision perceive a crocodile in the *svādhiṣṭhāna cakra*.* This *cakra* has water as its element, symbolizing the subterranean storehouse of innate tendencies, *vāsanās*, or impressions unconsciously left in the mind of a person by past *karma*, which impels us around in the world.

"Gaṅgā's carrier is no ordinary crocodile, for it is white, not brown, in color. The crocodile has two powers: to destroy and to redeem. When its mouth is open, it has the power to devour us, whereas Gaṅgā has made the crocodile's powers submissive to her command. She is able to stand on her vehicle and travel around according to her wishes, whereas the ordinary man is obedient to his sensual nature."

In the summary of the Eighth Canto, Chapter Two, of the *Śrīmad-Bhāgavatam*, *Gajendra-mokṣa* (the liberation of Gajendra) is briefly described as follows: "In the midst of the ocean of milk, there is a very high and beautiful mountain that has an altitude of ten thousand *yojanas*, or eighty thousand miles. This mountain is known as Trikūṭa. In a valley of Trikūṭa there is a nice garden named Ṛtumat, which was constructed by

*There are seven *cakras* or circular psychic centers in the human body. The second *cakra* is known as *svādhiṣṭhāna*. The vehicle for this *cakra* is the *makara*, or crocodile. As this crocodile moves with serpentine motion, it can arouse the sensuous nature in a person. A crocodile captures its prey through many tricks. It floats, dives deep in the water, and is strong in sexual power. These habits of hunting, trickery, floating, and fantasizing are qualities of a second *cakra* person.

Varuṇa, and in that area is a very nice lake. Once the chief of the elephants along with female elephants, went to enjoy bathing in that lake, and they disturbed the inhabitants of the water. Because of this, the chief crocodile in that water, who was very powerful, immediately attacked the elephant's leg. Thus there ensued a great fight between the elephant and the crocodile. This fight continued for one thousand years. Neither the elephant nor the crocodile died, but since they were in the water, the elephant gradually became weak whereas the power of the crocodile increased more and more. Thus the crocodile became more and more encouraged. Then the elephant, being helpless and seeing that there was no other way for his protection, sought shelter at the lotus feet of the Supreme Personality of Godhead."

Śrīla Prabhupāda then comments on *Śrīmad-Bhāgavatam* (8.2.30): "Now, from this we may take the lesson that in our fight with *māyā* we should not be in a position in which our strength, enthusiasm, and senses will be unable to fight vigorously. Our Kṛṣṇa consciousness movement has actually declared war against the illusory energy, in which all the living entities are rotting in a false understanding of civilization. The soldiers in this Kṛṣṇa consciousness movement must always possess physical strength, enthusiasm, and sensual power. To keep themselves fit, they must therefore place themselves in a normal condition of life. What constitutes a normal condition will not be the same for everyone, and therefore there are four social and spiritual divisions of *varṇāśrama—brāhmaṇa, kṣatriya, vaiśya, śūdra, brahmācārya, gṛhastha, vānaprastha*, and *sannyāsa*...That one has been found to be very weak in one place does not mean that he should stop fighting the crocodile of *māyā*."

Under most normal conditions, we conditioned souls cannot escape the powerful grips of the crocodile of material existence. Without a proper balanced spiritual program of Kṛṣṇa consciousness in our lives, we will only fall under the deadly grip of the crocodile's jaws, as did Gajendra, the king of the elephants. By the mercy of the Supreme Lord, Gajendra was able to remember his past devotional life, which saved him at the moment of death by inspiring him to offer prayers to the Lord. The Lord appeared and rescued him from the crocodile's deadly grip, freeing him from material existence.

Similarly, with the assistance of our merciful mother Gaṅgā, who uses a crocodile as her vehicle, the crocodile of *māyā* can easily be tamed. Her crocodile assists her in delivering the living entities within the three worlds from their material contamination. We should not wait until the jaws of death are directly facing us, but begin at once to take shelter of the Supreme Personality of Godhead, Śrī Kṛṣṇa, with the help of mother Gaṅgā, who is accompanied by her enchanting and merciful *makara*.

Book One
Chapter Two

Sources of Gaṅgā From Goloka
(Lord Kṛṣṇa's Abode)

Sources of Gaṅgā From Goloka (Lord Kṛṣṇa's Abode)

In the *Padma Purāṇa*, Śrīla Vyāsadeva says to Jaimini Ṛṣi, "It is possible to count the number of dust particles on the earth, but one cannot fully narrate the glories of Gaṅgā." Throughout the Vedic literatures, mother Gaṅgā's glories are narrated with the utmost respect and adoration. The narrations of her origin in the spiritual world and within this material universe are numerous and vary in the different Vedic literatures, especially the *Purāṇas*. Tradition accounts for this by placing the variations in different cycles of universal time, known as *kalpas*. The perpetual structure of Vedic time allows for repeated yet varied descents of the Lord and His associates, so details of the pastimes sometimes differ. Since Gaṅgā-devī is eternally serving the divine couple, Śrī Śrī Rādhā-Kṛṣṇa, in Goloka Vṛndāvana, she actually has no birth, origin, or source. Her original liquid manifestation is born from the bodies of the divine couple, from Lord Kṛṣṇa's (and Lord Nārāyaṇa's) melted body, or from her own transformation into water. Many of the following narrations have similar accounts that vary only in a few details, but regardless of her origin and these slight differences, she bestows her merciful love just the same upon everyone.

1) Śrī Śrī Rādhā-Kṛṣṇa become Gaṅgā

In the *Brahma-vaivarta Purāṇa* (*Prakṛti-khanda* 9), the great sage Nārada inquires from Nārāyana Ṛṣi about the pastime when the bodies of Śrī Śrī Rādhā-Krsna melted due to the music of Lord Śiva. Nārāyaṇa Ṛṣi replied, "Once, on the full moon of Kārtika, a festival honoring Śrīmatī Rādhārāṇī was being nicely celebrated. Śrī Kṛṣṇa was worshiping Rādhārāṇī in His *rāsa-mandala* (a secluded area where the Lord enjoys His pastimes) in Goloka, when many other exalted personalities, including the four Kumāras, demigods, demigoddess, sages, saints, and others arrived to also worship the beloved of Lord Kṛṣṇa. Sarasvatī-devī began singing and playing her *vīṇā* (stringed instrument) beautifully for Lord Kṛṣṇa and Śrīmatī Rādhārāṇī. Being pleased, Lord Brahmā presented Sarasvatī a precious gem necklace, while Siva offered her a beautiful jewel.

"Due to the encouragement of Lord Brahmā, Lord Śiva then began singing songs for the pleasure of Lord Kṛṣṇa in which each word was filled with pure nectar. Hearing Śiva's glorious singing, all the demigods fell unconscious. Upon regaining their consciousness, they saw that the entire *rāsa-maṇḍala* was flooded with water and Śrī Śrī Rādhā-Kṛṣṇa had disappeared. Lord Brahmā understood that the divine couple had transformed Themselves into that water, which became known as Gaṅgā.

"Everyone then began to offer their obeisances and prayed, 'O Lord, please allow us to have Your *darśana* once again.' Just then, a voice in the sky was heard, 'Both Myself, the Supreme Being, and Śrīmatī Rādhārāṇī, My pleasure potency, have transformed Ourselves into this water. What else do you want from Us? Following My instructions, Lord Śiva should compile the part of the *Vedas* known as the *Tantra-śāstra*. All desires will be fulfilled when these *mantras* are chanted. This *Tantra-śāstra* should not be introduced to the faithless. If Śiva agrees to compile this *śāstra*, then everyone will be able to have Our *darśana* at this very moment.'

"After invisibly speaking these words, Lord Kṛṣṇa became silent. Hearing His words, Brahmā discussed the instruction with Śiva; and upon understanding those words of Lord Kṛṣṇa, Śiva took the Gaṅgā water in his hand and took a *saṅkalpa* (oath) in order to follow that instruction. He thus began to compile the *Tantra-śāstra*. Then all of the sudden, Lord Kṛṣṇa and Śrīmatī Rādhārāṇī appeared. The demigods were all very happy and started offering prayers to the divine couple.

"O Nārada, I have spoken this most dear history to you. The water that has emanated from the bodies of Śrī Śrī Rādhā-Kṛṣṇa is the bestower of pure *bhakti*, which is why the entire universe worships Gaṅgā."

2) Śrī Kṛṣṇa, Śrīmatī Rādhārāṇī, and Gaṅgā-devī

Further along in the *Brahma-vaivarta Purāṇa* (*Prakṛti-khaṇḍa* 10), Nārada Muni continues to inquire from Nārāyaṇa Ṛṣi by asking, "How did Gaṅgā, who has also emanated from the lotus feet of Lord Kṛṣṇa, enter the *kamaṇḍalu* (waterpot) of Lord Brahmā? Please describe to me how this occurred."

Nārāyaṇa Ṛṣi replied, "O Nārada, previously Gaṅgā-devī was living in Goloka as a *gopī* (cowherd girl). Her form as water appeared from the limbs of Śrī Śrī Rādhā-Kṛṣṇa, and she is identical to Them. She then came in her liquid form to the earth. Previously in Goloka, there was no comparison of Gaṅgā-devī's beauty. Her body was filled with fresh youth, and she was decorated with beautiful ornaments. Her face blossomed like a lotus in the mid-afternoon of Śarat (the autumn season). Her complexion was like the yellow *campaka* flower, and she had a form of pure goodness. Her hair was decorated with sweet smelling *mālatī* flowers.

"As she once shyly sat near Lord Kṛṣṇa, her eyes became intoxicated drinking the nectar of Kṛṣṇa's beauty. Just then, Śrīmatī Rādhārāṇī arrived and also sat near Lord Kṛṣṇa. She was accompanied by innumerable *gopīs*. Her beauty put to shame the splendor of millions of moons. At that time, Rādhārāṇī's eyes began to appear like red lotuses as She exhibited Her pastime of anger. Her complexion was like molten gold, and She gazed like a drunken elephant. She was decorated with many beautiful ornaments, and She wore a garland of *pārijāta* flowers. Due to Her anger, Her lips started shaking as She sat closer to Kṛṣṇa.

"At that time, the *gopas* were extremely frightened. They all offered their obeisances to Rādhārāṇī and Kṛṣṇa. Gaṅgā also stood up and began offering prayers to Rādhārāṇī.

She was filled with fear and inquired about Rādhārāṇī's welfare. Within her mind, Gaṅgā-devī took shelter of the lotus feet of Kṛṣṇa. Then the Lord consoled Gaṅgā within her heart, so she became sober-minded. Gaṅgā then observed Rādhārāṇī sitting on the raised *āsana* (seat), Her body filled with transcendental effulgence. Her youthfulness was that of a sixteen year old. She is the mother of the universe and the life air of Lord Kṛṣṇa.

"O Nārada, seeing the beauty of Śrīmatī Rādhārāṇī, Gaṅgā was unable to take her eyes off Her effulgent form. Then Rādhārāṇī spoke to Lord Kṛṣṇa with pleasing words, 'Who is this Gaṅgā-devī, who is glancing at Your beautiful face without blinking? She is filled with the desire to be with You, as Your beauty has totally stunned her. Each of her limbs are filled with immense happiness. It has become her nature to gaze at You with such crooked eyes, and You are also engaged in the same way.'

"Rādhārāṇī wanted to say something to Gaṅgā, but Gaṅgā was able to understand everything. Thus Gaṅgā transformed herself into water and entered into the lotus feet of Lord Kṛṣṇa for protection. Understanding the secret between Kṛṣṇa and Gaṅgā, Rādhārāṇī wanted to drink the entire Gaṅgā. At that time water throughout the universes dried up. The entire creation was filled with various dead aquatic bodies. Lord Brahmā, Lord Śiva, and all the sages arrived to offer obeisances and prayers to Lord Kṛṣṇa. The Lord then began to speak, 'O Brahmā, I know why you are praying. You desire to take Gaṅgā with you, but she has now taken shelter of My lotus feet because Rādhārāṇī was ready to drink her up. I will be pleased to give her to you, but you must first make her fearless and peaceful.'

"O Nārada, hearing these words of Lord Kṛṣṇa, Brahmā began to smile. Then all the demigods started to praise Śrīmatī Rādhārāṇī. Brahmā said to Her, 'This same Gaṅgā had previously appeared from the bodies of both You and Kṛṣṇa, when You were both in the *rāsa-maṇḍala*. Gaṅgā is meant for Your worship. The Lord of Vaikuṇṭha is going to be her husband, and she will also be the wife of the ocean. Please allow this Gaṅgā, as she is in Goloka, to be distributed everywhere for the benefit of everyone. You are her mother, and she is eternally Your daughter.'

"Rādhārāṇī was pleased with Brahmā's prayers and accepted his request. Just then, Gaṅgā appeared from the toes of Lord Kṛṣṇa. Brahmā took that water into in his *kamaṇḍalu*, and Śiva accepted the same water on his head. This is why she is called Tripurāri-śirogṛha, or she who resides on the head of Śiva. Brahmā then initiated Gaṅgā into the *rādhā-mantra* of the *Sāma Veda* (one of the four original scriptures).

"Then Lord Kṛṣṇa instructed Brahmā, 'You accept Gaṅgā, and I will prepare *kāla* (time) again for creation. In Goloka, *kāla* does not act. Now, the universe is sunken into the waters of devastation. All the other Brahmās of other planetary systems have already entered within Me. Apart from Vaikuṇṭha, everything has merged into the waters. You proceed to begin creation again, then Gaṅgā will come to your abode. Now move foward and carry out this order.'

"O great sage, after Brahmā set forth creation again, Gaṅgā went wherever she was ordered to go by the Supreme Lord. Later on, Lord Kṛṣṇa Himself became Viṣṇu, and upon the request of Brahmā, He married Gaṅgā-devī."

(There are other narrations regarding Lord Brahmā's *kamaṇḍalu* in the next chapter.)

Also in the *Garga-saṁhitā* (3.9.9), we learn that Gaṅgā is nondifferent from the lotus feet of Kṛṣṇa: "Gaṅgā, who travels through the three material worlds, was born from the lotus feet of Lord Kṛṣṇa, who is the master of countless material universes and the ruler of the spiritual realm of Goloka."

3) Nārada's sweetness melts Śrī Kṛṣṇa into Gaṅgā

This narration from the *Śrī Garga-saṁhitā* (5.21-22) explains how Lord Kṛṣṇa's body became a river (the Gaṅgā) of spiritual water (the Kāraṇa-samudra).

Once Śrīmatī Rādhārāṇī inquired from the Supreme Personality of Godhead, Lord Śrī Kṛṣṇa, about the details of how His body became liquid. The Supreme Personality of Godhead replied, "The sages tell the ancient story of this pastime. When one hears this story, all sins are destroyed.

"After Lord Brahmā created the material universe, a saintly son named Nārada was born of him. Nārada was mad with love for Me, and he wandered throughout the three worlds singing My glories. One day, Lord Brahmā requested him to give up his wandering and become the father of many children. Upon hearing his words, Nārada said, 'Father, I am eager to acquire transcendental knowledge. I will not create any children. Creating children is the cause of bewilderment and grief. I will create loving devotional songs in glorification of Lord Kṛṣṇa. You should give up being a progenitor of children, which brings only suffering.' When Brahmā heard these words, his lips trembled in anger and he cursed Nārada, 'You fool, since you like to sing, then become a Gandharva (celestial singer) for one *kalpa* (one day of Brahmā).' Nārada then became Upabarhaṇa, the leader of Gandharvas, in the world of the demigods for one *kalpa*. One day, accompanied by many women, he returned to Lord Brahmā's planet. Since his mind was thinking of these beautiful women, he sang without proper *rāga* (melody). Again Brahmā cursed him, 'Fool, become a *śūdra* (laborer).' Nārada then became a maidservant's son.

"Eventually, Nārada Muni was born as Lord Brahmā's son once again. Still mad with love for Me, he wandered throughout the worlds, singing in glorification of Me. Nārada became the king of sages and the best of devotees. One day, as he was traveling and singing many songs, he came to the place named Ilāvṛta-varṣa. There he saw the city of Veda-nagara, which was filled with jeweled palaces inhabited by divine men and women. Then he saw that the men and women there were all deformed. Some had no feet, some had no ankles, some had no knees, and some had no legs. Various persons had twisted hips, emaciated thighs, disfigured torsos, loosened teeth, hunched shoulders, bowed heads, or no necks.

"Seeing them all like this, the great sage Nārada inquired, 'What is this wonder? You all have lotus faces and splendid, beautiful garments and ornaments. Are you *devas* or great *ṛṣis*? Why are you deformed? Please explain this to me.' Addressed in this way, all the deformed beings, who were unhappy at heart, replied, 'O sage, our bodies have suffered terribly. We will tell you how these sufferings may be relieved. We are the personified forms of *rāgas*, and we live in this city of Veda-nagara. O gentle and humble sage, please hear how we became deformed in this way. Lord Brahmā has a son named Nārada, who is mad with love for Lord Kṛṣṇa, but he sings the wrong melodies at the wrong times. He is a great sage who wanders the three worlds as he wishes, but his singing the wrong songs at the wrong time with the wrong notes and without proper rhythm has broken the limbs of our bodies.' Upon hearing these words, Nārada was astonished. Humbled and trying to smile, he asked, 'How can one obtain knowledge of the proper times and proper rhythms of music? Please tell me.'

"The *rāgas* replied, 'Goddess Sarasvatī is the dearest beloved of the master of Vaikuṇṭhaloka. One who learns from her will know the proper times of music.' After hearing their words, Nārada Muni went to Mount Subhra to obtain the mercy of goddess Sarasvatī.

"O Queen of Vraja, for one hundred celestial years, Nārada performed great austerities. Fasting from food and water, he meditated on goddess Sarasvatī. Purified by his austerities, Mount Subhra became known as Mount Nārada. When his austerities came to an end, Sarasvatī-devī, the splendid goddess of speech and the beloved of Lord Viṣṇu, personally appeared before him. At once Nārada recited many prayers glorifying her beauty, virtues, and sweetness, 'I offer my respectful obeisances to you, beautiful goddess Sarasvatī. You hold in your pure and splendid hands a *vīṇā* and a book, you grant the blessing of fearlessness, and you have come to this material world in your spiritual form. O goddess dressed in white silk tossed by graceful waves as you walk, O auspicious one, please give me knowledge of music. Make me the best of all musicians.'

"Being pleased, goddess Sarasvatī gave the great sage Nārada the *vīṇā* named Devadatta, which was decorated with spiritual sound. Then, the dearest beloved of the Lord of Vaikuṇṭha taught Nārada the different *rāgas* and *rāginīs*, their derivatives, the proper times and places for the different kinds of music, the different rhythms, the five hundred and sixty million divisions and numberless sub-divisions of scales, the various dances, the different musical instruments, and the different kinds of modulation. In this way, Sarasvatī made Nārada unrivaled in the circle of musicians. Then she returned to the spiritual world of Vaikuṇṭha.

"Nārada Muni then went to Gandharva-nagara and accepted the Gandharva named Tumburu as his student. Thereafter, as Nārada sweetly sang My glories, he thought to himself, 'Who is a suitable audience to hear the music I sing?' Nārada, accompanied by Tumburu, went to see Indra, Sūrya, Lord Brahmā, Lord Śiva, and finally Lord Nārāyaṇa, but they were all engaged in their respected pastimes and unable to appreciate Nārada's singing. Finally, Nārada and Tumburu flew over many millions of universes and went to the supreme realm of Goloka, which is beyond the world of matter. Crossing the wave-filled Virajā River, they came to the beautiful Vṛndāvana forest, which is filled with flowering vine cottages, pleasant breezes, and the humming of bees. Then they saw Govardhana Hill and finally they came to My own forest garden. Upon reaching My garden, some of the *gopīs* asked, 'Who are you two and from where have you come? What is your purpose here? Please tell us.' Nārada and Tumburu replied, 'O beautiful girls, we are two singers, expert at playing the *vīṇā*, and we are the best of poets. We have come here to play sweet music before Śrī Kṛṣṇa, the master of Śrīmatī Rādhārāṇī and the original Supreme Personality of Godhead. Please speak these words to Lord Kṛṣṇa.' The *gopīs* then informed Me of the two poet visitors, and I requested them to enter. The two poets saw You and Me sittting on a great lotus with millions of *gopī* friends under a pearl parasol. After bowing down, circumambulating Me, and offering prayers to Me, Nārada Muni approached to sing My glories. Playing his *vīṇā* named Devadatta and accompanied by Tumburu, Nārada sang sweet songs that had no equal anywhere. Being pleased and shaking My head, I praised his music. I then offered Myself to him as a gift and, melting with love, I became liquid. In that way, My body became a river of spiritual water* that flows through millions and millions of universes.

"O Rādhārāṇī, in this limitless spiritual water all the universes float like *indrāyaṇa* fruits. In this *manvantara* (the interval of a Manu), I broke an opening in the universe and the celestial river that removes all sins known as Gaṅgā entered. In the upper planets this river is called Mandākinī, in the middle planets, Bhāgīrathī, and in the lower planets, Bhogavatī. In this way, Gaṅgā flows in three paths. A person who chants the name 'Gaṅgā! Gaṅgā!' and travels the sixteen hundred mile length of the earthly Gaṅgā will become free of all sins and will enter the realm of Lord Viṣṇu. In Kali-yuga, one who sees Gaṅgā vanquishes the sins of a hundred births, one who drinks the water of Gaṅgā vanquishes the sins of two hundred births, and one who bathes in Gaṅgā vanquishes the sins of a thousand births. Those who see Gaṅgā attain the goal of life, while those who do not see Gaṅgā waste their lives."

(There is similar narration regarding the Lord's body melting in the next chapter.)

4) The River Virajā

As explained in the last narration, the river of spiritual water that came from Lord Kṛṣṇa's body is nondifferent from the River Gaṅgā and the Kāraṇa-samudra. The following narrations and quotations establish that the River Virajā and the Kāraṇa-samudra are also nondifferent. Also, the *Garuḍa Purāṇa* states the River Virajā is nondifferent to Lakṣmī. As mentioned earlier from the *Nārada Purāṇa*, there is no difference in these forms of Srimati Rādhārāṇī: Lakṣmī, Sāvitrī, Sarasvatī, and Gaṅgā. They are different manifestations of the same personality. Being "identical" or "nondifferent" also refers to their similarities in qualities, for they all simultaneously retain their distinct personalities. It is also mentioned in the *Garga-saṁhitā* that when the River Yamunā began her descent from Goloka Vṛndāvana to earth, the Rivers Virajā and Gaṅgā entered her waters.

In the *Śrī Brahma-vaivarta Purāṇa* (*Śrī Kṛṣṇa-janma-khaṇḍa*), there is a narration of the pastimes between Lord Kṛṣṇa and the *gopī* named Virajā. As Śrīmatī Rādhārāṇī was approaching the secluded area of Goloka where the Lord and Virajā were intimately speaking, Virajā-gopī, by her mystic *yoga* power, turned herself into the River Virajā in order to hide herself. Encircling Goloka in the spiritual sky, this river is filled with jewels and measures ten million *yojanas* (eighty million miles) in width and is ten times that in length.

The following quotation from *Śrī Caitanya-caritāmṛta* (*Madhya* 21.50-52) describes the Virajā River as situated between the spiritual world of Vaikuṇṭha and this material world: "Between the spiritual and material worlds is a body of water known as the River Virajā. This water is generated from the bodily perspiration of the Supreme Personality of Godhead, who is known as Vedāṅga. Thus the river flows. Beyond the River Virajā is a spiritual nature, which is indestructible, eternal, inexhaustible, and unlimited. It is the supreme abode consisting of three fourths of the Lord's opulences. It is known as *paravyoma*, the spiritual sky. On the other side of the River Virajā is the external abode, which is full of unlimited universes, each containing unlimited atmospheres."

The *Garuḍa Purāṇa* (*Brahma-kāṇḍa* 10.17-27) further describes the River Virajā

* The original Sanskrit word used here is *brahma-drava*, meaning liquid Brahma, or the liquid form of the Absolute Truth. In the *Gaṅgā-sahasra-nāma* one of the names of Gaṅgā is Brahmavidyā-taraṅgiṇī, or the river in the form of knowledge of the Absolute Truth. Another name for her is Brahmāṇḍa-koṭivyāptāmbu, or one whose waters (the Kāraṇa-samudra) have pervaded millions upon millions of Cosmic Eggs, or Golden Eggs.

as follows: "The River Virajā is the eighth enclosure around the creation. It flows between the spaces of ether. It is the most sacred river and awards freedom from rebirth. O lord of birds, the River Virajā does not disappear even at the time of dissolution. The River Virajā is identical with Lakṣmī; it has the function of destroying one's subtle body."

When Śrī Caitanya Mahāprabhu left Jagannātha Purī for Vṛndāvana, He passed through the Jhārikhaṇḍa forest, Vārāṇasī, and Prayāga, before reaching Lord Kṛṣṇa's abode, Śrī Vṛndāvana-dhāma. On His return journey, Caitanya Mahāprabhu again visited Prayāga and met Śrī Rūpa Gosvāmī. For ten successive days, Lord Caitanya instructed him on the basic principles of *bhakti*. Rūpa Gosvāmī later fully elucidated them in the *Bhakti-rasāmṛta-sindhu*, or *The Nectar of Devotion*.

During their discussions, Lord Caitanya explained that when one begins to practice devotional service, a seed is sown in the heart and one must become a gardener and take care of that seed. If the seed is properly watered by the process of *śravaṇa* and *kīrtana* (hearing and chanting), that seed will begin to sprout. As one continues his devotional service, or as one waters the seed, the creeper gradually grows to the point where it penetrates the coverings of this universe and goes beyond the River Virajā between the spiritual world and the material world. After attaining the *brahmajyoti* (spiritual light), it penetrates into the spiritual planet known as Goloka Vṛndāvana.

Śrīla Prabhupāda further elucidates in the *Śrī Caitanya-caritāmṛta* (*Madhya* 19.153, 15.172): "Devotional service is especially meant for the Supreme Personality of Godhead, and it is beyond this material range. There is a river, or causal ocean, between the spiritual and material natures, and this river is free from the influence of the three modes of material nature; therefore it is called Virajā. The word *vi* (*vigata*) means 'completely eradicated', and *rajaḥ* means 'the influence of the material world.'…It is to be understood that this side of the River Virajā is filled with material planets [universes] floating in the Causal Ocean. The name Virajā indicates a marginal position between the spiritual and material worlds, but this Virajā River is not under the control of material energy."

5) The Causal Ocean (Kāraṇa-samudra)

In another narration from the *Brahma-vaivarta Purāṇa* (*Prakṛti-khaṇḍa* 2-3), we learn how the Causal Ocean is nondifferent from Śrīmatī Rādhārāṇī. We also understand that only one drop of the Kāraṇa Ocean becomes the River Gaṅgā in this planetary system.

Nārāyaṇa Ṛṣi described the origin of Mahā-Viṣṇu and the Causal Ocean to Nārada Muni in the following words: "O Nārada, due to the intense enjoyment of loving exchanges between Śrī Kṛṣṇa and the most fortunate Śrīmatī Rādhārāṇī in the *rāsa-maṇḍala*, the body of Rādhārāṇī began to perspire and she started to breath heavily. The perspiration that appeared from Her glorious body turned into the Causal Ocean and Her breathing became the life-giving air throughout the universe. This air resides within and sustains all living entities. Vāyu, the personified form of air, manifested from this air of life. From Rādhārāṇī's left side was born Vāyupatnī, the wife of Vāyu, and from her the *pañca-prāṇas* (*prāṇa*, *apāna*, *vyāna*, *samāna*, and *udāna*), or the five life airs in the body, were born. Then the personified form of the ocean, Varuṇa, also manifested from Rādhārāṇī's perspiration, and from his left side manifested Varuṇānī, who became his consort. Then a radiant, beautiful golden child appeared, who contained within Himself the total power of maintaining the entire

universe. Śrīmatī Rādhārāṇī placed this child on the fathomless water of the Causal Ocean.

"Then from one portion of Lord Kṛṣṇa's body appeared Sadāśiva Mahādeva. His body was decorated with ornamental snakes. While holding a beautiful *mālā* (string of chanting beads), he chanted the sacred name of 'Kṛṣṇa' with his five mouths. Because he worships Lord Kṛṣṇa, who is feared by fear personified, Lord Śiva is also known as Mṛtyuñjaya.

"O Nārada, the golden child remained in the Causal Ocean for the lifetime of Brahmā. Then one part of that child, who was as effulgent as millions of suns together, expanded into a golden shining egg. The other part of the golden child became Mahā-Viṣṇu. Lord Kṛṣṇa then appeared and gave Him the *mantra 'oṁ kṛṣṇāya-svāhā'*, which is the cause of all success."

In the *Śrī Brahma-saṁhitā* (12-13), the innumerable universes that are floating in and scattered all over the Causal Ocean are referred to as golden eggs or sperms: "Mahā-Viṣṇu is spoken of by the name of Nārāyaṇa in this mundane world. From that eternal person has sprung the vast expanse of water of the spiritual Causal Ocean. The subjective portion of Saṅkarṣaṇa who remains in *paravyoma*, reposes in the state of *yoga-nidrā* (divine sleep) in the waters of the spiritual Causal Ocean. The spiritual seeds of Saṅkarṣaṇa existing in the pores of skin of Mahā-Viṣṇu, are born as many golden eggs or sperms. These eggs are covered with five great elements."

The *Śrīmad-Bhāgavatam* (3.20.15) further explains the next stage of one of these golden eggs: "For over one thousand years the shiny egg lies on the waters of the Causal Ocean in a lifeless state. Then the Lord enters into it as Garbhodakaśāyī Viṣṇu." Śrīla Prabhupāda elaborates further elsewhere in the *Śrīmad-Bhāgavatam* (2.5.33): "In a corner of the spiritual sky of *brahmajyoti* a spiritual cloud sometimes appears, and the covered portion is called the *mahat-tattva*. The Lord then, by His plenary portion as Mahā-Viṣṇu, lies down within the water of the *mahat-tattva*, and the water is called the Causal Ocean (Kāraṇa-jala). While Mahā-Viṣṇu sleeps within the Causal Ocean, innumerable universes are generated along with his breathing. These universes are floating, and they are scattered all over the Causal Ocean. They stay only during the breathing period of Mahā-Viṣṇu. In each and every universal globe, the same Mahā-Viṣṇu enters again as Garbhodakaśāyī Viṣṇu and lies there on the serpentlike Śeṣa incarnation. From His navel sprouts a lotus stem, and on that lotus, Brahmā, the lord of the universe, is born."

In the *Śrīmad-Bhāgavatam* (2.7.40) Śrīla Prabhupāda explains how the sacred Gaṅgā enters this universe: "He is known as Trivikrama because once, in His incarnation of Vāmana, He expanded His leg beyond the highest planetary system, Satyaloka, and reached the neutral state of the modes of nature called the covering of the material world. There are seven layers of material coverings over the material sky, and the Lord could penetrate even those coverings. With His toe He made a hole through which the water of the Causal Ocean filters into the material sky, and the current is known as the sacred Ganges, which purifies the planets of the three worlds."

From the following statement of the *Śrī Caitanya-caritāmṛta* (*Ādi* 5.54), we can try to understand how vast this Causal Ocean is when compared to the earthly River Gaṅgā: "The water of the Kāraṇa Ocean, which is the original cause, is therefore spiritual. The sacred Ganges, which is but a drop of this ocean, purifies the fallen souls."

Book One
Chapter Three

Other Origins of Gaṅgā

Other Origins of Gaṅgā

1) Lakṣmī, Sarasvatī, and Gaṅgā

In the *Brahma-vaivarta Purāṇa* (*Prakṛti-khaṇḍa* 6), when Nārada Muni inquired from Nārāyaṇa Ṛṣi about the argument between Lakṣmī, Sarasvatī, and Gaṅgā, where they counter-cursed one another to become rivers in Bhārata-varṣa, Nārāyaṇa Ṛṣi replied, "Listen, great sage Nārada, just after their cursing, Lord Viṣṇu appeared and took Sarasvatī close to Him. Hearing the reason of the cursing between the goddesses, who were all filled with sadness, Lord Viṣṇu spoke pleasingly according to the time and circumstance, 'Lakṣmī, you will expand yourself into the house of King Dharmadhvaja. You will appear directly on the earth without taking a human birth. A demon named Śaṅkhacūḍa will appear as a part of Me. You will become his wife and afterwards, you will have the privilege of becoming My wife. Then you will reside in the form of a sacred plant and throughout the three worlds you will be known as the most purifying *tulasī*. You will also transform yourself into the River Padmāvatī (Gaṇḍakī).* O most beautiful one, proceed to the land of Bhārata-varṣa, since you have already been cursed by Sarasvatī.'

"O Nārada, then Sarasvatī, who resides with Lord Viṣṇu in Vaikuṇṭha, came to Bhārata-varṣa in the form of a river. The River Sarasvatī is very auspicious, the giver of pious results, and meant to be served by religious persons. Saintly personalities should reside on her banks, for she is the goal of the *yogīs'* austerities. All sins are like dry wood, and she is like blazing fire. One who knows her glories and leaves his body on her bank will attain Vaikuṇṭha at once, residing there for eternity."

Nārada then asked, "How did Gaṅgā, who is eternally pure and the bestower of all pious results, curse Sarasvatī? The cause of the cursing of these divine effulgent goddesses must be very interesting for the ears. Therefore, please describe this history to me."

---

*In the *Padma Purāṇa*, it is stated that Tulasī's body transformed into the holy river named Gaṇḍakī and her hair became the *tulasī* plant, the leaves of which are sacred to the three worlds.

Nārāyaṇa Ṛṣi answered, "O Nārada, I will describe this ancient history to you. Lakṣmī, Sarasvatī, and Gaṅgā are the eternal consorts of Lord Viṣṇu. Once Sarasvatī suspected that the Lord loved Gaṅgā more than her. Thus Sarasvatī spoke a few harsh words to Lord Hari, and since she was angy with Gaṅgā, she started dealing harshly with her. Lakṣmī, the embodiment of compassion and peace personified, then tried to appease Sarasvatī. Considering that Lakṣmī had taken Gaṅgā's side, Sarasvatī cursed her to become a river and a plant. Upon hearing the curse of Sarasvatī, Lakṣmī did not show even the slightest anger towards her. She sat there peacefully, holding the hand of Sarasvatī. But Gaṅgā could not tolerate this. Gaṅgā cursed Sarasvatī, saying, 'One who has cursed my sister should also become a river and go down to Mṛtyuloka (earth), where sinful people reside.' Hearing such a curse, Sarasvatī then cursed Gaṅgā that she should also go down to earth and accept everyone's sins.

"Lord Viṣṇu then began to speak, 'O Gaṅgā, O most auspicious one, due to the prayers of Mahārāja Bhagīratha, you will have to go down to the earth and there you will be known as Bhāgīrathī. Following My order, you will become the wife of the ocean, who is My own expansion.' Then He spoke to Sarasvatī, 'O Bhāratī, by accepting the curse of Gaṅgā, one of your plenary portions will appear in Bhārata-varṣa, and afterwards you will go to the abode of Lord Brahmā and become his consort. As for Gaṅgā, part of her will go to the abode of Lord Śiva and become his consort. Only Lakṣmī will remain here with all her complete portions, because her nature is very peaceful; she never gets angry, and she has unflinching faith in Me. She is also the personification of truth.'

"Then speaking to them all, Lord Hari said, 'It is against Vedic injunction for three ladies and their relatives of opposing nature to stay together. If they stay in one place, their presence will not be auspicious. In the house where the woman acts like a man or where the man is controlled by a woman, one's spiritual life is fruitless and the place becomes inauspicious. For one whose wife is harsh in speech and in action and who loves to quarrel, the forest is more favorable than the home. Since it is easy to get water, fruits, and peace in the forest, it is considered more auspicious than being with a mean wife. Those who are puppets in the hands of their wives are never sanctified, even by cremation. A henpecked husband is not liable to receive the results of any auspicious activities that he performs. The demigods and people of earth always criticize him and he is bereft of fame and glory, so he should be considered dead, though living in the body. Therefore, O Gaṅgā, you go to Lord Śiva, and you, Sarasvatī, should go to Lord Brahmā. Lakṣmī will remain here with Me, because a chaste wife is the cause of happiness for her husband, both in the upper planetary system as well as on earth. She also becomes the cause of his liberation.'

"After saying this to His three wives, Lord Viṣṇu became silent. Then the three wives embraced one another and began to cry. Fear of lamentation was bringing pain to their hearts, and their bodies began trembling. Upon seeing Lord Viṣṇu, their only shelter, they began offering prayers. Sarasvatī began, 'O my Lord, please forgive this wretched one and tell me the attonement of my sins and this curse. How is it possible for a wife to be happy if a husband like You neglects her? O Lord, I will give up this body in Bhārata-varṣa through severe austerities.' Then Gaṅgā began pleading, 'O Lord of the universe, I will not remain alive. Why are You rejecting me?' Thereafter, Lakṣmī spoke, 'You are the embodiment of pure goodness, therefore it is very shocking to see grief arise in You. Please be merciful to Your wives, because a master is respected due to his compassion. I will appear with an expansion of myself in Bhārata-varṣa because of Sarasvatī cursing me, but how long do I have to live there? And when will I attain Your lotus feet? How will I be freed from my sins and be qualified to see You again? How long should I remain as Tulasī, the daughter of Dharmadhvaja? How long will it take before Sarasvatī and Gaṅgā return to You? You said that Sarasvatī should go to Brahmā and Gaṅgā to Śiva, but I beg You to please forgive them and not to punish them like this.'

"O Nārada, speaking like this, Lakṣmī fell at the lotus feet of Lord Viṣṇu, embraced His feet with her hair, and started crying again and again. Lord Viṣṇu, who is always compassionate to His devotees, embraced Kamalā (Lakṣmī) and smilingly spoke, 'O chief amongst the goddesses. O lotus eyed one. I will keep your words as well as Mine. One portion of Sarasvatī will go to Bhārata-varṣa in the form of a river, and another portion to Lord Brahmā, but in her complete form she will remain with Me. The same with Gaṅgā. One portion of her will appear with Bhāgīrathī and have the privilege of residing on the head of Lord Śiva, but her whole portion will also remain with Me. And for you Lakṣmī, when you go to the earth, you will be known as the River Padmāvatī and *tulasī*. At the end of Kali-yuga, you will return to Me.

"'O Kamalā, there is always cause for happiness and distress in the life of a person. Without tolerating disasters, one never becomes glorious. Now listen to the process by which you may be purified. Many saints will bathe in your waters, and when you touch them and have their *darśana*, you will become free of sins. O Sundarī, not only you, but all *tīrthas* are purified in the same way. This land of Bhārata-varṣa is extremely pious, because throughout this land many persons engage in worshiping Me by chanting the *mahā-mantra* (the great transcendental sound vibration: *Hare Kṛṣṇa, Hare Kṛṣṇa, Kṛṣṇa Kṛṣṇa, Hare Hare/Hare Rāma, Hare Rāma, Rāma Rāma, Hare Hare*). The aim of such devotees is to deliver everyone. Wherever My devotees wash their feet or reside, that place becomes a place of pilgrimage, or *tīrtha*. This, I assure you, is the truth. The greatest of sinners become delivered simply by the glance and touch of My devotees. Even born *brāhmaṇas* who are fallen, if they have *darśana* of My devotees, they will also become purified. The touch and *darśana* of My devotees is so powerful that the greatest sinners become delivered.'

"Then Lakṣmī said, 'O Lord of the devotees, will You now please explain the symptoms of Your devotees? Their *darśana* and touch purifies even those who are proud, hypocritical, most obstinate, devoid of *viṣṇu-bhakti* (devotion of Viṣṇu), or engaged in praising themselves. When Your devotees bathe in the *tīrthas*, the *tīrthas* become holy again. By the dust from Your devotees' feet, the agonies of Kali-yuga are removed from the earth. The residents of Bhārata-varṣa eagerly await the *darśana* of such great saints, because the devotees of Lord Viṣṇu are the bestowers of all auspiciousness. The sacred waters are not the real *tīrthas*, nor are the deities the real *tīrthas*, because only after a long purification process do they purify the worshiper, whereas the devotees of Viṣṇu purify one within a moment. Actually, they are the real gods.'

"Hearing this from Lakṣmī, Lord Viṣṇu smiled like a blossoming lotus. Then He spoke the great secret, 'O Lakṣmī, the glories of devotees are explained everywhere in the *śāstras*. The glories of devotees are that they can bestow *bhukti* and *mukti* (material enjoyment and liberation from material existence). One who has received the *mahā-mantra* from a bona fide spiritual master, who chants that *mantra*, and who accepts Me as all in all, that person is known to be the most fortunate of all disciples. By the birth of such a person, hundreds of generations, either in heaven or hell, become liable to attain liberation. One who is My devotee attains all of My qualities. His mind is always engaged in singing My glories. He hears and chants My glories in the form of *kathā* (recitation of the Lord's pastimes). He also attains the *aṣṭa-sāttvika-bhāva* (eight symptoms of love for God), and due to the pleasure of performing My devotional service, he disregards the five kinds of liberation. My devotee does not even think or dream of becoming an enjoyer in a different planetary system. O Kamalā, please do as you wish now, since I have answered your questions.'

"Then all the goddesses engaged in executing the orders of the Supreme Personality of Godhead, while He sat on His throne."

2) Lord Brahmā's *kamaṇḍalu* and Gaṅgā

In this narration from the *Brahma Purāṇa* (*Gautami-māhātmyam* 2-4) Lord Brahmā explains to Nārada Muni how he received his *kamaṇḍalu* from Lord Śiva: "Ten thousand years before Gaṅgā appeared in Satya-yuga, the demigods were harassed by the great demon, Tāraka, who usurped the *devas*' glorious positions and wealth. Thereafter, all the *devas* headed by Indra sought the shelter of Lord Viṣṇu. They prayed, 'O Lord Hari, we have no other refuge. Our positions have been taken away, our women have been disgraced, and we have been rendered homeless. O Lord, please protect us.' Lord Viṣṇu then asked them what danger had overwhelmed them. They replied, 'The *asura* (demon) Tāraka causes our hairs to stand on end, for we are incapable of killing him in battle. He will meet death only from a ten day old child. Therefore, O Lord, please take action with this child in mind.' Lord Viṣṇu replied, 'O *devas*, I am not very powerful. He cannot be killed by Me, nor by My child, nor by any of you. Tāraka, the scorcher of the worlds, will meet death from an extremely powerful child born of Lord Śaṅkara (Śiva). Hence, let us all await the marriage of Śiva and Pārvatī, the daughter of Himavān.'

"Thereafter all the *devas* went to the lord of the Himālayas, Himavān, and his consort, Menā. They explained their plan, and both of them became extremely enthusiastic to help execute the secret plot. As time passed, the beloved Gaurī (Pārvatī) was born in the abode of Himavān. For the pleasure of Lord Śiva, she engaged herself in great austerities and meditation, performing penances on the ridge of the Himālayan mountains, as instructed by the demigods. The *devas* then discussed with one another on how to arouse Lord Śiva's interest in marriage. On the advice of the intellegent Bṛhaspati Muni, they arranged to have Kāmadeva (Cupid), his consort Rati, and Vasanta (Spring) enter into Lord Śiva's *āśrama* (hermitage). The demigods thought, 'Since the arrows of the victorious Cupid have never been ineffective, Lord Śiva will certainly desire to marry!' As Cupid was standing in front of Lord Śiva, holding his bow and arrows, he thought to himself, 'Will Lord Śiva, who is the preceptor of the worlds, be pierced?' Just then Cupid was reduced to ashes by Lord Śiva's third eye! The demigods then approached Lord Śiva with folded hands, saying, 'The great fear of Tāraka has overwhelmed us. Please make the daughter of Himavān your wife.' When these words entered Lord Śiva's mind, he immediately acted in accordance with the demigod's plea.

"The wedding took place in the Himālaya Mountains, which are beautifully bedecked with different kinds of jewels, various trees, creepers, birds, rivers, lakes, and wells. These mountains are frequently visited by the demigods, celestial singers and dancers, yogīs, great ṛṣis, and learned sages. They are surrounded by mountains like Meru, Mandara, Kailāsa, and the golden colored Maināka.

"Several sages such as Vasiṣṭha, Agastya, Pulastya, and Lomaśa attended the celestial festivities. Viśvakarmā and his son Tvaṣṭṛ constructed the wedding altar, which was studded with jewels, bedecked with gold, and lined with columns of diamonds, rubies, and sapphires. Prajāpati Dakṣa's daughters Jayā, Lakṣmī, Kṣānti, Kīrti, and Puṣṭi attended, along with the beautiful divine cows such as Surabhi, Nandinī, Nandā, and Sunandā, who fulfill every desire. Even the oceans, rivers, serpents, and mothers of the world performed various services for the marriage ceremony, and the earth, herbs, Varuṇa, Kuvera, and Agni supplied whatever was needed.

"Lord Viṣṇu, as the honored guest, presided over the marriage, while Lord Brahmā performed the sacrifice. After the holy fire was set ablaze, the divine couple, Gaurī and Śaṅkara, circumambulated the altar. At that time Lord Viṣṇu encouraged Lord Śiva to touch the toe of the right foot of the beautiful goddess with his hand. While performing his duties, Lord Brahmā saw that foot of Gaurī and with his agitated mind committed a great offense that produced the Vālakhilyas (sixty thousand pigmy sages who reside in the solar region). Brahmā was overwhelmed with shame and began to leave the ceremony, but Lord Śiva called Brahmā to return in order to free him of the offense.

"Lord Śiva then extracted the sacred essence of the earth and the waters, and after creating a kamaṇḍalu from the earth, he poured the waters into this kamaṇḍalu, while consecrating them with sacred mantras and hymns. He then gave Brahmā this waterpot, which was the combination of the earth and waters that were the cause of creation, maintenance, and destruction. Lord Śiva then glorified Lord Brahmā's kamaṇḍalu by saying, 'It is here that Dharma (religious morality) is established. It is here that eternal sacrifice is established. It is here that enjoyment and salvation are established. By remembering this kamaṇḍalu, mental sins perish. By bathing, drinking, and performing offerings with this sacred water, physical sins perish. This alone is nectar; there is nothing more sacred than this. O Brahmā, take this kamaṇḍalu that has been consecrated by me with special mantras. Of all five elements, water is the greatest. This sacred water is the best of all waters. By touching, remembering, and seeing this water, which is very splendid and pure, one is liberated from all sins.'

"After Lord Vāmanadeva took His second step at Bali Mahārāja's sacrificial arena, Lord Brahmā washed Vāmanadeva's lotus foot with the sacred water from the kamaṇḍalu that Lord Śiva had given him. That water became the Gaṅgā, which fell on Meru Mountain, flowing to the earth in four different directions."

The Śrīmad-Bhāgavatam (8.21.4) also refers to the kamaṇḍalu of Lord Brahmā: "O King, the water from Lord Brahmā's kamaṇḍalu washed the lotus feet of Lord Vāmanadeva, who is known as Urukrama, the wonderful actor. Thus that water became so pure that it was transformed into the water of the Ganges, which went flowing down from the sky, purifying the three worlds like the pure fame of the Supreme Personality of Godhead."

3) The descent of Viṣṇupadī

The *Śrīmad-Bhāgavatam* describes Gaṅgā's direct association with the Lord's lotus feet and why she is known as 'Viṣṇupadī', or she who flows from Lord Viṣṇu's feet and who is able to award one the lotus feet of the Lord.

Lord Vāmanadeva (Viṣṇu) appeared in this world as the son of Kaśyapa and Aditi, completely equipped with conchshell, disc, club, and lotus. His bodily hue was blackish, and He was dressed in yellow garments. Lord Viṣṇu appeared at an auspicious moment on Śrāvaṇa-dvādaśī when the Abhijit star had risen. During that time all the demigods, the cows, the *brāhmaṇas*, and even the seasons were very happy because of the Lord's appearance. After His appearance, the Lord assumed the form of a dwarf (Vāmana).

As time passed, Lord Vāmanadeva went to the northern side of the Narmadā River, to the field known as Bhṛgukaccha, where *brāhmaṇas* of the Bhṛgu dynasty were performing *yajñas*. When the Lord appeared in the sacrificial arena of Mahārāja Bali, due to His transcendental effulgent presence, all the priests were diminished in their prowess, and thus they all stood to offer prayers to Lord Vāmanadeva. After washing the Lord's feet, Mahārāja Bali immediately accepted the water from the Lord's lotus feet on his head.

The *Śrīmad-Bhāgavatam* (8.18.27-28) then continues, "Thus offering a proper reception to the Supreme Personality of Godhead, who is always beautiful to the liberated souls, Bali Mahārāja worshiped Him by washing His lotus feet. Lord Śiva, the best of demigods, who carries on his forehead the emblem of the moon, receives on his head with great devotion the Ganges water emanating from the toe of Viṣṇu. Being aware of religious principles, Bali Mahārāja knew this. Consequently, following in the footsteps of Lord Śiva, Bali Mahārāja also placed on his head the water that had washed the Lord's lotus feet."

Śrīla Prabhupāda further comments on the *Śrīmad-Bhāgavatam* (8.18.28), "Lord Śiva is known as Gaṅgā-dhara, or one who carries the water of the Ganges on his head. On Lord Śiva's forehead is the emblem of the half-moon, yet to give supreme respect to the Supreme Personality of Godhead, Lord Śiva placed the water of the Ganges above this emblem. This example should be followed by everyone, or at least by every devotee, because Lord Śiva is one of the *mahājanas*. Similarly, Mahārāja Bali also later became a *mahājana*. One *mahājana* follows another *mahājana*, and by following the *paramparā* system of *mahājana* activities one can become advanced in spiritual consciousness. The water of the Ganges is sanctified because it emanates from the toe of Lord Viṣṇu. Bali Mahārāja washed the lotus feet of Vāmanadeva, and the water with which he did so became equal to the Ganges. Bali Mahārāja, who perfectly knew all religious principles, therefore took that water on his head, following in the footsteps of Lord Śiva."

Eventually, Bali Mahārāja requested the Lord to ask for anything He liked. The Lord then begged the King for three paces of land. The learned *brāhmaṇa* Sukrācārya instructed the King to withdraw his promise to the Lord, but Bali Mahārāja ultimately gave in charity everything he possessed. With His first step in the sacrificial arena, the Lord extended Himself into a universal form, covering the entire sky. With His hands He covered all directions, and with His second footstep He covered the entire upper planetary system. Therefore, there was no vacant place where He could place His third foostep.

This pastime is decribed in the *Śrīmad-Bhāgavatam* (8.20.34) as follows: "As the Lord

took His second step, He covered the heavenly planets. And not even a spot remained for the third step, for the Lord's foot extended higher and higher, beyond Maharloka, Janaloka, Tapoloka and even Satyaloka." Śrīla Prabhupāda comments on the same text: "When the Lord's footstep exceeded the height of all the *lokas*, including Marharloka, Janaloka, Tapoloka and Satyaloka, His nail certainly pierced the covering of the universe. The universe is covered by the five material elements (*bhūmir āpo 'nalo vāyuḥ kham*). As stated in the *śāstras*, these elements are in layers, each ten times thicker than the previous one. Nonetheless, the nail of the Lord pierced through all these layers and made a hole penetrating into the spiritual world. From this hole, the water of the Ganges infiltrated into this material world, and therefore it is said, *pada-nakha-nīra-janita-jana-pāvana* (*Śrī Daśāvatāra-stotra* 5). Because the Lord kicked a hole in the covering of the universe, the water of the Ganges came into this material world to deliver all the fallen souls."

Earlier in the *Śrimad-Bhāgavatam* (5.17.1), Sukadeva Gosvāmi describes the glories of the River Gaṅgā to Mahārāja Parīkṣit in the following words: "My dear King, Lord Viṣṇu, the enjoyer of all sacrifices, appeared as Vāmanadeva in the sacrificial arena of Bali Mahārāja. Then He extended His left foot to the end of the universe and pierced a hole in its covering with the nail of His big toe. Through the hole, the pure water of the Causal Ocean entered this universe as the Ganges River. Having washed the lotus feet of the Lord, which are covered with reddish powder, the water of the Ganges acquired a very beautiful pink color. Every living being can immediately purify his mind of material contamination by touching the transcendental water of the Ganges, yet its waters remain ever pure. Because the Ganges directly touches the lotus feet of the Lord before descending within this universe, she is known as Viṣṇupadī. Later she received other names like Jāhnavī and Bhāgīrathī. After one thousand milleniums, the water of the Ganges descended on Dhruvaloka, the topmost planet in this universe. Therefore, all learned sages and scholars proclaim Dhruvaloka to be Viṣṇupada ('situated on Lord Viṣṇu's lotus feet')."

4) Śrī Caitanya Mahāprabhu's Gaṅgā-devī

In the *Śrī Caitanya-maṅgala* (*Ādi-khaṇḍa* 5), another account is given on how the Lord's body melted into water: "Early one evening, when Śrī Caitanya Mahāprabhu and His friends went to take *darśana* of Gaṅgā-mayī, many *brāhmaṇas*, *sādhus* (holy persons), women, both young and old, were worshiping and appreciating the pure, beautiful waters of Gaṅgā-mayī. Due to her uncontrolled love for Caitanya Mahāprabhu, Gaṅgā-mayī flowed rapidly, spilling over her banks to gently touch the body of the Lord. All the people wondered why Gaṅgā was roaring with waves and flooding her banks, yet no storm was brewing. They all saw that Caitanya Mahāprabhu was overcome with love for Gaṅgā-devī. Gaṅgā's desire was still not fulfilled, so she splashed her waters across the Lord's lotus feet. In extreme ecstasy, Gaurāṅga Mahāprabhu chanted 'Hari bol!' Out of love, Mahāprabhu keeps Gaṅgā-devī in His heart, and her waters manifest in His tears of love. Her water flows from each hair of Śrī Caitanya Mahāprabhu's body, which is why the ocean of love overflows.

"While this pastime was being performed, one local *brāhmaṇa*, who was extremely devoted to Gaṅgā-devī, was able

to explain why Gaṅgā had overflowed her banks that day. He said, 'Once upon a time, Śiva was ecstatically singing the glories of Lord Nārāyaṇa, while Nārada Muni was playing the *viṇā* and Gaṇeśa was playing the *mṛdaṅga* (drum). The harmonious spiritual vibration pierced the universe, so the Lord came to see their concert. The Lord told Śiva that their music was so ecstatic that it was causing His body to melt! Then Śiva increased the rhythm, which only increased the mystical effect. Upon doing this, the Lord's body began to increasingly melt into water! Then Śiva stopped singing, and the Lord's body stopped melting. Brahmā preserved this sacred water, which is the rarest thing in the material world, in his *kamaṇḍalu*. When the Lord manifested Himself as Lord Vāmanadeva, Brahmā washed the lotus feet of Vāmanadeva with this water. Brahmā then worshiped the Lord's feet and honored that water, pouring the sacred Gaṅgā over his head. Gaṅgā is also called Tripada-sambhava, because she came from the lotus feet of Tripada, Lord Vāmanadeva.'

"'Now the same Lord has appeared as Śrī Caitanya Mahāprabhu. So when Gaṅgā-devī remembered this pastime, she overflowed her banks out of love. When Mahāprabhu lovingly looked upon Gaṅgā-devī, she noticed that the Lord's body was extremely sweet like nectar. Then, on the pretext of making waves, she tenderly caressed the Lord's lotus feet.'"

* * *

The following purport of Śrīla Prabhupāda from the *Śrīmad-Bhāgavatam* (8.21.4) is a summary-conclusion of three of the most accepted origins of Gaṅgā described in Vedic literatures: "Here we understand that the Ganges began when the water from Lord Brahmā's *kamaṇḍalu* washed the lotus feet of Lord Vāmanadeva. But in the Fifth Canto it is stated that the Ganges began when Vāmanadeva's left foot pierced the covering of the universe so that the transcendental water of the Causal Ocean leaked through. And elsewhere it is also stated that Lord Nārāyaṇa appeared as the water of the Ganges. The water of the Ganges, therefore, is a combination of three transcendental waters, and thus the Ganges is able to purify the three worlds. This is the description given by Śrīla Viśvanātha Cakravartī Ṭhākura."

5) Gautamī Gaṅgā's appearance

In the *Brahma Purāṇa* (*Gautamī-māhātmyam* 5.1-5), Nārada Muni learns from Lord Brahmā how Gaṅgā has two different forms: the Gautamī Gaṅgā and the Bhāgīrathī Gaṅgā.

Nārada Muni inquired, "Kindly tell me how the River Gaṅgā reached the mortal world from the matted hair of Lord Śiva." Lord Brahmā replied, "O highly intelligent one, in the matted hair of Maheśvara (Śiva) there are two divisions of water, divided according to the two persons who received them. One part that is well known in the world was brought by the *brāhmaṇa* Gautama, who performed holy rites, gave in charity, worshiped Lord Śiva, and practised meditation. O extremely intelligent one, the other part was taken away by the powerful Mahārāja Bhagīratha, after propitiating Śiva by means of penance and holy rites. Thus, O excellent sage, Gaṅgā has two different forms."

From the following adaption of the *Brahma* and *Nārada Purāṇas*, we learn the history of the appearance of Gautamī Gaṅgā, otherwise known as the River Godāvarī:

Once, during Satya-yuga, Lord Brahmā decided to perform a sacrifice for the benefit of the Viśvadevas, the ten sons of Viśvā. For this occasion, Lord Viṣṇu, all the demigods, demigoddesses, emperors, princes, princesses, sages, and mendicants gathered at Prayāga-rāja (Allahabad). On that auspicious day,

Lord Brahmā took his axe to strike the earth in order to lay the foundation for the *vedī* (altar). When the axe struck a heavy iron chest in the ground, all the guests began to worry, wondering what the chest contained. With the approval of Lord Viṣṇu and Lord Śiva, the box was opened, and to the amazement of everybody, a most beautiful, charming young damsel was found inside! Her unparalleled beauty was quite hypnotizing, and practically everyone attending the sacrifice wanted the young girl's hand in marriage! Even Lord Brahmā became a little bewildered! Then, as some of the guests began to fight, bloodshed became imminent. Lord Brahmā then began thinking how to avoid an all-round bloodbath that would lead nowhere. Finally, he suggested an alternative, "There will be a competition, and the winner will win the girl's hand. Whoever first completes a *bhu-pradakṣiṇa* (circumambulation of the earth) will be married to the damsel!"

Suddenly a marathon race began between kings, princes, demigods, and sages, all trying to outrun one another. One of the competitors was the great sage Gautama Ṛṣi, who was well known for his spiritual attainment. Even though he lagged behind the rest of the participants, he continued on with all hope. While he was slowly trodding along, he came upon a *kapila* (tawny-colored cow) giving birth to a calf. Gautama Ṛṣi immediately circumambulated the cow three times and returned to Lord Brahmā, who was bewildered on seeing Gautama Ṛṣi appear from the very direction that everyone had gone. He felt sad for the sage, who was huffing and puffing, thinking that he had dropped out of the race. But to Lord Brahmā's surprise, Gautama Ṛṣi loudly declared that he had won the race. Lord Brahmā did not believe him, and again the sage raised his voice, declaring he had won the race. Still, Lord Brahmā hesitated, until a heavenly voice proclaimed that Gautama Ṛṣi was indeed the winner, because circumambulation of a cow delivering a calf is equal to a *bhu-pradakṣiṇa*. Thus Lord Brahmā immediately solemnised the marriage between Gautama Ṛṣi and the young girl, named Ahalyā.

Soon all the other contestants began to return, with demigods, kings, and sages closely arriving one after another. When they discovered that Gautama Ṛṣi had already won the race and was married to the damsel, they all became furious. Demanding an explanation from Lord Brahmā, they found his answer difficult to accept, thinking it to be a foul trick, which would bring misfortune to Gautama Ṛṣi and his new wife. Then the sage requested Lord Brahmā for a safe home for himself and his wife. Thereupon, Lord Brahmā instructed Gautama Ṛṣi to visit Lord Śiva, who was residing on Brahmagiri. Eventually, Lord Śiva gave Gautama Ṛṣi and his wife a suitable spot to erect a small *āśrama* near Brahmagiri.

Meanwhile, high above the Himālayas on Mount Kailāsa, mother Pārvatī had a problem. Gaṅgā-devī, who resides in Lord Śiva's *jaṭā* (matted locks of hair), was also known for her beauty and charm. From time to time, Lord Śiva would have intimate affairs with her. Once, when Pārvatī caught them in the act, she became very angry and confided in her son, Gaṇeśa, the situation. Gaṇeśa became furious and decided to wait until his father was asleep and then cut off his *jaṭā*, thereby forcing Gaṅgā to leave! But when mother Pārvatī heard of this plan, she did not approve, fearful of Lord Śiva's reaction on finding himself minus his *jaṭā*. She and Gaṇeśa carefully thought of a scheme to get rid of Gaṅgā-devī, without arousing Lord Śiva's suspicion.

Gaṇeśa invited Lord Varuṇa to his aid and decided to use Gautama Ṛṣi as part of their game plan. The scheme was carefully planned, so no one would be deprived or cursed. They arranged a three-year drought on planet earth, except at Gautama Ṛṣi's *āśrama*. The famine conditions were so severe that all the sages and mendicants began searching for water and food, without success. Gradually everyone flocked to Gautama Ṛṣi's *āśrama*, which kept the *ṛṣi* extremely busy sowing, harvesting, and feeding the countless souls that kept coming and taking shelter at his *āśrama*. One day, while tending his fields, a large cow entered and began to eat the crops. Gautama Ṛṣi approached the cow with a handful of *kuśa* grass and threw it at her in order to drive her away. At that very moment the cow appeared to drop down dead! Gautama Ṛṣi had accidently hit the cow with the grass and committed the most horrible sin of *go-hatyā*, the killing of a cow.

When all the sages and mendicants heard of this news, they began to desert the *āśrama*, since they could not accept food or water from such a grave sinner. They also advised the sage to purify himself through the appropriate *prāyaścitta* (atonement). Then Gaṇeśa came there disguised as a sage named Gaṇeśa Ṛṣi. He comforted the worried sage over the *go-hatyā* that he had committed and informed him that the only one way to absolve himself of the grave sin was to take bath in the celestial waters of the Gaṅgā. Gaṇeśa Ṛṣi then instructed Gautama Ṛṣi to petition Lord Śiva to send Gaṅgā there. Gautama Ṛṣi thus began to perform great austerities for more than eighty-eight thousand years, keeping body and soul together only by *vāyu-bhakṣaṇa*, or eating air.

When Gaṅgā-devī heard of the news related to Gautama Ṛṣi, she was not very willing to leave her position with Lord Śiva. She therefore decided to disturb the sage's penance by seducing him. She sent several beautiful heavenly damsels, who sang, danced, and tried their best to entice the sage, but the great Gautama Ṛṣi was fixed in his determination and concentration. Then she made one last effort by sending her companion, Jaṭikā, who had supernatural powers. Gaṅgā asked her to take the form of Gautama Ṛṣi's wife, Ahalyā, and try to disturb his meditation. Jaṭikā just finished taking a bath and looked very charming and attractive, when she caught the attention of Gautama Ṛṣi. The sage, however, began to think, "How can my wife allow passion to overcome her common sense?" Then he used his supernatural powers and, after seeing through the disguise, he cursed Jaṭikā. Gautama Ṛṣi then continued on with his penance.

Eventually Lord Śiva was pleased with the great sage and appeared before him. The sage offered his obeisances and prayers and begged the Lord that he be absolved of the *go-hatyā* by bathing in the waters of Gaṅgā. Lord Śiva immediately ordered Gaṅgā to come out of his *jaṭā* and go down to the earth. She was still reluctant, so Lord Śiva loosened his *jaṭā* and thrashed his hair against a rock, forcing Gaṅgā to leave and appear on top of Brahmagiri. The appearance of Gaṅgā was welcomed by all the demigods and *ṛṣis*.

Then Lord Śiva said, "So be it. A holy place greater than this has never been, nor will there ever be. It is truth! It is truth! It is truth! It is well established in the *Vedas*. Gautamī Gaṅgā is the holiest of all rivers." After saying this, the Lord vanished. Then Gautama Ṛṣi showered flowers, while the leading *devas*, sages, *brāhmaṇas*, and *kṣatriyas* all came there and honored Gautama Ṛṣi with cries of "Victory!" They were all joyous.

Mother Pārvatī and Gaṇeśa were greatly pleased that their plan had finally succeeded, but Gautama Ṛṣi was still not at ease. Then, as soon as Lord Śiva disappeared, Gaṅgā-devī also vanished! She could not bear separation

from the Lord and did not want to oblige Gautama Ṛṣi. So the sage began praying and begging her to reappear. Eventually she was pleased with the sage's sincerity and reappeared at another location known as Gaṅgādvāra, near Brahmagiri. However, as soon as she reappeared, a demon named Kolhāsura opened his mouth and began to drink all the water! The distressed Gautama Ṛṣi then pleaded with mother Pārvatī, who assumed the form of Amba-devī and immediately beheaded the demon. Gaṅgā-devī then finally requested Gautama Ṛṣi to take his bath, but he was hesitant, thinking that since Gaṅgā was so greatly honored, being able to reside on Lord Śiva's head, he could not touch her with his feet. Again, the sage was uncertain and prayed to Lord Viṣṇu to help him. Since Gautama Ṛṣi was still hesitating, Gaṅgā disappeared once again.

Gautama Ṛṣi's sin was still not absolved, so he searched the entire Brahmagiri area until he finally discovered Gaṅgā at the base of the hill, in the southwestern corner. This time, he quickly spread *kuśa* grass around the stream and threatened Gaṅgā that if she disappeared again, he would curse her. Thus Gaṅgā contained herself and became a *kuṇḍa*, known as Kuśāvarta. Gautama Ṛṣi immediately bathed in her waters and was finally absolved of the *go-hatyā* sin.

Gautama Ṛṣi then sprinkled Gaṅgā water on the cow, who revived, pardoned the sage, and then disappeared. Because the river gave new life to the cow, it became known as Goda or Godāvarī. The river is also known as the Gautamī Gaṅgā, after the sage.

6) Mahārāja Bhagīratha's devotion for Lord Śiva and Gaṅgā-devī

In the following story from the *Nārada Purāṇa* (Chapters 15-16) we learn more about the austerities performed by Mahārāja Bhagīratha prior to his meeting with Lord Śiva and Gaṅgā-devī.

Just before King Bhagīratha retired to the Himālayan forest to perform austerities for bringing Gaṅgā-mayī to this planet, he met Lord Dharmarāja (Yamarāja), who explained several spiritual topics to him. He asked Dharmarāja how many types of *dharmas* (religious principles) exist, which regions are suitable for religious people, how many kinds of tortures there are in hell, which persons are to be chastised, and which persons are to be glorified.

Towards the end of their lengthy discussion, Dharmarāja explained in detail the various hellish tortures, which are very difficult for sinful persons to escape. Yet the worship of Gaṅgā-devī, Tulasī-devī, the devotees, and Lord Hari is enough to compensate any failure of one who has tried to follow the injunctions of any *dharma-śāstra* (scripture on religious principles). He then explained the various levels of *bhakti-yoga*, or devotional service, and ultimately stated, "Devotion to Lord Hari should always be pursued in accordance to your prescribed duty. Hence, worship the Lord with full love and devotion and you will attain eternal happiness."

Ultimately, Lord Dharmarāja explained why he had come to see King Bhagīratha: The King should perform penances in order to bring Gaṅgā down to this earth to redeem his sixty thousand grandfathers residing in hell. "O highly blessed King, deliver your forefathers with the waters of the Gaṅgā, which immediately purify anyone. Even those whose ashes are cast into her waters are liberated from all sins and taken to Lord Hari's abode." After speaking thus to Bhagīratha, Lord Dharmarāja disappeared. Then the King entrusted the care of his kingdom to his ministers and went to practise

austerities on a snowy Himālayan peak, about sixteen *yojanas* (128 miles) to the west of the hermitage of Nara and Nārāyaṇa.

In a very charming and auspicious holy center named Nadeśvara, the King bathed three times a day, ate only fruits and roots, performed fire sacrifices, and daily worshiped Lord Nārāyaṇa three times with leaves, flowers, and water. After some time, he began eating only withered leaves as he practised *prāṇāyāma*, or breath control, while meditating on Lord Nārāyaṇa for sixty thousand years. All the demigods became frightened when they saw a terrifying fire emanating from the King's nostrils, so they went to seek refuge of Mahā-Viṣṇu (Kāraṇodakaśāyī Viṣṇu). After praying to Lord Viṣṇu, the demigods offered their obeisances. The Lord then consoled them and agreed to visit the saintly King, who was performing such great austerities.

Then the Lord revealed Himself to King Bhagīratha, who offered prostrated obeisances on the ground. He was overwhelmed with ecstasy and his hairs stood on end as he cried out in a voice choked with emotion, "O Kṛṣṇa! O Kṛṣṇa! O Kṛṣṇa! O Śrī Kṛṣṇa!" Then the Lord expressed His happiness with the King and assured him that the sixty thousand sons of King Sagara would return to His abode. He also instructed the King to glorify Lord Śambhu (Śiva) by chanting hymns, and since Śiva is the bestower of happiness, he would immediately answer his prayers. When Lord Hari disappeared, Bhagīratha stood up and began to glorify Śambhu with many beautiful prayers, until Lord Śiva personally appeared in front of the King. After the King offered obeisances and glorified the name of Śambhu, Lord Śiva said he was very pleased and the King should ask for his desired boon. The King was also very delighted and bowed before him, saying, "O Maheśvara, if you are pleased with me, then please bring Gaṅgā to this earth for the purpose of liberating my forefathers." Lord Śiva replied, "Gaṅgā will be given to you by me. The highest destination will be awarded to your forefathers. Excellent salvation will be granted to you." Then he vanished.

In the following words from *Śrīmad-Bhāgavatam* (9.9.9-11) we learn that King Bhagiratha was eventually successsful in bringing Gaṅgā to the earth: "When King Bhagīratha approached Lord Śiva and requested him to sustain the forceful waves of the Ganges, Lord Śiva accepted the proposal by saying, 'Let it be so.' Then, with great attention, he sustained the Ganges on his head, for the water of the Ganges is purifying, having emanated from the toe of Lord Viṣṇu. The great and saintly King Bhagīratha brought the Ganges, which can deliver all the fallen souls, to that place on earth where the bodies of his forefathers lay burnt to ashes. Bhagīratha mounted a swift chariot and drove before mother Ganges, who followed him, purifying many countries, until they reached the ashes of Bhagīratha's forefathers, the sons of Sagara, who were thus sprinkled with water from the Ganges."

7) Lord Kṛṣṇa, Bhagīratha, and Gaṅgā

In the *Brahma-vaivarta Purāṇa* (*Prakṛti-khaṇḍa* 9), Nārada Muni inquires from Nārāyaṇa Ṛṣi, who is known as 'the supermost human being', "O crest jewel amongst the knowers of the *Vedas*, please be merciful to me and describe the glories of Gaṅgā, who is known as Sureśvarī, Viṣṇurūpā, and Viṣṇupadī. How and in which *yuga* (age) did she come to earth, and upon whose request? I want to hear these most auspicious and purifying descriptions, which uproot all sins."

Nārāyaṇa Ṛṣi then said, "O honorable sage Nārada, in Satya-yuga there was a great

emperor in the solar dynasty known as Sagara. His two wives, Śaibyā and Vaidarbhī, were most enchanting and beautiful. From Śaibyā, there was a son born by the name of Asamañjasa. Sagara's second wife, Vaidarbhī, worshiped Lord Śiva for begetting a son. After one hundred years of contemplation, a lump of flesh was born to her. Upon seeing the lump, she became very unhappy and again worshiped Lord Śiva. Śiva thus appeared there in the disguise of a *brāhmaṇa* and separated the lump into sixty thousand pieces, which in turn, became the sixty thousand sons of Queen Vaidarbhī. There was no limit to their power and prowess. They were so effulgent that they would cover the effulgence of the sun in the summer season. But all of those effulgent princes were burnt to ashes due to their offending Kapiladeva. Hearing this depressing news, King Sagara cried torrents of tears. The King then retired from his kingdom and entered into the forest.

"Afterwards, Sagara's son Asamañjasa performed austerities to bring Gaṅgā down to this planet in order to deliver his sixty thousand brothers, but due to time personified, his life came to an end. Asamañjasa's son, Aṁśumān, also performed penances for the same purpose, but his life also came to an end before attaining that goal. Then Aṁśumān's grandson, Bhagīratha, who was a great devotee and scholar with unfliching faith in Lord Kṛṣṇa and all the wonderful qualities of a Vaiṣṇava, also performed great austerities for a lengthy period. Eventually Lord Kṛṣṇa was pleased and personally appeared for the pleasure of Bhagīratha. When Lord Kṛṣṇa appeared, His transcendental body was as radiant and effulgent as millions of summer suns. He had the youthful form of a cowherd boy, with two arms holding a flute. Exquisite clothing and ornaments made of transcendental gems bedecked His body. Free from the qualities of material nature, Lord Kṛṣṇa, who is the observer of all, who is beyond *prakṛti* (material energy), and who always displays compassion on His devotees, appeared with a most charming smile in order to bestow mercy upon His devotee. Śrī Kṛṣṇa is the original Supreme Personality of Godhead, and He can assume any form He desires. At that time, Lord Viṣṇu, Śiva, Brahmā, and other sages also appeared to offer their prayers to Śrī Kṛṣṇa. Having this vision of Lord Kṛṣṇa, Bhagīratha offered obeisances and prayers again and again. Bhagīratha then received the boon that his ancestors would be delivered and that he would attain devotional service at Lord Kṛṣṇa's lotus feet.

"Then the personified form of Gaṅgā appeared there, and Lord Kṛṣṇa spoke to her, 'O Sureśvarī, O Queen of the demigods, because of the curse of Sarasvatī you must now descend to Bhārata-varṣa and deliver the sons of Mahārāja Sagara. Just by your touch, they will be delivered and go to My abode. Their bodies will also become like Mine. They will ride on celestial chariots and have the privilege of being My associates. They will be freed from the pangs and sufferings of material nature. Their sinful reactions of all their lifetimes will come to an end. *Smṛti* therefore says the sins of human beings in Bhārata-varṣa are all destroyed just by your touch. Simply by bathing on ordinary days, one's sins are eradicated. By bathing on auspicious days, there are greater results; and by bathing during the lunar eclipse, an immense amount of pious activity is accumulated. Even greater than bathing during a lunar eclipse is bathing during a solar eclipse.'

"After thus speaking to Bhagīratha Mahārāja and Śrī Gaṅgā-devī, the Supreme Lord Kṛṣṇa became silent. Then, with great humility, Gaṅgā said, 'O Lord, the curse of Sarasvatī is already on my head. You have also instructed me, and by the great austerities of this saintly Bhagīratha Mahārāja, I will now go to Bhārata-varṣa. But, my Lord, upon reaching there in my form of water, impious people will deposit their various sins with me. In this condition, how will I be freed from their sins? Please reveal the process to me. O Supreme Lord, how long will I have to stay in Bhārata-varṣa, and when will I again be qualified to return to Your transcendental abode? You are omniscient and there is nothing hidden from You.'

"Lord Kṛṣṇa then said, 'O Sureśvarī, O Gaṅgā, I understand all of your concerns. You are going as a river to Bhārata-varṣa, and My own expansion as the ocean will be your husband. Amongst Sarasvatī and all other rivers, you will be the most dear consort of the ocean. Due to the curse of Sarasvatī, you will have to remain in Kali-yuga for ten thousand years. You are Rasika, and I am in the form of the ocean as Rasikarāja. You will have eternal union with the ocean, and all the inhabitants of Bhārata-varṣa will worship you with the hymns composed and chanted by Bhagīratha Mahārāja. One who offers his obeisances to you will easily attain the result of an Aśvamedha-yajña. Although one may be hundreds of miles away, he will be freed from all sins and will attain Kṛṣṇaloka simply by uttering the name 'Gaṅgā'. All sins that enter you will be destroyed by the touch and bathing of My pure devotees. You will reside in Bhārata-varṣa and have the company of all the other great rivers. Wherever your glories are sung, that place turns into a *tīrtha*. By chanting your glories, one comes to My abode at the time of death. Even the relatives of one who remembers your glories at the time of death, though they may be in a lower species of life, are taken to Goloka.' After saying this, Lord Kṛṣṇa asked Bhagīratha to worship Gaṅgā with love and devotion. As Bhagīratha offered his obeisances to the Lord and began praising Gaṅgā, Lord Kṛṣṇa disappeared."

Nārada Muni continued to inquire from Nārāyaṇa Ṛṣi, by asking, "O great sage, O knower of the *Vedas*, by which *stotram* (prayer) did Bhagīratha Mahārāja worship Gaṅgā? Please explain this clearly to me."

Nārāyaṇa Ṛṣi replied, "After the King performed his daily duties, he controlled his mind and with great devotion worshiped Gaṇeśa to remove obstacles, Sūrya for good health, Agni for purity, Śiva for knowledge, Pārvatī for intelligence, and Viṣṇu for attaining liberation. In this way, he became qualified to worship Gaṅgā. He then prayed, 'O Gaṅgā, your complexion is white like the *campa* flower. You remove all sins from everyone. You are decorated in white clothing, and jewelled ornaments adorn your body. Millions of moons have bestowed their effulgence upon you. You always remain smiling, and your youth is never depleted. You are the beloved of Lord Kṛṣṇa and fortune is always with you. You wear a garland of *mālatī* flowers, and *kuṅkuma* smeared with sandlewood paste drops upon your head. Your lips look like the red *bimba* fruit, and your teeth resemble a string of pearls. Your eyes are very enchanting, and your chest is broad. The minds of great ascetics are like bumblebees at your feet. Your feet grant liberation to those who deserve it. You are able to award the lotus feet of Lord Kṛṣṇa.'

"Afterwards, Bhagīratha Mahārāja led Gaṅgā to the place where the sixty thousand sons of King Sagara lay in heaps of ashes. Then, by her touch, they went to Vaikuṇṭha. Because of Bhagīratha's endeavor to bring Gaṅgā, she is called Bhāgīrathī."

8) The origin of Bhāgīrathī Gaṅgā

The following narration from the *Śrīmad Vālmīki Rāmāyaṇa* (*Bāla-kāṇḍa* 35-44) gives a similar yet more complete account of Bhāgīrathī Gaṅgā's appearance as that found in the above narrations.

After the great sage Viśvāmitra Ṛṣi left Ayodhyā with Śrī Rāma and Lakṣmaṇa, they traveled to the confluence of the Gaṅgā and Sarayū Rivers. Viśvāmitra told Śrī Rāma that the source of the Sarayū was near Mount Kailāsa, where a great lake created by Lord Brahmā's mind, Mānasa-sarovara, was located. From there, Sarayū flows down, encircles Ayodhyā, and eventually joins the Gaṅgā. Viśvāmitra instructed Śrī Rāma to kill the demon named Tāraka, and later he instructed Rāma and Lakṣmaṇa in the art of *mantra* missile warfare. Then they all went to Siddhāśrama, where Lord Vāmanadeva appeared and where Viśvāmitra's *āśrama* was located. They then decided to travel north-east, in the direction of Mithilā (Janakapura). After reaching the bank of the River Śoṇa, Viśvāmitra narrated the story of the four sons of Kuśa Mahārāja. The next morning, they crossed the Śoṇa River and came to the Gaṅgā, where Śrī Rāma inquired from the great sage about the origin of the foremost of all rivers.

In a joyful mood, Śrī Rāma addressed Viśvāmitra, "I wish to hear about the holy river Gaṅgā, which travels a threefold course, and how she meets the ocean." Viśvāmitra replied as follows, "O Rāma, in the extreme north, the king of mountains, the Himālayas, are located. The deity presiding over the Himālayas is Himavān, and his consort is Menā, the daughter of Mount Meru. They had two extremely beautiful daughters, Gaṅgā and Umā. The demigods solicited Himavān to allow Gaṅgā to go with them, since they knew she would eventually purify the three worlds. The pious Himavān readily gave his daughter to the demigods, who left fully satisfied. As they rose in the heavenly regions, Gaṅgā took the form of the delightful Mandākinī (also known as Ākāśa Gaṅgā or the Milky Way). She later descended in the form of an earthly river, capable of eliminating the sins of the three worlds. The other daughter, Umā, practised extreme austerities for the attention of Lord Śiva, and Himavān happily gave her away to the Lord. Thus the two well-known daughters of Himavān were worshiped by the whole universe with great jubilation."

Śrī Rāma and Lakṣmaṇa were very happy to hear about Gaṅgā and Umā, the two daughters of Himavān. Now, they became interested in the details of Gaṅgā's celestial and earthly sojourn, her pastime of sanctifying the three worlds, how she became the foremost river, and what achievements she is associated with. So the great sage Viśvāmitra narrated the whole story as follows:

"After Lord Śiva and Umā (Pārvatī) were married, they engaged in delightful conjugal bliss for one hundred celestial years (thirty-six thousand earthly years)! Neither son nor daughter was born to them, so the demigods, headed by Lord Brahmā, interrupted their amorous sport. They were afraid that if a child were produced, that progeny would be extremely powerful and capable of burning the three worlds. Lord Śiva agreed to retain his vital seed and allow the three worlds to live in peace. However, his vital fluid had already been shaken from his heart, so he wondered who was capable of receiving it. The demigods told him that earth was capable of receiving it, so Lord Śiva dropped his seed, which covered the entire planet. Vāyu and Agnideva controlled the mighty seed of Lord Śiva, which was consolidated into a white mountain and eventually transformed into thick white reeds, illuminating like fire and the sun.

"The demigods were highly pleased, but when they approached Umā, she became angry and said, 'Since you deterred my desire to have a son with my spouse, you shall no longer be able to beget offspring through your respective consorts. Let your wives remain issueless from this day on.' She also cursed the earth saying, 'You will have an uneven surface and shall have many masters. You also will not enjoy the delight of having a son.' Lord Śiva and Umā then went to the summit named Himavatprabhava in the northern part of the Himālayas to perform austerities.

"After some time, the demigods, including Lord Indra and Agnideva, approached Lord Brahmā, seeking to secure a commander for their forces. Knowing that their commander would take birth from Lord Śiva's seed, they asked Brahmā what should be done next. Lord Brahmā instructed Agnideva to place Lord Śiva's seed within Gaṅgā-devī, then a son would be born who would be capable of becoming the commander of the celestial armies and subduing the enemies.

"Agnideva approached Gaṅgā and informed her of Lord Brahmā's request. She assumed an ethereal form, causing the seed to melt all around. Agnideva then impregnated her on all sides until her veins were saturated with the liquid form of Lord Śiva's seed. Gaṅgā began to feel burning sensations, and her mind became very agitated. She told Agnideva that it was impossible to bear Lord Śiva's seed, so Agnideva said she could discharge the seed on the side of the Himālayas. Gaṅgā expelled from her veins that most glorious seed, which shone as molten gold of the purest type. The residue that fell on earth turned into gold, silver, copper, iron, tin, and lead. The molten gold, which shone like fire, became known as Jātarūpa, because at that time, the splendid form of a young boy manifested! Lord Indra and the demigods brought the boy to Kṛttikā (the constellation presided over by six female deities), so that he would be breast-fed and considered their son. The demigods named Lord Śiva and Gaṅgā's mighty-armed effulgent son Skanda (meaning to flow), because he was brought down in the form of Śiva's seed and then flowed out of Gaṅgā's body. He was also known as Kārtikeya, since he had been nursed by the Kṛttikās. As time passed, the demigods and Agnideva installed him as the commander of the celestial forces."

Viśvāmitra continued to narrate to Śrī Rāma and Lakṣmaṇa the story of Gaṅgā: "Long ago, there was a great pious king named Sagara, who ruled over Ayodhyā. He had two wives, Keśinī, who was the daughter of King Vidarbha, and Sumati, who was the sister of Garuḍa, but he was without progeny. He decided to travel to the Himālayas along with his two wives and practise austerities at a place known as Bhṛgu-prasravana. After one hundred years of austerities, Bhṛgu Muni awarded the boon to King Sagara that one wife would bear a son who would continue his family dynasty and the other wife would give birth to sixty thousand sons. As time passed, Queen Keśinī gave birth to Asamañjasa and Queen Sumati gave birth to sixty thousand sons. The eldest son, Asamañjasa, used to throw some of the infants into the Sarayū River, openly and heartily laughing to see them drown. Due to this sinful activity, he was exiled from his father's kingdom.

"As time passed, King Sagara decided to perform a great Aśvamedha sacrifice in the region known as Āryāvarta. While the great sacrifice was being performed, Indra, disguised as a demon, stole the sacrificial horse of King Sagara. The King then requested his sixty thousand sons to go and search out the

thief, so that the sacrifice could be completed. He instructed them to scour the entire planet, with each son excavating one square *yojana* (64 square miles) so that no part was missed, until the horse was found. King Sagara blessed his sixty thousand sons so that prosperity and good fortune would be with them. The sons traversed the entire planet, yet they could not find the horse. They then began excavating with pikes and ploughshares as hard as thunderbolts, which disturbed mother earth. There was a loud roar from the Nāgas, demons, and other living beings that were killed in the course of the excavations. In this way, the sixty thousand sons of King Sagara excavated the entire Jambūdvīpa, including the mountains. Since as a result the demigods and demons were greatly agitated, they all proceeded to visit Lord Brahmā. They explained that so many souls and aquatic animals were being unnecessarily killed by King Sagara's sons, and they requested Lord Brahmā to take action.

"Lord Brahmā replied that the goddess of earth is a consort of Lord Viṣṇu, who would eventually assume the form of Kapiladeva, and by His yogic power all the sons would be consumed by the fire of His wrath. Thus there was no need to maintain grief on this account. All the demigods, Vasus, Rudras, Adityas, Nāgas, etc., then returned to their respective abodes extremely delighted. Meanwhile, the sixty thousand sons returned to their father's kingdom and informed him that they had thoroughly excavated the entire globe, killing so many demons, Nāgas, enemies, etc., yet they were unable to locate the sacrificial horse. King Sagara angrily replied that the earth should be excavated further still, until it broke open. So the sixty thousand sons continued digging until they reached Rasātala (one of the seven planets beneath the earth).

"While they were tunnelling their way to Rasātala, they saw a huge elephant named Virūpākṣa, who was supporting the eastern quarter of the planet. As they penetrated into the southern quarter, they came upon the great elephant supporting that quarter on his head. As they continued, they saw another great elephant named Saumanasa, who resembled a mountain as he guarded and supported the western quarter of the planet. Then in the northern quarter, they saw the beautiful, white snow-colored elephant Bhadra guarding that quarter. All the sixty thousand sons respectfully circumambulated the elephants and began to excavate the earth once more.

"As they proceeded in the northeastern direction, which was presided over by Lord Śiva, all the angry sons of King Sagara finally beheld the eternal Lord Viṣṇu, who had manifested in the form of the great sage Kapiladeva. They also saw the sacrificial horse peacefully grazing nearby. Thoughtlessly, they suspected that He was the thief and they angrily rushed towards Kapiladeva, carrying spades, ploughs, trees, and rocks, accusing Him of stealing the sacrificial horse and exclaiming, 'O evil-minded one!' The great sage Kapila uttered the sound, 'Hummm', and the next moment all sixty thousand sons of King Sagara were reduced to a heap of ashes!

"Perceiving that his sons had been away for a long time, King Sagara requested his grandson Aṁśumān (son of Asamañjasa) to trace the location of his sons and the person who had stolen the horse. The King instructed him to take a bow and sword, and offer respects to those who deserved to be greeted and kill those who came in his way. He was also told to return only after accomplishing his purpose. After being fully instructed by King Sagara, Aṁśumān immediately departed and soon came upon the underground passage his uncles had dug. He came upon one of the four elephants who was protecting his quarter and inquired about his lost uncles and the horse. The elephant said, 'Accomplished of purpose, O son of Asamañjasa, you will soon come back along with the horse.' Aṁśumān hastened to the place where the sons of King Sagara lay reduced to a heap of ashes. As he cried in great agony, he felt inclined to offer water to the spirits of the sixty thousand princes, but water was not available. He then caught sight of the sacrificial horse grazing nearby.

"As Aṁśumān looked further, he saw Garuḍa, the maternal uncle of his uncles. The mighty Garuḍa informed him that the death of the sixty thousand sons of King Sagara was conducive to the interests of the three worlds, for their death would result in the advent of the holy Gaṅgā to the terrestrial plane. He was told not to offer them ordinary water, for by the mercy of Gaṅgā their ashes would be soaked by her waters and the souls of the sixty thousand princes would then attain the celestial plane. Aṁśumān then took the horse back to his grandfather's sacrificial arena, where the sacrifice was successfully completed in accordance with the Vedic scriptures. Then King Sagara returned to his capital and meditated on how to bring Gaṅgā to the terrestrial plane, but he failed to do so within his thirty thousand year reign. He then departed to the heavenly kingdom.

"The citizens accepted the highly pious Aṁśumān as their next ruler, and he soon proved to be a great monarch. Aṁśumān had a son named Dilipa, who was equally great. After entrusting the kingdom to Dilipa, Aṁśumān went to a Himālayan peak to perform great austerities with the hope of calling Gaṅgā down to the terrestrial plane. After performing austerities for three million, two hundred thousand years, Aṁśumān left his body without attaining the mercy of Gaṅgā. Dilipa fell in great sorrow on hearing about his father's death, and he could not ascertain any way to bring Gaṅgā down. During this time, a most pious son by the name of Bhagiratha took birth in the house of Dilipa.

"King Dilipa also failed to arrange for the deliverance of his ancestors. Meanwhile, Bhagiratha was installed as the new king. King Bhagīratha was unable to have a male progeny to continue the race, so in the course of time he entrusted the kingdom to his ministers and left for the secluded Himālayan summit named Mount Gokarṇa with the intention of achieving Gaṅgā's mercy. There he performed great austerities by controlling his senses, exposing himself to five fires (the four directions and the sun), and eating only once a month. After one thousand years of performing these austerities, he was able to obtain Lord Brahmā's audience. Lord Brahmā approached Bhagīratha and awarded him great success. He informed Bhagīratha that Gaṅgā would descend to the earth, but since the earth could not sustain her fall, only Lord Śiva would be capable of supporting and sustaining Gaṅgā when she descends. After speaking to King Bhagīratha, Lord Brahmā ascended to his heavenly planet.

"After Lord Brahmā left, Bhagīratha waited one year for Lord Śiva, standing on one of his large toes. Finally, Lord Śiva appeared and said he was extremely pleased with his determination and that he would receive Gaṅgā on his head as she descended to the earth. Gaṅgā then swelled into a mighty stream with great force and descended from the celestial heavens on to the blessed head of Lord Śiva.

"Gaṅgā was enraged on leaving the heavenly regions and said to herself, 'I may as well enter Pātāla.' Perceiving her arrogance,

Lord Śiva decided to conceal her within the midst of his matted locks. As Gaṅgā fell on top of Lord Śiva's coils of matted hair, the sacred river could not reach the planet earth for several years. Bhagīratha saw the difficulty and therefore performed additional austerities to please Lord Śiva. Finally, when Lord Śiva was satisfied, he let Gaṅgā fall into Bindu-sarovara (Bindusara), a large lake in the Himālayas attributed to Lord Brahmā.

"While the river was being released, it split into seven streams. The Hlādinī, Pāvanī, and Nalinī ran in the easterly direction. The Cakṣu, Sītā, and the great Sindhu flowed in the westerly direction. The seventh and main branch of Gaṅgā followed the chariot of Bhagīratha. Mounted on a splendid chariot, the royal sage Bhagīratha drove ahead, with Gaṅgā following him. In this way, the holy river finally descended and came to earth.

"Gaṅgā maneuvered along with terrific noise. The earth appeared exceptionally charming with fishes, tortoises, snakes, and even sea elephants falling into the river. The demigods, celestial sages, Gandharvas, Siddhas, and others beheld Gaṅgā's descent from their aerial cars. They all came with great speed to see the glorious event, and the sky became illuminated as if by the brilliance of hundreds of suns. Gaṅgā flowed swiftly and winding, broadening out, narrowing down, tossing high in the air, and gliding down again. The host of sages, Gandharvas, and earthly inhabitants touched, sipped, and bathed in the glorious Gaṅgā, freeing themselves from all sins. They all then followed Gaṅgā's path, as she flowed at the heels of Bhagīratha's chariot, proceeding in whatever direction the glorious chariot went.

"As Gaṅgā traveled on, she inundated the sacrificial arena of the great sage Jahnu, who became enraged over Gaṅgā's pride. Thus by dint of his yogic power, he drank all the water of Gaṅgā! Highly astonished, all the demigods, Gandharvas, sages, and others began to glorify Jahnu Ṛṣi in order to pacify him and induce him to treat Gaṅgā as his own daughter. Being pleased by their prayers, the powerful sage discharged Gaṅgā through his ears! Thus Gaṅgā is also known as Jāhnavī, being a descendant of Jahnu Ṛṣi.

"Gaṅgā then resumed her course behind Bhagīratha's chariot, until after forcing their way into the subterranean region they reached Rasātala. Leading Gaṅgā with superhuman effort, Bhagīratha finally fainted as he beheld his great-granduncles who had been reduced to ashes. The sacred waters of Gaṅgā merged within the heap of their ashes and thereby redeemed King Sagara's sixty thousand sons, who all ascended to the spiritual world.

"After the ashes were inundated by Gaṅgā, Lord Brahmā arrived and spoke to Bhagīratha. He informed him that all sixty thousand sons had been delivered. Gaṅgā would be known as his eldest daughter, 'Bhāgīrathī'. She would also be known as 'Divya', because she comes from the heavenly realm, and as 'Tripathagā', because she follows a threefold path.

"Lord Brahmā then said to Bhāgīrathī, 'Offer water to all your great-granduncles in order to fulfill the vow undertaken by your forefathers. The ambition of bringing Gaṅgā down was not realized by your ancestors, Sagara, Aṁsumān, or even by your own father, Dilipa. O jewel amongst men, this vow has been realized only by you.' After speaking thus, Lord Brahmā ascended to his capital and King Bhagīratha returned to his kingdom, where all the citizens greatly rejoiced.

"In this way, O Śrī Rāma, I have narrated to you at length the origin of Gaṅgā. Whosoever listens to this blessed story of the descent of Gaṅgā to this mortal plane will be freed from all sins."

The *Śrīmad-Bhāgavatam* clarifies the actual cause behind the burning of King Sagara's sons: When the sixty thousand sons finally reached Kapiladeva's *āśrama*, they were all very angry and shouted, "Here is the man who has stolen the horse. He is staying there with closed eyes. Certainly he is very sinful. Kill him! Kill him!" When they approached the great sage, He opened His eyes to see what the disturbance was all about. Since the sons of King Sagara were indirectly influenced by Lord Indra, they had lost their intelligence and disrespected a great personality. Due to their great *mahad-vyatikrama* (offense and misbehavior), the fire within the bodies of all the sons became so hot, it burned them all to ashes! So, by their insulting a great personality, the fire of their own bodies killed them.

The *Śrīmad-Bhāgavatam* (9.8.12) establishes this point by describing the saintly qualities of the great sage Kapiladeva as follows: "It is sometimes argued that the sons of King Sagara were burned to ashes by the fire emanating from the eyes of Kapila Muni. This statement, however, is not approved by great learned persons, for Kapila Muni's body is completely in the mode of goodness and therefore cannot manifest the mode of ignorance in the form of anger, just as the pure sky cannot be polluted by the dust of the earth."

Concluding the latter section of this chapter, Lord Brahmā states in the *Brahma Purāṇa* (*Gautami-māhātmyam* 8.77): "Thus, the water stationed within the matter hair of Maheśvara attained two forms. To the south of the Vindhya Mountains, Gaṅgā is called Gautamī. To the north of the Vindhyas, she is called Bhāgīrathī."

Book One
Chapter Four

Pearls of Ganga's Nectar

PEARLS OF GANGA'S NECTAR

This chapter includes a variety of narrations found in different Vedic literatures. Each story distinctly varies from the next and, at the same time, Gaṅgā's nectarean glories remain the central theme.

1) The Kāśyapī Gaṅgā

In the *Padma Purāṇa* (*Uttara-khaṇḍa* 135), Lord Siva describes the greatness of a river known in Kali-yuga as Sābhramati (Sabarmati) to his eternal consort, Pārvatī. This river is also known as the Kāśyapī Gaṅgā, since Kasyapa Muni brought about her descent. The river has its source at Nandi-kuṇḍa in the Mewar hills of the Pāripātra mountain (Arbuda-parvata), which is part of the Aravalli range and is situated near Mount Abu, Sihori, Rajasthan.

Lord Mahādeva begins the narration by describing how the great Kaśyapa Muni performed severe austerities: "For many years the great sage practiced penances on the charming Arbuda mountain, which is full of various trees and where the sin destroying Sarasvatī flows. O goddess, one day he went to the Naimiṣa forest, where all the sages were hearing and chanting about the various pastimes of the Lord. The sages humbly requested him, 'O Kaśyapa, for our pleasure, please bring Gaṅgā here. O great one, that best of rivers will be known after you.' Having heard the request of the sages, Kaśyapa returned to the Arbuda forest and continued his severe austerities. After some time, I appeared before Kaśyapa and to grant him a boon.

"Kaśyapa said, 'O lord of the world, O you are able to grant anyone a boon, I humbly ask that you give me Gaṅgā, which is stationed on your head and which is pure and destroys all sins.' I then said, 'O best of *brāhmaṇas*, take her.' Then taking a hair from my matted locks, I gave him Gaṅgā. After receiving her, he gladly returned to his hermitage, named Kesarandhra. On merely seeing that excellent River Kāśyapī, the killer of a *brāhmaṇa* is freed from his sins."

Pārvatī then asked her lord, "Tell me about the greatness and religious benefits acquired by taking a bath in her or seeing her." Mahādeva replied, "I have heard about many holy places and sanctuaries from Lord

Viṣṇu. Due to His mercy, many sacred rivers flow into the ocean, such as the Gaṅgā, Yamunā, Revā, Tāpī, Mahānadī, Godāvarī, Tuṅgabhadrā, Kauśikī, Kāverī, Sarayū, as well as various other rivers that destroy all sins. The king of holy places, Prayāga, as well as Kāśī, Puṣkara, Naimiṣāraṇya, Amarakaṇṭaka, Dvārakā, Arbudāraṇya, and other such divine and sacred places have all appeared due to the will of the Lord. Upon my request, all of these *tīrthas* entered the River Sābhramati, which I gave to Kaśyapa. Since he is my devotee, he is always dear to me. That is why I gave her to him. Formerly, Mahārāja Bhagīratha desired to go to Lord Viṣṇu's abode, so when he meditated upon me, I offered him Gaṅgā. On the request of the sages at Naimiṣa, I again offered Gaṅgā, but to Kaśyapa this time. The Kāśyapī Gaṅgā is named after Kaśyapa Muni and will always remove all sinful diseases.

"O beautifuly lady, listen to the names by which she is known in each age. In Kṛta, or Satya-yuga, she is known as Kṛtavatī. In Tretā, she is called Girikarṇikā. She is named Candanā in Dvāpara, and she is known as Sābhramati in Kali-yuga. Those souls who everyday bathe in her are freed from all sins and go to Vaikuṇṭha. O goddess, this is the greatest river, since it purifies all the worlds. She is most blessed and pure, and she destroys all sins."

According to another narration in the *Padma Purāṇa*, the name Sābhramati is derived from the word *sambhrama*, which means agitation and alarm mixed with reverence. Once the great sage Vasiṣṭha was seated in contemplation, and in that state, with his powerful and penetrating eyes, he saw the sage Viśvāmitra. Because of Vasiṣṭha's extraordinarily powerful glance, two holes were pierced in the earth from which two rivers manifested: the Sarasvatī and the Sābhramati. The latter name is explained to have its origin in the glance of Vasiṣṭha towards Viśvāmitra with great *sambhrama*. Also, since 88,000 powerful sages once performed austerities and sacrifices on both banks of the River Sābhramati, the river's sanctity and purifying capacity increased.

2) Gaṅgā fills the Ocean

The following short story is adapted from the *Mahābhārata* (*Vana-parva* 102-109) and gives another account of why Gaṅgā appeared on this earth.

Agastya Muni was born from the great Ṛṣi Varuṇa. He possessed great powers due to his performance of severe penances. When Indra, the King of heaven, killed the demon Vṛtrāsura with the help of Lord Nārāyaṇa, the followers of Vṛtrāsura, named Kālakeyas, fled to the depths of the sea and hid themselves there. The Kālakeyas were despondent over the death of Vṛtrāsura and planned to destroy the *brāhmaṇas* in order to stop the performance of sacrifices, which gave strength to their enemies, the demigods. They would attack the hermitages of saintly persons in the dead of the night and after killing the residents would go back into the sea by daybreak. This created havoc in the universe. The demigods sought the protection of the Supreme Lord Nārāyaṇa, who informed them about the hideout of the Kālakeyas and advised them that Agastya alone was powerful enough to dry up the ocean, upon which they could kill the Kālakeyas. The demigods then went to Agastya Muni and requested him to help them by drinking up the ocean. Agastya Muni agreed and with his powers drank up the ocean. The demons, who were left without a hideout, were then massacred by the demigods. Thereafter, the demigods asked Agastya to fill up the ocean, but Agastya had already

digested the water. Lord Brahmā then predicted that the ocean would later be filled by King Bhagīratha when he brought Gaṅgā down to the earth on the strength of his penances, thus delivering the sixty thousand sons of Sagara.

3) Lord Śiva's Gaṅgā

These next two short stories are commonly told in the Himālayan villages. Such narrations are part of what is known as *Sthala Purāṇa*, or histories that have been passed down from generation to generation.

Once upon a time on Mount Kailāsa, Pārvatī closed the eyes of Lord Śiva with her hands. When Lord Śiva's eyes were closed, the sun, moon, and fire did not shine forth. This caused a great catastrophe in the world, as everything was plunged into darkness. Eventually, Lord Śiva opened his third eye, whereupon the sun, moon, and fire all began to shine once again and all darkness disappeared.

Meanwhile, Pārvatī became very frightened, so she removed her hands and perspiration began to drip from her fingers. This perspiration turned into ten Gaṅgās with innumerable branches. All these rivers and branches created a great disturbance in the world. Therefore Lord Viṣṇu, Lord Brahmā, and even Lord Indra all came to Lord Śiva and requested him to avoid another catastrophe.

Lord Śiva understood the problem and brought all the rivers and branches into one lock of his *jaṭā*. Lord Brahmā and Indra then requested Lord Śiva for a little Gaṅgā water for their own planets. Thus Gaṅgā became Mānasa-tīrtha in Brahmaloka and Deva Gaṅgā in Indraloka. Later, Mahārāja Bhagīratha brought Gaṅgā down from Brahmaloka to deliver the sixty thousand sons of Mahārāja Sagara.

4) Gaṅgā-devī's Mother

When Gaṅgā-devī, the daughter of Himavān, was about to leave her parent's home, her mother, Menā, could not bear her separation. She therefore prayed that Gaṅgā should be turned into water and flow in the Himālayan region. Her prayer was granted, and thus she was able to see her daughter, Gaṅgā-devī, everyday in the form of a river.

5) Agastya Muni directs the Suvarṇamukharī Gaṅgā

In the following narration from the *Skanda Purāṇa* (2.1.30), another manifestation of Gaṅgā-mayī that appeared in South India, far from the Himālayas and beyond the Vindhya mountains, is described.

After Himavān (the presiding deity of the Himālayas) agreed to the marriage of his daughter Pārvatī with Lord Śiva, all the demigods, ṛṣis, and other devotees gathered in the north for the grand ceremony. This gathering of practically everyone in the north caused a great imbalance of the earth, so Lord Śiva requested the sage Agastya to go south to offset the balance of the planet. The Lord also gave him the benediction that he would be able to see the marriage from wherever he was. The sage thus traveled south beyond the Vindhya mountains until he discovered a mountain peak that appeared like a treasure of illustrious gems and herbs. Upon climbing the peak, Agastya Muni was very pleased and decided to remain there, making that place his hermitage.

After a long time passed, many demigods and ṛṣis came to associate and live with the fortunate sage on his mountain peak, which became known as Agastya-śilā. One morning while Agastya was entering the temple to perform his worship of Lord Śiva, a divine voice said to him, "O Agastya, this

beautiful land is without a river. Please bring a river here for the welfare of the people. The demigods, *ṛṣis*, and *yogīs* will all be very pleased with you." After discussing the situation with the other sages, he began to perform great austerities for the satisfaction of Lord Brahmā. Eventually Brahmā appeared and understood the sage's desire. Brahmā then mentally requested Gaṅgā-devī to direct a part of her flow to Agastya Muni's hermitage. Gaṅgā-devī appeared before the sage and said, "O Agastya, this part of my waters will form a river for fulfilling your desire." The sage brought the river to the mountain and then directed her as to the proper path to be followed. All the demigods, *ṛṣis*, and *yogīs* praised Agastya for his actions. Thus the river became known as Suvarṇamukharī Gaṅgā.

6) The Rākṣasas, the Kaliṅga Brāhmaṇa, and Gaṅgā-mayi

This narration from the *Nārada Purāṇa* (Chapter 9) illustrates how the most sinful living entities known as *rākṣasas* (human flesh eaters) and *piśācas* (ghosts) are immensely benefited by contact with a few drops of Gaṅgā water and a single *tulasī* leaf.

Saudāsa, who was also known as Mitrasaha, was the son of King Sudāsa and the eighth descendant from Bhagīratha Mahārāja. When he became king, he was well known throughout the three worlds for his knowledge of the scriptures. He was most pious and pure, and he possessed all good qualities. He was blessed with sons and grandsons, and while he ruled the earth for thirty-eight thousand years, he continued to retain his youth.

Once, on a hunting expedition, King Mitrasaha and his ministers rested on the bank of the Narmadā River. The next day, after he had completed his early morning worship, the King went alone to the forest seeking animals to hunt. He came upon a deer and began to pursue the animal on horseback. While chasing the deer, he came across a cave wherein a tiger couple were having union. He slowly and carefully fit an arrow to his bow and shot the tigress. As soon as the tigress fell down dead, she transformed into a giant *rākṣasī* (female man-eater), who roared like the rumbling clouds and thunder. The *rākṣasī* angrily threatened the King, saying she would take revenge someday, and then vanished. The frightened King returned to join his camp in the forest. After reporting everything, he suspected the demon would attack, so he gave up hunting from that time on.

After a long time passed, the King began to perform an Aśvamedha-yajña (horse sacrifice) under the direction of Vasiṣṭha Muni and in the company of other great sages. Vasiṣṭha offered proper oblations to Lord Brahmā and the other demigods and then left the sacrificial arena for a short period. While Vasiṣṭha was gone, the demoness who was previously in the form of a tigress came there disguised as Vasiṣṭha Muni and instructed the King that he wanted to eat human flesh! The demoness then assumed the form of the royal cook, cooked flesh, and presented it to the King. The King preserved the meat in a golden vessel for his preceptor, Vasiṣṭha Muni. When Vasiṣṭha returned, he was served the meat in the golden vessel and was struck with wonder while considering why the King had served him prohibited food, which would only bring about his ruination. He then cursed the King, saying, "Let this human flesh be your regular diet, since it is food fit only for *rākṣasas*." He also cursed the King to assume the status of a *rākṣasa*, who is accustomed to eating this diet. Then the King, who was very agitated and

2) Gaṅgā fills the Ocean

6) The Rakṣaṣas, the Kaliṅga Brāhmaṇa, and Gaṅgā-mayī

7) The Vultures and Gaṅgā

8) Kālakalpa is blessed by Gaṅgā-mayī's touch

9) Lord Rāmacandra meditates on Gaṅgā-mayī

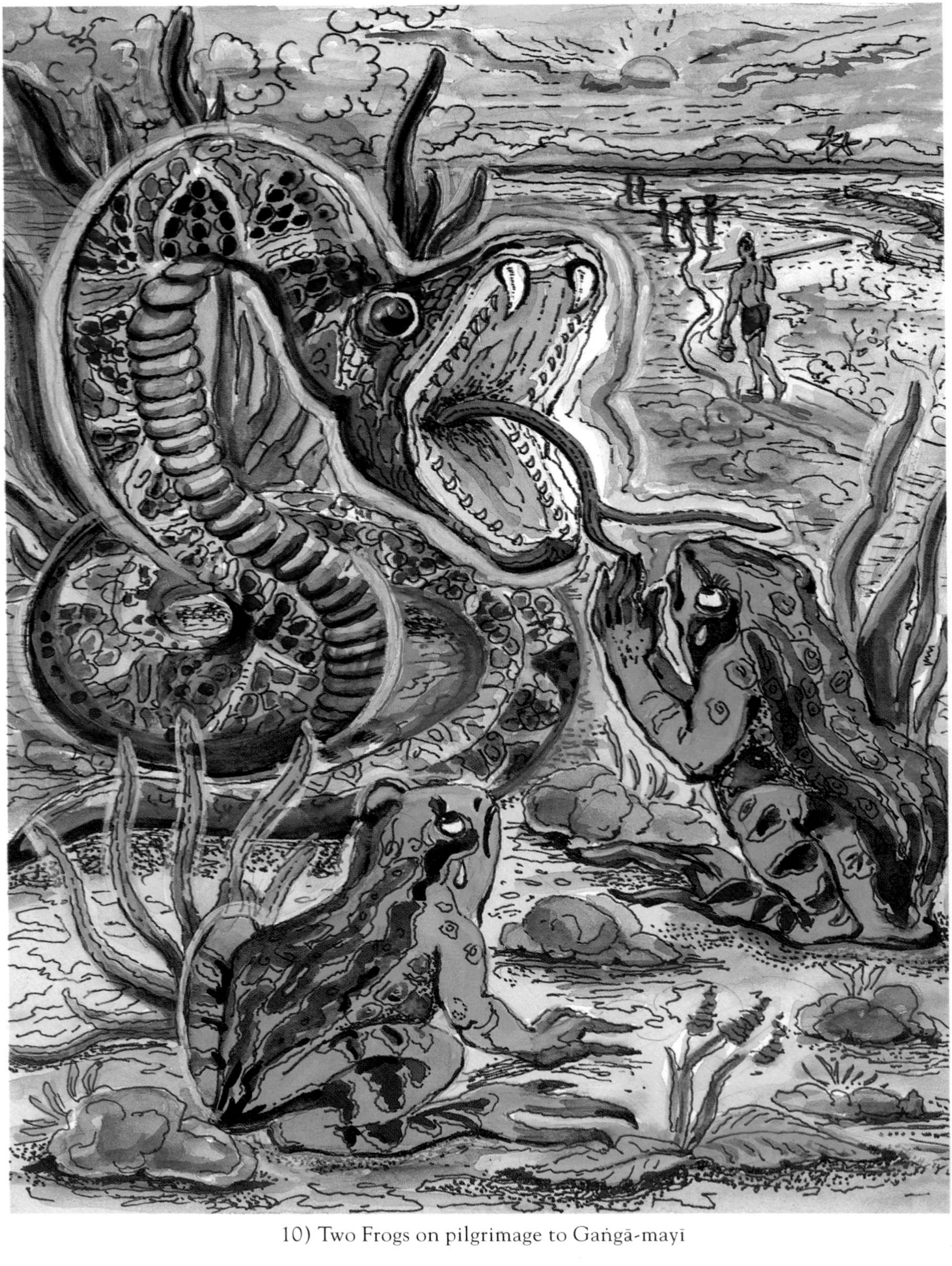

10) Two Frogs on pilgrimage to Gaṅgā-mayī

11) King Śantanu weds Gaṅgā-devī

12) Kṛṣṇa, Balarāma, the Vrajavāsīs, and Gaṅgā-devī

13) The Boatman and Mānasa Gaṅgā

14) Vyāsadeva bathes in Gaṅgā

19) Bhīṣmadeva glorifies his Mother Gaṅgā

21) Śrī Gaṅgā-mātā Gosvāminī

O Mohinī listen

Kalyāṇī begins to weep

The ten Pracetas

Gītā-māhātmyam

overwhelmed with fear, told Vasiṣṭha that it was he himself who had instructed him to cook the meat. With Vasiṣṭha's divine vision, he then understood that the King had been deceived. The King was just about ready to counter-curse his preceptor, when the King's wife, Madāyantī, intervened.

Queen Madāyantī requested the King to curb his anger, since everyone is forced to enjoy the results of one's *karma*. If he wanted to curse his preceptor, Vasiṣṭha, then he would take another birth as a *brahma-rākṣasa*. While being dissuaded by his wife in this way, the King appreciated her instructions and controlled his anger.

With humble submission, on his knees with palms joined in awe and reverence, he submitted, "O dear holy preceptor, please forgive me for everything that has happened, but the truth is that no offense or sin has been committed by me." Upon hearing this, the great sage Vasiṣṭha gave a deep sigh and considered his own thoughtlessness. He then told the King that he himself had not acted properly by thoughtlessly cursing him to become a *rākṣasa*. He then said that the curse would not be permanent, but would last for only twelve years. Then, after being sprinkled by the waters of the Gaṅgā, the King in the form of a *rākṣasa* would reassume his human form and return to rule his kingdom. Afterwards, when his sins were further vanquished through obtainment of perfect knowledge, he would be purely devoted to the service of Lord Hari and thus attain the highest spiritual position. Then Vasiṣṭha Muni returned to his *āsrama*. The King, who was filled with grief and anxiety, took the physical form of a *rākṣasa*.

As a *rākṣasa*, he was always oppressed with great hunger and thirst, and he was very furious. His complexion was like the dark night. He was terrifying in appearance, and he would kill various kinds of beasts, men, reptiles, birds, and even monkeys as he roamed through the forests. One day he was moving about on the banks of the Narmadā River, where he saw a sage and his wife speaking privately. He rushed at the sage with great force and strength, catching him like a hunter catches the fawn of a deer. On seeing her husband struggle in the hands of the *rākṣasa*, the sage's wife joined her palms in reverence and prayer.

The wife of the sage began to pray to the *rākṣasa*, begging him to spare the life of her husband, who was dearer to her than her own life's breath. She even knew that the *rākṣasa* was actually King Mitrasaha himself. She pleaded that a woman without her husband is considered a dead person and then spoke of the anxieties of being a widow at an early age. She had no father or mother, so her husband was her greatest treasure in life. Since the King knew all the *dharmas* (principles of religious morality), he should save her and the infant child in her arms from being deprived of her spouse. "The best charitable gift is that of saving one's life, so please give my husband's life as charity to me," the sage's wife prayed as she fell at the feet of the *rākṣasa*.

After her prayers, the *rākṣasa* devoured her *brāhmaṇa* husband, just like a tiger devours a baby spotted antelope. That chaste wife of the *brāhmaṇa* greatly lamented and angrily cursed the *rākṣasa*, though he had already been cursed. Since the *rākṣasa* had disturbed and interrupted her and her husband during their private talks, she cursed him saying, "The moment you have union with a woman you will die!" The sage's wife was still not happy and continued cursing him, "Since you have eaten my husband, you will permanently remain a *rākṣasa*."

On hearing these two curses, the *rākṣasa* flew into a rage, emitting sparks of fire due to his anger! He exclaimed, "O wicked woman, why have you cursed me twice in vain without proper reason?" The *rākṣasa* could understand being cursed once, but not for the second imprecation. He therefore cursed the sage's wife and child to be *piśācas*, and immediately they assumed ghostly forms. Since they had forms of ghosts, they were always distressed and hungry, and wherever their travels took them they would scream loudly. The *rākṣasa* and the ghosts roamed through the forests together, until they reached the bank of the Narmadā, where other *rākṣasas* were living. In a banyan tree at that place lived one great *brahma-rākṣasa*, who tormented the world. On seeing the other *rākṣasa* and the ghosts, he asked them why they had come and what sins they had committed in order to receive such forms. On hearing the *brahma-rākṣasa's* inquiry, the King and the sage's wife narrated their entire pastimes to him.

King Mitrasaha, in the form of a *rākṣasa*, then asked the *brahma-rākṣasa* about his previous activities. In reply, the *brahma-rākṣasa* happily spoke the following virtuous words, "I was formerly the well known *brāhmaṇa* named Somadatta. I lived in the country of Māgadha (the present districts of Patna and Gayā) and had mastered all the *Vedas*. I was devotedly engaged in the practices of *sanātana-dharma*, but due to great pride and arrogance from my learning, wealth, and youth, I ignored and offended my preceptor. Consequently I was forced to become a *brahma-rākṣasa*. Now I am deprived of all happiness, and I am always hungry and thirsty, even after devouring hundreds and thousands of *brāhmaṇas*. Disrespect and indifference to the preceptor leads one to become a *rākṣasa*. I have indeed experienced this. Therefore no one who is in knowledge should do the same."

The King inquired further because he was extremely curious to know the nature of a preceptor according to the *śāstras*. The *brahma-rākṣasa* said there was many categories of preceptors, all of them worthy of being worshiped and respectfully honored. "One who teaches the *Vedas* and their commentaries, one who instructs moral philosophy, one who initiates, one who explains the sacred *mantras*, one who dispels doubts in the scriptures, one who instructs in religious observances and vows, one who saves one from dangerous situations, one who provides food, the father-in-law, the maternal uncle, the eldest brother, the father—all are preceptors who deserve to be worshiped with great respect."

The King was fully pleased to hear what the *brahma-rākṣasa* had said, but he still wanted to know which preceptor was the most excellent. "Hence, O King, all the demigods and sages declare that the *Purāṇas* (historical supplements to the *Vedas*) constitute the essence of the meaning of all the Vedic passages. The expounder of the *Purāṇas* is therefore the greatest of all preceptors. The intellect of a person who always listens to the *Purāṇas* with great devotion becomes free from all impurities, and he devotes himself to *sanātana-dharma*. By listening to the *Purāṇas*, devotion towards Lord Viṣṇu, is re-established, and one becomes a devotee engaged in the Lord's service. If a person, knowingly or unknowingly, shows contempt and disrespect towards the preceptor, then intelligence, learning, wealth, and all holy observances vanish. O King, if you render service unto the preceptor with great respect, you will be blessed and endowed with devotional service."

Meanwhile, as the *brahma-rākṣasa*, the other *rākṣasa*, and the *piśācas* were discussing these spiritual topics sitting high in the banyan tree, one righteous *brāhmaṇa* from Kaliṅga (the present Orissa/Andhra coast) happened to walk by carrying Gaṅgā water on his shoulders. He was singing the names of Lord Viṣṇu, and the hairs on his body were standing on end. As he approached, the *rākṣasas* were eagerly waiting to enjoy him for their breakfast, but the potency of the *brāhmaṇa*'s recitation of the Lord's names forced the *rākṣasas* to stay at a distance. The *rākṣasas* then realized the purifying potency of the holy names of the Lord, which kept the *brāhmaṇa* safe and fearless of death. They informed the *brāhmaṇa* that even though they had devoured thousands and millions of *brāhmaṇas*, they were now feeling peace and tranquility by hearing the holy names of Acyuta (Viṣṇu). They then humbly requested the Kaliṅga *brāhmaṇa* to absolve them of all their sins by sprinkling Gaṅgā water over them.

The *rākṣasas* continued to glorify the name of Hari, realizing that it is the only remedy for all ills of this worldly existence and the easiest path to liberation. They said, "O excellent *brāhmaṇa*, whatever sacred and holy waters are there on the earth, are not equal in holiness to even a particle of Gaṅgā water. A drop of Gaṅgā water the size of a mustard-seed mixed with a *tulasī* leaf will definitely sanctify twenty-one generations. Hence, O you, who are expert in all scriptures, please protect us, who are embodiments of sinful acts, by bestowing upon us the water of the Gaṅgā."

After hearing this excellent discourse about the holy names and the greatness of Gaṅgā-mayī, that merciful Kaliṅga *brāhmaṇa* sprinkled the waters of Gaṅgā, which were mixed with a *tulasī* leaf, over the *rākṣasas* and *piśācas*. Those *rākṣasas* and *piśācas* then immediately gave up their forms and became as effulgent as demigods. The *brāhmaṇa* lady with her child, as well as her husband, were characterized by the symbols of Lord Viṣṇu (conch, discus, lotus, and mace). Then they glorified and thanked the Kaliṅga *brāhmaṇa*, before going to the abode of Lord Hari, Vaikuṇṭhaloka. King Mitrasaha then regained his royal form, but upon seeing those sinless *brāhmaṇas* being liberated, he began to think deeply. When the King felt extremely distressed and miserable, a mysterious voice spoke the following words, "O highly blessed King, it does not suit you to be miserable. At the end of your enjoyment of pleasures on earth you also will attain the highest liberation. There is no doubt that those who have purified themselves by pious activities and are engaged in devotional service to Lord Hari will reach the highest region of Vaikuṇṭhaloka."

After hearing these words of Bhāratī-devi, the demigoddess of speech, the King began to praise his preceptor, the Kaliṅga *brāhmaṇa*, and Lord Viṣṇu. After offering obeisances to the Kaliṅga *brāhmaṇa*, he immediately proceeded to Vārāṇasī while chanting the names of Viṣṇu. For six months he daily bathed in the Gaṅgā and had *darśana* of Kāśī Viśvanātha before returning to his capital. He was then re-crowned king by his noble preceptor, Vasiṣṭha Muni, and he proceeded to righteously protect his kingdom. Since King Mitrasaha could not beget a child with his queen, Madāyantī, on the King's behalf, Vasiṣṭha begot a son. Ultimately, the excellent King Mitrasaha attained the abode of Lord Viṣṇu.

From the *Śrīmad-Bhāgavatam* (9.9.39) we learn more about the child Vasiṣṭha Muni begot on behalf of King Mitrasaha: "Madāyantī bore the child within the womb for seven years and did not give birth. Therefore Vasiṣṭha struck her abdomen with a stone, and then the child was born. Consequently, the child was known as Aśmaka (the child born of a stone)."

7) The Vultures and Gaṅgā

This short story from the *Skanda Purāṇa* (*Kāsī-khaṇḍa* 28) illustrates Gaṅgā's potency to purify one whose single bone merely touches her waters.

Once there lived a very despicable character named Vāhika, who was addicted to gambling. He had also killed a cow and even kicked his own mother many times! One day Vāhika was killed in the forest by a tiger, and his soul was promptly brought before Lord Yamarāja, the superintendent of death, for final judgement. His sins were read off by the secretary, Citragupta, and there was not even a single virtue to balance any of his sins. He was therefore condemned to reside in several hells for millions of years. Meanwhile, Vāhika's body had been torn up by vultures, and one vulture flew away with a bone of his foot. While in flight, another vulture tried to take the bone away, and in the resulting struggle, the bone was dropped. That bone happened to fall into the River Gaṅgā, and as a result, Vāhika became qualified for liberation. While he was being sent off to hell, a celestial chariot arrived to take him to Vaikuṇṭha, the abode of Lord Viṣṇu.

8) Kālakalpa is blessed by Gaṅgā-mayī's touch

This long yet important narration from the *Padma Purāṇa* (*Kriyā-yoga-sāra-khanda* 7) explains how powerful and merciful a few drops of Gaṅgā water are. As the messengers of Lord Viṣṇu clearly said, "Gaṅgā water is like fire in the forest of sins."

Once, during Tretā-yuga, there lived a *brāhmaṇa* by the name Dharmasva. He was very righteous, peaceful, self-controlled, full of compassion, and a master of the *Vedas*. Not only was he truthful, free from anger, and a kind well-wishing friend to everyone, he was also a sincere devotee of Lord Kesava (Viṣṇu). On one auspicious festival day that best of *brāhmaṇas* went to the bank of Gaṅgā-mayī for taking bath.

After bathing and offering worship to Gaṅgā-mayi, Dharmasva filled a few pitchers with Gaṅgā-jala (Gaṅgā water) to take home with him. But as he proceeded along the road, he witnessed a most unusual event. One merchant named Ratnākara was just returning with his servants from a day of trade. Among his servants was one *brāhmaṇa* named Kālakalpa, who had committed numerous kinds of sins. This Kālakalpa was carrying a strong heavy staff, and when he saw one of Ratnākara's oxen taking rest out of fatigue, he struck the animal with the staff in various ways. Then, being angered by the beating, the ox got up and gouged Kālakalpa's chest and eyes with his sharp horns! Being intelligent and full of compassion, Dharmasva instantly took one *tulasi* leaf, placed it on the dead body, and then sprinkled several drops of Gaṅgā's water on the torn body. Then he continued on his way home.

While walking along chanting the names, "Gaṅgā! Gaṅgā!" the *brāhmaṇa* saw before him thousands upon thousands of Yamadūtas (messengers of Lord Yamarāja). Some of them had their legs cut off, others had their hands cut off, and still others had their ears torn off, while some others had their noses missing! Several also had their tongues missing, teeth broken, hair loosened, and their entire bodies were smeared with blood! Many were naked with their chests pierced, and many fingers and hands were tied up for support! Many others were crying in agony and running in dismay. When Dharmasva saw all of the Yamadūtas in such a horible state, his heart began to tremble and he fearfully became motionless.

After some time he gained enough courage to try and speak sweetly to the Yamadūtas, who appeared like savages. He inquired in wonder as to who had reduced them to such a pitiable condition. In reply, the Yamadūtas began to explain the reason behind the great chastisement they had received. They had been sent by their master, Yamarāja, to bring the sinful Kālakalpa to his court in Yamaloka (planet of Yamarāja) for punishment. They came and bound the most wicked-hearted *brāhmaṇa*, whose death had been caused by that angry ox, when Dharmasva had come walking by, chanting Gaṅgā's name, and had then sprinkled Gaṅgā-jala on the dead body. Thereupon Lord Viṣṇu had immediately sent His messengers, the Viṣṇudūtas, who spoke some angry words, "O noble ones, who are you? Why are you binding and taking this soul? Whose servants are you? Quickly run away from this place, otherwise we shall cut off your heads with our discs!"

Upon hearing these words from the messengers of Lord Viṣṇu, the Yamadūtas appreciated the effulgence and auspicious qualities of the Viṣṇudūtas. They wondered about the identity of these messengers, who wore garlands of *tulasī* blossoms, who had eyes like full grown lotuses, who were strong and handsome, who wore divine garments, and who had four arms holding conches, discs, clubs, and lotuses. They were also curious as to why the Viṣṇudūtas had come to take Kālakalpa. The Viṣṇudūtas had come to take him to Vaikuṇṭhaloka, so they told the Yamadūtas to quickly release Kālakalpa, who was a devotee of Lord Viṣṇu and free from sin.

The messengers of Yamarāja were furious upon hearing that Kālakalpa was sinless! They then re-counted all the numerous bad qualities he possessed and the sinful activities that he had committed. He had murdered thousands of *brāhmaṇas*, he was very ungrateful and evil-hearted, and he had killed cows and friends. He had stolen enough gold to equal the size of Mount Meru, kidnapped other men's wives, and had killed women. He even had incest with his mother and had caused abortions. He resembled a giant *yavana* (meat-eating barbarian) who had committed innumerable great sins, and his actions had not produced anything auspicious. Therefore, the Yamadūtas were firm in their decision to take Kālakalpa to the torturous hell, to be punished by Yamarāja. They could not understand why the Viṣṇudūtas wanted to take him to Vaikuṇṭha.

The messengers of Lord Viṣṇu understood and accepted as truth what the Yamadūtas had said. But they explained that since drops of Gaṅgā-jala had been sprinkled on that sinner, he had become pure and was fit to be taken to the spiritual world. As long as Gaṅgā-jala does not touch a person's body, sins will remain within that person. The Viṣṇudūtas further explained that even by merely remembering the names of Gaṅgā one is freed from all sins since, "Gaṅgā-jala is like fire in the forest of sins," and what to speak if one sees or touches her waters. Therefore, the servants of Yamarāja were warned to return to where they had come from. The Yamadūtas then began to laugh loudly. They could not believe that one is freed from sins by a few drops of water; rather, they explained that even after performing pious activities in millions of births a sinful person is not freed of his sins.

The Viṣṇudūtas quickly replied that the Yamadūtas were unaware of the mercy that is bestowed by Gaṅgā-mayī and that they were offensive and devoid of discrimination. As Lord Viṣṇu is eternal and self-manifested, so is Gaṅgā-mayī. When Lord Viṣṇu is pleased, there is no place for sins to remain. The Yamadūtas were further told that their present forms were due to past sinful lives, and they were questioned as to why they wished to continue performing sinful acts by censuring Gaṅgā-mayī as well as Lord Viṣṇu. Since their decision was wrong, the Viṣṇudūtas prepared to kill all the sinful Yamadūtas with their sharp discs!

They yelled, "Kill these mesengers of Yamarāja! Kill these messengers of Yamarāja!" Then a great battle began, as the joyful servants of Lord Viṣṇu blew their conchshells. The Yamadūtas showered trees, stones, and rocks upon the Viṣṇudūtas, but that only dispersed them temporarily. Then the servants of Lord Viṣṇu threw missiles, javelins, iron clubs, axes, knives, darts, swords, sharp arrows, and maces, as well as their discs. After thousands of Yamadūtas were killed, the remaining wounded servants ran away. Upon seeing their victory, the Viṣṇudūtas blew their conchshells once again. Then they freed the rope-bound Kālakalpa, placed him in an airplane, and they all went to Lord Viṣṇu's abode, Vaikuṇṭhaloka.

After the injured messengers of Yamarāja finished narrating the complete story of Kālakalpa to Dharmasva, they returned to the planet of Lord Yamarāja. Then that pious *brāhmaṇa* Dharmasva returned to the bank of Gaṅgā-mayī and took another bath. With folded palms he praised the greatly merciful Gaṅgā-mayī with the following prayer: "O dear Gaṅgā-devī, O mother of the entire world, you carry the dust from the lovely feet of Lord Kṛṣṇa, the enemy of Kaṁsa, and therefore I salute you, who destroys sins. O mother, who gives happiness to all, you are the best amongst rivers, and your mercy has been sung about by *brāhmaṇas* like Vyāsadeva. I salute your feet, which remove all sins. O daughter of Jahnu, I praise you for liberating the greatly sinful King Saudāsa, who murdered millions of *brāhmaṇas*. By your mercy please allow me to chant the names of the Lord, such as Nārāyaṇa, Acyuta, Janārdana, Kṛṣṇa, Rāma, and your own name also, while entering your waters. O goddess, what is the use of practising austerities, chanting Vedic *mantras*, giving charity, or even performing sacrifices, since by securing only a few drops of your water, the most sinful persons obtain liberation. May the dust from your feet be placed on my head, may my forehead be always decorated with the vertical lines of *tilaka* (auspicious clay markings on the body) made from the sands of your shore, and may I constantly chant your names with love and devotion. May my material attachments be removed by residing on your bank and may I drink and see your waters while remembering your pastimes. The spiritual world is difficult to obtain, but your waters are the staircase to the abode of Lord Viṣṇu. You are the chief of all rivers, for sins and diseases remain in the bodies of those who do not bathe in your waters. O you of uninterrupted flow, foolish people consider you an ordinary river, not knowing that you bestow the highest liberation. Lord Viṣṇu, Śiva, Brahmā, Indra, and others are easily reached by your kindness. Even though Śiva devotedly holds you on his head, he knows only part of your glories. Please nourish and protect me, your humble servant. I salute you, O giver of liberation, but how can I, whose mind is confused and bewildered, properly praise and worship you, the only real mother of this world?"

Suddenly Gaṅgā-devī appeared before Dharmasva with two arms, seated on her crocodile, white as a *kunda* flower, and adorned with all ornaments. He exclaimed, "O Gaṅgā! O Gaṅgā!" and offered her his full obeisances, touching his head to the ground. She smiled and said in a pleasing voice, "O *brāhmaṇa*, please choose a boon." Dharmasva requested that he be able to die in her waters while recollecting and chanting her names. He also asked her to award liberation to anyone who recited the hymn

of praise that he had composed. She replied that she was very pleased by his loving devotion, and that anyone who three times a day recited the prayer composed by him would be awarded the most excellent of all liberations. Then Gaṅgā-devī immediately vanished from the spot. After receiving that boon, the fortunate Dharmasva lived a long life on the beautiful bank of Gaṅgā-mayī. In due course of time, he met a happy death in her pure waters and reached the highest desired goal.

Śrīla Vyāsadeva concluded his narration of this story to the sage Jaimini with the following words, "Gaṅgā-jala, even though touched unintentionally, bears fruit. I do not know what would happen to those who touch it with devotion. I repeatedly say, there is no other holy place like Gaṅgā, since by touching a drop of her water, one attains the highest abode. Those who devotedly touch the waters of this excellent river are freed from the worst kinds of sins and go to the abode of Lord Viṣṇu."

9) Lord Rāmacandra meditates on Gaṅgā-mayī

The sacred place known as Koṭi-tīrtha, described in the following story from the *Skanda Purāṇa* (3.1.27), is presently located inside the famous Rāmeśvaram Temple on Pamban Island in the state of Tamil Nadu.

After killing the great demon Rāvaṇa in Laṅkā, Lord Rāmacandra came to the Gandhamādana Mountain on Setubanda (Rāmeśvaram). The Lord desired to atone for the sin of killing Rāvaṇa, who was a *brāhmaṇa*, so He established a *siva-liṅga* there. Then, desiring some fresh, pure water for bathing the *liṅga*, He dug into the earth with the *koṭi* (tip) of His bow. That tip went deep to Rasātala, one of the seven planets beneath the earth. While pulling His bow out of the ground, Lord Rāmacandra meditated on Gaṅgā-mayī, who gushed out of the hole, thereby fulfilling the Lord's desire to bathe the *liṅga*. Since then this holy place is known as Koṭi-tīrtha.

10) The Two Frogs on pilgrimage to Gaṅgā-mayī

Another narration from the *Padma Purāṇa* (*Kriyā-yoga-sāra-khaṇḍa* 9) glorifies the potency of Gaṅgā, by which one attains liberation simply by chanting her name while on pilgrimage to her shores, even if due to some serious accident one never actually reaches her waters.

At the junction of Tretā and Dvāpara-yugas, a most religious sweet-speaking king named Satyadharma lived with his beautiful highly devoted wife, Vijayā, for seven thousand years on this planet earth. They both happened to die at the same time and due to one grevious sin the Yamadūtas came and bound them and then took them to the abode of Lord Yamarāja. Seeing the couple, Yamarāja asked his secretary Citragupta about their irreligious activities and what punishment awaited them.

Citragupta explained to his lord the story behind the two who were awaiting judgement. Once, when King Satyadharma was in the forest with his entourage, a deer, frightened by some tigers, ran towards the King and his assembly for shelter. Yet when the deer approached the King, he took his sword and struck it down. Due to the cruel act of killing a deer that was seeking shelter, both he and his wife were to be punished.

Yamarāja then ordered that the King and his wife should be sent to the hell named Asi-patravana, where the trees have leaves as sharp as swords, and where each step is literally a painful hell. After living in Asi-patravana for millions of *yugas*, they were both sent to the hell named Vyāghrabhakṣya, where life is always full of difficulties and dangers, since one is constant prey for tigers. Then, after staying in Vyāghrabhakṣya for millions of *yugas* more, they were eventually reborn on earth as two frogs, who remembered their past lives, which only brought them more agony and pain. While living on the bank of a river, they had to eat insects.

On one auspicious day, while some men were on pilgrimage to the banks of the Jāhnavī (Gaṅgā), the two frogs saw them and began to re-collect how sinful they had been and how much pain they continued to suffer. Since the pilgrims were on their way to the Gaṅgā, which frees one of all sins, they thought of following in their footsteps and casting their frog bodies into the river, in order to end their unhappiness. They both agreed and began their pilgrimage while remembering Gaṅgā-mayī, who is the bestower of all auspiciousness. On their way to the Gaṅgā, they came across a hungry, poisonous, fearful serpent, who had not eaten for a long time.

The deadly serpent informed the two frogs that their time of death had arrived, for he was very hungry. The frightened couple then began to address the snake with reverence. They said that there was no need to be afraid of death. Remembering their former births as King Satyadharma and Queen Vijayā, they explained how much they had enjoyed one another, but by harming one deer they had been sent to Yamarāja's court. After a long term of suffering, they now had frog bodies and were on the way to the Gaṅgā to cast their bodies into her waters and thus be relieved of their miseries and sufferings. They told the serpent, "Give up your indiscrimination. How much pleasure would you obtain by devouring us? Since Lord Viṣṇu dwells in everyone's heart, why should there be any enmity? The wise know that they should never harm another living being, for someone who harms another living being factually harms Lord Viṣṇu as well as mother Lakṣmī. The body of a living being is the abode of Lord Viṣṇu. Therefore, one should avoid doing harm to anyone. The act of destroying another's life may give one a great amount of pleasure, but that pleasure is only temporary. An intelligent person is pained to see another living being in agony and happy to see another's happiness. In time, every living being on earth will receive the fruits of their pleasures and pains. Therefore, give up this idea of harming us and give us permission to continue our pilgrimage."

The serpent responded by asking, "Why is it that the supreme creator has created living beings who are prey and other living beings who eat them? You have spoken the truth that one should not harm others, but harm is not involved in the case of prey. Lord Viṣṇu is the truth; there is no doubt about that. He Himself has created the union of the prey and the hunter who eats the prey. Am I really able to kill you without the Lord's sanction? Lord Viṣṇu who created you also protects you, but He who is also all-devouring death kills you today with me as the instrument." Then with great hunger and zest the serpent ate the frogs as they chanted, "Gaṅgā! Gaṅgā!"

The results of chanting Gaṅgā's name while on pilgrimage to her bank are equal to numerous sacrificial fires. Thus the two frogs accumulated great credits of pious activity. Thus Lord Indra, accompanied by other demigods, their consorts, and several other celestial beings, appeared there on foot, carrying paraphernalia for worship. They all glorified the King and the Queen and welcomed them to the heavenly planets. Indra then worshiped the King, before placing him and his wife aboard his chariot. The heavens

were full of music and noise, reflecting the joyous occassion. Lord Indra shared half of his seat with King Satyadharma before departing for Indraloka (Lord Indra's abode). Due to Lord Viṣṇu's compassion, the King and Queen were able to enjoy all pleasures for millions of *yugas*, before boarding another chariot that took them to Vaikuṇṭhaloka.

As Śrīla Vyāsadeva spoke to Jaimini Ṛṣi, he concluded this narration by saying, "O *brāhmaṇa*, I have told you the entire pastime of one who goes on pilgrimage to the Gaṅgā. Philosophers, great sages, and even Nārada Muni all have declared that there are no restrictions regarding time for going to the bank of the Gaṅgā. If a man repeatedly commits sins, then Gaṅgā will not purify him. It is possible to count the number of dust particles on the earth, but one cannot narrate the entire glories of Gaṅgā. After considering all Vedic scriptures, I conclude that a person will receive liberation by taking just one bath in the Gaṅgā. Even if one thinks of Lord Viṣṇu and Gaṅgā, all of his afflictions and anxieties are destroyed. Due to the favor of mother Gaṅgā, she can help one go to the abode of Lord Viṣṇu."

11) King Śāntanu weds Gaṅgā-devi

This famous narration from the *Mahābhārata* (*Sambhava-parva* 46-50) explains why the celestial Gaṅgā-devī took a human birth and the historical events leading up to the birth of the famous great grandfather of the Kurus and the Pāṇḍavas, Bhiṣmadeva.

There was once a king named Mahābhiṣa, who belonged to the Ikṣvāku (Solar) dynasty. He was an excellent king, truthful in speech, and endowed with superior skills and abilities. By performing a thousand Asvamedhas and one hundred Rājasūyas (different forms of sacrifices), he pleased Lord Indra and attained the celestial heavens. One day, all the celestials had gathered to worship Lord Brahmā. King Mahābhiṣa was present along with many great *ṛṣis* and *munis*. Gaṅgā-devī, the queen of rivers, had also come to pay her respects and adorations to Lord Brahmā. At that time, Gaṅgā's beaming white garments were displaced by a strong gust of wind, which exposed her body, causing the celestials to shamefully turn their heads the other way. King Mahābhiṣa, however, rudely stared at Gaṅgā-devī. As a result, Lord Brahmā cursed him, "O wretched one, since you have forgotten yourself at the sight of Gaṅgā-devī, you shall be reborn on earth. You shall attain these celestial regions again only after my wrath has been pacified. Gaṅgā-devī shall also be born in the world of men and be the cause of your sufferings."

Mahābhiṣa thus desired to be born as the son of the great and kind-hearted King Pratīpa. As Gaṅgā-devī went her way, she met the eight Vasus, who were in a great predicament. They explained to her that they had been cursed by Vasiṣṭha Muni. Since one of the Vasus (Dyau) had stolen his cow, Nandinī, they all had to be born on earth. So the Vasus approached Gaṅgā-devī and requested her, "Since you have also been cursed to become a human female, please allow us to be your children. We are not willing to enter the womb of any human female." Gaṅgā-devī replied, "Let it be so, but who is that foremost of men willing to be your father" The Vasus replied that the famous King Pratīpa would have a son by the name of Śāntanu, who would be world famous. Gaṅgā-devī was pleased to hear this and promised to be very loyal and loving to Śāntanu. Since the Vasus were also anxious to return to the celestial regions as soon as possible, they instructed her to immediately throw the new-born babies into the River

Gaṅgā, so that they would be delivered quickly without having to live on earth for a lengthy period. She then answered, "I shall do as you have requested, but in order to keep Śāntanu content and not entirely fruitless, please allow at least one son to live." The Vasus replied, "We shall each contribute an eighth part of our respective energies, resulting in one son, but he will not produce any children on earth. Therefore, that son will be blessed with great energy and strength, but shall be childless." Thus the eight Vasus and Gaṅgā-devī went their ways.

The heroic King Pratīpa was kind-hearted to all living creatures. He performed great austerities at Gaṅgādvāra (Haridvāra). One day, the beautiful Gaṅgā-devī rose from her waters, approached the King, and sat on his right thigh. The King then asked her what she desired. She replied that her desire was to have him as her husband, since he was the foremost of the Kuru dynasty. She continued to say, "O King, to refuse a woman coming of her own accord is never appreciated by the wise. Refuse me not, O virtuous one!" King Pratīpa replied, "O heavenly damsel, you should know that this seat is for one's own children and daughters-in-law. The left thigh is for the wife, but you avoided this. Therefore, O best of woman, please be my daughter-in-law, and I will accept you on behalf of my son."

Gaṅgā-devī agreed to assist the King's son and increase his happiness and she told the King that his son would eventually return to the heavenly planets. She also glorified the celebrated Bharata dynasty and declared that she would maintain the respect of the race, which contained a lineage of most glorified and victorious monarchs on the earth. After everything was understood, Gaṅgā-devī disappeared and King Pratīpa awaited the birth of his son in order to fulfill his promise.

After some time, King Pratīpa of the Kuru race, the strongest amongst the *kṣatriyas*, along with his wife, engaged in austerities for the purpose of obtaining a child. As they both grew old, a boy was born who was none other than Mahābhiṣa. He was named Śāntanu because his father Pratīpa had controlled his passions through penances. When Śāntanu grew into a young man, his father Pratīpa addressed him, "O dear son, some time ago a celestial damsel approached me for your own interest. If you meet this beautiful being who will solicit you for children, then accept her as your wife." King Pratīpa then handed over the kingdom to his son, Śāntanu, and went to the forest to retire.

King Śāntanu possessed great intelligence and was equal to Indra in splendor. One day, while on a hunting trip in the woods, he was walking along the bank of Gaṅgā and came upon an area that was frequently visited by Siddhas and Cāraṇas. There he saw a lovely maiden of unparalleled beauty who reminded him of Lakṣmī, the goddess of fortune. Her limbs appeared faultless, she had pearly teeth, and she was bedecked with celestial ornaments and dressed in fine garments that resembled the beautiful texture of a lotus flower. The young King was surprised and appeared to drink her charming form with his unbroken gaze. The young maiden also observed the King's movements and reactions and felt great affection for him. While they both gazed at each other, King Śāntanu spoke, "O slender, beautiful one, are you from the race of Gandharvas (celestial singers and musicians), Apsarās (celestial dancers), Yakṣas (ghostly servants of Kuvera), Nāgas (celestial serpents), or of human origin? O you of celestial beauty, I propose that you be my wife."

After hearing the soft sweet words of the King, the young maiden replied, "O King, I shall become your wife and obey your orders, but you should not interfere with anything that I do, whether agreeable or disagreeable. I shall remain with you as long as you behave kindly, but as soon as you interfere or speak to me unkindly, I shall leave." The King agreed with everything she proposed. Thus they were married and enjoyed the fullest pleasures with each other. The great monarch became fully satisfied by her beauty, affection, love, music, and dance. In the course of time, seven beautiful, celestial children were born of them, but as soon as they were born, one after another, they were thrown into the river by their mother with the words, "This is for your own benefit." The King was not very pleased to see such conduct, but he remained quiet, afraid of losing his wife. But when the eighth child was born and she was about to throw it into the river, the distressed King addressed her with a desire to save the child, "Do not kill this child! Who are you and why are you killing your own children? Please stop this grievous crime!"

Then the King's wife informed her husband that their allotted time together had come to an end. She explained to him that she was Gaṅgā-devī, Jahnu's daughter, who is worshiped by all great sages in the celestial regions. She further explained that the death of their seven sons was due to an agreement she had made with the eight Vasus, who were thereby freed, from the curse of Vasiṣṭha Muni. She told the King that she would train their last child under strict, rigid vows and then return him to the King. After explaining the full details to the King, she named their son Gaṅgādatta, as well as Devavrata, and then disappeared with the boy to the heavenly regions. Thereafter the King returned to his capital with a sorrowful heart.

As time passed, King Śāntanu ruled and governed his kingdom with great expertise. All the citizens were completely happy since religiosity had increased greatly. He was free from anger and malice and was as handsome as Soma, the demigod of the moon. His splendor was like that of the sun and his valor like that of Vāyu, the demigod of the wind. His wrath was just like that of Yamarāja, the demigod of death, and his patience like that of the earth. During his rule, no deer, boars, birds, or other animals were unnecessarily slain. Truly there was never a king like Śāntanu. Eventually, after enjoying the domestic facilities for many years, he retired to the forest.

Thirty-two years later, while Śāntanu was wandering along the banks of the River Gaṅgā, he observed how the river had changed course and become shallow. Suddenly he saw a well-built youth, appearing like Lord Indra himself, checking the flow of the river with his celestial weapons. The King was very surprised to see someone check the flow of the river and could not realize that the youth was his own son. Since the King had only seen his son for a few moments after he had been born, he was unable to identify him. The youth, however, knew who Śāntanu was, and by his celestial powers of illusion, disappeared from his sight.

Reminded by that sight, the King called out to Gaṅgā-devī, "Please show me that child." Then Gaṅgā assumed a beautiful form, holding the boy with her right hand. Śāntanu, however, was unable to recognise his ex-wife who he had known before. Gaṅgā then spoke, "This is your eighth child who is conversant with all weapons. O King, I have reared him with care. Now you take him. He has studied the *Vedas* from Vasiṣṭha Muni. He is skilled in all weapons and is a mighty bowman, just like Indra in battle.

Both the demigods and demons showered favors on him. All the weapons and power known to Parasurāma are also known to him. O King of superior courage, take this heroic child that was born to you by myself. He is in knowledge of all laws and principles for being a king."

After speaking this, Gaṅgā-devī disappeared and King Śāntanu with his son returned to the capital. Upon summoning all the ministers together, the boy was installed as the heir to the throne. All members of the Bharata dynasty, the Paurava dynasty, and all the other subjects of the kingdom gave him a royal reception. King Śāntanu lived happily with his son, who eventually became the great general, grandfather, and devotee, Bhīṣmadeva.

In the chapter summary to *The Descendants of Ajamīḍha* (*Śrīmad-Bhāgavatam*, Canto 9, Chapter 22), Śrīla Prabhupāda describes other interesting events related with King Śāntanu: "The sons of Pratipa were Devāpi, Śāntanu, and Bāhlika. When Devāpi retired to the forest, his younger brother Śāntanu became the king. Although Śāntanu, being younger, was not eligible to occupy the throne, he disregarded his elder brother. Consequently, there was no rainfall for twelve years. Following the advice of the *brāhmaṇas*, Śāntanu was ready to return the kingdom to Devāpi, but by the intrigue of Śāntanu's minister, Devāpi became unfit to be king. Therefore Śāntanu resumed charge of the kingdom, and rain fell properly during his reign. By mystic power, Devāpi still lives in the village known as Kalāpa-grāma. In this Kali-yuga, when the descendants of Soma known as the Candra-vaṁśa (the lunar dynasty) die out, Devāpi, at the beginning of Satya-yuga, will re-establish the dynasty of the moon. The wife of Śāntanu named Gaṅgā gave birth to Bhīṣma, one of the twelve authorities. Two sons named Citrāṅgada and Vicitravīrya were also born from the womb of Satyavatī by the semen of Śāntanu, and Vyāsadeva was born from Satyavatī by the semen of Parāśara. Vyāsadeva instructed the history of the *Śrīmad-Bhāgavatam* (*Bhāgavata Purāṇa*) to his son Śukadeva. Through the womb of the two wives and the maidservant of Vicitravīrya, Vyāsadeva begot Dhṛtarāṣṭra, Pāṇḍu, and Vidura."

12) Kṛṣṇa, Balarāma, the Vrajavāsīs, and Gaṅgā-devī

These next two stories recount Lord Kṛṣṇa's pastimes near Govardhana Hill, where Gaṅgā-devī manifested as Mānasa-gaṅgā. Afterwards Gaṅgā-devī personally appeared for the *darsana* of Lord Kṛṣṇa and the residents of Vṛndāvana. The following stories have been adopted from *Mādhurya Dhāma*, by H.G. Padmalocana Prabhu.

One day Kṛṣṇa and Balarāma, along with Their cowherd boyfriends, were tending the cows in the pasture grounds near Govardhana Hill. A demon named Vatāsura came there disguised as a calf. With the evil intention of killing Kṛṣṇa, he mingled with the other calves. Kṛṣṇa, however, was aware that this demon was hiding amongst the calves, and He warned Balarāma. The transcendental brothers then sneaked up behind the demon calf. Kṛṣṇa suddenly caught him by his back legs, whipped him around with great force, and threw him up into a nearby tree. The demon gave up his life air, and his dead body fell to the ground. Then all the cowherd boys congratulated Kṛṣṇa.

Because Kṛṣṇa had killed a demon in the shape of a calf, however, the cowherd boys asked him to take bath in the River Gaṅgā in order to purify Himself. Not wanting to leave Vraja, Kṛṣṇa told the cowherd boys that He would call the River Gaṅgā to appear in Vraja. Kṛṣṇa then meditated and from within His mind the River Gaṅgā manifested before Him in the form of Mānasa-gaṅgā. *Mānasa* means "pertaining to the mind". In other words, the River Gaṅgā manifested from the mind of Lord Kṛṣṇa.

On another occassion, Nanda Mahārāja, mother Yasoda, and the residents of Vraja-dhāma were told a story about the glories of the River Gaṅgā. They heard that Garuḍa, the giant bird-carrier of Lord Viṣṇu, had been searching for food, when he came across a large snake. He immediately picked it up and flew away. When they passed over the Gaṅgā, the tail of the snake happened to touch the sacred water and, due to its touch, the snake immediately attained a four-armed form identical to the residents of Vaikuṇṭha. When Garuḍa saw this, he placed that glorious personality on his back and personally carried him to Vaikuṇṭha.

When Mahārāja Nanda and the residents of Vraja-dhāma heard of this event, they all desired to take a dip in the sacred waters of the Gaṅgā. Therefore they all prepared to leave immediately. When Kṛṣṇa saw all of the preparations going on, He inquired from His mother and father as to where they were planning to go. They informed Him they were going on pilgrimage to the River Gaṅgā. Thereupon Kṛṣṇa declared to them that there was no need to go out of Vraja-maṇḍala to visit any holy place, as all of the *tīrthas* throughout the three worlds were present in Vraja-dhāma itself.

The residents of Vṛndāvana thought that Kṛṣṇa was just a small child and did not fully understand these matters, but Lord Kṛṣṇa insisted again and again that there was no necessity for them to go and visit any other holy place. When He saw that they were not convinced, He led them to the shore of Mānasa-gaṅgā in the center of Govardhana Hill. There, in front of all of them, Gaṅgā-devī immediately appeared in her personified form and offered prayers to the Lord. When the residents of Vṛndāvana saw Gaṅgā-devī, they offered their respectful obeisances to her. They all took their baths in her sacred waters and offered her ghee-lamps.

This pastime took place on the dark moon night in the month of Kārtika. Up to the present time, that day is celebrated throughout India as Dīpāvalī, when people in every home light lamps with which they decorate their rooftops. Also, to this day, thousands of people gather at Mānasa-gaṅgā with small lamps in clay cups and float them on the sacred waters, thus lighting up the whole lake.

13) The Boatman and Mānasa-gaṅgā

Once in the evening, Śrīmatī Rādhārāṇī along with Her girlfriends arrived on the sandy banks of Mānasa-gaṅgā. They carried with them yogurt pots filled with various kinds of milk preparations. They wanted to cross the water, but they saw that there was only one very old boat in the care of a young boy with a peacock feather in His hair. When they inquired from Him if He would take them to the other bank, He agreed and inquired what His payment would be. They argued for some time over the fare and eventually settled the payment in sweets and butter. Thereafter, they got into the boat and the boatman started to row. After rowing for some distance, however, He stopped and just sat there. Śrīmatī Rādhārāṇī then had one of Her friends inquire from Him why He had stopped. He informed them that He was tired and hungry and that He could not go any further unless they fed Him. At first they refused, but when they saw that He was not going to take them, they relented and offered their pots of milk products to Him. After completely emptying their pots, He informed them that He was full and would have to take a little nap. Then He asked for two of them to massage His arms and two of them His legs. In reply to this, the friends of Rādhārāṇī told Him that certainly two of them would take His legs and two His arms and then throw Him overboard unless He started to row immediately.

On hearing these words, He began to row again. But after a little while, He stopped, and they again inquired from Him what was the problem. He told them that the boat was very old and water was beginning to come in because the load was too heavy. He said that unless they threw some of the articles overboard, they would certainly all drown. Eventually they all agreed and threw overboard all of their yogurt pots. When all of the yogurt pots had disappeared into the waters, He again told them that the weight was too much and that now they would have to throw all of their jewellery into the water. At first they refused, but when they saw that boat was still sinking, Rādhārāṇī told her friends to throw their jewellery overboard. But even after this, the boat still appeared to be sinking. So He then informed them that they would have to remove all of their clothing and throw it overboard. Upon hearing this, the cowherd girls told Him that they would throw Him overboad and solve the excess weight problem if He did not start to row. Hearing this, He again started to row.

After a short time, many dark clouds started to gather in the sky, the wind started to blow, and the waves became agitated. He could see that the cowherd girls, headed by Rādhārāṇī, were frightened, and to add to their fears, He started to rock the boat. At that point Rādhārāṇī became so frightened, thinking She might fall into the water, that she put her arms around the boatman. As soon as She did this, She realized that the boatman was in fact Her beloved Śyāmasundara (Kṛṣṇa). At that time the clouds cleared, the winds and waves became calm, and the moon came out. When the cowherd girls saw this scene, with Śrīmatī Rādhārāṇī embracing the boatman, they inquired from Her what the meaning of this was. In answer to their questions, She pulled Kṛṣṇa's flute out from under His covering cloth. When they saw the flute, they could immediately understand that the boatman was Kṛṣṇa Himself in disguise. Kṛṣṇa informed them that He had performed this pastime just so He could get the *darśana* of Śrīmatī Rādhārāṇī.

Thereafter they spent many hours boating from island to island in the Mānasa-gaṅgā. This pastime is known as Nauka-vihara, and it is described in Jīva Gosvāmī's *Gopāla-campu.*

14) Vyāsadeva bathes in Gaṅgā

In the material universal that we live, there is a continuous cycle of four *yugas*: Satya-yuga, Tretā-yuga, Dvāpara-yuga, and Kali-yuga. As the ages proceed from Satya to Kali, religion and the good qualities of mankind gradually diminish. The present age in which we live is Kali-yuga, the age of quarrel and hypocrisy, which began five thousand years ago and lasts a total of 432,000 years. According to the Vedic literatures, there is only one process of self-realization effective in this bleak age: chanting the holy names of Lord Kṛṣṇa. The *Viṣṇu Purāṇa* (6.3) reveals the following narration of Parāśara Muni, the father of Vyāsadeva, to Maitreya Muni, explaining why Kali-yuga is actually the best of all ages.

Parāśara Muni said, "Once upon a time a dispute arose amongst the great sages regarding which *yuga* yields the greatest results for the least religious performances and who is most qualified for executing those activities. In order to reach a conclusion, they went to visit my son, Vyāsadeva. They found the great literary incarnation of the Lord half

immersed in the waters of the Gaṅgā. While awaiting the completion of his purification rites, the sages remained on the banks of the sacred stream under the shelter of a grove of trees. As my son plunged down into the water and again rose up from it, the sages heard him exclaim, 'All glories to the age of Kali!' Again he dived under, and again rising, he exclaimed, 'All glories to the *śūdras*, who are happy!' Again he sank down, and as he once more emerged from the waters of Gaṅgā, they heard him say, 'All glories to the women, who are also happy and even more fortunate!'

"After this, my son finished his bath and welcomed the sages as they approached him. He then inquired, 'On what account have you come to me?' They replied, 'We came to you to clear our doubts, but after hearing you say, 'All glories to Kali-yuga! All glories to the *śūdras*! All glories to the women!' we now desire to know why you said this and why you called them happy. Then, we will reveal the question that is on our minds.'

"Being thus addressed by the sages, Vyāsadeva smiled and said to them, 'O great sages, please listen why I uttered the words, "All glories! All glories!" The results obtained by practicing austerities, self-control, meditation, and purity for ten years in Satya-yuga, for one year in Tretā-yuga, or for one month in Dvāpara-yuga are obtained in one day and night in Kali-yuga. Therefore, I exclaimed, 'Excellent is the age of Kali!' The reward that a person obtains in Satya by meditation, in Tretā by sacrifice, in Dvāpara by worship is easily attained in Kali by merely reciting the name of Lord Kṛṣṇa.'

"The sages then said to Vyāsadeva, 'The question we intended to ask has already been answered in your reply to our preceding inquiry.' On hearing this, Vyāsadeva laughed and said to the sages, 'I preceived the questions you intended to ask. In Kali-yuga, duty is discharged with very little trouble by mortals, whose numerous faults are washed away by their individual pious activites; by *śūdras*, simply by attentively serving the twice-born *brāhmaṇas*; and by women, through the slight effort of obeying their husbands. Therefore O sages, I expressed my admiration thrice for their happiness.'

"The sages then glorified Śrīla Vyāsadeva and after offering him their obeisances, they departed as they came."

15) Gaṅgā in the *Mahābhārata*

Throughout the great epic *Mahābhārata*, numerous episodes between the Pāṇḍavas and the Kauravas took place near the Gaṅgā, on the banks of the Gaṅgā, or actually in the Gaṅgā, particularly since the city of Hastināpura was located on her bank. From the very beginning of the *Mahābhārata*, when King Śāntanu married Gaṅgā-devī, up to when King Dhṛtarāṣṭra attained liberation on the bank of the Gaṅgā at Saptasrota (Gaṅgādvāra), mother Gaṅgā has served an important and vital role in this divine history of ancient India.

Throughout the *Mahābhārata* there are several narrations that exemplify mother Gaṅgā's contribution to this divine land. The Pāṇḍavas never went any place where the Gaṅgā or the holy names of the Lord were absent. The following are two short incidents from the *Mahābhārata* that are related with the Gaṅgā. Additional narrations from the *Mahābhārata* in which Gaṅgā serves in various roles will follow.

In the *Ādi-parva* it is stated: "On another day, Droṇācārya and his pupils went to the Gaṅgā to bathe in the sacred waters. When Droṇa entered the river, a crocodile seized him by the thigh. Although capable of killing the crocodile, he called to his students, 'Please kill this animal and rescue me!' Instantly, Arjuna released five arrows that struck the crocodile. This happened so fast that the others stood looking dumbfounded. The crocodile released Droṇa and died within the waters. When Droṇa emerged from the river, he embraced Arjuna and then pronounced blessings upon him by saying, 'There will never be an archer greater than yourself. You will never be defeated by any enemy, and your achievements will be recorded in the history of the world."

Again, from the *Ādi-parva*: "Since King Dhṛtarāṣṭra, as well as his son Duryodhana, were envious that the Pāṇḍavas were growing in power, influence, and popularity, they made a plan to send the Pāṇḍavas to the beautiful town of Vāraṇāvata on the pretext of a scenic visit. Then they summoned their counselor Purocana and ordered him to construct a residence for the Pāṇḍavas—a palace made of resin, oil, shellac, and other flammable materials.

"When the Pāṇḍavas arrived in Vāraṇāvata and inspected the newly built palace, Yudhiṣṭhira said to Bhīma, 'This house is certainly made of flamable materials. Our adversaries, by the aid of trusted artisans, have built this house with hemp, straw, and bamboos, all soaked in ghee. The wicked Purocana is also staying in this palace to burn us to death when we least expect it. Our well-wishing uncle Vidura has warned me that Duryodhana has constructed this house for our death.'

"After some time one of Vidura's friends, who was well skilled in excavation, arrived at the palace of the Pāṇḍavas. In private, he said, 'I have been sent to excavate a tunnel under this house. Purocana will set fire to this palace on the fourteenth day of the dark moon.' Yudhiṣṭhira replied, 'This large mansion has been made of inflammable materials and there are few doors. I want you to build a tunnel beginning from the center of the house and ending by the side of the River Gaṅgā.'

"After the tunnel had been built and the Pāṇḍavas had been living in Vāraṇāvata for one full year, Yudhiṣṭhira planned a festival in the palace. At the end of the festival all of the invited guests left, but Purocana had become so drunk that he lay on the floor unconscious. Suddenly a violent wind began to blow outside, and Yudhiṣṭhira instructed Bhīma to set fire to the house. Soon the whole mansion was ablaze, as the Pāṇḍavas and their mother escaped through the tunnel excavated by the miner. They came out near the bank of the Gaṅgā, and as they looked back, they could see in the distance the palace of shellac high in flames."

16) Bhīma's pastime in the Gaṅgā

The following narration from the *Mahābhārata*, *Ādi-parva*, explains why the Pāṇḍava Bhīma had the vitality of ten thousand elephants.

"The wicked Duryodhana built an opulent house on the bank of Gaṅgā. Not understanding Duryodhana's evil intentions, the Pāṇḍavas accompanied Dhṛtarāṣṭra's sons to the bank of Gaṅgā and inspected the newly constructed palace. Then they all sat down to a feast before swimming. Duryodhana brought Bhīma a cake filled with enough poison to kill one hundred men. After the feast, the boys began to play in the water, but Bhīma became fatigued from the poison so he came out of the water and laid down on the bank. Seizing this opportunity, Duryodhana and some of his brothers bound him with ropes and threw him into the Gaṅgā. Bhīma thus sank to the bottom of the river where the Nāga (snake) kingdom is situated. Thousands of Nāgas there began to bite him, and the poison from the cake was neutralized by the serpent's venom.

"On regaining consciousness, Bhīma broke his bonds and began killing the snakes that were biting him. The rest of the snakes

fled to their leader, Vāsuki, telling him about the events that had taken place. Vāsuki happened to be related to Bhīma through the wind-god, Vāyu, so upon hearing that Bhīma was present in his kingdom, he went to the spot and embraced him. Bhīma then told Vāsuki about the sinister plot to kill him with the poisoned cake. Wanting to protect him from future attacks, Vāsuki offered Bhīma eight bowls of nectar, which empowered a person with the strength of ten thousand elephants. Bhīma drank the first bowl in one breath, and after drinking all eight, he laid down on a bed prepared by the serpents.

"After eight days, Bhīma awoke from his deep sleep. The Nāgas glorified him and tended to his needs. 'O greatly powerful Bhīma,' they said, 'you are filled with the nectar of the heavenly gods. This will give you the vitality of ten thousand elephants. No one will be able to defeat you in battle. You must now return home, for your mother is in great anxiety over your absence.' The Nāgas then dressed him in fine silks and ornaments and returned him to the palace on the bank of Gaṅgā."

17) Karṇa afloat in the River Gaṅgā

In the *Udyoga-parva*, Karṇa's mother, Kuntī, affectionately tries to persuade him to become friends with his 'unknown' younger brother, Arjuna, but Karṇa resolutely states: "Either I will kill Arjuna, or Arjuna will kill me!"

"Just after Lord Kṛṣṇa spoke to Karṇa about the origin of his birth, the saintly Vidura spoke with Kuntī about the hopelessness of obtaining peace between the Kauravas and the Pāṇḍavas. Understanding the desperate situation, Kuntī decided to speak to Karṇa herself and disclose to him the fact that he was her first son. Kuntī thus went to the bank of the Gaṅgā to petition her son with maternal affection.

"Having reached the bank of the sacred Gaṅgā, Kuntī saw her son, Karṇa, sitting in meditation and performing his daily worship. She stayed behind him while he completed his prayers. When Karṇa felt the warmth of the sun's rays, he turned around and saw Kuntī standing between himself and the sun. He was surprised to see such a woman, and he greeted her with joined palms. He said, 'I am Karṇa, the son of Rādhā and Adhiratha. For what reason have you come here? Tell me what I can offer you, for I am a bestower of charity.' Kuntī then disclosed to Karṇa the truth of his birth, 'You are not actually the son of Rādhā and Adhiratha. Your birth is divine. You are not a *sūta* by birth. Your real father is Sūryadeva, the sun-god, whom you daily worship, and I am your mother.' Kuntī was standing in the rays of the sun, and Karṇa could not distinguish who she was. He therefore questioned her, 'Who are you?'

"'I am Kuntī, the mother of the Pāṇḍavas,' Kuntī replied. 'You are my first born son, before my marriage to Pāṇḍu. Because of disgrace associated with begetting a child while not married, I set you afloat in the River Gaṅgā. The Pāṇḍavas are my other sons. It is time to take your place next to your brothers and, after conquering the Kurus, enthrone yourself as king. Today, you can embrace your younger brother, Arjuna, and become the best of friends. If both of you are united, there is nothing in this world that you will not accomplish.' After Kuntī had spoken, the voice of the sun-god confirmed what she had said by saying, 'The words spoken by Pṛthā (Kuntī) are indeed true. O Karṇa, my son, act according to the instructions of your real mother. O tiger among men, you will infinitely prosper if you take your stand with the pious sons of Pāṇḍu.'

"After Karṇa heard the advice of his real mother and father, he did not waver from his position but replied, 'O blessed lady, I cannot agree with your statement, that to obey your command is my highest duty. O mother, you abandoned me as soon as I was born. This stain on my birth, being recognized as the son of a *sūta*, has darkened my achievements. I could have died in the River Gaṅgā after you set me afloat. If, indeed, I am *kṣatriya*, then I have been deprived of these rights by your neglect. What enemy could have done me a greater injury? Instead of having my birth rites performed, you abandoned me, and now, today, you would have me follow your command? Before today you never sought my welfare as my mother. Why are you now soliciting me except to benefit yourself? If I take up the Pāṇḍava's cause, everyone will think I am a traitor. If I assist your sons, then everyone will consider that I have left aside my friendship with Duryodhana for my personal fame. I cannot obey your instructions, however favorable they may be. But your request will not prove fruitless. Though I am able to kill all your sons except Arjuna, I promise that I will not do so. Arjuna, alone, I will fight. By killing him or being killed by him, I will achieve lasting fame. O blessed lady, the number of your sons will always remain not less than five. Either I will kill Arjuna, or Arjuna will kill me.'

"Hearing this promise, Kuntī, who was trembling from these true statements, embraced her son Karṇa. Yet he remained unmoved by her maternal emotions. She then requested him, 'O my son, you have granted the assurance of safety to four of your brothers. Please remember this promise at the time of the battle.' Karṇa replied, 'It shall be so.' Kuntī then left her son on the bank of the Gaṅgā and returned to Hastināpura."

18) Gaṅgā sends Swans to Bhīṣma

The *Bhīṣma-parva* recounts the pastime of how the celestial and auspicious water provided by his mother, Gaṅgā, gave Bhīṣmadeva the ability to control his life airs.

On the tenth day of the battle of Kurukṣetra, Arjuna, with the help of Sikhaṇḍī, completely pierced the great warrior Bhīṣma's body with arrows. There was not even a two-fingered breadth of space in his body without an arrow. Being thus pierced, Bhīṣma fell off his chariot, and the arrows that pierced him supported his body like a bed. At that time, Bhīṣma looked divine as the clouds poured a cool shower and the earth trembled. Seeing her son fallen from the chariot, Gaṅgā-devī sent *ṛṣis* from the heavenly realm in the form of swans. Circumambulating him, they requested him not to leave his body until the sun entered its northern course. He replied to them, "I will never pass from this world while the sun is in its southern course. I will proceed from this world only when the sun changes to its northern passage." The celestial swans then returned to the heavens and informed Gaṅgā-devī of her son's decision.

Then, upon Bhīṣma's request, Arjuna added more arrows under his head for support as a pillow. All the warriors present in the battle assembled around Bhīṣma to pay their respects to him. Bhīṣma felt very thirsty, so pots of cool water were brought to satisfy his thirst, but Bhīṣma refused. Arjuna then invoked the *parjanya* weapon and shot it into the earth near Bhīṣma. From that spot arose a jet of water, pure, auspicious, cool Gaṅgā-jala, resembling nectar with its celestial scent and taste. After drinking that ambrosial water, he controlled his life airs and waited for the sun to enter its northern course before leaving his body.

At the time of Bhīṣma's fall, the sun was in the south, which according to the scriptures is an inauspicious time to die. But Bhīṣma was able to delay his death because his father, Śāntanu, had blessed him with the words, "Death will approach you only when you wish to die." While the great Bhīṣmadeva was lying down on the bed of arrows at the close of the Battle of Kurukṣetra, he imparted instructions to King Yudhiṣṭhira on the subject of occupational duties. His passing away attracted the attention of all the contemporary elites; all of them assembled there to show their feelings of love, respect, and affection for the great soul Bhīṣma. The Supreme Personality of Godhead, Lord Śrī Kṛṣṇa, arrived driving Arjuna's chariot. Bhīṣma's brother, Vyāsadeva, was also present, as were all the Pāṇḍavas.

19) Bhīṣmadeva glorifies his Mother Gaṅgā

During his last discourse to King Yudhiṣṭhira, as recorded in the *Anusāsana-parva*, Bhīṣmadeva described the glories and greatness of his mother, Gaṅgā. Afterwards, Gaṅgā-devī received soothing and comforting words from Lord Kṛṣṇa upon learning of her son's death.

King Yudhiṣṭhira asked Bhīṣmadeva, "Which countries, which provinces, which *āśramas*, which mountains, and which rivers are the foremost in sanctity?" The great warrior replied by citing the following conversation between a *brāhmaṇa* and a *ṛṣi*. The *ṛṣi* said, "Those countries, provinces, *āśramas*, and mountains should be regarded as foremost in sanctity through which or by the side of which the most sacred of all rivers, Gaṅgā, flows. The result that a living entity is capable of attaining by austerities, by *brahmācārya* (celibacy), by sacrifice, or by practising renunciation is sure to be attained simply by living on the side of the Gaṅgā and bathing in her sacred waters. Those who plunge everyday into the sacred waters of Gaṅgā become equals with the great *munis*. Those who are devoid of humility and modest behavior and who are exceedingly sinful become righteous and good by having *darśana* of Gaṅgā. Gaṅgā is held to be identical with Pṛśni, the mother of Lord Viṣṇu. She is identical with the word of speech and is the embodiment of auspiciousness and prosperity. She is always ready to extend her mercy, and she is the best refuge for all creatures. Gaṅgā always bestows her grace upon those who are devoted to her with a humble heart. She also bestows every kind of happiness on such devotees. I pray that the greatly blessed Gaṅgā may always inspire my heart and mind with the qualities of righteousness."

King Yudhiṣṭhira, his brothers, and the assembled personages were all greatly pleased to hear his discourse, which was full of praise for Gaṅgā-mātā. Then Bhīṣma begged Lord Kṛṣṇa for His permission to leave this world. When the Lord consented, Bhīṣma's restrained life breath rose, pierced through his head, and, after rising high in the sky, became invisible. All the denizens of the upper planetary systems showered flowers upon the body of Bhīṣma. The Pāṇḍavas then took his body in a chariot to the bank of the River Bhāgīrathī (Gaṅgā), where they cremated the body and offered oblations of water unto Bhīṣma. Then goddess Gaṅgā rose from the river. She was weeping in distress due to the death of her son, Bhīṣma. Lord Kṛṣṇa consoled her with many soothing words and reminded her that Bhīṣma, who was one of the eight Vasus, had returned to heaven. After duly honoring Gaṅgā-devī, all those present received her permission to depart.

20) The Kuru Dynasty and Bhāgīrathī Gaṅgā

In this last narration from the *Mahābhārata* (*Āśrama-vasika-parva* 3-38), we hear of how Vidura left his body by entering the body of Yudhiṣṭhira and about the pastime of Dhṛtarāṣṭra, Gāndhārī, and Kuntī leaving their bodies in a forest fire at Gaṅgādvāra.

While regretting his foolish activities that lead to the battle of Kurukṣetra, fifteen years before, Dhṛtarāṣṭra requested King Yudhiṣṭhira's permission to leave for the forest with Gāndhārī to devote the rest of life to penances and austerities. On the advice of Kṛpa, Vidura, and Vyāsadeva, Yudhiṣṭhira reluctantly agreed. After taking permission from the residents of the kingdom and giving charity to the *brāhmaṇas* and *ṛṣis*, Dhṛtarāṣṭra, along with Gāndhārī, Vidura, and Sañjaya, prepared to depart for the forest. Kuntī, the mother of the Pāṇḍavas, persuaded her sons to allow her to join them. After performing some ceremonies on the banks of the Bhāgīrathī, which flowed by their capital of Hastināpura, they proceeded towards the forest in Kurukṣetra. There they took initiation from Vyāsadeva into the *vānaprastha* order of life. They then dwelt on the banks of the Yamunā, at the *āśrama* of Śatayūpa, the King of Kekaya, who was also in the *vānaprastha* order.

The Pāṇḍavas were already much aggrieved by the loss of their kinsmen and friends in the battle of Kurukṣetra. Therefore they were soon unable to bear separation from their mother and relatives, so they set out for Kurukṣetra with the other members of the Kuru dynasty. There they were once again united with the Kuru elders. Vidura, however, remained at a distance. At an opportune time, Yudhiṣṭhira went alone to meet him and found him leaning on a tree. As soon as Yudhiṣṭhira came before him, Vidura, with the aid of *yogic* power, united his senses and life breath and entered Yudhiṣṭhira's body, leaving behind his own body. The reason for this was that Vidura and Yudhiṣṭhira were both expansions of Yamarāja. Yudhiṣṭhira then returned to the *āśrama* and gave charity to all the *brāhmaṇas* and sages present there.

Amidst the festive gathering, everyone remembered those who had perished at the battle of Kurukṣetra, and thus lamentations soon filled the air. Vyāsadeva then directed them to the bank of the Bhāgīrathī. Fulfilling the request of Kuntī, Vyāsadeva, by his mystic potency, made all the warriors who had fallen in battle reappear from the waters of the Bhāgīrathī. Those persons who had died on the battlefield had thereafter attained heaven, where they became freed of all vices and pure in heart. Dhṛtarāṣṭra and Gāndhārī were provided with special vision so that they could also behold their sons, relatives, and others. Being merciful, Vyāsadeva said, "Those ladies who wish to join their husbands in their abodes should plunge quickly into the River Bhāgīrathī." When they heard this, the ladies immediately took permission from the elders present there, entered the river, and were reunited with their respective husbands. Dhṛtarāṣṭra, along with Yudhiṣṭhira and his entourage, then returned to the *āśrama* of Śatayūpa, near Kurukṣetra. With great difficulty, Dhṛtarāṣṭra persuaded the Pāṇḍavas and others to return to Hastināpura.

One day, two years later, Nārada Muni came to see King Yudhiṣṭhira, who offered Nārada Muni a seat and duly worshiped him. After Nārada Muni had rested awhile, the King inquired about his welfare and his travels. Nārada replied that he had been visiting all the holy places. Yudhiṣṭhira then earnestly inquired about his parents. Nārada

replied, "After your return from Kurukṣetra, Dhṛtarāṣṭra and the others proceeded to Gaṅgādvāra. Guided by Sañjaya and Kuntī, they all performed severe penances in the forest there. The sacrificial fire they used to perform their rites was abandoned and thrown in one corner of the woods, where it soon produced a huge conflagration. Your parents, who were weak from fasting, asked Sañjaya to escape. They then sat facing east and absorbed themselves in meditation, as the fire engulfed them and liberated them from their bodies. In this way, Dhṛtarāṣṭra, Gāndhārī, and Kuntī left this world. After this happened, Sañjaya left for the Himālayas."

On hearing this, everyone lamented very pitifully. All the Pāṇḍavas then went to the bank of the Gaṅgā and offered oblations to the departed souls. They also arranged for the proper cremation of the bodies of their parents at Gaṅgādvāra. On the twelveth day, after performing *srāddha* (anniversary ceremony for parents and grandparents), King Yudhiṣṭhira gave abundant gifts in charity to everyone and returned to his capital, where he continued ruling his kingdom.

There is a similar narration in the *Śrīmad-Bhāgavatam*, which gives a different account regarding how King Dhṛtarāṣṭra and Vidura left the planet. An account of this narration is found in Book Two, Chaper Three: *Travels With Gaṅgā*, under section 4:Gaṅgādvāra, *Mahātmā Vidura*.

21) Śrī Gaṅgā-mātā Gosvāminī

The following narration is adapted from *Gaura-pāriṣada-caritāvali* (*The Lives of the Saints*) by H.H. Bhakti Vidhāna Mahāyogi Swami.

Some four hundred years ago in the state of Bengal, there was a king named Naresh Nārāyaṇa. He had a daughter named Śacī-devī, who was a great devotee of the Lord Kṛṣṇa. Basic education did not attract her attention, for she was always completely immersed in studying the scriptures. As Śacī-devī came to age, her beauty charmed all the young boys, but she had no attraction for any of them. She was always absorbed in thoughts of Śrī Madana-gopāla (Kṛṣṇa). The King and Queen tried to arrange her marriage, but Śacī-devī told her parents, "I will not marry a mortal man born in this world of death." As time passed, they failed to marry Śacī-devī and eventually grew old and died.

After they died, the royal succession fell on Śacī-devī, so she duly accepted the responsibilities of governing the kingdom. One day, Śacī-devī decided to travel to the holy places of pilgrimage, so she appointed some relatives to govern the kingdom. Although she wandered here and there, she could not find satisfaction in her heart. She therefore decided to search for a bona fide spiritual master and traveled to Jagannātha Purī for that purpose. After having *darśana* of Lord Jagannātha one day, she got an inspiration to go to Vṛndāvana.

In Vṛndāvana, she had the good fortune of meeting a great devotee of Śrī Caitanya Mahāprabhu by the name of Haridāsa Paṇḍita Gosvāmī, who was a disciple of Ananta Ācārya. Upon seeing his spiritual power and austerity, Śacī-devī became filled with ecstasy. After several days, Haridāsa Paṇḍita gave shelter to Śacī-devī. She fell at his lotus feet with pouring tears and prayed for his mercy.

In order to test Śacī-devī's qualifications as a disciple, Haridāsa Paṇḍita said, "It is not possible for the daughter of a king to stay in Vṛndāvana and live as a poor devotee, constantly absorbed in *bhajana* (worship) with little to eat and no comforts. It will be better if you return to your kingdom and worship the Lord in your home." Yet she paid no attention to his words of discouragement. With fierce determination, renunciation, and austerity, she continued with her *bhajana*. Step by step, she eventually renounced her opulent dress and fine ornaments.

One day, Haridāsa Paṇḍita said to Śacī-devī, "If you like, you may give up all pride and fear by wandering throughout Vraja-maṇḍala and begging from place to place as a renounced devotee. You have my blessings." Upon hearing these words of her *guru*, Śacī-devī was overwhelmed. Freed from all false ego and her body covered only with rags, she went house to house, begging alms in the fashion of a bumblebee, who takes only a little pollen from each flower. In this way, she showed the intense renunciation and austerity of a highly advanced devotee. All the devotees of Vṛndāvana were astonished by her severe renunciation.

Gradually, Śacī-devī's body became frail and weak. Physically exhausted from her diligent service, she would sleep on the banks of the Yamunā River and rise early to cleanse the Lord's temple. Everyday she would circumambulate some holy places, observe the worship of the Deity, and listen to lectures on *Śrīmad-Bhāgavatam*. Seeing the intense renunciation of Śacī-devī, Haridāsa Paṇḍita's heart was filled with pity, and his mercy towards her increased. He smiled and said to her, "You are a princess; yet by seeing the renunication and austerity in your firm determination to worship Lord Kṛṣṇa, I have become supremely happy. Soon I shall give you initiation into the *mantra*."

Haridāsa Paṇḍita had one disciple named Lakṣmīpriyā, who used to chant three hundred thousand names of Lord Kṛṣṇa daily. When she arrived in Vṛndāvana one day, Haridāsa Paṇḍita instructed her to go and live with Śacī-devī, who was performing her daily *bhajana* on the banks of Rādhā-kuṇḍa. Thereafter Śacī-devī and Lakṣmīpriyā would daily circumambulate Govardhana Hill together. In this way, along with Lakṣmīpriyā, Śacī-devī continued her worship of Lord Kṛṣṇa with great determination.

One day, Haridāsa Paṇḍita instructed Śacī-devī to return to Jagannātha Purī and preach what she had learned of Lord Caitanya's teachings, since most of the personal associates of the Lord had returned to the spiritual world. On the order of her *guru*, Śacī-devī left Vṛndāvana and returned to Jagannātha Purī. Upon arriving, Śacī-devī went to Sārvabhauma Bhaṭṭācārya's old house, which was dilapidated and crumbling. There she engaged in performing *bhajana* and giving *Śrīmad-Bhāgavatam* classes. She also re-established the worship of the Dāmodara Śalagrāma that was once worshiped by Sārvabhauma. In a short time, her *Śrīmad-Bhāgavatam* classes became very famous, with faithful devotees daily coming from miles around in order to hear her wonderful explanations.

One day, the King of Jagannātha Purī, Mukunda Deva, came to hear *Śrīmad-Bhāgavatam* from Śacī-devī. Upon hearing her original explanations of the *Bhāgavatam*, the King was completely astounded. Out of appreciation for her devotion to Lord Kṛṣṇa, the King felt inspired to make a nice offering to Śacī-devī. That night the King had a wonderful dream in which Lord Jagannātha ordered him, "Offer Śacī-devī a place on the banks of the Gaṅgā (Śveta Gaṅgā)."* The next day, the King went to Śacī-devī and explained to her the instruction he had received from Lord Jagannātha to construct a place for her by the Gaṅgā. Śacī-devī did not want to accept any sort of wealth or comfortable situation, so refused the offer. But

* See explanation at end of Chapter.

the King did not want to violate Lord Jagannātha's order, so he issued a decree naming a holy *ghāṭa* by the side of the Śveta Gaṅgā tank after Śacī-devī.

One time, Śacī-devī wanted to bathe in the River Gaṅgā on the coming auspicious day of Mahāvāruṇī-snāna (the thirteenth day of the waning moon in the month of Vaiśākha), but her *guru* had instructed her to never leave Jagannātha Purī. Remembering her spiritual master's instruction, Śacī-devī gave up her desire to bathe in the River Gaṅgā. That night, however, Lord Jagannātha appeared to her in a dream and said, "Śacī-devī, do not give up your desire to bathe in the Gaṅgā. You must simply bathe in Śveta Gaṅgā instead. Gaṅgā-devī has been praying for your association, so you must bathe in Śveta Gaṅgā." Having had such a wonderful vision of Lord Jagannātha, Śacī-devī became very joyful.

The day of Mahāvāruṇī-snāna arrived and in the middle of the night, Śacī-devī went to the Śveta Gaṅgā tank to bathe. As she bathed, the current of the Gaṅgā picked her up and began moving her along. The waters of Gaṅgā eventually overflooded the tank and the current carried her into the Jagannātha temple. Seeing this, thousands and thousands of local inhabitants became ecstatic and took their bath in the flooding Gaṅgā.

In the midst of the commotion, the guards at the gate of Jagannātha's temple awoke. They were speechless on seeing the disturbance. The King also woke and ordered the gates of the temple opened. By some miracle, Śacī-devī was standing all alone inside the temple of Jagannātha. The priests and servants of Jagannātha concluded that Śacī-devī was a thief who had come to steal the valuable ornaments of the Lord. Immediately Śacī-devī was imprisoned in the dungeons to stand trial for theft. Śacī-devī's mind did not become weak or confused, rather she absorbed herself in constantly chanting the holy name of Lord Kṛṣṇa.

Late that night, King Mukunda Deva saw Lord Jagannātha in a dream. The Lord angrily told him, "Immediately release Śacī-devī from your dungeons. It was because I wanted to personally arrange for her holy feet to be washed that I had Gaṅgā bring her to My temple. If you want your life to be auspicious, then you better have the priests bow at her feet and pray for forgiveness. You yourself must take initiation from her." Seeing all of this in his dream, the King was repentant and immediately ordered the priests to release Śacī-devī and fall at her feet for forgiveness. The King also went before Śacī-devī and with great petition begged her to forgive his offense. At that time, the King explained to Śacī-devī how Lord Jagannātha had ordered him to accept her as his *guru* and take *mantra* initiation from her.

Understanding all of these things to be the loving pastimes of Lord Jagannātha, Śacī-devī became extremely happy and her heart filled with divine love for Lord Kṛṣṇa. Placing her hand on the Kings's head, she gave him her blessings. Afterwards, Śacī-devī initiated King Mukunda Deva into the eighteen syllable *rādhā-kṛṣṇa-mantra*. Along with the King, many of the priests also took shelter of Śacī-devī. From that day forward, Śrī Śacī-devī became known as Śrī Gaṅgā-mātā Gosvāminī.

According to the local tradition of Jagannātha Purī, it is understood that there is a hidden underground passage from the lotus feet of Lord Jagannātha, who resides inside the main temple, to the tank of Śveta Gaṅgā, which is located outside the temple about one hundred metres to the south. This supports another explanation of how Gaṅgā had brought Śacī inside the temple when the temple was closed.

*In *Śrī-kṣetra*, by Sundānanda Vidyāvinoda, it is stated: "In the *Skanda Purāṇa, Utkala-khaṇḍa*, it is described that in Tretā-yuga there was a king named Śveta who was a great devotee of Śrī Jagannātha-deva. Following the method of worship established by Mahārāja Śrī Indradyumna, he made daily arrangements for food offerings. Early one morning, while Śrī Jagannātha-deva was being worshiped, he saw thousands of offerings being presented by demigods. He thought to himself, "How can the same Śrī Jagannātha-deva whom the demigods worship with such divine offerings accept the offerings of a mere mortal like myself?" Contemplating in this way, the King bowed down to Lord Jagannātha, offered Him prayers, and then went to the Śrī Mandira. Standing by the doorway, he personally saw Śrī Lakṣmī-devī serving Śrī Jagannātha-deva the food offering he had made containing the six kinds of tastes. Moreover, he saw Lord Jagannātha was eating the offering with full satisfaction. On seeing this amazing scene, the King realized that he was very fortunate.

"King Śveta remained absorbed in the worship of Śrī Jagannātha-deva for many years. Extremely satisfied with his service, Lord Jagannātha offered King Śveta the benediction that in the 'field of liberation' (*mukti-kṣetra*) located halfway between the sea and the 'immortal banyan tree' (*akṣaya-vaṭa*) the King would become famous by the name Śveta Mādhava. In accordance with this name, Śveta Mādhava, this pond is called Śveta-gaṅgā. On the shore of this pond are the deities of Śveta Mādhava and Śrī Matsya Mādhava. There are also deities of the nine planets on one side of the pond."

This narration regarding Mahārāja Śveta is one explanation of how the Gaṅgā in Jagannātha Purī became known as Śveta Gaṅgā. Also, from historical accounts of the pastimes of Śveta Gaṅgā, we learn that on rare occasions the waters turn white like milk, and since *śveta* also means white, this may be accepted as another explanation for Śveta Gaṅgā's name.

Book One
Chapter Five

Gaṅgā-Māhātmyam
(The Glories of Gaṅgā)
Part I— All Glories to Gaṅgā-devī
Part II— But Be Well Informed

Gaṅgā-Māhātmyam
(The Glories of Gaṅgā)

Part I-All glories to Gaṅgā-mayī!

Māhātmyam means 'greatly glorified'; glorification of the Supreme Lord and His associates. This *Gaṅgā-māhātmyam* is a collection of various glorifications of Gaṅgā.

Lord Dhanvantari, the preceptor of Ayurveda, states: "When the body is afflicted by senility and diseases, the sacred waters of mother Gaṅgā are the medicine and Lord Viṣṇu, from whose lotus feet Gaṅgā emanates, is the great physician."

The *Garuda Purāṇa* (*Ācāra-kāṇda* 213) says: "Gaṅgā water is the best of all. Gaṅgā water removes all sins committed till death. Gaṅgā water is better than the water in Gayā or Kurukṣetra. It is the holiest."

Then the *Padma Purāṇa* (*Sṛṣṭi-khanda* 62.120) says: "Especially in this age of Kali, Gaṅgā is the bestower of liberation on mankind. Those lacking spiritual strength can obtain unlimited results of pious activities by practicing penances on the banks of the Gaṅgā."

And in the *Nārada Purāṇa* (6.27) it is stated: "One who recites the two syllables 'Gaṅ-gā', even once, becomes completely liberated from all sins and is taken to the abode of Lord Viṣṇu."

In the *Śrīmad-Bhāgavatam* (3.5.41) the glories of the Ganges River are narrated in the following words:

mārganti yat te mukha-padma-nīḍais
chandaḥ-suparṇair ṛṣayo vivikte
yasyāgha-marṣoda-sarid-varāyāḥ
padaṁ padaṁ tīrtha-padaḥ prapannāḥ

"The lotus feet of Lord Kṛṣṇa are by themselves the shelter of all places of pilgrimage. The great, clear-minded sages, carried by the wings of the *Vedas*, always search after the nest of Your lotus-like face. Some of them surrender to Your lotus feet at every step by taking shelter of the best of rivers (the Ganges), which can deliver one from all sinful reactions."

In his purport on this verse, Śrīla Prabhupāda writes: "The Lord is so kind that He has spread the River Ganges throughout the universe so that by taking bath in that holy river everyone can get release from the reactions of sins, which occur at every step. There are many rivers in the world which are able to evoke one's sense of God consciousness simply by one's bathing in them, and the River Ganges is chief amongst them. In India there are five sacred rivers, but the Ganges is the most sacred. The River Ganges and the *Bhagavad-gītā* are chief sources of transcendental happiness for mankind, and intelligent persons can take shelter of them to go back home, back to Godhead. Even Śrīpāda Śaṅkarācārya recommends that a little knowledge in *Bhagavad-gītā* and the drinking of a little quantity of Ganges water can save one from the punishment of Yamarāja."

The *Śrīmad-Bhāgavatam* (9.9.12) also states:

yaj-jala-sparśa-mātreṇa
brahma-daṇḍa-hatā api
sagarātmajā divaṁ jagmuḥ
kevalaṁ deha-bhasmabhiḥ

"Because the sons of Sagara Mahārāja had offended a great personality, the heat of their bodies had increased and they were burnt to ashes. But simply by being sprinkled with water from the Ganges, all of them became eligible to go to the heavenly planets. What then is to be said of those who use the water of mother Ganges to worship her."

Śrīla Prabhupāda comments as follows: "Mother Ganges is worshiped by the water of the Ganges: a devotee takes a little water from the Ganges and offers it back to the Ganges. When the devotee takes the water, mother Ganges does not lose anything, and when the water is offered back, mother Ganges does not increase, but in this way the worshiper of the Ganges is benefited. Similarly, a devotee of the Lord offers the Lord '*patram puṣpam phalam toyam*' (a leaf, flower, fruit or water) in great devotion, but everything, including the leaf, flower, fruit and water, belongs to the Lord, and therefore there is nothing to renounce or to accept. One must simply take advantage of the *bhakti* process because by following this process one does not lose anything, but one gains the favor of the Supreme Personality."

In his purport on *Śrīmad-Bhāgavatam* (4.21.31), Śrīla Prabhupāda writes: "In India, one can actually see that a person who takes a bath in the Ganges waters daily is almost free from all kinds of diseases. A very respectable *brāhmaṇa* in Calcutta never took a doctor's medicine. Even though he sometimes felt sick, he would not accept medicine from the physician but would simply drink Ganges water, and he was always cured within a very short time. The glories of Ganges water are known to Indians and to ourselves also. The River Ganges flows by Calcutta and sometimes within the water there are many stools and other dirty things which are washed away from neighbouring mills and factories, but still thousands of people take baths in the Ganges water, and they are very healthy as well as spiritually inclined. That is the effect of Ganges water. The Ganges is glorified because she emanates from the toes of the lotus feet of the Lord. Similarly, if one takes to the service of the lotus feet of the Lord, or takes to Kṛṣṇa consciousness, he is immediately cleansed of the many dirty things which have accumulated in his innumerable births. We have seen that in spite of the very black record of their past lives, persons who take to Kṛṣṇa consciousness become perfectly cleansed of all dirty things and make spiritual progress very swiftly."

The *Śrīmad-Bhāgavatam* (11.6.19) also states:

vibhvyas tavāmṛta-kathoda-vahās tri-lokyāḥ
pādāvane-ja-saritaḥ śamalāni hantum
ānuśravaṁ śrutibhir aṅghri-jam aṅga-saṅgais
tīrtha-dvayaṁ śuci-ṣadas ta upaspṛśanti

"The nectar-bearing rivers of discussions about You, and also the holy rivers generated from the bathing of Your lotus feet, are able to destroy all contamination within the three worlds. Those who are striving for purification associate with the holy narrations of Your glories by hearing them with their ears, and they associate with the holy rivers flowing from Your lotus feet by physically bathing in them."

The disciples of Śrīla Prabhupāda have commented on this verse as follows: "The other nectar described here is *caraṇāmṛta*, the nectarean waters that bathe the Lord's feet. Lord Vāmanadeva bathed His own lotus foot by kicking a hole in the universal covering so that the sacred Ganges water washed His toes and fell into the universe. The Yamunā River also washed Kṛṣṇa's lotus feet when the Lord appeared on this planet five thousand years ago. Kṛṣṇa sported daily with His boyfriends and girlfriends in the Yamunā River, and consequently that river is also *caraṇāmṛta*. One should therefore try to take bath in the Ganges or Yamunā."

Finally, Śrīla Prabhupāda writes in his commentary on *Śrīmad-Bhāgavatam* (5.17.1): "The water of the Ganges is called *patita-pāvanī*, the deliverer of all sinful living beings. It is a proven fact that a person who regularly bathes in the Ganges is purified both externally and internally. Externally his body becomes immune to all kinds of disease, and internally he gradually develops a devotional attitude toward the Supreme Personality of Godhead. Throughout India many thousands of people live on the banks of the Ganges, and by regularly bathing in her waters, they are undoubtedly being purified both spiritually and materially. Many sages, including Śaṅkarācārya, have composed prayers in praise of the Ganges, and the land of India itself has become glorious because such rivers as the Ganges, Yamunā, Godāvarī, Kāverī, Kṛṣṇā and Narmadā flow there. Anyone living on the land adjacent to these rivers is naturally advanced in spiritual consciousness."

Śrī Śaṅkarācārya's *Gaṅgāṣṭakam*

Śrī Ādi Śaṅkarācārya, the great exponent of Advaita Vedānta philosophy, composed the following eight beautiful verses glorifying Gaṅgā-mayī entitled *Śrī Gaṅgāṣṭakam*.

1

bhagavati bhava-līlā-mauli-māle tavāmbhaḥ
kaṇam aṇu-parimāṇaṁ prāṇino ye spṛśanti
amara-nagara-nārī-cāmara-grāhiṇīnāṁ
vigata-kali-kalaṅkātaṅkam aṅke luṭhanti

O goddess, O pastime garland on the head of Lord Bhava, any living being who simply touches a tiny drop of your water will find himself rolling on the laps of women from the heavenly cities who hold *cāmaras* (yak-tail whisk) in their hands. He will become free from the contamination and disease of Kali-yuga.

2

brahmāṇḍaṁ khaṇḍayantī hara-śirasi jaṭā-vallim ullāsayantī
svar-lokād āpatantī kanaka-giri-guhā-gaṇḍa-śailāt skhalantī
kṣoṇī-pṛṣṭhe durita-caya-camūr nirbharaṁ bhartsayantī
pāthodhiṁ pūrayantī sura-nagara-sarit-pāvanī naḥ punātu

You break through the shell of the universe and adorn the creeper-like matted locks on the head of Lord Hara. As you fall from Svargaloka, you glide down from the caves and cliffs of the golden mountain. On the surface of the earth, you severely chastise the army of difficulties. You fill the ocean and purify the rivers of the heavenly abodes. Please also purify us.

3

majjan-mātaṅga-kumbha-cyuta-mada-madirāmoda-mattāli-jālaṁ
snānaiḥ siddhāṅganānāṁ kuca-yuga-vigalat-kuṅkumāsaṅga-piṅgam
sāyaṁ prātar munīnāṁ kuśa-kusuma-cayaiś channa-tīra-stha-nīraṁ
pāyān no gāṅgam ambhaḥ kari-kara-makarākrānta-raṁhas taraṅgam

In your waters an elephant submerges himself, and from the prominences of his forehead pours the liquid *mada*, like an intoxicating wine, the fragrance of which drives swarms of bees wild. You become reddish by the contact of the *kuṅkumā* (red powder) falling from the breasts of the wives of the perfect sages who take bath in you. The water along your shore becomes covered in the early morning and evening by the *kuśa* grass and flowers offered by great sages. May your water—the force whose waves are impeded by crocodiles and the trunks of elephants—protect us.

4

ādāv ādi-pitāmahasya niyama-vyāpāra-pātre jalaṁ
paścāt pannaga-śāyino bhagavataḥ pādodakaṁ pāvanam
bhūyaḥ śambhu-jaṭā-vibhūṣaṇa-maṇir jahnor maharṣer iyaṁ
kanyā kalmaṣa-nāśinī bhagavatī bhāgīrathī pātu mām

At first you were the water used for ritual duties in the vessel of Brahmā, the first grandfather of the universe. Then you became the all-purifying water that washed the feet of the Personality of Godhead lying on the serpent bed. Then again you became the jewel adorning the matted locks of Lord Śambhu, and you became the daughter of Maharṣi Jahnu. May you, goddess Bhāgīrathī, who destroys all inauspiciousness, protect me.

5

śailendrād avatāriṇī nija-jale majjaj-janottāriṇī
pārāvāra-vihāriṇī bhava-bhaya-śreṇi-samutsāriṇī
śeṣāher anukāriṇī hara-śiro-vallī-dalākāriṇī
kāśī-prānta-vihāriṇī vijayate gaṅgā mano-hāriṇī

You descend from the king of mountains and uplift all people who immerse themselves in your waters. You enjoy your sports both on earth and in heaven. You eradicate all fear of material existence. Your movement imitates the serpent Śeṣa. You appear like the leaf of a creeper on the head of Lord Hara. You play on the side of Kāśī. O all-enchanting one, O Gaṅgā, all glories to you.

6

kuto 'vīci vīcis tava yadi gatā locana-pathaṁ
tvam āpītā pītāmbara-pura-nivāsam vitarasi
tvad-utsaṅge gaṅge patati yadi kāyas tanu-bhṛtām
tadā mātaḥ śāta-kratava-pada-lābho 'py ati-laghuḥ

If one has a glimpse of your waves, how can he deviate from the proper path? If someone drinks your waters, you grant him residence in the city of Lord Pītāmbara (Viṣṇu). If any conditioned soul's body falls dead into your lap, O Gaṅgā, then, O mother, there is no difficulty in his attaining even the position of Indra.

7

bhagavati tava tīre nīra-mātrāśano 'haṁ
vigata-viṣaya-tṛṣṇaḥ kṛṣṇam ārādhayāmi
sakala-kaluṣa-bhaṅge svarga-sopāna-saṅge
tarala-tara-taraṅge devī gaṅge prasīda

O goddess, I will sit on your shore, subsisting only on your water, and I will worship Kṛṣṇa without any desire for sense gratification. O destroyer of all contamination, association with you is the staircase to heaven. O goddess Gaṅgā, whose waves are always agitated, be pleased with me.

8

mātar jāhnavī śambhu-saṅga-milite maulau
tvat-tīre vapuṣo 'vasāna-samaye nārāyaṇāṅghri-dvayam
sānandaṁ smarato bhaviṣyati mama prāṇa-prayāṇotsave
bhūyād bhaktir avicyutā hari-harādvaitātmikā śāśvatī

O mother Jāhnavī, who associates with Lord Śambhu by residing on the crest of his head, when I leave my body on your shore while happily remembering the lotus feet of Lord Nārāyaṇa, then I will enjoy the festival of my life air's passing on. Please allow me to always have unfailing devotion for Hari and Hara as one and the same.

9

gaṅgāṣṭakam idaṁ puṇyaṁ
yaḥ paṭhet prayato naraḥ
sarva-pāpa-vinirmukto
viṣṇu-lokaṁ sa gacchati

Any person who attentively recites this auspicious *Gaṅgāṣṭakam* will be completely freed from sins and attain the abode of Lord Viṣṇu.

(*Śrī Gaṅgāṣṭakam* was translated by H.G. Gopīparāṇadhana Dāsa)

Śrīla Vyāsadeva speaks

In the *Padma Purāṇa* (*Kriyā-yoga-sāra-khaṇḍa* 7, 9), Jaimini Ṛṣi inquires from Śrīla Vyāsadeva about the importance of Gaṅgā. Vyāsadeva replies as follows, "I shall tell you the importance of the sacred Gaṅgā. During the morning, if a sinful person devoutly remembers the two syllables 'Gaṅ-gā', his sins will be destroyed just as darkness perishes at dawn. The sins of those who bathe in Gaṅgā leave their bodies and enter the bodies of those who do not bathe in Gaṅgā. It is very strange that many fools fall into hell, even though the name of Gaṅgā is there to purify them. Any *brāhmaṇa* who carries even a single drop of Gaṅgā water on his head is freed from great sins like *brahma-hatyā*, or the murder of a *brāhmaṇa*. That pious person who marks his forehead with the sand of Gaṅgā undoubtedly purifies the entire world. If a person sees someone who has just come from the bank of the Gaṅgā and offers him respect, the results of thousands of horse sacrifices will be obtained. If the name of Gaṅgā is remembered while bathing from a well, one obtains the same result as by bathing in the Gaṅgā. If at the time of death one receives even a single drop of Gaṅgā the size of a mustard seed, that person will obtain the highest position. Lord Viṣṇu is very pleased and awards fulfillment of all desires to that person who tells another, 'I am going to the bank of the Gaṅgā. You should also come with me.'"

Jaimini Ṛṣi then replied, "O dear preceptor, please tell me more of the excellent glories of Gaṅgā. Due to her sweetness, I desire to again drink the nectar of Gaṅgā's pastimes." Śrīla Vyāsadeva continued, "I will tell you since you are a devotee of Gaṅgā. The feet of men who go to the bank of the Gaṅgā are meritorious, the ears that hear the sound of Gaṅgā's waves are glorious, the tongues that taste the varieties of Gaṅgā's sweetness are fruitful, the eyes that see the charming ripples of the Gaṅgā are fortunate, the foreheads that wear the vertical marks of clay from Gaṅgā are admirable, the hands that are intent on worshiping Gaṅgā are praiseworthy, and the bodies that have bathed in the pure waters of Gaṅgā are superior.

"While on pilgrimage to the Gaṅgā, one should avoid eating flesh, having sex, riding on a horse or an elephant, and using shoes or an umbrella. The difficulties due to the fatigue of the journey should not be regarded as painful. One should also avoid eating twice, quarreling, criticizing others, laughing too much, or being overcome with greed, pride, anger, jealousy, or grief. One should sleep on the ground, and one should chant the names of Gaṅgā while traveling. The greatness of Jāhnavi-devī destroys all sins. One obtains happiness and liberation by calling out, 'O Gaṅgā, O goddess, O mother of the world, please reveal yourself to me.'

"Wise persons should not undertake any type of work during their pilgrimage to the Gaṅgā. Half of one's religious merit perishes if one engages in activities like trade or business on the banks of the Gaṅgā. Before going to the bank of the Gaṅgā, a wise person should say, 'All my small and great sins that were committed in numerous past births will perish due to your mercy, O Gaṅgā-devī.' Upon seeing mother Gaṅgā, one should pray, 'Today my existence is fruitful and my life well lived, since I am actually seeing you, O Gaṅgā-devī. All of my innumerable sins from millions of lifetimes have perished.' After praying in this way, one should with full love and devotion offer one's humble obeisances to Jāhnavī-devī by prostrating completely on the ground. Then with palms joined, being greatly delighted in a devotional mood, one should pray, 'O Gaṅgā-devī, O mother of the world, please forgive me if my feet touch your

water. O auspicious one, your water is the staircase to the spiritual world. Therefore, O Gaṅgā-devī, please forgive me again, as I repeatedly offer obeisances to you.' Then the wise should devotedly carry some Gaṅgā water on his head and, upon entering her water, call out, 'Gaṅgā! Gaṅgā!. One should then pray, 'I now smear my body with your mud, which is very soft and which destroys all sins. O mother Gaṅgā, please remove my sins.' O *brāhmaṇa* Jaimini, a wise person should then remember Gaṅgā and Lord Nārāyaṇa. While bathing in her waters, one should again pray, 'O Gaṅgā-devī, mother of the world, I am bathing in your pure waters. Please bestow upon me the merit that is mentioned in the scriptures.' Having thus bathed, one should clean his body with a cloth, without rinsing that cloth in the Gaṅgā. One should not brush his teeth in the Gaṅgā or wear a garment that was worn during the night while taking bath in the Gaṅgā.

"A wise person should also bathe a deity of Gaṅgā-devī, as well as a deity of Lord Viṣṇu, with the heavenly water of a coconut. In the absence of the deity, one should remember Gaṅgā in his heart while pouring the coconut water into the Gaṅgā. Then one should devotedly worship Śrī Gaṅgā-devī and Lord Viṣṇu with divine fragrances, ghee lamps, incense, beautiful flowers, ripened fruits, excellent eatables, and water for washing their feet and mouths. Afterwards one should circumambulate Gaṅgā-devī and Lord Viṣṇu three times and then make a solemn vow, promising to remain without food or sleep that day. If one is too weak, then fruits may be taken; but a complete meal should be avoided. After worshiping in the morning, charitable gifts should be given to a *brāhmaṇa*, according to one's wealth. Then, with a pure mind, one should pray, 'O best of rivers, may all that I have done for you be faultless and accepted through your mercy.' One should then break fast the next day.

"One who observes all that I have said will be freed from all sins committed during past births, and upon reaching Lord Viṣṇu's abode, he rejoices with the Lord Himself. There is no doubt that even one who meets death while on pilgrimage to the Gaṅgā will reach the highest abode in Vaikuṇṭhaloka."

O Mohinī listen

In the *Nārada Purāṇa* (*Uttara-bhāga* 38-39), Vasu, the sacrificial priest of King Rukmāṅgada, narrates the glories of Gaṅgā-mayī to Mohinī, Lord Brahmā's daughter. Vasu says, "Listen, Mohinī, I shall thoroughly narrate the characteristics of the holy places. On understanding them, any sinner can immediately obtain the highest liberation. The most excellent of all sacred places on the surface of the earth is the Gaṅgā. There is nothing else that destroys sins as effectively as the Gaṅgā."

When Mohinī, who had great reverence for bathing in the Gaṅgā, heard these words of her priest, Vasu, she offered her obeisances to him and said, "O holy respectable sir, O most excellent *brāhmaṇa*, kindly recount Gaṅgā's superior qualities, which are acknowledged by all the *Purāṇas*. After hearing the unparalleled qualities of Gaṅgā, I shall go with you to bathe in that holy river which destroys all sins. Those lands, countries, mountains, and hermitages are considered very holy if they are near the sacred Gaṅgā."

After hearing these words of Mohinī, Vasu, who is conversant with all the *Purāṇas*, retold the greatness of Gaṅgā-mayī, who is destructive of all sins. The great Vasu said, "Those persons who have committed sins early in their lives can later on still resort to the Gaṅgā and attain salvation. For living beings in this world whose minds are afflicted by misery and who are searching for salvation, there is no place superior to the Gaṅgā. Those who reside near the Gaṅgā are certainly equal to sages and demigods. The demigods, sages, and human beings resort to the Gaṅgā on every occassion for the sake of improving their prosperity. Gaṅgā even sanctifies blind, senseless, and poor people. In Satya-yuga, all sacred places are equal; in Tretā-yuga, Puṣkara lake is the greatest; in Dvāpara-yuga, Kurukṣetra is the holiest place; and in Kali-yuga, Gaṅgā is superior to all other holy places. In the age of Kali, all holy places and sacred rivers entrust their qualities and potency into Gaṅgā, but the divine Gaṅgā does not entrust it anywhere else. There is no doubt that Lord Janārdana, Viṣṇu, who is the all-pervading Supreme Lord, assumes this liquid form, which is called Gaṅgā.

"The murderer of a *brāhmaṇa*, the slayer of one's preceptor, the slaughterer of a cow, the thief, and the defiler of the preceptor's bed are also sanctified by the waters of Gaṅgā. No doubt need be entertained in this regard. The waters of Gaṅgā will drive away one's sins committed up to death, regardless if her waters are honored in a holy place or taken elsewhere, either in hot or cold weather. Even if a person does not fulfill all the procedures laid down for the performance of pilgrimage, full benefit will be bestowed on him due to the mercy of Gaṅgā's waters. Those who sprinkle Gaṅgā water on *śālagrāma-śilās* (Deity incarnation in the form of stones) will shine like the sun that dispels dense darkness at the time of rising. There is no doubt that a person engulfed in various sins originating from or committed by his mind, words, or body becomes purified just by seeing Gaṅgā. One who partakes of alms sprinkled with Gaṅgā water, sheds off all sins like a serpent casting off its skin.

"O daughter of Brahmā, those persons who continuously reside on the banks of the Gaṅgā and who drink her waters will be liberated from all their previously accumulated sins. Verily, one who resorts to Gaṅgā and fearlessly stays there deserves to be worshiped by the demigods, great sages, and mortals. Of what value is *aṣṭāṅga-yoga* (the eightfold path of yoga), of what use are austerities, and of what advantage are sacrifices? Residence on the banks of the Gaṅgā is certainly superior to all of these in every respect. Even after performing hundreds of sacrifices it is not possible to obtain the benefit that one receives by being devoted to the service of Gaṅgā for half a day. Devotion to Gaṅgā certainly redeems unlimited family members from the ocean of worldly existence. The devotee of Gaṅgā attains contentment, great power, prosperity, knowledge of the Absolute Truth, happiness of the soul, humility, and good conduct. Only by resorting to Gaṅgā does a person become content and blessed. There is no doubt that even after death such a person will be a devotee absorbed in loving feelings. One who devotedly touches and drinks her waters obtains the means of liberation without any difficulty.

"O Mohinī listen! I shall recount to you the glorious benefits of seeing and remembering Gaṅgā, as mentioned in the *Purāṇas*. Just as serpents become impotent at the sight of Garuḍa, one also becomes liberated from sins at the sight of Gaṅgā. By seeing, touching, drinking her waters, or by glorifying the name of Gaṅgā, a person sanctifies hundreds and thousands of his family members. Enjoyment of sense gratification, vices, sins, ruthlessness, violence towards others, crookedness, fault-finding, and hypocrisy all perish by the mere sight of Gaṅgā. By seeing the Gaṅgā one attains the same pious results as one receives by the digging and construction of tanks, wells, lakes, hermitages, temples, etc. By looking at Gaṅgā with devotional feelings one attains the same

benefit as by seeing Paramātmā. The great sages all say that in Kali-yuga, by just glancing at Gaṅgā, a person obtains the same benefit as bathing or touching the sacred waters in Naimiṣāraṇya, Kurukṣetra, Narmadā, and Puṣkara. One who constantly remembers Gaṅgā while waking, standing, sleeping, meditating, walking, eating, laughing, or crying becomes liberated from material bondage. By glorifying Gaṅgā one is liberated from sins, and by seeing her one derives auspiciousness. One who sincerely contemplates, 'When shall I see Gaṅgā, or when shall I be able to bathe in Gaṅgā?' redeems a hundred family members. The merit of bathing at midday is ten times greater than in the morning. Bathing in the evening has one hundred times the merit. Wherever you perform oblations to Gaṅgā, the benefit is the same as by performing oblations at any sacred place, but one receives more benefit when bathing at Haridvāra, Prayāga, and the Gaṅgā's confluence with the sea. Even Sūryadeva says, 'O Gaṅgā, those who take bath in your waters, which are heated by my rays, will attain salvation.' And once Varuṇa said to Gaṅgā, 'One who glorifies you even while taking bath in his house will go to Vaikuṇṭha.'

"O gentle blessed lady, thus the excellent greatness, glories, and qualities of Gaṅgā have been recounted to you. A person who reads or listens to this narration will attain the greatest region, the abode of Lord Viṣṇu."

Sanaka-kumāra explains

In the *Nārada Purāṇa* (Chapter 6), when Nārada Muni and the four Kumāras were bathing in the Gaṅgā before going to see Lord Brahmā, Nārada inquired from Sanaka-kumāra about the glories of Gaṅgā-mayī. The great spiritual master replied to Nārada, "The goddess Gaṅgā, who originated from Lord Viṣṇu's lotus feet and is respectfully held on the head by Lord Śiva, deserves to be resorted to by all sages and demigods, so what to speak of the unfortunate human beings? Even sinners who take bath in the Gaṅgā become completely absolved of all sins and proceed to Vaikuṇṭhaloka in a wonderful airplane. The mud from the root of *tulasī*, the dust from the feet of a *brāhmana*, and the sand from the bed of Gaṅgā all award *sārūpya-mukti*, or obtaining the same form of the Lord. The Gaṅgā, *tulasī*, pure unalloyed devotional service to Lord Hari, and attachment to the *guru* are extremely rare indeed. Amongst all holy rivers such as Godāvarī, Bhīmarathī, Kṛṣṇā, Revā, Sarasvatī, Tuṅgabhadrā, Kāverī, Kālindī, Bāhudā (Rāmagaṅgā), Vetravatī, Tāmraparṇī, and Sarayū, Gaṅgā is remembered as the holiest of all. Gaṅgā is all-pervading and destroys all sins. There is no other sacred water like the Gaṅgā, there is no other Deity like Viṣṇu, and there is no other primary principle like the spiritual master. As the *brāhmaṇas* are the most excellent of all social and spiritual orders, as the moon is the best of all constellations, and as the ocean is the best of all bodies of water, so Gaṅgā is remembered as the greatest river.

"Gāyatrī is the mother of all Vedic metres, and Gaṅgā is the mother of the world. Both of them destroy all sins. If anyone is favored by Gāyatrī, then Gaṅgā is also pleased. Both of them possess the potency of Viṣṇu. Rare indeed and very difficult to attain are Gāyatrī, Gaṅgā, *tulasī*, and pure devotion to Hari. That fortunate person who is sprinkled with at least one drop of Gaṅgā is liberated from all sins and attains the highest region, Vaikuṇṭhaloka."

* * *

The *Śrīmad-Bhāgavatam* further narrates the glories of the Ganges in the following two verses:

eṣu snānaṁ japo homo
vrataṁ deva-dvijārcanam
pitṛ-deva-nṛ-bhūtebhyo
yad dattaṁ tad dhy anasvaram

"During these periods of seasonal change, if one bathes in the Ganges, in Yamunā or in another sacred place, if one chants, offers fire sacrifices or executes vows, or if one worships the Supreme Lord, the *brāhmaṇas*, the forefathers, the demigods and the living entities in general, whatever he gives in charity yields a permanently beneficial result." (*Bhāg.* 7.14.25)

na hy etat paraṁ āścaryaṁ
svardhunyā yad ihoditam
ananta-caraṇāmbhoja-
prasūtāyā bhava-cchidaḥ

"Because mother Ganges emanates from the lotus toe of the Supreme Personality of Godhead, Anantadeva, she is able to liberate one from material bondage. Therefore whatever is described herewith about her is not at all wonderful." (*Bhāg.* 9.9.14)

In his purport on *Śrīmad-Bhāgavatam* (9.9.14), Śrīla Prabhupāda writes as follows: "It has actually been seen that anyone who regularly worships mother Ganges simply by bathing in her waters keeps very good health and gradually becomes a devotee of the Lord. This is the effect of bathing in the water of the Ganges. Bathing in the Ganges is recommended in all Vedic *śāstras*, and one who takes to this path will certainly be freed from all sinful reactions. The practical example of this is that the sons of Mahārāja Sagara went to the heavenly planets when water from the Ganges merely touched the ashes of their burnt bodies."

The *Śrīmad-Bhāgavatam* (11.7.29) further states:

janeṣu dahyamāneṣu
kāma-lobha-davāgninā
na tapyase 'gninā mukto
gaṅgāmbhaḥ-stha iva dvipaḥ

"Although all people within the material world are burning in the great forest fire of lust and greed, you remain free and are not burned by that fire. You are just like an elephant who takes shelter from a forest fire by standing within the water of the Ganges River"

In their purport on this verse, Śrīla Prabhupāda's disciples have written: "Śrīla Bhaktisiddhānta Sarasvatī Ṭhākura explains that within the Ganges flow great currents of water, capable of extinguishing a blazing fire. If an elephant maddened by sex desire stands within the Ganges, its powerful, cooling currents extinguish his lust, and the elephant becomes pacified. Similarly, ordinary human beings trapped in the cycle of birth and death are constantly harassed by the enemies of lust and greed, which never allow the mind to be completely peaceful. But if, following the example of the elephant, one situates oneself within the cooling waves of transcendental bliss, then all material desire will soon be extinguished, and one will become *śānta*, or peaceful. As described in *Śrī Caitanya-caritāmṛta*: *kṛṣṇa-bhakta niṣkāma ataeva śānta*. Thus, everyone should take to the movement of Śrī Caitanya Mahāprabhu and cleanse himself in the cooling waters of Kṛṣṇa consciousness, our real, eternal consciousness."

And finally, Śrīla Prabhupāda comments on *Śrī Caitanya-caritāmṛta* (*Antya* 1.37 and 4.98) as follows: "Formerly when a person died it was commonly said that he had attained the shelter of mother Ganges, even if he did not die on the bank of the Ganges. It is customary among Hindus to carry a dying person to a nearby bank of the Ganges, for if one dies on the bank of the Ganges, his soul is considered to reach the lotus feet of Lord

Viṣṇu, wherefrom the Ganges flows...In every part of India, and especially in the holy places of pilgrimage, even an ordinary uneducated man is inclined toward Kṛṣṇa consciousness, and as soon as he sees a Kṛṣṇa conscious person, he offers obeisances. India has many sacred rivers like the Ganges, Yamunā, Narmadā, Kāverī and Kṛṣṇā, and simply by bathing in these rivers people are liberated and become Kṛṣṇa conscious."

PART II-BUT BE WELL INFORMED

As warned in the Vedic literatures, *tīrthas*, including rivers, absolve all sins of the living beings, but one should not continue sinning, thinking atonement is nearby, and then shamelessly take bath in the Gaṅgā or other holy places. We are also warned that sometimes *tīrthas* do not allow certain sinful persons to even enter their purifying waters.

There is a warning in the *Brahma-vaivarta Purāṇa* (*Prakṛti-khaṇḍa* 9) that says: "Anyone who takes Gaṅgā water into his hands and makes a promise, but does not execute that promise, goes to the Kālasūtra hellish planet for the duration of Brahmā's lifetime." And the *Padma Purāṇa* (as quoted in *Śrimad-Bhāgavatam* 4.21.12 purport) says: "One who thinks the Deity in the temple to be made of wood or stone, who thinks of the spiritual master in the disciplic succession as an ordinary man, who thinks of the Vaiṣṇava in the Acyuta *gotra* (traditional family line) to belong to a certain caste or creed, or who thinks of *caraṇāmṛta* or Ganges water as ordinary water is taken to be a resident of hell."

Also in the *Padma Purāṇa* (*Sṛṣṭi-khaṇḍa* 62.74), we are warned: "Those persons with confused and bewildered minds who severely criticize Gaṅgā go to such a terrible hell that it is very difficult to return. Those persons who have not gone to Gaṅgā become blind, crippled, or incapacitated through miscarriage, being born in this proud worldly existence. The knowledge of dull-headed persons who do not glorify Gaṅgā will not bear any success." The *Padma Purāṇa* (*Kriyā-yoga-sāra-khaṇḍa* 8.7-13) further states: "That person who discourages one from going to the bank of the Gaṅgā goes along with a million members of his family to the hell named Raurava. The atonement for those who urinate or excrete on the bank of the Gaṅgā is unknown even after hundreds of millions of *kalpas*. The person who drops phlegm, spittle, rheum, tears, or dirt on the bank of the Gaṅgā will become a resident of hell and acquire the sin of killing a *brāhmaṇa*. Any sin that a foolish man commits on the bank of Gaṅgā will indeed be perpetual and is not destroyed by visiting other holy places. A sin committed at another holy place is destroyed in the Gaṅgā, but a sin committed in the Gaṅgā is destroyed nowhere. Therefore, those who are learned in Vedic knowledge should not commit sins in the Gaṅgā."

Also in the *Devī Purāṇa*, the great sage Cyavana instructs Prahlāda with the following words: "Only those pure in heart will receive the benefit of visiting sacred places. The banks of Gaṅgā are crowded with villages and cities. Many types of people like fishermen, Vaṅgas, Khasas, Hūṇas, and Mlecchas live there. They bathe in the holy river and drink the holy water, but they do not get salvation because their minds and hearts are not clean."

Finally, Śrīla Prabhupāda warns us in his commentary on the *Śrimad-Bhāgavatam* (10.10.4) as follows: "People generally go to the Ganges to be purified of the effects of sinful life, but here is an example of how foolish persons enter the Ganges to become involved in sinful life. It is not that everyone becomes purified by entering the Ganges. Everything, spiritual and material, depends on one's mental condition."

Śrī Yādavaprakāśa's envy

This short story relating the plot to kill Rāmānujācārya by his spiritual master has been condensed from *The Life of Rāmānujācārya*, by H.G. Naimiṣāraṇya Dāsa.

Śrī Yādavaprakāśa, who was the spiritual master of Śrīmān Rāmānujācārya during his youth, proposed a plot to kill Rāmānuja, since he was refuting all of Śaṅkarācārya's commentaries. After discussing this matter with his other students, Yādavaprakāśa began considering how to secretly kill Rāmānuja, without anyone discovering their crime. Eventually Yādavaprakāśa made a proposal, "Let us go on pilgrimage to bathe in the Gaṅgā at Vārāṇasī. On the way, there are many remote areas where we can put an end to this heretic, without anyone knowing anything about it. By bathing in the sacred Gaṅgā, we will free ourselves from the sin of killing a *brāhmaṇa*, and when we return, we will simply say he fell sick and died on the journey."

During the pilgrimage, Rāmānuja's cousin heard about Yādavaprakāśa's plot and informed Rāmānuja. After hearing about the plot, Rāmānuja left to return home to Kāñcīpuram alone, through dense forests that were infested with robbers and wild animals. On his way, he met a fowler couple who assisted and guided him in his journey. He realized later that the couple were none other than mother Lakṣmī and Lord Nārāyaṇa!

As time passed, Rāmānuja accepted *sannyāsa* and became the local *ācārya* in Kāñcīpuram. During this time, Yādavaprakāśa had a dream, where an effulgent personality instructed him to take initiation from Rāmānuja. The next day Rāmānuja's ex-teacher, who had once plotted to kill him, became his initiated disciple, receiving the name Govinda dāsa.

Regarding Yādavaprakāśa's mentality, if one expects Gaṅgā-mayī to neutralize one's sins while continuing to sin, that may be compared with the seventh offence in the chanting of the Hare Kṛṣṇa *mahā-mantra*, which warns us against misusing the potency of the holy name of the Lord. The seventh offense in chanting the holy names is to commit sinful activities on the strength of the holy name of the Lord. It should not be taken that, because chanting the holy name of the Lord frees one from all kinds of sinful reaction, one may continue to act sinfully and then chant Hare Kṛṣṇa to neutralize his sins. Such a dangerous mentality while chanting the holy name of the Lord or while bathing in the Gaṅgā is very offensive and should be avoided.

Poor Dhanañjaya's mother

The following short account from the *Skanda Purāṇa* (*Kāśī-khaṇḍa* 30) concerning Dhanañjaya's mother illustrates that not everyone is qualified to reach the shores of Gaṅgā at the time of death.

Dhanañjaya's mother led a very sinful life. When she died, Dhanañjaya properly performed all the ritualistic rites and prayed that she would go to the heavenly planets. He took her ashes, tied in some leaves, and went to Kāśī (Vārāṇasī) with the intention of throwing the ashes into the Gaṅgā. Unfortunately, the ashes were mistakenly taken away and thrown into a forest. Dhanañjaya eventually found the man who had taken them, and they both searched several forests, but were unable to find the ashes. Dhanañjaya therefore returned home feeling very sad because he was not able to place his mother's ashes in the Gaṅgā. He did not realize that Kāśī Viśveśvara (Śiva) was not allowing his mother to reach the shores of Gaṅgā because of her sinful life.

Kalyāṇī begins to weep

In the following account from the *Śrī Śaila-māhātmyam*, we hear of an exemplary pastime of Gaṅgā's mercy upon one appealing soul named Kalyāṇī.

Once there lived in Avantīpura (Ujjain) an unmarried *brāhmaṇa*, who was forty years of age. He was a great scholar, with full knowledge of the *Vedas*; he performed all the proper religious functions and was very devoted. One day, a relative from the *brāhmaṇa's* village visited him and requested him to marry one girl. The relative insisted that a man without a son is not eligible for *mokṣa*, or liberation. After contemplating the issue, the *brāhmaṇa* accepted the marriage proposal. The *brāhmaṇa* then went to the King of Avantīpura to explain his future marriage plans and request the King for financial assistance. The King happily agreed to help the *brāhmaṇa*, which made him very pleased.

The marriage took place in the village and was attended by all the relatives, as well as the King and his servants. After the marriage, the new bride, Kalyāṇī, followed her new husband back to Avantīpura, where they lived for some time. Later, due to a great famine, they moved to Kāśī, where the young bride matured and all their necessities were nicely arranged by friends and well-wishers.

One day, the damsel Kalyāṇī felt very inconvenienced and cursed for having an old husband. During her daily morning walk to the Gaṅgā, she met a young, handsome, charming man, who attracted her very much. After they both exchanged sweet words with one another, they went to a secluded place to fulfill their desires. Afterwards, Kalyāṇī returned to the Gaṅgā to bathe, but as soon as she stepped into the sacred water, Gaṅgā-devī appeared and strongly objected, saying Kalyāṇī should not take bath in her waters. Gaṅgā-devī blamed her for deceiving her devoted husband by having contact with a *caṇḍāla* (low-class person). Upon realizing her mistake, Kalyāṇī began to weep and beg Gaṅgā-devī to excuse her and allow her to become pure again by taking bath.

Gaṅgā-devī was eventually pleased with her appeal and told her why the incident had taken place. She narrated the story of her past life as a tribal lady. Once she was wandering in a forest, wherein she came upon a handsome *brāhmaṇa*. Astonished by his handsome features, she began to look upon him with desires, but the *brāhmaṇa* simply cursed her, saying that she would have contact with a *caṇḍāla* in her next life. She then fell at his feet and begged forgiveness for her evil thoughts. Since he felt sorry for her, he agreed to be that *caṇḍāla* in his next life.

After hearing all of this from Gaṅgā-devī, Kalyāṇī again appealed for her blessings. When she finally took a bath to purify herself, her husband became youthful again, and they both lived peacefully from then on. Meanwhile, Gaṅgā-devī traveled throughout the three worlds to get rid of Kalyāṇī's sin, but wherever she went, she was unsuccessful. Finally Gaṅgā-devī came to Śrī Śailam Mahākṣetram, where the River Kṛṣṇāveṇyā flows. Gaṅgā-devī plunged into those waters to absolve herself of Kalyāṇī's sin. As a result, that place on the banks of the Kṛṣṇāveṇyā became known as Pātāla Gaṅgā.

Kāverī-mayī bestows her mercy

In the *Skanda Purāṇa* (*Kārtika-māsa-māhātmyam* 4.51-65), we hear that sometimes Gaṅgā herself has to take shelter of another river for purification.

Once Nārada Muni went to Satyaloka to inquire from Lord Brahmā about the glories of the Kāverī River and how Gaṅgā-devī took shelter of her. Brahmā explained to

Nārada how Gaṅgā was born from the lotus feet of Lord Viṣṇu and how she resides in the northern region. She is worshiped by the three worlds, as she destroys all sins. Once, however, she became doubtful about her great burden of people's sins and thought to herself, "So many people come and leave their sins with me; how can these sins be dispelled?" With this thought worrying her, she went to Mount Kailāsa to inquire from Lord Śiva. After meeting Mahārudra (Śiva) there, Gaṅgā submitted, "O Mahārudra, all obeisances to you. All people come to me and discharge their sins in me. O lord of Pārvatī, it is impossible for me to bear these sins. Please tell me the means by which those sins will not trouble me."

Upon hearing these words of Gaṅgā-devī, Lord Parameśvara (Śiva) replied, "O gentle lady, who is worried and in distress. You appeared from the lotus feet of Lord Padmanābha (Viṣṇu) in order to dispel everyone's sins. The responsibility for destroying sins has been allotted to you by Lord Viṣṇu. Now I shall tell you the means of dispelling those sins, which are polluting you. Due to the power given to her by Lord Hari, the River Kāverī is the most excellent of all. She has the power to dispel those sins. One who takes a holy bath in Kāverī during Kārtika is freed from all sins and goes to the supreme abode of Viṣṇu. Hence, O gentle lady, go to the River Kāverī, and you will be liberated from all sins." Being thus advised by Lord Śiva, Gaṅgā went to Kāverī during the month of Kārtika. Merely by touching her waters, Gaṅgā-devī became free from all sins and then returned to her own abode.

Every year during the month of Kārtika, Gaṅgā-devī comes to the River Kāverī in order to take a bath with great devotion and to dispel her sins.

The *brāhmaṇa* named Satyaketu

The following short story from the *Sthala Purāṇa* about the *brāhmaṇa* named Satyaketu illustrates the importance of giving food in charity.

Satyaketu did not find time to go to the Gaṅgā due to his vow of offering food to all pilgrims who passed by his door. Once a pious pilgrim named Satyajit refused to accept food from Satyaketu because he had not performed his oblations to Gaṅgā. Then, when Satyajit went to bathe in the Gaṅgā, she disappeared! Satyajit began to pray, and Gaṅgā soon instructed him to take food from Satyaketu first and then return for his bath.

The River Vaitaraṇī

Mother Gaṅgā, in the form of a river, mercifully flows from the abode of Goloka throughout the three worlds for the purpose of purifying all sinful living entities. Anyone who bathes in her waters becomes purified, both internally and externally, even of the greatest sins like *go-hatyā* (killing of a cow) and *brahma-hatyā* (killing of a *brāhmaṇa*). By continuously bathing in her waters, one will become purified and acquire the taste to chant Lord Kṛṣṇa's name and obtain His lotus feet. For those persons who do not approach and bathe in Gaṅgā in this lifetime, in their next lifetime they will be thrown into Gaṅgā's more fearful form of Vaitaraṇī, which acts as a moat around the region of hell.

The *Mādhurya Dhāma* says: "When a sinful man is thrown into the River Vaitaraṇī, the aquatic animals there immediately begin to devour him. But because of his extremely sinful life, he does not leave his body. He constantly remembers his sinful activities and suffers terribly in that river." (See also Book Two, Chapter Four: Gaṅgā's Final Destination)

* * *

This section is concluded with quotes from Śrīla Prabhupāda, the first from his purport on the *Śrīmad-Bhāgavatam* (3.5.38), wherein he writes: "The Lord is equal to every living entity, just like the flowing Ganges. The Ganges water is meant for the purification of everyone, yet the trees on the banks of the Ganges have different values. A mango tree on the bank of the Ganges drinks the water, and the *nimba* tree also drinks the same water. But the fruits of both trees are different. One is celestially sweet, and the other is hellishly bitter. The condemned bitterness of the *nimba* is due to its own past work, just as the sweetness of the mango is also due to its own *karma*. The Lord says in *Bhagavad-gītā* (16.19): 'Those who are envious and mischievous, who are the lowest among men, I perpetually cast into the ocean of material existence, into various demoniac species of life.' Demigods like Yamarāja and other controllers are there for the unwanted conditioned souls who always engage in threatening the tranquility of the kingdom of God. Since all the demigods are confidential devotee-servitors of the Lord, they are never to be condemned."

The following extract from *Conversations with Śrīla Prabhupāda*, London, July 11, 1973, illustrates the final purpose of *yoga* as explained by Śrīla Prabhupāda.

Pradyumna: "To practice *yoga*, one should go to a secluded place."

Prabhupāda: Now, first of all you have to find out secluded place. *Yoga* practice is not possible in a hotel or in a public place. It is not possible. You have to find out a secluded place. First condition. Then?

Pradyumna: "...and should lay *kuśa* grass on the ground and then cover it with a deerskin and a soft cloth."

Prabhupāda: Then there is process of making the *āsana* (seat or sitting place), deerskin, *kuśāsana*, then cloth. You have to sit down in that *āsana*. *Āsana, dhyāna, dhāraṇā, pran*... Then?

Pradyumna: "The seat should neither be too high nor too low."

Prabhupāda: Yes, everything is there. "It should not be too high nor too low." Then?

Pradyumna: "And should be situated in a sacred place."

Prabhupāda: A sacred place. Just like formerly those who were practicing *yoga*, they were going to Gaṅgotrī where the Ganges is coming down, in the Himālaya, in Haridvāra, in a secluded, sacred place. These are the condition, first condition. So where you are getting these conditions fulfilled? You cannot practice *yoga* in a hotel or in a club. That is not possible.

Student (2): How do you decide whether a place is sacred or not?

Prabhupāda: Sacred place, generally we take as a lonely place, solitary place. If it is not solitary, it is not sacred.

Student (2): Is sacred the same as solitary?

Prabhupāda: Yes, they used to sit down in the Himālaya where the Ganges is coming. That is a sacred place. If you go simply on the Ganges's side on the bank of the Ganges, Yamunā, you will immediately purify your mind, immediately. Or on a seaside where there is nobody disturbing. These are sacred places. Then?

Pradyumna: "The *yogī* should then sit on it very firmly."

Prabhupāda: Then *yogī* has to sit down very firmly like this. Yes, straight, perpendicularly. Then?

Pradyumna: "And should practice *yoga* by controlling the mind and the senses."

Prabhupāda: Then he has to practice meditation for controlling the mind and the senses. First of all *āsana* place, sacred place, now, *āsana*, secluded place, alone. That is stated. These are the *yogic* process. First of all...First of all thing is the, what is the aim of practicing *yoga*? So to achieve that end, that purpose, you have to control the mind because mind is very flickering, going here, there, there, there. So first of all you must know what is the purpose of practicing *yoga*, why you should practice *yoga*. So in order to achieve that goal, you have to concentrate your mind, and therefore you have to control the mind going here and there. That is control. Mind business is acceptance and rejecting. This is mind's business. Immediately I accept, "It is very good;" again, next moment, "No, no it is not good. Reject it." This is called flickering mind. So by *yoga* practice you have to make your mind in such a way that whatever you decide, that is correct, not the state of rejecting and accepting. So first of all, you have to know why you are practicing *yoga*. As you asked the question, "Why control of mind?" Then the next question will be "Why you are practicing? What is your aim?" You are going to practice *yoga*. Why? What is the aim?

Student (1): Is it to realize God?

Prabhupāda: That's nice. Therefore you must have to concentrate upon God; therefore you have to control the mind. You have to withdraw your mind from any other engagement, only concentrate on God…And that is Kṛṣṇa. So if you concentrate your mind on Kṛṣṇa, that is *yoga*. That is first-class *yoga*. That is stated. You...List the last..." *yoginām api sarveṣāṁ mad-gatenāntar-ātmanā śraddhāvān bhajate yo māṁ sa me yuktatamo mataḥ*". He is first-class *yogi* who is always concentrating his mind on Kṛṣṇa.

Student (1): Why Kṛṣṇa?

Prabhupāda: Yes. Only on Kṛṣṇa. That is...*Yoginām api sarveṣāṁ*. You read the translation.

Pradyumna: "And of all *yogis*, he who alw ays abides in Me with great faith, worshiping Me in transcendental loving service, is most intimately united with Me in *yoga* and is the highest of all."

Prabhupāda: That's it. This is the highest *yoga*. So to concentrate your mind on Kṛṣṇa, that is highest perfection of *yoga*.

And finally from the *Bhagavad-gītā* (6.11-12), Śrīla Prabhupāda offers us the best instruction in this age of Kali: "'Sacred place' refers to places of pilgrimage. In India the *yogis*, the transcendentalists or the devotees, all leave home and reside in sacred places such as Prayāga, Mathurā, Vṛndāvana, Hṛṣīkeśa and Hardiwar and in solitude practice *yoga* where the sacred rivers like Yamunā and the Ganges flow. But often this is not possible, especially for Westerners. The so-called *yoga* societies in big cities may be successful in earning material benefit, but they are not at all suitable for the actual practice of *yoga*. One who is not self-controlled and whose mind is not undisturbed cannot practice meditation. Therefore, in the *Bṛhan-nāradīya Purāṇa* it is said that in Kali-yuga (the present age), when people in general are short-lived, slow in spiritual realization and always disturbed by various anxieties, the best means of spiritual realization is chanting the holy name of the Lord.

harer nāma harer nāma
harer nāmaiva kevalam
kalau nāsty eva nāsty eva
nāsty eva gatir anyathā

"'In this age of quarrel and hypocrisy the only means of deliverance is chanting the holy name of the Lord. There is no other way. There is no other way. There is no other way.'"

Book One
Chapter Six

The Conclusion
Part I— The Pure Devotees
Part II— The Purified, Absolute Vision of *Bhagavad-gītā*

The Conclusion

Part I-The Pure Devotees

In this chapter, we hear various references, mainly from Śrīla Prabhupāda's purports on the *Śrīmad-Bhāgavatam*, about the spiritual potency of pure devotees of the Lord. These references are summarized by Srila Prabhupada with the words: "Devotees and saintly persons advanced in the renounced order can deliver even the Ganges."

In the *Padma Purāṇa*, it is stated:

guroḥ pāda udakaṁ putra tīrtha koṭi phala pradāṁ
tasya bhāgīrathī snānam ahany ahani jāyate

"The water that washes the feet of the pure spiritual master is equal to the water of ten million places of pilgrimage and gives the merit of regularly bathing in Bhāgīrathī (Gaṅgā)."

In the *Prārthanā* (*Vaiṣṇave Vijñapti*), Narottama dāsa Ṭhākura has stated:

gaṅgāra paraśa hoile paścate pāvana
darśane pavitra koro—ei tomāra guṇa

"After bathing in the waters of sacred Gaṅgā many times, one becomes purified, but just by the sight of you (Vaiṣṇava Gosvāmī), the fallen souls are purified. This is your great power."

The *Śrīmad-Bhāgavatam* (1.1.15) confirms the potency of pure devotees as follows:

yat-pāda-saṁśrayāḥ sūta
munayaḥ praśamāyanāḥ
sadyaḥ punanty upaspṛṣṭāḥ
svardhuny-āpo 'nusevayā

"O Sūta, those great sages who have completely taken shelter of the lotus feet of the Lord can at once sanctify those who come in touch with them, whereas the waters of the Ganges can sanctify only after prolonged use."

In his purport on this verse, Śrīla Prabhupāda writes: "Pure devotees of the Lord are more powerful than the waters of the sacred River Ganges. One can derive spiritual benefit out of prolonged use of the Ganges waters. But one can be sanctified at once by the mercy of a pure devotee of the Lord. In *Bhagavad-gītā* it is said that any person, regardless of birth as *śūdra*, woman, or merchant, can take shelter of the lotus feet of the Lord and by so doing can return to Godhead. To take shelter of the lotus feet of the Lord means to take shelter of the pure devotees. The pure devotees, whose only business is serving, are honored by the names Prabhupāda and Viṣṇupada, which indicate such devotees to be representatives of the lotus feet of the Lord. Anyone, therefore, who takes shelter of the lotus feet of a pure devotee by accepting the pure devotee as their spiritual master can be at once purified. Such devotees of the Lord are honored equally with the Lord because they are engaged in the most confidential service of the Lord, for they deliver out of the material world the fallen souls whom the Lord wants to return home, back to Godhead. Such pure devotees are better known as vice-lords according to revealed scriptures. The sincere disciple of the pure devotee considers the spiritual master equal to the Lord, but always considers himself to be a humble servant of the servant of the Lord. This is the pure devotional path."

Vidura leaves home

Prior to the fratricidal war of Kurukṣetra, the great soul Vidura repeatedly implored his elder brother Dhṛtarāṣṭra to do justice to the Pāṇḍavas, but his brother did not like any interference, which only insulted Vidura. Thus Mahātmā Vidura left home for pilgrimage. During his travels he met the great sage Maitreya, who imparted various instructions to Vidura. After understanding that the ultimate goal of life was *bhakti* (devotional service) unto Lord Govinda (Kṛṣṇa), Vidura left his spiritual master Maitreya and returned to Hastināpura. In the *Śrīmad-Bhāgavatam* (1.13.9-10), Mahārāja Yudhiṣṭhira inquires from Vidura how he had maintained himself during his pilgrimage and glorifies his exalted position: "While traveling on the surface of the earth, how did you maintain your livelihood? At which holy places and pilgrimage sites did you render service? My Lord, devotees like your good self are verily holy places personified. Because you carry the Personality of Godhead within your heart, you turn all places into places of pilgrimage."

Śrila Prabhupāda comments on the latter verse as follows: "The Personality of Godhead is omnipresent by His diverse potencies everywhere, just as the power of electricity is distributed everywhere within space. Similarly, the Lord's ompipresence is perceived and manifested by His unalloyed devotees like Vidura, just as electricity is manifested in an electric bulb. A pure devotee like Vidura always feels the presence of the Lord everywhere. He sees everything in the potency of the Lord and the Lord in everything. The holy places all over the earth are meant for purifying the polluted consciousness of the human being by an atmosphere surcharged with the presence of the Lord's unalloyed devotees. If anyone visits a holy place, he must search out the pure devotees residing in such holy places, take lessons from them, try to apply such instructions in practical life and thus gradually prepare oneself for the ultimate salvation, going back to Godhead. To go to some holy place of pilgrimage does not mean only to take a bath in the Ganges or Yamunā or to visit the temples situated in those places. One should also find representatives of Vidura who have no desire in life save and except to serve the Personality of Godhead. The Personality of Godhead is always with such pure devotees because of their unalloyed service, which is without any tinge of fruitive action or utopian speculation. They are in the actual service of the Lord, specifically by the process of hearing and chanting. The pure devotees hear from the authorities and chant, sing and write of the glories of the Lord. Mahāmuni Vyāsadeva heard from

Nārada, and then he chanted in writing; Śukadeva Gosvāmī studied from his father, and he described it to Parīkṣit; that is the way of *Śrīmad-Bhāgavatam*. So by their actions the pure devotees of the Lord can render any place into a place of pilgrimage, and the holy places are worth the name only on their account. Such pure devotees are able to rectify the polluted atmosphere of any place, and what to speak of a holy place rendered unholy by the questionable actions of interested persons who try to adopt a professional life at the cost of the reputation of a holy place."

(See also Book Two, Chapter Three: *Travels With Gaṅgā*, under section 6: Vidura Kutir.)

The ten Pracetās

In the *Śrīmad-Bhāgavatam*, Lord Śiva, the topmost Vaiṣṇava, prays to Lord Kṛṣṇa for the benediction of association with pure devotees.

When the sons of King Prācīnabarhi (Barhiṣat), known as the ten Pracetās, left home to practise austerities and penances in the depths of the ocean, they met Lord Śiva, who instructed them regarding the execution of austerities. Lord Śiva was very pleased with them and said, "Any person who is surrendered to the Supreme Personality of Godhead, Kṛṣṇa, the controller of everything—material nature as well as the living entity—is actually very dear to me...You are all devotees of the Lord, and as such I appreciate that you are as respectable as the Supreme Personality of Godhead Himself. I know in this way that the devotees also respect me and that I am dear to them. Thus no one can be as dear to the devotees as I am." (*Bhāg*. 4.24.28, 30)

Because Lord Śiva loved the Pracetās, as well as all other devotees, he chanted a very transcendental, pure, and auspicious prayer for the benefit of everyone who aspires to attain the ultimate goal of life. Lord Śiva addressed the Supreme Personality of Godhead, Śrī Kṛṣṇa, as the all-pervading Vāsudeva, the predominating Deity Saṅkarṣaṇa, the master of intelligence Pradyumna, and the supreme directing Deity Aniruddha. Lord Śiva prayed that the Lord be kind on him so that his mind would always be in a perfect state of cleanliness, which would enable him to engage in devotional service. He also prayed for strength and freedom from all obligations to the forefathers, demigods, general living entities, and saintly persons by being completely engaged in loving service to the Lord.

Lord Śiva then described the wonderful, superexcellently beautiful features of the Lord, which can perfectly satisfy all the demands of the senses. He explained that one must realize the position of the Supreme Personality of Godhead by the practice of *bhakti-yoga*, then real perfection of life will be attained. He continued to pray that it is very difficult to attain the lotus feet of the Lord by any method other than *bhakti-yoga*. Then Lord Śiva stated that without being blessed by a pure devotee, no one can be fully satisfied, nor can anyone understand the transcendental position of the Supreme Personality of Godhead.

Lord Śiva then prayed, "My dear Lord, Your lotus feet are the cause of all auspicious things and the destroyer of all the contamination of sin. I therefore beg Your Lordship to bless me by the association of Your devotees, who are completely purified by worshiping Your lotus feet and who are so merciful upon the conditioned souls. I think that Your real benediction will be to allow me to associate with such devotees." (4.24.58)

Śrīla Prabhupāda comments on the above verse as follows: "The Ganges water is celebrated as being able to eradicate all kinds

of sinful reactions. In other words, when a person takes his bath in the Ganges, he becomes freed from all life's contaminations. The Ganges water is celebrated in this way because it emanates from the lotus feet of the Supreme Personality of Godhead. Similarly, those who are directly in touch with the lotus feet of the Supreme Personality of Godhead, and who are absorbed in the chanting of His glories, are freed from all material contaminations. Such unalloyed devotees are able to show mercy to the common conditioned soul. Śrīla Vṛndāvana dāsa Ṭhākura has sung that the devotees of Lord Caitanya are so powerful that each one of them can deliver a universe. In other words, it is the business of devotees to preach the glories of the Lord and deliver all conditioned souls to the platform of *śuddha-sattva*, pure goodness. Here the word *su-sattva* means *śuddha-sattva*, the transcendental stage beyond material goodness. By his exemplary prayers, Lord Śiva teaches us that our best course is to take shelter of Lord Viṣṇu and His Vaiṣṇava devotees."

While the Pracetās underwent austerities for ten thousand years within the ocean during the age of Satya-yuga, they chanted and repeated the *mantras* that Lord Śiva had given them. By so doing they were able to satisfy Lord Viṣṇu, the Supreme Personality of Godhead, and the Lord rewarded their austerities by personally appearing before them. Lord Viṣṇu, possessing eight arms, appeared on the shoulder of Garuḍa and His bodily effulgence dissipated all the darkness of the universe. The Lord then expressed His great satisfaction for the mutual cooperation between the ten sons, since they were all occupied in devotional service. He also mentioned that anyone who remembers the activities of the Pracetās every evening will become friendly with all living entities, and those who chant the prayers composed by Lord Śiva, both in the morning and evening, will receive full benedictions. Lord Viṣṇu also instructed the Pracetās to marry the daughter of the sage Kaṇḍu, and since the daughter was also on the same level of devotional service, they should create progeny through her. After enjoying all the facilities of this world and the heavenly kingdom for one million celestial years, all the Pracetās developed pure, unadulterated devotional service, freed from any material contamination, and then returned home, back to Godhead, the abode of Lord Viṣṇu.

In an ecstatic, faltering voice, the Pracetās prayed to the Lord, who was before them face to face. They offered their humble obeisances, realizing that only by His causeless mercy can He be attained, not by any other method. They prayed, "Even a moment's association with a pure devotee cannot be compared to being transferred to heavenly planets or even merging into the Brahman effulgence in complete liberation. For living entities who are destined to give up the body and die, association with pure devotees is the highest benediction...The Supreme Lord, Nārāyaṇa, is present among devotees who are engaged in hearing and chanting the holy name of the Supreme Personality of Godhead. Lord Nārāyaṇa is the ultimate goal of *sannyāsīs*, those in the renounced order of life, and Nārāyaṇa is worshiped through this *saṅkīrtana* (congregational chanting) movement by those who are liberated from material contamination. Indeed, they recite the holy name again and again. Dear Lord, your personal associates, devotees, wander all over the world to purify even the holy places of pilgrimage. Is not such activity pleasing to those who are actually afraid of material existence?" (4.30.34, 36-37)

In his purport on verse 37 quoted above, Śrīla Prabhupāda states: "When a pure devotee goes to a place of pilgrimage, he desires to purify that holy place of pilgrimage. Many sinful men bathe in the holy waters of the places of pilgrimage. They take their baths in the waters of the Ganges and Yamunā at places such as Prayāga, Vṛndāvana and Mathurā. In this way sinful men are purified, but their sinful actions and reactions remain at the holy places of pilgrimage. When a devotee comes to take his bath at those places of pilgrimage, the sinful reactions left by the sinful men are neutralized by the devotee. *Tīrthī-kurvanti tīrthāni svāntaḥ-sthena gadābhṛtā* (*Bhāg*. 1.13.10). Because the devotee always carries the Supreme Personality of Godhead within his heart, wherever he goes becomes a place of pilgrimage, a holy place for understanding the Supreme Personality of Godhead. It is therefore the duty of everyone to associate with a pure devotee and thus attain freedom from material contamination. Everyone should take advantage of the wandering devotees, whose only business is to deliver conditioned souls from the clutches of *māyā*."

Devotees can deliver even Gaṅgā

In the *Śrīmad-Bhāgavatam* (9.9.3-6), after King Bhagīratha completed his severe austerities to bring Gaṅgā down to this planet, Gaṅgā-devī personally appeared before Bhagīratha and said, "I am very satisfied with your austerities and am now prepared to give you benedictions as you desire. When I fall from the sky to the surface of the planet earth, the water will certainly be very forceful. Who will sustain that force? If I am not sustained, I shall pierce the surface of the earth and go down to Rasātala, the Pātāla area of the universe. O King, I do not wish to go down to the planet earth, for there the people in general will bathe in my water to cleanse themselves of their sinful deeds. When all these sinful reactions accumulate in me, how shall I become free from them? You must consider this very carefully."

Then Bhagīratha said, "Those who are saintly because of devotional service and are therefore in the renounced order, free from material desires, and who are pure devotees, expert in following the regulative principles mentioned in the *Vedas*, are always glorious and pure in behavior, and are able to deliver all fallen souls. When such pure devotees bathe in your water, the sinful reactions accumulated from other people will certainly be counteracted, for such devotees always keep in the core of their hearts the Supreme Personality of Godhead, who can vanquish all sinful reactions."

In his purport on *Śrīmad-Bhāgavatam* (9.9.5 and 6), Śrīla Prabhupāda elaborates on how we should always respectfully honor a saintly person: "One who is very powerful is not affected by any sinful activity. But here we see mother Ganges fears being burdened with the sins of the people in general who would bathe in her waters. This indicates that no one but the Supreme Personality of Godhead is able to neutralize the reactions of sinful deeds, whether one's own or those of others. Sometimes the spiritual master, after accepting a disciple, must take charge of that disciple's past sinful activities and, being overloaded, must sometimes suffer—if not fully, then partially—for the sinful acts of that disciple. Every disciple, therefore, must be very careful not to commit sinful activities after initiation. The poor spiritual master is kind and merciful enough to accept a disciple and partially suffer for that disciple's sinful activities, but Kṛṣṇa, being merciful to His servant, neutralizes the reactions of sinful deeds for the servant who engages in preaching His glories. Even mother Ganges feared the sinful reactions of the people in general and was anxious about how she would counteract the burden of these sins.

"Mother Ganges is available to everyone for bathing. Therefore, not only will sinful persons bathe in the Ganges water, but in Haridwar and other holy places where the Ganges flows, saintly persons and devotees will also bathe in the waters of the Ganges. Devotees and saintly persons advanced in the renounced order can deliver even the Ganges. *Tīrthī-kurvanti tīrthāni svāntaḥ-sthena gadābhṛtā*. Because saintly devotees always keep the Lord within the core of their hearts, they can perfectly cleanse the holy places of all sinful reactions. Therefore, people in general must always respectfully honor saintly persons. It is ordered that as soon as one sees a Vaiṣṇava, or even a *sannyāsī*, one should immediately offer respects to such a holy man. If one forgets to show respect in this way, one must observe a fast for that day. This is a Vedic injunction. One must be extremely careful to refrain from committing offenses at the lotus feet of a devotee or saintly person."

Also in the *Śrīmad-Bhāgavatam* (3.29.11-12), we hear how the pure devotee cannot stop devotional service by any means, just as the flow of the Gaṅgā cannot be stopped: "The manifestation of unadulterated devotional service is exhibited when one's mind is at once attracted to hearing the transcendental name and qualities of the Supreme Personality of Godhead, who is residing in everyone's heart. Just as the water of the Ganges flows naturally down towards the ocean, such devotional ecstasy, uninterrupted by any material condition, flows towards the Supreme Lord."

In the purport to these verses, Śrīla Prabhupāda writes: "The basic principle of this unadultlerated, pure devotional service is love of Godhead. *Mad-guṇa-śruti-mātreṇa* means 'just after hearing about the transcendental qualities of the Supreme Personality of Godhead.' These qualities are called *nirguṇa*. The Supreme Lord is uncontaminated by the modes of material nature, therefore He is attractive to the pure devotee. There is no need to practise meditation to attain such attraction; the pure devotee is already in the transcendental stage, and the affinity between him and the Supreme Personality of Godhead is natural and is compared to the Ganges water flowing towards the sea. The flow of the Ganges water cannot be stopped by any condition; similarly, a pure devotee's attraction for the transcendental name, form and pastimes of the Supreme Godhead cannot be stopped by any material condition. The word *avicchinna*, 'without interruptions', is very important in this connection. No material condition can stop the flow of the devotional service of a pure devotee."

Elsewhere in his purport on the *Śrīmad-Bhāgavatam* (10.4.20), Śrīla Prabhupāda explains how the pure devotee is unaffected by material conditions: "One may argue that we may see a person who is spiritually engaged twenty-four hours a day but is still suffering from disease. In fact, however, he is neither suffering nor diseased; otherwise he could not be engaged twenty-four hours a day in spiritual activities. The example may be given in this connection that sometimes dirty foam or garbage is seen floating on the water of the Ganges. This is called *nira-dharma*, a function of the water. But one who goes to the Ganges does not mind the foam and dirty things floating in the water. With his hand, he pushes away such nasty things, bathes in the Ganges and gains the beneficial results. Therefore, one who is situated in the spiritual status of life is unaffected by foam and garbage—or any superficial dirty things. This is confirmed by Śrīla Rūpa Gosvāmī: 'A person acting in the service of Kṛṣṇa with his body, mind and words is a

liberated person, even within the material world.' (*Bhakti-rasāmṛta-sindhu* 1.2.187). Therefore, one is forbidden to regard the *guru* (spiritual master) as an ordinary human being (*gurusu nara-matir...naraki sah*). The spiritual master, as *ācārya*, is always situated in the spiritual status of life. Birth, death, old age and disease do not affect him. According to the *Hari-bhakti-vilāsa*, therefore, after the disappearance of an *ācārya*, his body is never burnt to ashes, for it is a spiritual body. The spiritual body is always unaffected by material conditions."

And finally in *Śrīmad-Bhāgavatam* (3.1.45), Śrīla Prabhupāda points out in his purport that the Lord always desires to remain where His glories are chanted by His devotees: "The purpose of pilgrimages is to remember the Lord constantly, and therefore the Lord is known as *tīrtha-kīrti*. The purpose of going to a place of pilgrimage is to get the chance to glorify the Lord. Even today, although times have changed, there are still pilgrimage sites in India...The beauty of such a pilgrimage site is that automatically one remembers the holy glories of the Lord. His name, fame, quality, form, pastimes and entourage are all identical to the Lord, and therefore chanting the glories of the Lord invokes the personal presence of the Lord. Anytime or anywhere pure devotees meet and chant the glories of the Lord, the Lord is present without any doubt. It is said by the Lord Himself that He always stays where His pure devotees chant His glories."

Traveling with Śrīla Bhaktivinoda Ṭhākura

In 1898, during the period of his service to the Tripura Royal Government, Śrīla Bhaktisiddhānta Sarasvatī traveled with his father, Śrīmad Bhaktivinoda Ṭhākura, to Kāśī, Prayāga, and other holy places. The ideal *ācārya*, Śrīla Bhaktisiddhānta Sarasvatī, clearly taught us by touring the holy sites in close allegiance with Śrīla Bhaktivinoda that the holy places are to be seen by following the pure devotee, then the actual glory of the holy places can be realized. The only gain in traveling to different holy places without adherence to a Vaiṣṇava is only the effort involved. Observing the touring of holy places by people devoid of faithful adherence to a Vaiṣṇava, Śrī Narottama Ṭhākura has sung: *tīrtha-yātrā pariśrama kevala manera bhrama sarva-siddhi govinda-caraṇa*—"The struggle to travel to various holy places of pilgrimage is simply the mind's mistake, because to make spiritual advancement all one actually needs is the lotus feet of Lord Govinda."

If the holy places are seen in the association of a Vaiṣṇava, one gets the good fortune of realizing all the pastimes of Godhead and His devotees. Those pastimes are the life-breath of the holy places, and by their audience, the heart is cleansed of all impurities. The various holy places impart inspiration to all those pastimes in the pure heart of devotees. In reality, the pure heart is the living holy place. Śrīla Bhaktisiddhānta Mahārāja gathered many facts about all the holy places, which were later incorporated in his commentary on the *Śrī Caitanya-caritāmṛta* called *Anubhāṣya*.

The following quotes from the *Śrīmad-Bhāgavatam* (10.86.52) and the *Śrī Caitanya-caritāmṛta* (*Madhya* 22.54) conclude this first part of the chapter by glorifying the pure-hearted devotees of the Lord:

devāḥ kṣetrāṇi tīrthāni
darśana-sparśanārcanaiḥ
śanaiḥ punanti kālena
tad apy arhattamekṣayā

"One can gradually become purified by seeing, touching and worshiping temple deities, places of pilgrimage and holy rivers. But one can attain the same result immediately simply by receiving the glance of exalted sages."

'sādhu-saṅga', 'sādhu-saṅga'-sarva-śāstre kaya
lava-mātra sādhu-saṅge sarva-siddhi haya

"The verdict of all revealed scriptures is that by even a moment's asociation with a pure devotee, one can attain all success."

PART II-THE PURIFIED, ABSOLUTE VISION OF *BHAGAVAD-GĪTĀ*

Again, in the following quotes from the *Śrīmad-Bhāgavatam*, Śrīla Prabhupāda compares the water of the Ganges to the *Bhagavad-gītā*. The verse, translation, and purport of *Śrīmad-Bhāgavatam* (3.20.5) state:

tayoḥ saṁvadatoḥ sūta
pravṛttā hy amalāḥ kathāḥ
āpo gāṅgā ivāgha-ghnīr
hareḥ pādāmbujāśrayāḥ

"Saunaka inquired about the conversation between Vidura and Maitreya: There must have been many narrations of the spotless pastimes of the Lord. The hearing of such narrations is exactly like bathing in the water of the Ganges, for it can free one from all sinful reactions."

"The water of the Ganges is purified because it pours forth from the lotus feet of the Lord. Similarly, *Bhagavad-gītā* is as good as the water of the Ganges because it is spoken from the mouth of the Supreme Lord. So it is with any topic on the pastimes of the Lord or the characteristics of His transcendental activities. The Lord is absolute; there is no difference between His words, His perspiration or His pastimes. The water of the Ganges, the narrations of His pastimes and the words spoken by Him are all on the absolute platform and thus taking shelter of any one of them is equally good. Śrīla Rūpa Gosvāmī has enunciated that anything in relationship with Kṛṣṇa is on the transcendental platform. If we can dovetail all our activities in relationship with Kṛṣṇa, then we do not stand on the material platform, but always on the spiritual platform."

In the purport to *Śrīmad-Bhāgavatam* (3.32.28) he writes: "*Bhagavad-gītā* confirms that they are fools who, simply upon seeing Kṛṣṇa, consider Him a common man. They do not know the unlimited knowledge, power and opulence of the Supreme Personality of Godhead. Material sense speculation leads to the conclusion that the Supreme is formless. It is because of such mental speculation that the conditioned soul remains in ignorance under the spell of the illusory energy. The Supreme Person has to be understood by the transcendental sound vibrated by Him in *Bhagavad-gītā*, wherein He says that there is nothing superior to Himself, the impersonal Brahman effulgence is resting on His personality. The purified, absolute vision of *Bhagavad-gītā* is compared to the River Ganges. Ganges water is so pure that it can purify even the asses and cows. But anyone who, disregarding the pure Ganges, wishes to be purified instead by the filthy water flowing in a drain, cannot be successful. Similarly, one can successfully attain pure knowledge of the Absolute only by hearing from the pure Absolute Himself."

And in the purport to *Śrīmad-Bhāgavatam* (2.1.1) he writes: "In the *Bhagavad-gītā* it is stated that simply by understanding the transcendental nature of Lord Kṛṣṇa's appearance, disappearance, and activities, one can immediately return home, back to Godhead, and never come back to this miserable condition of material existence. It is very

auspicious, therefore, to hear always about Kṛṣṇa. So Mahārāja Parīkṣit requested Śukadeva Gosvāmī to narrate the activities of Kṛṣṇa so that he could engage his mind in Kṛṣṇa. The activities of Kṛṣṇa are nondifferent from Kṛṣṇa Himself. As long as one is engaged in hearing such transcendental activities of Kṛṣṇa, he remains aloof from the conditional life of material existence. The topics of Lord Kṛṣṇa are so auspicious that they purify the speaker, the hearer and the inquirer. They are compared to the Ganges waters, which flow from the toe of Lord Kṛṣṇa. Wherever the Ganges waters go, they purify the land and the person who bathes in them. Similarly, *kṛṣṇa-kathā*, or the topics of Kṛṣṇa, are so pure that wherever they are spoken, the place, the hearer, the inquirer, the speaker and all concerned become purified."

* * *

By an impartial study of the *Gītā-māhātmyam*, as quoted below from the *Bhagavad-gītā As It Is* introduction, we can learn that the *Bhagavad-gītā* is more important than the water of the Ganges.

maline mocanaṁ puṁsāṁ
jala-snānaṁ dine dine
sakṛd gītāmṛta-snānaṁ
saṁsāra-mala-nāśanam

"One may cleanse himself daily by taking a bath in water, but if one takes a bath even once in the sacred Ganges water of *Bhagavad-gītā*, for him the dirt of material life is altogether vanquished." (3)

gītā su-gītā kartavyā
kim anyaiḥ śāstra-vistaraiḥ
yā svayaṁ padmanābhasya
mukha-padmād viniḥsṛtā

"Because *Bhagavad-gītā* is spoken by the Supreme Personality of Godhead, one need not read any other Vedic literature. One need only attentively and regularly hear and read *Bhagavad-gītā*. In the present age, people are so absorbed in mundane activities that it is not possible for them to read all the Vedic literatures. But this is not necessary. This one book, *Bhagavad-gītā*, will suffice, because it is the essence of all Vedic literatures and especially because it is spoken by the Supreme Personality of Godhead." (4)

bhāratāmṛta-sarvasvaṁ
viṣṇu-vaktrād viniḥsṛtam
gītā-gaṅgodakaṁ pītvā
punar janma na vidyate

"One who drinks the water of the Ganges attains salvation, so what to speak of one who drinks the nectar of *Bhagavad-gītā*? *Bhagavad-gītā* is the essential nectar of the *Mahābhārata*, and it is spoken by Lord Kṛṣṇa Himself, the original Viṣṇu. *Bhagavad-gītā* comes from the mouth of the Supreme Personality of Godhead, and the Ganges is said to emanate from the lotus feet of the Lord. Of course, there is no difference between the mouth and the feet of the Supreme Lord, but from an impartial study we can appreciate that *Bhagavad-gītā* is even more important than the water of the Ganges." (5)

sarvopaniṣado gāvo
dogdhā gopāla-nandanaḥ
pārtho vatsaḥ su-dhīr bhoktā
dugdhaṁ gītāmṛtaṁ mahat

"This *Gītopaniṣad*, *Bhagavad-gītā*, the essence of all the *Upaniṣads* (philosophical treatises of the *Vedas*), is just like a cow, and Lord Kṛṣṇa, who is famous as a cowherd boy, is milking this cow. Arjuna is just like a calf, and learned scholars and pure devotees are to drink the nectarean milk of *Bhagavad-gītā*." (6)

ekaṁ śāstraṁ devakī-putra-gītam
eko devo devakī-putra eva

eko mantras tasya nāmāni yāni
karmāpy ekaṁ tasya devasya sevā

"In this present day, people are very much eager to have one scripture, one God, one religion, and one occupation. Therefore, *ekaṁ śāstraṁ devakī-putra-gītam*: let there be one scripture only, one common scripture for the whole world—*Bhagavad-gītā. Eko devo devakī-putra eva*: let there be one God for the whole world—Srī Kṛṣṇa. *Eko mantras tasya nāmāni yāni*: and one hymn, one *mantra*, one prayer—the chanting of His name: *Hare Kṛṣṇa, Hare Kṛṣṇa, Kṛṣṇa Kṛṣṇa, Hare Hare/ Hare Rāma, Hare Rāma, Rāma Rāma, Hare Hare. Karmāpy ekaṁ tasya devasya sevā*: and let there be one work only—the service of the Supreme Personality of Godhead." (7)

Book Two
Chapter One

Following in the Footsteps of Gaṅgā-devī
(From Mukhwa to Gaṅgotrī)

BOOK TWO

Pastimes in the Sacred Places

Chapter One

Following in the Footsteps of Gaṅgā-devī (From Mukhwa to Gaṅgotrī)

Gaṇgā-devī Temple in Mukhwa

Above:
Lord Śiva, known as Someśvāra, on his palanquin before the procession

Left:
Gaṅgā-devī on procession in her palanquin at Mārkeṇḍeya

Far Right:
The procession enroute to Gaṅgotrī

Right:
Bhāgīrathī Gaṅgā near Mukhwa

Above:
Procession
resting place
midway
between
Mukhwa and
Gaṅgotrī

Above: Himalayan peaks surrounding Gaṅgotrī Valley

Left:
Bhāgīrathī
Gaṅgā near
Mārkeṇḍeya

Right:
Mallā-devī
on the bank
of Bhāgīrathī
Gaṅgā

Below:
Gaṅgā-devī Temple on opening day in Gaṅgotrī

Below: A *brāhmaṇa* performs Gaṅgā worship for a pilgrim

Chapter Two
Retracing the Footsteps of Gaṅgā-devī (From Gaṅgotrī to Mukhwa)

Bhāgīrathī below the Durgā-devī Temple

Opposite page:
Durgā-devī Temple where the procession halts for the evening before proceeding to Mukhwa

Top Left:
Gaṅgā-devī's procession leaves Gaṅgotrī

Middle Left:
Bhagīratha-śilā at Gaṅgotrī

Left:
Road from Gaṅgotrī

Right:
View from Gaṅgotrī

The procession between Mārkeṇḍeya and Mukhwa

Below: Gaṅgā-devī enroute to Mārkeṇḍeya

Right: Gaṅgotrī Temple on closing day

Following in the Footsteps of Gaṅgā-devī

(From Mukhwa to Gaṅgotrī)

After serving on ISKCON's Saṅkīrtana Padayātrā in India for eleven years (1985 to 1996), it was glorious to finally arrive in Śrīdhāma Māyāpur during the 1996 Gaura Pūrṇimā festival, Śrī Caitanya Mahāprabhu's appearance day celebration on the full moon day in the month of Phālguna. During the five week visit, I was inspired by hearing about Śrī Caitanya Mahāprabhu's Māyāpur pastimes, which have been revealed to us by Śrīla Prabhupāda. Everywhere one looks and anywhere one goes, the love of Śrī Caitanya Mahāprabhu and Śrīla Prabhupāda is all around, especially with all of our Godbrothers and sisters gathered together from around the world. Their *sat-saṅga* (association) is something rare and merciful.

During this festival I was in anxiety over my future, since an eleven year career on the road had come to an end. After leaving Māyāpur, New Delhi was the next destination, with a short stop-over in Vārāṇasī. Over the years on Padayātrā, we had visited Vārāṇasī several times. But to visit this holy abode without being in charge of the Padayātrā and the corresponding responsibilities involved was a relaxing change.

Daily I would visit the various *ghāṭas* (bathing places) spread along the bank of the Gaṅgā. The area where Lord Viṣṇu resides, named Pañca-gaṅgā-ghāṭa, which is the confluence of five sacred rivers (Gaṅgā, Yamunā, Sarasvatī, Dhūtapāpā, and Kiraṇā), was my favorite *ghāṭa*. Every day I spent several hours bathing, reading, chanting, and meditating on Gaṅgā-devī's merciful pastimes at Pañca-gaṅgā-ghāṭa, otherwise known locally as Viṣṇupurī. Caitanya Mahāprabhu also bathed and lived near this place, which is just below the famous Bindu-Mādhava temple. Here Gaṅgā's waters are low, calm, peaceful, and merciful, especially since Gaṅgā-mayī manifests from the lotus feet of Lord Viṣṇu and then returns to His lotus feet here at Viṣṇupurī, which is a place a devotee should aspire to visit, return to, or even reside at.

On the last day of my two week visit to Vārāṇasī, I took one last bath and asked Gaṅgā-devī, "When will I see you again?" Then I departed for ISKCON's Centennial House in New Delhi.

After one week in New Delhi, I was feeling restless and indecisive about what to do next when my Godbrother Badarī Viśāla Prabhu from Haridvāra suddenly appeared. He invited me to attend the opening day ceremony at Gaṅgotrī, which falls on Akṣaya-tṛtīyā (the third day after the new moon in the month of Vaiśākha—April/May) each year. This *yātrā* (pilgrimage) would include a two day walk with Śrī Gaṅgā-devī. Only have a few days remained for us to meet Gaṅgā-devī in her winter abode, a small village named Mukhwa (sometimes called Mukhāra), some 22 kilometres before Gaṅgotrī. So I quickly packed and we (including a Swiss devotee named Param Tattva Prabhu) set off for Haridvāra on the midnight bus.

Before I realized it, we were bathing in the Gaṅgā at the Lokanātha Brahmacārī-ghāṭa in Haridvāra. I sincerely appreciated Gaṅgā-mātā's mercy, especially since only a week before I had asked her in Vārāṇasī, "When will I see you again?" I recalled a conversation in the *Nārada Purāṇa* between Sanaka-kumāra and Nārada Muni, where Sanaka says, "He who ardently desires and yearns, 'When shall I go to Gaṅgā? When shall I see that river?' goes to the region of Lord Viṣṇu." I just sat on the steps of the *ghāṭa* without words or any more thoughts. Her waters were perfectly chilled, relieving one of the early summer heat.

Shortly afterwards we were in Rishikesh (340 metres above sea level) boarding a bus to Tehri (770 m.), and then a bus to Uttarkāśī (1158 m.), which is the district headquarters. Two of the four most important holy places in the Garhwal Himālayas, Yamunotri (3185 m.) and Gaṅgotrī (3140 m.), are situated within this district. After *darśana* of Kāśī Viśvanātha Mahādeva and Lord Paraśurāma in Uttarkāśī the next morning, we took a jeep a few kilometres to a small hillside village named Netala, just after the Gaṅgā dam project at Maneri (1524 m.). Badarī Viśāla Prabhu arranged morning *prasāda* for us with a *brāhmaṇa* friend, Yamuna Prasad Semwal, who was going to guide us to Mukhwa, Gaṅgā-devī's winter abode. After honoring delicious *prasāda* and appreciating the Himālayan hospitality, we eventually started for Mukhwa. Between trying to stop a bus and its eventual mechanical breakdown, the occasional rain, a crowded jeep, windy hilly roads, and the early evening darkness, we finally arrived at a village named Dharāli. This village is just opposite and below Mukhwa and is situated on the bank of the River Bhāgīrathī Gaṅgā, a few kilometres after Harsil (2620 m.). Hiring a coolie to carry some of the luggage, we slowly descended some 50 metres before crossing a 30 metre long foot-bridge over the Bhāgīrathī. Then we ascended a wet, slippery, rock-loose footpath about 200 metres to the simple village of Mukhwa at 2800 metres, the winter abode of Śrī Gaṅgā-devī.

* * *

During our journey to Mukhwa, I recalled a visit in 1995 to one part of the Bhāgīrathī valley, between Tehri and Dharāsu, that we passed on the way. The following is a portion of that recollection.

Since the transcendental waters of Gaṅgā-mayī are generally described as coming from three sources—from Lord Brahmā's *kamaṇḍalu*, from the Causal Ocean, and from Lord Kṛṣṇa's (Nārāyaṇa's) melted body—she is able to purify the three worlds. Also, Lord Brahmā says in the *Padma Purāṇa*, "Having observed her to be great, I held her in my waterpot. Since she has risen from the lotus feet of Viṣṇu and is held on the head of Śiva, she is united with us three: Viṣṇu, Śiva, and Brahmā. Due to her contact with us, she is purified and thus purifies the three worlds." Since Gaṅgā-mayī undertakes a threefold path, traveling from the heavenly planetary

systems to this planet earth and onwards to the lower planetary systems, she is called Tripathagā. She is also known as Trailokya-pāvanī-puṇyā, the holiest of all rivers sanctifying the three worlds.

Reflecting on Gaṅgā-mayī's threefold path, I began to reminisce on my three journeys into the Himālayas with Padayātrā in the previous years: 1987, 1992, and 1995. As soon as one approaches the Tehri area from Rishikesh, Bhāgīrathī Gaṅgā comes into clear view—a *darśana* that captivates and overwhelms the heart with awe, reverence, and inspiration. She spreads out vast and wide, navigating a zig-zag course greater than any snake.

As we passed the Tehri-Bhaldiyana-Barethi region, just before entering the Bhāgīrathī Gaṅgā valley that leads towards Uttarkāśi, Harsil, and then to Mukhwa, I truly appreciated the scenic beauty for which the Himālayas are famous. The following words were recorded in my Padayātrā Journal at Bhaldiyana (900 m) on the 22nd of June, 1995: "Although it was a full day of nonstop rain, we covered a long distance. This Bhāgīrathī valley road is on the southern bank of the river, which has some spectacular U-shape turns, stretching the imagination about the course taken by King Bhagīratha in his chariot as he turned this way and that while Gaṅgā-devī followed behind. Many small villages are dotted throughout the valley on both sides. But with the rain and overcast skies, the naturally beautiful Himālayan scenery appeared dull, though still very enliven. Many villagers were actively cultivating the fields, taking advantage of the continuous flow of rain water.

"By Kṛṣṇa's mercy we had very nice shelter in the local high school, a bit outside the small township, perched on top of a small ridge overlooking the mighty Bhāgīrathī some 100 metres below. It is not possible to explain in a few words the intense, mystical environment that hovers over the entire region where Gaṅgā-mayī is mercifully flowing. All I can say is that I am extremely grateful to be able to visit her and her surroundings once again. What have I done to deserve her mercy again, considering my continuous offenses day in and day out? Dear Gaṅgā-devī, I thank you again and again. BHĀGĪRATHĪ GAṄGĀ KI JAI!"

The next afternoon, the 23rd of June, 1995, I wrote the following from Barethi (840 m): "What a pleasant day! Such a clear, blue sky. Every single leaf, stone, plant, tree, house, field, and person appeared three-dimensional through the pure, clear, fresh air, a result of the rains yesterday. The sun's rays enhanced the various mountain colors into striking, sharp pictures, especially the bright green rice fields and the pine trees. I was so completely absorbed in mother nature's Himālayan scenery that I did not even find a moment to rest. My book distribution in the small villages and towns was disturbed, since I was so anxious to be back out in the country, along the most merciful, flowing Bhāgīrathī Gaṅgā. Even the bright sunshine was welcome on top of my head, compared to yesterday's constant rainfall. Some of the other *padayātrīs* (walking members of Padayātrā), however, complained that it was too hot.

"Presently I am very, very tired and ready to go out like a light switch! I feel completely content and self-satisfied by appreciating Lord Kṛṣṇa's majestic creation here on this insignificant planet earth. Just now, the local children are happily dancing and chanting in the Gaura-ārati *kīrtana* (evening worship with song and dance). They are so enthusiastic and excited to chant, the result of taking birth and living in an environment so conducive for spiritual life, immersed in and surrounded by *sattva-guṇa* (the quality of goodness). HARE KṚṢṆA!"

Let's return to our visit to Mukhwa, which is high above the Bhāgīrathī Gaṅgā and which has a full panoramic view of the snow-capped Himālayas, including the mighty 6140 metre high Śrī Kānta Parvata. When we arrived during the evening darkness, confusion overcame us since we did not know where we were being taken. We had passed numerous villages on the roadside, and now we were hiking up an unknown trail to an unfamiliar village. Since it was the day after Amāvasyā (new moon) and the sky was overcast, there was no helpful, guiding light from the moon or stars. After reaching the village, we were relieved to sit but still unsure of what to expect next. Then we were directed even higher through the uppermost part of the mountainside village to practically the last house. This was to be our halting spot for the night.

We were introduced to the owner, who is one of the *brāhmaṇas* of Gaṅgotrī, Mr. Bharosa Rama Semwal. He is now the high school headmaster at the nearby town of Harsil. He was very happy to receive two foreign devotees of Lord Kṛṣṇa into his home. He specially welcomed Badarī Viśāla Prabhu, since he is a native of Deoprayāga, which is also in the Himālayas on the Rishikesh-Badarinath Road. While they were discussing the arrangements for late evening *prasāda*, Param Tattva Prabhu and I were led into Mr. Semwal's guest room on the first floor so that we could adjust and feel at home. Meanwhile, the *mātājīs* (women) began preparations for the meal in the room next door. Due to physical exhaustion, we just lay down and took rest until *prasāda* was ready. Upon being woken up, a delicious Himālayan home-made meal, offered to Their Lordships Śrī Śrī Badarī-Nārāyaṇa, as well as to Gaṅgā-devī, awaited us. It was a pleasure to receive such hospitality from the devotees of Gaṅgā-devī.

Param Tattva Prabhu was amazed at the genuine spiritual hospitality that was offered to us. He was truly grateful. Later, we slept soundly, keeping warm under the heavy blankets and quilts in the thin, cold, mountain spring air.

I awoke early, as usual, finding my way outside to answer nature's call, before securing a warm seat on the upper veranda with a 180 degree panoramic view of the mountainous snow-clad peaks directly surrounding Śrī Kānta Parvata. Since it was still the *brāhma-muhūrta* hour (auspicious time before sunrise), the dark early morning hours were slightly aglow from the star's and planet's reflections. As the sun began its slow ascent, the beautiful, white, snowy peaks began to shine. From the golden-red reflection of the rising sun's rays, the snowy peaks began to look even more majestic and prominent, demanding a great amount of respect. Yet they were graceful, bestowing on humankind plentiful amounts of merciful purification. As it is said in the *Skanda Purāṇa*: "He who thinks of the Himālayas is greater than he who performs all worship in Kāśī (Vārāṇasī). As the dew is dried up by the morning sun, so are the sins of mankind by the sight of the Himālayas."

While the sun was rising, I continued my *japa-mālā* (chanting on beads). Afterwards, I recalled a particular text from the *Śrīmad-Bhāgavatam* (1.12.22), comparing the superexcellent qualities of Emperor Parīkṣit to the lion and the Himālayas: "This child (Emperor Parīkṣit) will be as strong as a lion, and as worthy a shelter as the Himālaya Mountains. He will be forbearing like the earth, as tolerant as his parents." Śrīla Prabhupāda comments: "The Himālayan mountains are famous for all richness. There are innumerable caves to live in, numberless trees of good fruits to eat, good springs to drink water from and profuse drugs and

minerals to cure diseases. Any man who is not materially prosperous can take shelter of these great mountains, and he will be provided with everything required. Both the materialist and the spiritualist can take advantage of the great shelter of the Himālayas." Also by appreciating the essential quality of these mountains, one can see Lord Kṛṣṇa, the Immovable, as He says in the *Bhagavad-gītā* (10.25), "Of immovable things I am the Himālayas."

My mind pondered what lay beyond this limited eyesight of mine that was observing these mountains. So much spiritual wealth of self-realization was deeply engraved throughout the Himālayas. I recollected how many pilgrims, *sādhus*, devotees like the Pāṇḍavas, *ācāryas*, *munis*, *ṛṣis*, demigods, demigoddesses, *avatāras*, as well as Lord Viṣṇu, Śiva, and Brahmā had spent countless years performing various severe austerities and elaborate sacrifices for our benefit. With the results of their hard devotional work, they were passing their blessings down for the benefit of all future generations, dynasties, races, etc. Where would we be without their prayers, guidance, mercy, and love?

Meanwhile, the other devotees and family members slowly rose to begin their day. I remained fixed in my comfortable, warm seating arrangement, thinking ahead to when Śrī Gaṅgā-devī would be taken from the temple that served as her winter abode, onto a palanquin, along with her companions, Sarasvatī-devī and Annapūrṇā-mātā (Pārvatī). The whole festival was to begin around 2:00 p.m., when the procession would leave Mukhwa and proceed to Mārkaṇḍeya, Mārkaṇḍeya Ṛṣi's *tapo-bhūmi* (place of austerities), then onwards to Laṅkā, crossing Jādh-Gaṅgā (Jāhnavī) to Bhaironghāṭi, where the walking procession-cum-pilgrimage would halt for the evening. Then the next morning Gaṅgā-devī would arrive at Gaṅgotrī, where she would remain for the six months of summer, monsoon, and autumn, before returning to Mukhwa in the month of Kārtika (October/November) on Amāvasyā, the day after Dīpāvalī.

The time came for a refreshing cold bath. The only water supply within the village was a pipe-faucet system, which supplied the drinking water for the entire village. Since the pipe-faucet was being used by the village *mātājis*, we decided to walk outside the village to a beautiful waterfall for our early morning bath. I quickly braved the steep, slippery terrain to the waterfall and shot under the forceful freezing water, which woke my entire existence through and through! The other devotees took their bath at a lower level of the waterfall. Thereafter we all greatly appreciated the rising sun's warm rays as we sat on some rocks that overlooked the entire Bhāgīrathī Gaṅgā valley down below. While we walked back through the village, all the local villagers were able to have *darśana* of their new guests, especially the foreigners! Meanwhile, we observed the unique style of architecture and appreciated the simple mountain lifestyle, especially how the village was located with a view of the surrounding Himālayan peaks, overlooking Gaṅgā-mayī flowing peacefully far below. Returning to the house, we found awaiting us another delicious meal of *prasāda*, which we thoroughly honored and enjoyed as the mercy of Gaṅgā-devī.

Resuming the comfortable seat on the veranda, I wrote the following words on the 19th of April, 1996: "Due to the mercy of Śrī Gaṅgā-devī, somehow or other we are presently sitting in this small mountainside village, just east of Harsil (Hari-śilā). We are waiting to participate in the yearly two-day pilgrimage from this village of Mukhwa to Gaṅgotrī. During the winter months, the

golden face of Gaṅgā-devī is brought here so that her worship and *darśana* can continue without interruption throughout the year. Then she is taken back again to Gaṅgotrī on every Akṣaya-tṛtīyā, which marks the opening day of the holy *dhāma* (Lord's abode) for the general pilgrims and tourists and which falls this year (1996) on the 20th of April. While traveling here yesterday, we encountered rain, which just increased my anxieties, since we had not properly prepared ourselves for this last minute Himālayan journey. This morning, however, as a result of yesterday's showers, the snow-capped, majestic Himālayan peaks stood out sharply with the clear blue sky as a background, and Sūrya (the demigod of the sun) shone brightly above. I cannot begin to describe the peaceful setting—the people with their children, animals, and land; the eternal echo of Gaṅgāmayī below us; and the natural countryside manifest by Kṛṣṇa's external energy. It is difficult to believe I am here, since only three days back I was in Delhi, and now I find myself in heaven!

"The procession will begin around 2:00 p.m., when an expected five hundred devoted villagers will participate. Today's walk will be on the northern side of Gaṅgā-mayī, along a local foot-trail, just opposite the side traveled by the bus *yātrīs* (pilgrims on journey). The procession should take about 4 to 5 hours, arriving at Bhaironghāṭi in the early evening. Tomorrow we will arrive in Gaṅgotrī for the official opening of Gaṅgā-devī's temple. This jouney is completely under the control of Gaṅgā-devī, so I am anxious to participate in the upcoming walk. GAṄGĀ-DEVĪ KI JAI! HARE KṚṢṆA!"

During this writing spree, Badarī Viśāla Prabhu and our host, Mr. Semwal, were happily sitting in the warm morning sun in the front courtyard, stringing raisins and cashews into garlands to be offered for the pleasure of Gaṅgā-devī before the procession began. Afterwards, Param Tattva Prabhu and myself took additional rest as most of the villagers gathered near the Gaṅgā-devī temple, which was located on the lower level of Mukhwa. The villagers were busy cleaning and dressing themselves in their best clothing for the annual festival. As midday approached, some preliminary ritualistic activities began, preparing Gaṅgā-devī for the walking pilgrimage, which was to start in about two hours time. Mr. Semwal and his family were about ready to join the ceremonies down on the lower level. He decided to go ahead of them, accompanying us for *darśana* of Gaṅgā-devī, just before she is taken out of her winter abode and placed onto her palanquin for the pilgrimage.

As we walked down through the village, many other villagers welcomed us. Upon arriving at the temple, we were brought to the front entrance for *darśana*; but, since so much activity was taking place within the temple's inner sanctum, we could not properly see Gaṅgā-devī. I therefore began to browse around the ceremonial functions. Below Gaṅgā-devī's temple I could see two other palanquins, both of Lord Someśvara (Śiva), one from Mukhwa and the other from Dharāli, that were to join the procession with Gaṅgā-devī. The palanquins were decorated with bright, colorful reddish cloth, fully covering Lord Śiva, except for a small opening for his face.

Many other residents from neighbouring villages began to arrive. Everyone was dressed in their best. Even the Indian Army's musical regiment from Harsil appeared to accompany the procession with the sounds of their bagpipes! The army has devotedly contributed to and assisted in the Gaṅgā-devī *yātrā*, but the sight and sound of the bagpipes seemed out of place in the Himālayas. The participation of bagpipes is

a local tradition that is difficult to understand! Just the same, they began playing their bagpipes, while I slowly walked around taking a few photos. While the music was being played, Gaṅgā-devī's palanquin was being decorated with fine silken clothes and a miniature silver replica of the Gaṅgotrī temple, which was placed in the center.

Then Sarasvatī-devī, also from Mukhwa, was placed within the miniature temple on the same palanquin. While all this was taking place, the devotees were trying to approach as close to the palanquin as possible, some fanning the deities with *cāmaras* (yak-tail whisks), others simply enthralled by just being present. Finally, Gaṅgā-devī was taken from her winter abode temple to her palanquin. Reflecting her splendid beauty, the pure golden face of Gaṅgā-devī is just a few inches in height and circumference, but so brilliant in appearance! I recalled her description from the *Nārada Purāṇa* (*Uttara-bhāga* 41.33-35): "She is clad in white garments, she is bedecked in pearls and jewels, she is pleased, her face is splendid, and her lotus-like heart melts with pity."

As she made her appearance, I tried capturing her with a photo; but an elderly *pūjārī* (priest) objected, so I casually walked away. The air was filled with the jubilant sound of drums and bugles as well as the army's tune on its bagpipes and the exclamations of all the gathered devotees. Gaṅgā-devī was placed in the middle of the Gaṅgotrī temple replica, her head barely raised above all her clothing, flowers, decorations, and offerings. Then it was time to begin the annual pilgrimage to Gaṅgotrī.

Since I was carrying my own rucksack (backpack), it would have been too much of an effort to move ahead of the *yātrā* for the purpose of taking photos, so staying behind seemed more practical and relaxing. As the pilgrimage began its two-day, 22 kilometre *yātrā*, the entire village along with the playful, colorful, mountain children and neighbours from the surrounding areas followed the footsteps of Gaṅgā-devī. The music continued to resound throughout the Himālayan slopes, the forest trail, and the Bhāgīrathī Gaṅgā valley far in the distance beyond. It was absolutely wonderful being able to trek in the Himālayan forests again, following Śrī Gaṅgā-devī and her devotees, while simultaneously walking parallel to her liquid form down below.

The procession took us directly to the first neighbouring village of Mārkaṇḍeya, also known as Mārkaṇḍeya-kṣetra, just two kilometres away. Here, Mārkaṇḍeya Ṛṣi performed austerities in his *āśrama* alongside the branching Puṣpabhadra Gaṅgā. His *āśrama* was located at the bottom of the village, right above the rocky banks of the Bhāgīrathī. The *yātrā* brought Gaṅgā-devī to the temple of Annapūrṇā-mātā, who was to accompany Gaṅgā-devī to Gaṅgotrī and reside with her for six months before returning here for the winter. While we took a little rest, I pondered whether or not this was the actual location where Mārkaṇḍeya Ṛṣi had *darśana* of Lord Śrī Hari in His forms of Nara (the best of human beings) and Nārāyaṇa Ṛṣis (the Supreme worshipable Deity) and the place where he saw the illusory energy within the Supreme Personality, Lord Śrī Hari, who appeared to him as a small child floating on top of a banyan leaf. Some say this pastime took place near Badarīnātha or at Pulahāśrama (Śalagrāma, Gaṇḍakī). Regardless of the actual location, just being here inspired me to refer to the *Śrīmad-Bhāgavatam*, Twelfth Canto, Chapters Eight and Nine, regarding the extraordinary activities of this rare, great *ṛṣi* (sage) who performed *tapasya* (austerities) on the lap of Gaṅgā-mayī.

* * *

Because of Mārkaṇḍeya Ṛṣi's powerful practice of *tapasya*, he was able to live through the lifetimes of six Manus (approximately 1,851,428,500 years). Then, during the lifetime of the seventh Manu (the present one), Lord Indra became fearful of his mystic potency. He therefore sent Kāmadeva, Apsarās, Gandharvas, Vasanta, as well as Greed and Intoxication personified to entice the great *ṛṣi*. They all tried their utmost to distract the *ṛṣi* in whatever way possible. Then Cupid himself drew his five-headed arrow, but his shot upon the *ṛṣi* failed to seduce him. Eventually all these disturbing agents stopped their nonsense, since they felt themselves being burnt alive by the *ṛṣi's* potency, just like children who have aroused a sleeping snake! Lord Indra became astonished and embarassed, not realizing that for great devotees like Mārkaṇḍeya Ṛṣi to tolerate such temptations is not at all surprising.

In order to bestow His blessings upon the saintly Mārkaṇḍeya Ṛṣi, the Supreme Personality of Godhead, Lord Viṣṇu, personally appeared to him in the forms of Nara and Nārāyaṇa, both the best of sages. As mentioned in the *Śrīmad-Bhāgavatam* (12.8.33-34), these two sages were direct personal forms of the Supreme Lord: "One of Them was of a whitish complexion, the other blackish, and They both had four arms. Their eyes resembled the petals of blooming lotuses, and They wore garments of black deerskin and bark, along with the three-stranded sacred thread. In Their hands, which were most purifying, They carried the mendicant's waterpot, straight bamboo staff and lotus-seed prayer beads, as well as the all-purifying *Vedas* in the symbolic form of bundles of *darbha* grass. Their bearing was tall and Their yellow effulgence the color of radiant lightning. Appearing as austerity personified, They were being worshiped by the foremost demigods."

When Mārkaṇḍeya Ṛṣi saw the two great personalities, he immediately fell down to the ground like a stick to offer obeisances at Their lotus feet. In a voice choked with ecstasy, he continued to repeat: "I offer You my humble obeisances." After bathing Their feet and making various offerings, Mārkaṇḍeya Ṛṣi began to glorify these two most worshipable sages. Nara and Nārāyaṇa told Mārkaṇḍeya Ṛṣi that he was the best of the learned *brāhmaṇas* and that They were very pleased with his lifelong celibacy. They then urged the *ṛṣi* to choose whatever benediction he desired. Mārkaṇḍeya Ṛṣi replied that he could not imagine the extent of his good fortune in being able to see Their personal forms before him, which was the only benedicton he wanted. Although he was satisfied simply by seeing Them, Mārkaṇḍeya Ṛṣi expressed his eagerness to see how the Lord's *māyā* (illusory energy) works. Thus satisfied by Mārkaṇḍeya's praise and worship, Nara and Nārāyaṇa smiled and replied, "So be it", and then departed for Their hermitage at Badarikāśrama.

One evening, when the great *ṛṣi* was performing his worship on the bank of Puṣpabhadra Gaṅgā, a great wind suddenly arose. It created a terrible sound and brought with it fearsome clouds that poured down torrents of rain, with lightning and roaring thunder on all sides. Then he saw from his *āśrama* four great oceans, terrible sea monsters, and all the inhabitants of the universe, including himself, tormented within and without. As the whole earth flooded, he grew perplexed and fearful. Rain continued to pour down, creating a vast sea, its waters whipped into terrifying waves by hurricanes. The water eventually inundated the entire earth, outer space, heaven, and the celestial region. The great sage wandered alone, as if dumb and blind, his matted hair dishevelled. He was tormented by hunger and thirst and

attacked by monstrous fish. Being battered by the mighty waves, he lost all sense of direction. Sometimes he felt lamentation, bewilderment, misery, happiness, or fear, and at other times he felt such terrible illness and pain that he felt himself dying. Millions of years passed as Mārkaṇḍeya wandered around in that deluge, bewildered by the illusory energy of Lord Viṣṇu. While wandering in the water, he came upon a small island on which stood a young banyan tree full of flowers and fruits. In the northeast part of that tree, upon a branch, he saw an infant boy lying upon a leaf.

Later on, in the *Śrīmad-Bhāgavatam* (12.9.22-25), a description of that boy lying on a leaf is given as follows: "The infant's dark-blue complexion was the color of a flawless emerald, His lotus face shone with a wealth of beauty, and His throat bore marks like the lines on a conchshell. He had a broad chest, a finely shaped nose, beautiful eyebrows, and lovely ears that resembled pomegranate flowers and that had inner folds like a conchshell's spirals. The corners of His eyes were reddish like the whorl of a lotus, and the effulgence of His corallike lips slightly reddened the nectarean, enchanting smile of His face. As He breathed, His splendid hair trembled and His deep navel became distorted by the moving folds of skin on His abdomen, which resembled a banyan leaf. The exalted *brāhmaṇa* watched with amazement as the infant took hold of one of His lotus feet with His graceful fingers, placed a toe within His mouth and began to suck."

The great spiritual master, Śrīla Viśvanātha Cakravartī Ṭhākura, comments on these verses, "The young child was Lord Śrī Kṛṣṇa, who wondered, 'So many devotees are hankering for the nectar of My lotus feet. Therefore, let Me personally experience that nectar.' Thus the Lord, playing like an ordinary baby, began to suck on His toes."

After Mārkaṇḍeya Ṛṣi saw the child, all his troubles and worries vanished. Since he was confused about the identity of the infant, the sage approached Him. Just then the child inhaled, drawing the *ṛṣi* into His body. Once inside, the sage was amazed to see the entire universe as it was before the annihilation, as well as the Himālaya mountains, the Puṣpabhadra Gaṅgā, and his own *āśrama*, where he had had *darśana* of the sages Nara-Nārāyaṇa. Then he was hurled back into the ocean of annihilation as the infant exhaled. Realizing that the child was none other than Lord Śrī Hari (Lord Kṛṣṇa), he tried to embrace the Lord, but at that very moment Lord Śrī Hari suddenly disappeared. Thereafter, Mārkaṇḍeya found himself back in his own hermitage, just as before.

Afterwards, when Lord Śiva was traveling in the sky, his wife, Pārvatī, requested that they visit the *āśrama* of Mārkaṇḍeya Ṛṣi. They were both very pleased with the *ṛṣi's* austerities and requested him to choose whatever benediction he desired. Mārkaṇḍeya begged for unflinching devotion to the Supreme Lord, Śrī Hari, to the devotees of the Supreme Lord, and also to Lord Śiva himself. Then Lord Śiva granted the great sage the boons of renown, freedom from old age and death until the time of universal dissolution, knowledge of the three phases of time, renunciation, realized knowledge, and the position of a teacher of the *Purāṇas*. Hence, Mārkaṇḍeya Ṛṣi was blessed with a lifetime that would last until the time of universal dissolution.

This pastime of the great exalted Mārkaṇḍeya was one of the last narrations in the *Śrīmad-Bhāgavatam* by Sūta Gosvāmī, after Śrī Śaunaka Ṛṣi and the other sages urged Sūta Gosvāmī to continue reciting *Śrīmad-Bhāgavatam*. It is interesting to note that this jewel of all the *Purāṇas*, the *Śrīmad-Bhāgavatam*, was originally compiled by

Vyāsadeva in his hermitage high above the Badarikāśrama area of the Himālayas near Keśava-prayāga in an area called Śamyāprāsa on the western bank of the River Sarasvatī where it joins the River Alakanandā (Gaṅgā). The ending narration about Mārkaṇḍeya Ṛṣi also took place in the Himālayas, but near the confluence of the Puṣpabhadra Gaṅgā and the Bhāgīrathī Gaṅgā. It appears that by dint of his *tapasya* and the fact that he has already lived through the lifetimes of seven Manus, Mārkaṇḍeya Ṛṣi is as immovable as the mighty Himālayas.

* * *

Returning to the small village of Mārkaṇḍeya, the procession was about to resume. Gaṅgā-devī's palanquin was picked up again by two servants and taken to the front of the procession. However, instead of resuming the pilgrimage on the foot trail, they entered the dry, rocky bed of the Bhāgīrathī Gaṅgā. Since it is spring, Bhāgīrathī's water level is at a minimum. Although at this particular spot her bed is some 100 metres wide, her waters were flowing only along the opposite bank. The palanquin of Lord Someśvara followed Gaṅgā-devī's palanquin. He was brought onto the riverbed where he offered oblations to Gaṅgā-devī by being rocked back and forth very vigorously. He was then carried back to his place of residence. We all continued on, walking over the dry rocks and sand, though I felt somewhat offensive for walking on mother Gaṅgā's bed. After a short distance of about one kilometre, we all quickly scrambled up the side of the mountain slope (some 50 metres) to a famous Durgā temple.

On either sides of the wide sprawling Bhāgīrathī Gaṅgā reside two manifestations of Durgā-devī, both facing in the direction of Gaṅgotrī, protecting the holy *dhāma* against inauspiciousness. Practically every Himālayan village has at least one *devī* (demigoddess) whom the villagers worship, such as Nandā-devī, Anasūyā-devī, Kuñjapurī-devī, Santoṣī-devī, Caṇḍeśvarī-devī, Surkhaṇḍā-devī, Jvālpā-devī, etc. She protects their village and the surrounding areas against demoniac intruders and influences. I immediately remembered visiting this same location one year earlier when Padayātrā was returning from Gaṅgotrī on its way to Harsil. On that particular day I had walked alone on this same trail, purposely avoiding the vehicle route in order to have a quiet day in solitude. The other *padayātrīs* walked on the opposite bank, and we all eventually met in Harsil.

Looking back through my Padayātrā Journal, recorded at Harsil (2620 m.) on the 26th of July, 1995, I recollected that day more vividly: "Another most relishable trek, as I had the good fortune to take the inside foot trail, opposite the bus route. Most of the trail is hardly used, except by a few villagers grazing their animals. Every step was sheer ecstasy as the sun was shining brightly, revealing every beautiful part of the Himālayan scenery. Bhāgīrathī begins to spread her waves, as she broadens out into a more open area. From Gomukha to Jhangla, she is bound deep between high narrow cliffs and gorges, but from this point up to Deoprayāga she is more free to spread out and dance about. I did not want the day's trek to end, for I was relishing walking alone with nature, carefully observing everything within my limited sight. I can just imagine being able to reside here; what a joy to be able to observe the various seasons change!"

During this solitary walk, I had stopped at this very same Durgā temple for *darśana* and for a little rest on the veranda of the *dharma-śālā* (pilgrim's rest house). So returning to this same location with the Gaṅgā-devī *yātrā*, when Gaṅgā-devī herself takes *darśana* of Durgā-devī, was a very special moment.

Then, after a very short rest, many of the *yātris* began to return to their homes, and from this point on, only the full-time *pūjārīs* and *paṇḍitas*, who would serve and worship Gaṅgā-devī in Gaṅgotrī for the next six months, continued on the pilgrimage. The *yātrā* now numbered only about fifty out of the original five hundred villagers who had participated during the initial formal ceremony in Mukhwa.

As we continued walking through the Himālayan forests, the drums and bugles echoed in the distance. The trail moves along the small rolling shoulders of the Himālayan slopes, sometimes as high as 100 metres above Bhāgīrathī and sometimes right along her merciful bank. Around midway, near a huge cave-like shelter that is used by the large herds of sheep and goats, we all took a break with Gaṅgā-devī, who was placed down upon a large, salient boulder. I took this opportunity to take a few close-up photos of the beautifully decorated palanquin.

Then a slight drizzle began to fall, but not enough to deter the *yātrā*. The procession continued, while I stayed behind for a few photos of the procession in motion. The drizzle turned into more of a rainfall, and this upset me, since I had not come prepared. At any given time, regardless of the season, it can rain anywhere in the Himālayas. Most pilgrims, *sādhus*, and locals usually carry a small piece of plastic to cover themselves, otherwise a few umbrellas are sometimes at hand. As the rain continued, we just kept on walking regardless of the situation. My mind returned to the last two visits Padayātrā had made to the mountains in 1992 and 1995. Both treks had been in the middle of the monsoon season and had included many days of trekking in the heavy forest rains on so many wet trails, over numerous river crossings, on top of slippery rocks, along with occassional slips and falls, and finding innumerable leeches sucking our blood!

As we trekked on, Badarī Viśāla Prabhu saw a few friendly young yaks (Tibetan cows) grazing. He snapped a few photos as I sat down near one who was grazing on the sweet, wet mountain grass. He slowly approached me and curiously smelled my hand and then continued on with his late afternoon snack. After another photo, we finally joined the motorable road at Jhangla, some 10 kilometres past Mukhwa. From Jhangla, the road ascends about 200 metres by-passing an army road work-camp before reaching Laṅkā at an altitude of 2780 metres. Before 1984, the year "the highest bridge over a riverbed in the world" was built, this hill station named Laṅkā was the last stop for vehicles. From here one continued on foot, descending 100 metres, crossing Jādh Gaṅgā by means of a rope foot-bridge, and then ascending up the other side to Bhaironghāṭī (Bhairava-ghāṭī), where another vehicle would be waiting for the pilgrims to take them to Gaṅgotrī, about 10 kilometres away. In order to introduce vehicles on the other side of the river, some vehicles had been completely taken apart, carried over to the other side piece by piece, and then re-assembled at Bhaironghāṭī! Now, a sturdy, well-built, motorable bridge stands over the mighty deep canyon and the deep, blue waters of Jādh Gaṅgā, some 130 metres below.

Somewhere in this area (some say near Jhangla), possibly near the *saṅgama* (confluence) of Jādh Gaṅgā and Bhāgīrathī Gaṅgā, where the blue foaming Jādh Gaṅgā unites with Bhāgīrathī, was the sacrificial arena and *āśrama* of the great Jahnu Ṛṣi.

In the *Śrīmad-Bhāgavatam* (9.15.2-3), we learn about the great sage Jahnu: "The son of Bhīma was Kāñcana; the son of Kāñcana was Hotraka; and the son of Hotraka was

Jahnu, who drank all the water of the Ganges in one sip." Also in the *Viṣṇu Purāṇa* (4.7) it is stated: "The sage Jahnu, whilst performing a sacrifice, saw the whole arena flooded by the waters of Gaṅgā. Highly offended at this intrusion and with his eyes red with anger, he united the sacrifice within himself by the power of his devotion and swallowed the river." And the *Nārada Purāṇa* (*Uttara-bhāga* 41.37) says: "It was on the seventh day in the bright half of the month of Vaiśākha that Gaṅgā was formerly drunk up by Jahnu out of anger and cast off later on through his right ear."

In addition to this *āśrama* of Jahnu Ṛṣi, he had five other *āśramas* along the Gaṅgā: Kānyakubja (Kannauj), north of Kanpur (Uttar Pradesh); Jahāngīr in Sultāngañj, west of Bhagalpur (Bihar); Sahibganj near Rampur Boalia (Bihar); Gour near Maldah (West Bengal); and Jannagara (Jahnagar), west of Navadvīpa, Nadia (West Bengal).

By the time I reached Laṅkā, I was soaking wet and alone. Crossing the Jādh Gaṅgā in the cold, wet rain did not help remind me of Jahnu Ṛṣi and Gaṅgā-mayī's pastime! After reaching Bhaironghāṭi, I located the other devotees, who had taken shelter on a veranda of the local *dharma-śālā*. Although the entire area was completely crowded with the additional locals who had joined the pilgrimage upon its arrival there, Gaṅgā-devī was nicely situated on the first floor of the *dharma-śālā*, where the devotees could easily have her *darśana*. The cooks were just beginning to prepare the late evening *prasāda* meal. Most of the pilgrims, visitors, and *sādhus* were busy in their own respective groups, resting, smoking, drinking tea, chatting, chanting, performing *pūjā* (worship), or simply searching for a warm dry place to sleep. As the early evening darkness approached, a mystical, damp fog hovered over us, while the forest crickets and the echoes of both Jādh and Bhāgīrathī filled the ether with their musical tunes.

I was in a little anxiety, since I did not have a secure, peaceful resting place. Even the only government rest house was full of local villagers. Our small group secured a small floor space in the corner of the veranda. The only space left was sufficient enough, but it was right in the middle of a short pathway. After re-visiting and inspecting the government rest house, I was able to secure, at the end of the inner hallway, a folding bed that was leaning-up against the wall. A difficult time followed trying to convince the acting-in-charge, but eventually I was allowed to rest there, warm, dry, and very peaceful. I was very tired and not interested in staying awake for the meal at 10:00 p.m. So, after thanking Gaṅgā-devī for this most merciful, eventful, and inspiring day, I quickly fell asleep, while more rain began to clatter on the rooftop overhead.

I woke up as usual at 3:00 a.m., fulfilled the demands of my body, and chanted on my *japa-mālā*. *Pūjā* for Gaṅgā-devī began at 5:00 a.m., but due to the damp, cold weather and my absorption in *japa*, I just remained in my warm comfortable situation. Before I realized it, the whole Gaṅgā-devī *yātrā* had returned to the road with the sound of the horns and drums at the head. Since I was feeling a bit lazy and had not yet packed, I laid back and decided to remain behind and walk the remaining 10 kilometres to Gaṅgotrī later at a slower pace. Knowing that I would not be with the procession when Gaṅgā-devī arrived in Gaṅgotrī made me feel disheartened, but walking in the warm sun under cloudless blue skies somehow took priority. Before setting off into the beautiful, bright, shining day, I had *darśana* of Śrī Bhairava-nātha, who also guards the entrance to Gaṅgotrī from any negative influences and intruders.

After walking in the rain yesterday with Gaṅgā-devī and her devotees, this morning's crystal clear weather was most welcome. The vision of the surrounding snow-capped mountains that line the Gaṅgotrī valley was a rare treat. When we were here last year during the month of July, there wasn't any snow to be seen. As I looked towards the snow-capped mountains, I continually exclaimed, "O Kṛṣṇa! O Kṛṣṇa!" at the sight of such unparalleled beauty. Kṛṣṇa was certainly exhibiting His artistic stroke and proving over and over again to insignificant persons like me that He was indeed the Himālayas.

As the road gently ascended and curved around the various slopes, Bhāgīrathī Gaṅgā appeared more and more distant. As I rounded each turn, I constantly tried capturing with my camera the scenic beauty, which seemed to increase at each and every step. This was my fourth trek through this part of the mountains, and it was by far the most beautiful I had experienced. By the time I reached Gaṅgotrī, Gaṅgā-devī had just taken *darśana* of the River Gaṅgā near the spot where Bhagīratha Mahārāja had performed great austerities to win the favor of Gaṅgā-devī.

The *brāhmaṇas* had placed Gaṅgā-devī on the temple veranda so that everyone could have long, unrestricted *darśana*. The doors of the Gaṅgotrī temple remained locked and sealed. The actual opening of the temple doors along with many ritualistic ceremonies and the final *pūjā* to welcome Gaṅgā-devī back to her summer abode, was scheduled for around midday, I joined the other *yātrīs* and devotees on the bank of the Bhāgīrathī. They had just finished their auspicious, freezing baths on this sacred Akṣaya-tṛtīyā day. I was surprised to see the river's level and speed, which was shallow and gentle compared to the monsoon period, when the rushing river is capable of sweeping away anyone or anything in her path. Her color was very refreshing—somewhere between emerald and blue—whereas the monsoons leave the river a muddy color—full of sand, rocks, mud, and debris. Since I arrived late, I had not yet bathed. So off with the rucksack and on with the gamcha (Indian towel). As I quickly entered the soothing, purifying, yet freezing waters of Gaṅgā-mātā, I begin to meditate and recite the *Śrī Gaṅgā Praṇāma*:

sadyaḥ pātaka-saṁhantrī
sadhyo duḥkha-vināśinī
sukhadā mokṣadā gaṅgā
gaṅgaiva paramā gatiḥ

"O Gaṅgā, you immediately destroy all sins and miseries. You bestow the ultimate happiness and the supreme liberation, for you are the ultimate shelter."

* * *

Afterwards, I remembered another prayer from the *Padma Purāṇa* (*Sṛṣṭi-khaṇḍa* 62.58-60): "O Gaṅgā-devī, all thirty-five million sacred places on heaven, earth, and in the intermediate region are situated in you. O Gaṅgā, you who have risen from the lotus feet of Lord Viṣṇu, O you who flow in a threefold path, O you who are known as having meritorious water, please remove my sins. You belong to Viṣṇu. You are honored by Viṣṇu. Therefore, protect me from the sins committed from birth up to death. O great goddess, O Bhāgīrathī, O you who are full of religious merit, purify me with faith and with your immortal rich potency."

The unlimited benefits one receives by giving charitable gifts on the auspicious day of Akṣaya-tṛtīyā are also mentioned in the *Nārada Purāṇa*. If one worships Lord Viṣṇu, Lord Śiva, and Gaṅgā-devī with feelings of great devotion throughout the night, offering such items as cooked barley grains, gingelly seeds, fragrant flowers, saffron, sandalwood

paste, *tulasī* leaves, incense, citrus-like fruits, ghee lamps, and *naivedya* (food), that person will go to the world of Lord Viṣṇu on a divine aerial chariot. And if someone donates the gift of cow ghee on the banks of the Gaṅgā, he will go to the world of Lord Brahmā along with his ancestors for billions and trillions of years. And for the gift of a cow, that person will be honored in the heavenly world for as many years as there are hairs on the body of that cow. Then he will return to earth in a very pious family, blessed with good conduct, learning, wealth, and fame. After being blessed with sons and grandsons, that person will eventually attain freedom from *saṁsāra* (cycle of birth and death) and return to the abode of Lord Viṣṇu. And finally, one who gives sixteen *māṣas* (one *māṣa* is approximately equal to one gram) of gold to a leading *brāhmaṇa* on this Akṣaya-tṛtīyā day, that person will be honored and worshiped throughout the three worlds. This day is also important for the Vaiṣṇavas, since it is the first day of Candana-yātrā, which lasts for twenty-one days, when sandalwood paste is applied on the body of the Lord. Finally, it is also Lord Paraśurāma's appearance day.

* * *

As I sat on one large boulder along the river's stone wall, appreciating the warm rays of the sun, I wrote the following on the 20th of April, 1996: "Wow! What a majestic day! Śrī Gaṅgā-devī punctually arrived in her summer abode, as the winter's snows slowly melt and the Gaṅgā slowly swells. The locals all came with their prayers and offerings, which include an ice-cold bath in her waters. Some women even behaved in a manner that seemed 'mad' to me. They were rolling on the ground in ecstasy, uttering sharp exclamations, and it appeared they were on the verge of losing consciousness.

"Such a difference with most of the *āśramas* (monasteries) and shops closed! The season started a bit earlier this year, and some of the locals were anticipating a rush of pilgrims, *sādhus*, and tourists. Several local *sādhus* (about twenty-five) who live in the surrounding areas are fortunate enough to reside here throughout the entire year. From total isolation to maddening rush, and then into the wet monsoons. How can I ever thank you for bringing me here again? Such an idea would have never come into this restless mind. I thank you for sending Badarī Viśāla Prabhu, otherwise I would still be in New Delhi, wondering what to do next! HARE KṚṢṆA!"

* * *

Badarī Viśāla Prabhu returned to Haridvāra the next day, after another refreshing, freezing bath! Param Tattva Prabhu and I remained in Gaṅgotrī for an extra day and a half, trying to absorb the heavenly Gaṅgotrī environment, including the great baths. We had learnt from one of the *paṇḍitas* of Mukhwa that when Gaṅgā-mayī was released from the top of Lord Śiva's head down to this planet, she had also appeared in her personal form so that Bhagīratha Mahārāja could have *darśana* of her. When she disappeared, she left behind a tall black *śilā* (a self-manifested natural stone) that was placed deep within the rocks, with about two metres projecting above the ground, so that her personal *pūjā* could commence.

Gaṅgotrī is at an altitude of 3200 metres. The present day temple there was erected in the eighteenth century by Gorkha General Amar Singh Thapa. Many other temples existed before, and many more will be renovated, destroyed, and constructed in the future generations. Yet regardless of the external building conditions, the self-manifested *śilā* that Gaṅgā-devī personally left behind is and always will be the main center of *pūjā*. On top of the front portion of the *śilā* is the golden face of Gaṅgā-devī,

which is used for the processions and the winter *pūjā* in Mukhwa. Also included within the inner sanctum are deities of Yamunā-devī, Jāhnavī-devī, Mahārāja Bhagīratha, Sarasvatī-devī, Annapūrṇā-mātā, Mahā-lakṣmī, Mahā-durga, Gaṇapati (Gaṇeśa), Himavān (King of the Himālayas and father of Gaṅgā-devī), and Ādi Śaṅkarācārya.

Some 18 kilometres east of Gaṅgotrī is Gomukha (3892 m.), the present origin of the River Bhāgīrathī Gaṅgā. In past *yugas*, the source of Gaṅgā used to be near the Bhagīratha-śilā in Gaṅgotrī. Due to the effect of Kali-yuga, it has receeded some 18 kilometres higher up the Bhāgīrathī valley. The Gomukha glacier is approximately 32 kilometres long, 2-4 kilometres wide, and 100-300 metres high. At the glacier's base, from the bluish-grey icy walls, Gaṅgā-devī emerges in her liquid form to begin her long, merciful journey through this land of Bhārata-varṣa into the Bay of Bengal.

Above Gomukha, some 5-6 kilometres away and 500 metres above the glacier, one arrives at Tapovan (4500 m.), where the Ākāśa Gaṅgā flows by a small hermitage in a lush meadow, which is full of beautiful varieties of flowers during the monsoon season. Nearby, but at a tremendous height, Lord Śiva resides at Shivling, a natural mountain peak in the form of a *liṅga* (phallus of Lord Śiva) some 6540 metres high. Beyond Tapovan, 5-6 kilometres away, is Nandavan (4500 m.), from where one can go further ahead to the Bhāgīrathī Parvatas I, II, and III (6510 m., 6450 m., 6860 m.). Then comes Vāsuki Parvata (6700 m.), and eventually one arrives at the lotus feet of Śrī Śrī Badarī Viśāla in Badarīnātha.

For centuries, sages in the past have used this Tapovan area as a central base. The four sacred places of Yamunotri, Gaṅgotrī, Kedāranātha, and Badarīnātha are all near this central point, separated by massive mountain ranges. One single priest used to offer prayers at all four shrines, shuttling between the *tīrthas* frequently!

* * *

More words, dated the 21st of April 1996, from my journal which is now of great assistance to me in recalling several pastimes during our Gaṅgotrī *yātrā*: "It is such a wonderful experience being able to bathe in Bhāgīrathī, near the spot where Bhagīratha Mahārāja performed his *tapasya*. As it is spring, her waters are very shallow and relatively calm; and the quick, sudden dips are incredibly freezing, fresh, and purifying. Just as we completed our bath and offering, another *devī-yātrā* arrived to have *darśana* of Gaṅgā-devī and perform *pūjā* on the banks of the Gaṅgā. During special auspicious days like Akṣaya-tṛtīyā, Śrī Gaṅgā or Jahnu-saptamī, and Śrī Gaṅgā-duṣharā, the villagers have the fortune of bringing their *devī* to Gaṅgotrī for *darśana*, bathing, *pūjā*, etc. This particular *devī* was named Mallā-devī. She resides in the Bhatwari area, 70 kilometres from Gaṅgotrī, on the Uttarkāśī road.

"My mind wonders and wanders throughout the day and night as it contemplates whether or not I will ever be able to reside in the Himālayas for a lengthy period, especially through the winter. That would really be a number-one challenge for the mind! Maybe this lifetime, or possibly another, or possibly I may already have! So many *sādhus* are residing here. Some are first-class, while others 'appear' last-class; but we really do not know who these rare souls are. External appearance is one thing, but where have they been, what they have done, and what are they doing now? Besides, where will they go once they leave this holy *dhāma*? We are not *trikālajña* (one who can see into the past, present, and future), so we should approach them cautiously and with respect, otherwise we may leave with an offensive attitude,

which will only disturb our advancement in spiritual life.

"The weather is overcast and drizzling, giving a strong indication of coming snow. The morning was splendid, warm and clear, just perfect for a bath. Just some twenty days ago, the snow was one metre deep on the southern bank. There are still many patches of snow scattered throughout the mountainside forests. How can one live inside for four to five months, completely surrounded, captured, and surrendered to the will of the snowfall? When the tourists and pilgrims arrive, they only see the beautiful, breathtaking, comfortable Himālayan environment that captures everyone's heart. They remain unaware of the few *sādhus* and *yogis* who reside here throughout the year, year after year. Time to hide under heavy quilts and warm up a bit, since the afternoon chills, breeze, and rain are still continuing. HARE KṚṢṆA!"

* * *

This desire to live in the Himālayas someday made me reflect on a verse from the *Śrīmad-Bhāgavatam* (7.9.44), one of the prayers offered to Lord Nṛsiṁhadeva by Prahlāda Mahārāja, just after the Lord killed the great demon Hiraṇyakasipu: "My dear Lord Nṛsiṁhadeva, I see that there are many saintly persons indeed, but they are interested only in their own deliverance. Not caring for the big cities and towns, they go to the Himālayas or the forest to meditate with *mauna-vrata* (vow of silence). They are not interested in delivering others. As for me, however, I do not wish to be liberated alone leaving aside all these poor fools and rascals. I know that without Kṛṣṇa consciousness, without taking shelter of Your lotus feet, one cannot be happy. Therefore, I wish to bring them back to shelter at Your lotus feet."

Śrīla Prabhupāda writes in his summary on the *Śrīmad-Bhāgavatam*, Seventh Canto, Ninth Chapter: "Those interested in silently worshiping the Lord in solitary places may be eligible for liberation themselves, but a pure devotee is always aggrieved to see others suffering. Therefore, not caring for his own liberation, he always engages in preaching by glorifying the Lord. Prahlāda Mahārāja, therefore, had tried to deliver his class friends by preaching and had never remained silent. Although being silent, observing austerities and penances, learning the Vedic literature, undergoing ritualistic ceremonies, living in a solitary place and performing *japa* and transcendental meditation are all approved means of liberation, they are meant for nondevotees or for cheaters who want to live at the expense of others. A pure devotee, however, being freed from all such deceptive activities, is able to see the Lord face to face. Thus the Kṛṣṇa conscious person avoids all kinds of pseudo spiritualists, transcendentalists, meditators, monists, philosophers and philanthropists."

Śrīla Prabhupāda's strong purport is something to reflect on. At the same time, all living entities need to realize their original Kṛṣṇa conscious position with the Lord, including the pseudo spiritualists, transcendentalists, meditators, monists, philosophers, and philanthropists. One can try to give *hari-nāma* (Kṛṣṇa's holy name), some *kṛṣṇa-prasāda*, or one of Śrīla Prabhupāda's books, not only to the common masses, but to everyone, including the so-called saintly personalities who are interested only in their own deliverance. The loving compassion that Prahlāda Mahārāja expressed in his prayer is something very rare and special, something that Śrīla Prabhupāda fully possessed, and something that he passed down to us all. We may not associate with these external

spiritualists, but within one's own limited capacity, one may try to give them some Kṛṣṇa consciousness.

I recall the words of Śrīla Bhaktivinoda Ṭhākura, who stressed: "By reading the book of Nature, one can attain God consciousness and realize the spiritual world." Also in H.H. Satsvarūpa dāsa Goswami's *Journal and Poems*, Śrīla Prabhupāda is quoted as saying: "From Nature we can study so many things, very instructive. Kṛṣṇa has made Nature in such a way that any intelligent man, if he studies Nature without going to school or college, he becomes a very learned man. If he has got the capacities to study Nature." Then Satsvarūpa Mahārāja comments, "In His most intimate, original feature, Kṛṣṇa chooses to live in a natural, rural setting. Our own attraction for rural peace and beauty is actually an expression of the spirit soul's original desire to live in Vṛndāvana."

* * *

On our last morning, Param Tattva Prabhu and I had one last *darśana* of Gaṅgā-devī in her temple. I was fortunate enough to spend a few moments with the Mukhwa *brāhmaṇa* who was acting as the temple administration secretary. The *brāhmaṇas'* positions within the temple administration are rotated amongst the qualified *brāhmaṇa* families of Mukhwa. This one had heard of Śrīla Prabhupāda, his books, and of ISKCON, and was very happy to host us, the first foreign devotees in recent history to participate in the annual Gaṅgā-devī *yātrā*. I presented him with some of Śrīla Prabhupāda's books, as well as some Padayātrā information. He was very pleased and invited us to attend the Dīpāvalī *yātrā*, when Gaṅgā-devī returns to her winter home in Mukhwa. We thanked him and requested him to please pray to Gaṅgā-mātā for us, so that we will be able to return, participate in the procession, and associate with the fortunate devotees of Śrī Gaṅgā-devī.

After *darśana* and before one last exhilirating bath, which was taken one kilometre upstream from Gaṅgotrī, I noted down the following words on the 22th of April, 1996, as a conclusion to our stay in the abode of Gaṅgā-devī: "It took Sūrya a while to break through the heavy overcast morning skies, but he is now shining very brightly throughout the Gaṅgotrī valley. Several laborers are working hard in the riverbed, trying to re-position the boulders to direct Gaṅgā-mayī's course during her upcoming rush from Gomukha. It is really amazing to witness her during this period, as she gently flows in, around, and through the miniature dams and walls. In a few months the monsoons will arrive, and she will rush down so fiercely that she will carry away the rocks and boulders. When will the day come when I will be able to reside on your merciful banks? Please, please fulfill my simple prayer some day, since without your causeless mercy, how will I ever qualify to understand the more confidential pastimes of the Himālayas, especially here in Śrī Gaṅgotrī-dhāma."

Book Two
Chapter Two

Retracing the Footsteps of Gaṅgā-devī
(From Gaṅgotrī to Mukhwa)

Retracing the Footsteps of Gaṅgā-devī
(From Gaṅgotrī To Mukhwa)

Six months later, on Dīpāvalī, my friend Haresh and I returned to Gaṅgotrī to participate in the procession with Gaṅgā-devī again; this time from Gaṅgotrī to Mukhwa. We first arrived in Mukhwa before heading for Gaṅgotrī, where the procession originates. The following was recorded upon arriving in Mukhwa on the 7th of November, 1996: "As I sit viewing the snow-clad peak of Śrī Kānta (6140 m.), just opposite us to the southeast, I am still appreciating how we reached Gaṅgā-devī's village, Mukhwa, without any major difficulties. Sitting on the veranda of our kind host, we were directly facing this majestic peak, which by this late afternoon hour of 4:45 p.m. was the lone, solitary peak that gloriously reflected the rays of the setting sun off its dazzling white slopes. Five months back, when I was in the hospital, I never imagined being here in Mukhwa so soon again. I am sure the surgeon would be very angry to know that I was in the mountains so soon after my double hernia operation, but what can I do when Gaṅgā-devī is calling me so persistently? Thanking you, Gaṅgā-mayī! HARE KṚṢṆA!"

Due to the mercy of Lord Śrī Kṛṣṇa, Śrīla Prabhupāda, and my dearest Guru Mahārāja, Śrīla Lokanātha Swami, I was able to return to the Himālayas, particularly to the Gaṅgotrī area, to attend the closing ceremony of Śrī Gaṅgotrī-dhāma and walk behind Śrī Gaṅgā-devī to her winter abode, Mukhwa, also known as Mukti-maṭha. Upon reaching Mukhwa, I was incredibly happy just to see the simple school children play, the villagers cultivating their fields, and the householders busy with their domestic chores. Despite my mental anxieties over additional luggage, everything actually went very smoothly, right up to the door-step of our dear friend, Bharosa Rāma Semwal and his family. His wife and children were very happy to receive us, regardless of the fact that we (Haresh Prabhu and I) arrived unexpectedly in the late afternoon around 4:30 p.m.. Bharosa Rāma was still in nearby Harsil at his school-master's job. He arrived a little later and happily received his unexpected guests. He was also eager to know about our program. We expressed our desire to spend a couple of nights with him before going onto

Gaṅgotrī to participate in the annual Dīpāvalī and Amāvasyā festivals and then walk back down to Mukhwa with Gaṅgā-devī and the other villagers and pilgrims. He was delighted and quickly made us feel at home.

During the evening, he confided to us some of the difficulties he and his family had encountered since my last visit in April. His main anxiety was over family health problems, which had troubled him for several months and had forced him to travel between Mukhwa and Rishikesh-Dehra Dun several times without any positive or encouraging news from any doctor. He then asked if I would be able to help him and his family when I returned to New Delhi early next year. I replied that I would help him in whatever way possible. Yet I stressed the importance of chanting the Hare Kṛṣṇa *mahā-mantra* in addition to his regular, traditional worship, since chanting is the best medicine for all problems. Then, with great delight, I presented him a litre of the Sahasra Tīrtha Jala (one thousand sacred waters) along with the accompanying book, for his daily *pūjā* and other religious activities. I had also brought a complete set of *Śrīmad-Bhāgavatam* in Hindi to present to Gaṅgā-devī and the villagers when she returns in a few days. With great delight, he informed me that his prayers had been answered, since he had long desired to read the *Śrīmad-Bhāgavatam*. Very soon, after his family shifted to another location near Uttarkāśī for the snowy winter, he would continue to reside alone in Mukhwa and would have the time (at least two months) to read the entire *Bhāgavatam* and to meditate upon and appreciate the wonderful and inconceivable activities of Lord Śrī Kṛṣṇa.

Since it was the first week of November, the early winter snows had yet to arrive; but the thin, cool air of the early mornings and late evenings made it appear as if the snow had already fallen. It was much colder now than in April; but the mountainside scenery was much more colorful with its mixture of yellowish-brown apple tree leaves, the barren fields, the snowy peaks, and the clear, deep dark blue skies, as well as the Gaṅgā, far down at the bottom of the valley, which appeared like an endless embroidery of sparkling bluish colors that continually changed with each weaving turn.

The next morning, which was Rāma Ekādaśī, Haresh and I decided to take a small trek to Harsil, some 3 kilometres away, to visit the ancient Śrī Śrī Lakṣmi-Nārāyaṇa temple, located at the *saṅgama* of the Bhāgīrathī Gaṅgā and the Jālandhari Gaṅgā. This is one of the sites—another being in Śalagrāma (Gaṇḍakī, Nepal)—where the pastimes of Lord Viṣṇu, Lord Śiva, Mahārāja Jālandhara, and Vṛndā-devī are said to have taken place.

The name Harsil is derived from Hari-śilā, or "Lord Hari in the form of a stone", which manifests in a pastime between Lord Viṣṇu and Vṛndā-devī. The ancient Lakṣmī-Nārāyaṇa temple is situated near Hari-prayāga, where the Jālandhari Gaṅgā meets the Bhāgīrathī Gaṅgā. Jālandhara was the husband of Vṛndā-devī. Lord Viṣṇu appeared in the form of Jālandhara and had union with Vṛndā-devī, with the result that Jālandhara was killed in battle by Lord Śiva. Vṛndā-devī eventually realized that she had been deceived by Lord Viṣṇu and hence cursed the Lord, who thus became Hari-śilā. The self-manifested *śilā* is under the water at the *saṅgama* and not normally visible, except around Janmāṣṭamī, when the tide is low.

We were able to reach the *saṅgama* easily, since the river's level is very low at this time of the year. Yet upon accepting water on our heads at the *saṅgama*, we began to wonder where the *śilā* was actually located. Just the same, this location is unique, since

it is actually the *saṅgama* of three rivers, the third being the Kakora Gaṅgā, which flows through the township of Harsil. It is mentioned in the following words from the *Skanda Purāṇa*, "Nearby is the *tīrtha* named Hari-prayāga. Those who have bathed there, even the most debauched, go to Viṣṇuloka." We were particularly fortunate to visit this *tīrtha* on Ekādaśī.

After a short rest and a snack of fruits and dates, we ventured further down the valley to Bhaguri, a Tibetan township with a Buddhist monastery. The inhabitants are mostly traders, though many produce hand-woven woolen products. But since it was the beginning of the winter season, nearly 90% of the town was locked and deserted, like a forgotten "ghost town"! We then returned to Harsil through the military camp and onto the foot trail that leads to Mukhwa. Gaṅgā-mayī appeared absolutely captivating as she curved in and around, shimmering against the setting sun's reflections. It felt wonderful being able to walk again through the Himālayas, absorbing Kṛṣṇa's external energy (mother nature, at her loving best). Despite my physical limitations after the operation, just the fact that we were in the mountains helped me transcend my physical handicaps. At a small junction in the trail we split up, walking our own directions, one steeper but shorter trail compared to the other easier but longer one. Eventually we both returned to the warm, homey atmosphere of Bharosa Rāma's home and settled in for the evening.

The next morning we walked down and crossed the bridge over the Bhāgīrathī Gaṅgā to Dharāli, where the bus to Gaṅgotrī halts. While waiting for the bus, we decided to visit Tapovan Mātājī, who was residing in Dharāli. This elderly woman is originally from Uḍupī, Karnataka, yet because she lived in Tapovan (above the Gomukha glacier at 4500 m.) for the last eight years without leaving, she has received the name Tapovan Mātājī (her actual name is Subhadrā-devī). After locating her, we happily spent over an hour in her association, discussing various matters including her drastically poor health, which had obliged her to be carried down. I inquired why she had left the most attractive Lord Kṛṣṇa of Uḍupī, and she replied, "He is the one who sent me to the Himālayas!"

She then described the beauty of the Tapovan area and recounted several of her experiences and realizations. Like almost all her visitors, we inquired from her, "How do you pass your time? Doesn't it get boring up there all alone in the solitude?"

She replied, "It all depends upon one's mind. With the mind at peace, there are not enough hours in each day for me to complete my service,"

One pilgrim had once asked her if she had acquired any *siddhi* (perfection) up there. She had replied, "Just to obtain a few *chapatis* (flat bread) up there in the snow is a great achievement and a *siddhi*!"

I presented her with several of Śrīla Prabhupāda's books, a few *Padayātrā Worldwide* newsletters, and the *Sahasra Tīrtha Jala* book, and I explained how the water collection program had taken two years to complete. I particularly pointed out that we had also collected *jala* (water) from Ākāśa Gaṅgā in Tapovan (our Padayātrā team had visited her last year during the water collection). She was very pleased to receive the gifts, and she offered us a drink and some fruit *prasāda*.

Then she went into the other room to bring a photo of her Guru Mahārāja. To my surprise it was none other than H.H. Śrī Viśveśa Tīrtha Svāmī, of Pejavar Maṭha, who is a dear friend and well-wisher of our ISKCON Society. He travels often and has been our guest in Māyāpur, Vṛndāvana, and Mumbai (Bombay). When Padayātrā visited

Uḍupī in 1985 and 1991, he had hosted us and taken special care of us, especially by offering us plenty of Uḍupī Kṛṣṇa *prasāda*! To my amazement I realized that I was sitting in front of an unknown Godsister, albeit a distant one, since our Gauḍīya-sampradāya (disciplic succesion) is directly connected to Madhvācārya and the eight monasteries that he established in Uḍupī. Her kindness, humility, and hospitality was very dear, loving, and special. As the bus arrived, we offered our obeisances and best wishes and then boarded the bus for the short 22 kilometre beautiful drive to Śrī Gaṅgotrī-dhāma.

While riding on the bus, I recollected a narration from the *Skanda Purāṇa* (*Kedāra-khaṇḍa* 38): "Once during Satya-yuga in Brahmaloka, Lord Brahmā and all the other great demigods and sages were assembled. At that time Nārada Muni arrived singing the glories of Śrī Gaṅgotrī-dhāma. After he paid his most humble obeisances to Lord Brahmā, Brahmā inquired from him where he had been traveling, since he had not seen him for a long time. Nārada replied, 'I have been roaming here and there before reaching Gaṅgotrī, situated on the snowy peaks of the Himālayas, which are full of forests and beautiful flowers. The entire area vibrates with enchanting sounds of many wonderful birds.

"It was in Gaṅgotrī that Gaṅgā-devī, who originated from the lotus feet of Lord Viṣṇu, descended from the celestial world and appeared to mankind for the first time. The shining, sacred, famous *silā* on which Mahārāja Bhagīratha sat and performed severe austerities is situated there. I took bath in the sacred Bhāgīrathī Gaṅgā, worshiped her with love and devotion, and praised the goddess with a thousand names. Then I came here singing the glories of Śrī Gaṅgotrī-dhāma, which is the best of all holy *tīrthas*.'"

Nārada Muni continued to glorify the holy *dhāma* (Lord's abode) in many beautiful ways. But as we arrived by bus, it was difficult to immediately see the beauty described in the *sāstras*. Gaṅgotrī is now lined with numerous *āsramas*, hotels, guest-houses, stores, temples, and ramshackle huts on both sides of her shores. Before the roads and bridges were constructed, only very sincere pilgrims would be able to walk the long difficult trail from the Rishikesh/Haridvāra area. Today, Kali-yuga and its accompanying negative influences are there, although on a more subtle level than in a larger town or city. Still, Gaṅgotrī rejuvenates and rekindles past glories as Gaṅgā-mayī gracefully flows down her long merciful path, through the most majestic and serene Himālayas.

We quickly got down from the bus and were fortunate to meet a kind-hearted resident from Mukhwa, who carried my luggage. We crossed the bridge over the Gaṅgā to our friend's hermitage, Kṛṣṇa Āśrama. Brahmacārī Ātmā Svarūpa, who is incharge, was in Uttarkāśī for the day and would return later. Just the same, we settled into the *sādhu* quarters and tried to make ourselves comfortable. Due to the extremely cold weather and the high altitude, that night's sleep was very restless, and we woke to subzero temperatures that froze the water in the bucket outside!

The Kṛṣṇa Āśrama is named after one great *mauna-vrata* (vow of silence) *yogi*, H.H. Kṛṣṇa Svāmī, who lived some one hundred and fifty years, most of which were in a small cave at Gaṅgotrī. In memory of him a small temple with a life-like *mūrti* (statue) stands above that cave just next to the foot trail. He is depicted with a bluish complexion, which he acquired after performing great austerities throughout the years. Hence, he received the name "Kṛṣṇa". His *mūrti* faces towards Gaṅgā-mayī and Gaṅgā-devī's temple on the other side of the river.

Since it was so cold in the room where we had tried to sleep, I surrendered to the shelter of Kṛṣṇa Svāmī's small temple room, where there is just enough space for keeping one person a little warm. As I chanted on my beads, I kept observing Kṛṣṇa Svāmī's posture, sitting in *yogāsana* (crossed leg position) without any clothes on, keeping very content in the middle of the snowy winter. And there I was in my Norwegian sleeping bag, Badarīnātha woollen blanket, and a Tibetan wool hat, still feeling cold! I felt his presence there, and after chanting a few rounds of *mālā*, I slowly became warmer and warmer. I thanked him for his merciful comfort.

During the month of November, the sun shines in the valley surrounding Gaṅgotrī for no more than four hours a day. The sun appears over a peak in the southeast around 10:30 a.m. and then swiftly races across the sky in a short arc to disappear behind a neighbouring peak in the southwest around 2:30 p.m. This short period is the only time a bath can be somewhat appreciated. Observing a daily bath in Gaṅgotrī is only practical when the sun is shining. Pilgrims generally visit Gaṅgotrī for a brief period, so they often have to take a bath at any time of day. However, if one desired to maintain a daily bath in the freezing waters of the Gaṅgā, one would want to depend on the sun's mercy. But a little bit of mustard oil also warms the skin and reduces the icy water's sharp bite. It is especially beneficial to bath in Gaṅgotrī, for it is mentioned in the *Skanda Purāṇa* that the closer to Gaṅgā's source one takes bath, the more benefit one receives.

We then went to Gaṅgā-devī's temple on the other side of the river for *darśana* and to sit in the warm sunshine. This northwestern side of the valley receives the sun earlier than the side we were staying on. While relaxing in the open courtyard directly in front of the temple, the secretary of the Gaṅgotrī temple administration, Ravindra Semwal, approached me. He remembered me from the time I had attended the opening ceremony in April. We exchanged warm greetings before he expressed his happiness that I had returned to attend the closing Dīpāvalī ceremony and walk to Mukhwa with Gaṅgā-devī. Haresh Prabhu and I began to inquire about different details on some of the pastimes of Gaṅgā-devī, and he began quoting various *ślokas* (texts) from the *Kedāra-khaṇḍa* of the *Skanda Purāṇa*, as well as the *Rāmāyaṇa*. He then inquired about our accommodations, and we replied that we were taken care of for that evening. But with the next day being Dīpāvalī, the day before the temple closes, we preferred to stay the night in the temple guest house. He offered to reserve a room for us and, as we thanked him, he replied, "It is my duty."

During this second day in Gaṅgotrī, I was happy to meet several foreigners who were on a spiritual holiday. One Japanese lady had been on a Buddhist walking pilgrimage in Japan that covered eighty-eight temples. She was very attracted to chant and sing the various names of the Lord that she had learnt from spiritual *sat-saṅgas* (associations) in Japan and India. Her genuine humility and kindness were inspiring and heart-warming. There were also two visitors from Austria who had met Śrīla Prabhupāda and knew some of the earlier devotees in the German temples. They were convinced about Śrī Caitanya Mahāprabhu's prophecies related to Śrīla Prabhupāda's and the devotees' spreading *hari-nāma* (Kṛṣṇa's holy name) around the world. Later on in the day, a busload of members from the International Śivānanda Yoga Vedānta Society arrived. It was nice seeing so many foreigners who practised some part of Vedic culture through

hatha-yoga (one of the eightfold paths of *aṣṭāṅga-yoga*). That same evening, some of us gathered around a warm fire in the Kṛṣṇa Āśrama and chanted *kīrtanas* (devotional songs), glorifying the Lord and His associates, including Gaṅgā-devī. It was an atmosphere conducive to exchanging spiritual realizations, especially the numerous pastimes that have occurred on Padayātrā. It was to be a pleasure able to inform them of the Sahasra Tīrtha Jala program, especially the water collection and book project, as well as to present them with some of Śrīla Prabhupāda's literature.

The next day being Dīpāvalī, a good day for feeding *sādhus*, pilgrims, and other visitors in Gaṅgotrī, the Śivānanda Yoga Vedānta Society sponsored a delicious, well prepared feast, which was a thoroughly surprising treat at such an altitude in the Himālayas. It was certainly the arrangement of Gaṅgā-mātā, as it was arranged in an *āśrama* located just above her right bank. This gathering presented me with another excellent opportunity to speak more on the Sahasra Tīrtha Jala project and offer general Kṛṣṇa conscious literature to the main host and the other visitors. Then Haresh and I walked up Gaṅgā's bed about one kilometre to the same location that is photographed on the front cover of the *Sahasra Tīrtha Jala* book. The conditions were slightly different than in April, except the water level appeared the same. The skies were perfectly clear blue and there was no ice around, but the sun was quickly leaving and shadows were rapidly forming. This particular spot proved once again to be our favorite private bathing location, thanks to the mercy of Śrīla Prabhupāda's Sahasra Tīrtha Jala program. After a quick bath, Haresh returned to Gaṅgotrī and I proceeded to the Śrī Rāma temple, which is located on the Gomukha trail.

When Padayātrā was here last in July 1995, returning from Gomukha, Upananda, Prabhu and I had stopped at the Śrī Rāma temple, which is two kilometres from Gaṅgotrī. We were surprised at the warm welcome and *prasāda* that we were offered, both to our full satisfaction. Afterwards, we met Bal Gaṅgā Mahārāja, who happens to be a Vrajavāsī (born inhabitant of Vraja-Vṛndāvana, Mathurā). He has spent sixty years in this area. Forty-five of these were spent down below in a cave near the bank of Gaṅgā. Then after he became blind, he relocated to the Śrī Rāma temple, which is higher-up near the foot trail that leads to Gomukha. During all these years he has never left the Gaṅgotrī area. He was happy to meet two Hare Kṛṣṇa devotees, and he immediately began to glorify Śrīla Prabhupāda for what he had done, especially giving *kṛṣṇa-prema* (love of Kṛṣṇa) to everyone. He then remarked, "Now Vṛndāvana is in the U.S.A." We spoke briefly about our water collection and Padayātrā mission, which pleased him more. Then we happily departed, leaving a few of Śrīla Prabhupāda's books for Mahārāja's servants.

Now I desired to visit that same Śrī Rāma temple again. So I scrambled up the steep, rocky hillside that was a short-cut to the Gomukha foot trail. Upon arriving, Mahārāja was basking in the sun and narrating the *Rāmāyaṇa* by memory to a few visitors. I was very inspired by his sharp memory, which appeared more clear due to his being blind. His facial expression was of sheer ecstasy from reciting Lord Rāmacandra's pastimes. I wondered what he was experiencing within. I did not interrupt, but was greeted warmly by the young *pūjārī* (priest), who offered prostrated obeisances. After *bhoga* (food) offering and a short *ārati* (worship), we sat down to relish a feast of puris, sabji, and sweet rice! Even though I had just

honored a delicious feast a few hours before in Gaṅgotrī, I felt it would be offensive to refuse the *prasāda*. The *pūjāri*'s serving mood was so enthusiastic, it overwhelmed me.

Then, to my surprise, another Vrajavāsī introduced himself to me. He was from Nandagram and had come here for a more solitary lifestyle in the Himālayas, accepting some sort of *sannyāsa* initiation. But he was not very happy associating with the other *sādhus*, who he said were impersonal and hard like the surrounding rocks! He was hankering to go back to that special Vraja atmosphere and the pastimes of Śrī Śrī Rādhā-Kṛṣṇa, Nanda Mahārāja, the cows, and the *gopas* (cowherd boys). He was incredibly pleased to meet a Hare Kṛṣṇa *bhakta* (devotee) and asked me whether or not I had a photo of Rādhā-Kṛṣṇa. I searched my bag and found the beautiful, colorful photo on the front of the *Hare Kṛṣṇa Yuga* booklet in Hindi. I also offered him a beautiful photo of Śrī Śrī Nitāi-Gaurasundara, the famous Lordships traveling on Padayātrā India. Then I recited the *Srī Kṛṣṇa Praṇāma mantra:he kṛṣṇa karuṇā-sindho dīna-bandho jagat-pate/gopeśa gopikā-kānta rādhā-kānta namo 'stu te* ("O my dear Kṛṣṇa, You are the friend of the distressed and the source of creation. You are the master of the *gopīs* and the lover of Rādhāraṇī. I offer my respectful obeisances unto You.) He was overjoyed and said, "Just like a Vrajavāsī!" Then he asked me to spend the night. However, due to prior agreements, I had to politely decline the nice offer and promised to return another time. This Vrajavāsī was anxious to return to the Vṛndāvana area during the winter time, while the *pūjāri* would continue performing his *pūjā*, cooking, and serving in several ways during the winter months, in his fifth consecutive year. After snapping a few photos, I slowly savored the short two kilometre walk back down to Gaṅgotrī.

Returning to Gaṅgotrī, the early evening darkness was slowly approaching as I stopped by the temple administration guest house to see if a room was available for us. Since it was, I returned to Kṛṣṇa Āśrama, where the few residents were sitting snug and warm around the fire, in order to collect my belongings and bring Haresh to the guest house. Ātmā Svarūpa Prabhu had returned from Uttarkāśī and invited me to sit down and relax. He had assisted the original water collection team in June 1994 by offering advice, shelter, and *prasāda*. Then during Padayātrā's third Himālayan Char-dhāma-yātrā, he had again provided us with comfortable accommodation and more information for our water collection. Now the *āśrama* was about to close for the winter season, and he was just about to pack, seal, and lock up all the rooms and the temple. He has visited our ISKCON centers in Mumbai, Vṛndāvana, and Māyāpur, so he understands something about Śrīla Prabhupāda's society. He was impressed with the Śrīdhāma Māyāpur project. He had met Kṛṣṇa Svāmī, his Guru Mahārāja, some fifteen years ago, just before Mahārāja had left this mortal world. He has been in Gaṅgotrī ever since, usually moving to the lower altitudes for the winter, or traveling to other holy places in India.

We all sat around the blazing fire discussing various subjects related to Gaṅgotrī, such as the few *sādhus* who remain behind during the winter months, the influx of tourists and pilgrims, the changing weather conditions, the *anna-kṣetras*, or *āśramas* that offer free *prasāda* meals to the visitors, different aspects of the *Vedas*, *slokas* from various scriptures, and on, and on, and on. I was feeling very much at home, warm and protected from the cold environment outside, and moving to the temple guest house seemed too much of an effort. Ātmā Svarūpa

wanted us to stay and share *prasāda* with him, but we had to shift our residence to the other side of Gaṅgotrī. Besides, I was full after already relishing two feasts, so I humbly declined and moved onwards. Before leaving, I presented a litre of Sahasra Tīrtha Jala to Kṛṣṇa Svāmī in his temple, which pleased Ātmā Svarūpa Prabhu. We thanked him and the other guests for their association, hoping to see them all the next day for the final closing ceremony, when Gaṅgā-devī begins her journey back to Mukhwa.

Once we were settled on the other side, near Gaṅgā-devī's temple, I felt even more at home, since I was able to associate with the Mukhwa-vāsīs, or residents of Muhkwa, who are the dear loving servants of Śrī Gaṅgā-devī. Since this was the evening before Gaṅgā was to depart, several other Mukhwa-vāsīs, pilgrims, and guests, with relatives and friends, began to arrive and settle into different accommodations. After seeing that so may visitors had arrived, I was appreciating having a room close to the temple.

A large crowd gathered in the open courtyard just in front of the temple for the last evening *ārati* of the year. Since it was Dīpāvalī, several candles were lit and placed around the temple complex, while the *brāhmaṇas* and priests chanted *mantras*, which enhanced the already auspicious atmosphere. Despite the cold everyone appeared in a festive mood, rushing ahead to queue for *darśana*, receive *caraṇāmṛta* (holy water), or offer something to Gaṅgā-devī. Then several of the Mukhwa-vāsis gathered inside the temple administration office, where the secretary, Ravindra Semwal, led everyone in *bhajanas* (devotional songs) glorifying Gaṅgā-mātā. While he played the harmonium, others played tabla (small drums) and a bell instrument, which created a rhythmical beat. That most of the songs were sung in their local Garhwali language added an extra sweetness to the air. As more and more devotees gathered tightly in the small room, the already spiritual atmosphere became more holy and warm.

Haresh and I sat snugly in a corner of the room next to Bharosa Rāma's son, Prem Vallabha, and his friends. Some of the leading devotee *mātājīs* of Mukhwa sang their favorite *bhajanas*, with their high-pitched Garhwali voices echoing far beyond any mundane level. That was a new sound for both of us. I was thoroughly appreciating this rare opportunity to observe a special form of devotion that is only found in the Garhwal Himālayas. The Mukhwa-vāsīs' intimacy with one another and their devotion to Śrī Gaṅgā-devī is something that must be experienced, something very difficult to record in words.

Then Jyoti Mātājī arrived and participated in the *bhajanas*. She is German born and has spent the past ten years (six months each year) in Gaṅgotrī, living as a *sādhu-sannyāsinī* (female renounced holy person). Since she is well known amongst the Mukhwa-vāsīs, she was invited to chant: *gaṅgā rāṇī gaṅgā rāṇī gaṅgā rāṇī rakṣa mām/ bhāgīrathī bhāgīrathī bhāgīrathī pāhi mām*—O Queen Bhāgīrathī Gaṅgā, please protect and maintain me. This was easy enough even for me to follow, and the entire room followed with the chorus, chanting to our full satisfaction the glories of Bhāgīrathī Gaṅgā. The *bhajanas* continued on and on, resumed in their local fashion, until a special Mahā-Lakṣmī *pūjā* was performed in the temple, followed by a late night *prasāda* meal of rice, dahl, and halva and then more *bhajanas* until midnight.

Early the next morning I met Ravindra Semwal and gave him one litre of Sahasra Tīrtha Jala along with the accompanying

book for offering to Śrī Gaṅgā-devī before she departs. He was pleased to receive this auspicious gift and said that the Sahasra Tīrtha Jala would be used for the morning *abhiṣeka* (bathing) before Gaṅgā-devī left for Mukhwa. Upon offering the gift, I recalled Śrīla Prabhupāda's explanation of how, while taking bath in Gaṅgā, a devotee takes some Gaṅgā-jala and offers it back to Gaṅgā. Similarly, we had begun the Sahasra Tīrtha Jala project at Gomukha, the source of Gaṅgā, and now by presenting this sacred *jala* back to Gaṅgā-devī, not only had Gaṅgā-jala been offered back to her, but more than a thousand other sacred waters were being presented for the pleasure of Śrī Gaṅgā-devī. Then we spoke of Śrīla Prabhupāda's *mahā-abhiṣeka* that took place in Calcutta on the 6th of September this year and about the morning schedule of the final closing ceremonies of the temple.

The *yātrā* was to start around 2:00 p.m. this afternoon. Meanwhile, more and more pilgrims, devotees, and visitors arrived throughout the morning, paying their respects and offering gifts to Gaṅgā-devī on her last day here in Gaṅgotrī. Special *abhiṣeka* and *pūjās* were performed throughout the morning, while in between all the activities visitors queued to have her *darśana* one last time.

During the morning I was fortunate to meet Jyoti Mātājī again. As we discussed various holy places of pilgrimage throughout the country, I discovered that she had practically traveled longer and further than I had. Meeting her was like meeting an old-time traveling partner, very much like one's own self.

Since it was too early and cold for a morning bath and the sun's rays were yet to be seen, I had to forfeit my bath. Moreover I did not want to miss any of the ceremonial functions. Several large carpets had been spread out on the front courtyard of the temple, and the *pūjārīs* began to assemble and decorate Gaṅgā-devī's beautiful silver palanquin with colorful cloth and flowers. While this was going on, about eighty to a hundred soldiers from the Fifth Gorkha regiment stationed at Harsil arrived. They have been participating in this annual pilgrimage for the last fifteen years. Some of them came just for a bath, others desired to walk with the rest of the *yātrīs*, while the rest were part of the musical bag-pipe entourage that would acompany Śrī Gaṅgā-devī. As the army arrived, a few soldiers, as well as a few of the wives of the *brāhmaṇas* from Mukhwa, braved the freezing morning weather for a quick dip and *darśana* of Gaṅgā-mayī. I was sitting on top of some rocks in the distance, observing with great awe and reverence these rare devotees tackling the natural winter elements, regardless of the time of day.

As the morning slowly but sweetly progressed, more and more devotees, *sādhus*, and other guests arrived. Many *sādhus* that came are not usually seen in public, since many of them live a life of semi-seclusion. Yet they happily attend the final day of Gaṅgā-devī's *darśana* and socialize with the other *sādhus* who they do not meet very often. Then a few V.I.P.s arrived with police escort for one last blessing. Around 11:00 a.m., *prasāda* was served in the *prasāda* hall, next to the kitchen, just behind the temple. Everyone rushed to be in the first group to be served hot rice, dahl, and special halva. In between serving and honoring *prasāda*, more and more people gathered around the entire temple complex, while Gaṅgā-devī's palanquin was made ready for her arrival, together with Annapūrṇā-devī and Sarasvatī-devī.

Once Gaṅgā-devī and her associates were placed within the temple replica, standing in the middle of the palanquin, the main temple doors were locked and anticipation grew for the upcoming departure. Crowds

gathered in front and around the side entrance, where Gaṅgā-devī and her palanquin waited. From the distance, the intermingling of the *brāhmaṇas*, *pūjāris*, devotees, *sādhus*, pilgrims, visitors, and army personnel appeared like a natural, colorful integration of fortunate souls who have gathered for one common cause, to be with Śrī Gaṅgā-devī, either for the entire pilgrimage or just up to the front gate. Gaṅgā-devī's mercy seemed to be shining brighter than the rays of the sun.

Eventually, the time approached for departure, so I took a bird's-eye-view from the top of a flight of steps to capture a few photos. Then the army bag-pipers began their traditional tune, the palanquin bearers took their positions, and they lifted Gaṅgā-devī onto their shoulders. The march was led by the musicians, including the horn and drum players, then came Gaṅgā-devī, who was followed by some two hundred participants, all cheering with joy as they left the temple complex, not to return for six months. After taking the photos, I remained behind for one last *darśana* of Gaṅgā-mayī, the Bhagīratha-śilā, and the front doors of Śrī Gaṅgā-devī's locked temple. Then as I left the front gates of the temple complex, I turned around and prayed, "O dear Gaṅgā-mātā, please allow me to return with you next season."

Every time I have walked out of Gaṅgotrī, the weather has been superbly wonderful; and this day, when Gaṅgā-devī had just left her winter abode, it appeared beyond any description. In fact, throughout our entire journey during this *yātrā* in the Himālayas the weather had been absolutely perfect, without a trace of clouds anywhere. Just crystal clear, deep azure skies. So when Sūryadeva shone in all his glory, it increased the beauty a thousandfold. As I followed far behind the *yātrā*, I met several of the local *sādhu* residents on their way back to Gaṅgotrī. Many of them walked with Gaṅgā-devī only the first kilometre before returning. Being able to personally thank some of them for my pleasurable and most merciful short visit to Śrī Gaṅgotrī-dhāma was nice. After a short exchange of words, I was alone walking down the winding motorable road, trying to appreciate the vast, endless beauty that the Himālayas present. After some time, a few army vehicles passed by, filled with many of the guests and visitors who were not into walking. Along the way the army nicely organized a couple of *prasāda* stops for the devotees and pilgrims who were walking. Yet by the time I arrived at the first one at Bhaironghāṭi, everyone had left already and all the *prasāda* was finished except for a few crumbs left over from the *pakoras*! The army personnel were packing up their equipment and offered me a ride, but I just thanked them and continued walking.

After having *darśana* of Śrī Bhairava-nātha, I crossed the towering bridge at Laṅkā that crosses the Jādh Gaṅgā. I stopped on the bridge to have *darśana* of the Bhāgīrathī and Jāhnavī *saṅgama*, far down below, and remembered the time last year when Sanaka Sanātana Prabhu and I were bathing at that same spot. We had sat on top of a mammoth boulder right at the *saṅgama's* junction, basking in the warm sun and chanting *japa*. This day, however, sufficient sunshine was not there to entertain even the thought of taking a bath or relaxing at that same spot. Instead, I just wrapped myself snugly with my woollen blanket, while the cold afternoon breeze blew, and crossed the bridge to the other side.

Laṅkā marks the halfway point between Gaṅgotrī and Mukhwa, and only a few more kilometres remained on the road before the route enters a foot trail at Jhangla (Jangala). Just before Jhangla is Helang, where another *prasāda* stop had been organized. Even though I arrived late, some warm, tasty halva

was waiting for me. After sharing it with one large, matted hair Himālayan dog, I continued on for the remainder of the *yātrā*. By this time, dusk had arrived along with the evening coolness, and since I had started so late from Gaṅgotrī, I still could not catch up with the fast-paced *yātrā*. Moreover, due to my recent surgery, I was forced to slow down my usual fast strut and take several rests along the way. Finally, I reached the foot trail, which is one of the nicest areas for trekking, but since the evening's darkness had arrived, instead of the visual beauty, a different kind of appreciation was to be experienced.

While walking in the dark through the thick forest trail parallel to Gaṅgā's flowing waters, I recalled our first attempt to visit Sapta Ṛṣi-kuṇḍa, which is above Yamunotri, in 1992. When we returned it was very late at night. Due to our anxieties, being without lights, and our immaturity, the whole trek had almost resulted in a nightmare! But now, while walking alone in the dark alongside Gaṅgā-mayī, I felt completely safe, sound, and warm, even without seeing the next step. In fact, the entire walk on the foot trail was without a single stumble or fault, only sheer joy in being able to experience something new and different, without the anxieties.

The evening halt was at the Durgā temple, just two kilometres before Mukhwa, making the first day's total trek about 20 kilometres. The area surrounding this temple, the nearby village of Mārkaṇḍeya, and Mukhwa are described in the *Skanda Purāṇa* (*Kedāra-khaṇḍa* 38) as follows: "Amongst all the monasteries or hermitages upon the earth, this is the chief dwelling place of Śrī Gaṅgā-devī. Whatever auspicious activity is performed here will bestow the desired result, because it was here that the great sage Mārkaṇḍeya Ṛṣi performed his *tapasya*. This place is known as Mukti-maṭha." By the time I arrived, complete exhaustion had overtaken my mind, body, and words, but it was also a very special feeling to be one of the *yātrīs* who had completed the trek on foot. Even during the dark trek in the forest I had passed a few other *yātrīs* who were resting on a rock. When I arrived, many of the locals welcomed me to their particular blazing campfire that they were gathered around, but I just greeted them and continued onto find a quiet resting spot on the veranda of the small *dharma-śālā*. After finding my luggage, which had been carried with the *pūjārī's* luggage on mules from Gaṅgotrī, I just sat back, rested my cold aching body, and thanked Śrī Gaṅgā-devī for allowing me to be there with all her devotees, the Mukhwa-vāsīs and the Mārkaṇḍeya-vāsīs.

After relaxing for some time, I noticed that one of the *pūjārīs* was building a large fire directly in front of Gaṅgā-devī, who was inside the small inner sanctum with Durgā-devī. After shifting there, I sat with two or three other *yātrīs* around this fire, which was very much appreciated, since it instantly warmed my tired body and muscles. I was too tired to speak very much, so I simply meditated on the warmth of the fire kindly supplied by Agnideva (demigod of fire). As one of the kind-hearted *pūjārīs* kept the fire blazing, I observed how expertly these mountain people handled and maintained those burning logs. Then Ravindra Semwal arrived on foot from Mukhwa. He wanted to know how the *yātrā* with Gaṅgā-devī had gone and if I was all right. He informed me that some of the other devotees were inside the *dharma-śālā* chanting and singing *bhajanas* and invited me to go along. I thanked him, but for the time being, I was satisfied being near the hot fire, in front of Gaṅgā-devī. He proceeded on having *darśana* and then greeted the other

locals who were sitting around various other fires, just behind the temple.

The freezing evening turned out to be very warm because of several fires ablaze on top of this small mountainside plateau, and the hours slowly and peacefully drifted by in spite of the loud talking, the devotees' chanting, and the firewood crackling. While Bhāgīrathī Gaṅgā flowed nearby, just below the short plateau, the kitchen team was at the fires, one outside and the other inside the kitchen, cooking a hearty mountain meal for Gaṅgā-devī and her devotees. I slowly drifted over to the *dharma-śālā* to listen to the Garhwali *bhajanas*, but it was so cold inside I just snuggled up in one corner on top of someone's bed-roll, trying to keep warm, especially since I had just come in from the warm fire outside. Since I was overwhelmed with exhaustion and now also cold, I just could not appreciate the chanting at 10:00 at night. Then someone yelled, "*Prasāda*!" which struck the right note, so we all quickly found a place around the outdoor fires, where we were served chapatis, potato sabji, and hot halva. During the meal, one *pūjāri* distributed small ball-shaped pieces of butter as Gaṅgā-devī's *mahā-prasāda*, which tasted celestial on the hot chapatis. The mood around the fires, as the devotees sat honoring *prasāda*, was a strong feeling of unity and fraternity; so I thanked the Lord from my tired, yet grateful heart for allowing me to share in it.

Next, where to sleep? Every space appeared to be taken or reserved, but when I went down the trail for some water next to a small waterfall and stream (some say that this is the Puṣpabhadra Gaṅgā), I noticed one small, empty, single-roomed hut made from earth, rocks, and tin sheets. I then returned to inquire from Ravindra Semwal about the possibility of sleeping there for the night. He informed me that the small structure belonged to the temple committee, and I was welcome to use it if I liked. Thanking him, I quickly arranged my sleeping area, immediately lay down and fell asleep.

Upon waking, nicely rested but slightly cold and stiff, I appreciated the natural surroundings, especially at dawn bordering the entire Bhāgīrathī Gaṅgā valley After the usual morning rituals and spiritual practices, I went for *darśana* and found a warm fire to sit next to. The mules and handlers were already on the scene, loading everyone's luggage to be taken to the village of Mukhwa. After everything was packed, loaded, and sent off, the sun began to shine gently over the distant peaks. Then about a dozen *brāhmaṇas* and I scrambled down the rocks to the shore of Gaṅgā-mayī. Due to a sharp breeze in the air a deep chill made bathing incredibly austere. As I entered the freezing water, a sharp pain ran up my legs and body up to my head. It was extremely difficult to submerge completely in the water, and after doing so, I almost lost my balance. One *brāhmaṇa*, who was on the shore performing *pūjā* and *japa*, motioned for me to come out. But due to my stubborn nature, I just had to complete the three prescribed dunks in the water, which almost knocked me down! Reaching the shore on my knees was a blessing, as the blowing wind dried my shaking wet body. Then I seated myself comfortably on top of some rocks lying in the riverbed and chanted a few more rounds of *japa*, facing the direction of Gaṅgotrī.

As we continued with our own program alongside the Gaṅgā, many residents of the nearby Mārkaṇḍeya and Mukhwa villages began to assemble up above at the Durgā temple. Gaṅgā-devī was carried out of the temple in her palanquin and placed outside facing the warm sun. The silver temple replica was removed from the top of the palanquin, and the most beautiful pure golden

face of Śrī Gaṅgā-devī, together with the sweetly smiling silver face of Sarasvatī-devī, was exposed for the pleasure of everyone. As time passed, most of the bathers went back up to the temple to join and associate with the other locals, including a few visitors from the police department, and, of course, the army musicians, who had also arrived! While the sun increased in warmth, more and more local devotees, with their offerings for Gaṅgā-devī, began to queue for her *darśana*. Everyone had on their best dress on, especially the *mātājīs* in their bright, colorful dresses. Then another meal was ready to be served to the walking *yātrīs* only. After relishing that hearty, spicy hot meal, this time only rice, dahl and sabji, we were almost ready to begin the concluding part of Gaṅgā-devī's *yātrā*.

While I rushed several metres ahead on the trail in order to capture a few photos of the *yātrā* leaving from the temple, the music began to play again and the palanquin bearers took their place. At least two hundred fortunate souls had gathered to walk, during the middle of such a beautiful day, the last two kilometres to Mukhwa, where Gaṅgā-devī would reside until next Akṣaya-tṛtīyā (9 May, 1997). As one Mukhwa-vāsī so aptly commented, "Today, Mukhwa becomes glorious, since Gaṅgā-devī is returning home." It certainly appeared that way, observing the large turn-out of followers who were walking with their goddess of the three worḷds, known as Vaiṣṇavī, Jāhnavī, Viṣṇupadī and, of course, well known to all of us as our dear loving, merciful mother, Śrī Gaṅgā-devī.

The *yātrā*, which appeared to be one kilometre long, weaved in and out along the hillside trail, which eventually leads to Mukhwa. Just after the Durgā temple and just before Mukhwa is the small village of Mārkaṇḍeya, and below it, near the river's bed, are two temples dedicated to Annapūrṇā-devī and Sarasvatī-devī. Upon the arrival of Gaṅgā-devī, she is met by two forms of Lord Śiva, both known as Someśvara Mahādeva. They were handsomely dressed and decorated in their own respective palanquins, happily awaiting the arrival of Gaṅgā-devī. As soon as she arrives, her palanquin is taken to the temple of Annapūrṇā-devī, who has accompanied Gaṅgā-devī and Sarasvatī-devī from Gaṅgotrī. This is the final destination for Annapūrṇā-devī, who resides throughout the winter in Mārkaṇḍeya. While the *yātrā* rested and all the devotees were busy having *darśana* or simply appreciating the auspicious day, I happened to meet Tapovan Mātājī again. This was her first outing since she had been brought down from Tapovan. She appeared a little tired from the long five kilometre hike up the mountainside from Dharāli. We were happy to meet each other, but since I was a little busy strolling around shooting photos, I was unable to spend much time with her. After the *yātrā* left Mārkaṇḍeya for Mukhwa, I saw her walk alone, splitting off from the main trail onto the short-cut path down to the bridge that returns to Dharāli.

Upon arriving in Mukhwa, the entire central ground in front of Someśvara Mahādeva's temple was completely jammed with so many people that it was difficult to move. Gaṅgā-devī's palanquin was brought up the stairs in front of her temple, where she was placed for everyone to have *darśana*. Down below on the next level some sort of pastime was being enacted between the two forms of Someśvara Mahādeva and the local citizens. Trying to understand their relationship with the Lord was difficult. Without inquiring, I just observed the pastimes with great pleasure. Meanwhile, more and more devotees came forward with their offerings for Gaṅgā-devī. Then one of Lord Someśvara Mahādeva's palanquins came up and circumambulated Gaṅgā-devī's temple before stopping in front of her for *darśana.* Then the *pūjārīs* made their offerings as the deity of Someśvara Mahādeva was rocked strongly back and forth before the *pūjārīs*, who stood there undisturbed, privately speaking to Someśvara. Then the other Someśvara palanquin proceeded up to Gaṅgā-devī's temple and repeated the same procedure as the first one. I was amazed at how strongly and closely the palanquins were rocked in front of the *pūjārīs* without actually hitting them. It was a pastime beyond my limited understanding.

Then I asked Ravindra Semwal whether I could offer the *Śrīmad-Bhāgavatam* set to Śrī Gaṅgā-devī at this most appropriate and auspicious time. He gave me permission, adding that it would have to be done very soon, since she would be entering her temple shortly. So I requested Prema Vallabha to quickly run up to the other side of the village to his house and bring four or five volumes of the set. He returned quickly, however Gaṅgā-devī had already decided to enter her temple. Nevertheless, Ravindra Semwal made the necessary arrangements for us to enter with the offering. I presented the volumes to the *pūjārīs*, who anointed them with *tilaka* and placed them before Śrī Gaṅgā-devī within the inner sanctum. Then my name and *gotra* (traditional family line) were given as they recited several *mantras* to accompany the offering. The four volumes were then returned to Ravindra Semwal, who took them outside to look at. Then two of the *pūjārīs* came forward with Ravindra Semwal and myself, and we all gathered for a photo in front of Gaṅgā's temple, each holding open one of the four volumes of the *Śrīmad-Bhāgavatam*. Many of the surrounding locals were wondering what was happening as they curiously watched us present the beautiful, well-printed, colorful volumes. Once the word about our gift spread, the local devotees were impressed and full of great admiration and reverence. Since my original intention had been to have Bharosa Rāma Semwal read the *Bhāgavatam* set first, the entire set was entrusted in his care. Later, he would arrange some system whereby any interested person in the village would be given the opportunity to read these beautiful volumes presented by Śrīla Prabhupāda. Then Ravindra Semwal, who was speaking on behalf of Gaṅgā-devī and the temple administration, said that after two months the *Bhāgavatam* set must be returned to the temple committee. Then I promised him that next year, when I came for the opening ceremony, I would arrange for more of Śrīla Prabhupāda's books to be donated to the temple's library in Gaṅgotrī. This pleased everyone. We then handed all the volumes over to Bharosa Rāma Semwal.

The festive activities continued awhile in the village's central ground; but since I was still feeling tired from the pilgrimage, I decided to return to Bharosa Rāma's home to rest and settle in for the evening. The next morning we boarded the crowded bus full of *yātrīs* returning to their mountainside villages and headed to Ṛṣi-kuṇḍa at Gangnani, where the Sapta Ṛṣis performed austerities and where Parāśara Muni, the father of Vedavyāsa, had his *āśrama.* This *tīrtha* is famous for its hot-water tank and waterfall. The hot bath was a perfect ending to our long, cold, difficult but inspiring journey to Gaṅgotrī.

"JAI GAṄGĀ-MAYĪ!"

Book Two
Chapter Three

Travels With Gaṅgā
(From the Causal Ocean to the Bay of Bengal)

Travels With Gaṅgā
(From the Causal Ocean to the Bay of Bengal)

This chapter describes Gaṅgā's arrival in this universe from the Causal Ocean, her travels through the heavenly planetary systems, her descent in the Himālayas onto Lord Siva's head, and the glories of the sacred places along her banks as she flows through three states of India: Uttar Pradesh, Bihar, and West Bengal.

Gaṅgā flows from the Causal Ocean

In his introduction to the *Śrī Caitanya-caritāmṛta*, Śrīla Prabhupāda summarizes the history of Gaṅgā, the most sacred water of Lord Viṣṇu, in the following words: "When it is necessary to create the material universe, Viṣṇu expands Himself as Mahā-Viṣṇu. This Mahā-Viṣṇu lies down on the Kāraṇa-samudra (Causal Ocean) and breathes all the universes from His nostrils. Thus from Mahā-Viṣṇu and the Causal Ocean all the universes spring, and all these universes float in the Causal Ocean. In this regard, there is the story of Vāmana, who, when He took three steps, stuck His toe through the covering of the universe. Water from this Causal Ocean flowed through the hole which His toe made, and it is said that that flow of water became the River Ganges. Therefore the Ganges is accepted as the most sacred water of Viṣṇu, and is worshiped by all Hindus from the Himālayas down to the Bay of Bengal."

The River Gaṅgā first descends to Dhruvaloka, the topmost planet in this universe, before falling onto Bhārata-varṣa. Her descent is described in the *Śrīmad-Bhāgavatam* (5.17.4-9) as follows: "After purifying the seven planets near Dhruvaloka [the polestar], the Ganges water is carried through the spaceways of the demigods in billions of celestial airplanes. Then it inundates the moon [Candraloka] and finally reaches Lord Brahmā's abode atop Mount Meru. On top of Mount Meru, the Ganges divides into four branches, each of which gushes in a different direction [east, west, north and south]. These branches, known by the names Sītā, Cakṣu, Bhadrā and Alakanandā, flow down to the ocean. The branch of the Ganges known as Sītā flows through Brahmāpurī atop Mount Meru, and from there it runs down to the nearby peaks of the Kesarācala mountains, which stand almost as high as Mount Meru itself. These mountains are like a bunch of filaments around Mount Meru. From the Kesarācala mountains, the Ganges falls to the peak of Gandhamādana Mountain and then flows into the land of Bhadrāśva-varṣa. Finally it reaches the ocean of salt water in the east.

The branch of the Ganges known as Cakṣu falls onto the summit of Mālayavān Mountain and from there cascades onto the land of Ketumāla-varṣa and this way also reaches the ocean of salt water in the west. The branch of the Ganges known as Bhadrā flows from the northern side of Mount Meru. Its waters fall onto the peaks of Kumuda Mountain, Mount Nīla, Śveta Mountain and Śṛṅgavān Mountain in succession. Then it runs down into the province of Kuru and, after crossing through that land, flows into the salt water in the north. Similarly, the branch of the Ganges known as Alakanandā flows from the southern side of Brahmapurī [Brahma-sadana].

Passing over the tops of mountains in various lands, it flows down with fierce force upon the peaks of the mountains Hemakūṭa and Himakūṭa. After inundating the tops of these mountains, the Ganges falls down onto the tract of land known as Bhārata-varṣa, which she also inundates. Then the Ganges flows into the ocean of salt water in the south. Persons who come to bathe in this river are fortunate. It is not very difficult for them to achieve with every step the results of performing great sacrifices like the Rājasūya and Aśvamedha *yajñas*."

The *Śiva Purāṇa* (*Umā-saṁhitā* 17.29,32) also confirms the travels of Gaṅgā already mentioned from the *Śrīmad-Bhāgavatam*: "Issuing from Lord Viṣṇu's lotus feet, the River Gaṅgā falls in that city of Brahmā flowing through the sphere of the moon...Thus flowing along three paths, the holy River Gaṅgā flows into the great ocean in the four quarters after crossing all the mountains."

Gaṅgā reaches the Himālayas

As mentioned earlier from the *Śrīmad-Bhāgavatam*, after Gaṅgā travels through the heavenly planetary system, she eventually reaches Candraloka (the moon) before landing on top of Lord Brahmā's abode on Mount Meru, which is located on Ilāvṛta-varṣa, one of the other *varṣas* (tracts of land) that are situated within Jambūdvīpa (one of the seven islands or planets that comprise the totality of Bhu-maṇḍala). These other *varṣas* are beyond the perception of the residents of this planet. From Meru, Gaṅgā splits into four branches, one of which falls on Hemakūṭa Mountain in Hari-varṣa, before arriving in the Himālayas here on Bhārata-varṣa, where she is known as the River Alakanandā.

Many of the *tīrthas*, rivers, mountains, and other geographical locations found in the *Purāṇas* are located on other planets or *varṣas*, or even on this planet, but are described during different *kalpas* and not the present one in which we are living. Sometimes the *tīrthas* on other planets have a replica manifestation on this planet. For example, there are also mountains identified as Mount Meru on this planet. One such mountain is the great Pamir of Asia, in the highland of Tartary, north of the Himālayas. Other such mountains are listed as the Rudra Himālaya in Garhwal, the Hindukush mountain, and the Karakoram range.

The following description found in the Motilal Banarsidass edition of the *Liṅga Purāṇa* as a footnote in the chapter entitled: *Geography of the World*, explains how Gaṅgā falls onto this earthly Mount Meru: "The *Purāṇas* describe the three stages in the evolution of Gaṅgā: (1) It is a starry river

(Ākāśa Gaṅgā, the Milky Way) in the form of snow; (2) As the snow falls on the high plateau of Pamir (Meru) and also on the high ridges and ranges which surround and radiate from the Pamir region, it is still snowy Gaṅgā; (3) As the snow melts, it divides into four main rivers of Asia [Sītā is the River Hoangho in China and also known as Sirdaria, which rises from the plateau south of Issykkul lake in the Tutanshan; Cakṣu is the River Oxus, or Amu Daria, which rises in the Pamir lake, and is also called Sari-kul, located at a distance of three hundred miles south of Jaxartes; Bhadrā is the River Oby in Siberia and is also known as the Rivers Yarkand and Zarafshan; and Alakanandā flows from Nārāyaṇa Parvata in Badarīnātha], which radiate in different directions. Gaṅgā at this stage becomes a stream, or rather streams of water. After passing through thousands of mountains, valleys, forests, and caves, it falls into the southern sea."

HER VOYAGE THROUGH INDIA

Gaṅgā-mayī travels far beyond our understanding and reach, but from a practical viewpoint, we can understand her more reasonably by observing her descent onto this planet in the Himālayas and her course through three states of India, as well as Bangladesh. In the *Padma Purāṇa* it is stated that the area within three *yojanas* (24 miles) on either side of Gaṅgā's banks is considered Siddha-kṣetra, where one can easily attain perfection and return to the spiritual world, Vaikuṇṭhaloka. Regardless of where one may perform worship, prayer, or bath, practically every square metre is as sacred as the next, from the beginning in Gomukha to Gaṅgā-sāgara, where she meets the Bay of Bengal. Śrīla Prabhupāda had commented on how foolish it was that the residents of Calcutta travel all the way to Haridvāra for a bath, when Gaṅgā is already flowing through Calcutta! If one has the proper consciousness to meditate on Gaṅgā-mayī, wherever that person may be, it is as good as being within Siddha-kṣetra.

Gaṅgā is known as Mandākinī or Ākāśa Gaṅgā while she travels through the heavenly planets, before falling on the mountain known as Hemakūṭa, which is located in Hari-varṣa. There is also a sacred peak in the Himālayas known as Hemakūṭa, which is located north of Mānasa-sarovara near Mount Kailāsa (which represents the Ladakh Kailāsa Trans Himālayan chain). Śrīla Prabhupāda comments that the water of Gaṅgā rests and remains for one thousand milleniums on the head of Lord Śiva, who is an incarnation of the Supreme Personality of Godhead, who sustains the entire universe by different potencies. According to the commentary called *Śrī Bhāgavata-candra-candrikā* by Śrī Vīrarāghava Ācārya, Gaṅgā flows through Mount Kailāsa because she comes from the hair of Lord Śiva.*

In the *Mahābhārata*, it is mentioned that while Gaṅgā was going to Mount Kailāsa, Vasiṣṭha Muni diverted some of her waters into Mānasa-sarovara, but Gaṅgā broke the bank of the lake and flowed forth as the River Sarayū. This short narration from the *Mahābhārata*, as well as other spiritual references, brings us to localities on this planet—Mount Kailāsa, Mānasa-sarovara, and Bindusara—which are located in the Tibetan (Chinese) Himālayas. After coming from a spot named Gaṅgā-mahādvāra in the Mount Kailāsa region through the mercy of Lord Śiva, Gaṅgā branches into seven main

* From the *Varāha Purāṇa* (Chapter 144), we learn more about Gaṅgā's travels: "Three streams fell down from the three streaks of Lord Śiva's hair. These three streams are known as Gaṅgā, Yamunā, and Sarasvatī. They fell from Śiva's mattted hair when he was sitting in yogic contemplation in the place known as Śalagrāma, where he was meditating on Lord Viṣṇu and imparting knowledge to his devotees on how to end *saṁsāra* (the cycle of birth and death)."

rivers. These seven sacred streams, also known as Sapta Samudrik Tīrtha or Divya Gaṅgās, are listed differently in the various *Purāṇas* and Vedic literatures. According to the *Padma Purāṇa,* the names of these seven streams are Vaṭodakā, Nalinī, Sarasvatī, Jambunadī, Sītā, Gaṅgā, and Sindhu. The *Rāmāyaṇa* and the *Matsya Purāṇa* refer to these seven rivers as Hlādinī, Nalinī, Pāvanī, Cakṣu, Sītā, Gaṅgā, and Sindhu. According to the *Mahābhārata* they are Vasvokāsarā, Nalinī, Pāvanī, Jambu, Sītā, Gaṅgā, and Sindhu. Another reference lists the rivers as Yamunā, Sarasvatī, Vitastā, Sarayū, Gomatī, Gaṅgā, and Gaṇḍakī Rivers. And a local Himālayan version is Alakanandā, Dhaulī, Nandākini, Pinder, Mandākinī, Nayar, and Bhāgīrathī. Whichever reference is accepted, our main and common concern is the River Gaṅgā or Bhāgīrathī.

UTTAR PRADESH

There are twenty-eight states and a number of Union territories in India, and in every district of every state there are innumerable major and local *tīrthas,* where the resident devotees and visiting pilgrims can visit, take bath, offer charity and prayers, receive blessings, associate with *sādhus,* gain inspiration, and ultimately try to obtain the favor of the Supreme Lord. In this state of Uttar Pradesh alone there are more prominent *tīrthas* than in any other state of India, which is why Uttar Pradesh is also known as the Land of *Tīrthas*. It is also the most populated state, with two hundred million people, and the fourth largest in size.

Throughout the most auspicious land of India, referred to in the scriptures as Bhāratavarṣa, every single step is considered holy due to the innumerable pastimes performed therein by the Lord and His associates. But due to the Lord's sweet will, certain *tīrthas* have a special prominence over others, regardless of whether their locations are in cities, towns, villages, on river banks, on top of mountains, or near oceans. The *Garuḍa Purāṇa,* the *Mahābhārata,* and other Vedic literatures list seven sacred cities known as *sapta-purīs* or *mokṣa-purīs* (*tīrthas* wherein one easily attains liberation from material bondage)—Ayodhyā, Mathurā, Māyāpurī (Haridvāra), Kāśī (Vārāṇasī), Kāñcī, Avantī (Ujjain), and Dvāravatī (Dvārakā)—the first four of which are in the state of Uttar Pradesh. Also, of the seven most sacred rivers of India—Gaṅgā, Yamunā, Sarasvatī, Godāvarī, Narmadā, Sindhu, and Kāverī—the first three flow through this state. Other principal rivers in Uttar Pradesh are Sarayū, Gomatī, and Rāmagaṅgā. According to the *Skanda Purāṇa,* there are over one *crore* (ten million) Gaṅgās in the Himālayas alone. Some of the major Himālayan branches include the Alakanandā, Kedāra Gaṅgā, Jādh Gaṅgā (Jāhnavī), Dhaulī Gaṅgā, Nandākini, Piṇḍār, Mandākinī, Sone Gaṅgā, Bhilangnā, Kālī Gaṅgā, Madhyameśvara Gaṅgā, and Hanumān Gaṅgā. And of the four Kumbhamelās, each of which are held once every twelve years, in Prayāga-rāja (Allahabad), Haridvāra, Naśika, and Ujjain, the first two are in Uttar Pradesh.

In the list of 108 Śrī Vaiṣṇava Divya Deśams, or 108 Viṣṇu *tīrthas,* there are eight self-manifested holy places, or Svayamvyakta-kṣetras, where the Lord desires to appear out of His own will—Śrī Raṅgam, Tirumala, Śrī Muṣṇam, Vānamāmalai, Puṣkara, Śalagrāma, Naimiṣāraṇya, and Badarikāśrama—the last two of which are located in Uttar Pradesh. Lord Śiva's residence is particularly celebrated in twelve *tīrthas* known as Jyotir-liṅgas—Kedāreśvara (Kedāranātha), Visveśvara (Viśvanātha), Somanātha, Mallikārjuna, Mahākāleśvara, Oṁkāreśvara, Bhīmeśvara, Tryambakeśvara,

Photo by Ashok Dilwali

Kailāsa-parvata — The sacred mountain abode of Lord Śiva where Gaṅgā descends to this planet from Sumeru-parvata, or Mount Meru. Above: the North face. Below: the South face.

Photo by Ashok Dilwali

Photo by Ashok Dilwali

1. Gomukha: The peaks of Bhāgīrathī-parvata on the left and Śivaliṅga on the right form the two horns of the cow's face

1. Bhāgīrathī Gaṅgā before reaching Gaṅgotrī

Photo by Ashok Dilwali

1. Gaṅgotrī with Sudarśana-parvata in the far distance

2. Deoprāyaga, where the Bhāgīrathī and Alakanandā Rivers meet to form the Gaṅgā

Photo by Ashok Dilwali

Photo by Ashok Dilwali

2. Vasanta-pañcamī, the first day of spring at Deoprāyaga

4. Below: Sapta-sarovara, Gaṅgādvāra, where the Seven Ṛṣis performed austerities

3. Śrīla Prabhupāda crossing the Gaṅgā by boat at Rishikesh

4. Gaṅgā-devī at Sapta-sarovara-ghāṭa, Haridvāra

4. Gaṅgā-devī at Birla-ghāṭa, Haridvāra

5. Śukadeva Gosvāmī at Śuka-tāla

7. Yudhiṣṭhira Mahārāja at Hastināpura

6. Mahātmā Vidura at Vidura Kutir

4. Left: Gaṅgā-devī at the entrance of Haridvāra

8. Gaṅgā-devī at Garhmuktesar

9. Sūkara-kṣetra, the famous Gṛdhra-vaṭa, or Banyan tree

10. Durgā-devī at Kānyakubja

9. Opposite: Near Soro-kṣetra, where Caitanya Mahāprabhu converted the Pāṭhāna Muslim soldiers into Vaiṣṇava mendicants

11. The great sage Vālmīki at Biṭhūr

12. Triveṇī, the confluence of the Gaṅgā, Yamunā, and Sarasvatī

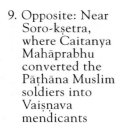

11. Biṭhūr, where Sītā-devī gave birth to Kuśa and Lava

12. Right: Gaṅgā-devī at the Fort, Prayāga-rāja

12. Daśāśvamdha-ghāṭa at Prayāga

13. Vallabha Ācārya's house at Āḍaila-grāma

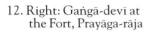

14. *Brāhmaṇas* on the bank of the Gaṅgā at Kāśī

13. Left: While crossing the Yamunā at Prayāga, Caitanya Mahāprabhu became bewildered with ecstatic love

14. Gaṅgā and Maṇikarṇikā-ghāṭa at Vārāṇasī

14. Golden Temple of Kāśī Viśvanātha, Vārāṇasī

14. Gaṅgā-devī at Pañcagaṅgā-ghāṭa, Vārāṇasī

14. Ādi Keśava Temple near the confluence of the Rivers Gaṅgā and Varaṇā, Vārāṇasī

14. Lord Buddha delivering his first sermon at Sārnātha, Vārāṇasī

15. Sunset over the Gaṅgā near Buxar
Insert—Rāma-rekhā-ghāṭa at Siddhāśrāma, Buxar

16. Harikṣetra, Sonepur, where the Rivers Gaṇḍakī and Gaṅgā meet

17. Caitanya Mahāprabhu at Gai-ghāṭa, Patna City

19. The site of the ancient Buddhist University at Vikramaśīla

18. Jahāngīr, the *āśrama* of Janhu Ṛṣi

19. Rāma Temple at Pātharghāṭā-ghāṭa

19. Opposite: Sūrya Nārāyaṇa at the *āśrama* of Vasiṣṭha Muni, Pātharghāṭā

20. Caitanya Mahāprabhu on the road to Kānāi-nāṭaśālā

20. Sunrise over the Gaṅgā at Kānāi-nāṭaśālā

20. Kānāi-nāṭaśālā, the lotus footprints of Caitanya Mahāprabhu

Vaidyanātheśvara, Nāgeśvara, Rāmeśvaram, and Ghuśmeśvara—the first two of which are also in this state. Finally, there are four Kingdoms of God (Char Dhāmas), representing the spiritual planets—Jagannātha Purī, Rāmeśvaram, Dvārakā, and Badarīnātha—of which Badarīnātha is also in Uttar Pradesh.

1) GOMUKHA (GAṄGOTRĪ)

The *Skanda Purāna* (*Kedar-khaṇḍa* 38) glorifies Gomukha as the most exalted *tirtha* related to our dear mother Gaṅgā: "O dear mother, this extremely fascinating and most wonderful place is more pious than the pious, the best *tirtha* amongst *tirthas*, since this *tīrtha* has been born from the lotus feet of Lord Viṣṇu. In order to attain the Lord's mercy, one must bathe at the aperture of the icy-cave (Gomukha) with single-minded devotion on the Lord and His pastimes. Gomukha is the original place of Śrī Gaṅgāmayī. O Śrī Gomukha! O Gaṅgā! Please accept our prostrated obeisances to you through our mind, body and speech. We accept that by offering homage to you and by bathing in your clear, nectar, pious waters, our births have been blessed. We are blessed, extremely blessed, to offer you obeisances again and again. We are incredibly grateful for having the opportunity to worship you."

According to the *Skanda Purāṇa*, Gaṅgā appeared at the place known as Bhagīrathaśilā where Mahārāja Bhagīratha performed his austerities. (This place was the original site of the Gomukha glacier, which due to the influence of Kali-yuga has receded some 18 kilometres from Gaṅgotrī.) Both Gaṅgā-devī and Yamunā-devī simultaneously appeared before Mahārāja Bhagīratha. They were both extremely beautiful, bedecked with various ornaments and jewels, smiling very sweetly with lotus eyes, and sitting together on a golden throne. They were surrounded by celestial women, and Lord Indra was fanning them. It is also mentioned in the *Kedāra-khaṇḍa* that Gaṅgā-devī always resides here along with her constant companion, Yamunā-devī. According to the *Mahābhārata*, Mahārāja Bhagīratha also performed his austerities at another location known as Bindusaras, which was created by a few drops of Gaṅgā that fell on earth from Lord Śiva's head, which is located north of Mount Kailāsa.

From Gomukha (Gaṅgotrī) to Devaprayāga, several other famous sub-branches of the Gaṅgā join the main Bhāgīrathī Gaṅgā. Right at Gaṅgotrī, Kedāra Gaṅgā, originating from Kedāra Tal (5,000 m.), near the mountains adjacent to Śrī Kedāranātha-dhāma, meets Bhāgīrathī Gaṅgā, before she joins Rudra Gaṅgā (Rudradhara), which originates from a mountain named Rudrageru (5,820 m.), where the eleven Rudras reside. Then the famous Jādh (Jāhnavī) Gaṅgā meets her near the *āśrama* of the great sage Jahnu, before she is joined by a small stream named Kumkum (Gungum Nāla). From here, Bhāgīrathī Gaṅgā passes near the *tapo-bhūmi* (place of austerities) of Mārkandeya Ṛṣi, then Mukhwa, before she joins the Kṣira Gaṅgā, which reflects the ocean of milk. Then at Harsil (Hari-śilā), the Kakora and Jālandhari Gaṅgās join her, and nearby she is joined by the dark beautiful waters of Śyāma Gaṅgā. As Bhāgīrathī Gaṅgā passes the district town of Uttarkāśī, the Asī and Varaṇā Gaṅgās join her, thereby forming the Himālayan Kāśī-dhāma. Then, passing through Tehri, the mighty Bhilangnā Gaṅgā meets her at Gaṇesa-prayāga. Finally at Deva-prayāga, the Bhāgīrathī Gaṅgā meets the Alakanandā Gaṅgā and thereafter becomes known simply as "Gaṅgā", for then all the Himālayan branches and sub-branches of the Gaṅgā have become the one famous river.

2) DEVA-PRAYĀGA (DEOPRAYĀGA)

Where the Bhāgīrathī meets the Alakanandā

According to the *Skanda Purāṇa*, during Satya-yuga a great sage named Deva Sharma Ṛṣi meditated and performed austerities to obtain Lord Viṣṇu's *darśana*. After the Lord appeared to Deva Sharma Ṛṣi, various *devas* and *devīs* also came for Lord Viṣṇu's *darśana* and a bath at the *saṅgama* of the Bhāgīrathī Gaṅgā and the Alakanandā Gaṅgā, thus the town was named Deva-prayāga, or Deoprayāga. Lord Vāmanadeva also came here to Deva-prayāga to perform austerities in a cave after His pastimes with Bali Mahārāja. And, in Tretā-yuga, Lord Rāmacandra and Lakṣmaṇa performed austerities and a sacrifice here to atone for killing the great demon Rāvaṇa.

An exquisitely beautiful five-metre tall *mūrti* of Lord Raghunāthajī (Rāmacandra), along with Sītā-devī, was installed here by Ādi Śaṅkarācārya some 1,250 years ago; and, according to the *Nārada-pañcarātra*, this holy shrine is one of Bhārata-bhūmi's 108 Divya Deśams and was also glorified by Periyālvār. In front of this hilltop *mandira* (temple), Garuḍa resides in a small shrine, and Annapūrṇā-devī (Pārvatī) resides in her own temple outside on the Lord's right side. Up a few steps just behind the *mandira*, a small cave where Lord Vāmanadeva performed His austerities is located. Around the other side of the *mandira* is a small temple with a *mūrti* of Śaṅkarācārya, and nearby is the stone-throne used by Lord Rāmacandra. Deva-prayāga is considered the second most important confluence in India, next to Prayāga-rāja (Allahabad, U.P.), and is the first of the five river *saṅgamas* of Alakanandā going up from Hṛṣīkeśa to Badarīnātha. The other four *saṅgamas* are Rudra-prayāga (where the Alakanandā meets the Mandākinī), Karṇa-prayāga (where the Alakanandā meets the Pinder), Nanda-prayāga (where the Alakanandā meets the Nandākinī), and Viṣṇu-prayāga (where the Alakanandā meets the Dhaulī). Surrounding this "Timeless Village" of Deva-prayāga are three mountains named: Gṛdhrācala, Narasiṁhācala, and Daśarathācala.

3) HṚṢĪKEŚA (RISHIKESH)

The hair of the ṛṣi

In the *Skanda Purāṇa* (*Kedāra-khaṇḍa*), there is this narration about Raibhya Ṛṣi, a great sage who performed austerities on the bank of Gaṅgā.

Once upon a time a powerful sage named Raibhya Ṛṣi was living in his *āśrama* on the banks of Gaṅgā. He had a massive growth of *jaṭā* (matted locks of hair) that was placed on top of his head. Once, when he was returning from his early morning bath during *brāhma-muhūrta* (time before sunrise), his son Sharma accidently hit and killed him, mistaking him to be a wild animal. The son performed several ritualistic activities and austerities to atone for his father's death; and since he had performed them with such great precision and repentance, several demigods appeared and inquired as to his intentions. The son requested that his father be brought back to life, and his wish was eventually granted.

Afterwards, Raibhya Ṛṣi made inquiries about the mysteries of death and the means of salvation. He and his son performed great austerities for a lengthy period, which resulted in their having Lord Viṣṇu's *darśana*. When the Lord appeared, the powerful sage requested the Lord to show him His *māyā*

(illusory potency) in its various forms. After understanding the intricate diversities of the Lord's illusory energy, the *ṛṣi* requested the Lord to kindly free all human beings from the bondage of *māyā*. Lord Viṣṇu replied, "Since you have performed these austerities by controlling your senses, let this place be known as Hṛṣīkeśa (named after Lord Hṛṣīkeśa, master of all senses), and during Kali-yuga, one of my incarnations will be known as Bharata Mahārāja. Anyone who follows religious principles and takes bath in Māyā-kuṇḍa while residing here will be free from worldly bondages."

According to the *Sthala Purāṇa*: "Raibhya Ṛṣi preferred the sanctity of the place where Lord Viṣṇu appeared, so he remained there in the form of dense green vegetation on top of the surrounding mountains, which resemble his matted locks. In consideration of this and the spiritual qualities of Raibhya Ṛṣi, the area also became known as Ṛṣi-keśa (Rishikesh), or the hair of the *ṛṣi*."

Rāmacandra, Lakṣmaṇa, Kaṇva, and Śivānanda

Before Lord Rāmacandra and His younger brother Lakṣmaṇa visited Devaprayāga, They performed austerities and sacrifices to atone for killing Rāvaṇa here. They also bathed in Ṛṣi-kuṇḍa on the bank of Gaṅgā. Some six kilometres from here is the hermitage of Kaṇva Ṛṣi, who adopted the rejected daughter of Viśvāmitra and Menakā, Śakuntalā, who eventually married Duṣyanta. This hermitage is situated amidst the beautiful Himālayan forests on the banks of the River Mālinī, a tributary of the Gaṅgā. It is located between Hṛṣīkeśa and Kothdwar.

Śivānanda Swami is a well-known and respected name in the Hṛṣīkeśa area, particularly at Muni-ki-reti, the abode of *ṛṣis*. This saintly person's love for Gaṅgā-mātā was unprecedented, and he lived on her holy banks for more than three decades. It was only from there that he was able to commune with mother Gaṅgā always, day and night. He glorifies Gaṅgā with the following words: "Gaṅgā-mayī is the form of Lord Viṣṇu. The sight of her is soul stirring and elevating. She flows in the valleys and lives by the side of her younger sister, Pārvatī, the other daughter of Himavān. How magnificent she is when she flows in the valley of Hṛṣīkeśa. She has a blue color like that of the ocean. Her water is extremely clear and sweet, and it is taken in big copper vessels to far off places in India. To have a look at Gaṅgā in Hṛṣīkeśa is soul elevating. To sit a few minutes on a rock by the side of Gaṅgā is a blessing. To stay for some months in Hṛṣīkeśa on the banks of Gaṅgā and do *anuṣṭhāna* (accepting vows) or *puraścaraṇa* (regularly practising vows) is a great austerity, which will take the aspirant to the abode of Lord Hari."

Śrīla Prabhupāda at 'Gaṅgā Darshan'

The following story from *Śrīla Prabhupāda-līlāmṛta* (Vol. 6, Chapters 7-8), tells of Śrīla Prabhupāda's activities while staying at 'Gaṅgā Darshan' in Hṛṣīkeśa during the month of May in 1977.

"Śrīla Prabhupāda occasionally talked of traveling to a place better for his health. It was May, and Bombay was hot. Soon the monsoons would come. He had considered going to Kashmir, because the air and water were reputedly good for health; but no suitable accommodations could be found there, and the weather was too cool. Then one day he received a visit from Śrīman Narayan, the former governor of Gujarat. 'You should take care of your health,' said Śrīman Narayan. 'I hope you get better.'

"'Oh, this is just an old machine,' Prabhupāda laughed. 'The more you cure it, the more it gets worse. But my work never stops. That keeps on going. My main work is to write these books, and that is going on.' Several other Indian guests were present, and they at once began recommending good places for health: Srinagar, Kashmir, Dehradun, Mussoorie, Shimla, Haridwar. 'Yes, the water in Hardwar is good,' said Śrīman Narayan, 'but better than that would be in Hṛṣīkeśa, where the Ganges flows. Whatever places are on the bank of the Ganges, the water will be very good. Pure Ganges water.'

"Śrīla Prabhupāda took these remarks seriously and turned to his disciples. 'Yes, then we can go to Hṛṣīkeśa. This time is very good. Let us arrange for that.' From that moment, going to Hṛṣīkeśa became a definite plan, and Prabhupāda prepared to leave Bombay within a week. The devotees in Hṛṣīkeśa had been in high spirits, and so had Śrīla Prabhupāda. While crossing the Ganges by boat, Prabhupāda had requested drinking water to be fetched from the center of the river. He had liked the lodge [named 'Gaṅgā Darshan'], provided by his host, and he had even gone into the kitchen to show his disciples how to cook. Word had spread through the pilgrimage-tourist town that A.C. Bhaktivedanta Swami was present, and Prabhupāda had agreed to hold a *darśana* from five to six p.m. daily. The room had always been crowded at that hour with forty to fifty people, including Western hippies and seekers as well as Indians on pilgrimage or vacation. Although Śrīla Prabhupāda's voice had been extremely faint, he had spoken with force, stressing *Bhagavad-gītā* as it is.

"Only a few disciples were with Prabhupāda in Hṛṣīkeśa, and they had deemed it a wonderful treat. Not only had Prabhupāda directed the cooking, but he had told stories while cooking. He had said that only a lazy man couldn't cook, and then he told a Bengali story—the story of a lazy man—to illustrate. There was a king, who decided that all lazy men in his kingdom could come to the charity house and be fed. So many men came, all claiming, 'I am a lazy man.' The King then told his minister to set fire to the charity house, and all but two men ran out of the burning building. One of the two said, 'My back is becoming very hot from the fire.' And the other advised, 'Just turn over to the other side.' The King then said, 'These are actually lazy men. Feed them.'

"But on the evening of May 15, Śrīla Prabhupāda could neither sleep nor work at his dictation. The storm, a harbinger of the monsoon season, knocked out all electric power in Hṛṣīkeśa. Since the fans were not running and the window shutters had to be closed because of the wind, the room became very hot. Suddenly, at one-thirty a.m., Prabhupāda rang his bell, and Tamāla Kṛṣṇa and Kṣīracorā-gopīnātha responded. From beneath his mosquito net he said, 'As I was telling you, the symptoms are not good. I want to leave immediately for Vṛndāvana.' If it was time for him to pass away, he said, then let it be in Vṛndāvana. Since he wanted to leave immediately, the devotees stayed up all night, packing and preparing to leave. Train reservations were not available, however, so they decided to go by car."

4) Gaṅgādvāra (Haridvāra)

We begin this section with a quote from the *Skanda Purāṇa*, wherein Gaṅgādvāra and Gaṅgā are glorified as follows: "There is no *tīrtha* equal to Gaṅgādvāra, no mountain equal to Kailāsa, no Lord equal to Vāsudeva, and no river equal to the Gaṅgā." Then the *Garuḍa Purāṇa* (*Ācāra-kāṇḍa* 81.29) continues:

"He who takes a holy dip at Gaṅgādvāra, Kuśāvarta, and Kanakhala is not born again."

Even Lord Brahmā, who has four heads, cannot narrate all the qualities of Gaṅgā, what to speak of all the numerous pastimes that have been performed on her banks since time immemorial, especially here in Gaṅgādvāra (Haridvāra). Whether one remembers this sacred area as Māyāpurī, Māyādvāra, Mokṣadvara, Brahmāpurī, or even Kapilasthāna (where Kapila Muni once resided), the pastimes appear to be never ending, resembling a spiritual theatrical performance, highlighting Lord Viṣṇu (Nārāyaṇa) and all His associates, especially all the great devotees, down to the simple humble pilgrim.

Śrīla Prabhupāda mentions that what makes a holy place spiritualized is the land and the pastimes that were performed there. Haridvāra generates a very high spiritual, energetic atmosphere due to the numerous pastimes. However, most of the credit must be awarded to the presence of our dear mother Gaṅgā. Otherwise, why would the Lord and His associates choose this particular place to enact so many wonderful pastimes for the benefit of everyone? And why have so many great personalities visited this most auspicious *tīrtha*, which is also considered the birthplace or source of the River Gaṅgā? It is here that Gaṅgā enters the earth, or plains of India. Therefore this place is considered the "Gateway to Gaṅgā", whether one travels to the Himālayas or in the opposite direction towards Bhārata-varṣa.

Sapta Gaṅgā

Again from the *Nārada Purāṇa* (*Uttara-bhāga* 66.32-35), we hear the priest of King Rukmāṅgada, Vasu, narrate the glories of Gaṅgādvāra (Haridvāra) to Lord Brahmā's daughter, Mohinī, as he explains the glories of Sapta Gaṅgā (also known as Saptasrota, Sapta-dhara, or Sapta-sarovara): "Similarly, O gentle lady, in the northern quarter there is the famous *tīrtha* known as Sapta Gaṅgā, which destroys all sins. The holy hermitages of the seven sages are there. By taking a holy bath in each *tīrtha* and by performing the rite of *tarpana* (water offerings) to the demigods and forefathers, one obtains the eternal world of the sages. O highly intelligent lady, when the divine River Gaṅgā was being brought to earth by King Bhagiratha, Gaṅgā, thanks to her love and fondness for the seven sages, flowed in seven currents. Therefore, this *tīrtha* became famous as Sapta Gaṅgā."

Please see Book Two, Chapter Seven, SAPTA ṚSIS (The Seven Sages)

Nārada, Śveta, Pratīpa, Gaṅgā-devī, and Dattātreya

The following narration from the *Padma Purāṇa* (*Sṛṣṭi-khaṇḍa* 62) describes Gaṅgādvāra as one of the places where Nārada Muni performed austerities.

Once Nārada Muni went to visit Lord Brahmā, and after offering his humble obeisances, he inquired, "O Father, what have you created on earth that is approved by even Lord Viṣṇu and Śiva and which is beneficial and auspicious for all living beings?" Lord Brahmā was pleased to hear this question of Nārada and replied, "Formerly when I was creating the world, I instructed the illusory energy, Māyā, to be the first energy to manifest, and from her I would create. After hearing this, she divided herself into seven parts: Gāyatrī, Vāk, Svarlakṣmī, Umā, Śaktibīja, Varṇikā, and Dharma-dravā. Māyā, in the form of Dharma-dravā, has taken shelter in all moral conduct. She has emanated from the lotus feet of Lord Viṣṇu and is held on the head of Lord Śiva. She is united with all three of us. Dharma-dravā is also known to be the water in my waterpot, which has risen from the sacrifices of Bali Mahārāja. Formerly the almighty, powerful Lord Viṣṇu tricked Bali by occupying the entire universe with two steps and simultaneously pierced the covering of the universe. As the Lord stood before me, I worshiped His foot with the water in my pot.

"After washing the Lord's foot, the water fell onto Hemakūṭa and then took refuge within Lord Śiva's matted hair. Then Mahārāja Bhagīratha propitiated Śiva and brought the best elephant, Airāvata, to the earth to be worshiped daily by his austerities. Then Airāvata forcibly made three holes in the mountain with his three tusks. Thus Gaṅgā flowed through the three holes and hence she is known in the world as having three streams. Due to her contact with Lord Viṣṇu, Śiva, and myself, she is purified and she purifies the three worlds. The highest position can only be obtained by serving Gaṅgā, since there is no greater means for accomplishing religious merit than this. Therefore, O Nārada, go to her and obtain the religious merit available in the three worlds." After hearing this, Nārada Muni, the best of sages, went to Gaṅgādvāra and practiced austerities on her bank.

The following narration about an ancient *kuṇḍa* in Gaṅgādvāra is from the *Skanda Purāṇa* (*Kedāra-khaṇḍa*).

At Gaṅgādvāra, King Śveta of Kāśmīra once performed great austerities for one million years for the pleasure of Lord Brahmā. When the King eventually captured Brahmā's attention, Brahmā said to him, "O fortunate King, whatever boon you desire will be fulfilled. There is nothing that is unavailable to you within the three worlds." The King then requested, "O dear Lord Brahmā, allow this area to be famous by your name, and may you always reside here with Lord Viṣṇu and Lord Śiva. Whoever takes bath here on the bank of Gaṅgā (known as Brahmāpurī or Brahma-kuṇḍa, near Hari-ki-pari) will be awarded the highest position, engagement in devotional service."

As mentioned earlier, it was at Gaṅgādvāra that King Pratīpa performed austerities on the bank of Gaṅgā, when Gaṅgā-devī personally appeared to him and requested him to be her husband. He accepted her as his daughter-in-law, and she eventually married his son, Śāntanu. Also, Dattātreya, the son of Atri Ṛṣi and Anasūyā, performed great austerities for ten thousand years by standing on one leg on the bank of Gaṅgā at Gaṅgādvāra. One day, Gaṅgā-mayī flowed with her usual force past the place where Dattātreya was performing austerities. By providence, the *kuśa* grass that he was using for his rituals was washed away. Knowing the damage that had been caused to his sacred *āśrama*, he became very angry and was just about to burn up the Gaṅgā. Realizing the predicament, Lord Brahmā descended along with other demigods to pacify the angry sage. After being pleased, Dattātreya forgave the offense and requested them to remain in his hermitage forever. They all agreed and since then this sacred place within Gaṅgādvāra is called Kuśāvarta.

The famous Droṇācārya

From the *Mahābhārata* (*Ādi-parva*), we learn about the birth of the great military teacher Droṇācārya at Gaṅgādvāra.

Once the great sage Bharadvāja traveled on pilgrimage to Haridvāra, where the sacred River Gaṅgā flows. On the bank of that holy river, Bharadvāja, who was always strict in his vows of spiritual life, began a sacrifice. After lighting the sacrificial fire by *mantra*, he suddenly beheld an Apsarā named Ghṛtācī, who had just finished bathing in the Gaṅgā. She was intoxicated and careless of her dress. Suddenly, a wind blew away her garments and exposed her faultless youthful form. The sage Bharadvāja could not control himself and discharged his semen onto the ground. After realizing what he had done, he carefully picked up his life fluid and placed it in an earthen pot. Miraculously, a child developed in the pot, and when a boy was born, Bharadvāja named him Droṇa, which is a Sanskrit word for pot. This child later became the famous learned scholar of the *Dhanur Veda* known as Droṇācārya, the military teacher of Arjuna and the other Pāṇḍavas, as well as the commander-in-chief of the Kauravas on the battlefield of Kurukṣetra.

Ulūpī and Arjuna

Also from the *Mahābhārata* (*Ādi-parva* 217), we see how the Pāṇḍava Arjuna entered the deep waters of the Gaṅgā at Gaṅgādvāra in order to fulfill the desires of Ulūpī.

After Arjuna obtained permission from his elder brother, Yudhiṣṭhira, he prepared himself for a one year pilgrimage in the forest. Upon arriving where Gaṅgā enters the plains (Gaṅgādvāra), the mighty hero thought of settling there, because it was a most exceedingly beautiful area. While taking up his residence on the banks of the sacred Gaṅgā, Arjuna and his entourage performed innumerable Agnihotra fire sacrifices.

One day, after Arjuna entered the Gaṅgā to perform his oblations, he was about to return to the bank when he was dragged to the bottom of the water by the daughter of the king of the Nāgas. Arjuna was carried into the king's beautiful mansion, where he saw a sacrificial fire already ignited for himself. After he performed his rites, he approached the King's daughter and addressed her smilingly, "O attractive girl, who is the master of this beautiful region, who are you, and who is your father?"

Hearing these words of Arjuna, she replied, "This region belongs to the Nāga named Kauravya, who was born in the line of Airāvata. I am the daughter of Kauravya, and my name is Ulūpī. O tiger among men, I was deprived of reason by Kāmadeva, the lord of desire, and I am still unmarried. Afflicted as I am by the lord of desire, please gratify me today by giving thyself to me." Arjuna pleaded that since a vow of celibacy had been forced upon him for twelve years, she would have to wait. She then explained that the vow was limited, referencing only to Draupadī, because Arjuna had violated the agreement between the five brothers by entering Draupadī's room when she was with one of the other Pāṇḍavas. As he listened to her, he understood that she was in a distressed condition and was seeking protection, otherwise she was willing to end her life.

Making virtue his motive and with the understanding that one should accept a women who desires marriage, Arjuna did everything she desired. After spending the night in the mansion, Arjuna rose with the morning sun and returned to Gaṅgādvāra accompanied by Ulūpī. Before returning to her own abode, Ulūpī granted Arjuna the boon of being invincible in water by saying, "Every aquatic creature shall, without doubt, be vanquishable by thee." Afterwards, she begot a son by the name of Irāvān.

Mahātmā Vidura

Just before the battle of Kurukṣetra was to begin, Lord Kṛṣṇa had visited Hastināpura to try to negotiate a peaceful settlement between the Kauravas and the Pāṇḍavas, but He had left after failing in His attempt. King Dhṛtarāṣṭra then invited his younger brother, the saintly and wise Vidura (who was an incarnation of Lord Yamarāja), for consultation. When Vidura informed the King that his dynasty was doomed if he fought with Lord Kṛṣṇa and the Pāṇḍavas, the King's wicked son, Duryodhana, interrupted and spoke harshly to the gentle Vidura, "Who asked for advice from this son of a maidservant? He is so unchaste that he spies in the interest of our enemy even though he has grown up in our support. We should throw him out of the palace immediately and leave him with only the clothes he is wearing!" Afflicted to the core of his heart by his nephew's cruel words, Vidura left his brother's palace for good. He gave up his royal dress and left Hastināpura to travel on pilgrimage, for he did not want to see the outcome of the fratricidal war.

By his devotional credits, Vidura took full advantage of traveling on pilgrimage with a desire to advance in devotional life. He traveled to numerous holy places, where thousands of transcendental forms of the Lord are situated. While traveling alone, dressed as a mendicant with matted hair, and thinking only of Lord Śrī Kṛṣṇa, his travels eventually brought him to Ayodhyā, Dvārakā, Mathurā, Prabhāsa-kṣetra, and then proceeding west, he came to the sacred River Sarasvatī. He was now free of all political intrigue and he constantly sanctified himself by taking bath in holy rivers. Afterwards, he traveled through the wealthy provinces of Surat, Sauvira, and Matsya, before reaching the bank of the River Yamunā, where he met Uddhava, the great devotee of Lord Kṛṣṇa. After embracing one another, Vidura asked for news about the family of Lord Kṛṣṇa. Uddhava began to narrate the wonderful pastimes of Lord Kṛṣṇa in Vṛndāvana, Mathurā, and Dvārakā, as well as the Lord's final disappearance pastime. Uddhava also expressed his desire to fulfill the Lord Kṛṣṇa's instruction to go to the Himālayas and serve His incarnations, Nara and Nārāyaṇa Ṛṣis, in Badarikāśrama. Then Uddhava told Vidura that he might take lessons from the great learned Maitreya Ṛṣi, who was residing nearby on the bank of the Gaṅgā in Haridvāra. Maitreya was personally instructed by Lord Kṛṣṇa, when He was about to leave this mortal world.

In the *Śrīmad-Bhāgavatam* (3.4.36 and 3.5.1), we read that Vidura eventually arrived in Haridvāra: "After passing a few days on the bank of the River Yamunā, Vidura, the self-realized soul, reached the bank of the Ganges, where the great sage Maitreya was situated...Vidura, the best amongst the Kuru dynasty, who was perfect in devotional service to the Lord, thus reached the source of the celestial Ganges River (Haridwar), where Maitreya, the great fathomless learned sage of the world, was seated. Vidura, who was perfect in gentleness and satisfied in transcendence, inquired from him."

Śrīla Prabhupāda then explains in the *Śrīmad-Bhāgavatam* (3.5.1) how Vidura reached perfection by practice of devotional service: "Vidura was already perfect due to his unalloyed devotion to the infallible Lord. The Lord and living entities are all qualitatively the same by nature, but the Lord is quantitatively much greater than any individual living entity. He is ever infallible, whereas the living entities are prone to fall under the illusory energy. Vidura had already surpassed the fallible nature of the living entity in conditional life due to his being *acyuta-bhāva*, or legitimately absorbed in the devotional service of the Lord. This stage of life is called *acyuta-bhāva-siddha*, or perfection by dint of devotional service. Anyone, therefore, who is absorbed in the devotional service of the Lord is a liberated soul and has all admirable qualities. The learned sage Maitreya was sitting in a solitary place on the bank of the Ganges at Haridwar, and Vidura, who was a perfect devotee of the Lord and possessed all good transcendental qualities, approached him for inquiry."

Later in the *Śrīmad-Bhāgavatam* (3.8.2) we learn of the first subject matter disclosed by the enthusiastic Maitreya to Vidura: "Let me now begin speaking on the *Bhāgavata Purāṇa*, which was directly spoken to the great sages by the Personality of Godhead for the benefit of those who are entangled in extreme miseries for the sake of very little pleasure."

Further on in the *Śrīmad-Bhāgavatam* (3.20.4), Śaunaka Ṛṣi inquires from Śrī Sūta Gosvāmī about Mahātmā Vidura: "Vidura was purified of all passion by wandering in sacred places, and at last he reached Haridwar (Kuśāvarta), where he met the great sage who knew the science of spiritual life, and inquired from him. Saunaka Ṛṣi therefore asked: What more did Vidura inquire from Maitreya?"

Śrīla Prabhupāda then comments from the same text of the *Śrīmad-Bhāgavatam* on the importance of visiting the holy places of pilgrimage: "Here the words *virajās tīrtha-sevayā* refer to Vidura, who was completely cleansed of all contamination by traveling to places of pilgrimage. In India there are hundreds of sacred places of pilgrimage, of which Prayāga, Haridwar, Vṛndāvana and Rāmeśvaram are considered principal. After leaving his home, which was full of politics and diplomacy, Vidura wanted to purify himself by traveling to all the sacred places, which are so situated that anyone who goes there automatically becomes purified. This is especially true in Vṛndāvana; any person may go there, and even if he is sinful he will at once contact an atmosphere of spiritual life and will automatically chant the names of Kṛṣṇa and Rādhā. That we have actually seen and experienced. It is recommended in the *śāstras* that after retiring from active life and accepting the *vānaprastha* order, one should travel everywhere to places of pilgrimage in order to purify himself. Vidura completely discharged this duty, and at last he reached Kuśāvarta, or Haridwar, where the sage Maitreya was sitting.

"Another significant point is that one must go to sacred places not only to take bath there, but to search out great sages like Maitreya and take instructions from them. If one does not do so, his traveling to places of pilgrimage is simply a waste of time. Narottama dāsa Ṭhākura, a great *ācārya* of the Vaiṣṇava sect, has, for the present, forbidden us to go to such places of pilgrimage because in this age, the times having so changed, a sincere person may have a different impression on seeing the behavior of the present residents of the pilgrimage sites. He has recommended that instead of taking the trouble to travel to such places, one should concentrate one's mind on Govinda, and that will help him. Of course, to concentrate one's mind on Govinda in any place is a path meant for those who are the most spiritually advanced; it is not for ordinary persons. Ordinary persons may still derive benefit from traveling to holy places like Prayāga, Mathurā, Vṛndāvana and Haridwar."

After Vidura retired from putting questions to Maitreya Muni, who thoroughly educated him in transcendental knowledge, he returned to Hastināpura, where he was welcomed by all the inhabitants, especially by Mahārāja Yudhiṣṭhira. They all exchanged obeisances and welcomed one another with embraces. Vidura then ate sumptously and took sufficient rest. Afterwards, as stated in the *Śrīmad-Bhāgavatam* (1.13.9), King Yudhiṣṭhira inquired from him as follows: "While traveling on the surface of the earth, how did you maintain your livelihood? At which holy places and pilgrimage sites did you render service?"

Śrīla Prabhupāda gives further details on the same text of the *Śrīmad-Bhāgavatam*:

"Vidura went out from the palace to detach himself from household affairs, especially political intrigues...This preparatory stage is called *vānaprastha-āśrama*, or retired life for traveling and visiting the holy places on the surface of the earth. In the holy places of India like Vṛndāvana, Haridwar, Jagannātha Purī and Prayāga, there are many great devotees, and there are still free kitchen houses for persons who desire to advance spiritually. Mahārāja Yudhiṣṭhira was inquisitive to learn whether Vidura maintained himself by the mercy of the free kitchen houses (*chatras*)."

The great Mahātmā Vidura gradually described everything he had personally experienced during his pilgrimage. Though he had accepted the renounced order of life on the authority of Maitreya Muni, he did not return to the capital to enjoy material comforts. His actual reason was to deliver his elder brother, Mahārāja Dhṛtarāṣṭra, who was too much materially attached. He said to Dhṛtarāṣṭra, "My dear King, please get out of here immediately. Do not delay. Just see how fear has overtaken you." Vidura explained the influence of supreme *kāla* (eternal Time), under the influence of which everyone must eventually surrender their most dear life. He instructed his elderly brother to leave for the North without informing his relatives.

The *Śrīmad-Bhāgavatam* (1.13.29-30) further elaborates how King Dhṛtarāṣṭra finally left his comfortable lifestyle in Hastināpura: "Thus Mahārāja Dhṛtarāṣṭra, the scion of the family of Ajamīḍha, firmly convinced by introspective knowledge (*prajña*), broke at once the strong network of familial affection by his resolute determination. Thus he immediately left home to set out on the path of liberation, as directed by his younger brother Vidura. The gentle and chaste Gāndhārī, who was the daughter of King Subala of Kandahar (or Gāndhāra), followed her husband, seeing that he was going to the Himālaya Mountains, which are the delight of those who have accepted the staff of the renounced order like fighters who have accepted a good lashing from the enemy."

When Mahārāja Yudhiṣṭhira discovered that both his uncles, Dhṛtarāṣṭra and Vidura, along with Gāndhārī, had left the palace, naturally his doubts arose, and he conjectured that they had drowned themselves in the waters of the Gaṅgā. While Yudhiṣṭhira and Sañjaya were trying to determine the location of their missing relatives, Nārada Muni appeared on the scene carrying his *vīṇā*. After he was properly received, Mahārāja Yudhiṣṭhira inquired about the whereabouts of his uncle and aunt. Nārada informed him not to lament for anyone, for everyone is under the control of the Supreme Lord, and they are all bound by different Vedic injunctions and are conditioned to obey the orders of the Supreme.

In the *Śrīmad-Bhāgavatam* (1.13.51-59) Śrī Nārada Muni gives an account of the final passing of Dhṛtarāṣṭra as follows: "O King, your uncle Dhṛtarāṣṭra, his brother Vidura, and his wife Gāndhārī have gone to the southern side of the Himālaya Mountains, where there are shelters of the great sages. The place is called Saptasrota (divided by seven) because there the waters of the sacred Ganges were divided into seven branches. This was done for the satisfaction of the seven *ṛṣis*. On the banks at Saptasrota, Dhṛtarāṣṭra is now engaged in beginning *aṣṭāṅga-yoga* (eightfold path) by bathing three times daily, by performing the Agnihotra sacrifice with fire and by drinking only water. This helps one control the mind and the senses and frees one completely from thoughts of familial affection. One who has controlled the *yogic āsanas* (sitting postures) and the breathing process can turn the senses toward the Absolute Personality of Godhead,

and thus become immune to the contaminations of the modes of material nature, namely mundane goodness, passion and ignorance.

"Dhṛtarāṣṭra will have to amalgamate his pure identity with intelligence and then merge into the Supreme Being with knowledge of his qualitative oneness, as a living entity, with the Supreme Brahman. Being freed from the blocked sky, he will have to rise to the spiritual sky. He will have to suspend all the actions of the senses, even from the outside, and will have to be impervious to interactions of the senses, which are influenced by the modes of material nature. After renouncing all material duties, he must become immovably established, beyond all souces of hindrances on the path. O King, he will quit his body, most probably on the fifth day from today. And his body will turn to ashes. While outside observing her husband, who will burn in the fire of mystic power along with his thatched cottage, his chaste wife will enter the fire with rapt attention. Vidura, being affected with delight and grief, will then leave this place of sacred pilgrimage."

After speaking this to Mahārāja Yudhiṣṭhira, Nārada Muni ascended into outer space, glorifying the Lord with his transcendeantal *vīṇā*. Yudhiṣṭhira, realizing that the demise of his relatives was imminent, kept Nārada's instructions in his heart and rid himself of all lamentation. When Dhṛtarāṣṭra left his body, Vidura departed from the Saptasrota area in the foothills of the Himālayas and traveled west towards the ocean on pilgrimage.

And finally from the *Śrimad-Bhāgavatam* (1.15.49), we learn of Vidura's departure from this planet: "Vidura, while on pilgrimage, left his body at Prabhāsa. Because he was absorbed in thought of Lord Kṛṣṇa, he was received by the denizens of Pitṛloka planet, where he returned to his original post."

Dakṣa's sacrifice at Kanakhala

In the *Nārada Purāṇa* (*Uttara-bhāga* 66.25-26) the glories of Kanakhala are mentioned as follows: "The devotee should go to the *tīrtha* named Kanakhala (also known as Dakṣasthāna), south of Gaṅgādvāra. By observing fast for three nights and taking a holy bath in this *tīrtha*, one is liberated from all sins. He who gives a cow there to a *brāhmaṇa* who has mastered the *Vedas* will never see the River Vaitaraṇī nor Yamarāja."

While Vidura was at Kuśāvarta (Haridvāra) hearing *Śrīmad-Bhāgavatam* from the great sage Maitreya, he asked Maitreya, "Why was King Dakṣa envious of Lord Śiva and why did he neglect his daughter Satī?" Maitreya wanted to clarify the cause of the misunderstanding between Lord Śiva and Dakṣa and why Satī gave up her body.

Then the great sage explained that the leaders of the universal creation, such as Marīci, Dakṣa, and Vasiṣṭha, had performed a great sacrifice, wherein all the demigods, including Lord Brahmā and Lord Śiva, had assembled with their followers. When Dakṣa entered the sacrificial assembly, everyone stood to offer him respect, except Lord Brahmā and Lord Śiva. Dakṣa was very much offended seeing Lord Śiva sitting. He then became greatly angry, and with his eyes glowing, he began to speak very strongly against Lord Śiva. After speaking harshly to Śiva, Dakṣa washed his hands and mouth and cursed him. Upon understanding that Lord Śiva had been cursed, one of his principal associates, Nandīśvara, countered the curse by saying, "Dakṣa has accepted the body as all in all. Therefore, since he has forgotten the knowledge of Lord Viṣṇu, and is attached to sex life only, within a short time he will have the face of a goat." As a reaction to Nandīśvara's curse, the sage Bhṛgu condemned the followers of Lord Śiva with a very strong brahminical curse.

While this cursing and countercursing was going on between Lord Śiva's followers and the parties of Dakṣa and Bhṛgu, Lord Śiva became very morose. Not saying anything, he left the arena of the sacrifice. The sacrifice was executed for thousands of years, and upon the completion of the sacrifice, all the demigods went to the confluence of the Rivers Gaṅgā and Yamunā and took their baths. After becoming purified in heart, they all departed for their respective abodes.

Meanwhile, the tension between the father-in-law, Dakṣa, and the son-in-law, Lord Śiva, continued for a considerably long period. After Dakṣa was appointed the chief of all the Prajāpatis by Lord Brahmā, he decided to commence a sacrifice named *vājapeya*, which was followed by another great sacrifice named *bṛhaspati-sava*, on the banks of the River Gaṅgā at Kanakhala. With the exception of Lord Brahmā and Lord Śiva, great personalities such as Kaśyapa, Atri, Vasiṣṭha, Pulastya, Pulaha, and Sanaka, as well as all the demigods, the eight Vasus, the Aśvinī-kumāras, the Gandharvas, the Vidyādharas, and the Yakṣas were all cordially invited to the great sacrifice.

Satī, Lord Śiva's young wife, strongly desired to attend her father's sacrifice. Yet Lord Śiva tried to persuade her not to attend, because Dakṣa and his followers were envious of him, and due to this envy, they had insulted him with cruel words, even though he was innocent. Finally Lord Śiva said, "If in spite of this instruction you decide to go, neglecting my words, the future will not be good for you. You are most respectable, and when you are insulted by your relative, this insult will immediately be equal to death."

Satī felt very sorry at being forbidden to attend her father's sacrifice. Crying, shaking, and being very much afflicted, Satī left her husband. When she reached the arena, no one received her properly, except her mother and sisters, but Satī did not reply to their reception. She noted that there were no oblations offered to her husband, Lord Śiva, and her father, Dakṣa, had not received her. She then became extremely angry, so much so that she looked at her father as if she were going to burn him with her eyes. The followers of Lord Śiva were ready to kill Dakṣa, but Satī stopped them. She then began to condemn the process of the sacrifice, as well as her father in the presence of all.

In the *Śrīmad-Bhāgavatam* (4.4.11,14, 23), we learn of Satī's desire to give up her bodily relationship to her father Dakṣa: "The blessed goddess said: 'Lord Śiva is the most beloved of all living entities. He has no rival. No one is very dear to him, and no one is his enemy. No one but you could be envious of such a universal being, who is free from all enmity...My dear father, you are committing the greatest offense by envying Lord Śiva, whose very name, consisting of two syllables, *śi* and *va*, purifies one of all sinful activities. His order is never neglected. Lord Śiva is always pure, and no one but you envies him...Because of our family relationship, when Lord Śiva addresses me as Dākṣāyaṇī, I at once become morose, and my jolliness and my smile at once disappear. I feel very much sorry that my body, which is just like a bag, has been produced by you. I shall therefore give it up.'"

After Satī spoke to her father in the arena of sacrifice, she sat down on the western bank of Gaṅgā at Śaunaka (also known as Satī-kuṇḍa) and faced north. Dressed in saffron garments, she sanctified herself with water and closed her eyes to absorb herself in the process of mystic *yoga*. She carried the life air upwards, placing it in an equilibrium position near the navel. Then mixed with intelligence, she raised her life air to the heart, gradually towards the pulmonary passage and then between her eyebrows.

Further in the *Śrīmad-Bhāgavatam* (4.4.27), we see how Satī left her body: "Satī concentrated all her meditation on the holy lotus feet of her husband, Lord Śiva, who is the supreme spiritual master of all the world. Thus she became completely cleansed of all taints of sin and quit her body in a blazing fire by meditation on the fiery element."

Śrīla Prabhupāda elaborates on the same text of the *Śrīmad-Bhāgavatam*: "According to Śrī Jīva Gosvāmī, that Satī quit her body means that she gave up within her heart her relationship with Dakṣa. Śrī Viśvanātha Cakravartī Ṭhākura also comments that since Satī is the superintendent deity of external potency, when she quit her body she did not get a spiritual body, but simply transferred from the body she had received from Dakṣa. Other commentators also say that she immediately transferred herself into the womb of Menakā [Menā], her future mother. She gave up the body she had received from Dakṣa and immediately transferred herself to another, better body, but this does not mean that she got a spiritual body."

After Satī passed away, the news was conveyed by Nārada Muni to Lord Śiva. When Lord Śiva heard that his chaste wife was dead, he became exceedingly angry. He pressed his lips and immediately snatched from his head a strand of hair, which blazed like fire. Laughing like a madman, Lord Śiva dashed the hair to the ground. Then a fearful black demon as high as the sky and as bright as three suns was created. He had teeth like razors and hair like burning fire, as well as thousands of arms, all equipped with various weapons. When the giant demon, named Vīrabhadra, asked Lord Śiva, "What shall I do?" he replied, "Because you are born from my body, you are the chief of all my associates. Therefore, kill Dakṣa and his soldiers at the sacrifice."

Vīrabhadra, who was fearless enough to kill even Death, and the followers of Lord Śiva proceeded to Dakṣa's sacrificial arena. They completely destroyed the entire arena as all the attendants were very disturbed and began to flee in different directions. Vīrabhadra tore off the mustache of Bhṛgu, then forcibly put out the eyes of Bhaga, and then knocked out the teeth of both Dakṣa and Pūṣā. He tried to separate Dakṣa's head from his body with sharp weapons but was unsuccessful.

The *Śrīmad-Bhāgavatam* (4.5.24, 26) then describes how Dakṣa's head was removed: "Then Vīrabhadra saw the wooden device in the sacrificial arena by which the animals were to have been killed. He took the opportunity to use this facility to behead Dakṣa...Vīrabhadra then took the head and with great anger threw it into the southern side of the sacrificial fire, offering it as an oblation. In this way, the followers of Lord Śiva devastated all the arrangements for sacrifice. After setting fire to the whole arena, they departed for their master's abode, Kailāsa."

All of the defeated and injured priests, demigods, and other members of the devastated sacrifice approached Lord Brahmā and explained the situation. Brahmā and Lord Viṣṇu purposely did not attend the sacrifice, since they both knew the disastrous outcome between Lord Śiva and Dakṣa. Nevertheless, Lord Brahmā listened to all the members and then replied, "You cannot be happy in executing a sacrifice if you blaspheme a great personality and thereby offend his lotus feet." He then explained that even he himself, and what to speak of the demigods and sages, do not know how powerful Lord Śiva really is. Then Lord Brahmā instructed everyone to go to Mount Kailāsa and beg Lord Śiva's pardon.

On behalf of all those concerned, Lord Brahmā offered prayers to Lord Śiva and asked him to show mercy upon everyone who had been injured and let the sacrifice be completed. Then Lord Śiva said, "I do not mind the offenses by the less intelligent demigods, and since Dakṣa's head has already been burned, he will receive the head of a goat. The demigod Bhaga will be able to see again through Mitra, the demigod Pūṣā will be able to chew through the teeth of his disciples, and Bhṛgu will have the beard from the goat's head." After everyone was fully satisfied with Lord Śiva's benedictions, Bhṛgu Muni invited him to attend the arena and revive the sacrificial fire. There is a common phrase: "*śiva-hina-yajña*", any sacrifice without the presence of Lord Śiva is baffled. This was clearly illustrated here.

In the *Śrīmad-Bhāgavatam* (4.7.8) we learn of what new head Dakṣa received: "After everything was executed exactly as directed by Lord Śiva, Dakṣa's body was joined to the head of the animal (a goat) to be killed in the sacrifice." When the goat's head was attached to Dakṣa's body, he was immediately brought back to consciousness, and as he awoke, he saw Lord Śiva standing before him. Since Dakṣa now saw Lord Śiva with devotion and reverence, he was immediately purified from his past offenses. He began to pray, glorifying the auspicious qualities of Lord Śiva, but at the same time he realized his mistake, not fully understanding his position. So with a humble heart he thanked him for his mercy. After being pardoned by Lord Śiva, and with the permission of Lord Brahmā, Dakṣa again began the performance of the sacrifice. As soon as Dakṣa offered the ghee (clarified butter) while reciting *mantras* from the *Yajur Veda,* Lord Viṣṇu appeared there in His original form as Nārāyaṇa, seated on the shoulder of Garuḍa. As soon as Lord Viṣṇu was visible to everyone, including Lord Brahmā and Lord Śiva, they all immediately offered their respectful obeisances by falling down straight before Him. Everyone present became fearful with awe and veneration and prepared to offer their prayers to the Supreme Personality of Godhead. The *brāhmaṇas* concluded the prayers by saying, "We pray unto You, therefore, to be pleased with us. Simply by chanting Your holy name, one can surpass all obstacles. We offer our respectful obeisances unto You in Your presence."

After Lord Viṣṇu was glorified by everyone, Dakṣa arranged to again begin the sacrifice. Lord Viṣṇu was satisfied with His share of the sacrifice and the offerings. Then, in the *Śrīmad-Bhāgavatam* (4.7.50-54), Lord Viṣṇu addresses Dakṣa in the following pleasing words: "Brahmā, Lord Śiva and I are the supreme cause of the material manifestation. I am the Supersoul, the self-sufficient witness. But impersonally there is no difference between Brahmā, Lord Śiva and Me. My dear Dakṣa-dvija, I am the original Personality of Godhead, but in order to create, maintain and annihilate this cosmic manifestation, I act through My material energy, and according to the different grades of activity, My representations are differently named. One who is not in proper knowledge thinks that the demigods like Brahmā and Śiva are independent, or he even thinks that the living entities are independent. A person with average intelligence does not think the head and other parts of the body to be separate. Similarly, my devotee does not differentiate Viṣṇu, the all pervading Personality of Godhead, from anything or any living entity. One who does not consider Brahmā, Śiva, Viṣṇu or the living entities in general to be separate from the Supreme, and who knows Brahman, actually realizes peace; others do not."

Śrīla Prabhupāda comments on Lord Viṣṇu's statement in his purport on *Śrīmad-*

Bhāgavatam (4.7.54): "Lord Brahmā, Lord Śiva, and Lord Viṣṇu, they are three, and therefore they are separate, but at the same time they are one. This is the philosophy of simultaneous oneness and difference, which is called *acintya-bhedābheda-tattva*. The example given in the *Brahma-saṁhitā* is that milk and yogurt are simultaneously one and different; both are milk, but the yogurt has become changed. In order to achieve real peace, one should see everything and every living entity, including Lord Brahmā and Lord Śiva, as nondifferent from the Supreme Personality of Godhead. No one is independent. Every one of us is an expansion of the Supreme Personality of Godhead. This accounts for unity in diversity. There are diverse manifestations, but, at the same time, they are one in Viṣṇu. Everything is an expansion of Viṣṇu's energy."

Having been instructed by Lord Viṣṇu, Dakṣa then worshiped Him, as well as Lord Brahmā and Lord Śiva. After finishing all his sacrificial activities, as well as pleasing the demigods and other assembled guests, Dakṣa-dvija finally took bath and was fully satisfied.

Maitreya Muni continued to narrate this pastime about Dakṣa's sacrifice to Vidura, telling him that he had heard Dākṣāyaṇī (Satī) had taken birth in the kingdom of the Himālayas as the daughter of Menā. He also said that Ambikā (Durgā), who was known as Dākṣāyaṇī, again accepted Lord Śiva as her husband. Finally, in the *Śrīmad-Bhāgavatam* (4.7.61), Maitreya concludes: "If one hears and again narrates, with faith and devotion, this story of the Dakṣa sacrifice as it was conducted by the Supreme Personality of Godhead, Viṣṇu, then certainly one is cleared of all contaminations of material existence, O son of Kuru."

According to the *Skanda Purāṇa*, after Dakṣa regained consciousness with the head of a goat, he offered the following prayer to Lord Śiva: "O Mahādeva, may I always serve and worship your lotus feet." Lord Śiva then replied, "O Prajāpati Dakṣa, since this whole incident has occurred from envy, or the illusory energy known as Māyā, this sacred land will be known as Māyāpurī. Anyone who sees or remembers this *tīrtha*, will be liberated from all sins." Then Lord Indra said, "There is no area as holy as Māyāpurī amongst the thirty-five million *tīrthas* on this earth."

Again from the *Nārada Purāṇa* (*Uttara-bhāga* 66.49-56), Vasu continued his narration of the glories of Gaṅgādvāra by saying to Mohini: "Hari-tīrtha is that holy place where the omniscient Lord Viṣṇu, also known as Yajñeśvara, was glorified by Dakṣa and the demigods. The person who duly takes a holy bath there at Haripada (Hari-ki-pauri), O chaste lady, shall obtain the blessings of Lord Viṣṇu." Vasu then concluded the narration as follows, "One who remembers Gaṅgādvāra, wherever he may be, will attain the same result as remembering Lord Hari at the time of death. The Deity of the Lord, if worshiped with a pure heart at Haridvāra, will become greatly delighted and fulfill all desires. The place where Gaṅgā entered the earth is itself a place of *tapasya* (austerity), excellent for *japa* (chanting), and *homa* (sacrifice). The person who controls his senses and, after taking bath, three times daily recites the thousand names of Gaṅgā will not take another material birth. O blessed lady, one who devotedly listens to the *Purāṇas* at Gaṅgādvāra with full attention and sincerity will attain the permanent abode of the Supreme Lord, Viṣṇu. That fortunate person who listens to or reads about the glories of Haridvāra with great devotion shall acquire the same benefit as obtained by bathing there."

Exalted Visitors

As mentioned earlier, Gaṅgādvāra (Haridvāra) resembles a spiritual theater where unlimited pastimes of the Lord and His associates have been performed. Numerous important personalities have traveled through and resided in the Gaṅgādvāra area. A few prominent spiritual masters who have visited within the past one thousand years are described below.

Śrī Rāmānujācārya

Some 950 years ago, Śrī Rāmānujācārya had traveled here during the third of his four *padayātrās* (foot journeys), which eventually covered the entire country. During this particular *yātrā*, he traveled with seventy-four of his chief disciples and followers, spreading the glories and names of Lord Nārāyaṇa, as well as refuting the impersonalists' false doctrines. His *visiṣṭādvaita-vāda* (philosophy of qualified oneness) was strongly presented to defeat Śaṅkarācārya's impersonal *advaita-vāda* (philosophy of one undifferentiated, changeless Brahman).

After leaving Śrī Raṅgam (Tamil Nadu), Rāmānuja and his party went to Kāñcipuram to have *darśana* of Lord Varadarāja and then went onto Kumbhakonam. While in Madurai, he was able to convince a large assembly of *paṇḍitas* to become devotees. Then, continuing the journey, they came to the Kerala coast at Trivandrum (Thiruvananthpuram), where they enjoyed the exquisite *darśana* of the most beautiful Lord Ananta Padmanābha. From there they traveled up the western coast to Dvārakā, relishing the pastimes of Lord Kṛṣṇa. They then went inland to Puṣkara (Rajasthan), Mathurā, and Vṛndāvana, before visiting Naimiṣāraṇya and Śaketa, the capital city of northern Kośala. Eventually Rāmānuja came to the bank of the River Gaṅgā at Haridvāra on his way to Badarikāśrama. Everywhere Śrī Rāmānujācārya traveled, he preached the Vaiṣṇava doctrine of the *Śri-bhāṣya*, which establishes the supremacy of Lord Viṣṇu and the glories of devotional service.

Śrī Madhvācārya

Some 300 years after Śrī Rāmānujācārya, the great Śrī Madhvācārya passed several times through the area of Haridvāra on his way to Badarīnātha. After traveling and preaching in South India, Madhvācārya desired to tour North India to continue spreading his *dvaita* (dualism) philosophy. The holy *tīrtha* of Badarīnātha attracted him irresistably. He had a great desire to visit Śrī Śrī Badarī Viśāla and Nara-Nārāyaṇa Ṛṣis, as well as to present his *Bhagavad-gītā* commentary as a tribute to Śrīla Vyāsadeva at his hermitage. Once there, he observed a vow of strict silence for forty-eight days and daily bathed in the River Alakanandā (Gaṅgā). After returning to South India, he undertook the task of writing a commentary on the *Brahma-sūtras*.

After spending some time in the Uḍupī vicinity, Madhvācārya wrote *bhāṣyas* (commentaries) on many important Vedic literatures, including ten *Upaniṣads* and forty hymns of the *Ṛg Veda*, as well as the treatise entitled *Bhāgavata-tātparya*. Before he returned to Badarīnātha, he reinstalled and re-established the Uḍupī Kṛṣṇa Deity, which was originally made by Lord Kṛṣṇa for Rukmiṇī Mahārāṇī in Dvārakā.

Once, when Madhvācārya was crossing the Gaṅgā, he was stopped by Muslim soldiers and their ruler, who were eventually astounded by his truthful, bold words. The King begged Madhvācārya to reside permanently in his kingdom, but he rejected the offer and continued onwards with his *daṇḍa* (*sannyāsī* rod) in hand. Then one day on the road to the Himālayas, his party was attacked by a band of robbers. He silenced them all after a fierce fight and said, "One should cultivate strength of the body on the same level as strength of the mind. It is impossible for a weak body to have a strong mind." He always encouraged his disciples to cultivate bodily strength along with their Vedāntic lessons.

Once in Badarīnātha, Madhvācārya again had *darśana* of Badari Viśāla, Nara-Nārāyaṇa Ṛṣis, and Vyāsadeva before he traveled to Kurukṣetra, where he excavated and wielded the buried mace of Bhīma in front of his disciples and then reburied it.

Madhvācārya eventually initiated eight of his chief disciples into the *sannyāsa* order and established eight different *maṭhas* (Vedic institutes) for preaching purposes. At the age of seventy-nine, he left all his responsibilites to his disciples and without any thought or care, proceeded in the year 1317 for the last time to Badarīnātha, where he left this mortal world.

Śrī Advaita Ācārya

Before the advent of Śrī Caitanya Mahāprabhu, Advaita Ācārya left Śāntipura in Bengal and went on a long pilgrimage. He first went to see Kṣīra-corā-gopīnātha in Remuṇā, before continuing onto Nābhi-gayā (Yājapura), Jagannātha Purī, Godāvarī River, Śiva-kāñcī, Viṣṇu-kāñcī, Kāverī River, Madurai, Setubandha, Dhanus-tīrtha, Rāmeśvaram, and Uḍupī, where He met His future spiritual master, Mādhavendra Purī. He then resumed His pilgrimage through the Daṇḍakāraṇya forest, Nāsika, Dvārakā, Prabhāsa-tīrtha, and Puṣkara, until He eventually arrived at Kurukṣetra.

As He continued His pilgrimage, He went to Haridvāra to take bath in the Gaṅgā.

Thereafter He visited Śrī Badarikāśrama, the topmost holy place, where He had *darśana* of Nara-Nārāyaṇa Ṛṣis and Śrīla Vyāsadeva. After He danced in ecstasy and offered obeisances, He continued on with His travels. Then He went to the River Gaṇḍakī, where *śālagrāma-śilās* (Deity incarnation in the form of stones) are found. He took bath there and after resting, He incessantly chanted the holy name of the Lord. He found a *śālagrāma-śilā* marked with a *cakra* (disc) and other auspicious marks, and He devotedly took it with Him when He left.

Lord Nityānanda

Before Lord Śrī Nityānanda Prabhu met Śrī Caitanya Mahāprabhu in Śrīdhāma Māyāpur (Navadvīpa) some 500 years ago, He traveled for eight years on pilgrimage to all the major *tīrthas*. In the *Śrī Caitanya-bhāgavata* (*Ādi* 9.127-128, 196), Vṛndāvana dāsa Ṭhākura has described Lord Nityānanda's travels.

"After bathing in the sacred rivers Gomatī, Gaṇḍakī, and Śoṇa, Lord Nityānanda climbed the summit of Mahendra Parvata, where He offered obeisances to Lord Paraśurāma. Then Lord Nityānanda traveled to Haridvāra, the birthplace of Gaṅgā-mayī. He again visited Māyāpurī (Haridvāra), then Avantī (Ujjain), and the holy River Godāvarī. After taking bath, the Lord went to Jiyaḍa-Nṛsiṁha (Siṁhācala-kṣetra)."

Vṛndāvana dāsa Ṭhākura concludes this chapter by praying that Lord Nityānanda's lotus feet always remain impressed upon his heart and that his desire to study the *Śrīmad-Bhāgavatam* in the Lord's presence be fulfilled. Lord Nityānanda's pilgrimage was part of His transcendental pastimes, and anyone who hears these descriptions of Lord Nityānanda's travels to the holy places will attain the great wealth of pure love for Lord Śrī Kṛṣṇa.

Śrīla Prabhupāda in Haridvāra

While Śrīla Prabhupāda was in Bombay during the month of April, 1977, he planned a trip to Hṛṣikeśa. After taking advice from the former governer of Gujarat, Śrīla Prabhupāda boarded a train headed for Haridvāra. Yadubara Prabhu received Śrīla Prabhupāda at the Haridvāra train station in a red Ambassador car, expecting to drive Śrīla Prabhupāda straight to his destination in Hṛṣikeśa. Before leaving Haridvāra, however, Śrīla Prabhupāda said that there was a famous *kacauri* (fried savory snack) shop he wanted to visit. He therefore asked Yadubara and the other devotees to try to find it. They drove around town for some time under Śrīla Prabhupāda's direction but could not find the shop, much to everyone's disappointment.

* * *

The *Śrīmad-Bhāgavatam* (6.2.39-44) gives the following information about Ajāmila leaving his body at Haridvāra: "Because of a moment's association with devotees [the Viṣṇudūtas], Ajāmila detached himself from the material conception of life with determination. Thus free from all material attraction, he immediately started for Haridwar. In Haridwar, Ajāmila took shelter at a Viṣṇu temple, where he executed the process of *bhakti-yoga*. He controlled his senses and applied his mind in the service of the Lord. Ajāmila fully engaged in devotional service. Thus he detached his mind from the process of sense gratification and became absorbed in thinking of the form of the Lord. When his intelligence and mind were fixed upon the form of the Lord, the *brāhmaṇa* Ajāmila once again saw before him four celestial persons. He could understand that they were those he had seen previously, and thus he offered them his obeisances by bowing down before them. Upon seeing the Viṣṇudūtas, Ajāmila gave up his material body at Haridwar on the bank of the Ganges. He regained his original spiritual body, which was a body appropriate for an associate of the Lord. Accompanied by the order carriers of Lord Viṣṇu, Ajāmila then boarded an airplane made of gold. Passing through the airways, he went directly to the abode of Lord Viṣṇu, the husband of the goddess of fortune."

To conclude, let us take advantage of Śrīla Prabhupāda's comments on the *Śrīmad-Bhāgavatam* (6.2.39) regarding spiritual advancement: "The word *mukta-sarvānubandhanaḥ* indicates that after this incident, Ajāmila, not caring for his wife and children, went straight to Haridwar for further advancement in his spiritual life. Our Kṛṣṇa consciousness movement now has centers in Vṛndāvana and Navadvīpa (Māyāpur) so that those who want to live a retired life, whether they be devotees or not, can go there and with determination give up the bodily concept of life. One is welcome to live in those holy places for the rest of his life in order to achieve the highest success by the very simple method of chanting the holy name of the Lord and taking *prasāda*. Thus one may return home, back to Godhead. We do not have a center in Haridwar, but Vṛndāvana and Śrīdhāma Māyāpur are better for devotees than any other place. The Śrī Caitanya Candrodaya temple (in Māyāpur) offers one a good opportunity to associate with devotees. Let us all take advantage of this opportunity."

5) Śukara-tāla (Śuka-tāla)

In the *Padma Purāṇa* (*Uttara-khaṇḍa* 119), Śukara-tāla is glorified as follows: "By bathing just once at Śukara-tāla, at Triveṇī, or at the confluence of the Gaṅgā and the ocean, a man removes the sin of the murder

of a *brāhmaṇa*." Also in the *Padma Purāṇa* (*Yamunā-māhātmyam*) it is said: "The River Yamunā (Kālindī) flows from the mountain Kalinda and flows to Mathurā. The River Gaṅgā (Bhāgīrathī) at Śukara-tāla flows westwards. The confluence of the Yamunā and Bhāgīrathī is known as the *saṅgama*. By bathing at any of these places one achieves highly pious results."

Śuka-tāla is located on the southwestern bank of Gaṅgā, approximately 50 kilometres east of the district town of Muzzaffarnagar. Generally it is said that Mahārāja Parīkṣit took shelter on the bank of Gaṅgā at this location, whereupon Śukadeva Gosvāmī recited the *Śrīmad-Bhāgavatam* to him.

The literary incarnation of God, the *Śrīmad-Bhāgavatam*

In the *Śrīmad-Bhāgavatam* (1.3.40) it is stated: "The *Śrīmad-Bhāgavatam* is the literary incarnation of God, and it is compiled by Śrīla Vyāsadeva, the incarnation of God. It is meant for the ultimate good of all people, and it is all-successful, all-blissful and all-perfect."

The following short account from *A Ray of Viṣṇu* describes Bhaktisiddhānta Sarasvatī Mahārāja's visit to Śukara-tāla: "In November of 1931, Śrīla Bhaktisiddhānta Sarasvatī Ṭhākura sent the preachers from his Delhi *maṭha* with a spiritual message to the then Viceroy of India, Lord Willingdon. Śrīla Sarasvatī later delivered some lectures in Delhi in the latter part of that year and glorified the *Śrīmad-Bhāgavatam* at Śukara-tāla, the place where Śukadeva Gosvāmī delivered the *Bhāgavatam* to Mahārāja Parīkṣit five thousand years earlier." Also, mentioned in *Prabhupāda Śrīla Sarasvatī Ṭhākura*: "Śrīla Sarasvatī Ṭhākura also went to Badarinārāyaṇa, the site of the first *Śrīmad-Bhāgavatam* recitation; to Śukara-tāla, the site of the second recitation of the *Bhāgavatam*; and to Naimiṣāraṇya, the site of the *Bhāgavatam's* third recitation, and he preached the glories of these places. The facts that were discovered by Śrīla Sarasvatī in the course of uplifting these concealed holy places stand as priceless gems in the realm of spiritual research."

In the Introduction of the *Śrīmad-Bhāgavatam* (One Volume Edition), the following history explains the importance of the *Bhāgavatam* that was recited on the bank of Gaṅgā: "The timeless wisdom of India is expressed in the *Vedas*, ancient Sanskrit texts that touch upon all fields of human knowledge. Originally preserved through oral tradition, the *Vedas* were first put into writing five thousand years ago by Śrīla Vyāsadeva, the 'literary incarnation of God.' After compiling the *Vedas*, Vyāsadeva set forth their essence in the aphorisms known as *Vedānta-sūtras*. *Śrīmad-Bhāgavatam* (*Bhāgavata Purāṇa*) is Vyāsadeva's commentary on his own *Vedānta-sūtras*. It was written in the maturity of his spiritual life under the direction of Nārada Muni, his spiritual master. Referred to as 'the ripened fruit of the tree of Vedic literature,' *Śrīmad-Bhāgavatam* is the most complete and authoritative exposition of Vedic knowledge.

"After compiling the *Bhāgavatam*, Vyāsa impressed the synopsis of it upon his son, the sage Śukadeva Gosvāmī. Śukadeva Gosvāmī subsequently recited the entire *Bhāgavatam* to Mahārāja Parīkṣit in an assembly of learned saints on the bank of the Ganges at Hastināpura. Mahārāja Parīkṣit was the emperor of the world and was a great *rāja-ṛṣi*, or saintly king. Having received a warning that he would die within a week, he renounced his entire kingdom and retired to the bank of the Ganges to fast until death

and receive spiritual enlightenment. The *Bhāgavatam* begins with Emperor Parīkṣit's sober inquiry to Śukadeva Gosvāmī: 'You are the spiritual master of great saints and devotees. I am therefore begging you to show the way of perfection for all persons, and especially for one who is about to die. Please let me know what a man should hear, chant, remember and worship, and also what he should not do. Please explain all this to me.'

"Śukadeva Gosvāmī's answer to this question, and numerous other questions posed by Mahārāja Parīkṣit, concerning everything from the nature of the self to the origin of the universe, held the assembled sages in rapt attention continuously for the seven days leading to the King's death. The sage Sūta Gosvāmī, who was present on the bank of the Ganges when Śukadeva Gosvāmī first recited *Śrīmad-Bhāgavatam*, later repeated the *Bhāgavatam* before a gathering of sages in the forest of Naimiṣāraṇya. Those sages, concerned about the spiritual welfare of the people in general, had gathered to perform a long, continuous chain of sacrifices to counteract the degrading influence of the incipient age of Kali. In response to the sages' request that he speak the essence of Vedic wisdom, Sūta Gosvāmī repeated from memory the entire eighteen thousand verses of *Śrīmad-Bhāgavatam*, as spoken by Śukadeva Gosvāmī to Mahārāja Parīkṣit."

Once upon a time, as Mahārāja Parīkṣit was hunting in a forest, he became exhausted, hungry, and thirsty. As he was searching for water, he came upon the *āśrama* of the well-known Śamika Ṛṣi. Upon entering his *āśrama*, where the sage was deep in meditation, the King expected a formal welcome by means of being offered a sitting place, water, and a few sweet words. But due to the supreme will of the Lord, the King was neglected by the sage. Since the King felt that he was coldly received, he countered those feelings by placing a dead snake on the shoulder of the sage. King Parīkṣit then left, but was contemplating as to whether the sage in meditation had actually seen him enter his *āśrama* or not.

Meanwhile, Śamika Ṛṣi's son, Śṛṅgi, heard that his father had been insulted by Mahārāja Parīkṣit and with his youthful brahminical power cursed the King to die in seven days from the bite of a snake-bird. When his father heard of the curse against the King, he only repented by saying, "Alas! What a great sinful act has been performed by my son. He has awarded heavy punishment for an insignificant offense." The sage regretted the sin committed by his own son and did not take the insult paid by the King very seriously. Since Mahārāja Parīkṣit was a self-realized devotee, he was not afraid of meeting death. So, instead of begging pardon for his minor insult, he decided to prepare himself for his imminent death and find out the way to return to the spiritual world.

The *Śrīmad-Bhāgavatam* (1.19.5-7) furthers elucidates how Mahārāja Parīkṣit prepared himself for his death: "Mahārāja Parīkṣit sat down firmly on the banks of the Ganges to concentrate his mind in Kṛṣṇa consciousness, rejecting all other practices of self-realization, because transcendental loving service to Kṛṣṇa is the greatest achievement, superseding all other methods. The River Ganges carries the most auspicious water, which is mixed with the dust of the lotus feet of the Lord and *tulasī* leaves. Therefore that water sanctifies the three worlds inside and outside, and even sanctifies Lord Śiva and other demigods. Consequently, everyone who is destined to die must take shelter of this river. Thus the King, the worthy descendant of the Pāṇḍavas, sat on the Ganges' bank to fast until death and give himself up to the lotus

feet of Lord Kṛṣṇa, who alone is able to award liberation. So, freeing himself from all kinds of associations and attachments, he accepted the vows of a sage."

Śrīla Prabhupāda explains in his purports on the *Śrīmad-Bhāgavatam* (1.19.5-7) how Mahārāja Parīkṣit took shelter of the River Yamunā instead of Gaṅgā: "For a devotee like Mahārāja Parīkṣit, none of the material planets, even the topmost Brahmaloka, is as desirable as Goloka Vṛndāvana, the abode of Lord Śrī Kṛṣṇa, the primeval Lord and original Personality of Godhead...The devotee always desires to go back home, back to Godhead, just to become one of the associates of the Lord in the capacity of servitor, friend, parent or conjugal lover of the Lord, either in one of the innumerable Vaikuṇṭha planets or in Goloka Vṛndāvana...

"Modern scientists are very eager to reach the moon by material arrangements, but they cannot conceive of the highest planet of this universe. But a devotee like Mahārāja Parīkṣit does not care a fig for the moon or, for that matter, any of the material planets. So when he was assured of his death on a fixed date, he became more determined in the transcendental loving service of Lord Kṛṣṇa by complete fasting on the bank of the transcendental River Yamunā, which flows down by the capital Hastināpura. Both the Ganges and Yamunā are *amartyā* (transcendental) rivers, Yamunā being still more sanctified for the following reasons.

"Mahārāja Parīkṣit, after receiving the news of his death within seven days, at once retired from family life and shifted himself to the sacred bank of the Yamunā River. Generally it is said that the King took shelter on the bank of the Ganges, but according to Śrīla Jīva Gosvāmī, the King took shelter on the bank of the Yamunā. Śrīla Jīva Gosvāmī's statement appears to be more accurate because of the geographical situation. Mahārāja Parīkṣit resided in his capital Hastināpura, situated near present Delhi, and the River Yamunā flows down past the city. Naturally the King would take shelter of the River Yamunā because she was flowing past his palace door. And as far as sanctity is concerned, the River Yamunā is more directly connected with Lord Kṛṣṇa than the Ganges. The Lord sanctified the River Yamunā from the beginning of His transcendental pastimes in the world. While His father, Vasudeva, was crossing the Yamunā with baby Lord Kṛṣṇa for a safe place at Gokula on the other bank of the river from Mathurā, the Lord fell down in the river, and by the dust of His lotus feet the river at once became sanctified.

"It is especially mentioned herein that Mahārāja Parīkṣit took shelter of that particular river which is beautifully flowing, carrying the dust of the lotus feet of Lord Kṛṣṇa, mixed with *tulasī* leaves. Lord Kṛṣṇa's lotus feet are always besmeared with *tulasī* leaves, and thus as soon as His lotus feet contact the water of the Ganges and Yamunā, the rivers become at once sanctified. The Lord, however, contacted the River Yamunā more than the Ganges.

"According to the *Varāha Purāṇa*, as quoted by Śrīla Jīva Gosvāmī, there is no difference between the water of the Ganges and Yamunā, *but when the water of the Ganges is sanctified one hundred times, it is called Yamunā.* Similarly, it is said in the scriptures that one thousand names of Viṣṇu are equal to one name of Rāma, and three names of Lord Rāma are equal to one name of Kṛṣṇa.

"The water of the Ganges sanctifies all the three worlds, including the gods and the demigods, because it emanates from the lotus feet of the Personality of Godhead, Viṣṇu. Lord Kṛṣṇa is the fountainhead of the principle of *viṣṇu-tattva*, and therefore shelter of His lotus feet can deliver one from all sins, including an offense committed by a king unto a *brāhmaṇa*. Mahārāja Parīkṣit, therefore, decided to meditate upon the lotus feet of Lord Śrī Kṛṣṇa, who is Mukunda, or the giver of liberations of all descriptions. The banks of the Ganges or Yamunā give one a chance to remember the Lord continuously. Mahārāja Parīkṣit freed himself from all sorts of material association and meditated upon the lotus feet of Lord Kṛṣṇa, and that is the way of liberation..."

Just as Mahārāja Parīkṣit decided to fast until death on the bank of the Gaṅgā (Yamunā), all the great minds and thinkers, along with their disciples, as well as the great sages, arrived there. These great souls could verily sanctify any place of pilgrimage, but they arrived on the plea of making a pilgrim's journey. Outwardly, these great souls came to Gaṅgā on pilgrimage, but actually they arrived because they could foresee that the *Śrīmad-Bhāgavatam* would be spoken by Śukadeva Gosvāmī. Also many demigods, kings, and other royal orders arrived for this great occasion. After Mahārāja Parīkṣit greeted everyone with folded hands, he explained his decision to fast until death and surrender unto the lotus feet of Lord Śrī Kṛṣṇa. He then said to the assembled devotees, "Just accept me as a completely surrendered soul, and let mother Gaṅgā, the representative of the Lord, also accept me in that way, for I have already taken the lotus feet of the Lord into my heart. Let the snake-bird bite me at once. I only desire that you all continue singing the deeds of Lord Viṣṇu."

To conclude this section, the *Śrīmad-Bhāgavatam* (1.19.17, 25, 29) describes the meeting of Mahārāja Parīkṣit and Sukadeva Gosvāmi, just prior to the narration of the *Śrīmad-Bhāgavatam*, in the following words: "In perfect self-control, Mahārāja Parīkṣit sat down on a seat of straw, with the straw-roots facing the east, placed on the southern bank of the Ganges, and he himself faced the north...At that moment there appeared the powerful son of Vyāsadeva, who traveled over the earth disinterested and satisfied with himself. He did not manifest any symptoms of belonging to any social order or status of life...Mahārāja Parīkṣit, who is known as Viṣṇurāta (one who is always protected by Viṣṇu), bowed his head to receive the chief guest, Śukadeva Gosvāmī. Receiving respect from all, Śukadeva Gosvāmī took his exalted seat."

Today in Śuka-tāla, an extraordinarily large banyan tree, which dates back to Dvāpara-yuga, sprawls on top of a small hill within the Śrī Śukadeva Āśrama Sevā Samiti. According to the local tradition, this sacred tree marks the location where Mahārāja Parīkṣit listened to the *Śrīmad-Bhāgavatam* from Śukadeva Gosvāmī. Presently, the main branch of Gaṅgā is about three to four kilometres away from this location, but a smaller branch flows just below the hilltop, where one Gaṅgā-ghāṭa has been established.

The entire area has an incredibly peaceful atmosphere, which is conducive for living a spiritual life and especially for reading the *Śrīmad-Bhāgavatam*. Yearly, there are two large *Bhāgavata-saptaha* Melās (organized recitals of *Śrīmad-Bhāgavatam*) at Śuka-tāla, where some one hundred thousand devotees and pilgrims attend.

The same spot that marks the place where the *Bhāgavatam* was supposely narrated also bears witness to the death of Mahārāja Parīkṣit, when he was finally bitten by the snake-bird, Takṣaka. Local tradition claims that anyone who is bitten by any snake within this area will certainly meet death without any chance of survival. Will they receive the same result as Mahārāja Parīkṣit did?

There appears to be a difference of opinion regarding where the *Śrīmad-Bhāgavatam* was actually spoken, but nevertheless the *Śrīmad-Bhāgavatam* was recited to Mahārāja Parīkṣit by Śukadeva Gosvāmī for the spiritual welfare of the people in general in this fallen age of Kali.

(Please refer to the following section on Hastināpura)

6) VIDURA KUTIR (DARANAGAR)

Love and devotion

In the *Vidura Niti* (1.26), Mahātmā Vidura says: "One who is humble and soft spoken is praised as a leader [noble person] by all people. On account of his clean mind and self-control, he becomes very effulgent. Such a person is as brilliant as the sun."

As mentioned in the *Mahābhārata*, after Mahātmā Vidura was insulted by Duryodhana by "being pierced by arrows through his ears that afflicted the core of his heart", Vidura placed his bow at the door and left his brother's palace. He then crossed the River Gaṅgā and established an *āśrama* on the eastern bank. Due to his sincere performance of austerities and devotional service unto Lord Kṛṣṇa, the Lord Himself visited and stayed with Vidura rather than accept the royal hospitality of King Dhṛtarāṣṭra and his son Duryodhana. Because of the simple, austere surrounding conditions, Vidura had only *bathuwa sāk* (wild green spinach) to offer and feed the Lord.

This particular type of *sāk* is most ordinary, since it grows wild and is readily available. Just as Lord Kṛṣṇa accepted the simple, humble offering of chipped-rice from Sudama Vipra in Dvārakā, because it was filled with love and devotion, similarly, Lord Kṛṣṇa was very pleased to accept the simple loving offer of *sāk* from His devotee Vidura.

The footprints of Lord Kṛṣṇa remain here to memorialize His visit, and *bathuwa sāk* is perpetually growing in this area, near the shrine of Vidura, at the Vidura Sevā Āśrama.

7) HASTINĀPURA (MAWANA)

The ancestral kingdom of the Pāndavas and Kauravas

In the *Śrīmad-Bhāgavatam* (9.21.20-21), we learn of the ancestral kingdom from King Hastī: "Bṛhatkṣatra had a son named Hastī, who established the city of Hastināpura. From King Hastī came three sons, named Ajamīḍha, Dvimīḍha and Purumīḍha. The descendants of Ajamīḍha, headed by Priyamedha, all achieved the position of *brāhmaṇas*."

As mentioned in the *Śrīmad-Bhāgavatam*, another name for Hastināpura is Gajahvayam. In the Ninth Canto, Twenty-Second Chapter, entitled *The Descendants of Ajamīḍha*, the long lineage of great personalities and their dynasties who were connected to the Hastināpura kingdom are described. The following is a paraphrase of a portion of that chapter: "Another son of Ajamīḍha was named Ṛkṣa. From Ṛkṣa came a son named Saṁvaraṇa, and from Saṁvaraṇa came Kuru, the King of Kurukṣetra. One of King Kuru's sons was called Jahnu, then nine more generations followed up to the son of Devatithi, who was also named Ṛkṣa, and his son was Dilipa, whose son was Pratīpa. King Pratīpa had three sons, one of whom was Śāntanu, who had been King Mahābhiṣa in his previous birth. From Śāntanu, through the womb of Gaṅgā-devi, Bhīṣma, one of the twelve *mahājanas* (Vaiṣṇava authorities) was born. Two other sons, Citrāṅgada and Vicitravīrya, were also born by the semen of Śāntanu, from the womb of Satyavatī, and Vyāsadeva was born from Satyavatī by the semen of

Parāśara. Vyāsadeva instructed the history of the *Bhāgavatam* to his son Śukadeva. Through the two wives and maidservant of Vicitravīrya, Vyāsadeva begot Dhṛtarāṣṭra, Pāṇḍu, and Vidura. Dhṛtarāṣṭra had one hundred sons, headed by Duryodhana, and Pāṇḍu had five sons, headed by King Yudhiṣṭhira."

Since most readers are already familiar with the pastimes in the *Mahābhārata*, which are centered in and around the kingdom of Hastināpura (including Kurukṣetra), it is not the intention of this book to repeat those glorious, historical pastimes. A few pastimes that are directly related to Gaṅgā have already been narrated in Book One, Chapter Four of this book. It is generally accepted that the location of Hastināpura city was on the southern bank of the Gaṅgā at the place still known as Hastināpura, northeast of Mawana in Meerut District, some 170 kilometres northeast of New Delhi. Śukatāla is aproximately 40 kilometres north of this present day Hastināpura.

According to the *Mahābhārata*, the Pāṇḍavas were given half the kingdom of Hastināpura, wherein they established their capital, Indraprastha. After the Kurukṣetra war came to an end, the Pāṇḍavas returned to the city of Hastināpura, which was in the other half of the kingdom of Hastināpura. Afterwards, Yudhiṣṭhira was coronated as the new ruler of the ancestral kingdom of Hastināpura. A.C. Bhaktivedanta Swami Prabhupāda has already stated in his purports from the previous section on Śuka-tāla, that the ancient capital of Hastināpura was located where New Delhi is presently situated. In reference to this, the following passage from *KṚṢṆA*, chapter entitled: *Ill-motivated Dhṛtarāṣṭra*, which is a summary study of the *Śrīmad-Bhāgavatam*, Tenth Canto, states that the ancient capital of Hastināpura was located where New Delhi, the present capital of India, stands.

"Thus being ordered by the Supreme Personality of Godhead, Śrī Kṛṣṇa, Akrūra visited Hastināpura. Hastināpura is said to be the site of what is now New Delhi. The part of New Delhi, which is still known as Indraprastha, is accepted by people in general as the old capital of the Pāṇḍavas. The very name Hastināpura suggests that there were many *hastis*, or elephants. Because the Pāṇḍavas kept many elephants in the capital, it was called Hastināpura."

Lord Balarāma's prowess

Further on in the Tenth Canto of the *Śrīmad-Bhāgavatam*, the story of *The Marriage of Samba*, Lord Kṛṣṇa's son, is narrated. The following is a paraphrase of that chapter: Samba, who was the son of Jāmbavatī, kidnapped the daughter of Duryodhana, Lakṣmaṇā. In response, the Kauravas joined together to arrest him. After seizing Samba, the Kauravas brought both him and Lakṣmaṇā back to Hastināpura. When King Ugrasena heard of Samba's capture, he instructed the Yādavas to retaliate. Lord Balarāma tried pacifying them, hoping to avoid a fight between the Kuru (Kaurava) and Yadu (Yādava) dynasties. Then the Lord went to Hastināpura along with several *brāhmaṇas*, some Yādava elders, and the great devotee Uddhava.

The party of Yādavas had set up camp outside the city, while Lord Balarāma sent Uddhava to ascertain King Dhṛtarāṣṭra's frame of mind. The Kaurava court properly received and worshiped Uddhava, as well as Lord Balarāma, whom the Kauravas went to see. When the Lord conveyed King Ugrasena's demand for Samba's release, the Kauravas became very angry. They were

amazed and just laughed at Ugrasena's order. After deriding the Yādavas, the Kauravas returned to the city and Lord Balarāma decided that the only way to deal with such persons who were maddened by false prestige was through brute punishment.

Then the Lord exhibited His prowess as described in the *Śrīmad-Bhāgavatam* (10.68.41-42, 54): "The Lord angrily dug up Hastināpura with the tip of His plow and began to drag it, intending to cast the entire city into the Ganges. [The *Viṣṇu Purāṇa* states the River Bhāgīrathī] Seeing that their city was tumbling about like a raft at sea as it was being dragged away, and that it was about to fall into the Ganges, the Kauravas became terrified…Even today the city of Hastināpura is visibly elevated on its southern side along Ganges, thus showing the signs of Lord Balarāma's prowess."

In the last paragraph of *KṚṢṆA*, chapter entitled: *The Marriage of Samba*, A.C. Bhaktivedanta Swami Prabhupāda writes: "It is confirmed by Śukadeva Gosvāmī that the site of Hastināpura is now known as New Delhi, and the river flowing through the city is called Yamunā, although in those days it was known as the Ganges. From authorities like Jīva Gosvāmī it is also confirmed that the Ganges and Yamunā are the same river flowing in different courses. The part of the Ganges which flows through Hastināpura to the area of Vṛndāvana is called Yamunā because it is sanctified by the transcendental pastimes of Lord Kṛṣṇa. The part of Hastināpura which slopes towards the Yamunā becomes inundated during the rainy season and reminds everyone of Lord Balarāma's threatening to cast the city into the Ganges."

In Vedic culture, it is not uncommon for the River Yamunā to be called Gaṅgā, since they are actually the same river flowing in different courses. The Vedic literatures instruct us to consider all water as Gaṅgā water.

Gaṅgā's inundation of Hastināpura

Again from the Twenty-second Chapter of the Ninth Canto, the descendants of Ajamīḍha are further described as follows: "The son of Arjuna, through the womb of Subhadrā, was Abhimanyu, whose son was Mahārāja Parīkṣit. Mahārāja Parīkṣit had four sons, one of them being Janamejaya. From Janamejaya, Śatānīka was born, then Sahasrānīka, Aśvamedhaja, and Asīmakṛṣṇa, whose son was Nemicakra."

In the same chapter of the *Śrīmad-Bhāgavatam* (9.22.40), we learn that the ancient capital of Hastināpura was flooded: "When the town of Hastināpura is inundated by the river (Gaṅgā), Nemicakra will live in the place known as Kauśāmbī." According to this text and ancient historical geography, Hastināpura was flooded by the Gaṅgā, and King Nemicakra, also known as Nicakṣu, transferred his capital to Kauśāmbī, which was located near the present town of Kosam, on the bank of the River Yamunā, approximately 50 kilometres southwest of Allahabad (Prayāga-rāja). It has been suggested that the ancient remnants of this glorious capital are on the bank of a smaller stream known as Budhi Gaṅgā, which connects with the main branch of Gaṅgā some 10 kilometres away. The present position of the Budhi Gaṅgā represents the old bed of the Gaṅgā, and excavations carried on by archaeologists in 1950 and 1952 reveals evidence of this historical inundation of Hastināpura by the River Gaṅgā.

During the 1952 excavations, the following sites of Hastināpura were claimed to be discovered: Vidura-ka-tila (Vidura's palace); Draupadī-ki-rasoi (Draupadī's kitchen); and Draupadī-ghāṭa (the pond where Draupadī bathed). After Hastināpura flooded, it did not flourish again until after Lord Buddha's visit.

Today, according to local tradition, there is one small Pandaveśvara Mahādeva (Śiva) temple, which is said to be one of the Pāṇḍava's places of worship; and the Draupadeśvara Mahādeva temple, where Draupadī worshiped Lord Śiva. This location also marks the place where the Pāṇḍavas began their thirteen year exile. Also, the nearby town of Mawana was supposedly the main entrance to the city of Hastināpura.

And finally, from the *Śrī Caitanya-bhāgavata*, *Ādi-khaṇḍā*, Chapter Nine, we learn about Lord Nityānanda's visit in Hastināpura: "Nityānanda offered His obeisances to Mandana-gopāla and then went to Hastināpura, the abode of the Pāṇḍavas. Seeing the home of those devotees, Nityānanda began to cry. The local people, however, could not understand the Lord's sentiments due to their lack of devotion. As Nityānanda remembered Balarāma's glorious activities in Hastināpura, He exclaimed, 'O Haladhara, please save Me!' and then offered obeisances."

8) GARHMUKTEŚVARA (GARHMUKTESAR)

Where the Vasus were thrown into Gaṅgā

In the *Nārada Purāṇa* (*Uttara-bhāga* 66), while narrating the glories of Gaṅgādvāra to Lord Brahmā's daughter, Mohinī, Vasu explains the glories of the *tīrtha* named Śāntanu, which is located near Garhmukteśvara.

"Thereafter, the devotee should go to the excellent *tīrtha* known as Śāntanu. By taking a holy bath there and performing the rite of *tarpaṇa* in accordance with spiritual injunctions, the devotee attains liberation. It was here that Gaṅgā-devī assumed a human form and became the wife of Śāntanu. After giving birth to the eight Vasus year after year, she threw seven of them into the river here. Where the bodies were cast off, medicinal trees grew. By the mercy of the goddess Gaṅgā, anyone who takes birth there and eats part of these trees will never live a misfortunate life."

Although this place was originally named Śiva Vallabhapuri, after Lord Śiva's *gaṇas* (attendants) installed Mukteśvara Mahādeva here, the area became known as Gaṇa Mukteśvara or Garhmukteśvara. Others say that Lord Paraśurāma installed Mukteśvara Mahādeva and King Yudhiṣṭhira performed atonement here. Due to the change of Gaṅgā's course, Garh Gaṅgā is situated some six kilometres from Garhmuktesar. Nearly one hundred years ago, Gaṅgā-mayī flowed next to this town and touched the eighty-five steps that lead to the famous Gaṅgā-devī temple there. The town of Garhmuktesar is located on the western bank of Gaṅgā, 70 kilometres east of New Delhi.

9) SŪKARA-KṢETRA (SORO-KṢETRA / SORON)

The appearance of Lord Varāha

While Lord Brahmā was engaged in the process of creation, the earth was inundated by a deluge and sank down into the depths of the ocean. Brahmā became preplexed over what to do, but since he had full faith in the Supreme Personality of Godhead, he did not become discouraged. While Brahmā was thinking like this, the Supreme Personality of Godhead, Lord Viṣṇu, assumed the form of a small boar and came out of Brahmā's nose! The boar was not more than the size of the upper portion of a thumb, but within a few moments, He became as large as a stone, then as big as an elephant, and soon He became the size of a giant mountain.

The appearance of the boar incarnation of the Supreme Lord is elaborated in the *Śrīmad-Bhāgavatam* (3.13.28,30-33,46-47) as follows: "He was personally the Supreme Lord Viṣṇu and was therefore transcendental, yet because He had the body of a hog, He searched after the earth by smell. His tusks were fearful, and He glanced over the devotees engaged in offering prayers. Thus He entered the water...Lord Boar penetrated the water with His hooves, which were like sharp arrows, and found the limits of the ocean, although it was unlimited. He saw the earth, the resting place for all living beings, lying as it was in the beginning of creation, and He personally lifted it. Lord Boar very easily took the earth on His tusks and got it out of the water. Thus He appeared very splendid. Then, His anger glowing like the Sudarśana wheel, He immediately killed the demon, Hiraṇyākṣa, although he tried to fight with the Lord. Thereupon, Lord Boar killed the demon within the water, just as a lion kills an elephant. The cheeks and tongue of the Lord became smeared with the blood of the demon, just as an elephant becomes reddish from digging in the purple earth. Then the Lord, playing like an elephant, suspended the earth on the edge of His curved white tusks...The Lord, touched the earth with His hooves and placed it on the water. In this manner the Personality of Godhead, Lord Viṣṇu, the maintainer of all living entities, raised the earth from within the water, and having placed it afloat on the water, He returned to His own abode."

In his purports on the *Śrīmad-Bhāgavatam* (3.13.31 and 3.19.31), Śrīla Prabhupāda further explains the appearance of Lord Varāha as follows: "According to Śrīla Jīva Gosvāmī, the Vedic literatures describe the incarnation of Lord Varāha (Boar) in two different devastations, namely the Cākṣuṣa devastation and the Svāyambhuva devastation. This particular appearance of the boar incarnation actually took place in the Svāyambhuva devastation, when all the planets other than the higher ones—Jana, Mahar, and Satya—merged in the water of devastation.This particular incarnation of the boar was seen by the inhabitants of the planets mentioned above. Śrīla Viśvanātha Cakravartī suggests that the sage Maitreya [who narrates this chapter] amalgamated both the boar incarnations in different devastations and summarized them in his description to Vidura...Thus He became *ādi-sūkara*, the original boar. In the material world a boar or pig is considered most abominable, but *ādi-sūkara*, the Supreme Personality of Godhead, was not treated as an ordinary boar. Even Lord Brahmā and the other demigods praised the Lord's form as a boar."

The Jackal and the Vulture

The *Padma Purāṇa* identifies the place where Lord Varāha rescued the earth when it sank in the ocean of universal devastation as Śaukara-purī, or Sūkara-kṣetra. In the *Varāha Purāṇa* (Chapters 137-138), Lord Varāha narrates the glories of Śaukara to Bhūmi (the earth) and in the course of the narration describes an incident between a jackal and a vulture and, later on, the pastime of one small long-tailed bird, the wagtail.

The earth inquired, "Which holy place brings pleasure to the devotees?" Lord Varāha then said, "Listen, O Bhūmi, the most sanctified spot for the devotees is a most confidential subject, but Śaukara, where I raised you from the underworld and where the River Gaṅgā flows, releases one from *saṁsāra* (the cycle of birth and death)." She then asked, "To which worlds do those who die in Śaukara go? What are the benefits of bathing there? What are the sacred *tīrthas* in Śaukara? You should tell me all of this for the sake of establishing *dharma*."

Answering her questions, the Lord replied, "Those who die in Śaukara liberate seven generations of their ancestors and fourteen generations of their descendants. By merely going there and seeing Me, one takes birth for seven lives in the families of devotees. He who resides there without committing any offense until death is awarded a four-armed form, holding conch, disc, club, and lotus, and is taken to Vaikuṇṭha. One also acquires enormous religious merit by bathing in Cakra-tīrtha, where My *cakra* is installed. By taking a ritualistic bath there on Dvādaśī in the month of Vaisākha (April/May), one becomes a great devotee dedicated to My service. And when that person dies there, he receives a form similar to Mine and excels in My world."

Hearing these words of the Lord, the earth folded her hands and said, "In the *tīrtha* Śaukara, Soma (moon) propitiated You. Please tell me about this, since I am eager to know." Lord Varāha spoke to her in a voice like thunder, "Listen, O earth. I shall tell you the reason why I was worshiped by him. When I was pleased with him, I revealed to him My original form, but Soma could not stand the effulgence of that form and fell down senseless. Seeing his condition, I spoke to him in sweet words, 'O Soma, with what aim do you perform this severe *yoga*?' Then Soma, the lord of the luminaries, said, 'O great Lord, master of *yoga* and Lord of *yogīs*, may I have firm and eternal devotion for You as long as these worlds exist. May this form You have given me be visible on all seven islands of the earth. On the new moon day when I am weak, let there be oblations for the forefathers, and may I become pleasant to look at after that. Let my mind never turn to what is unrighteous. Let me be the lord of all herbs. If You are pleased, may this be granted to me.' Hearing the words of Soma, I granted him the boons and then disappeared. In this way Soma performed penance and received the supreme attainment at Soma-tīrtha, which is rare to get.

"Now I shall tell you about a *tīrtha* called Vaivasvata, where Sūrya (the sun) performed great austerities for seventeen thousand years in order to beget a son. Since I was very much pleased with him, I asked him to seek a boon. He then spoke to Me in sweet words. 'If You are pleased with me, then bless me with the benediction of begetting a child.' I was glad to hear this by him in all purity, seriousness, and devotion. 'You will beget twins, Yama and Yami (Yamunā),' I said, then I disappeared and he returned to his own abode.

"Now I shall tell you another pastime that illustrates the wonderful greatness of Śaukara. By the prowess of this place of Mine, a female jackal who was without any desire when she happened to die there was born as a beautiful princess. On the eastern side is the *tīrtha* called Gṛdhra-vaṭa, where a vulture died without any desire and became a virtuous prince." Hearing these words of Lord Varāha, the holy earth spoke for the welfare of the devotees of the Lord, "What power does this *tīrtha* possess, by which two beings in animal bodies, namely a jackal and vulture, attained human forms. O Janārdana, tell me what destination is attained by those who die there without any desire?"

Hearing the words of the earth, Lord Varāha spoke to her in sweet words, "Listen, O earth. At the beginning of Tretā-yuga, a virtuous king by the name of Brahmadatta was ruling in the city of Kāmpilya, the capital of southern Pañcāla. He had a handsome and righteous son named Somadatta. Once the prince went hunting in a forest full of tigers and lions for the sake of his father. While wandering, he came across a female jackal. The prince hit her with an arrow, and she fell down in great pain. Being wounded and tormented by the heat of the sun, she wandered to a *sakhotaka* tree in Śaukara and then gave up her life without any desire in Somatirtha. The jackal was born as the daughter of the King of Kāñcī.

"Meanwhile, the prince felt thirsty and reached Gṛdhra-vaṭa for taking rest. He saw a vulture on the branch of that banyan tree and hit it with an arrow. Being pierced in its heart, the vulture fell down dead. The prince was delighted and plucked out its wings to feather his arrows and then went home. The vulture died there without any desire, and after awhile, was born as the son of the King of Kaliṅga.

"O earth, due to My favor, the kingdoms of Kāñcī and Kaliṅga became very friendly and closely attached with each other. In due course, the marriage of the prince of Kaliṅga with the princess of Kāñcī was performed. They delighted themselves everywhere they went and lived every moment together. Their mutual love steadily grew and their intimacy was like that of Indra and Śacī. In due coarse, they begot five children, who were all resplendent like the sun. Then one day, the loving princess made a request to her husband, 'I wish to sleep for awhile without being seen by anybody.' Hearing the words of his wife, the prince of Kaliṅga agreed to her request.

"Meanwhile, as time passed, the aging King of Kaliṅga installed his son on the throne. As he then ruled the kingdom happily and free from trouble, seventy-seven years passed. In the seventy-eighth year, the aging King thought, 'Who is my wife worshiping, and what is her vow to sleep alone? A vow ordaining a woman to sleep is not heard of anywhere. This is not established by Lord Viṣṇu or Śiva, nor is it found in the *Dharma-śāstra* of Manu, Bṛhaspati, or even Yama. Certainly my wife will be angry if I see her, but I should know what vow she is practicing. Perhaps she wants to acquire the Kinnaras' power of attraction, or she wants to become a *yogeśvarī*, or maybe she is having sexual urge for another person.'

"The King went to the place where his beloved wife was executing her vow. He found her crying with severe headaches. The shy beautiful lady then held her husband's feet and told him, 'O King, my dear husband, please do not ask me any questions. My former life was full of bad deeds, but since you are virtuous, glorious, and most dear, I should certainly tell you. Still, I do not wish to speak because it may cause sorrow to you. O noble King, you are my god, preceptor, husband, sacrifice, *dharma*, wealth, desire, fame, and heaven. When you ask me anything, I should tell you the truth. That is the duty of all obedient wives. But the husband's happiness should not be disturbed by a wife. Therefore, please do not ask me about my pain.' Hearing the words of his wife, the King became distressed and said, 'Happy or unhappy, the husband should be told what he asks. No virtuous wife will hide from her husband any matter, private or public, good or bad. Even if it is a sin committed out of passion, if the wife hides it, she is never considered virtuous. Considering all this, O great lady, tell me the truth. You will not be committing any sin by telling me the truth.'

"Hearing the words of her husband, who was standing on *dharma*, she replied, 'If I should not keep any secret, then come with me to the place called Śaukara.' Hearing the words of his wife, the King of Kaliṅga agreed to her proposal. Then the King and Queen left that place and started for Śaukara. After a long journey, they reached Śaukara and gave large gifts of money and grain.

"O earth, as time passed, they became more and more purified. One day the King sweetly said to the Queen, 'Now a thousand years of my life has passed, please tell the secret which I have asked you before.' Then, holding his hand as in wedlock, she spoke sweetly, 'O my lord, formerly I was a female jackal and I was hit by the arrow of Somadatta when he was hunting. See here the stump of the arrow well lodged in my head, as a result of which I have developed headaches. I was then born in the Kāñcī royal family, and I was given to you in marriage. By the prowess of this place, I attained all this.' Upon hearing this, the King recollected his previous life and said, 'I was a vulture who was also hit by a single arrow of the same Somadatta. Then I was born in the kingdom of Kaliṅga. All of this was because I died without any desire in this holy place.'

"By their death in this *tīrtha*, the jackal and vulture were relieved of their sins. Once they gained memory of their formal lives, they finally went to Vaikuṇṭha. The devotees of Lord Viṣṇu and all the other people there who heard this pastime began to perform devotional activities without any personal motivation. In time, those who died in Śaukara without any desire also went to Vaikuṇṭha with four-armed forms, similar to Mine.

"Thus I have told you about the greatest benefits of dying in Śaukara."

The Wagtail

The goddess Bhūmi continued, "How great Your *tīrtha* known as Śaukara is. I have heard that any being that dies there takes a human birth. Please narrate another story about Śaukara in this regard." Hearing the words of the earth, Lord Varāha began to speak, "O fair goddess, I shall tell you what you wish to know. In Śaukara, a wagtail bird once ate too many worms, and as a result it suffered from indigestion. Some boys then came there, took the bird for playing, and then began quarelling among themselves over who should keep the bird. Eventually one of the boys took the bird and threw it into the River Gaṅgā, saying that it was of no use to them. The wagtail happened to fall in the Gaṅgā at Āditya-tīrtha, where it died. As a result of this, the bird was born as the beautiful son of a wealthy *vaiśya* (farmer or merchant member of the third social division in Vedic society).

"After twelve years passed, that intelligent, pure boy, who was devoted to Me, bowed to his parents and requested, 'If I am dear to you, please grant me a boon.' The parents were happy to hear these words of their son and replied to him, 'Whatever you say and whatever you have in your mind, we will certainly fulfill it.' The parents then offered him various boons, such as different occupations of trade, aristocratic girls, facilities for performing sacrifices, opportunities for farming and rearing cattle, as well as facilities to give in charity, especially feeding the *brāhmaṇas*. Hearing the offers of his parents, the virtuous boy held their feet and said, 'There is only one thing that I desire and that is to go to Śaukara, the place of Lord Nārāyaṇa.'

"The mother then said, 'How is it that you think of Lord Nārāyaṇa now? This is of course good, but at your young age! I still run after you to make you eat, and now you think of going to Śaukara. My breasts are still filled with milk, and during your sleep you still call out 'Mother! Mother!' I do not find any reason for your renunciation.' The boy then spoke to his mother in sweet words,

'I have always been attached to you. During pregnancy, I was in your womb. As a child, I played over your shoulder. I have suckled your breasts, and while sitting on your lap, soiled your whole body. O mother, be kind to me and give up the grief of parting with me. People come and go. When once gone, they are not to be seen again. From where is one born? What relation has he? Who is a mother or father? I happened to fall into your womb and thereby into the ocean of *samsāra*. There are thousands of fathers and mothers, and hundreds of sons and wives in numerous lives. Who are they, and who are we? Therefore, O mother, do not feel sorry.' The parents were surprised to hear all of this and said, 'What great secret is it that you speak about.' The boy replied, 'If you think that there is a secret in what I said, then ask me about that secret at Śaukara.' They agreed and resolved to go to Śaukara.

"All arrangements were made for the journey to Śaukara. Meditating on Lord Nārāyaṇa throughout the journey, they reached the *tīrtha* on the Dvādaśī day in the month of Vaiśākha. During their stay, the boy's father daily gave in charity thousands of cows, as well as gifts of money and gems. When autumn was over and the month of Kārtika (October/November) started, the parents took their bath and then spoke to their son, 'We have now stayed here for six months and the auspicious Dvādaśī day has come. Please tell us the secret that you have been hiding from us.' The dutiful son then said, 'What you say is true. Tomorrow morning I shall tell you this secret. My dear parents, this Dvādaśī is particularly dear to Lord Viṣṇu and is very auspicious for the well being of the Lord's devotees. By offering gifts on this day, one is able to cross the dreadful ocean of *samsāra*.' As he was speaking in this way to his parents, the night came to a close.

"After taking bath and worshiping the Lord during the early morning hours of Dvādaśī, the boy held the feet of his parents and said, 'I shall tell you the purpose of our coming here. It is to reveal to you the mysteries of this Śaukara. Formerly I was born as a wagtail bird. I ate numerous flies and worms and then suffered from indigestion. Because I was unable to move, some boys grabbed me and started to play with me. One of them carried me away and threw me into Gaṅgā. That happened to be at Āditya-tīrtha, where I finally left the bird's body. O mother, since I died there without any desire, by the power of that place, I was born on this holy day as your son. Thirteen years have passed since then, and I have been hiding this truth from you all the time. I have now told the purpose of our coming here. I shall now engage myself in the worship of Lord Viṣṇu. I bow to you, O father, be pleased to return home.'

"The parents then said, 'Whatever deeds you will do to propitiate Lord Viṣṇu, we shall do the same.' Thus they all became My devotees and performed actions recommended for liberation from *samsāra*. In the course of time, they died there, and due to their determination and by the power of Śaukara, they were liberated and attained Vaikuṇṭha. Thus I have told you about this great story."

The Pāṭhāna Vaiṣṇavas

When Śrī Caitanya Mahāprabhu, Balabhadra Bhaṭṭācārya, and their associates were on their way from Vṛndāvana to Prayāga, they stopped in Soro-kṣetra (Soron), where they took bath in the River Gaṅgā. Somewhere in between Vṛndāvana and Soro-kṣetra, the following pastime occurred between Śrī Caitanya Mahāprabhu and the Pāṭhāna Vaiṣṇavas.

When Caitanya Mahāprabhu had to leave Vṛndāvana to resume His pilgrimage, one local Sanoḍiyā *brāhmaṇa* requested to travel with Mahāprabhu along the banks of the Gaṅgā to Prayāga, since it would be a very pleasurable journey. He also said they could stop in Soro-kṣetra for bathing in the Gaṅgā, before reaching Prayāga in time for the Makara-saṅkrānti (when the sun enters Capricorn). Balabhadra Prabhu, who was feeling tired from the constant crowds, favored the idea of traveling along the banks of the Gaṅgā to Prayāga. Although the Lord had no desire to leave Vṛndāvana, He fulfilled the desires of His devotees and they began their journey.

While walking, they became fatigued and took rest beneath a tree, where Caitanya Mahāprabhu fell unconscious due to ecstatic love for Lord Śrī Kṛṣṇa. At that time ten cavalry soldiers from the Mohammedan Pāṭhāna military arrived. Seeing Mahāprabhu unconscious, they instantly thought that the four associates of the Lord were rogues who had killed this *sannyāsī* with poison and had stolen His wealth! Thinking this, the soldiers decided to kill all four persons. Then, during an argument between the soldiers and devotees, Caitanya Mahāprabhu regained His normal senses. Mahāprabhu explained to the soldiers that these four persons were His associates, and that He Himself was a begging *sannyāsī*.

Among the Mohammedans was a saintly scholarly person who wanted to speak with the Lord to establish impersonal Brahman on the basis of the *Koran*. As narrated in the *Śrī Caitanya-caritāmṛta* (*Madhya* 18.189-190, 193, 196), Caitanya Mahāprabhu refuted all the arguments of the learned scholar as follows: "The *Koran* has certainly established impersonalism, but at the end it refutes that impersonalism and establishes the personal God. The *Koran* accepts the fact that ultimately there is only one God. He is full of opulence, and His bodily complexion is blackish...The Lord is the Supreme Truth worshipable by everyone. He is the cause of all causes. By engaging in His devotional service, the living entity is relieved from material existence...In the *Koran* there are descriptions of fruitive activity, speculative knowledge, mystic power and union with the Supreme, but ultimately everything is refuted as the Lord's personal feature and His devotional service is established."

The saintly Mohammedan admitted to the Lord that everything He said was true. He also mentioned that their own scholars can never understand or accept what has been written in the *Koran*. He then accepted Śrī Caitanya Mahāprabhu as the Supreme Personality of Godhead Himself, and the holy name of Kṛṣṇa (Hare Kṛṣṇa *mahā-mantra*) appeared on his tongue. He fell at the lotus feet of Śrī Caitanya Mahāprabhu, who said, "Please get up. You have chanted the holy name of Kṛṣṇa; therefore the sinful reactions you have accrued for many millions of lives are now gone. You are now pure."

The Lord then instructed all the other Mohammedans to chant the holy name of Kṛṣṇa, and everyone became overwhelmed with ecstatic love. The saintly scholar became known as Rāmadāsa, and King Vijulī Khān and the other Mohammedans became mendicants. Later, these Pāṭhānas became celebrated as the Pāṭhāna Vaiṣṇavas, and they toured all over the country, chanting the glorious activities of Śrī Caitanya Mahāprabhu.

In the *Śrī Caitanya-caritāmṛta* (*Madhya* 18.214-215), the Lord's visit is described: "Śrī Caitanya Mahāprabhu next went to a holy place of pilgrimage called Soro-kṣetra. He took bath in the Ganges there and started for Prayāga on the path along the banks of the Ganges. At Soro-kṣetra the Lord requested the Sanoḍiyā *brāhmaṇa* and Rājaputa

Kṛṣṇadāsa to return home, but with folded hands they said, 'Let us go to Prayāga with You. If we do not go, when shall we again get the association of Your lotus feet?'"

* * *

Since the time of the British, the River Gaṅgā has changed her course and is 5 to 10 kilometres away (depending on which route) from the center of Sūkara-kṣetra, or Soron as it is known today, which is 125 kilometres east of Mathurā. When Gaṅgā started to move away, the British constructed a large rectangle water tank in the center of town, which is connected through an underground canal leading directly to the main branch of the Gaṅgā. This tank became known as Hari-ki-pauri, and surrounding the banks of this tank are numerous temples and *āsramas*, including a Gauḍīya Maṭha (Vaiṣṇava monastery preaching center) that was established by H. H. Śrīmad Bhakti Sāraṅga Goswami Mahārāja. Within this temple on the eastern bank of the tank reside the Deities of Śrī Śrī Lakṣmī-Varāhadeva, Lord Narasiṁhadeva, and Śrī Caitanya Mahāprabhu.

A short distance outside of town is Gṛdhra-vaṭa, one of the famous banyan trees described in the scriptures. It was here that Somadatta killed the vulture with his arrow. Also, Lord Rāmacandra visited this place to perform *piṇḍa-dāna* and *śrāddha* (anniversary ceremonies for parents and grandparents). He also made an offering here to Jaṭāyu, the famous bird that tried to stop Rāvaṇa from kidnapping Sitā-devī and died after a fierce fight with Rāvaṇa. Nearby is the *yajña-sthala* (sacrificial arena) of Mahārāja Somadatta. And near to that is Candra-kūpa (Soma-tīrtha), the place where the Moon performed his austerities. It is said that on Rāma-navamī (the appearance day of Lord Rāma) the water in this *kūpa* (well) turns to milk. Gautama Ṛṣi performed penance here. Also, there is Sūrya-kuṇḍa, or Yajña-kuṇḍa (Āditya-tīrtha), where the sun performed austerities and sacrifices for the pleasure of Lord Varāhadeva after He killed Hiraṇyākṣa. As mentioned in the *Varāha Purāṇa*, this entire area is known as *yoga-mārga*, the place or path where one reaches perfection in *yoga*.

In the *Skanda Purāṇa*, it mentions that when Lord Varāha rescued the earth from the great deluge, He pierced the earth with one of His tusks at Prabhāsa-kṣetra (Somnātha, Gujarat). Because that tusk was smeared with *kardama* (mud), the sacred *kuṇḍa* (tank or pond) it formed became known as Kardamāla-tīrtha. Another narration from the same *Purāṇa* says that Kardamāla-tīrtha is located at Dvārakā. In the *Padma Purāṇa*, Lord Mahādeva describes the creation of Varāha-tīrtha to Pārvatī as follows: "O daughter of the Himālayas, please listen. After the Supreme Lord took the form of a boar for the pleasure of the demigods, He uplifted the divine earth, which was supported by His tusk at the place called Kardamāla. O beautiful lady, a great holy place thus manifested there. A man who bathes there receives salvation." According to some of the *paṇḍitas* in Sūkara-kṣetra, Lord Varāha's tusk pierced the earth at Sūkara-kṣetra.

On the Dvādaśī day in the bright half of the month of Mārgaśīrṣa (November/December) more than two million pilgrims visit Sūkara-kṣetra to celebrate the pastimes of Lord Varāhadeva, who killed Hiraṇyākṣa (on Ekādaśī, the day before) and then left His boar body at Varāha-ghāṭa in Sūkara-kṣetra before returning to Vaikuṇṭha. In the *Śrīmad-Bhāgavatam*, *Padma Purāṇa*, *Agni Purāṇa*, etc., it mentions only that the Lord returned to His own abode. Yet, according to the *Liṅga Purāṇa*: "When Lord Varāha returned to the ocean of milk after relinquishing His form as a boar, the earth shook again." But the place where the Lord left His boar's form is not mentioned. As stated in the *Nārada Purāṇa* (*Uttara-bhāga* 40.30-31): "There is the highly meritorious holy center named Śaukara wherein formerly Acyuta manifested Himself in the form of a Divine Boar. By visiting this holy center and bathing therein a man attains the benefit of a hundred Agnihotra sacrifices." The Gauḍīya Vaiṣṇavas celebrate the appearance of Lord Varāhadeva on the Dvādaśī day in the bright half of the month of Māgha (January/February).

In the Chulakiya area, a short distance from the town of Soron, is a small unkept temple, which Śrī Caitanya Mahāprabhu is said to have visited. At one time, Lord Narasiṁhadeva resided there, but He was eventually moved to the Gauḍīya Maṭha on the bank of Hari-ki-pauri. Ādi Śaṅkarācārya and Vallabha Ācārya both visited Sūkara-kṣetra, and their *baitakas* (seats) are located just outside the town. Also, the great Mughal emperor Akbar, who was ruling from his capital at Agra, used to drink Gaṅgā water with his Hindu wife. Daily that water was brought by servants traveling all the way from Agra to Soron (approximately 250 kilometres). The famous Rāma-bhakta Gosvāmī Tulsidas was born here in Soron. As Soron was his *janma-bhūmi* (birthplace); Rajapur (Banda District of Uttar Pradesh, which is located on the bank of River Yamunā) was his *tapo-bhūmi* (place of austerities); and Vārāṇasī was his *mukti-bhūmi* (place of liberation).

One popular local *brāhmaṇa* by the name Gaṅgā Purohita Paṇḍita Rāma Kishore Dubey (Salone) had a strong realization one day, some thirty-five years ago, when he was thirty years old. As he was taking bath in the Gaṅgā and praying to her for some material benedictions, he saw several pots of gold and other valuable jewels and gems floating in the river. This made him understand that Gaṅgā can fulfill all desires, either material or spiritual, but ultimatley she can deliver anyone from *saṁsāra* and lead that person to the lotus feet of Lord Viṣṇu.

Painted on the walls in the waiting room of the small country metre gauge train station in Soron (Shukarkshetra) are verses from the *Varāha Purāṇa* describing the glories of Sūkara-kṣetra and Gaṅgā-mayī. What more can be said? "Sūkara-kṣetra ki jai!"

10) KĀNYAKUBJA (KANNAUJ)

Ajāmila's life and the birth of Viśvāmitra

In the Introduction Summary of the Sixth Canto, First Chapter, of the *Śrīmad-Bhāgavatam*, Śrīla Prabhupāda describes the history of Ajāmila as follows: "To prove the strength of devotional service, Śukadeva Gosvāmī describes the history of Ajāmila. Ajāmila was a resident of Kānyakubja (the modern Kannauj). He was trained by his parents to become a perfect *brāhmaṇa* by studying the *Vedas* and following the regulative principles, but because of his past, this youthful *brāhmaṇa* was somehow attracted by a prostitute, and because of her association he became most fallen and abandoned all regulative principles. Ajāmila begot in the womb of the prostitute ten sons, the last of whom was called Nārāyaṇa. At the time of Ajāmila's death, when the order carriers of Yamarāja came to take him, he loudly called the name Nārāyaṇa in fear because he was attached to his youngest son. Thus he remembered the original Nārāyaṇa, Lord Viṣṇu. Although he did not chant the holy name of Nārāyaṇa completely offenselessly, it acted nevertheless. As soon as he chanted the holy name of Nārāyaṇa, the order carriers of Lord Viṣṇu immediately appeared on the scene. A discussion ensued between the order carriers of Lord Viṣṇu and those of Yamarāja, and by hearing that discussion Ajāmila was liberated. He could then un-

derstand the bad effect of fruitive activities and could also understand how exalted is the process of devotional service."

In the *Śrīmad Vālmīki Rāmāyaṇa* (*Bāla-kāṇḍa* 32), the birth of the great sage Viśvāmitra is narrated as follows: "King Kuśa was the son of Lord Brahmā. He begot through the womb of Queen Vaidarbhī four sons: Kuśāmbu, Kuśanābha, Asūrtarajasa, and Vasu. King Kuśa advised his sons to protect all of the citizens according to *śāstra* and to establish separate kingdoms for themselves. Kuśāmbu made the city known as Kauśāmbī his capital. Kuśanābha selected Mahodayapura as his capital. Asūrtarajasa chose Dharmāraṇya, while Vasu made Girivraja (Rajgir) his capital.

"The second son of King Kuśa, Kuśanābha, begot one hundred daughters in the Apsarā Ghṛtācī. Lord Vāyu tried to marry all of his daughters, but when they refused, Lord Vāyu cursed them by entering their limbs and distorting them into hunch-backs. Because the hundred *kanyakās* (girls) became *kubjās* (hunch-backs), Mahodayapura became known as Kānyakubja (or present day Kannauj). King Gādhi was one of the sons of Kuśanābha, and Viśvāmitra was born in Mahodayapura as the son of Gādhi. Viśvāmitra's elder sister was Satyavatī, who married the great sage Ṛcīka."

In the *Skanda Purāṇa* (6.166), the pastime between Viśvāmitra's elder sister and Bhṛgu Muni's son is described: "The sage Bhṛgu Muni had a son named Ṛcīka, who was a great ascetic. Once he went to Bhojakaṭam, which is a pilgrimage place on the bank of the River Kauśikī (Kosī). While sitting there performing austerities, he saw King Gādhi's beautiful daughter, Satyavatī, who was worshiping mother Pārvatī for a suitable husband. He was attracted to her and immediately went to King Gādhi for permission to marry her. The King did not want his daughter to marry a poor *brāhmaṇa*, but at the same time, he did not want to offend the *brāhmaṇa* and be cursed. So the King said there was a traditional marriage fee of one hundred and seven white horses each with one black ear and having the speed of wind. Ṛcīka promised to bring that fee and then went to Kānyakubja on the bank of Gaṅgā. There he sat down and began reciting the hymn, known as *Aśvavodha*, to Lord Varuṇa. As he chanted the hymn, all the horses of the above description, including the riders, came out of the River Gaṅgā. The horses were given to the King, and the princess was married to Ṛcīka. Since then, this place on the bank of the Gaṅgā in Kānyakubja is known as Aśva-tīrtha. Anyone who bathes there receives the same results as performing an Aśvamedha sacrifice."

In the *Mahābhārata* (*Ādi-parva* 191) it is stated that Mahārāja Gādhi's father had a different name: "O best of the Bhāratas, in the city of Kānyakubja there once lived a famous king known as Gādhi, the son of Kuśika." Mahārāja Kuśika was a very famous monarch in the Puru dynasty and is also considered the grandfather of Viśvāmitra. Further on in *Śānti-parva* (49), there is the narration of when Kuśika once performed austerities to beget a son that would be equal to Lord Indra and could not be killed by anyone. Since Indra was pleased with his penances, he voluntarily took birth as Mahārāja Kuśika's son, known as Gādhi.

Tāladhvaja, the imaginary husband of Nārada Muni

In the *Devī Purāṇa* (*Aṣṭama-skanda*), we hear the following unique pastime of Nārada Muni: "Once Nārada Muni went to visit Mahā-Viṣṇu in Vaikuṇṭha and inquired about Māyā. Nārada requested that he be shown Māyā, so the Lord took Nārada and left Vaikuṇṭha on the back of His carrier,

Garuḍa. They crossed forests, rivers, cities, lakes, villages, and mountains until they reached Kānyakubja. After locating a beautiful lake, Garuḍa landed, and Mahā-Viṣṇu and Nārada got down. They walked around the shore of the lake for awhile, and then they took rest beneath one tree.

"After some time, Mahā-Viṣṇu asked Nārada to take a bath in the lake. Pleased at His command, Nārada placed his *vīṇā* and deerskin on the shore. He first washed his face and feet, he performed *ācamana* (sipping water for purification) with *kuśa* grass in his hand, and then he stepped into the water for his bath. While Mahā-Viṣṇu was standing nearby and watching him bathe, Nārada instantly turned into the most beautiful woman! She then approached the shore and began to look around at the surroundings, remembering nothing of her past.

"Then one King named Tāladhvaja came riding horseback near the lake. He addressed the woman as Saubhāgya-sundarī (the most attractive and beautiful) and began talking with her. Within a few hours, they were married, and then Tāladhvaja took her to his palace, where they happily spent their honeymoon. After twelve years passed, Saubhāgya-sundarī became pregnant and in due coarse of time begot a son named Vīravarmā. After two more years, she begot another son named Sudharma. In this way she delivered a son every two years for twenty-four years and thus became a mother of twelve sons. After some time she gave birth to eight more sons. When all twenty sons came of age, they were married according to Vedic rites, and eventually these sons begot their own sons. Thus Tāladhvaja and Saubhāgya-sundarī became the heads of a large family of children and grandchildren and lived very happily.

"One day, a king from another country along with his army suddenly came and surrounded Kānyakubja. A great battle was fought wherein the sons and grandsons of King Tāladhvaja and Saubhāgya-sundarī were killed. Tāladhvaja then left the battlefield and returned to his palace. Saubhāgya-sundarī was in great distress. When the enemy left the battlefield, she secretly went there to have a last look at her sons and grandsons lying dead. The sight terrified her. They laid there without heads, hands, or legs, with eyes protruded, stomachs cut open, intestines hanging out, and blood oozing forth from everywhere. She then fell to the ground and wept bitterly. Then Mahā-Viṣṇu appeared there disguised as a old *brāhmaṇa* and began to comfort her. He began giving her instructions on the truths of life. Saubhāgya-sundarī then called her husband, and they both went to the old lake to take a bath as instructed by the old *brāhmaṇa*. Just as she entered the lake to bathe, she became Nārada Muni again!

"When Nārada came out of the lake, Mahā-Viṣṇu was still standing next to his *vīṇā* and deerskin smiling at him. At the sight of Mahā-Viṣṇu, Nārada Mini fully realized what had happened. He stood there and recollected everything, beginning with when he had asked Mahā-Viṣṇu to show him Māyā, all the way through the whole life of Saubhāgya-sundarī, to the old *brāhmaṇa* on the battlefield, and the last bath in that same lake. As he stood there, Nārada just pondered over everything. Then Mahā-Viṣṇu called out, 'Please hurry, Nārada. What is taking you so long? What are you thinking about?'

"Tāladhvaja was puzzled to find a *sannyāsī* coming from the same place where his beautiful wife had just taken bath. He approached Nārada and inquired, 'O best of the sages. Where is my wife, and where did you come from?' Even before receiving a reply, the King began to cry over the loss of his wife. Then

Mahā-Viṣṇu consoled him by explaining that human relationships are only ephemeral. He then instructed the King to take a bath in the lake. After taking bath, Tāladhvaja became disgusted with worldly life, and after performing great austerities in the forest, he attained liberation."

King Harṣavardhana

The *Historical Geography of Ancient India* gives an account of a great Buddhist king named Harṣavardhana, who also resided in Kānyakubja: "When the Chinese pilgrim, Hiuen Tsang, visited Kānyakubja in the seventh century A.D., King Harṣavardhana was the reigning sovereign and was known to be just in his administration and precise in the discharge of his duties. Harṣavardhana devoted his heart and soul to the performance of good works. He erected many Buddhist monasteries on the bank of Gaṅgā. He brought the monks together for examination and discussion, and he was known as a Sanskrit poet. His compositions include *Nāgānanda*, *Ratnāvali*, and *Priyadarśikā*. He also made inspection visits throughout his dominion. The King's day was divided into three parts, of which one was given to the affairs of government and two were devoted to religious works.

"Hiuen Tsang saw one hundred Buddhist establishments at Kānyakubja and, according to him, the River Gaṅgā was on the west side of Kannauj, not the east. The kingdom had a dry ditch around it with strong lofty towers. The kingdom contained flowers, forests, lakes, and ponds. The citizens were all well off and content. The climate was agreeable and soft. For clothing, they used ornamented and bright shining fabrics. They were also fond of learning. They were all followers of Lord Buddha."

And in the *Śrī Caitanya-bhāgavata* (*Ādi* 9.147), we learn of Lord Nityānanda's visit: "Śrī Nityānanda traveled to the town of Kānyakubja and saw the beautiful deity of Durgā-devī."

11) BIṬHŪR

The birth of Kusa and Lava

The following pastime, from the *Śrīmad Vālmīki Rāmāyaṇa* (*Uttara-kāṇḍa* 42-49, 64-66, 70-72, 93-97), describes the birth of Sītā-devī's two sons: "After Lord Rāmacandra's coronation, Sītā-devī and the Lord went to their recreation garden, known as the Aśoka grove. They spent two years in that beautiful forest, which was decorated with various trees, bushes, creepers, flowers, bees, birds, and ponds. Their grove compared to Lord Indra's Nandana gardens and Kuvera's Caitraratha gardens. Attendants, singers, and dancers entertained Śrī Rāma and Sītā-devī. One day, Śrī Rāma noticed the auspicious signs of pregnancy in His consort and became immeasurably happy, exclaiming, 'Very fine! very fine!'

"In the course of time, the Lord heard various wise and humorous stories narrated by His friends. When Śrī Rāma inquired about the talk-of-the-town amongst the citizens of the kingdom, Badra informed the Lord of the malicious talk about the character of Sītā, who had lived in the palace of Rāvaṇa. Lord Rāma was most annoyed with the ill report about Sītā, so He instructed Lakṣmaṇa to take her to the forest hermitage of the great sage Vālmīki, on the bank of the River Gaṅgā.

"Thus Lakṣmaṇa instructed the charioteer, Sumantra, to get the chariot ready to take Sītā-devī to the sage's *āśrama*. On the way, they rested on the banks of the River Gomatī, before reaching the Gaṅgā. Upon reaching the Gaṅgā, Lakṣmaṇa began to weep, since He had not yet informed Sītā of the reason why she was being sent away from

Ayodhyā. She then asked Lakṣmaṇa to take her across the river, so He summoned the boatmen to take them to the other side of Gaṅgā. Once reaching the other side, Lakṣmaṇa told Sītā-devī the truth about her banishment, which deeply depressed the consort of Lord Rāma. She even thought of drowning herself in the waters of Jāhnavī (Gaṅgā). Lakṣmaṇa then offered His obeisances and circumambulated Sītā with tears in His eyes before departing from the forest hermitage. With a burdened, sorrowful heart, Lakṣmaṇa boarded the chariot, which was waiting on the northern bank of Gaṅgā, and returned to Ayodhyā.

"All of the ascetics and their sons who were residing in Vālmīki's *āśrama* ran out to the crying Sītā-devī, who was on the bank of the Gaṅgā. Then Vālmīki also went to the shore of the river and beheld Sītā lamenting there helplessly. After speaking sweet words to her, Vālmīki informed Sītā that she would be under his care, and the female ascetics living nearby would take care of her like a child. He told her to accept his offer and to remain calm and free from all anxieties, as if entering her own home. He then instructed the female ascetics to care for Lord Rāmacandra's consort with the greatest affection and respect. Then, after handing over Sītā-devī to the female ascetics, Vālmīki returned to his own hermitage.

"Afterwards, in Ayodhyā, Śrī Rāma instructed Śatrughna and his army to proceed to the forest of Madhupurī (Mathurā), in order to kill the demon Lavaṇa. After traveling for two nights, Śatrughna came to the great sage Vālmīki's residence on the bank of the Gaṅgā. After welcoming the brother of Śrī Rāma, Vālmīki narrated to him the story of Kalmāṣapāda, the son of King Sudāsa. During the evening of that full moon day of the month of Śrāvaṇa (July/August), Sītā-devī gave birth to two sons. At midnight, the young ascetics informed Vālmīki about the auspicious motherhood of Lord Rāma's wife. Thus the great sage began making symbols to protect the new-born sons from inauspicious *bhutas* (ghosts) and *rākṣasas* (man-eaters). Vālmīki took a handful of the top portion of *kuśa* grass along with the lower portion (*lava*) and performed the protection ceremony. He then said, 'He who was born first should be cleansed with the *kuśa* grass. After being purified with *mantras*, he will be known as Kuśa. He who was born later should be carefully cleansed with *lava* by the elderly women, and he will be known as Lava. These two twins, named Kuśa and Lava, will become famous bearing the names I have given them.'

"After killing the demon Lavaṇa, Śatrughna remained in Madhupurī for twelve years to re-establish the city. During the twelfth year, Śatrughna, His attendants, and His army all proceeded towards Ayodhyā, passing through Vālmīki's *āśrama* once again. Meanwhile, Kuśa and Lava were brought up as hermit boys, as the pupils of the sage Vālmīki. After Śatrughna stayed with Śrī Rāma in Ayodhyā for one week, He again returned to Vālmīki's *āśrama* before heading once more to Madhupurī.

"After a while, Kuśa and Lava were brought to Ayodhyā, where they recited the entire narrations of their father's pastimes (*Rāmāyaṇa* of 24,000 verses). Thereafter the Lord requested Sītā-devī and Vālmīki to come to Ayodhyā. Upon arriving, Sītā took an oath that she was pure, and Vālmīki supported her. She stated, "I do not know anyone except Śrī Rāma." She then prayed to the goddess of the earth, Mādhavī, to allow her entrance. Then a divine throne arose from the earth. As Sītā-devī sat upon it, she entered the nether world."

According to the *Rāmāyaṇa*, this last pastime occurred in Ayodhyā, but presently in Biṭhūr there is a monument installed by

Śrī Rāmānujācārya marking the place where Sītā entered the earth. The great sage Vālmīki had his *āśrama* in three different places: on the bank of Gaṅgā at Biṭhūr; at the confluence of the Rivers Tamasā (Tons) and Gaṅgā, a few kilometres southwest of Prayāga; and in Citrakūṭa.

12) Prayāga-rāja (Triveṇī)

Prayāga-rāja is also known as Tīrtha-rāja, or the king of all holy places. Prayāga is glorified in numerous Vedic literatures, a few of which are cited as follows.

In the *Garuḍa Purāṇa* (*Arca-kāṇḍa* 81.2) it stated: "Prayāga is a very holy place conducive to worldly enjoyment and liberation for those who die there. By taking bath there, all sins are dispelled." The *Ṛg Veda* (*Khila-āśvalāyana*) says: "Those who bathe at the confluence of the white waters of the Gaṅgā and the black waters of the Yamunā go to the celestial heavens, and those having a steady mind who give up their bodies here attain the eternal abode." The *Mahābhārata* (*Vana-parva*) states: "The land between the Gaṅgā and Yamunā is called the waist, or middle part, of the earth; and Prayāga, which is the most sacred and prosperous place, is the fertile part of mother earth. This Prayāga is the *madhya*, or middle, of the five *vedis*, or sacrificial altars, on earth. The other *vedīs* are Kurukṣetra, Gayā, Virajā, and Puṣkara. Prayāga is also known as Prajāpati-kṣetra."

In the *Varāha Purāṇa* (Chapter 144) Prayāga is glorified as follows: "In Prayāga, there is the Triveṇī (the confluence of three rivers: the Ganges, Yamunā and Sarasvatī), where Lord Śiva resides and is known by the names Śūlaṭaṅka and Someśvara. Lord Viṣṇu is known there as Veṇī-Mādhava, and the Rivers Gaṅgā, Yamunā, and Sarasvatī meet. By bathing there one goes to heaven, and by dying there one gets liberation. It is the king of all *tīrthas* and is dear to Lord Viṣṇu." And in the *Śrīmad-Bhāgavatam* (7.14.30-33) Prayāga is considered one of the most sacred places: "The sacred lakes like Puṣkara and places where saintly persons live, like Kurukṣetra, Gayā, Prayāga, Pulahāśrama, Naimiṣāraṇya, the banks of the Phalgu River, Setubandha, Prabhāsa, Dvārakā, Vārāṇasī, Mathurā, Pampā, Bindu-sarovara, Badarikāśrama, the places where the Nandā River flows, the places where Lord Rāmacandra and mother Sītā took shelter, such as Citrakūṭa, and also the hilly tracts of land known as Mahendra and Malaya—all of these are to be considered most pious and sacred...."

In his purports on the *Śrīmad-Bhāgavatam* (7.14.29 and 5.17.9), Śrīla Prabhupāda comments on the holy places of pilgrimage as follows: "According to Vedic civilization, therefore, the holy places of pilgrimage are considered most sacred, and still there are hundreds and thousands of holy places like Jagannātha Purī, Vṛndāvana, Haridwar, Rāmeśvara, Prayāga, and Mathurā. India is the place for worshiping or for cultivating spiritual life. The Kṛṣṇa consciousness movement invites everyone from all over the world, without discrimination as to caste or creed, to come to its centers and cultivate spiritual life perfectly.

"Most people in India are still inclined to bathe in the Ganges, and there are many places where they can do so. At Prayāga (Allahabad), many thousands of people gather during the month of January to bathe in the confluence of the Ganges and Yamunā. Afterward, many of them go to the confluence of the Bay of Bengal and the Ganges to take bath there. Thus it is a special facility for all the people of India that they can bathe in the water of the Ganges at so many places of pilgrimage."

The sacred *tīrthas*

In the *Padma Purāṇa* (*Sṛṣṭi-khaṇḍa* 90), we hear of the power the holy places have to destroy sins, but Prayāga has unlimited power in destroying sins: "Once upon a time in the assembly of Lord Indra, the King of heaven, a debate was going on regarding the sancitity of various holy places. All of a sudden, Nārada Muni appeared there, shining like the sun. After being formally worshiped and welcomed, Lord Indra inquired from him as to the reason for his arrival. The great sage then addressed Indra and the assembly, 'After bathing in all the holy places and sacred regions with great faith, as well as worshiping all deities, I have come from earth to see you, O Indra.'

"Then Lord Indra inquired from him about which sacred place would deliver the killer of a *brāhmaṇa*, the drunkard, the cow-killer, the killer of a woman, or the gold thief. Nārada Muni replied, 'I do not know the details regarding the destruction of sins by the holy places. I only know that all great holy places are very auspicious and divine.' After hearing these words, Indra ordered all the holy places on earth to appear before him in their personal forms. As all the personified divine forms of the sacred *tīrthas* appeared, adorned with beautiful garments, ornaments, and garlands, they resembled the sun's luster, with the complexion of gold and pearls. Some of the great personified holy rivers that appeared in Indra's assembly were Gaṅgā, Narmadā, Candrabhāgā, Sarasvatī, Sindhu, Kāverī, Soṇa, Veṇā, and Godāvarīmayī. The holy places that appeared there were lead by Prayāga, Puṣkara, Vārāṇasī, Dvārakā, Prabhāsa, Avantī, Nimiṣa, Māyāpurī, and Mathurā. All these and innumerable other holy places and rivers offered obeisances to Lord Indra with their heads bent down.

"Then all the holy places inquired, 'O lord of the heavens, why have you called us? Please tell us the reason.' Then Indra asked, 'Which holy place is able to remove the sins of murdering a *brāhmaṇa*, a cow or a woman; and which place can deliver one from the sins of plotting against one's master, drinking liquor, causing abortion, making treachery, destroying pasture land for cows, burning a dwelling, having illicit sex, changing the deity, or running away from the battlefield? After properly deciding, you may all speak.' After consultation, the personified sacred *tīrthas* replied, 'Listen, O Indra, we shall tell you. All holy places destroy sins, but not every place is able to destroy the very fearful and strong sins which you have mentioned. Only Prayāga, Puṣkara, Aghatīrtha, and Vārāṇasī are able to destroy the sins you have mentioned. These four holy places have unlimited power to destroy sins. O Lord Indra, these holy places as well as all others have been created by the Supreme Creator, Lord Viṣṇu.'

"After hearing these words, Lord Indra was full of joy and thus praised all the sacred *tīrthas*."

Nārada Muni inquires

In the *Nārada Purāṇa* (Chapter 6), Sanaka-kumāra glorifies Prayāga for the benefit of Nārada Muni: "Once the four Kumāras, Sanaka, Sanandana, Sanātana, and Sanat, were heading towards Mount Meru to the assembly of Lord Brahmā. On their way they saw the sacred River Gaṅgā, which originates from the lotus feet of Lord Viṣṇu. Just as they were about to take bath, their younger brother, Nārada Muni, arrived there. Upon seeing his brothers, he bowed before them and began to invoke the holy names of Lord Viṣṇu. Then with great pleasure they all bathed together in the Gaṅgā.

"Afterwards, Sanaka, who is the master of spiritual knowledge and philosophy, began to glorify devotional service to the Lord and describe the life of Mārkaṇḍeya Ṛṣi. Nārada then asked him what was the most excellent and sacred of all places of pilgrimage. Sanaka-kumāra replied, 'O *brāhmaṇa*, listen to this confidential secret regarding which sacred *tīrtha* destroys all the effects of evil, is conducive to virtue, and destroys all sins. This should also be understood by even the demigods and sages, for this *tīrtha* wards off the influence of evil planets, subdues all ailments, and awards longevity. Great sages say that the confluence of the Gaṅgā and Yamunā is the most sacred of all sacred places. All the divine personalities, headed by Lord Brahmā, as well as all the sages, Manus, and demigods resort to this sacred confluence of white and dark waters. O *brāhmaṇa*, Gaṅgā should be known as the most pure and holy river, since she emanates from the lotus feet of Lord Viṣṇu, and Yamunā is born from the sun. Hence their confluence is bound to be most auspicious. O great sage, the holy place called Prayāga should be known as the most sacred and meritorious of all the holy places on earth, which is bound by the oceans. It was there that Lord Brahmā performed a sacrifice to propitiate Viṣṇu, the Lord of goddess Lakṣmī. All sages have also performed similar sacrifices for His pleasure. It is stated in the scriptures that the pious inclination for listening to the *Purāṇas* is equal to offering oblations to Gaṅgā, and devotion to the spiritual master is comparable to bathing at Prayāga.'"

Prayāga-māhātmyam

Again from the *Nārada Purāṇa* (*Uttara-bhāga* 63), Vasu, the sacrificial priest of King Rukmāṅgada, narrates to Lord Brahmā's daughter, Mohinī, the greatness of Prayāga-rāja: "Listen, O Mohinī, I shall narrate the glories of Prayāga to you, as approved in the *Vedas*. One who takes bath there in accordance with spiritual injunctions becomes pure. Bathing at Kāśī (Vārāṇasī), where Gaṅgā flows north, is one hundred times more beneficial than at other places. But the place where the Gaṅgā mingles with the Yamunā is one hundred times more beneficial than at Kāśī. When Gaṅgā mingles with Kālindī (Yamunā), they destroy more sins than can be accumulated in hundreds of *kalpas*. The continuous flow of the braided currents of the Gaṅgā and the Yamunā is said to be like nectar. When the sun is in the sign of Makara (Capricorn) during the month of Māgha, all *tīrthas* on earth come to take bath at the Triveṇī, where Gaṅgā, Yamunā, and Sarasvatī meet. Not only the *tīrthas*, but Lord Viṣṇu, Mahādeva, Lord Brahmā, the Rudras, Adityas, Maruts, Gandharvas, Yakṣas, Kinnaras, Guhyakas, and Siddhas, along with their consorts such as Lakṣmī, Pārvatī, Brahmāṇī, Śacī, Aditi, and all the other demigod's wives, even the celestial damsels like Ghṛtācī, Menakā, and Urvaśī, come to Prayāga in the month of Māgha.

"During Satya-yuga (Kṛta-yuga), all these *tīrthas* and great personalities usually appeared personally, but in Kali-yuga they all appear in disguise or in invisible form. Due to contact with sinners, *tīrthas* become black, but after bathing in Prayāga during the month of Māgha, they again become white in color. The benefit of bathing in a lake is twice that of bathing in a tank. In a natural pond the benefit multiplies tenfold, and in a river it increases one hundredfold. At the confluence of two great rivers, the benefit is four hundred times more. But when one bathes in Gaṅgā at Prayāga when the sun is in Capricorn, it is considered one thousand times more beneficial.

"O gentle lady, your father created this Prayāga to reduce the accumulated sins on earth, for the benefit of mankind. In some places the waters are whitish and in other places they are blackish. Lord Brahmā has shown us the way to his own abode by taking bath at Triveṇī, where the flow of currents that are white and black is blended and braided together by the Sarasvatī. The holy waters at Prayāga are actually like a forest fire for the fuel of sins. This *tīrtha* destroys rebirth, for by glorifying the waters there, one attains liberation and the abode of Lord Viṣṇu.

"By entering Prayāga, all sins immediately perish. A person who remains pure in mind and body, refrains from violence, and maintains faith will go to the highest region. There are many holy places, shrines, and sacred mountains residing in Prayāga. There are ten thousand *tīrthas* and three hundred million shrines that radiate the glories of Prayāga. Lord Vāyu says that there are thirty-five million additional holy shrines in Prayāga.

"The area of Prayāga extends from Pratiṣṭhāna (Jhunsi) up to the two Nāgas (Kambala and Aśvatara) and then to Bhogavatī, the pool of Vāsuki. This area is known as the *vedi*, or sacrificial altar, of Lord Brahmā. O beautiful lady, there is no holy center more meritorious in the three worlds. The power of this *tīrtha* is superior to that of all other *tīrthas*. Māyā-devī, who is created by Lord Viṣṇu, is impossible to overcome. Even the demigods are bound by her. But, O daughter of Brahmā, in the month of Māgha at Prayāga, Māyā's bonds are burnt. Even Citragupta, the secretary of Yamarāja, does not adequately know the extent of merit that a person receives from taking bath in Sitāsita (the confluence of Gaṅgā and Yamunā) during the month of Māgha when the sun is in Capricorn.

"The confluence of the Gaṅgā and the Yamunā is well known in the three worlds, and it is also called Kāmika-tīrtha, or the place where one's desires are fulfilled. Whatever one desires will be realized here by taking bath with devotion. If the devotee desires a worldly kingdom, the heavenly planets, or salvation in the spiritual world, Prayāga-tīrtha satisfies him. O lady of beautiful eyes, by taking a holy bath in Haridvāra, Prayāga, or at the confluence of the Gaṅgā and the ocean, the devotee shall go to the abodes of Lord Brahmā, Mahādeva, and then Lord Viṣṇu."

Kumbha-melā

In India, there are four Kumbha-melās, which are the largest spiritual gatherings on the face of this world. They are held at Prayāga, Haridvāra, Naśika (Trimbak), and Ujjain. These Kumbha-melās rotate every twelve years. The following passages from the *Purāṇas* elaborate on the pastime associated with these *melās*.

Long ago, during Satya-yuga, Durvāsā Muni cursed the demigods, thereby depriving them of their heavenly kingdoms, giving them to the *asuras*. The demigods went along with Lord Brahmā and Lord Śiva to the shore of the ocean of milk and offered prayers to Kṣīrodakaśāyī Viṣṇu. After Lord Viṣṇu was pleased by the prayers of Lord Brahmā and Lord Śiva, He advised them and the demigods to make a truce, whereupon the demigods and demons could churn the ocean of milk, with hope of producing nectar. The rope would be the largest serpent, Vāsuki, and the churning rod would be Mandara mountain, which is made of gold. The Lord warned the demigods not to fear or be attracted to the things produced of the churning, as well as not to become angry. They were also instructed to make peace with Bali Mahārāja, the King of the demons. They then started towards the ocean of milk carrying Mandara mountain with them. Since the mountain was extremely heavy, the Lord

placed it on Garuḍa, who placed it in the middle of the ocean. After some time, the mountain sunk and then the Lord assumed the shape of a tortoise. He lifted the mountain on His back, which extended for one million two hundred-eighty thousand kilometres, like a large island.

The demons began pulling the serpent-rope from the mouth and the demigods held the tail. With great force, they pulled the serpent in both directions, thus producing the following: Kālakūṭa (the poison that Lord Śiva drank), a Surabhi cow (to obtain ghee for sacrifices), a horse named Uccaiḥśravā (for Bali Mahārāja), the king of elephants named Airāvata (and eight she-elephants), the Kaustubha and Padmarāga gems (for Lord Viṣṇu), a *pārijāta* flower (which fulfilled everyone's desires), the Apsarās, Lakṣmī, Vāruṇī (the goddess of drink), Dhanvantari (the plenary portion of Lord Viṣṇu, who was carrying the *kumbha*, or jug, filled with nectar), and finally Mohinī-mūrti (the woman incarnation of Lord Viṣṇu who bewildered the demons).

When Dhanvantari appeared with the *kumbha* of nectar, the demons immediately snatched it away by force. They fought amongst themselves saying: "You cannot drink it first. I must drink it first. Me first, not you!" Then Mohinī-mūrti appeared to fool the demons, and they ultimately delivered the *kumbha* of nectar into her hands. She then distributed the nectar only to the demigods, thus cheating the demons out of their share. Then Lord Viṣṇu, who appeared as a woman, disclosed His original form and returned to His abode on the back of Garuḍa.

Somewhere in the middle of all this churning and struggling for the nectar, when the demons and demigods were fighting amongst themselves, a few drops of nectar fell onto this planet. In the *Śrīmad-Bhāgavatam* there is no clear description regarding how the nectar fell onto this planet. However, the *Padma Purāṇa*, *Brahma Purāṇa*, and other *Purāṇas* give the following explanation.

Fourteen jewels were created from the churning of the ocean of milk: Lakṣmī, Kaustubha, Pārijāta, Sūrya, Dhanvantari, Cāndrāya, Garal, Puṣpaka, Airāvata, Pāñcajanya, Śaṅkha, Rambhā, Kamadhenu, and Amṛta. After the demons obtained the fourteenth jewel (*amṛta*), they learned that if they drank the *amṛta*, they would live forever, and thus be able to fearlessly disturb the demigods. The demigods feared the demons and told Lord Indra's son, Jayanta, to escape with the *kumbha* of *amṛta*, or nectar. So the demigods and demons fought and struggled for twelve days. During this fight, some drops of nectar fell onto this planet earth. In order to secure the *amṛta*, the demigods gather together in the form of *sādhus* and saints and attend the Kumbha-melās every twelve years, the equivalent of twelve days in the heavenly planets, at each of the four places where the nectar fell: Prayāga, Haridvāra, Naśika (Trimbak), and Ujjain.

Lord Rāmacandra and the sage Bharadvāja

As narrated in the *Śrīmad Vālmiki Rāmāyaṇa* (*Ayodhyā-kāṇḍa* 50, 52, 54), when Lord Rāmacandra began His journey into exile from Ayodhyā, He boarded His chariot and crossed the lovely kingdom of Kośala until He was able to see the celestial soothing Gaṅgā. Lord Rāma was delighted on seeing the blessed river with its cool waters and numerous *ṛṣis* dwelling in hermitages along her banks. He said, "Gaṅgā is always blessed by the presence of demigods, Gandharvas, Kinnaras, and Nāgas, along with their consorts. This well known river is surrounded by hundreds of pleasing mountains (the Himālayas) and is adorned by celestial gardens. At some places the waters of Gaṅgā form the shape of braided locks, in other places they are very still and deep, and at other places they are disturbed with great agitation.

"Singing swans and cranes hover over her waters, and trees grow like garlands along her banks. Beds of lotuses are carpeted along her shores, and wild elephants are guarding the interior part of the forest. She is not only devoid of sins, but the celestial river dispels all sins, since she flows from the lotus feet of Lord Viṣṇu. The depths of her waters are infested with sharks and crocodiles, as well as the snakes that have fallen from Lord Śaṅkara's head."

As Śrī Rāma, Lakṣmaṇa, and Sītā-devī proceeded on their way, they finally reached the bank of Gaṅgā, in the vicinity of Śṛṅgaverapura (near Prayāga). Upon reaching the northern bank, Lord Rāma decided to take shelter under one Ingudi tree and rest there for the evening. Meanwhile, Mahārāja Guha, who was the king of the territory and a friend of Śrī Rāma, heard about the Lord's arrival and hastened to the bank of the Gaṅgā. Upon meeting and embracing one another, King Guha said to Śrī Rāma, "This principality of Śṛṅgaverapura is as much Yours as Ayodhyā. How can I serve You, O Rāma?" After offering proper prayers and worship to Lord Rāma, Guha made everyone comfortable for their evening stay. The Lord fasted that night in due reverence to Gaṅgā.

The next morning, Śrī Rāma and Lakṣmaṇa adopted the dress and hair style of ascetic sages. Then, boarding a boat that King Guha had arranged, Rāma, Lakṣmaṇa, and Sītā carefully departed from the shore of Gaṅgā. They all properly honored the celestial river by sipping her waters and offering obeisances. While the propelled boat was in the middle of the Gaṅgā, Sītā-devī joined her palms and spoke the following words, "O mother Gaṅgā, please protect this son of the wise Emperor Daśaratha, so that Lord Rāma may fulfill His fourteen years in exile. When the day arrives when Rāma and Lakṣmaṇa return here in safety and cross your water again, then all my desires will be fulfilled and I shall worship you with great delight. O goddess, who flows through the three worlds, I, Sītā, greet and praise you and await that day when we return. Then I will give garments, *prasāda*, and one hundred thousand cows in charity to the *brāhmaṇas*, just with the intention of pleasing you. When I return to Ayodhyā, I shall worship you with a thousand and one articles that are not even available to the demigods. I shall also worship all the deities that have their abodes along your banks, as well as all the sacred places. O sinless goddess, may the sinless Rāma re-enter Ayodhyā from the forest along with Lakṣmaṇa and Myself."

After praying in this way, they arrived at the southern bank and entered the happy and prosperous region known as Vatsa, the land situated between the Gaṅgā and Yamunā. Lord Rāma and Lakṣmaṇa engaged in sporting activities there, before they all took rest for the evening. The next morning they went towards the confluence of the Rivers Gaṅgā and Yamunā, where they saw and smelt the fragrant smoke rising near Prayāga. From this, Lord Rāma concluded that the hermitage of the great sage Bharadvāja was at hand, so they slowly approached the outskirts of the sage's dwelling.

Lord Rāma politely introduced Himself and the others to Bharadvāja and stated their intentions. Since the great sage was already expecting them, he welcomed them with full respect and worship. Then Lord Rāma inquired from the sage about a secluded place in the forest where they could dwell.

Bharadvāja described one place where a sacred mountain stood, 30 *krośas* (96 kilometres) from Prayāga, which would be conducive for their abode. The mountain was inhabited by great *ṛṣis* and infested with long-tailed monkeys, apes, and bears. It was known as Citrakūṭa and was as beautiful as Gandhamādana Mountain. The sage considered Citrakūṭa to be very secluded and comfortable for living, but if that did not appeal to the Lord, he offered them his own hermitage for the period of their exile.

After spending the evening at Bharadvāja's *āśrama*, Lord Rāma asked him for blessings and guidance to their future abode in Citrakūṭa. The great sage said, "O Rāma, proceed in joy to Citrakūṭa, which abounds in honey, roots, and fruits. It is adorned with clusters of trees of every description and is regularly visited by the Kinnaras and Nāgas. The whole area is charmed by the calls of the peacocks and elephants, and deer roam about freely there. Your mind will be pleased by beholding the rivers, cascades, peaks, caves, and streams, as well as by listening to the tittibha and cuckoo birds. O Rāma, proceed and take up Your abode on Citrakūṭa Mountain."

Prince Bharata follows Śrī Rāma

The following narration is also taken from the *Śrīmad Vālmīki Rāmāyaṇa* (*Ayodhyā-kāṇḍa* 79-80, 83, 86-92). When Lord Rāmacandra left Ayodhyā, His younger brother, Bharata, was requested to accept the throne, but He refused and planned instead to bring Śrī Rāma back to Ayodhyā. Under the guidance of Bharata's ministers, a broad passage was constructed from Ayodhyā to the bank of the Gaṅgā, making it easier for trekking. Eventually the pathway, which was adorned with flowers, trees, and birds and sprinkled with sandlewood paste, reached the shore of Gaṅgā. Then Bharata and His entourage started out and eventually reached the bank of the Gaṅgā at Śṛṅgaverapura, where He performed the *śrāddha* and *tarpana* ceremonies for His deceased father, King Daśaratha. During the entire journey, Bharata thought only of how to bring Śrī Rāma back to Ayodhyā.

The King of Śṛṅgaverapura, Guha, welcomed Bharata and His entire entourage with the utmost care and respect. Guha described all the pastimes recently performed by Śrī Rāma there at Śṛṅgaverapura. When Bharata was told how Rāma and Lakṣmaṇa accepted the dress of ascetics, He fell unconscious to the ground! Guha assured everyone of Rāma's safety and then showed them the *kuśa* grass on which Rāma and Sītā had taken rest, that had been prepared by Lakṣmaṇa. The contrast between the royal luxury in Ayodhyā and the simple bed of *kuśa* grass made everyone lament. Then Bharata decided to also adopt mendicant dress, live in the forest, and live the austere life-style of Śrī Rāma.

After spending the evening at the same place where Śrī Rāma had rested on the bank of Gaṅgā, Bharata requested King Guha to prepare their journey across the Gaṅgā. More than five hundred boats were assembled to carry Bharata, Śatrughna, Vasiṣṭha, Kauśalyā, Kaikeyī, Sumitrā, and all the other royal members, along with their army and other members of the entourage, across the Gaṅgā to the forest that encircles Prayāga. Upon reaching the other side, Bharata and His counsellors set out for the hermitage of the family priest of the demigods, that great sage Bharadvāja. Upon their meeting, Bharadvāja informed Bharata where Śrī Rāma, Lakṣmaṇa, and Sītā-devī were dwelling, and then he invited Bharata and His entire entourage to spend the evening at his hermitage.

Bharadvāja wondered why Bharata did not bring His entire entourage to his hermitage and instead left them behind near the bank of Gaṅgā. Bharata felt that if He had brought everyone, including the animals, the secluded peaceful hermitage, which was a place for study and austerities, would be disturbed and damaged. But Bharadvāja insisted that every single person and animal should be treated with the fullest hospitality. He invoked the architect of the demigods, Viśvakarma, as well as Yamarāja, Varuṇa, and Kuvera, to provide hospitality for the whole army of Bharata. He also summoned all the sacred rivers to meet in Prayāga. The Gandharvas, the Apsarās, and the dancing girls who serve Lord Brahmā were also requested to come to his hermitage. He instructed Soma to provide various meals and drinks. Then Bharadvāja greeted Prince Bharata and His entourage.

Within a very short time, the entire stretch of land within a radius of sixty-five kilometres was transformed into a heavenly city. Carpets of fresh green grass manifested, trees of all varieties sprang up, white mansions and palaces stood on the bank of Gaṅgā, and stables were prepared for the elephants and horses. Lord Brahmā, Lord Indra, and Kuvera each sent twenty thousand women to serve the entire army. Under the instructions of Bharadvāja, the chiefs of the Gandharvas began to sing and dance for the pleasure of Bharata, and the muddy streams bordering the banks of Gaṅgā turned into thickened sweet rice!

The animal keepers fed the elephants, horses, donkeys, bullocks, and camels sugarcane and ghee-fried grains, soaked in honey. In fact, the animals were groomed and fed so nicely and opulently that the animals did not recognize their handlers and the handlers did not recognize their own animals! Everyone was so completely intoxicated with the celestial hospitality that they neither desired to return to Ayodhyā nor to proceed towards Citrakūṭa in the Daṇḍakāraṇya forest! After they were all fed with ambrosial food, they retired for the evening. All the soldiers were smeared with sandalwood and aloe paste and adorned with beautiful celestial garlands, which eventually became strewn and crushed as they slept. Then all the demigods, Gandharvas, sacred rivers, and lovely women returned to their respective abodes.

The next morning, Bharata was given directions to Citrakūṭa by Bharadvāja, who also described the beautiful characteristics of that uninhabited forest dwelling, situated near the River Mandākinī. Queens Kauśalyā, Sumitrā, and Kaikeyī expressed their heartfelt appreciation for his hospitality and grasped the feet of the sage before circumambulating him. The great Bharadvāja understood their unhappiness due to the plight Śrī Rāma might be in while living in the forest, so he said, "Do not feel guilty for Śrī Rāma's banishment. Only good and happiness will prevail from the exile of Śrī Rāma, not only for you, but for all the demigods and *ṛṣis* who meditate on the Supreme Lord." Then Prince Bharata offered His obeisances to the great sage and prepared to depart. The huge army, full of elephants and horses, marched on like a burst cloud. After traveling to the confluence of the Rivers Gaṅgā and Yamunā, the forces followed the flowing Yamunā to the west, which took them through forests that were inhabited with deer and birds, as well as over mountains and rivers. The birds scattered everywhere when the huge entourage proceeded into the dense forest, as the elephants led the way to Citrakūṭa.

Bharata returns to Bharadvāja's *āśrama*

Continuing from the *Śrīmad Vālmīki Rāmāyaṇa* (*Ayodhyā-kāṇḍa* 112-113): Once Bharata arrived in Citrakūṭa, He was warmly and affectionately greeted by Lord

Rāmacandra, who remained fixed in His vow to live in exile for the entire fourteen year period. Since Bharata's attempts to bring Śrī Rāma back to Ayodhyā failed, He placed a new pair of wooden sandals that were bedecked with gold in front of the Lord. Śrī Rāma stood on them, thus blessing the sandals to represent Him on the throne of Ayodhyā during His absence. Bharata vowed to live as an ascetic outside Ayodhyā in Nandigrāma and to enter the fire if Śrī Rāma did not return exactly the day after His fourteen year exile was over.

Then, placing the wooden sandals on His head, Bharata and His entire entourage departed from Citrakūṭa and returned to the hermitage of Bharadvāja. After crossing the Rivers Gaṅgā and Yamunā at Prayāga, they proceeded once again to the town of Śṛṅgaverapura, before returning to Ayodhyā.

Śrī Rāma returns to Ayodhyā

To conclude from the *Śrīmad Vālmiki Rāmāyaṇa* (*Yuddha-kāṇḍa* 121-125): After Lord Rāmacandra completed His pastimes in Laṅkā, Vibhīṣaṇa invoked Puṣpaka, the aerial vehicle of Kuvera, to appear to take Śrī Rāma, Lakṣmaṇa, Sītā-devī, Sugriva, Hanumān and other monkeys, as well as himself, to Ayodhyā. During the course of their flight, Śrī Rāma pointed out to Sītā-devī the various places where their pastimes had been enacted, such as Laṅkā, Setubandha, Kiṣkindhā, Mount Ṛṣyamūka, Pampā lake, Godāvarī River, and Citrakūṭa.

They arrived at the hermitage of that great sage Bharadvāja on the fifth day of the month of Āśvina-śukla (September/October), when the fourteenth year of exile was completed. After offering their obeisances to the great sage, Śrī Rāma inquired from him about the condition of Ayodhyā during His absence. Then the Lord dispatched Hanumān to travel ahead to Śṛṅgaverapura, on the other bank of Gaṅgā, and inform King Guha of His arrival. He also instructed Hanumān to find Bharata, who was living in Nandigrāma, and tell Him that they were at the hermitage of Bharadvāja at Prayāga.

The sage Bharadvāja requested Śrī Rāma to remain at his hermitage for the evening and then offered Him water to wash His hands. "You shall go to Ayodhyā tomorrow morning," said Bharadvāja. The Lord then requested the following boon, "Let all the trees on the way from Prayāga to Ayodhyā bear fruits and flow with honey. Let the fruits be filled with the fragrance of nectar. Let it be so!" The next day, Lord Rāmacandra returned to Ayodhyā.

Today, a *mūrti* of the sage Bharadvāja is situated in an impressive temple in Colonel Gunj at the University of Allahabad, which is said to be the site of this great personality's hermitage.

Pulastya Muni and Bhīṣma

The *Mahābhārata* (*Vana-parva* 81-85) tells that when Bhīṣma was observing his *pitrya-vrata* (vow to forefathers) and studying the *Vedas* amongst ascetics near the sacred region at the source of the Gaṅgā, the great Pulastya Muni appeared. Upon noticing that Bhīṣma was observing his vows perfectly, Pulastya offered to grant him whatever he desired. Bhīṣma then requested Pulastya to remove some doubts he had regarding the *tīrthas*. The great *muni* began describing the merits that are attached to the various *tīrthas* and why one should take refuge of the *tīrthas*. He explained that if one is without sin and acts without motivation, fasts and then eats simply, controls the senses, gives up anger, speaks truthfully, firmly executes his vows, regards all other creatures as one's own self, and gives in charity, then he enjoys the fullest benefit from the *tīrthas*.

Pulastya Muni then described in detail to Bhīṣma nearly three hundred *tīrthas*, beginning with Puṣkara and including such *tīrthas* as the Narmadā River, Prabhāsa, Dvārakā, the *saṅgama* of the Sindhu River and the ocean, Kurukṣetra, Vāsuki-tāla, the sources of the Yamunā and Sindhu Rivers, Naimiṣāraṇya, Vārāṇasī, Gayā, the Mahānadī River, the Gaṇḍakī River, Salagrāma, Mahendra Parvata, Kanyākumārī, Gokarṇa, the Godāvarī River, Daṇḍakāraṇya, and at last, Prayāga.

"Then, O great Bhīṣma, one should proceed to Prayāga, whose praises have been sung by *ṛṣis* and where all the demigods dwell with Lord Brahmā. The Lokapālas, the Siddhas, the Pitṛs, the four Kumāras, the Nāgas, the Suparṇas, the rivers, the seas, the Gandharvas, the Apsarās, and even Lord Hari, all reside there. In that region is the world purifying daughter of the sun, Yamunā, who is celebrated throughout the three worlds, and who unites with Gaṅgā. The land between Gaṅgā and Yamunā is regarded as the most celebrated in the world, and Prayāga is the foremost part of that region. Prayāga, Pratiṣṭhāna, Kambala, Aśvatara, and Bhogavatī are the sacrificial platforms of Lord Brahmā. The learned say that of all these *tīrthas*, Prayāga is the most sacred, in fact, it is the foremost *tīrtha* in the three worlds. By visiting this *tīrtha*, by singing its praises, or by taking a little earth from it, one is cleansed from all sins. The wise say that six hundred million ten thousand *tīrthas* exist at Prayāga. Having committed a hundred sins, he who bathes in Gaṅgā will wash away his sins as fuel is consumed by fire. He who recites the name Gaṅgā is purified, and he who bathes in her or drinks her water will sanctify seven generations of his family. There is no *tīrtha* like Gaṅgā, there is no Lord like Keśava, and there is no class like the *brāhmaṇas*. O great Bhīṣma, the region through which Gaṅgā flows should be regarded as a sacred hermitage, and any spot of land that is on Gaṅgā's banks should be regarded as favorable to the attainment of an ascetic's success."

Pulastya concluded his *tīrtha* narration by informing Bhīṣma that one should recite these descriptions only to one who is pious, who is one's son, friend, disciple, or dependent, because such narrations are auspicious and sacred. They destroy one's enemies and sharpen one's intellect. Of the *tīrthas* described by Pulastya, some are easily accessible, while others are difficult to reach. But one who is inspired with the desire to see all the *tīrthas* should make the effort, even if it is only in imagination.

Yudhiṣṭhira Mahārāja's lamentation

The *Nārada Purāṇa* (*Uttara-bhāga* 63.43) describes how after the Battle of Kurukṣetra, Yudhiṣṭhira Mahārāja became the Emperor of Bhārata-varṣa from Hastināpura. He was extremely aggrieved over the destruction of his family and cousins, as well as Bhīṣma, Droṇācārya, and Karṇa. The only main survivors were the five Pāṇḍavas and Lord Kṛṣṇa. Yudhiṣṭhira felt a sense of guilt, sin, and frustration. Meanwhile, the great sage Mārkaṇḍeya Ṛṣi was in Vārāṇasī when he heard about King Yudhiṣṭhira's sadness. He came to Hastināpura to console the King and advise him to undertake a journey to Prayāga, where he could atone for any sin and obtain mental peace. The great sage said that every step taken in Prayāga by the faithful devotee was as rewarding as the performance of an Aśvamedha (horse sacrifice).

"The devotee who has taken sacred vows should bathe at the confluence of the Gaṅgā and Yamunā, which is equal in benefit to both the Rājasūya and Aśvamedha sacrifices."

The chastisement of Choṭa Haridāsa

In the *Śrī Caitanya-caritāmṛta* (*Antya-līlā*, Chapter 2) it is described that when Śrī Caitanya Mahāprabhu was residing at Jagannātha Purī, He took *prasāda* at the houses of various devotees. One of them was Bhagavān Ācārya. One day when Bhagavān Ācārya was cooking lunch for Caitanya Mahāprabhu, he requested Choṭa Haridāsa, a singer in the assembly of Mahāprabhu, to get some white rice from Mādhavī-devī, the sister of Śikhi Māhiti. Mādhavī-devī was an advanced devotee and was considered one of the intimate devotees of Caitanya Mahāprabhu. After Choṭa Haridāsa brought the rice, Bhagavān Ācārya cooked many preparations and also obtained *mahā-prasāda* from Lord Jagannātha's temple for the pleasure of Caitanya Mahāprabhu.

When Mahāprabhu was eating, He asked, "Where did you get such fine rice?" Bhagavān Ācārya replied that Choṭa Haridāsa had brought it on his request from Mādhavī-devī. Then after returning to his residence, Mahāprabhu ordered His servant Govinda, "From this day onward, do not allow Choṭa Haridāsa to come here." When Haridāsa heard this, he was very unhappy and fasted for three days. The other devotees approached Mahāprabhu and said, "What great offense has Haridāsa committed that he has been forbidden to come to your door? He has been fasting for three days." Mahāprabhu replied, "Icannot tolerate seeing the face of a person who has accepted the renounced order of life but who still talks intimately with a woman."

The Lord then said, as stated in the Manu-saṁhitā (2.215) and *Śrīmad-Bhāgavatam* (9.19.17) "One should not sit closely with one's mother, sister or daughter, for the senses are so strong that they may attract even a person advanced in knowledge." Saying this, He angrily entered His room. The next day, all the devotees again begged Mahāprabhu to pardon Choṭa Haridāsa for his small offense and said that he would not repeat it in future. The Lord refused to hear one more word on this matter. He warned that He would leave the place if they persisted. Then the devotees approached Śrī Paramānanda Purī, a senior devotee, and requested him to pacify the Lord.

Although Caitanya Mahāprabhu respected Paramānanda Purī, He did not listen and was about to leave for Ālālanātha. Paramānanda Purī humbly persuaded the Lord to stay and said, "You are the Supreme Personality of Godhead. You are completely independent and can do whatever You like. Who can say anything above You?" The devotees then advised Haridāsa to break his fast and be patient. Choṭa Haridāsa would stand far away and gaze at the Lord when He would go to the temple of Lord Jagannātha. Śrī Caitanya Mahāprabhu is the ocean of mercy. When He chastises His devotees, He does so to reestablish the principles of religion. In this way, one year passed, but there was no change in the Lord's attitude toward Haridāsa.

One night, Choṭa Haridāsa conclusively decided to attain the lotus feet of Mahāprabhu and departed for Prayāga. He gave up his life by entering into the water of the confluence of the Gaṅgā, Yamunā, and Sarasvatī at Triveṇī. Attaining his spiritual body resembling that of a Gandharva, Choṭa Haridāsa would sing at night for the Lord to hear, although invisible. Only the Lord knew this. One day when the Lord's associates went to bathe in the sea at Jagannātha Purī, they heard Haridāsa singing, but could not see him. They speculated that he had committed suicide by swallowing poison. Later a devotee arrived from Prayāga and gave the details of Choṭa Haridāsa's suicide. When the devotees related the news to Caitanya Mahāprabhu, He said, "If with sensual intentions one in the renounced order looks at women, this is the only process of atonement." Then the devotees understood that Choṭa Haridāsa had attained the shelter of the Lord by commiting suicide at the confluence of the Rivers Gaṅgā and Yamunā at Prayāga.

Suicide in Triveṇī

Śrī Caitanya Mahāprabhu used Choṭa Haridāsa as a perfect example for understanding the seriousness of accepting *sannyāsa*, the renounced order of life, especially in this present age of Kali. Situated within an underground temple in the fort of Allahabad is the famous Akṣaya-vaṭa, or immortal banyan tree. There was an ancient tradition of committing religious suicide at Triveṇī or at the Akṣaya-vaṭa. In the *Dharma-śāstras*, suicide in general is forbidden. Both homicide and suicide are condemned and considered equal offenses. Even Manu, who is the father of mankind and who wrote the code of conduct (*Manu-smṛti*) for a harmonious existence of social life, condemns suicide and denies *udaka-kriya* (water libations) to those who commit suicide. Other Vedic texts also condemn anyone who commits suicide as an *ātmāhan* (killer of the soul), but still the practice persisted in spite of the scriptural warnings.

Though suicide in general is discouraged, certain exceptions are tolerated and even recommended. Persons who commit grave sins should perform *prāyaścitta*, or religious rites performed as atonement for sins, which sometimes recommend suicide. Those unable to perform their religious duties or those suffering from incurable diseases took to this course. Old and incapacitated people, those having no further ambition, those convinced of the impermanence of the world, and of course Satī, also followed this path. Suicide could be committed in various ways: by jumping from a cliff, by entering a fire prepared from cowdung cakes, or by starting on an endless journey on foot in the Himālayas, as done by the Pāṇḍavas. It could also be achieved by drowning in Triveṇī (Gaṅgā, Yamunā, and Sarasvatī) head first, fasting unto death, falling from the Akṣaya-vaṭa, or even cutting off parts of one's body and throwing them to the birds! This tradition of religious suicide at Prayāga was extended to other *tīrthas*.

In Vārāṇasī, there used to be another famous ritual called "Kāśī-karvat", or changing your side in Kāśī. This was another religious style of committing suicide. A person would voluntarily lie on a platform jutting out over the water of Gaṅgā in such way that his head would be facing the water. Then a priest would ask that person to change his side, and at that moment amidst the chanting of *mantras*, a heavy sharp edged iron blade would fall on the neck of the person lying on his side, hacking his head off into the Gaṅgā! In this way, the person who was willing to die would do so with the scene of the rippling waves of Gaṅgā secured in his eyes, and then death would throw his head in the lap of mother Gaṅgā, ensuring his liberation. Though this gory pratice was stopped during the British Raja, there are still many old believers who would love to end their life in this way.

EXALTED VISITORS

Since time immemorial, Prayāga-rāja has been considered one of the most sacred *tīrthas* on this planet. Numerous great personalities have visited and bathed at Triveṇī, the confluence of the Gaṅgā, Yamunā, and Sarasvatī Rivers. Listed below are only a few pastimes associated with some of those personalities.

The Pāṇḍavas

When the Pāṇḍavas, the heroic sons of Mahārāja Pāṇḍu, began their *tīrtha-yātrā* (sacred pilgrimage), they first went to Naimiṣāraṇya and bathed in the River Gomatī. Proceeding onwards, they reached the sacrificial region of the demigods known as Prayāga. There they bathed in the confluence of the Gaṅgā and Yamunā Rivers and then resided there practising austerities of great merit. Those truthful Pāṇḍavas bathed in that *tīrtha* and cleansed themselves of every sin before traveling onwards to Vedī-tīrtha, which is sacred to Lord Brahmā and adored by all ascetics.

Lord Balarāma

After Lord Balarāma left Dvārakā to visit the various holy places of pilgrimage, He eventually arrived in Naimiṣāraṇya. Various sages, ascetics, *brāhmaṇas*, and scholars had gathered there in a meeting. Upon the Lord's arrival, they all received Him with great respect, except Romaharṣaṇa (Sūta Gosvāmī's father), who remained sitting on the *vyāsāsana* (the seat of Vyāsadeva or his representative). Seeing Romaharṣaṇa's deficiency in self-realization, Lord Balarāma chastised him for being too proud by killing him with a blade of grass. To atone for this act, Lord Balarāma was advised by the assembled *brāhmaṇas* first to kill the demon Balvala, who was contaminating the sacred place of sacrifice in Naimiṣāraṇya, and then continue to visit all the holy places of pilgrimage for twelve months. After the Lord killed Balvala, the *brāhmaṇas* offered Lord Balarāma prayers and gave Him a ceremonial bathing, new clothing, ornaments, and then garlanded Him before He continued His pilgrimage.

In the *Śrīmad-Bhāgavatam* (10.79.9-10), part of Lord Balarāma's pilgrimage is described in these words: "Then, given leave by the sages, the Lord went with a contingent of *brāhmaṇas* to the Kauśikī River, where He bathed. From there He went to the lake (Mānasa-sarovara) from which flows the River Sarayū. The Lord followed the course of the Sarayū, then He came to Prayāga, where He bathed and then performed rituals to propititate the demigods and other living beings. Next He went to the *āśrama* of Pulaha Ṛṣi."

Śrī Ādi Śaṅkarācārya

The following are some of the features of Śaṅkarācārya's life: He was born in Kāladi, Kerala, in a family of Nambūdiri *brāhmaṇas*; he left home as a boy to accept the life of a *sannyāsī*; he wrote scholarly commentaries on the *Vedānta-sūtras*, ten principal *Upaniṣads*, and the *Bhagavad-gītā*; he traveling all over India vigorously refuting Buddhist doctrines; he left four principal disciples to continue his mission (Padmapāda, Sureśvara, Toṭaka, and Hastāmalaka); he established centers of Advaitic learning; and he passed away at the early age of thirty-two, most likely at Kedāranātha in the Himālayas.

Śaṅkarācārya's profound teachings were at that time "powerful like the currents of the Gaṅgā augmented by strong winds, flowing majestically, carrying away the accumulated dirt of false doctrines of perverse notions of Dharma." His teachings also constitute a mighty river "whose sanctifying waters are the *Upaniṣads*, and whose torrential flow is irresistible like the heavenly River Gaṅgā rushing from the matted locks of Lord Śiva with its waters overflowing its bank."

At the age of eight years, Śaṅkarācārya accepted the renounced order of life. From that point on he traveled extensively throughout India, preaching and accepting disciples. His travels brought him to Sṛṅgeri,

Oṁkāranātha on the River Narmadā, Kāśī, Badarī, Uttarkāśī, Prayāga, Māhiṣmatī, Śrī Śailam, Rāmeśvaram, Śrī Raṅgam, Kāñcī, the west coast to Gokarṇa, Ujjain, Dvārakā, Kāmākhyā of Assam, Kāśmīra, and Kedāranātha.

After traveling from the southern Vindhya mountains, Śaṅkarācārya visited Prayāga, where the blue waters of the Yamunā meet the sparkling clear waters of the Gaṅgā. When he arrived, there were swans residing where the water was shining, while *cakravaka* birds found it convenient to stay where the water was dark.

After Śaṅkarācārya took his bath along with his disciples, he recited the following verses in praise of this special *tirtha*: "O Sanctifier! Thou hast the experience of being imprisoned in Lord Śiva's matted locks, and yet, by sanctifying the numbers of people who bathe in thee into holy beings, thou art enhancing for thyself the danger of being imprisoned in the locks of all of them. O mother! Thy waters being of such transcendent purity, why is it that thou receivest into thee so much of unclean matter like human bones? Thou rousest into the wakefulness of the Spirit, those who are wrapt in the sleep and dullness of ignorance. Thou art reputed also for converting men who have abandoned all hankering for sense objects into *dhūrta* bedecked beings (*dhūrta* is a particular flower with which Lord Śiva is decorated). All glories to you!" After praising Triveṇī and while resting on the shores refreshed by fragrant and cool breezes, he also remembered his own mother and prayed for her purification.

Śrī Advaita Ācārya

Advaita Ācārya traveled from Vārāṇasī until He arrived at Prayāga, where He had His head shaved. He then bathed in the confluence of the holy rivers, Gaṅgā, Yamunā, and Sarasvatī, and devotedly offered oblations to His forefathers according to regulations. Next He went and offered prayers and obeisances to Veṇī-Mādhava, and then He saw Bhīma's club at Kurukṣetra, which He repeatedly glorified.

Śrī Advaita Prabhu then left for Mathurā, the site of Lord Kṛṣṇa's eternal pastimes. When He arrived at the transcendental abode of the Lord, He manifested ecstatic feelings and cried out, "O Kṛṣṇa!" After relishing the transcendental abode of Śrī Vraja-dhāma, He returned to Śāntipura in Bengal.

Lord Nityānanda

As mentioned in the *Śrī Caitanya-bhāgavata* (*Ādi-khaṇḍa* 9.109, 123-125), when Lord Nityānanda was on His way to Mathurā during the earlier portion of His pilgrimage, He bathed at the confluence of the Gaṅgā and Yamunā and visited the nearby Śṛṅgaverapura. "In Prayāga, the Lord bathed at the river's confluence in the early chilled morning during the month of Māgha. Then He proceeded to Mathurā where He had appeared in the previous *yuga* as Lord Balarāma. There He visited Lord Kṛṣṇa's birthplace... Then Śrī Nityānanda traveled to the tribal kingdom of King Guhaka (Guha), Śṛṅgaverapura. King Guhaka reigned during the time of Lord Rāmacandra. When Śrī Nityānanda thought of His devotee, the tribal King Guhaka, He entered an ecstatic trance for three days. Nityānanda Prabhu then visited the different forests in which the Supreme Lord Rāmacandra once roamed. His feeling of separation from the Lord made Him roll on the ground in anguish."

Śrī Caitanya Mahāprabhu

After attending the Ratha-yātrā ceremony of Lord Jagannātha in Purī, Śrī

Caitanya Mahāprabhu decided to start for Vṛndāvana. His associates selected a *brāhmaṇa* named Balabhadra Bhaṭṭācārya to personally assist Him. Early in the morning, before sunrise, the Lord started for the town of Kaṭaka (Cuttack), then He traveled to the Jhārikhaṇḍa forest, where He engaged many animals, including tigers and elephants, in chanting the Hare Kṛṣṇa *mahā-mantra*. Whenever the Lord had a chance to visit a village, He would beg alms and acquire some rice and vegetables. Otherwise, He would collect some wild spinach from the forest to eat. In this way, the Lord and Balabhadra passed their way, finally reaching Vārāṇasī and then Prayāga, before arriving in Vṛndāvana.

The Lord's travels are described in the *Śrī Caitanya-caritāmṛta* (*Madhya* 17.149-151) as follows: "Śrī Caitanya Mahāprabhu then went to Prayāga, where He bathed at the confluence of the Ganges and Yamunā. He then visited the temple of Veṇī-Mādhava (Bindu-Mādhava) and chanted and danced there in ecstastic love. As soon as Śrī Caitanya Mahāprabhu saw the River Yamunā, He threw Himself in it. Balabhadra Bhaṭṭācārya hastily caught the Lord and very carefully raised Him up again. The Lord stayed at Prayāga for three days. He delivered the holy name of Kṛṣṇa and ecstatic love. Thus He delivered many people."

In his purports on the *Śrī Caitanya-caritāmṛta* (*Madhya* 17.149 and 18.145), Śrīla Prabhupāda emphasises the importance of Prayāga, which is also known as Tīrtha-rāja, the king of all places of pilgrimage.

"The city of Prayāga is situated a few miles from the city of Allahabad. The name Prayāga is given due to successful sacrifices performed there. It is said: *prakṛṣṭaḥ yāgaḥ yāga-phalaṁ yasmāt*. If one performs sacrifices at Prayāga, he certainly gets immediate results without difficulty. Prayāga is also called Tīrtha-rāja, the king of all places of pilgrimage. This holy place is situated on the confluence of the Rivers Ganges and Yamunā. Every year a fair takes place there known as Māgha-melā, and every twelve years a Kumbha-melā is also held. In any case, many people come to bathe there every year. During Māgha-melā, people from the local district generally come, and during Kumbha-melā people come from all over India to live there and bathe in the Ganges and Yamunā. Whoever goes there immediately feels the places' spiritual influence. A fort located there was constructed by the Emperor Akbar about five hundred years ago, and near the fort is the place called Triveṇī. On the other side of Prayāga is an old place known as Pratiṣṭhāna-pura. It is also well known as Jhuṅsi. Many saintly people live there, and consequently it is very attractive from the spiritual point of view."

"Bathing at the confluence of the Ganges and Yamunā near the fort at Allahabad, Prayāga, is mentioned in revealed scriptures:

māghe māsi gamiṣyanti
gaṅgā-yāmuna-saṅgamam
gavāṁ śata-sahasrasya
samyag dattaṁ ca yat-phalam
prayāge māgha-māse vai
tryahaṁ snātasya tat-phalam

'If one goes to Prayāga and bathes at the confluence of the Ganges and Yamunā in the month of Māgha, he attains the result of giving hundreds and thousands of cows in charity. Simply by bathing for three days there, he attains the results of such a pious activity.' Generally *karmīs* (fruitive laborers) take advantage of bathing there during the month of Māgha, thinking that they will be rewarded in the future. Those who are situated in devotional service do not very strictly follow this *karma-kāṇḍiya* process."

After Śrī Caitanya Mahāprabhu visited Vṛndāvana, He returned to Prayāga and stayed for ten days. The *Śrī Caitanya-caritāmṛta* (*Madhya* 18.222) states: "Śrī Caitanya Mahāprabhu finally arrived at Prayāga and for ten successive days bathed in the confluence of the Rivers Yamunā and Ganges during the festival of Makara-saṅkrānti [Māgha-melā]."

Later in the *Śrī Caitanya-caritāmṛta* (*Madhya* 19.37-43), some of Śrī Caitanya Mahāprabhu's pastimes in Prayāga are described as follows: "Śrī Rūpa Gosvāmī and Anupama Mallika (Śrī Vallabha) went to Prayāga, and they were very pleased to hear news that Śrī Caitanya Mahāprabhu was there. At Prayāga, Śrī Caitanya Mahāprabhu went to see the temple of Bindu-Mādhava, and many hundreds of thousands of people followed Him just to meet Him. Some of the people following the Lord were crying. Some were laughing, some dancing and some chanting. Indeed, some of them were rolling on the ground, exclaiming, 'Kṛṣṇa! Kṛṣṇa!' Prayāga is located at the confluence of two rivers—the Ganges and Yamunā. Although these rivers were not able to flood Prayāga with water, Śrī Caitanya Mahāprabhu inundated the whole area with waves of ecstatic love for Kṛṣṇa. Seeing the great crowd, the two brothers remained standing in a secluded place. They could see that Śrī Caitanya Mahāprabhu was ecstatic to see Lord Bindu-Mādhava. The Lord was loudly chanting the holy name of Hari. Dancing in ecstatic love and raising His arms, He asked everyone to chant 'Hari! Hari!' Everyone was astounded to see the greatness of Śrī Caitanya Mahāprabhu. Indeed, I cannot properly describe the pastimes of the Lord at Prayāga."

While in Prayāga, Śrī Caitanya Mahāprabhu would take His meals in a South Indian *brāhmaṇa's* house. One day, Śrī Rūpa and Śrī Vallabha came to meet Him. When the two brothers saw the Lord, they immediately fell down to the ground, offering their humble obeisances. The Lord was very pleased to once again see Rūpa and Vallabha, so He embraced both brothers. After receiving the causeless mercy of the Lord, they both folded their hands and in great humility offered the following prayer, quoted from the *Śrī Caitanya-caritāmṛta* (*Madhya* 19.53):

namo mahā-vadānyāya
krsna-prema-pradāya te
krsnāya krsna-caitanya-
nāmne gaura-tviṣe namaḥ

"O most munificent incarnation! You are Kṛṣṇa Himself appearing as Śrī Kṛṣṇa Caitanya Mahāprabhu. You have assumed the golden color of Śrīmatī Rādhārāṇī, and You are widely distributing pure love of Kṛṣṇa. We offer our respectful obeisances unto You."

The main reason why Śrī Caitanya Mahāprabhu returned to Prayāga was to teach the science of devotional service to Śrī Rūpa Gosvāmī. The following narration is in the *Śrī Caitanya-caritāmṛta* (*Madhya* 19.114-115,135, 237): "Due to the great crowds in Prayāga, Śrī Caitanya Mahāprabhu went to a place called Daśāśvamedha-ghāṭa. It was there that the Lord instructed Śrī Rūpa Gosvāmī and empowered him in the philosophy of devotional service. Śrī Caitanya Mahāprabhu taught Śrīla Rūpa Gosvāmī the ultimate limit of the truth about Lord Kṛṣṇa, the truth about devotional service, and the truth about transcendental mellows, consumating in conjugal love between Rādhā and Kṛṣṇa. Finally He told Rūpa Gosvāmī about the ultimate conclusions of *Śrīmad-Bhāgavatam*...For ten days Śrī Caitanya Mahāprabhu stayed at Prayāga and instructed Rūpa Gosvāmī, empowering him with the necessary potency...After saying

this, Śrī Caitanya Mahāprabhu embraced Śrīla Rūpa Gosvāmī. The Lord then decided to go to the city of Benares [Vārāṇasī]."

Śrīla Rūpa Gosvāmī has personally spoken about the mercy of Śrī Caitanya Mahāprabhu in the auspicious introduction to his book *Bhakti-rasāmṛta-sindhu*.

Pastimes of Śrīla Prabhupāda

The next four passages are paraphrases from the *Śrīla Prabhupāda-līlāmṛta*. They describe A.C. Bhaktivedanta Swami Prabhupāda's pastimes in Prayāga, which is also known as Allahabad.

The first narration is from the First Volume, Third Chapter: In 1923, Abhay Charan and his wife and child moved to Allahabad, a twelve-hour train ride northwest from Calcutta. The British had once made Allahabad the capital of the United Provinces. Europeans and affluent Indian families like the Nehrus lived in a modern, paved, well-lit section of town. Many Bengalis resided there, and it was there that Abhay decided to settle his family.

He had chosen Allahabad, traditionally known as Prayāga, as a good location for business, but it was also one of India's most famous places of pilgrimage. Situated at the confluence of the three holiest rivers of India—the Ganges, Yamunā, and Sarasvatī—Allahabad was the site of two of India's most widely attended spiritual events, the annual Māgha-melā and the Kumbha-melā, which took place every twelve years. In search of spiritual purification, millions of pilgrims from all over India would converge here each year at the time of the full moon in the month of Māgha and bathe at the junction of the three sacred rivers.

Abhay's home at 60 Badshahi Mundi consisted of a few rented rooms. For his business he rented a small shop in the commercial center of the city at Johnston Gunj Road, where he opened his dispensary, Prayag Pharmacy. It so happened that both Motilal Nehru and his son Jawaharlal were customers at Prayag Pharmacy. Because Jawaharlal would always order Western medicines, Abhay thought he must have felt that Indian ways were inferior. Once, Jawaharlal approached Abhay for a political contribution, and Abhay donated, being a conscientious merchant. For five years Abhay traveled widely out of Allahabad, and when he was home he put in long hours at the dispensary. But he also spent time with his wife and played with his children.

It was Kumbha-melā, January 1928. Bhaktipradīpa Tīrtha Mahārāja of the Gauḍīya Maṭha had come to Allahabad with a few men. One day he walked unannounced into the Prayag Pharmacy, and all of a sudden Abhay was seeing them again, after so many years. "Oh, these are the people I saw before!" he thought. "Gauḍīya Maṭha. Yes, come in."

Bhaktipradīpa Tīrtha Svāmī was the same *sannyāsī* who had visited Narendranath Mullik in Calcutta, a visit that had led to Abhay's going to visit Bhaktisiddhānta Sarasvatī. Folding his palms in a humble gesture, standing before Abhay in simple saffron khadi robes, his head shaven, with a tuft of *sikha* in the back, his forehead marked with Vaiṣṇava *tilaka*, Tīrtha Mahārāja said to Abhay, "We are new here. We are going to establish a temple in Allahabad. We have heard your name, so we have come to you. Please help us." Abhay was joyful: "Yes, I will help you." He contributed what money he could and then introduced Tīrtha Mahārāja to Dr. Ghosh, who also contributed.

After Kumbha-melā, Pradīpa Tīrtha Svāmī left, but five or six *brahmacārī* disciples of Bhaktisiddhānta Sarasvatī stayed on in Allahabad, maintaining a small *maṭha* headquarters. They worshiped the Deity, held an evening program of *kīrtana* and lecture, and preached actively to the local people. The devotee in charge, Atulānanda Brahmacārī, would visit the homes of Allahabad citizens, trying to solicit subscriber members for the *maṭha*; for half a rupee per month, a person would receive a subscription to the Gauḍīya magazine.

After several visits and hours of discussion on the activities and philosophy of Gauḍīya Vaiṣṇavism, Atulānanada brought Mr. De to the Allahabad *āśrama*. Shortly thereafter, the *maṭha* relocated to a rented house on South Mallaca Street near Ram Bagh, just a short walk from Abhay's house. Now it was possible for Abhay to visit every evening. After work, he would attend the *maṭha*, where he would play the *mṛdaṅga* (sacred drum), surprising the *brahmacārīs* with his already developed *mṛdaṅga* playing skills. He sang *bhajanas* with them and sometimes took the lead part in the congregational singing. He would also bring important persons from Allahabad to visit the *maṭha*. For the *brahmacārīs*, Abhay seemed to give new life to their *āśrama*, and for Abhay new life had come to him in his reunion with the disciples of Bhaktisiddhānta Sarasvatī.

The second narration is from the First Volume, Fourth Chapter: Abhay was again anticipating an imminent meeting with Śrīla Bhaktisiddhānta, this time at Allahabad. Abhay had only recently returned from Vṛndāvana to his work at Prayag Pharmacy when the devotees at the Allahabad Gauḍīya Maṭha informed him of the good news. They had secured land and funds for constructing a building, the Śrī Rūpa Gauḍīya Maṭha; and Śrīla Bhaktisiddhānta would be coming on November 21, 1932, to preside over the ceremony for the laying of the cornerstone. Sir William Malcolm Haily, governor of the Uṇited Provinces, would be the respected guest, and in a grand ceremony, would lay the foundation stone in the presence of Śrīla Bhaktisiddhānta. When Abhay learned that there would also be an initiation ceremony, he asked if he could be initiated. Atulānanda, the *maṭha's* president, assured Abhay that he would introduce him to Śrīla Bhatisiddhanta Sarasvatī.

On the day of the ceremony, Bhaktisiddhānta Sarasvatī met with his disciples at the Allahabad Gauḍīya Maṭha on South Mallaca Street. While he was speaking *hari-kathā* (narrations of Lord Hari) and taking questions, Atulānanda Brahmacārī took the opportunity to present several devotees, Abhay amongst them, as candidates for initiation. The Allahabad devotees were proud of Mr. De, who regularly attended the *maṭha* in the evening, and led *bhajanas*, listened to the teachings and spoke them himself, and often brought respectable guests. He had contributed money and had induced his business colleagues to do so. With folded palms, Abhay looked up humbly at his spiritual master. He and Śrīla Bhatisiddhanta were now face to face, and Śrīla Bhaktisiddhānta recognized him and was visibly pleased to see him. He already knew him. "Yes," he said, exchanging looks with Abhay, "he likes to hear. He does not go away. I have marked him. I will accept him as my disciple."

As the moment and the words became impressed into his being, Abhay was in ecstasy. Atulānanda was pleasantly surprised that his Gurudeva was already in approval of Mr. De. Other disciples in the room were also pleased to witness Śrīla Bhaktisiddhānta Sarasvatī's immediate acceptance of Mr. De as a good listener. Some of them wondered when or where Śrīla Bhaktisiddhānta had arrived at such an estimation of the young pharmacist. Abhay basked in the presence of his Gurudeva. "Yes, he likes to hear", the words of his spiritual master and his glance of recognition had remained with Abhay. Abhay would continue pleasing his spiritual master by hearing well. "Then," he thought, "I will be able to speak well."

Finally, Śrīla Bhaktisiddhānta called for Abhay to come forward and receive the *harināma* initiation by accepting his beads. After offering prostrated obeisances, Abhay extended his right hand and accepted the strand of *japa* beads from the hand of his spiritual master. At the same time, he also received the sacred brahminical thread, signifying second initiation. Usually, only after some time, when he was satisfied with the progress of the disciple, would Śrīla Bhaktisiddhānta give the second initiation. But he offered Abhay both initiations at the same time. Now Abhay was a full-fledged disciple, a *brāhmaṇa*, who could perform sacrifices, such as this fire *yajña* for initiation; he could worship the Deity in the temple and would be expected to discourse widely. Śrīla Bhaktisiddhānta added *aravinda* (lotus) to his name; now he was Abhay Caraṇāravinda.

In the Fourth Volume, Fifth Chapter, the Ardha-kumbha-melā of January of 1971 is described as follows: Kumbha-melā is the greatest congregation of human beings on earth. Every twelve years in Allahabad, *sādhus* and pilgrims from all over India gather at the Triveṇī. At an auspicious time that assures the worshiper liberation from the cycle of birth and death, as many as fifteen million people enter the sacred waters. A smaller version, the Māgha-melā, takes place annually during the month of Magh. Halfway through this twelve year cycle from one Kumbha-melā to the next, the Melā is known as Ardha-kumbha-melā. Knowing that millions would attend the Ardha-kumbha-melā in January of 1971, Śrīla Prabhupāda decided to take advantage of the opportunity for preaching by attending the Melā with his disciples.

While his disciples took the train from Surat to Allahabad, Prabhupāda, accompanied by Tamāla Kṛṣṇa, Haṁsadūta, Nanda Kumāra, and others, went briefly to Bombay and then to Calcutta, where he satisfied himself that his shipment of books from Dai Nippon was safely stored at a Scindia warehouse. He also purchased twenty-four inch brass Rādhā-Kṛṣṇa Deities to take with him to Allahabad. On January 11 he wrote: "Tomorrow morning we are going to Allahabad to attend the Ardha-kumbha-melā festival. We shall be going all forty strong devotees and there are an expected seven million going by there also for the month of Māgha."

The devotees were in the midst of a great religious festival and human spectacle, and without Prabhupāda most of them were bewildered by the strange sights and sounds. *Yogīs* sat all day in the same posture, while crowds stood watching. Trident-carrying Śaivites, with simple red cloth, *rudrākṣa* beads, and matted hair, sat smoking *gañjā* (marijuana). A procession of elephants, followed by two long files of naked *sādhus*, strode by. An ascetic lay on a bed of thorns. And there were still others, extreme renunciants rarely seen by the rest of civilization. And, of course, the various Hindu sects abounded, their chants and prayers rising into the air to mingle with the morning mist and the smoke from the ten thousand campfires that clouded the sky above the city of tents.

Sitting in his tent with disciples, Prabhupāda explained the significance of Ardha-kumbha-melā. For millions of years, he said, this had been among the most sacred places in India. During the appearance of the tortoise *avatāra*, when the demons and demigods had been churning immortal nectar, a drop of that nectar had fallen here. Since then, every six and twelve years certain auspicious planets form a jug, and this jug, filled with immortal nectar, is said to pour that nectar upon the Triveṇī. Lord Rāmacandra and Hanumān visited Prayāga, and here Lord Caitanya taught Rūpa Gosvāmī the science of devotional service. Prabhupāda said he had also lived in Allahabad with his wife and family, and Śrīla Bhatisiddhanta Sarasvatī had initiated him at Allahabad's Rūpa Gosvāmī Gauḍīya Maṭha in 1932. As for the Melās, anyone who came and bathed at the auspicious times when the *prāṇa* (life airs) were pouring down from the heavens was guaranteed either promotion to the heavenly planets or liberation.

Prabhupāda said that although most of the saints and *sādhus* present were inauthentic, many were perfect *yogīs*, some of them three and four hundred years old. These *yogīs*, from remote parts of India, would come out for the Melā and then return to seclusion. "I have personally seen," he said, "that they take bath in the Ganges and come up in the seven sacred rivers. They go down in the Ganges and come up in the Godāvarī River. Then they go down and come up in the Kṛṣṇa River, and go down, like that." The devotees, therefore, should respect everyone who attended the Melā.

"So actually it's true," one of the devotees inquired, "that just by bathing here they are liberated?" "Yes," Prabhupāda said, "it's true. They come here for liberation. But we have not come for liberation. We have come to preach. Being engaged in Kṛṣṇa's unalloyed devotional service, we are already liberated. We are not interested in liberation. We have come to preach devotional service."

After *kīrtana* Prabhupāda lectured on *Śrīmad-Bhāgavatam* resuming the story of Ajāmila. This particular story, with its glorification of the Lord's holy name, seemed especially relevant. The holy name was so powerful that by chanting only once Ajāmila had been saved. Chanting, therefore, was far more beneficial than the *prāṇa* coming down from the constellations.

As a result of the devotee's *kīrtana*, thousands would stream into ISKCON's large paṇḍāl to see the Rādhā-Kṛṣṇa Deities and take *prasāda*. ISKCON had the only Kṛṣṇa Deity at the whole Melā, and thousands would line up to see Him. Prabhupāda would speak in English in the morning and in Hindi at night, and his evening *kīrtanas* in the paṇḍāl became a great success. The Western *sādhus* with women and little children were a great curiosity to behold.

Prabhupāda also arranged for mass *prasāda* distribution. He had assigned Revatīnandana and a few helpers to cook almost nonstop over two small wood fires in the kitchen shed. Some nights the devotees would cook vegetables and halava or vegetables and puris for as many as seven hundred people. ISKCON's impact on the Melā pleased Prabhupāda.

He wrote: "In the meantime our program for touring India has been going with all success in every place we are invited. Now we have come to the Ardha-kumbha-melā at Prayāga (Allahabad) and we have got undisputed prominence amongst all groups here in the large gathering."

And finally from the Sixth Volume, Seventh Chapter, the main Kumbha-melā of January of 1977 is described as follows: Śrīla Prabhupāda wanted to travel with a group of his disciples by train to Allahabad. But when a devotee went to buy tickets, he discovered that all seats had long been purchased; there was no chance of making reservations for Allahabad so close to Kumbha-melā. One of Śrīla Prabhupāda's Bombay friends, however, a Mr. Gupta, held a high position with the Central Railway of India, and at Prabhupāda's request, arranged for a special, private car, exclusively for Prabhupāda and his disciples, on a train to Allahabad.

Early on the morning of January 11, 1977, Śrīla Prabhupāda embarked on the twenty-

four-hour-plus train ride from Bombay to Allahabad. He was sharing his first-class compartment with Rāmeśvara Swami, Jagadiśa, and Hari Śauri, and even as the train pulled out of the station, Prabhupāda was preaching.

They arrived at nine a.m., and half a dozen of Śrīla Prabhupāda's *sannyāsī* disciples, along with a *kīrtana* party of about fifty devotees, were there to greet him. They had brought Prabhupāda's car down from Delhi, and he rode the short distance from the station to the Melā site. Thousands of pilgrims, on foot and in rickshas, crowded the streets, making Prabhupāda's progress by car slow. Finally the road ended, but the traffic continued onto the sandy flats surrounding the Triveṇī. Here, within a few days, a city of tents had sprung up. Two million had camped already, with millions more arriving daily. Every spiritual group in India had its bamboo-fenced compound of tents.

As the car inched along, Prabhupāda smiled to see a group of his disciples strolling among the camps and performing *hari-nāma-kīrtana*. But not until he passed through the congested main area of camps to the far end of the Triveṇī did he reach the ISKCON camp. The ISKCON tents, most of which had been erected about half an hour before Śrīla Prabhupāda's arrival, were located near a railway bridge on an island called Gaṅgādvipa; and the Triveṇī bathing area was a twenty minute walk away.

The devotees crowded into Śrīla Prabhupāda's tent for *guru-pūjā* (worship of the spiritual master) and *Śrīmad-Bhāgavatam* class. They had no garland for him, but he said nothing about it. By the time he had ended his short lecture, the sun had risen. He asked Hari Śauri to put his cot outdoors, where he rested and later took massage in the sunshine. During his massage, Prabhupāda looked over at the railroad bridge and said that he remembered this bridge from his former days in Allahabad. He said that his father had been cremated under the bridge on the same island of Gaṅgādvipa in 1930.

January 14, Śrīla Prabhupāda's third day in Allahabad, was the first day of Kumbha-melā bathing and would be a special opportunity for book distribution. An ISKCON chanting party of about fifty men and several Indian *gurukula* boys was very well received as they traveled throughout the Melā area. At one-thirty p.m., the time of auspicious bathing, the *kīrtana* party made its way to the Triveṇī. As they approached, the police cleared a path for them all the way to the water. By evening they had distributed eight thousand books, and, for the first time since they had arrived, Prabhupāda expressed his pleasure at their success. He ordered some of the *sannyāsīs* to stay at the Melā until all the books were distributed.

The next morning, despite ill health, Prabhupāda took a walk. Surrounded by about twenty-five disciples, he walked slowly. Although he was a small figure surrounded by tall *sannyāsīs*, the Kumbha-melā pilgrims were easily able to recognize his preeminent position, and they would break through the ranks of devotees and offer *dandavats* (obeisances) before him. When Prabhupāda saw people approaching, he would stop walking and let them touch his feet, despite the objections of his disciples. He was already sick, and he had explained in his books that a devotee can become ill if sinful people touch his feet. Still, he did not object.

Śrīla Prabhupāda was scheduled to stay at the Melā through January 21, but his disciples pressed him to go to a place more suitable for his health. Rarely had any of them seen him so sick, and they worried. "But my only ambition," said Prabhupāda, "is that so many people can become enlightened."

13) Āḍāila-grāma (Alarkpur/Arail)

Vallabha Ācārya

As mentioned in the *Śrī Caitanya-caritāmṛta* (*Madhya* 19.60-61), during Śrī Caitanya Mahāprabhu's second visit of Prayāga, the great learned scholar of Vaiṣṇavism, Vallabha Ācārya, went to see the Lord at Triveṇī: "Śrī Caitanya Mahāprabhu selected His residence beside the confluence of the Ganges and Yamunā at a place called Triveṇī. The two brothers, Śrī Rūpa and Śrī Vallabha, selected their residence near the Lord's. At that time, Vallabha Ācārya was staying at Āḍāila-grāma, and when he heard that Śrī Caitanya Mahāprabhu had arrived, he went to His place to see Him."

Śrīla Prabhupāda comments on the *Śrī Caitanya-caritāmṛta* (*Madhya* 19.61) about the glories and pastimes of Vallabha Ācārya: "Vallabha Ācārya was a great learned scholar of Vaiṣṇavism. In the beginning he was very much devoted to Śrī Caitanya Mahāprabhu, but since he thought that he could not receive proper respect from Him, he later joined the Viṣṇusvāmī sect and became *ācārya* of that sect. His sect is celebrated as the Vallabhācārya-sampradāya...Āḍāila-grāma, where he was staying, was near the confluence of the Rivers Ganges and Yamunā on the other side of Yamunā, about one mile from the river...

"Vallabha Ācārya was originally from a place in southern India called Trailaṅga. There is a railway station there called Nidāḍābhalu. Sixteen miles from that station is a village called Kāṅkaḍabāḍa, or Kākuṅrapādhu...In someone else's opinion, Vallabha Ācarya appeared near the village named Cāṅpā-jhāra-grāma, which is near the railway station named Rājima in Madhya Pradesh...After studying for eleven years at Vārāṇasī, Vallabha Ācārya returned home...After that, he traveled throughout India thrice on trips lasting six years each. Thus he passed eighteen years and became victorious in his discussions of the revealed scriptures. When he was thirty years old, he married Mahā-Lakṣmī...Near Govardhana Hill he established a Deity in the valley. Finally he came to Āḍāila, which is on the other side of Prayāga.

"Vallabha Ācārya had two sons, Gopīnātha and Viṭhṭhaleśvara, and in his old age he accepted the renounced order. In 1452 Śakābda Era, he passed away from the material world at Vārāṇasī. His book known as *Ṣoḍaśa-grantha* and his commentaries on *Vedānta-sūtra* (*Anubhāṣya*) and *Śrīmad-Bhāgavatam* (*Subodhinī*) are very famous. He has written many other books besides."

Once meeting Śrī Caitanya Mahāprabhu, Vallabha Ācārya offered his obeisances to Him, and the Lord embraced him. They then discussed the transcendental topics of Lord Kṛṣṇa. After the discussions, Vallabha Ācārya invited the Lord to his house for lunch. He then placed the Lord and His associates aboard a boat that crossed the River Yamunā. As soon as Śrī Caitanya Mahāprabhu saw the Yamunā, He immediately jumped into her water. Everyone aboard pulled the Lord out of the water. As soon as He was on the boat's platform, the Lord began to dance! Because of the Lord's dancing and heavy weight, the boat began to rock and fill with water and so appeared to be on the verge of sinking! Śrī Caitanya Mahāprabhu tried to restrain His ecstatic love, but it could not be checked. After some time, the Lord understood the circumstances and finally began to calm down, and thus the boat reached Āḍāila safely.

Upon arriving at the house, the Lord was properly received and then offered lunch

prasāda. While Vallabha Ācārya was massaging the Lord's legs, one respectable scholarly devotee by the name of Raghupati Upādhyāya arrived. He was requested by the Lord to describe Lord Kṛṣṇa with some verses that he had personally composed. Upon hearing them, Śrī Caitanya Mahāprabhu was overwhelmed with ecstatic love. The Lord asked him, "According to your decision, who is the foremost being?" Raghupati replied, "Lord Śyāmasundara is the Supreme Form." The Lord then asked, "Of all Kṛṣṇa's abodes, which do you think is the best?" The learned scholar answered, "Madhupurī, or Mathurā-dhāma, is certainly the best." Śrī Caitanya Mahāprabhu continued questioning, "Of the three ages of Kṛṣṇa (childhood, boyhood, and fresh youth), which do you consider best?" The respectable gentleman answered, "Fresh youth is the best age." Finally, the Lord asked, "Among all the mellows, which do you consider best?" The great devotee replied, "The mellow of conjugal love is supermost." Śrī Caitanya Mahāprabhu concluded by saying, "You have certainly given first class conclusions." The Lord then embraced Raghupati Upādhyāya, and they both began to dance.

Again from the *Śrī Caitanya-caritāmṛta* (*Madhya* 19.111-113), we learn of the Lord's return to Prayāga: "Vallabha Ācārya then decided not to keep Śrī Caitanya Mahāprabhu at Āḍāila because the Lord had jumped in the River Yamunā in ecstatic love. Therefore he decided to bring Him to Prayāga. Vallabha Ācārya said: 'If anyone likes, he can go to Prayāga and extend invitations to the Lord.' In this way he took the Lord with him and departed for Prayāga. Vallabha Ācārya avoided the River Yamunā. Putting the Lord on a boat in the River Ganges, he went with Him to Prayāga."

According to the *Śrī Caitanya-caritāmṛta*, the village where Vallabha Ācārya lived when Śrī Caitanya Mahāprabhu visited him was called Āḍāila-grāma. According to the present local residents at the house of Vallabha Ācārya, the Āḍāila-grāma area was known as Alarkpur. Vallabha Ācārya lived at this residence between the ages of nineteen and fifty-two, before leaving this mortal world at Vārāṇasī. At the time of Vallabha Ācārya, the Alarkpur area was eight kilometres in diametre. Today, the entire area is known as Arail and has been divided into eight separate villages. Vallabha Ācārya's residence, which is known as Prabhu-baitaka, is presently located in the village known as Deorakh. It is approximately 3 kilometres south of Arail-ghāṭa, which is near Triveṇī, on the bank of the River Yamunā.

As already mentioned, Vallabha Ācārya left this planet at Vārāṇasī (120 kilometres east of Prayāga), but there are different versions regarding how he disappeared. According to the version told in Arail, at the age of fifty-two, Vallabha left Prayāga and went to Hanumān-ghāṭa in Vārāṇasī, where he spoke on *Śrīmad-Bhāgavatam* for fifteen days and then entered the River Gaṅgā, not to be seen again. Another version is that one day he went to bathe at Hanumān-ghāṭa and the local people saw a brilliant light ascending the sky from the earth. In the presence of a host of spectators, he ascended the sky and disappeared. That pastime took place in the year 1531 A.D. Also, some people say his *samādhi* is in Gokula near Vṛndāvana.

14) Kāśī (Avimukta/Vārāṇasī)

In the *Śrīmad-Bhāgavatam* (12.13.17) the city of Kāśī is glorified as one of the most exalted *tīrthas*: "O *brāhmaṇas*, in the same way that the city of Kāśī is unexcelled among holy places, *Śrīmad-Bhāgavatam* is supreme among all the *Purāṇas*." In the *Śiva Purāṇa*

(*Koṭi-rudra-saṁhitā* 23.14) it is stated: "People of all castes and of all stages of life—whether children, youths, or aged—if they die in my city of Kāśī, they are undoubtedly liberated." Also, in the *Padma Purāṇa*: "Varaṇā and Asī are two rivers and in between them is a *kṣetra* (holy place) that has no equal in excellence on earth."

In the *Kūrma Purāṇa*: "Vārāṇasī is the city between the Rivers Varaṇā and Asī." According to the *Skanda Purāṇa*: "These two rivers were created and placed in position to guard against the entrance of evil. One is named Varaṇā (the avertor) and the other, Asī (the sword)."

The *Vāmana Purāṇa* says: "Those two rivers originated from the primeval Puruṣa at the beginning of creation. The Varaṇā was created from the right foot of the Lord, and the Asī from the left foot. The tract of land lying between them is the best place of pilgrimage in the three worlds and is potent enough to destroy all sins. It has qualities that do not exist in heaven, earth, or the nether world."

And finally, in the *Brahma-vaivarta Purāṇa*, it is mentioned: "All *tīrthas*, cities, rivers, streams, lakes, oceans, sages, and demigods desire to reside in Kāśī. The minds of those who have worshiped Kāśī will not be pleased in any other *tīrtha*."

Lord Viṣṇu's perspiration

Long before the appearance of Gaṅgāmayī, just after the great deluge, the Supreme Personality of Godhead, Lord Viṣṇu, sent Lord Śiva and the goddess Śakti (Pārvatī) to this planet, where they created a beautiful, radiant, auspicious city. Upon the request of Lord Śiva, Mahā-Viṣṇu came there to perform austerities in order to create the rest of the universe. Mahā-Viṣṇu first made a beautiful *puṣkariṇī* (lotus pond) with his *cakra*, which eventually filled up with His own perspiration. When Lord Śiva saw all the water, he shook his head in wonder and one of his earrings fell into the water. Mahā-Viṣṇu then said, "O Lord, by virtue of the dropping of your pearl earring here, let this holy spot become the greatest of all holy spots that grant salvation. O mighty Lord, since that brilliance, which cannot be adequately described, shines here, let this abode be known as Kāśī." Thus Cakra-puṣkariṇī became known as Maṇikarṇikā.

Other narrations say that either Lord Śiva's crest-jewel or Pārvatī's earring fell into the *kuṇḍa* while they were bathing. All narrations, however, describe Maṇikarṇikā as the world's first *tīrtha*, dug out by Mahā-Viṣṇu's *cakra* and filled with His own perspiration.

Lord Brahmā's fifth head

The *Purāṇas* mention that Kāśī was first the abode of Lord Viṣṇu. No one can obtain liberation in a sacred place without Lord Viṣṇu's mercy. This city was formerly the abode of Lord Viṣṇu, who is the bestower of salvation to all creatures and who destroys everyone's sins. The following narration from the *Nārada Purāṇa* (*Uttara-bhāga* 29), explains how Lord Śiva cut off the fifth head of Lord Brahmā.

"Once upon a time, Lord Śaṅkara went to see Lord Brahmā. After Śiva offered his obeisances, he was extremely delighted to hear the four *Vedas* being chanted by four of Brahmā's five beautiful heads. Upon observing the fifth head to be very impudent and arrogant, Śiva became very malicious. Then the three-eyed Lord, who was born of anger, could not control his own daring anger, so with the tip of his nail he cut off the fifth head of Brahmā! That head of Brahmā stuck to Śiva's left hand and remained fixed there. Lord Brahmā became very sad and stared at Lord Śiva. Śiva therefore became ashamed and quickly left the abode of Lord Brahmā.

"Lord Śiva tried every possible way to remove the head, but it was impossible, which only made him perturbed and perplexed. In a worried condition, he remembered Lord Viṣṇu, who is always carried by Garuḍa. At that moment, Lord Viṣṇu manifested Himself before him. Upon seeing Viṣṇu, Śiva became pale and offered his humble obeisances. Then Lord Viṣṇu began to console Lord Śiva and spoke the following words, 'In as much as the head of Lord Brahmā has been cut off, O Śambhu, you have committed a grave sin. Therefore, you must experience the results of such an act for a short period. *Karma* (action) performed by one, whether auspicious or inauspicious, must be realized. *Karma* does not perish without being experienced. What can I do? On seeing your miserable condition, my *prāṇas* are agitated and dispirited. In My opinion, even the most serious sins are not equal to *brahma-hatyā*. You are the spiritual master of the world and one of the *mahājanas*, but since this sin has been incurred, you are not peaceful. The terrible personified form of *brahma-hatyā* smells; she is senile and sickly, and she captures all offenders. Hence, you should not stay anywhere for a long time, but for your own benefit, you must wander on pilgrimage continuously for twelve years. You must wander with the skull, begging for alms, washing your left hand in all the holy rivers and *kuṇḍas*. Then, O Lord of the *devas*, you will become pure and liberated from this sin.' Thus being instructed by Lord Viṣṇu, Lord Śiva began his journey.

"Lord Śiva washed his left hand at every holy place he visited, and then after wandering for three years, he came to the abode of Nara and Nārāyaṇa Ṛṣis in Badarikāśrama. He begged alms from Nārāyaṇa Ṛṣi and then remained there for three years. Afterwards, Lord Śiva went to Kurukṣetra and remained under the waters of Brahma-hrada for three

more years. Then he prayed to Lord Viṣṇu, who eventually appeared and told Śiva to continue wandering until he reached Kāśī. Upon reaching Kāśī, Lord Śiva observed that the personified *brahma-hatyā* was not following him anymore, since she was not allowed inside Kāśī.

"Lord Śiva began to feel very satisfied being in a *tirtha* belonging to Lord Viṣṇu. Thereafter, Lord Śiva chanted very enthusiastically the following prayer, 'All glories and victories, O Lord of the universe, O Lord Viṣṇu, who is knowable only through the *Vedas*. O suppressor of the demon Madhu, O Nṛsiṁha, O Lord who rides on Garuḍa, O Mādhava, O primeval Lord, O Rāma, the lover of the Vrajavāsīs, O Lord of Rādhā, O Kṛṣṇa, O ocean of kindness. O destroyer of anguish, O lotus-eyed one, O expert in lifting the mountain Govardhana. O Paraśurāma, O Buddha, O Kalki, O Lord of sacred flame and name, O Lord of the Raghus, O Lord of the Yādavas, O Lord having the luster of fresh rain clouds, O Lord of the goddess of fortune. O Lord who was bound with a rope by Your mother, O Lord fond of fresh butter, O Lord of the *gopas* (cowherd boys), O destroyer of the demons Agha, Baka, Vṛṣa, Keśī, and Pūtanā, O friend of Sudhama, O bestower of boons, I seek refuge in Your lotus feet, which destroy all sins. Please protect me. There is no one else who can grant liberation other than You, the original Puruṣa. Be pleased with me and fulfill my request.' Upon hearing these words, Lord Viṣṇu, who always favors His devotees, suddenly appeared before Lord Śambhu (Śiva).

"Lord Viṣṇu then said to Śiva, 'Choose a boon. I am very pleased with your prayer.' Then Lord Śiva replied, 'I wish to stay in Your holy center, since the *brahma-hatyā* is restricted from entering here. O Lord of Garuḍa, be merciful to me and grant me the gift of residing here, otherwise the sin of *brahma-hatyā* will harass me. Being stationed here, I will be worshiped by the three worlds.' Lord Viṣṇu accepted Lord Śiva's request by saying, 'Let it be so'. The devotees know this ancient holy place as Keśava. Tears gushed out of the eyes of Lord Viṣṇu, who was overwhelmed with compassion, thus creating the lake named Bindu-saras. Upon the request of Lord Viṣṇu, Śiva took his bath, and then the skull of Brahmā finally fell from his hand. That sacred lake became famous by the name Kapāla-mocana. Since Lord Viṣṇu was captured by the sincere devotional attitude of Śiva, He stationed Himself nearby under the name of Bindu-Mādhava, and gave His own abode to Śiva, the trident-bearing Lord."

Gaṅgā-māhātmyam

The following glorification of Gaṅgā is from the *Skanda Purāṇa* (*Kāśī-khaṇḍa* 27) and is translated by H.G. Gopiparāṇadhana Dāsa.

1

skanda uvāca
vārāṇasīti prathitaṁ
yathā cānanda-kānanam
tathā ca kathayāmiha
deva-devena bhāṣitam

Skanda said: I will now recount how the "forest of bliss" became famous by the name Vārāṇasī. This was described by the chief of the demigods, Lord Śiva.

2

īśvara uvāca
niśāmaya mahā-bāho
viṣṇo trai-lokya-sundara
prāptaṁ vārāṇasīty ākhyām
avimuktaṁ yathā tathā

Lord Śiva said: O might-armed Viṣṇu, beauty of the three worlds, please hear how the place Avimukta became known as Vārāṇasī.

3-4

nirdagdhān sāgarāñ chrutvā
kapila-krodha-vahninā
aśvamedhāśva-saṁyuktān
pūrvajān svān bhagīrathaḥ

sūrya-vaṁśe mahā-tejā
rājā parama-dhārmikaḥ
arirādhayiṣur gaṅgāṁ
tapase kṛta-niścayaḥ

Bhagīratha was a very potent king of the Sūrya dynasty. He was supremely religious. When he heard that his predecessors, accompanied by the sacred horse of the Aśvamedha sacrifice, had been burned to death by the fire generated from the anger of Lord Kapila, he decided to perform austerities for the purpose of worshiping Gaṅgā.

5

himavantaṁ naga-śreṣṭham
amātya-nyasta-rājya-dhūḥ
jagāma yaśasāṁ rāśir
uddidhīrṣuḥ pitāmahān

Wanting to deliver his forefathers, that repository of great fame turned over to his ministers the anxieties of ruling the kingdom and went to the best of mountain ranges, the Himālayas.

6

brahma-śāpāgni-nirdagdhān
mahā-durgati-gān api
vinā tri-mārga-gāṁ viṣṇo
ko jantūṁs tri-divaṁ nayet

Without the help of the one who travels through the three worlds (Gaṅgā), how can anyone expect to deliver to heaven those living beings who have been burned to ashes by a brahminical curse and have fallen into a situation of horrible distress?

7

mamaiva sā parā-mūrtis
toya-rūpā śivātmikā

brahmāṇḍānām anekānām
ādhāraḥ prakṛtiḥ parā

She is my own transcendental body in the form of water. Her substance is all-auspicious. She is the transcendental source of creation and the foundation of countless universes.

8

śuddha-vidyā-svarūpā ca
tri-śaktiḥ karuṇātmikā
ānandāmṛta-rūpā ca
śuddha-dharma-svarūpiṇī

Her essential nature is pure knowledge. She contains the three energies of matter and is full of compassion. Her form is that of blissful nectar, She is the embodiment of the pure principles of religion.

9

yām etāṁ jagatāṁ dhātrīṁ
dhārayāmi sva-līlayā
viśvasya rakṣaṇārthāya
para-brahma-svarūpiṇīm

As my own pastime, I carry this mother of the worlds—who is nondifferent from the Supreme Absolute Truth—in order to protect the entire universe.

10-12

trai-lokyeyāni tīrthāni
puṇya-kṣetrāṇi yāni ca
sarvatra sarve ye dharmāḥ
sarva-yajñāḥ sa-dakṣiṇāḥ

tapāṁsi viṣṇo sarvāṇi
śrutiḥ sāṅgā catur-vidhā
ahaṁ ca tvaṁ ca kaś cāpi
devatānāṁ gaṇāś ca ye

puruṣārthāś ca sarve vai
śaktyo vividhāś ca yāḥ
gaṅgāyāṁ sarva evaite
sūkṣma-rūpeṇa saṁsthitāḥ

O Viṣṇu, within Gaṅgā reside in subtle form all the pilgrimage places and holy sites of the three worlds, all the principles of religion, all sacrificies with the rewards for their priests, all austere penances, the *Vedas* with their four divisions and secondary texts, myself, You, Lord Brahmā, all the demigods in their various groups, all the goals of human endeavor, and the various universal energies.

13

sa snātaḥ sarva-tīrtheṣu
sarva-kratuṣu dīkṣitaḥ
cīrṇa-sarva-vrataḥ so
'pi yas tu gaṅgāṁ niṣevate

One who serves Gaṅgā has bathed in all the holy places, has been initiated into all the Vedic sacrifices, and has undertaken all pious vows.

14

tapāṁsi tena taptāni
sarva-dāna-pradaḥ sa ca
sa prāpta-yoga-niyamo
yas tu gaṅgāṁ niṣevate

One who serves Gaṅgā has executed all difficult austerities, given all kinds of charity, and perfected the regulative practices of *yoga.*

15

sarva-varṇāśramebhyaś ca
veda-vidbhyaś ca vai tathā
śāstrārtha-pāragebhyaś
ca gaṅgā-snāyi viśiṣyate

One who has bathed in Gaṅgā is better than all the followers of the *varṇāśrama* system, all knowers of the *Vedas*, and all who have become expert in the purports of various scriptures.

16

mano-vāk-kāya-jair doṣair
duṣṭo bahu-vidhair api

vīkṣya gaṅgāṁ bhavet pūtaḥ
puruṣo nātra saṁśayaḥ

Although a person may be contaminated by many kinds of faults of the body, mind, and speech, if he just sees Gaṅgā he becomes completely purified, without a doubt.

17

kṛte sarvatra tīrthāni
tretāyāṁ puṣkaraṁ param
dvāpare tu kuru-kṣetraṁ
kalau gaṅgaiva kevalam

In Kṛta-yuga holy places are found everywhere. In Tretā-yuga the only holy place is Puṣkara. In Dvāpara-yuga the only holy place is Kurukṣetra. And in Kali the only holy place is Gaṅgā.

18

pūrva-janmāntarābhyāsa-
vāsanā-vaśato hare
gaṅgā-tīre nivāsaḥ syān
mad-anugrahataḥ parāt

O Hari, one can take up residence on the shore of Gaṅgā only on the strength of the accumulated credits of many auspicious practices in previous lives and only after obtaining my favor.

19

dhyānaṁ kṛte mokṣa-hetus
tretāyāṁ tac ca vai tapaḥ
dvāpare tah vayaṁ yajñāḥ
kalau gaṅgaiva kevalam

In Kṛta-yuga meditation is the cause of liberation. In Tretā austerities are. In Dvāpara persons like us perform sacrifices. But in Kali the only cause of liberation is Gaṅgā.

20

yo deha-patanād yāvad
gaṅgā-tīraṁ na muñcati
sa hi vedānta-vid yogī
brahmācārya-vratī sadā

One who never leaves the shore of Gaṅgā until his body falls dead is a *yogī* who perfectly knows *Vedānta*, and he perpetually follows the vow of celibacy.

21

kalau kaluṣa-cittānāṁ
para-dravya-ratātmanām
vidhi-hīna-kriyāṇāṁ ca
gatir gaṅgāṁ vinā na hi

In Kali-yuga there is no salvation other than Gaṅgā for those whose minds are full of contamination, who are eager to take the property of others, and who act without regard to regulative principles.

22

alakṣmīḥ kāla-karṇī ca
duḥsvapno durvicintitam
gaṅgā gaṅgeti japanāt
tāni nopaviśanti hi

If one simply chants "Gaṅgā! Gaṅgā!" he will never experience poverty, misfortune, evil dreams, or anxious thoughts.

23

gaṅgā hi sarva-bhūtānām
ihāmutra phala-pradā
bhāvānurūpato viṣṇo
sadā sarva-jagad-dhitā

Gaṅgā rewards the fulfillment of every creature's desires—according to their specific wishes—in both this world and the next. She always acts for the benefit of the whole world.

24

yajña-dāna-tapo-yoga-
japāḥ sa-niyamā yamāḥ
gaṅgā-sevā-sahasrāṁśaṁ
na labhante kalau hare

O Hari, in Kali-yuga the combined practices of sacrifice, charity, austerity, *yoga*, chanting, regulative disciplines, and ethical principles cannot yield one thousandth of what is achieved by serving Gaṅgā.

25

kim aṣṭāṅgena yogena
kim tapobhiḥ kim adhvaraiḥ
vāsa eva hi gaṅgāyāṁ
brahma-jñānasya kāraṇam

What is the value of the eightfold practice of *yoga*, of severe penances, and of Vedic sacrifices? Simply residing by Gaṅgā is enough to result in attaining knowledge of Brahman.

26

api dūra-sthitasyāpi
gaṅgā-māhātmya-vedinaḥ
ayogyasyāpi govinda
bhaktyā gaṅgā prasīdati

O Govinda, if someone learns about the glories of Gaṅgā—even if he lives far away from her and is otherwise disqualified—his devotion will satisfiy her.

27

śraddhā dharmaḥ paraḥ sūkṣmaḥ
śraddhā jñānaṁ parantapaḥ
śraddhā svargaś ca mokṣaś ca
śraddhayā sā prasīdati

Faith is the topmost, subtlest principle of religion, O conqueror of Your enemies. Faith is true knowledge. Faith is heaven and liberation. By faith, Gaṅgā is satisfied.

28

ajñāna-rāga-lobhādyaiḥ
puṁsāṁ sammūḍha-cetasām
śraddhā na jāyate dharme
gaṅgāyāṁ ca viśeṣataḥ

Persons whose minds are bewildered by ignorance, attachment, greed, and so on never develop faith in religion in general and in Gaṅgā in particular.

29

bahiḥ-sthitaṁ jalaṁ yadvan
nārikelāntare sthitam
tathā brahmāṇḍa-bāhya-sthāṁ
para-brahmāmbu jāhnavī

Just as the same water found outside is also present within a coconut, so the water of the Absolute Truth found outside the egg of the universe is also present within as Jāhnavī (Gaṅgā).

30

gaṅgā-lābhāt paro lābhaḥ
kvacid anyo na vidyate
tasmād gaṅgām upāsīta
gaṅgaiva paramaḥ pumān

If one achieves Gaṅgā, no other gain remains to be achieved. Therefore Gaṅgā should be worshiped, because Gaṅgā is nondifferent from the Supreme Person.

31

śaktasya paṇḍitasyāpi
guṇino dāna-śīlinaḥ
gaṅgā-snāna-vihīnasya
hare janma nirarthakam

One may be competent, learned, virtuous, and charitable, but if he has never bathed in Gaṅgā, O Hari, his life is wasted.

32

vṛthā kulaṁ vṛthā vidyā
vṛthā yajñā vṛthā tapaḥ
vṛthā dānāni tasyeha
kalau gaṅgāṁ na yo bhajet

If someone does not worship Gaṅgā in Kali-yuga, his good birth, education,

sacrifices, austerities, and charitable acts
are all useless.

33

guṇavat-pātra-pūjāyāṁ
na syād vai tādṛśaṁ phalam
yathā gaṅgā-jala-snāna-
pūjane vidhinā phalam

One cannot obtain the same benefit
from worshiping the most deserving person
as he can from bathing in Gaṅgā and worshiping her according to prescribed
procedures.

34

mama tejo-'gni-garbheyaṁ
mama vīryāti-saṁvṛtā
dāhikā sarva-doṣāṇāṁ
sarva-pāpa-vināśinī

She is a reservoir of the fire of my energy and is totally encompassed by my
potency. She burns away all faults and destroys all sins.

35

smaraṇād eva gaṅgāyāḥ
pāpa-saṅghāta-pañjaram
śatadhā bhedam āyāti
girir vajra-hato yathā

If a person simply remembers Gaṅgā, the
cage of his accumulated sins is smashed into
a hundred pieces, just like a mountain struck
by Indra's thunderbolt.

36

gaṅgāṁ gacchati yas tv eko
yas tu bhaktyānumodayet
tayos tulyaṁ phalaṁ prāhur
bhaktir evātra kāraṇam

It is said that the results of traveling
alone to Gaṅgā and of praising that endeavor
with devotion are equal. The actual cause of
approaching Gaṅgā is devotion.

37

gacchaṁs tiṣṭhañ japan dhyāyan
bhuñjañ jāgrat svapan vadan
yaḥ smaret satataṁ gaṅgāṁ
sa hi mucyeta bandhanāt

One who constantly remembers Gaṅgā
while moving, standing, chanting, meditating, eating, staying awake, sleeping, and
speaking will certainly become freed from all
bondage.

38-39

pitṝn uddiśya yo bhaktyā
pāyasaṁ madhu-saṁyutam
guḍa-sarpis-tilaiḥ sārdhaṁ
gaṅgāmbhasi vinikṣipet

tṛptā bhavanti pitaras
tasya varṣa-śataṁ hare
yacchanti vividhān kāmān
parituṣṭāḥ pitāmahāḥ

If one offers for the sake of his forefathers condensed milk mixed with honey and
gur, ghee and sesame seeds, throwing this
mixture into Gaṅgā, then his forefathers become pleased with him. For one hundred
years, O Hari, these satisfied ancestors fulfill all his desires.

40

liṅge sampūjite sarvam
arcitaṁ syāj jagad yathā
gaṅgā-snānena labhate
sarva-tīrtha-phalaṁ tathā

In the same way as the entire universe
is worshiped by worshiping the Śiva-liṅga,
so by bathing in Gaṅgā one gets the results
of visiting all holy places.

41

gaṅgāyāṁ tu naraḥ snātvā
yo liṅgaṁ nityam arcati
ekena janmanā muktiṁ
parāṁ prāpnoti sa dhruvam

And a man who both bathes in Gaṅgā and regularly worships the Śiva-liṅgā is certain to obtain ultimate liberation in a single lifetime.

42

agnihotraṁ ca yajñāś ca
vrata-dāna-tapāṁsi ca
gaṅgāyāṁ liṅga pūjāyāḥ
koṭy-aṁśenāpi no samāh

Offerings of oblations, ritual sacrifices, vows, charity, and penances are all not as effective as one millionth of the effect of worshiping a Śiva-liṅga near Gaṅgā.

43

gaṅgāṁ gantuṁ viniścitya
kṛtvā śraddhādikaṁ gṛhe
sthitasya samyak saṅkalpāt
tasya nandanti pūrva-jāḥ

If one performs the *śraddhā* ceremony and its corrolaries in his home and decides to travel to Gaṅgā, his forefathers are delighted by his intention even if he remains home.

44

pāpāni ca rudanty āśu
hā kva yāsyāma ity alam
lobha-mohādibhiḥ sārdhaṁ
mantrayanti punaḥ punaḥ

His sins quickly cry out, "Alas, where can we go?" Together with his greed, delusion, and so on, they go on commisserating among one another.

45

yathā na gaṅgāṁ yāty eṣa
tathā vighnaṁ prakurmahe
gaṅgāṁ gato yathā caiṣa
na ucchittiṁ vidhāsyati

"As long as he never went to Gaṅgā we were able to create disturbances from him, but now that he has gone to Gaṅgā he is going to eradicate us."

46

gṛhād gaṅgāvagāhārthaṁ
gacchatas tu pade pade
nirāśāni vrajanty eva
pāpāny asya śarīrataḥ

If one goes from his house to take bath in Gaṅgā, at every step of his walking sins leave his body, having lost all hope to influence him.

47

pūrva-janma-kṛtaiḥ puṇyais
tyaktvā lobhādikaṁ hare
vyudasya sarva-vighnaughān
gaṅgāṁ prāpnoti puṇya-vān

After having put aside greed and other vices on the strength of one's pious works in previous lives and having abandoned all the entanglements that obstruct one's spiritual progress, only then a pious person achieves Gaṅgā.

48

anuṣaṅgena maulyena
vāṇijyenāpi sevayā
kāmāsakto 'pi vā martyo
gaṅgā-snāto divaṁ vrajet

If a mortal bathes in Gaṅgā—whether rendering this service circumstantially, for payment, in the course of doing business, or with strong attachment to material desires—he will go to heaven.

49

anicchayāpi saṁspṛṣṭo
dahano hi yathā dahet
anicchayāpi saṁsnātā
gaṅgā pāpaṁ tathā dahet

In the same way as a fire burns even if touched unintentionally, so Gaṅgā burns one's sins even if bathed in unintentionally.

50

tāvad bhramati saṁsāre
yāvad gaṅgāṁ na sevate
saṁsevya gaṅgāṁ no jantur
bhava-kleśaṁ prapaśyati

One has to wander in the cycle of birth and death as long as he has not served Gaṅgā. But after serving Gaṅgā a living being no longer will have to experience the suffering of material existence.

51

yo gaṅgāmbhasi nisnāto
bhaktyā santyakta-saṁśayaḥ
manuṣya-carmaṇānaddhaḥ
sa devo nātra saṁśayaḥ

A person who takes bath in the water of Gaṅgā with devotion, giving up all doubts, becomes a demigod even while covered with the skin of a human body. There can be no doubt about this.

52

gaṅgā-snānārtham udyukto
madhye mārgam mṛto yadi
gaṅgā-snāna-phalaṁ so 'pi
tad āpnoti na saṁśayaḥ

If someone intends to bath in Gaṅgā but dies while on the road, he still achieves the results of bathing in Gaṅgā, without a doubt.

53

māhātmyaṁ ye ca gaṅgāyāḥ
śṛṇvanti ca paṭhanti ca
te 'py aśeṣair mahā-pāpair
mucyante nātra saṁśayaḥ

Those who hear and chant the glories of Gaṅgā become free from the effects of all the worst sins, without a doubt.

54

durbuddhayo durācārā
haitukā bahu-saṁśayāḥ
paśyanti mohitā viṣṇo
gaṅgām anya-nadīm iva

Persons whose intelligence and behavior are corrupt, who are mental speculators, and who are full of doubts, O Viṣṇu, see Gaṅgā in their delusion as if it were some ordinary river.

55

janmāntara kṛtair dānais
tapobhir niyamair vrataiḥ
iha janmani gaṅgāyāṁ
nṛṇāṁ bhaktiḥ prajāyate

Only by charity, austerities, regulative practices, and vows of previous lives can people develop faith in Gaṅgā during this life.

56

gaṅgā-bhakti-matām arthe
mahendrādi-pureṣu ca
harmyāni ramya-bhogāni
nirmitāni svayambhuvā

For those who have faith in Gaṅgā, self-born Brahmā has constructed special palaces with wonderful facilities for enjoyment in the heavenly cities of Mahendra and other demigods.

57-58

siddhayaḥ siddhi-liṅgāni
sparśa-liṅgāny anekaśaḥ
prāsādā ratna-racitās
cintāmaṇi-gaṇā api

gaṅgā-jalāntas tiṣṭhanti
kali-kalmaṣa-bhītitāḥ

ata eva hi saṁsevyā
kalau gaṅgeṣṭa-siddhi-dā

Out of fear of the contamination of Kali-yuga, all mystic perfections take up residence within the water of Gaṅgā, along with the symptoms of such perfections and the symptoms of material enjoyment, and also palaces constructed of gems and many *cintāmaṇi* stones. Therefore it is very desirable to serve Gaṅgā in Kali-yuga, when she can bestow all desired perfections.

59-60

sūryodaye tamāṁsiva
vajra-pāta-bhayān nagāḥ
tārksyekṣaṇād yathā sarpā
meghā vātāhatā iva

tattva-jñānād yathā mohaḥ
siṁhaṁ dṛṣṭvā yathā mṛgāḥ
tathā sarvāṇi pāpāni
yānti gaṅgekṣaṇāt kṣayam

As darkness goes away with the rising of the sun, mountains flee out of fear of being struck by lightning, delusion is dispelled by knowledge of the truth, and animals run away upon seeing a lion, so all sins are destroyed just by seeing Gaṅgā.

61-62

divyauṣadhair yathā rogā
lobhena ca yathā guṇāḥ
yathā grīṣmoṣma-sampattir
agādha-hrada-majjanāt

tūla-śailaḥ sphuliṅgena
yathā naśyati tat-kṣaṇāt
tathā doṣāḥ praṇaśyanti
gaṅgāmbhaḥ-sparśanād dhruvam

As diseases are immediately destroyed by medicines with divine potency, good character is immediately destroyed by greed, the heat of the summer is immediately destroyed by bathing in a deep lake, and a mountain of cotton is immediately destroyed by a single spark of fire, so upon simply touching the water of Gaṅgā all one's faults are certainly destroyed.

63-64

krodhena ca tapo yadvat
kāmena ca yathā matiḥ
anayena yathā lakṣmīr
vidyāmānena vai yathā

dambha-kauṭilya-māyābhir
yathā dharmo vinaśyati
tathā naśyanti pāpāni
gaṅgāyā darśanena tu

As the power of austerities is destroyed by anger, determination is destroyed by lust, the appearance of injustice destroys prosperity, and religion is destroyed by hypocrisy, duplicity, and fraud, so all sins are destroyed by seeing Gaṅgā.

65

mānuṣyaṁ durlabhaṁ prāpya
vidyut-sampāta-cañcalam
gaṅgāṁ yaḥ sevate so 'tra
buddheḥ pāraṁ paraṁ gataḥ

One who has attained this rare human life, which is as unsteady as a flash of lightning, has achieved the perfection of intelligence in this life if he serves Gaṅgā.

66

vidhūta-pāpā ye martyāḥ
paraṁ-jyotiḥ-svarūpiṇīm
sahasra-sūrya-pratimāṁ
gaṅgāṁ paśyanti te bhuvi

Those mortals who view Gaṅgā on this earth as having a divine form of transcendental light, equal to thousands of suns, are certainly free of all sins.

67

sādhāraṇāmbhasā pūrṇāṁ
sādhāraṇa-nadīm iva
paśyanti nāstikā gaṅgām
pāpopahata-locanāḥ

But faithless persons whose vision is ruined by sin consider her an ordinary river filled with ordinary water.

68

saṁsāra-mocakaś cāhaṁ
janānām anukampayā
gaṅgā-taraṅga-rūpeṇa
sopānaṁ nirmame divaḥ

Out of compassion for the people in general, I, the deliverer from material existence, produced this staircase to heaven in the form of Gaṅgā's waves.

69

sarva eva śubhaḥ kālaḥ
sarvo deśas tathā śubhaḥ
sarvo jano dāna-pātraṁ
śrīmatī-jāhnavī-taṭe

On the shores of Śrīmatī Jāhnavī, all times are auspicious, all places are auspicious, and every person is a fit receiver of charity.

70-73

yathāśvamedho yajñānāṁ
nagānāṁ himavān yathā
vratānāṁ ca yathā satyaṁ
dānānām abhayaṁ yathā

prāṇāyāmaś ca tapasāṁ
mantrāṇāṁ praṇavo yathā
dharmāṇām apy ahiṁsā ca
kāmyānāṁ śrīr yathā varā

yathātma-vidyā vidyānāṁ
strīṇāṁ gaurī yathottamā
sarva-deva-gaṇānāṁ ca
yathā tvaṁ puruṣottama

sarveṣām eva pātrāṇāṁ
śiva-bhakto yathā varaḥ
tathā sarveṣu tīrtheṣu
gaṅgā-tīrthaṁ viśiṣyate

As the Aśvamedha is the best of sacrifices, the Himālayas are the best of mountains, truth is the best of vows, fearlessness is the best of gifts, *prāṇāyāma* is the best austerity, *oṁ* is the best *mantra*, nonviolence is the best religious principle, the favor of the goddess of fortune is the best of blessings, the science of the self is the best of sciences, Gaurī is the best of women, You, O Supreme Personality, are the best of all the gods, and a devotee of Śiva is the best recipient of charity, so Gaṅgā-tīrtha is the best of holy places.

74

hare yaś cāvayor bhedaṁ
na karoti mahā-matiḥ
śiva-bhaktaḥ sa vijñeyo
mahā-pāśupataś ca saḥ

O Hari, one should be considered a devotee of Śiva, a great Pāśupata, who is intelligent enough not to see any difference between the two of us.

75

pāpa-pāṁsu-mahā-vātyā
pāpa-druma-kuṭhārikā
pāpendhana-davāgniś ca
gaṅgeyaṁ puṇya-vāhinī

This Gaṅgā, full of piety in her current, is like a mighty wind blowing away the dust of sin, an axe to cut down the tree of sin, or a forest fire to consume the dry wood of sin.

76

nānā-rūpāś ca pitaro
gāthā gāyanti sarvadā
api kaścit kule 'smākaṁ
gaṅgā-snāyī bhaviṣyati

The elevated forefathers in their various forms are always singing this song: "May someone take birth in our family who will bathe in Gaṅgā."

77-78

devarṣīn parisantarpya
dīnānāthāṁś ca duḥkhitān
śraddhayā vidhinā snātvā
dāsyate salilāñjalim

api naḥ sa kule bhūyāc
chive viṣṇau ca sāmya-dṛk
tad-ālaya-karo bhaktyā
tasya sammārjanādi-kṛt

"May such a descendant faithfully bathe in Gaṅgā following the prescribed rules, offering her a palmful of water after placating the demigods and sages, and also the poor, homeless, and miserable. May he see Lords Śiva and Viṣṇu as equal, and may he construct for them temples, which he will serve by cleaning and so on."

79

akāmo vā sa-kāmo vā
tiryag-yoni-gato 'pi vā
gaṅgāyāṁ yo mṛto martyo
narakaṁ sa na paśyati

If any mortal dies by Gaṅgā—be he free from desires, full of desires, or even in an animal species—he will not have to see hell.

80

tīrtham anyat praśaṁsanti
gaṅgā-tīre sthitāś ca ye
gaṅgāṁ na bahu manyante te
syur niraya-gāminaḥ

If those who are on the shore of Gaṅgā praise some other holy place and disregard the importance of Gaṅgā, they will be sure to go to hell.

81

māṁ ca tvāṁ caiva yo dveṣṭi
gaṅgāṁ ca puruṣādhamaḥ
svakīyaiḥ puruṣaiḥ sārdhaṁ
sa ghoraṁ narakaṁ vrajet

That lowest of men who envies me, You, and Gaṅgā will go to a horrible hell along with all his family and associates.

82

ṣaṣṭir gaṇa-sahasrāṇi
gaṅgāṁ rakṣanti sarvadā
abhaktānāṁ ca pāpānāṁ
vāse vighnaṁ prakurvate

There is an army of sixty thousand attendants who constantly guard Gaṅgā. They attack the homes of nondevotees and sinful persons.

83

kāma-krodha-mahā-moha-
lobhādini śitaiḥ śaraiḥ
ghnanti teṣāṁ manas tatra
sthitiṁ cāpanayanti ca

With sharp arrows of lust, anger, delusion, greed, and other enemies, they overwhelm the minds of these nondevotees and sinful persons.

84

gaṅgāṁ samāśrayed yasa
sa muniḥ sa ca paṇḍitaḥ
kṛta-kṛtyaḥ sa vijñeyaḥ
puruṣārtha-catuṣṭaye

Anyone who takes shelter of Gaṅgā is a sage and a scholar. He should be understood to be a completely successful person, one who has already achieved the four goals of human endeavor.

85

gaṅgāyāṁ ca sakṛt snāto
hayamedha-phalaṁ labhet

tarpayaṁś ca pitṝn tatra
tārayen narakārṇavāt

If one just once bathes in Gaṅgā, he receives the fruit of performing one hundred horse sacrifices. If he placates his forefathers there, he will be delivered from countless hells.

86

nairantāryeṇa gaṅgāyāṁ
māsaṁ yaḥ snāti puṇya-vān
śakra-loke sa vasati
yāvac chakraḥ sa pūrva-jaḥ

The pious person who bathes in Gaṅgā every day for a month will reside on the planet of Indra as his elder brother for as long as Indra lives.

87

abdaṁ yaḥ snāti gaṅgāyāṁ
nairantaryeṇa puṇya-bhāk
viṣṇor lokaṁ samāsadya
sa sukhaṁ saṁvasen naraḥ

If a pious person bathes in Gaṅgā every day for a year, he will achieve the planet of Viṣṇu and live there happily.

88

gaṅgāyāṁ snāti yo martyo
yāvaj jīvaṁ dine dine
jīvan-muktaḥ sa vijñeyo
dehānte mukta eva saḥ

A mortal who bathes in Gaṅgā every day for his entire life is to be understood as liberated even while in this body, and at the end of this body he becomes actually liberated.

89

tithi-nakṣatra-parvādi
nāpekṣyaṁ jāhnavī-jale
snāna-mātreṇa gaṅgāyāṁ
sañcitāghaṁ vinaśyati

In approaching the water of Jāhnavī, there are no calculations of proper date, lunar signs, or junctures of the month. Simply by bathing in Gaṅgā all one's accumulated sins are destroyed.

90

paṇḍito 'pi sa mūrkhaḥ
syāc chakti-yukto 'py aśaktikaḥ
yas tu bhāgīrathī-tīraṁ
sukha-sevyaṁ na saṁśrayet

Even a scholar is actually a fool and even a powerful person is actually powerless if they do not take shelter of Bhāgīrathī's shores, which are so easy to resort to.

91

kiṁ vāyuṣāpy arogeṇa
vikāsinyātha kiṁ śriyā
kiṁ vā buddhyā vimalayā
yadi gaṅgāṁ na sevate

What is the use of one's long life, good health, expansive prosperity, or purified intelligence if he never serves Gaṅgā?

92

yaḥ kārayed āyatanaṁ
gaṅgā-pratikṛter naraḥ
bhuktvā sa bhogān pretyāpi
yāti gaṅgā-salokatām

A man who builds a temple for the deity of Gaṅgā will after leaving his body join Gaṅgā on the planet where she resides and enjoy wonderfully.

93

śṛṇvanti mahimānaṁ ye
gaṅgāyā nityam ādarāt
gaṅgā-snāna-phalaṁ teṣāṁ
vācaka-prīṇanād dhanaiḥ

Those who regularly hear with respect the glories of Gaṅgā obtain the results of

bathing in Gaṅgā, especially if they gratify the speaker with donations.

94

pitṝn uddiśya yo liṅgaṁ
snapayed gāṅga-vāriṇā
tṛptāḥ syus tasya pitaro
mahā-niraya-gā api

If on behalf of one's forefathers one bathes a Śiva-liṅga with Gaṅgā water, the forefathers will be satisfied even if they have gone to the worst hell.

95

aṣṭa-kṛtvo mantra-japtair
vastra-pūtaiḥ su-gandhibhiḥ
procur gāṅga-jalaiḥ snānaṁ
ghṛta-snānādhikaṁ budhāḥ

Intelligent authorities have declared that taking Gaṅgā water that has been strained through a cloth and mixed with fragrant substances and bathing with it eight times while quietly chanting *mantras* is more auspicious than bathing with ghee and all the other auspicious baths.

96-97

aṣṭa-dravya-vimiśreṇa
gaṅgā-toyena yaḥ sakṛt
māgadha-prastha-mātreṇa
tāmra-pātra-sthitena ca

bhānave 'rghaṁ pradadyāc ca
svakīya-pitṛbhiḥ saha
so 'ti-tejo-vimānena
sūrya-loke mahīyate

If one once offers *arghya* to the sun-god with Gaṅgā mixed with eight auspicious substances in a copper pot the size of one *māgadha-prastha*, he will be taken in an most effulgent airplane to the sun and there be elevated to a glorious life.

98-99

āpaḥ kṣīraṁ kuśāgrāṇi
ghṛtaṁ madhu gavāṁ dadhi
raktāni karavīrāṇi
rakta-candanam ity api

aṣṭāṅgārgho 'yam uddiṣṭas tv
atīva-ravi-toṣaṇaḥ
gāṅgair vārbhiḥ koṭi-guṇo
jñeyo viṣṇo 'nya-vāritaḥ

This *arghya* offering should include eight auspicious substances: water, milk, the tips of *kuśa* grass, ghee, honey, yoghurt from cow's milk, red *karavīra* leaves, and red sandalwood pulp. This is considered very pleasing to the sun-god. When mixed with Gaṅgā water, O Viṣṇu, it should be understood as millions of times superior to all other waters.

100

gaṅgā-tīre sva-śaktyā yaḥ
kuryād devālayaṁ su-dhīḥ
anya-tīrtha pratiṣṭhāto
bhavet koṭi-guṇaṁ phalam

An intelligent person who constructs a temple according to his capacity on the bank of Gaṅgā will obtain millions of times the benefit as he would for building a temple in any other holy place.

101-102

aśvattha-vaṭa-cūtādi-
vṛkṣāropeṇa yat phalam
kūpa-vāpī-taḍāgādi-
prapā-satrādibhis tathā

anyatra yad bhavet puṇyaṁ
tad gaṅgā-darśanād bhavet
puṣpa-vāṭyādibhiś cāpi
gaṅgā-sparśaṁ tato 'dhikam

The pious credit gained by planting trees like the *aśvattha*, *vaṭa*, and *cūṭa*, by digging wells, bathing tanks, lakes, and other bodies of water, and by other pious activities are all gained simply by seeing Gaṅgā. One gains more credit by touching Gaṅgā than from constructing flower gardens and other pious works.

103

kanyā-dānena yat puṇyaṁ
yat puṇyaṁ go-'nna-dānataḥ
tat puṇyaṁ syāc chata-guṇaṁ
gaṅgā-gaṇḍūṣa-pānataḥ

The pious credit of giving a daughter or a cow and grains in charity is gained a hundred times multiplied by drinking a palmful of Gaṅgā water.

104

cāndrāyaṇa-sahasreṇa
yat puṇyaṁ syāj janārdana
tato 'dhika-phalaṁ gaṅgā
amṛta-pānād avāpnuyāt

O Janārdana, by simply drinking the nectar of Gaṅgā one gains more pious credit than obtained from performing the *cāndrāyaṇa* fast a thousand times.

105

bhaktyā gaṅgāvagāhasya
kim anyat phalam ucyate
akṣayaḥ svarga-vāso 'pi
nirvāṇam atha vā hare

And how can one even describe, O Hari, the additional piety one acquires by bathing in Gaṅgā with devotion? One gains unending residence in heaven or even final liberation.

106

gaṅgāyāḥ pādukā-yugmaṁ
nityam arcati yo naraḥ
āyuḥ puṇyaṁ dhanaṁ putrān
svarga-mokṣau ca vindati

A person who regularly worships a deity of Gaṅgā's two feet obtains a long life, pious credits, wealth, sons, heaven, and liberation.

107

nāsti gaṅgā-samaṁ tīrthaṁ
kali-kalmaṣa-nāśanam
nāsti mukti-pradaṁ kṣetram
avimukta-samaṁ hare

There is no holy place like the Gaṅgā, which can destroy the contamination of Kali-yuga, and there is no holy city, O Hari, like Avimukta.

108

gaṅgā-snāna-rataṁ martyaṁ
dṛṣṭvaiva yama-kiṅkarāḥ
diśo daśa palāyante
siṁhaṁ dṛṣṭvā yathā mṛgāḥ

If the servants of Yamarāja see a mortal who is dedicated to bathing in the Gaṅgā, they run away in the ten directions like animals who have seen a lion.

* * *

Additional glorification of Kāśī (also known as Avimukta) is found throughout the Vedic literatures. In the *Skanda Purāṇa* (*Kāśī-khaṇḍa* 6.70-71) it is stated: "Avimukta excels Prayāga, the foremost among holy spots. Undoubtedly nowhere else can salvation be acquired as in Avimukta. If one does not get released from *saṁsāra*, even after reaching Kāśī, he cannot get salvation even if he visits millions of other holy places." Also, in the *Śiva Purāṇa* (*Koṭi-rudra-saṁhitā* 23.22) it says: "Hence this holy center is known as Avimukta. It is greater than Naimiṣa and all other *tīrthas* in yielding liberation to the deceased." In the *Sanat-kumāra-saṁhitā* it is stated: "One may be a *brāhmaṇa* or a *caṇḍāla*, learned or unlearned—all are equally entitled to liberation after bathing at Maṇikarṇikā." And in the *Garuḍa Purāṇa* (*Ācāra-kāṇḍa* 81.3): "Vārāṇasī is the holy place where Lord Keśava has taken the form of Viśveśvara (Lord Śiva)."

Again, in the *Nārada Purāṇa* (*Uttara-bhāga*, Chapters 48, 51), Avimukta is further glorified by Vasu, as he describes the various holy centers to Mohinī. When Mohinī requests Vasu to narrate the glories of Kāśī, he replies, "May it be heard that the city of Kāśī is blessed and auspicious. Lord Maheśvara (Śiva) is blessed. Liberation awaits anyone who continuously takes shelter in Kāśī. This city was related to Lord Viṣṇu, and then Lord Śiva requested the city from Him. Lord Śiva remains there worshiping Lord Hṛṣīkeśa, and all the *devas* and devotees worship Lord Śiva. Kāśī is a beautiful city and is the essence of the three worlds. Persons who have committed various sins become free from all blemishes and shine like demigods when they visit this holy center, which is a mystical secret place. Kāśī is conducive to happiness for all living beings and bestows liberation upon all creatures. This *tīrtha* is dear to both Lord Viṣṇu and Lord Śiva. Those pious persons who reside in Kāśī, whether they are devotees of Hari or Hara, if they worship their deity with great loving respect and are as pure and saintly as Śambhu, become free from fear, sorrow, and sin. Thus they cut the thick net of *saṁsāra*.

"This great holy center is traditionally known as Avimukta. It will never be abandoned or given up by either Lord Viṣṇu or Lord Śiva. In this holy place the attainment of liberation is possible without any strain, more easily than in other holy places such as Prayāga. If a man or woman, knowingly or unknowingly, commits some inauspicious act through evil intellect, then that sin is instantly reduced to ashes upon entering Avimukta. The liberation attained by residing in Avimukta cannot be attained by residing at Kurukṣetra, Gaṅgādvāra, or in Puṣkara.

"O auspicious-looking Mohinī, whether willingly or unwillingly, if one abandons one's life at Avimukta, he shall attain liberation without a doubt, even in the case of animals. At the time of death in Avimukta, Lord Śiva himself offers the sacred *tāraka-mantra* of Lord Rāmacandra into the right ear of the dying person, who thus becomes liberated. Maṇikarṇikā is the most excellent *tīrtha* of all because Lord Viṣṇu and Lord Śiva perpetually reside there.

"The River Varaṇā, which meets Jāhnavī (Gaṅgā), is sacred and destroys all sins. At this confluence, an excellent *liṅga* was installed by Lord Brahmā. That *liṅga* is well known throughout the entire universe as Saṅgameśvara. There is no fear of rebirth for a person who takes a holy bath in the confluence of these two divine rivers and who worships Saṅgameśvara, the lord of the confluence. Keśava Himself stands to the east of Lord Śiva, and to the east of Keśava (Ādi-keśava) is this well-known Saṅgameśvara."

Vasu concludes by describing the glories of Gaṅgā as she flows through Kāśī: "O beautiful lady, all of the *tīrthas* in the three worlds exclusively resort to Gaṅgā, which flows through Kāśī. One who takes bath at Daśāśvamedha-ghāṭa and has *darśana* of Lord Visveśvara (Viśvanātha) shall immediately become freed from sins. Every part of the Gaṅgā is sacred and dispels the sin of *brahma-hatyā*, but especially in Kāśī. And by taking bath at the confluence of the River Asī and Gaṅgā, one is liberated without a doubt. The Rivers Dhūtapāpā and Kiraṇā dispel multitudes of great sins when they meet the Rivers Sarasvatī, Gaṅgā, and Yamunā. Hence, this holy confluence is well known throughout the three worlds as Pañcanada, or Pañca Gaṅgā. One who bathes at this confluence will not acquire another physical body consisting of the five elements. One certainly attains in a single day of bathing in Pañcanada at Kāśī the same benefit obtained by bathing at Prayāga throughout the month of Māgha.

"A single drop of water from Pañcanada is superior to one hundred and eight pots of *pañcāmṛta* (nectarean drink). By taking bath at Pañcanada, one attains one hundred times the benefit acquired by performing the Rājasūya and Aśvamedha sacrifices. There is no other *tīrtha* on the whole earth like Dhūtapāpā. In Saṭya-yuga (Kṛta-yuga), Dharmanada is the holy *tīrtha*; in Tretā-yuga, Dhūtapāpā is the *tīrtha*; in Dvāpara-yuga, Bindu-tīrtha is very sacred; and in Kali-yuga, it is Pañcanada. No one is competent enough to describe adequately the endless glories of Pañcanada-tīrtha. O gentle lady, thus the excellent greatness of Avimukta, otherwise known as Kāśī, has been recounted to you. If this narration is imparted to a devotee of Lord Viṣṇu or Lord Śiva, one shall attain the benefit of a holy bath in this *tīrtha*."

When Gaṅgā disappears

Although the *Brahma-vaivarta Purāṇa* states that Gaṅgā will foresake this planet after 10,000 years of Kali-yuga have passed, according to the following narration from the *Skanda Purāṇa* (*Kārtika-māsa-māhātmyam* 4) Gaṅgā will disappear from sight after 5,000 years of Kali-yuga have passed.

In this narration, Sūryadeva (the sun-god) is speaking to his charioteer, Aruṇa: "If one takes bath in cold water during the month of Kārtika, one obtains ten times greater benefit than by taking bath with hot water. If the bath is taken with water from a small outdoor well, there is one hundred times more benefit. If the bath is taken in a *kuṇḍa*, there is one thousand times greater benefit, and that benefit is increased ten times by bathing in a lake. By taking a bath in a stream, one obtains ten times greater benefit than by bathing in a lake, and one obtains even greater benefit by bathing in a river, especially at a *tīrtha*. Finally, ten times more benefit is attained when bathing at the confluence of two rivers, and there is no end to the benefit attained by taking bath at the confluence of three rivers.

"The following *tīrthas* are very difficult to visit for a bath during Kārtika: Sindhu, Kṛṣṇā, Yamunā, Sarasvatī, Godāvarī, Vipāśā (Beas), Narmadā, Mahī, Kāverī, Sarayū, Śiprā, Vitastā (Jhelum), Śoṇa, Vetravatī (Betwa), Gaṇḍakī, Gomatī, Brahmaputrā, the excellent lakes Mānasa and Nārāyaṇa, and Badarikāśrama. Ayodhyā is superior to Badarikāśrama and Gaṅgādvāra is superior to that. Greater than that is Kanakhala and better still is Madhupurī (Mathurā). If someone resides in Mathurā for the month of Kārtika and takes bath daily in the River Yamunā, he remains in Vaikuṇṭha. Śrī Śrī Rādhā-Dāmodara also take bath in Yamunā, hence Madhupurī is the most excellent, especially the River Yamunā. Dvārakā is also very excellent because Lord Kṛṣṇa used to bathe there with His sixteen thousand wives and the Yādavas. One who applies *gopī-candana tilaka* at Dvārakā is certainly known to be a liberated soul.

"When ten thousand years of Kali-yuga passes, Lord Viṣṇu will forsake the earth. With regards to the water of the Jāhnavī, the period is half of that, and regarding the demigods, half of that again. As long as Gaṅgā remains, all the *tīrthas* will also remain. When Gaṅgā herself disappears, the *tīrthas* will go beneath the surface of the earth. More excellent than all is Kāśī, since this *tīrtha* has no destruction. Kāśī and Gaṅgā support one another to dispel sins. There is no destruction of Kāśī, even if Brahmā passes

away. It is because of the sight of Kāśī that Gaṅgā began to flow north. In Gaṅgā, the *tīrtha* named Pañcanada is well known. At the advent of the month of Kārtika, Tīrtha-rāja (Prayāga) goes to Pañcanada for his holy bath. Even if a hundred thousand sins have been committed, they are all immediately destroyed by taking bath at Pañcanada and by worshiping Bindu-Mādhava. If anyone takes his holy bath at Pañcanada *tīrtha*, the pious merit shall be millions of times more than that of a holy bath in all the other *tīrthas*."

Lord Śiva leaves Kāśī

Here is a story from the *Skanda Purāṇa* (*Kāśī-khaṇḍa* 44-53) about how Lord Śiva had to leave his own abode that he loved so much and the long ordeal it took for him to regain his Kāśī.

"Once, when the world was plagued with a drought, Lord Brahmā called upon one retired king named Ripuñjaya, who was performing austerities in Kāśī. Lord Brahmā had to beg the King to reassume the kingship of the earth, but the King made one condition first: That all the demigods must return to their heavenly abodes, so that there would not be any interference from them. Lord Brahmā instructed all the demigods, including Lord Śiva, that they must leave. Ripuñjaya eventually became known as Divodāsa, the servant of heaven. Lord Śiva was not very pleased to leave, but in order to respect Lord Brahmā's request and his word to Divodāsa, Śiva left Kāśī to reside on Mandara-parvata.

"King Divodāsa ruled and governed his kingdom with expert leadership, all under the religious principles of *varṇāśrama-dharma* (Vedic social and spiritual system), but the demigods felt threatened and tried to create trouble. Nonetheless, due to the King's previous austerities, he was able to continue his leadership without losing the citizen's confidence. Meanwhile, Lord Śiva and Pārvatī greatly lamented being away from Kāśī and thus planned a way to reduce the King's righteous power. Since the King was immune to disease, old age, and death, Lord Śiva sent sixty-four *yoginīs* (female *yogīs*), who were expert with the power of *māyā* (illusory potency). They tried many enchanting ways to deceive the King, but ultimately failed. Since Kāśī was so beautiful and well loved, the *yoginīs* decided to remain there.

"Then after awhile, Lord Śiva sent Sūryadeva to Kāśī to find some faults in the King or within the kingdom. But after struggling in so many ways to instigate doubt and confusion, Sūryadeva was unsuccessful. He too decided to remain in Kāśī and took the vow of *kṣetra-sannyāsa*, never to leave the *dhāma* of Kāśī. He then divided himself into the twelve Adityas. Due to his great attachment and love for Kāśī, Lord Śiva then asked Lord Brahmā to go to Kāśī. Brahmā agreed to assume the form of a *brāhmaṇa*, with a plan to perform ten elaborate Aśvamedhas (horse sacrifices), with the hope that the King would make a mistake in executing *varṇāśrama-dharma*. But all the sacrifices were performed without fault, and the King remained in control of his perfect kingdom. Lord Brahmā found no fault with King Divodāsa, so he decided to remain and reside at the place where the ten horse sacrifices were performed, otherwise known as Daśāśvamedha-tīrtha.

"Lord Śiva became disturbed when Lord Brahmā did not return. So he then sent all of his *gaṇas* (attendants) to Kāśī. But upon arriving, they were overwhelmed with the unique spiritual atmosphere of the city, so they also decided to remain there and establish *liṅgas* in honor of Lord Śiva. After realizing that anyone he sent to Kāśī would not return, Lord Śiva smiled and then sent his chief *gaṇa*, Gaṇeśa. When Gaṇeśa arrived, he took the form of a *brāhmaṇa* fortune-teller. He was able to satisfy all the citizens, even one of the King's queens, Līlāvatī, who told Divodāsa about this famous fortune-teller. The King invited the *brāhmaṇa* to the palace and inquired from him, 'What is the result of all the good work I have performed here in Kāśī?' The fortune-teller said that he could not answer the question, but he could foresee that in eighteen days a wiser *brāhmaṇa* would arrive to answer this question. Gaṇeśa had Lord Viṣṇu in mind to complete the final task of removing Divodāsa, but meanwhile, he also decided to remain in Kāśī by dividing himself into forty-six other forms, to await the arrival of Lord Śiva.

"When Lord Viṣṇu understood the situation, He arrived in Kāśī at the place where the River Varaṇā meets the Gaṅgā and first took bath. This confluence became known as Pādodaka, the place where Ādi-Keśava washed His lotus feet. From there, He sanctified the entire area up to the center of Kāśī. Then Lord Viṣṇu transformed Himself into a Buddhist monk, Puṇyakīrti, Śrī-devī (Lakṣmī) became a Buddhist nun named Vijñānakaumudī, and Garuḍa became Puṇyakīrti's disciple. The three of them traveled throughout the entire kingdom of Kāśī. Everywhere they went, they preached Buddhist philosophy, which caused a great disturbance amongst the citizens. These Buddhists successfully created faults in the perfect kingdom of Divodāsa, and hence, his popularity began to decrease. The King patiently waited for that eighteenth day, as the fortune-teller had predicted.

"Meanwhile, Lord Viṣṇu assumed the form of that wise *brāhmaṇa* and appeared in the court of Divodāsa on the eighteenth day. The King expressed his feelings of exhaustion in ruling and asked the *brāhmaṇa*, 'How can I eliminate the reactions of *karma* and attain salvation?' The *brāhmaṇa* replied, 'Because of your excellent rule, you are free. Although you interfered with the demigods, you protected the religious principles. The only sin you occurred was expelling Lord Śiva from Kāśī. In order to remove that sin, you must establish a *liṅga* for him, then you will reach the celestial planets.'

"King Divodāsa then turned the kingdom over to his son and established a great *śiva-liṅga* known as Divodāseśvara, which he worshiped with all the proper rituals. Finally a chariot arrived to take Divodāsa to the heavenly kingdom. Meanwhile, Lord Viṣṇu also wanted to reside in Kāśī, so He decided to remain at Pañcanada-tīrtha, where the five Gaṅgās meet.

"When Lord Śiva heard of Lord Viṣṇu's success, he was overwhelmed with joy and made preparations to return to Kāśī. A great beautiful chariot was created for Śiva's travel. The Rivers Gaṅgā and Yamunā became the shafts of the chariot; the winds, morning, and evening became the wheels; the sky was the umbrella; the heavenly stars were the nails holding the chariot together; *dakṣiṇa* became the axle; *praṇava oṁkāra* was the seat; Gāyatrī was the foot-rest; Sūrya and Candra guarded the chariot; and Mount Meru became the flagpole. After a glorious *pūjā* was conducted for him, Lord Śiva returned to Śrī Kāśī-dhāma, accompanied by the seven oceans, all the rivers, mountains, and trees."

King Pauṇḍraka confronts Lord Kṛṣṇa

This short account taken from *KṚṢṆA*, chapter entitled: *Deliverance of Pauṇḍraka and the King of Kāśī*, shows how foolish they are when proud men claim they can kill the Supreme Personality of Godhead, Lord Kṛṣṇa.

Once there was a very proud king named Pauṇḍraka, who claimed to be the Supreme Lord in front of Lord Kṛṣṇa. When Lord Kṛṣṇa finally decided to kill Pauṇḍraka, that foolish king was living in Kāśī with his friend, the King of Kāśī. Eventually Lord Kṛṣṇa killed both kings, but He specifically arranged to throw the head of the King of Kāśī into the city, so his family members could see it. The King's son, Sudakṣiṇa, vowed to kill Lord Kṛṣṇa in order to liquidate his debts to his father. He began performing austerities and worshiping Kāśī Viśvanātha Mahādeva for the benediction to kill any enemy.

While performing these black art rituals, out of the sacrificial fire came Dakṣiṇāgni, a great demoniac form, whose hair, beard, and mustache were exactly the color of hot copper. This huge fierce demon, along with hundreds of ghostly companions, proceeded towards the city of Dvārakā. The fiery demon was about to burn the whole city when Lord Kṛṣṇa ordered His Sudarśana *cakra* to appear and freeze the demon. This defeated the demon's attempt and forced him to return to Kāśī.

According to the black-art *mantras* described in the *Tantras*, if a *mantra* fails to kill the enemy, it kills the original creator, since it must kill someone. Since Sudakṣiṇa was the originator, he was burned to ashes. Because the city of Kāśī was filled with so much opulence, and since the King of Kāśī and his son were against Lord Kṛṣṇa, the Sudarśana *cakra* entered Kāśī and devastated the whole city by burning every important place.

Kāśī's Gaṅgā

Kāśī's glories have already been exemplified throughout this section, but with the presence of Gaṅgā-mayī, the entire *dhāma* becomes even more famous and praiseworthy.

We find in the *Nārada Purāṇa* (*Uttara-bhāga*, 48.29): "That Kāśī became even more glorious and meritorious since Gaṅgā began to flow north through the middle of this holy center." In the *Skanda Purāṇa* (*Kāśī-khaṇḍa*, 28.23) it is stated: "All holy places in the three worlds that bestow cherished desires resort to Gaṅgā, which flows towards the north at Kāśī." Also in the *Skanda Purāṇa* (*Kāśī-khaṇḍa*) it is mentioned: "This is certainly known: Where the celestial River Gaṅgā flows in Lord Śiva's Ānandavana (forest of bliss), liberation awaits, without a doubt." And in the *Śiva Purāṇa* (*Koṭi-rudra-saṁhitā* 23.48): "If after reaching Kāśī a man takes his ceremonial bath in the Gaṅgā, the two types of *karma*, present and past, are destroyed."

In Kāśī today, there are some ninety *ghāṭas* that had, or are having, an important role in the pastimes of Kāśī-dhāma and Gaṅgā. Since her arrival, Gaṅgā-mayī has bestowed her mercy upon countless conditioned souls, making her glorious pastimes unlimited. She has mercifully expanded her greatness in Kāśī. Every *ghāṭa* has a very rich, deep-rooted history, but five of them hold the greatest prominence: Asī, Daśāśvamedha, Maṇikarṇikā, Pañca-gaṅgā, and Ādi-Keśava. There is a very popular "Pañca-tīrthī pilgrimage", which allows the pilgrims to visit all the *ghāṭas*, take bath at these five major ones, and finally have *darśana* of Kāśī Viśvanātha Mahādeva. The day long pilgrimage is extremely satisfying, for it enables one to constantly see, feel, and appreciate the greatness of Gaṅgā-mayī and the ancient history of Kāśī.

Asī-ghāṭa is at the confluence of the River Asī and Gaṅgā. Lord Śiva resides here as Asī-saṅgameśvara (lord of the confluence at Asī). It is said in the *Kāśī-khaṇḍa*: "All the other *tīrthas* that surround the earth are not equal to a sixteenth part of Asī-saṅgama-tīrtha." It is said that Kāśī includes all other *tīrthas*, including the *sapta-puris* (seven sacred cities): Ayodhyā, Mathurā, Māyāpurī (Haridvāra), Kāśī, Kāñci, Avantī (Ujjain), and Dvārakā. Asī-ghāṭa is considered the Haridvāra of Kāśī. Local Kumbha-melās are

also held and honored at this most auspicious confluence.

When Lord Brahmā came to Kāśī to perform ten horse sacrifices, that area was known as Rudra-sāra, or Rudra-sārovara (the nectar of Rudra, or the lake of Rudra), which then became known as Daśāśvamedha-ghāṭa, or old Rudra-sārovara. Nearby is Prayāga-ghāṭa, where Tīrtha-rāja (Prayāga) resides and bestows the same benefits as in Allahabad. Lord Brahmā installed a *liṅga* known as Brahmeśvara, and Lord Śiva is also known at Daśāśvamedha-tīrtha as Śulaṭaṅkeśvara and Daśāśvamedheśvara.

Near Maṇikarṇikā-ghāṭa is the original Cakra-puṣkariṇī established by Lord Viṣṇu. This *kuṇḍa* has an independent source from the Gaṅgā, an underground river that flows directly from Gomukha in the Himālayas. Lord Śiva and Pārvatī, Lord Brahmā, Lakṣmī, Indra, and several other demigods and sages all come to Cakra-puṣkariṇī-tīrtha for their bath. This *tīrtha* is so powerful that all other *tīrthas* come here at midday to bathe their over burden of sins away, becoming pure again.

Just below Śrī Bindu-Mādhava is the confluence of Pañca Gaṅgā, or Pañcanada-tīrtha, where two small streams, Dhūtapāpā and Kiraṇā meet, becoming Dharmanada. These rivers join the Gaṅgā, Yamunā, and Sarasvatī, which have already met in Prayāga.

Ādi-Keśava-ghāṭa (Rāja-ghāṭa), located near the confluence of the Rivers Varaṇā and Gaṅgā, is where Lord Viṣṇu's footprints are located. Near this confluence Lord Śiva resides as Saṅgameśvara, a four-faced *liṅga* established by King Sagara. Kāśī represents the five parts of Lord Viṣṇu's body: Asī is His head, Daśāśvamedha is His chest, Maṇikarṇikā is His navel, Pañcanada is His thighs, and Ādi-Keśava His feet.

In addition to the five most prominent *ghāṭas* along the bank of the Gaṅgā, Hariścandra-ghāṭa, named after the legendary king, also has great importance. A short account of this famed king is as follows: Once upon a time, the great sage Viśvāmitra asked King Hariścandra for the fee for performing a Rājasūya sacrifice. Due to the King's generosity, he offered his entire kingdom and everything he owned, but still Viśvāmitra was not pleased. He still pressured the King, but there wasn't anything left to offer. Instead of breaking his promise, the King came, totally impoverished, to Kāśī, where he sold his wife and son into slavery. He then sold himself into bondage to work the cremation grounds in order to pay Viśvāmitra's debt. One day, his wife, who was worn with hardship, came to the cremation grounds carrying their son's dead body. He had died from a snake bite and they were so poor, they could not even provide a blanket to cover the corpse. This great test of Hariścandra's character eventually proved his strength during the worse times. Then the demigods rewarded Hariścandra by reinstalling him on the throne, as well as bringing his dead son back to life.

EXALTED VISITORS

As in Gaṅgādvāra and Prayāga-rāja, several illustrious personalities have visited and played an important role in the history of Kāśī (Vārāṇasī). What would Kāśī be today without the contributions these great personalities offered?

Lord Buddha

Some 2,600 years ago, in the forest of Uruvelā (Bodhgayā), on the banks of the River Nirañjanā, Prince Siddhārtha sat cross-legged, facing east, under a *bodhi* (pipal) tree and made this final resolution: "Blood may become exhausted, flesh may decay, bones may fall apart, but I will never leave this

place until I find *sama-sam-bodhi* (the way to enlightenment)." Then during the full moon of Vaiśākha (April/May), at the age of thirty-five, the prince became Lord Buddha (Śākya Muni). From Bodhgayā, Lord Buddha went to Ṛṣipatana, also known as Isipatana (deer park, Sārnātha) in the Vārāṇasī district. There he met the five mendicants who had lived with him in Uruvelā. After the Lord delivered His first sermon, they regained faith in the Lord and became His first disciples. He then established Ariyasaccani (the four noble truths) and Aṣṭāṅgika-marga (the eightfold path), an act known as Dharma-cakra-pravartana (turning the wheel of law).

Śrī Śaṅkarācārya

After accepting initiation from his spiritual master, Śrī Govindāpāda, who was residing in a cave near Oṁkāranātha on the River Narmadā, Śaṅkarācārya traveled to Vārāṇasī. At that time, Vārāṇasī was adorned with numerous sacrificial pillars of gold and had a forest of *nimba* trees in its neighborhood. Śaṅkarācārya saw before him the Gaṅgā, which in the form of a river is a blessing mankind received as the fruit of Mahārāja Bhagīratha's great austerities and which is an ornament that adorns the locks of Lord Śiva. As Śaṅkarācārya stood on her bank, he began to contemplate, "Is it because of Gaṅgā's contact with Lord Viṣṇu, or because she flows from the crown of moon-crested Śiva, or because she originates in the snow of the Himālayas that her waters are flowing in their crystalline clearness? Was the maiden of this river singing through the humming bees hovering over lotuses crowding her waters? Was she dancing as that expanse of lotuses that were tossed in the winds? Was she smiling through the white foam released from her surface? And was she lifting up her hands to embrace her beloved by the high waves rising on her bosom?" As Śaṅkarācārya

lifted his head from bathing in Gaṅgā, his shining face looked like the crescent moon that had fallen down from Lord Śiva's matted locks. His frame, with drops of the holy waters dripping all over, looked like a *candrakanta* stone from the moon.

Afterwards, before meeting his first disciple, Sanandana (later known as Padmapāda), Śaṅkarācārya resided in Vārāṇasī for some time and worshiped Kāśī Viśvanātha. While the pleasant afternoon breeze blew and the surroundings were calm, with only the swirl of Gaṅgā echoing, Śaṅkarācārya gave his first discourse to Sanandana and a few other disciples, as they sat in the dry sands of along the Gaṅgā.

Śrī Rāmānujācārya

During Śrī Rāmānujācārya's third preaching tour of India, he visited Kāśmīra a second time. After he defeated all the scholars there, they became very envious and angry. They resorted to black magic and tried to kill him, but the spell had reverse effects and they all became sick and nearly died. After the Kāśmīra King pleaded with Rāmānuja to cure the scholars, they all became well again. Leaving Kāśmīra, Rāmānujācārya traveled continuously until reaching Vārāṇasī, where he spent several months preaching.

Śrī Advaita Ācārya

With great delight, Advaita Ācārya arrived in Mithilā, the birthplace of Sītā-devī, before traveling to the eternal abode of Śrī Rāma in Ayodhyā. As He took bath in the River Sarayū, He remembered the pastimes of Lord Rāma's bathing. Eventually, Advaita Prabhu arrived in Vārāṇasī, where He took bath in the River Gaṅgā at Maṇikarṇikā-ghāṭa. When He saw the Deity of Ādi-Keśava, Advaita blissfully offered His obeisances and many prayers. Advaita Prabhu then chanted and danced before Bindu-Mādhava in ecstatic love. His ecstatic feelings grew as He repeatedly offered more obeisances and prayers.

Then, in an ecstatic mood, Advaita Ācārya entered the temple of Visveśvara (Viśvanātha) in order to instruct people how to worship Lord Śiva. Advaita Prabhu requested Lord Śiva for the benediction of devotional service. He offered prayers and then chanted and danced with raised arms. After offering His obeisances, Advaita went to the temple of Annapūrṇā-devi and offered prayers to the goddess. Advaita Prabhu then went to visit various other holy places in Vārāṇasī, where He had *darśana* of Lord Viṣṇu, the demigods, and Gaṅgā-mayī.

Lord Nityānanda Prabhu

When Lord Nityānanda began His eight year pilgrimage throughout Bhārata-bhūmi, the first holy place He visited was Vakreśvara-tīrtha (West Bengal), and then He had *darśana* of Lord Śiva, otherwise known as Vaidyanātheśvara, in the forests of Vaidyanātha (Devgarh, Bihar). From there He proceeded to Viṣṇupada in Gayā before arriving in Kāśī, where He had *darśana* of Lord Siva, who is known there as Visveśvara. Lord Nityānanda became cheerful by drinking and bathing in the waters of the Gaṅgā.

Śrī Caitanya Mahāprabhu

In the *Śrī Caitanya-caritāmṛta* (*Madhya* 17.82-83, 86), Śrī Caitanya Mahāprabhu's visit to Kāśī is nicely elaborated: "Finally the Lord with great happiness arrived at the holy place called Kāśī. There He took His bath in the bathing *ghāṭa* known as Maṇikarṇikā. At that time, Tapana Miśra was bathing in the Ganges, and he was astonished to see the Lord there...Tapana Miśra then took Śrī Caitanya Mahāprabhu to visit the temple of Visveśvara. Coming from there, they saw the lotus feet of Lord Bindu-Mādhava."

Śrila Prabhupāda explains in his purports on the *Śrī Caitanya-caritāmṛta* (*Madhya* 17.82,86) some historical details related to Kāśī: "Kāśī is another name for Vārāṇasī (Benares). It has been a place of pilgrimage since time immemorial. Two rivers named Asiḥ and Varuṇā merge there. Maṇikarṇikā is famous because, according to the opinion of great personalities, a bejeweled earring fell there from the ear of Lord Viṣṇu. According to some, it fell from the ear of Lord Śiva. The word *maṇi* means 'jewel,' and *karṇika* means 'from the ear.' According to some, Lord Viśvanātha is the great physician who cures the disease of material existence by delivering a person through the ear, which receives the vibration of the holy name of Lord Rāma. Because of this, this holy place is called Maṇi-karṇikā. It is said that there is no better place than where the River Ganges flows, and the bathing ghat known as Maṇikarṇikā is especially sanctified because it is very dear to Lord Visvanātha.

"In the *Kāśī-khaṇḍa* it is said: *saṁsāri-cintāmaṇir atra yasmāt tārakaṁ sajjana-karṇikāyām. śivo 'bhidhatte saha-sānta-kāle tad gīyate 'sau maṇi-karṇiketi. mukti-lakṣmī mahā-pīṭha-maṇis tac caraṇābjayoḥ. karṇikeyaṁ tataḥ prāhur yāṁ janā maṇi-karnikām*. According to the *Kāśī-khaṇḍa*, if one gives up his body at Maṇikarṇikā, he is liberated simply by remembering Lord Śiva's name...

"This Bindu Mādhava is the oldest Viṣṇu temple in Vārāṇasī. Presently this temple is known as Veṇi Mādhava, and it is situated on the banks of the Ganges. Formerly five rivers converged there, and they were named Dhūtapāpā, Kiraṇā, Sarasvatī, Gaṅgā and Yamunā. Now only the River Ganges is visible. The old temple of Bindu Mādhava, which was visited by Śrī Caitanya Mahāprabhu, was later dismantled by

Aurangzeb, the great Hindu-hating emperor of the Mogul dynasty. In the place of this temple, he constructed a big *majīda*, or mosque. Later, another temple was constructed by the side of the mosque, and this temple is still existing. In the temple of Bindu Mādhava there are Deities of four-handed Nārāyaṇa and the goddess Lakṣmī."

Lord Śrī Caitanya Mahāprabhu stayed at Tapana Miśra's house, where He rested and would bathe daily at nearby Daśāśvamedha-ghāṭa. There He met His maternal uncle, Candraśekhara Vaidya. He related to the Lord the importance and appreciation of another devotee's association, especially being in Vārāṇasī, where there were only *Vedānta* philosophical discussions. Due to the requests of Tapana Miśra and Candraśekhara, Lord Caitanya remained in Vārāṇasī for ten days.

During this time, one local *brāhmaṇa* went to the Māyāvādī *sannyāsī*, Prakāśānanda Sarasvatī, who was teaching *Vedānta*, in order to describe the wonderfully auspicious features of Caitanya Mahāprabhu. The *brāhmaṇa* told Prakāśānanda Sarasvatī, "His tongue is always chanting the holy names of Kṛṣṇa, and from His eyes tears incessantly fall like the flowing Gaṅgā. Sometimes He dances, laughs, sings, and cries, and sometimes He roars like a lion. His name, Kṛṣṇa Caitanya, is all-auspicious to the world. Everything about Him, His name, form, and qualities, are unparalleled." Prakāśānanda just laughed and joked upon hearing the Lord's description. He then offended the Lord by saying that His activities were that of a *loka-pratāraka*, a first class pretender. "I know that His name is Śrī Kṛṣṇa Caitanya and He is accompanied by many sentimentalists. His followers dance with Him, and He tours from country to country and village to village. This Caitanya is a *sannyāsī* in name only, but actually He is a magician. In any case, His sentimentalism cannot be very much in demand here in Kāśī."

The *brāhmaṇa* returned to Caitanya Mahāprabhu and described what the famous Māyāvādī *sannyāsī* had said. The Lord then said that the holy name cannot manifest in the mouths of Māyāvādīs, because they are great offenders unto Lord Kṛṣṇa. He then continued to describe the wonderful attributes of the holy name of Kṛṣṇa, "I have come here to sell my emotional ecstatic sentiments in this city of Kāśī, but I cannot find any customers. I have brought a heavy load to sell in this city and to take it back again is a very difficult job. Therefore, if I get but a fraction of the price, I shall sell it here in this city of Kāśī." After saying this, Śrī Caitanya Mahāprabhu started for Mathurā.

Śrī Caitanya Mahāprabhu then went to Prayāga and finally reached Lord Kṛṣṇa's land in Vṛndāvana, Mathurā. On His return journey to Jagannātha Purī from Vṛndāvana, the Lord visited Soro-kṣetra and Prayāga, before returning to Vārāṇasī, described in *Śrī Caitanya-caritāmṛta* (*Madhya* 19.244): "After walking and walking, Śrī Caitanya Mahāprabhu finally arrived at Vārāṇasī, where He met Candraśekhara, who was waiting outside the city."

The Lord stayed at Candraśekhara's home this time, but accepted lunch *prasāda* at the home of Tapana Miśra. Then Mahāprabhu waited for the arrival of Sanātana Gosvāmī, who was escaping from the imprisonment of the Nawab Hussain Shah. After a few days, Sanātana Gosvāmī arrived at Vārāṇasī. He was very pleased hearing about Śrī Caitanya Mahāprabhu's arrival there. Since Sanātana Gosvāmī was dressed like a Muslim mendicant, Candraśekhara had difficulty recognizing that such an exalted Vaiṣṇava personality was sitting beside the door of his house. As Sanātana went inside, Lord Caitanya immediately got up and embraced him with overwhelming ecstatic love. Then Caitanya Mahāprabhu kept touching Sanātana Gosvāmī's body saying, "Saints of your caliber are themselves places of pilgrimage. Because of their purity, they are constant companions of the Lord, and therefore they can purify even the places of pilgrimage."

Afterwards, for two consecutive months, Lord Caitanya personally instructed Sanātana Gosvāmī on the science of the Absolute Truth; the opulence and sweetness of Lord Śrī Kṛṣṇa; life's ultimate goal: love of Godhead; along with the sixty-one explanations of the *Śrīmad-Bhāgavatam ātmārāma* verse. The Lord then gave Sanātana a synopsis of *Hari-bhakti-vilāsa*, which Sanātana later developed into the guiding principle of all Vaiṣṇavas.

During the Lord's visits to Vārāṇasī, He was always being blasphemed by the Māyāvādī *sannyāsīs* and never mixed or accepted invitations from them. But one day, a *brāhmaṇa* devotee of the Lord, invited Caitanya Mahāprabhu and all the Vārāṇasī *sannyāsīs* to his home, and Mahāprabhu accepted in favor of His devotee. Prakāśānanda Sarasvatī placed Mahāprabhu in a seat in the midst of their assembly and said, "You are a *sannyāsī*. Why then do you indulge in chanting, dancing, and engaging in your *saṅkīrtana* movement in the company of fanatics?" Śrī Caitanya Mahāprabhu replied that His own spiritual master had considered Him to be a fool. He had chastised the Lord, saying He was not qualified to study *Vedānta*, so He must always chant the holy name of Kṛṣṇa, which is the essence of all *mantras* and Vedic hymns. Mahāprabhu continued to explain the reasons and conclusions of chanting the *mahā-mantra* to all the Māyāvādī *sannyāsīs*. "In this age of Kali there is no alternative, there is no alternative, there is no alternative for spiritual progress than the holy name, the holy name, the holy name of the Lord."

After hearing Caitanya Mahāprabhu speak, the Māyāvādī's minds changed and they began to speak with pleasing words. They agreed that only when one is favored by fortune is attaining love of Godhead possible. Their minds had become greatly satisfied by Mahāprabhu's words. Then the Lord began to speak of *Vedānta-sūtra*. When the Māyāvādī *sannyāsīs* heard the explanation of *Vedānta-sūtra* from the Lord, their minds changed, and, on the instruction of Caitanya Mahāprabhu, they too chanted "Kṛṣṇa! Kṛṣṇa!" Caitanya Mahāprabhu excused all their offenses and criticism and mercifully blessed everyone with *kṛṣṇa-nāma*. The Lord then returned to His residence, where many other Māyāvādī *sannyāsīs* visited Him. In this way the entire city of Vārāṇasī began to praise Him. The crowd at the door of His residence was so great that it numbered hundreds and thousands, and when the Lord went to visit the temple of Kāśī Viśvanātha, hundreds and thousands of people assembled to see Him.

Afterwards, when Lord Caitanya went to see the beautiful form of Bindu-Mādhava, He began to dance in the temple's courtyard. Other devotees joined Him dancing and chanting, *haraye namaḥ kṛṣṇa yādavāya namaḥ/ gopāla govinda rāma śrī-madhusūdana*. Hundreds and thousands of people gathered from all directions and filled the air with the auspicious sound of "Hari! Hari!" Even Prakāśānanda and tens of thousand of his disciples all joined in dancing and chanting with Śrī Caitanya Mahāprabhu. All the residents of Vārāṇasī were simply astonished on seeing the Lord's jubilation and humility and in hearing His ecstatic talks. Mahāprabhu then offered prayers to Prakāśānanda, who immediately gripped the Lord's lotus feet. "My dear Sir, You are the spiritual master of

the whole world. Therefore, You are most worshipable. Formerly, I have committed many offenses against You by blaspheming You, but now the effects of my offenses are counteracted by my touching Your lotus feet."

Then Prakāśānanda Sarasvatī requested Śrī Caitanya Mahāprabhu to briefly explain the purpose and purport of the *Brahma-sūtra* (*Vedānta-sūtra*). In this way the Lord was again requested to explain the sixty-one meanings of the *ātmārāma* verse. Upon hearing this, everyone was completely struck with wonder. They concluded that Caitanya Mahāprabhu was none other that Lord Śrī Kṛṣṇa.

Again from the *Śrī Caitanya-caritāmṛta* (*Madhya* 25.165,167), the Lord's visit to Kāśī comes to a blissful end: "All the inhabitants of Kāśī [Vārāṇasī] began chanting the Hare Kṛṣṇa *mahā-mantra* in ecstatic love. Sometimes they laughed, cried, chanted, and sometimes danced...Śrī Caitanya Mahāprabhu then returned to His residence, with His personal associates. Thus He turned the whole city of Vārāṇasi into another Navadvīpa [Nadīyā-nagara]."

Śrī Caitanya Mahāprabhu embraced all His associates and proceeded on His way through the Jhārikhaṇḍa forest once again, before arriving in Jagannātha Purī.

Raghunātha Bhaṭṭa Gosvāmī

Upon the request of Śrī Caitanya Mahāprabhu, Tapana Miśra settled in the city of Vārāṇasī two years before the birth of his son, Raghunātha Bhaṭṭa. When Caitanya Mahāprabhu visited Vārāṇasī on His return from Vṛndāvana, Raghunātha was nine years old.

During this visit, Mahāprabhu stayed at the house of Candraśekhara but accepted His daily lunch at Tapana Miśra's house, where the young Raghunātha was able to render the Lord some menial service. He massaged the Lord's legs and washed His dishes, which gave the young boy a relishable taste of devotional service during Caitanya Mahāprabhu's two month stay.

During Raghunātha Bhaṭṭa's twentieth year, he went to Jagannātha Purī to see Caitanya Mahāprabhu. For eight months the Lord personally instructed Raghunātha in the eternal truths of Vedic literature, while he performed personal service to the Lord. During this time, Raghunātha Bhaṭṭa became an expert cook. All of his preparations tasted like "the nectar of the gods," and Caitanya Mahāprabhu ate them to His full satisfaction.

Raghunātha Bhaṭṭa was then instructed to return to Vārāṇasī to serve his elderly parents, remain unmarried, and study the *Śrimad-Bhāgavatam* under a pure Vaiṣṇava. He faithfully followed Caitanya Mahāprabhu's instructions, and when his parents eventually died, Raghunātha Bhaṭṭa left Vārāṇasī and returned to Jagannātha Purī to see Caitanya Mahāprabhu again. Afterwards, he proceeded to Vṛndāvana, where he associated with the other Gosvāmīs.

Jīva Gosvāmī

After Jīva Gosvāmī met Lord Nityānanda in Navadvīpa, the Lord personally took Śrī Jīva on a complete tour of Navadvīpa-maṇḍala. Afterwards, the Lord instructed Jīva Gosvāmī to go to Vṛndāvana, after studying in Vārāṇasī under a great learned disciple of Sārvabhauma Bhaṭṭācārya by the name of Madhusūdana Vācaspati.

Arriving in Vārāṇasi, Jīva Gosvāmī quickly met the Vācaspati and became his student. In a short time, Śrī Jīva learned all aspects of *Vedānta* philosophy and earned the reputation as a well known scholar, an authority on all branches of learning. To this day, the Benares Hindi University (B.H.U.) honors Śrī Jīva Gosvāmī by dedicating an entire department to the study of his works.

Śrīla Bhaktisiddhānta Sarasvatī

On the 16th of December, 1924, Śrīla Bhaktisiddhānta Sarasvatī Mahārāja traveled to Vārāṇasī and gave a lecture about "the place of the Vaiṣṇava philosophy in the religious world" at the Benares Hindu University. Then he went on *parikramā* (pilgrimage) to the various places where Caitanya Mahāprabhu had performed His pastimes. He returned to Kāśī in 1926 and installed Rādhā-Kṛṣṇa (Śrī Śrī Vinodā-Vinoda) at the Śrī Sanātana Gauḍīya Maṭha in the Belpura area.

Then, during September of 1927, he went on a long preaching pilgrimage tour, visiting Kāśī, Kanpur, Lucknow, Jaipur, Puṣkara, Dvārakā, Sudāmāpuri, Prabhāsa, Ujjain, Mathurā, Kurukṣetra, and finally Naimiṣāraṇya. In October of 1929, he visited Vārāṇasī again, lecturing on the teachings that Caitanya Mahāprabhu gave to Sanātana Gosvāmī. And in December of 1933, Bhaktisiddhānta Sarasvatī opened the gates of the Paramarthika Exhibition in the Michira Pokra area.

Pastimes of Śrīla Prabhupāda

In the *Śrīla Prabhupāda-līlāmṛta* (Vol. 4, Chapter 5), we hear of Śrīla Prabhupāda's preaching activities in Vārāṇasī: "Mr. Gourkishore was counting heavily on Prabhupāda's participation in the upcoming celebrations on February 6, 1971. The climax of the week-long observance of Lord Caitanya's visit to Vārāṇasī would be a parade, Mr. Gourkishore said, and Prabhupāda and his disciples had an important part in it. Newspaper articles, handbills, and loudspeaker carts had announced throughout the city the presence of Śrīla Prabhupāda and his foreign disciples. The devotees sensed they were being treated like entertainers, expected to perform as if under contract, but without salary.

"On the day of the procession Prabhupāda rode in a silver chariot, the kind customarily used in extravagant wedding processions. The chariot was pulled by a pair of white horses, wearing silver crowns and decorative blankets. The leading float in the parade bore a two metre statue of Lord Caitanya in yellow neem wood. Next followed a file of decorated elephants. One elephant carried a banner reading '*Harer Nāma Eva Kevalam*', one carried actors dressed as Lord Rāma and Sītā, another carried two actors dressed as Rādhā and Kṛṣṇa, who waved to the crowds, and another a picture of Lord Caitanya and His associates performing *saṅkīrtana.* Next came a decorated flatbed truck with children protraying Lord Caitanya and Lord Nityānanda, chanting and dancing. Then followed a series of professional *kīrtana* groups and Prabhupāda's foreign disciples dancing and performing *kīrtana*."

Mahā-śmaśāna

The present Kāśī Viśvanātha (Viśveśvara) *mandira* is just opposite the Jñānavāpī mosque (built by Raziyyat-ud-din and also known as Razia mosque), but Lord Śiva's carrier, Nandi the bull, still faces in the direction where the original temple once stood, bearing witness to the past.

The original Viśveśvara-liṅga was thrown into the Jñānavāpī (well of knowledge) during the temple's desecration by Aurangazeb in 1669. The original Bindu-Mādhava *mūrti* was thrown into the Gaṅgā by Aurangazeb during the destruction of that temple. The present Bindu-Mādhava *mūrti* manifested from the River Gaṇḍakī in the Himālayas before one *sādhu*, who eventually brought Him to Kāśī. Today, the temple of Bindu-Mādhava is located in an inconspicuous building in the shadow of the large mosque that Aurangazeb constucted on the temple's original location. Most of the *ghāṭas* are more or less in their original locations, with slight changes due to Gaṅgā's seasonal tide. There was also one Caitanya-vaṭa, a banyan tree under which Śrī Caitanya Mahāprabhu used to rest after taking His lunch. Today, the tree is no longer there. The place where it once stood is now called Jatana-bata on "Caitanya Road", where there is a small temple of Śrī Ṣaḍbhuja (a six-armed form of Lord Caitanya), allowing us to recollect the Lord's pastimes in Vārāṇasī. Nearby is the *baitaka* (seat) of Vallabha Ācārya. The homes of Tapana Miśra and Candraśekhara no longer exist, but they were formerly in the area now called Chaitan-ghar.

Kāśī is known as the "city of light", since this is where truth and reality are revealed and where Lord Śiva externally resides, bestowing the enlightening wisdom of liberation. Kāśī is a famous place in which to die. People from all over India make their final pilgrimage here. To die here is most glorious, since Yamarāja has no jurisdiction in Kāśī. It is a common sight to see a funeral procession accompanied by the familiar chant: *Rāma nāma satya hai! Rāma nāma satya hai!*: "Lord Rāma's name is truth! Lord Rāma's name is truth!" Kāśī is also known as Mahā-śmaśāna (the great cremation ground), and literally speaking, one can cremate the dead anywhere! The whole of Kāśī is a cremation ground! The most popular places to cremate bodies are at Maṇikarṇikā-ghāṭa and Hariścandra-ghāṭa. To sit and watch a body burn and smell the flesh and hair burn really gives one a sharp realization about our own bodies, reminding us that someday our turn is next!

There are numerous *Purāṇas* and Vedic literatures that describe the glories of Kāśī, but as mentioned in many *māhātmyams* (glorifications), the greatest glory is to leave one's body here and attain *mukti* (liberation) from the cycle of birth and death: *kāśyāṁ maraṇaṁ muktiḥ*. Anyone who may live, work, visit, or just come here to die will attain that liberation from the material world. But as explained by the famous saint from Vṛndāvana, Bilvamaṅgala Ṭhākura: *muktiḥ svayaṁ mukulitāñjali sevate 'smān*. Mukti herself is standing with folded palms, waiting to serve the devotee. So this *mokṣa*, or *mukti*, for which most Hindus are hankering for is automatically attained by the Vaiṣṇava devotee of the Lord, who is ready to serve the Supreme Personality of Godhead, Lord Kṛṣṇa, birth after birth, regardless of time or place, in any circumstance.

To conclude this section on Kāśī, the *Skanda Purāṇa* (*Kāśī-khaṇḍa* 35.7-10) is quoted as follows: "Of the many holy places on this earth, which of them would equal in the balance one speck of Kāśī's dust? Of the many rivers flowing to the sea, which of them is like the Gaṅgā in Kāśī? Of the many places that grant liberations on earth, which one equals the smallest part of Kāśī, the city never forsaken by Śiva? What wonder is there in that the glory of liberation is achieved where the three—Gaṅgā, Viśvanātha, and Kāśī—are found?"

BIHAR

The history of Bihar is rich and inspiring, as at Bihar there is verily a confluence of different religious faiths. Various paths of Hinduism, Buddhism, Jainism, and Sikhism have found millions of adherents in Bihar. The whole of northern Bihar is pratically saturated with devotees and their love for Śrī Rāmacandra and Sītā-devī, because the birthplace of Sītā in Mithilā, also known as Janakapura, Nepal, borders the Bihar districts of Sitamarhi and Madhubani. Also, the ancient kingdom of Māgadha, formerly ruled by the great King Jarāsandha, who was eventually killed by Lord Kṛṣṇa and Pāṇḍava Bhīma, later became a popular *tīrtha* for the Buddhists and Jains. Then there is Gayā, with its deep history that dates back to the beginning of creation and which is still the most popular *tīrtha* where people perform *piṇḍa-dāna* (offering to forefathers) at the famous Viṣṇupada Mandira (the temple that contains the lotus footprint of Lord Viṣṇu). Just south of Gayā is Bodhgayā, where Prince Siddhārtha became known as Lord Śākya Muni Buddha after he obtained *nirvāṇa* (freedom from material existence) under the Mahabodi tree. Bodhgayā is the foremost *tīrtha* for all Buddhists worldwide. On several different occassions Śrī Caitanya Mahāprabhu also visited Bihar, particularly the areas of Gayā, Patna, Mandara Hill, Kānāi-nāṭaśālā, and the section of the Jhārikhaṇḍa forest known as Choṭanagpura (Chhota Nagra), which is near the popular Lord Jagannātha temple in Jagannāthapura (Singhbhum district). He also passed through the Bundu and Tamar sections of the Ranchi District before proceeding on the ancient pilgrimage route to Jagannātha Purī. Due to His mercy, Bihar has embraced the Vaiṣṇavism of West Bengal and Orissa.

15) SIDDHĀŚRAMA (BUXAR)

The *āśrama* of Viśvāmitra

In the *Śrīmad Vālmīki Rāmāyaṇa* (*Bāla-kāṇḍa* 29-30), we hear the history of the famous hermitage of the great sage Viśvāmitra.

After Viśvāmitra instructed Śrī Rāma to kill the demon named Tāraka, the Lord and His younger brother Lakṣmaṇa accompanied Viśvāmitra to his *āśrama*, known as Siddhāśrama, which was situated on the bank of the Gaṅgā. In reply to Śrī Rāma's inquiry, Viśvāmitra explained that Lord Viṣṇu had spent hundreds of *yugas* performing austerities and *yoga* here at Siddhāśrama. During that time, the demigods requested the Lord's assistance to fight against the demons, because they foresaw His future *avatāra* as Lord Vāmanadeva, the dwarf *brāhmaṇa* incarnation of the Supreme Lord Viṣṇu. It was also here at Siddhāśrama that the Supreme Personality of Godhead appeared before Aditi and benedicted her that He would appear as her son. He then entered within Kaśyapa Muni and the great sage then transfered his potency into the womb of Aditi.

Viśvāmitra continued explaining to Śrī Rāma and Lakṣmaṇa that only through his own devotional service to Lord Viṣṇu here at Siddhāśrama was he able to obtain this hermitage. He then offered Śrī Rāma his hermitage, by saying, "The site of this *āśrama* is as much Yours as mine, since You are none other than Lord Viṣṇu." The great *ṛṣi* then instructed Śrī Rāma and Lakṣmaṇa to prepare themselves for the ceremony of sanctification, which was to initiate a six day sacrifice, during which Śrī Rāma and Lakṣmaṇa had to keep continuous vigil without sleep in order to protect Viśvāmitra's sacrificial arena from the demons Mārīca and Subāhu. On the sixth day, when the Soma juice (drink of immortality) was being extracted from the sacrifice, Rāma and Lakṣmaṇa prepared with eagerness for Their confrontation with the two demons.

Suddenly the demons appeared in the sky and began to rain torrents of blood, flesh, and pus on the sacrificial altar. Śrī Rāma then employed the Mānavāstra (the missile presided over by Svāyambhuva Manu), hurling it at the breast of Mārīca. The demon was flung one hundred *yojanas* (800 miles) into the middle of the ocean. Then the missile presided over by Agnideva, the demigod of fire, was employed on Subāhu, killing him instantly. Another missile presided over by

Vāyu, the demigod of the wind, was released towards the remaining *rākṣasas*, eliminating all of them.

Viśvāmitra then praised Śrī Rāma for protecting the sacrificial proceedings by saying, "I stand accomplished of my purpose, O mighty-armed Rāma. The name of this Siddhāśrama has now been justified." The next morning, Viśvāmitra, Śrī Rāma, and Lakṣmaṇa prepared to leave towards Mithilā (Janakapura), to witness the bow sacrifice of King Janaka.

Siddhāśrama is also known as Siddharāmapura. In the *Brahmāṇḍa Purāṇa* it is mentioned that this area in the former kingdom of Karūṣadeśa was called Vedagarbhapurī, Malada, or Aṅgamalaja.

16) Sarayū, Soṇa, and Gaṇḍakī-saṅgamas with the Gaṅgā

In and around the Patna area of Bihar there are three important rivers joining with the Gaṅgā. The following are a few pastimes related to these three significant rivers.

Sarayū

As stated in the *Nārada Purāṇa* (*Uttarabhāga* 40. 38-39): "Thereafter is the holy center called Veṇirājya where the highly meritorious Sarayū joins the holy Gaṅgā like a sister meeting with her sister. The Gaṅgā has become the celestial river inasmuch as it washes the right foot of Hari resembling a lotus. The Sarayū born of the Mānasa lake originates from his left foot."

In the *Śrīmad Vālmīki Rāmāyaṇa* (*Bālakāṇḍa* 23-24) we learn about the place where Lord Śiva performed austerities when he was disturbed by the lord of desire, Kāmadeva, otherwise known as Cupid.

After performing their morning devotional activities, Śrī Rāma, Lakṣmaṇa, and the great Viśvāmitra Ṛṣi proceeded on their way from Ayodhyā. While traveling onwards, Śrī Rāma and Lakṣmaṇa sighted the celestial River Gaṅgā and her blessed confluence with the River Sarayū. At that *saṅgama*, they also beheld the hermitages of various *ṛṣis* who had performed great austerities for thousands of years. Then Śrī Rāma inquired, "Whose holy hermitage is this? What personage dwells here?" Viśvāmitra then began to describe whose former residence it was.

"At this place, Kandarpa, who is also known as Kāmadeva, foolishly disturbed Lord Śiva, who was uninterruptedly performing great austerities and was absorbed in deep meditation. Then, with the glance of Lord Śiva's fierce third eye, all the limbs of the capricious Kāmadeva were burnt, and he became bodiless. Afterwards, Kāma became known as Anaṅga (bodiless) and this tract of land became known as the Aṅga territory. This holy hermitage belongs to Lord Śiva, and these sages performing austerities are his disciples. O Rāma, let us all halt here for the evening and tomorrow morning we will cross the holy Gaṅgā. After we bathe and offer oblations into the sacred fire, we will then be welcomed into their hermitages."

The next morning, Viśvāmitra and the two sons of King Daśaratha boarded a boat and proceeded to cross the River Gaṅgā. In the middle of the river, Śrī Rāma became perplexed by the great noisy agitation of the river waves striking one another. Śrī Rāma then inquired from Viśvāmitra, "What is the cause of this incredible noise?" Viśvāmitra then replied, "Near Mount Kailāsa is a great lake created by Lord Brahmā's mind known by the name Mānasa. This River Sarayū has her source from that lake and encircles Ayodhyā. This unparalled sound is produced by the turbulent meeting of this river with the Jāhnavī (Gaṅgā). O Rāma, You should therefore offer Your obeisances to these two rivers where they meet."

It is also mentioned in *Mahābhārata* (*Anuśāsana-parva*) that the River Sarayū originates from Mānasa-sarovara (Mānasa-saras), which is situated at the foot of Vaidyuta-giri, near Mount Kailāsa. In the *Tīrthaprakāsa* of *Vikramāditya*, the waters of Sarayū are described as very sacred. There are many saintly hermitages on her banks. A mere bath in her waters is stated to destroy sins equivalent to that of *brahma-hatyā* (killing of a *brāhmaṇa*). One is prescribed to bathe in her waters with a pure mind and then worship Lord Viṣṇu. One must also offer gifts of *anna* (grains), perform *homa* (sacrifice) and *japa*, and also feed the *brāhmaṇas*. A bath in the *saṅgama* of Sarayū and Gaṅgā is highly meritorious, especially on Ekādaśī.

It is recommended to perform pilgrimage of all the holy places situated on Sarayū's bank at Ayodhyā, which was originally established by King Manu. The River Sarayū was like the common mother for the various rulers of the Ikṣvāku dynasty. The bank of Sarayū was her lap, and her waters were like mother's milk.

Also in the *Mahābhārata* it is mentioned that the great sage Bhṛgu Muni had his *āśrama*, known as Bhṛgu-tīrtha, at the confluence of the Rivers Sarayū and Gaṅgā. It was here that Paraśurāma regained his lost energy and strength, which had been taken away by Lord Rāmacandra. The *Skanda Purāṇa* mentions another *āśrama* of Bhṛgu Muni, known as Bhṛgukacha-tīrtha, which was located on the northern bank of the River Narmadā. There was yet another *āśrama* located near the Himālayan peak known as Bhṛgutuṅga, which is situated on the eastern bank of the River Gaṇḍakī.

Śoṇa

As quoted in the *Garuḍa Purāṇa* (*Ācāra-kāṇḍa* 81.12): "Śoṇa is a great holy river."

Again, from the *Śrīmad Vālmīki Rāmāyaṇa* (*Bāla-kāṇḍa* 34-35), we now hear of Viśvāmitra's personal background. The confluence of the Śoṇa and Gaṅgā is the place where Viśvāmitra narrated to Lord Rāmacandra the origin of the Bhāgirathī Gaṅgā.

After Śrī Rāma vanquished the demons Mārīca and Subāhu, Viśvāmitra blessed everyone at his Siddhāśrama by saying, "May all blessings be bestowed upon all. Since my purpose has been accomplished, I shall proceed from Siddhāśrama to the Himālayan mountains on the northern bank of the holy Gaṅgā after first visiting the Śoṇa-saṅgama." Then Viśvāmitra, Rāma, Lakṣmaṇa, and several sages proceeded a long distance, until they arrived at the bank of the River Śoṇa near Gaṅgā. After bathing and performing oblations at sunset, everyone sat around the wise and learned Viśvāmitra. Śrī Rāma began to inquire about the particular tract of land where they were now residing.

In reply, Viśvāmitra first narrated the story of King Kuśa (of whom he himself was a descendent from the second of Kuśa's four sons, Kuśanābha), "O Śrī Rāma, after Kuśanābha married his one hundred daughters to Brahmadatta, he performed a sacrifice to procure a son. While the sacrifice was being performed, King Kuśa prophesied to Kuśanābha that a most pious son by the name of Gādhi would be born to him. That extraordinary pious man, Gādhi, was my father. I am known as Kauśika and also have an elder sister named Satyavatī, who was given away to the sage Ṛcīka.

Following the wishes of her husband throughout her life, my sister ascended to the celestial world and later transformed into the most beneficial and delightful River Kauśikī (Kośī). She flows by the side of the Himālayas, where her waters confer merit, and she is engaged in pious activities for others.

I have been leading a self-disciplined life in the Himālayas on the bank of Kauśikī. That pious and highly blessed lady, Satyavatī, who was established in the virtue of truthfulness, is still present in the form of Kauśikī, one of the foremost of all rivers. Leaving that river, I came down to the plains to perform that sacrifice at Siddhāśrama, where You, O Rāma, have assisted in fulfilling my purpose. In this way, I have told you about my birth from the loins of Gādhi, the genesis of my race from Kuśa, and about the history of this land of Girivraja (Rajgir), which extends along the bank of the River Śoṇa."

The next morning, after a beautiful sunrise, Viśvāmitra and his entourage began their journey onwards. Then Śrī Rāma asked, "Which of the two river fords in the holy Śoṇa should we wade through?" Viśvāmitra indicated the proper direction to lead them to the bank of the Gaṅgā, the place where he narrated the origin of the Bhāgīrathī Gaṅgā to Śrī Rāma.

In the *Śrīmad-Bhāgavatam* (10.79.15) and in the *Śrī Caitanya-bhāgavata* (*Ādi-khaṇḍa* 9.127) the accounts of Lord Balarāma's and, later, Lord Nityānanda's bathing in the River Śoṇa are given: "After Lord Balarāma bathed in the Rivers Gomatī, Gaṇḍakī and Vipāśā, He immersed Himself in the River Śoṇa before going to Gayā." "Thereafter, Lord Nityānanda bathed in the Gomatī, Gaṇḍakī, and Śoṇa Rivers."

The River Śoṇa (Sone) originates from the Amarakaṇṭaka plateau in the Maikāla mountain in Gondwana in the state of Madhya Pradesh, nine kilometres east of the source of the River Narmadā. In the *Skanda Purāṇa* (*Vidyeśvara-saṁhitā*), Amarakaṇṭaka is mentioned as a very sacred place where numerous *tīrthas* abide. It is considered very auspicious for the purpose of performing *śrāddha*. The River Śoṇa first flows north and then east for nearly eight hundred kilometres before she meets the Gaṅgā, opposite the *saṅgama* of the Sarayū and Gaṅgā, near Patna. The Rivers Sarayū and Śoṇa join Gaṅgā between Singhi and Harji Chhapra. The River Śoṇa is also called Māgadhī-nada, since it flowed through the five hills encircling Girivraja, the capital city of the Māgadha kingdom, and formed the kingdom's western boundary. It is a masculine river (*nada*), not feminine (*nadī*). There are seven rivers referred to as *nadas*: Śoṇa, Sindhu, Hiraṇyavatī (Little Gaṇḍakī), Kokā, Lauhityā (Brahmaputrā), Ghargharā (Sarayū), and Śatadru (Sutlej). It is also stated that the Rivers Śoṇa and Narmadā originated from two tears of Lord Brahmā dropped on opposite sides of the Amarakaṇṭaka plateau.

Gaṇḍakī

The sanctity of the Gaṇḍakī River is mentioned in the *Varāha Purāṇa* (145.112-114) as follows: "The place where the Gaṇḍakī flows is very holy, because Gaṇḍakī is the best of all rivers. Then there is Harikṣetra where Gaṇḍakī mingles with the Bhāgīrathī (Gaṅgā). The sacredness of the place where Gaṇḍakī joins Gaṅgā cannot be fully known, not even by the demigods."

The *Śrīmad-Bhāgavatam* (8.2-4) narrates the liberation of Gajendra, the king of elephants, otherwise known as Gajendra-mokṣa. This pastime occured in the midst of the ocean of milk, where there is a mountain named Trikūṭa. In a valley of Trikūṭa is a beautiful garden called Ṛtumat. In this area is a very nice lake, wherein Gajendra was bathing with some female elephants. While bathing and enjoying in the water, they disturbed the chief crocodile, who attacked Gajendra's leg. Thus a great fight went on for a thousand years, during which the elephant became weaker and the crocodile's strength increased. Being in a helpless condition, Gajendra sought shelter at the lotus feet of the Supreme Personality of Godhead, Nārāyaṇa, and began to offer prayers of surrender. Being satisfied with his prayers, the Lord appeared on the scene and pulled both the elephant and the crocodile out of the water. Then the Lord killed the crocodile with his disc and rescued Gajendra, who was awarded *sārūpya-mukti*, or liberation of receiving a spiritual body exactly like that of Lord Nārāyaṇa.

In Gajendra's past life, he was King Indradyumna, who was cursed by Agastya Muni to become a dull elephant. The crocodile was King Huhu, who insulted Devala Ṛṣi and was cursed to become a crocodile. In this way, both the elephant and the crocodile were delivered from their curses by Lord Nārāyaṇa Himself.

Obviously this pastime occured on another planet. But on this planet, there was a similar pastime that took place at one *tīrtha* named Harikṣetra, just outside a town called Sonepur on the bank of the Gaṇḍakī. At this *tīrtha*, which is near to where the Gaṇḍakī meets Gaṅgā-mayī, the following events narrated in the *Padma Purāṇa* (Uttara-khaṇḍa 110) occured.

"Kardama Muni and his wife Devahūti formerly gave birth to two sons. The elder one was Jaya by name, and the younger, Vijaya. Both were always fully engaged in the devotional service of Lord Viṣṇu. By controlling their senses, they were disposed to virtue, and everyday they chanted, 'Oṁ Namo Nārāyaṇāya'. Since they strictly observed their vows, Lord Viṣṇu would personally appear to them during their daily worship.

"One day, a *brāhmaṇa* named Marutta invited Jaya and Vijaya to perform a sacrifice. Since both of them were skilled in performing sacrifices, they accepted the invitation. Upon arriving at the arena, they were well received by all the divine sages who were participating in the sacrifice. Jaya became the *brahma* (officiating) priest and Vijaya became the *hotra* (sacrificing) priest. After the sacrificial rites were perfectly completed, Marutta and others took bath and gave Jaya and Vijaya their share of wealth for their participation in the sacrifice.

"Later in their hermitage, both Jaya and Vijaya desired to utilize the wealth in the worship and service of Lord Viṣṇu, but they differed on how the wealth should be divided. Jaya said, 'Let it be divided into equal parts', but Vijaya said, 'Whatever is received by one is one's own share.' Then Jaya, whose mind was agitated, angrily cursed Vijaya by saying, 'Since you have received the wealth and are not sharing it, therefore become a crocodile!' Due to arrogance, Vijaya countered the curse by saying, 'You become an elephant!'

"During the time of their daily worship, when Lord Viṣṇu appeared as usual, the brothers related to Viṣṇu what had happened and requested the Lord to render the curses ineffective, 'O dear Lord, how shall we, who are Your devotees, become a crocodile and an elephant? O ocean of kindness, please nullify the curses.' Then Lord Viṣṇu said, 'The words of my devotees shall never prove false, even I cannot change those words. Formerly, due to Prahlāda's words, I appeared in a pillar. Therefore, after undergoing the curses you pronounced, you will both attain My eternal abode.' After saying this, Lord Viṣṇu disappeared.

"Then Jaya and Vijaya took birth as an elephant and a crocodile respectively on the bank of Gaṇḍakī. They remembered their past lives and continued worshiping Lord Viṣṇu from within. One day during the month of Kārtika (October/November), the elephant went to the Gaṇḍakī for a bath. Just then, the crocodile remembered the cause of the curse and seized the elephant. While the two were struggling, the elephant remembered Lord Viṣṇu, who appeared holding His conch, disc, and mace. Then the Lord emancipated both the elephant and crocodile by using His disc and took them to Vaikuṇṭhaloka.

"Since then, that place became known as Harikṣetra,* and even now the mark of the Lord's disc is visible on some stones there. Jaya and Vijaya, who were very dear to the Lord, assumed their positions as His doorkeepers. It is further concluded that one should always bathe in Gaṇḍakī during the morning when the sun is in Libra (Tula-saṅkrānti, October), in Capricorn (Makara-saṅkrānti, January), or in Aries (Mesha-saṅkrānti, April), maintain a tulasī grove, and observe Ekādaśī-vrata. One should also worship the brāhmaṇas, cows, and Lord Viṣṇu's devotees."

According to the Padma Purāṇa, after the great demon Śaṅkhacūḍa was killed by Śiva through the help of Lord Viṣṇu's deceiving Tulasī, her body became the River Gaṇḍakī and Viṣṇu became śālagrāma-śilās (Deity incarnation in the form of stones). The Varāha Purāṇa states that Gaṇḍakī was formed from the sweat of the gaṇḍa (cheeks) of Lord Viṣṇu, who performed austerities at the source of the river. And in the Skanda Purāṇa it is mentioned that Gaṇḍakī was formed from the sweat of both Lord Viṣṇu and Lord Śiva. According to the Mahābhārata, Gaṇḍakī is also known as Nārāyaṇī, Śālagrāmī, Hiraṇvatī, Cakranadī, and Hiraṇyavatī. The Gaṇḍakī is also known as one of the seven branches of the Gaṅgā. The earthly source of Gaṇḍakī is Dāmodara-

kuṇḍa, located in the Dhaulāgiri range of the Himālayas, twenty-five kilometres from the sacred tīrtha Muktinātha in Nepal.

Also, near Harikṣetra is the town of Sonepur, that is situated on the eastern bank of the River Gaṇḍakī. Lord Śiva resides here as Hariharanātha, so Sonepur is also known as Hariharakṣetra. The origin of Hariharanātha remains shrouded in mystery. Many traditional Hindus believe that the original temple was built by Lord Rāmacandra, when He was on His way to Janakapura to win the hand of Sītā-devī. However, there is no reference to this in the Rāmāyaṇa, even though Lord Rāma did pass this way. During the month of Kārtika, especially during Pūrṇimā (the full moon), millions of pilgrims visit Sonepur (Harikṣetra and Hariharakṣetra) for bathing in the Gaṇḍakī and Gaṅgā. During this time, the world's second largest cattle melā (fair) is held, which brings even more visitors to this area. The Sonepur melā also includes the trading of horses, camels, sheep, and elephants.

17) PĀṬALIPUTRA (PATAN-DEVĪ / PATNA)

A stick, a pair of sandals, and a pot.

In the Kathāpīṭhalambaka (Kathāsarit-sāgara), there is a very interesting story of how Pāṭalī and Putraka were married, and how they then created a city named Pāṭaliputra, which was the ancient name of Patna, the present capital of Bihar.

There is a sacred place named Kanakhala (Haridvāra) on the banks of the River Gaṅgā. Once a brāhmaṇa from Dakṣiṇa-bhārata (South India) came with his wife to Kanakhala and started practising severe austerities. In the course of time, three sons were born of them, and the parents died. The three sons then went to Rājagṛha and studied there, but being very poor, they left

---

* According to the Varāha Purāṇa, Jaya and Vijaya were the sons of the sage Tṛṇabindu. After they had cursed one another, they became a crocodile and elephant at a sacred place named Triveṇikṣetra, high in the Himālayas. This is where the three rivers—Gaṇḍakī, Devikā, and Brahmatanayā—meet. It was here that Lord Viṣṇu appeared and smashed the mouth of the crocodile with His Sudarśana cakra (disc). This tīrtha is also known as Mukti-kṣetra and is the place where the great sages Pulastya and Pulaha had their hermitages.

in order to perform penance for the pleasure of Lord Subramaṇya (Kārtikeya). On their way, they entered the house of a *brāhmaṇa* named Bhojika, who lived by the sea coast. Bhojika had three daughters, and after learning more about his three guests, he gave his daughters to them, along with his wealth. Bhojika then went to perform austerities, while the three *brāhmaṇa* boys lived with their wives in that house.

One time later on there was a famine, and the three *brāhmaṇa* boys left their house and wives behind. The second wife was pregnant at the time, so she and her sisters went to the house of a friend of their father named Yajñadatta. In due course of time, she delivered a son and all three sisters looked after the child as their common son.

Lord Śiva and Pārvatī were once traveling in the air and upon seeing this child, Śiva said, "I am blessing this boy. This boy in his previous birth, along with his wife, worshiped me with great devotion. They are now born again to enjoy life. His wife in his previous life was born as the daughter of King Mahendra. Her name was Pāṭali, and she will again be the wife of this boy in this life." That night, Lord Śiva appeared to the mother of the boy and told her, "You must name this boy Putraka. Every morning when he rises, one hundred thousand gold coins will fall to the ground from his head."

Therefore, she named the boy Putraka, and every morning she and her sisters would collect and store all the gold coins that fell from his head. When Putraka grew up, he was immensely rich and started giving away his riches to *brāhmaṇas* as gifts. The news of this spread far and wide, so *brāhmaṇas* from all regions began to flock to his house.

One day, Putraka's father and two brothers came to his house. The father and brothers felt envious of his extraordinary wealth and fame, so they cleverly took Putraka to a lonely place in the heart of the Vindhya mountains to kill him. After engaging some murderers to kill him, they left that place. Then Putraka bribed the murderers with his costly dresses and ornaments and escaped from there. There was then a great storm, but Putraka continued to walk through it. On his way, he met the two sons of Mayāsura quarrelling over three items left to them by their father. The paternal property consisted of a stick, a pair of sandals, and a pot, all of which possessed some mystic powers. If one drew on the ground any object with the stick, whatever he drew would immediately appear on that spot. If the sandals were worn, one could travel in the air. And if one put his hand in the pot, he would receive full nourishment.

Putraka immediately thought of a plan and addressed the quarrelling brothers by saying, "Why do you fight like this? It is better to decide by competing in a race together. Whoever wins the race will be entitled to these three items." The two brothers agreed and after leaving the items with Putraka, began running their race. When the brothers had gone a long distance, Putraka put on the sandals, took the stick and pot, and flew away in the air! He landed at a city far away and began living in the house of an old woman. The king of that province had a daughter named Pāṭalī. When the old lady described to Putraka the beauty and good qualities of Pāṭalī, Putraka wanted to marry her. So one night, when everyone was asleep, Putraka put on the sandals and entered the room of Pāṭalī through the window. When Pāṭalī woke up, she immediately married Putraka according to the *gandharva-vidhi* (a Vedic marriage rite). Then they both went out of the palace through the air and landed at a place on the shore of Gaṅgā. Then at the request of Pāṭalī, Putraka made a city with the help of the stick and they named it

Pāṭaliputra, and the pot provided them full nourishment.

Before Pāṭaliputra became the capital, Rājagṛha (Rajgir) was the capital of Māgadha, which was once under the control of Jarāsandha, who was eventually killed by the Pāṇḍava Bhīma. Thereafter, King Bimbisāra made Rājagṛha his capital, which was frequently visited by Lord Buddha. Later, when King Ajātaśatru ruled Rājagṛha, he was worried that his capital was not properly situated for offensive and defensive operations. He wanted his capital shifted to the junction of the Rivers Sarayū, Soṇa, and Gaṇḍakī with the River Gaṅgā, leaving behind Rājagṛha, which was protected only by seven surrounding hills.

When Lord Buddha was traveling from Nālandā (Rajgir) to Vaiśālī, just before His *pari-nirvāṇa* (disappearance), He passed through Pāṭaliputra and was invited as an honored guest by two ministers. The place where Lord Buddha passed along the Gaṅgā became known as Gautama-ghāṭa. On this occasion, Lord Buddha made the following prophecy: "This Pāṭaliputra will grow as the chief Āryan city of Bhārata-varṣa and will be the center of trade and prosperity. But be warned, it will be destroyed by fire, floods, and treachery."

Emperor Aśoka also reigned from Pāṭaliputra for forty years, but he completely changed the appearance of the city. He replaced wooden walls with masonry and constructed ramparts, palaces, monuments, and monasteries. The renowned Canakya Paṇḍita had also lived here and was well honored as a *brāhmaṇa* advisor and the prime minister of King Candragupta Maurya. Canakya Paṇḍita mentions this city in his book *Artha-śāstra*.

In the *Vāyu Purāṇa*, Pāṭaliputra is also called Kusumapura. It is also mentioned that the word "Pāṭali" refers to the trumpet flower, and another narration says that Pāṭalī was the daughter of King Gādhi and another sister of Viśvāmitra. Because of her desire, the sage Kauṇḍinya created the city of Pāṭalī by mystic *yoga*.

The name Patna was derived from two Patan-devī temples: Bari Patan Devī (in Maharajganj) and Choti Patan Devī (in City chowk). According to one narration, during Dakṣa's sacrifice at Kanakhala, when Lord Śiva became angry upon learning of Satī's death, he took her dead body upon his shoulder and began to perform *tāṇḍava-nṛtya* (a dance) around the three worlds. All the *devas* were extremely frightened and requested Lord Viṣṇu to intervene. Lord Viṣṇu carefully followed Lord Śiva and started to cut the body of Satī into pieces with His *cakra* (disc). Wherever the major limbs fell became *mahāpīṭhas* (major holy places), and where the minor limbs fell became *upapīṭhas* (minor holy places). As mentioned in the *Cudamaṇi-tantra*, some portion of Satī's right thigh and cloth (*pat*) fell in Māgadha, supposedly near the Maharajganj and City chowk areas. Thus, Bari Patan and Choti Patan are derived from Satī's *pat*, or cloth. According to the locals, Patan means "town", and Patna refers to a big place of export and import.

Śrī Caitanya Mahāprabhu's visit

In the year 1506, after Śrī Caitanya Mahāprabhu's father, Jagannātha Miśra, left this mortal world, Nimāi Paṇḍita (Mahāprabhu) and many student friends proceeded from Navadvīpa on a pilgrimage to Śrī Gayā-dhāma. As they traveled on the various paths, Lord Caitanya made every village and town a holy place with the touch of His lotus feet. On their way, they visited Mandara Hill and had *darśana* of Lord Madhusūdana, and at Rajgir they bathed in Brahma-kuṇḍa. Finally they arrived in Gayā.

As they entered the temple containing Lord Viṣṇu's right footprint (Viṣṇupada), they listened to the *brāhmaṇas* chant the glories of the Lord, known as Gadādhara Viṣṇu, as follows: "Lord Śiva, the master of Kāśī, holds these feet close to his heart. These feet are the life and soul of goddess Lakṣmī. The Lord placed these feet on Bali Mahārāja's head. Yamarāja has no jurisdiction over a person who meditates on these feet for half a moment. The masters of *yoga* find these feet very difficult to attain. From these feet, Gaṅgā has manifested. The servants of the Lord never renounce these feet, they keep them always in their hearts. These very dear feet rest on the bed of Ananta Śeṣa. O fortunate people, please gaze upon these feet."

During his visit, Mahāprabhu performed *srāddha* and offered *piṇḍa-dāna* to His ancestors at each of the various sixteen Gayās (Preta, Rāma, Yudhiṣṭhira, Bhima, Śiva, Brahmā, etc). Then Caitanya Mahāprabhu met Īśvara Purī, who eventually gave Him initiation. On His return journey to Navadvīpa, Mahāprabhu rested at a place called Gai-ghāṭa, near the River Gaṅgā in Patna city.

Later, Srī Gopāla Bhaṭṭa Gosvāmī's disciple, Śrīnivāsa Ācārya, constructed the Caitanya Mandira near Gai-ghāṭa and installed Śrī Śrī Gaura-Nitāi Deities. Various Gauḍīya-Vaiṣṇava Bābājīs maintained the worship of the temple until 1714, when a Bengali family accepted the management. In 1740, Radhalal Gosvāmī established the Caitanya Pustakalaya (library), which contains some very rare handwritten copies of the works of Rūpa and Sanātana Gosvāmīs, Kṛṣṇa dāsa Gosvāmī, Vṛndāvana dāsa Ṭhākura, Caraṇa dāsa Bābājī, and Haladhara Dāsa. In addition, there is a collection of more than three hundred miniature paintings of the pastimes of Śrī Caitanya Mahāprabhu.

Śrila Bhaktisiddhānta Mahārāja's visit

On the 14th of November, 1933, by the mercy of Śrīla Bhaktisiddhānta Sarasvati Ṭhākura, the gates to the Patna Sat-sikṣā Exhibition (spiritual or theistic diorama exhibitions) were opened by the honorable Mahārājādhirāja Shri Kamesvara Singh Bahadur. On this occasion, many respectable people came from universities throughout Bihar and received instructions from this unprecedented Sat-sikṣā exhibition.

Srīla Bhaktisiddhānta Mahārāja also propagated theistic displays and diorama exhibitions in Kurukṣetra in 1928, 1933, and 1936; in Māyāpur during 1930; in Calcutta in 1930 and 1931; in Dhaka and Kāsī in 1933; and also in Prayāga in 1936. These free exhibitions described the *līlās*, or pastimes, of Lord Kṛṣṇa, Lord Caitanya, etc. with the help of toys, dolls, pictures, writings, and even mechanical devices for moving the dolls. Generally these exhibitions lasted for a fortnight, but according to popular demand they occasionally lasted longer.

By the desire of Srīla Bhaktisiddhānta Mahārāja, a festival was held at the Patna Gauḍīya Math (Bankipura, Kadamakuya) on the 14th of August, 1934, when he installed Their Lordships Srī Srī Vinodā-Govindānanda. After the installation, three huge *hari-nāma-saṅkirtana* processions went throughout the city. Since then, one street in the city of Patna was named "Exhibition Road," after Bhaktisiddhānta Mahārāja's Sat-sikṣā Exhibition.

Harmandira, the birthplace of Guru Govind Singh

Close to the bank of Gaṅgā-mayī in the City chowk area near Choti Patan Devī is the birthplace of the tenth and the last *guru* (spiritual master) of the Sikhs, Guru Govind Singh, who was born the 22th of December,

1666. A beautiful temple has been constructed at Harmandira ki Gali. In this temple, Guru Govind Singh's cradle, dagger, arrows, comb, shoes, and other personal paraphernalia are preserved. The Śrī Guru Granth Sahib, the holy religious book, which represents the final words spoken by all of the Sikh *gurus*, that was presented by Guru Govind Singh himself, is also preserved here. He personally signed his name in this Granth Sahib with an arrow. He impressed upon the Sikhs the importance of military discipline, initiating them into the Khalsa (The Master's Own) by assigning the five signs: *keśa* (uncut hair), *kāṅgā* (comb), *kacchā* (a pair of shorts), *kaḍa* (an iron bracelet), and *kirapāna* (a sword), and he introduced the surname "Singh".

Guru Govind Singh strongly prohibited the killing of cows. Moreover, he was considered a poet, well versed in Hindi, Persian, and Sanskrit. This temple is highly revered by all Sikhs. Every morning, at the beginning of *brāhma-muhūrta* (time before sunrise), the birthsite of Guru Govind Singh is bathed with Gaṅgā-jala. Their first Guru, Śrī Nanak Deva, had also spent several months in the same area.

18) JAHĀNGĪR (SULTĀNGAÑJ)

Jahnu Ṛṣi's *āśrama*

Jahāngīr was formerly one of the six *āśramas* of the great Jahnu Ṛṣi. This *āśrama* was once a center of cultural education. It was located on a large rock-island in the middle of the River Gaṅgā. As previously mentioned in the *Nārada Purāṇa*, Gaṅgā-mayī had purposely disturbed the meditating sage, Jahnu, and was swallowed up by him. She was later released through his right ear after Bhagīratha Mahārāja had pacified the sage.

This pastime is said to have occured near Gaṅgotrī in the Himālayas, in Śrī Navadvīpa-dhāma (West Bengal), as well as here. Other narrations state that Gaṅgā-mayī was released through both of his ears, his thigh, his knee, or his body. Regardless of where this pastime actually took place or how he released her (the narrations vary slightly since the pastime occured in different ages), Gaṅgā became known as Jāhnavī, the daughter or descendent of Jahnu Ṛṣi.

Jahāngīr is derived from Jahnu Ṛṣi's *giri* (hill) and his *gṛha* (abode). Situated today on the island that was formerly Jahnu Ṛṣi's *āśrama* is an ancient temple dedicated to Lord Śiva, who is known here as Ajgaivinātha, otherwise known as Gaivinātha Mahādeva. It is said that Lord Śiva received his bow known as Ajgav here. Nearby on Murli hill was a beautiful temple dedicated to mother Pārvatī, which was later replaced with a mosque. On one side of the island, Gaṅgā's strong, high flooding currents are slowly wearing away the decaying granite rocks. The small village of Jahāngīr forms a part of the town of Sultāngañj.

In Bihar there are three prominent Śiva temples: Lord Vaidyanātha at Devgarh, Lord Vāsukinātha at Dumka, and Lord Ajgaivinātha at Sultāngañj. During their respective annual festivals, thousands of devotees and pilgrims chant various *mantras* as they walk hundreds of kilometres to bring Gaṅgā-jala to these temples to bathe Lord Śiva. The rainy season provides a very attractive scene as the Gaṅgā swells and washes the feet of the temple of Lord Ajgaivinātha with her waters.

19) VIKRAMAŚĪLA (ANTICHAK/ PĀTHARGHĀṬĀ HILL)

Lord Buddha's University

In 560 B.C. (about 2,560 years ago), Prince Siddhārtha Gautama took birth as the son of King Śuddhodana at the foot of Mount Palpa (in the Himālayan foothills) in a grove known as Lumbinī, near the city of Kapilavastu (Nepal). Some thirty-five years later, after performing great austerities along the bank of the River Nirañjanā in Bodhgayā (Bihar), the Prince became "The Enlightened One", otherwise known as Lord Buddha or Śākya Muni. For forty-five years, Lord Buddha traveled and preached throughout the main Gangetic region. Once when Buddha was traveling from Rajgir (Nālandā, Bihar) to Śrāvastī (Gonda, U.P.), he had to cross the Gaṅgā. The King of Māgadha and his entourage, who were with Lord Buddha, had to cross Gaṅgā by boat. Buddda and his devoted student, Ānanda, crossed the river on a bridge formed by the hoods of Nāgas that had especially appeared to serve the Enlightened One. Other main sacred places associated with Lord Buddha are Sārnātha (Vārāṇasī, U.P.), Sāṅkāśya (Farrukhabad, U.P.), Pāṭaliputra (Patna), Vaiśālī (Bihar), and especially Kuśinagara (Deoria, U.P.), where the Lord left the planet in 480 B.C.

During the time of King Aśoka (268-232 B.C.), who was the third ruler of the Maurya kingdom, the teachings of Lord Buddha were spread throughout the entire country and beyond its boundaries to places such as Syria, Egypt, Kyrene, Macedonia, Epeiros, and Laṅkā-dvīpa.

Nearly one thousand years later, during the 8th century A.D., King Dharmapāla founded the great University of Vikramaśīla (also known as Vikramaśīla-saṅghārāma or Śīla-saṅgama) at Antichak, situated near the summit of Pātharghāṭā Hill, which overlooks the River Gaṅgā. The university buildings accommodated and maintained 108 residential professors and their students. A huge *vihara* (monastery) was constructed in the center of the university quarters, where a large Buddhist temple was erected, surrounded by 108 smaller temples.

On the walls of the university buildings were painted images of learned *paṇḍitas* who were the products of the university. Six colleges were affiliated to this university, and each of them had a staff of 108 professors. Distinguished scholars of the Vikramaśīla University went to foreign countries, particularly to Tibet, where they were respectfully invited to give the benefit of their learning and scholarship. These learned scholars of the university did such wonderful work in Tibet that some of these scholars were worshiped as saints. The Tibetian monk, Nag Tsho Lotsava, was sent by the Tibetian ruler to Vikramaśīla to persuade the very learned scholar, Dīpaṅkara-śrījñāna-asīta, to come to Tibet and preach Buddhism. Asīta was the best professor of that time. When Nag Tsho Lotsava arrived, there were eight thousand monks at Vikramaśīla, of whom Vidya Kokila was the head. Thus Vikramaśīla was one of the best known universities in India and abroad, and it continued to flourish for a period of four hundred years, until it was destroyed by the Muslims in 1203 A.D.

The main remnant of the Vikramaśīla University at Antichak today is the Mahā-vihara, which was located in the center of the university complex. Gaṅgā-mayī is now three kilometres away from Antichak, near a village named Orip and the summit of Pātharghāṭā Hill. Along the bank of the Gaṅgā and below Pātharghāṭā Hill are several caves, which constituted the *āśrama* of Vasiṣṭha Muni and other sages and which are known as Caturasi (eighty-four) Muni's *āśrama*. Outside this *āśrama* Lord Śiva resides as Vateśvara Mahādeva, one of the 108 rare Śiva-liṅgas mentioned in the *Śiva Purāṇa*. Nearby Lord Vateśvara is a modern Sītā-Rāma temple, founded by Nāga-bābājī

Mahārāja, located on a tip of the riverbank with a spectacular one hundred-eighty degree *darśana* of the vast, sprawling River Gaṅgā.

20) Kānāi-nāṭaśālā (Kānāiyasthāna)

The dancing place of Lord Kṛṣṇa

While in Gayā, after Śrī Caitanya Mahāprabhu performed *śrāddha* and offered *piṇḍa-dāna* to His ancestors, He approached Īśvara Purī for *mantra-dīkṣā* (spiritual initiation). Upon receiving initiation and being embraced by Īśvara Purī, Lord Caitanya began to reveal His true identity. Day by day the glory of His devotional love grew greater and greater, as He plunged into the nectar of *prema-bhakti-rasa*, loving devotional service unto the Supreme Personality of Godhead. He then took permission from Īśvara Purī and departed from Gayā. While returning to Navadvīpa, He passed through Gai-ghāṭa (Patna) and came to a village named Kānāi-nāṭaśālā, the dancing place of Lord Kṛṣṇa.

After Śrī Caitanya Mahāprabhu returned to the Navadvīpa area, He began exhibiting ecstatic symptoms to the other devotees. During one such occasion He recalled His visit at Kānāi-nāṭaśālā, as described in the *Śrī Caitanya-bhāgavata* (*Madhya-khaṇḍa*, Chapter 2): "'In that place was a handsome boy, dark like a *tamāla* tree. His charming hair was decorated with new *guñja* (small sacred berry). Above that was a splendid peacock feather, and He wore a necklace of glistening jewels. I have no power to describe Him. In His hands He held a very beautiful flute, and very charming anklets decorated His feet. Decorated with jeweled ornaments, His arms defeated sapphire pillars. Both the Śrīvatsa mark and the Kaustubha jewel shone on His chest. How can I describe His yellow garments, sharklike earrings, and lotus eyes? He smiled as He approached Me, and after embracing Me, He ran away.' While speaking in this way, Viśvambhara lost consciousness and fell to the ground exclaiming, 'O Kṛṣṇa!'"

There was once a great devotee of Śrī Caitanya Mahāprabhu named Śrī Nṛsiṁhānanda Brahmacārī, who became very pleased upon hearing that Mahāprabhu would be going to Vṛndāvana. Although he had no material wealth, he nevertheless began to construct within his mind a very attractive path for the Lord to travel. He contemplated an extensive road starting from Kuliyā-grāma (the present township of Navadvīpa). That road was decorated with coral, pearls, gold, various gems, stemless flowers, *bakula* trees, and several transcendental lakes with blossoming lotus flowers. Various birds were chirping, and the waters appeared exactly like nectar. The surcharged cool breezes carried sweet fragrances from a variety of flowers.

In his mind, Nṛsiṁhānanda Brahmacārī constructed this road only as far as Kānāi-nāṭaśālā (approximately 250 kilometres north of Kuliyā), situated on the western bank of Gaṅgā. He could not understand why the road's construction could not be completed and became astonished. He concluded that Caitanya Mahāprabhu would not be going to Vṛndāvana, but only up to Kānāi-nāṭaśālā.

Meanwhile, Śrī Caitanya Mahāprabhu left Kuliyā and proceeded to Rāmakeli-grāma to meet the two brothers Dabira Khāsa and Sākara Mallika. During His time there, Mahāprabhu performed *hari-nāma-saṅkīrtana* and danced until He lost external consciousness. When the Muslim King of Gauḍa (Bengal), Nawab Hussain Shah, heard of Mahāprabhu's influence in attracting everyone, he ordered the magistrate, "Do not disturb this Prophet. Allow Him to do as He desires."

Mahāprabhu came to Rāmakeli only to meet His two eternal servants, bestowing on them the names, Śrī Rūpa Gosvāmī and Śrī

Sanātana Gosvāmī. After listening to their humble prayers, the Lord said, "Now please abandon your humility, for My heart is breaking to see you both so humble. Birth after birth you have been My eternal servants. I am sure that Lord Kṛṣṇa will deliver you both very soon." After all the devotes saw the mercy of Lord Caitanya upon the two brothers, they all began to chant "Hari! Hari!"

The *Śrī Caitanya-caritāmṛta* (*Madhya* 1.227) describes the Lord's further pastimes as follows: "In the morning the Lord left and went to a place known as Kānāi-nāṭaśālā. While there, He saw many pastimes of Lord Kṛṣṇa." During the evening, Caitanya Mahāprabhu considered Sanātana Gosvāmī's proposal that He should not go to Vṛndāvana followed by so many people (some say up to fifteen hundred devotees followed Mahāprabhu from Rāmakeli). Then the Lord concluded that He would rather go to Vṛndāvana alone or at most with one person, instead of so many followers, which would only disturb the atmosphere. The *Śrī Caitanya-caritāmṛta* (*Madhya* 1.231) then describes the Lord's change-of-plans: "Thinking like this, the Lord took His morning bath in the Ganges and started for Nīlācala (Jagannātha Purī), saying 'I shall go there.'"

Mahāprabhu's lotus footprints

Śrīla Bhaktisiddhānta Sarasvatī Mahārāja desired to establish 108 altars of Śrī Caitanya Mahāprabhu's footprints at the various holy places the Lord visited. The first place where he established the Lord's footprints was at Kānāi-nāṭaśālā on the 13th of October, 1929. Afterwards, Bhaktisiddhānta Mahārāja and his followers traveled from Rājmahal to Bhagalpur, Nālandā, Rajgir, and other places in Bihar. Eventually arriving in Kāśī, he explained the teachings that Caitanya Mahāprabhu imparted to Sanātana Gosvāmī there.

Other altars containing the sacred footprints of Śrī Caitanya Mahāprabhu were installed by Śrīla Bhaktisiddhānta Sarasvatī Mahārāja at the following locations:

2) Mandara Hill (Bihar) 15th October, 1929
3) Yājapura (Orissa) 25th December, 1930
4) Śrī Kūrma-kṣetra (Andhra Pradesh) 26th December, 1930;
5) Siṁhācala (Andhra Pradesh) 27th December, 1930;
6) Kovvur (Andhra Pradesh) 29th December, 1930
7) Maṅgalgiri (Andhra Pradesh) 31st December, 1930;
8) Chatrabhoga (West Bengal) 3rd April, 1933

ISKCON Kānāi-nāṭaśālā

The ISKCON center at Kānāi-nāṭaśālā sits on top of a small hill, nestled amongst banyan, tamāla, pipal, neem, campa, and mango trees and overlooking the swift flowing currents of Gaṅgā-mayī. The lotus footprints of Lord Kṛṣṇa and Śrīmatī Rādhārāṇī are enclosed in a small shrine that is adjacent to the shrine enclosing the lotus footprints of Śrī Caitanya Mahāprabhu that was built by Śrīla Bhaktisiddhānta Sarasvatī Mahārāja in 1929. In between the two shrines, resides Lord Rāma's devotee, Hanumān, standing strong and ready to serve the Lord and His devotees.

The present Śrī Śrī Rādhā-Kānāilala temple there was built by Tulasī dāsa Bābāji and his disciple Garib Dāsa, some one hundred and fifty years ago. This temple stands next to the shrine constructed by Bhaktisiddhānta Mahārāja. Just outside the present temple compound wall are ruins of an ancient temple, wherein the original Deities of Rādhā-Kānāilala resided. This was where Śrī Caitanya Mahāprabhu had *darśana* of Their Lordships and Their lotus footprints. Afterwards, during the reign of

Aurangzeb, the temple was destroyed, but the Deities were kept safe and the footprints remained untouched.

The responsibility of serving Their Lordships Śrī Śrī Rādhā-Kānāilala was taken by a line of local Gauḍīya Vaiṣṇava Bābājīs, beginning with Bhagavān Dāsa, then Rama-dayal Dāsa and Ramdin Dāsa, before Tulasī dāsa Bābājī and his disciple Garib Dāsa took over. During their tenure, as they were relocating the lotus footprints of Rādhā-Kānāilala, a Deity of Ugra-Narasiṁhadeva was found below the three metre rock slab on which the footprints are imprinted. This Narasiṁhadeva Deity was eventually installed between the temple of Rādhā-Kānāilala and the shrine containing Lord Caitanya's footprints. Near the ancient temple ruins is one large *pipal* tree, whose base and roots form of a cave. Caitanya Mahāprabhu took rest under this tree, which was later used by the local Gauḍīya Bābājīs as their *bhajana-kutira* (place of spiritual practice).

As time passed, the next Vaiṣṇava to inherit the temple compound of Rādhā-Kānāilala was Narasiṁha dāsa Bābājī. Some time during the monsoon season of 1992, the original Deities of Rādhā-Kānāilala, which are made of *aṣṭa-dhatu* (eight different metals: gold, silver, copper, tin, zinc, black lead, iron, and mercury) were stolen. After that, some time in 1993, Narasiṁha Dāsa contacted the ISKCON Māyāpur officials with the desire that ISKCON take care of and maintain the service for Śrī Śrī Rādhā-Kānāilala. Eventually, on the first of June, 1995, the final agreement was completed and everything was transferred in the care of ISKCON. Then Narasiṁha dāsa Bābājī returned to his native village, Kanaily (in the Ara district of Bihar), where he left his body on the 10th of October, 1995.

Since then, ISKCON's Bhaktivedanta Swami Charity Trust (BVSCT) has rennovated the existing temples and shrines and constructed a new kitchen, *prasāda* hall, and additional rooms for devotees. During April of 1997, new marble Deities of Śrī Śrī Rādhā-Kānāilala and Śrī Caitanya Mahāprabhu were installed by ISKCON, and a celebration was held for the "return" of Their Lordships to this beautiful, sparkling jewel-of-a-hilltop *tīrtha* overlooking mother Gaṅgā.

WEST BENGAL

Now we will follow Gaṅgā-mayī through West Bengal until she reaches the Bay of Bengal at Gaṅgā-sāgara. At that point, Gaṅgā-mayī disappears from our vision as she enters the Bay of Bengal and begins her travels to the lower planetary system, where she is known as Bhogavatī, and then she flows at the threshold of Yamaloka (abode of Yamarāja) as the Vaitaraṇī River. Before she reaches that point, Gaṅgā-mayī again becomes known as Bhāgīrathī-mayī as she flows through the nine islands of the *gupta-tīrtha* (hidden holy place) of this age of Kali, Śrī Navadvīpa-dhāma. Here she performs wonderful loving pastimes with Śrī Caitanya Mahāprabhu and Śrī Nityānanda Prabhu, who are nondifferent from Lord Kṛṣṇa and Lord Balarāma.

Geographically, Gaṅgā-mayī enters West Bengal just after Sahibganj, Bihar, as she changes coarse to a southerly direction along the border of the Maldah District. Just before she enters Bangladesh, she bifurcates near Jangipur in the Murshidabad District, becoming a minor stream named Bhāgīrathī. The River Jalaṅgī joins Bhāgīrathī near Navadvīpa town, thus becoming the River Hughli, until reaching the Bay of Bengal. The main branch of Gaṅgā-mayī enters Bangladesh and assumes the name Padmā: there the River Brahmaputrā, which originates from Mānasa-sarovara, joins this main branch of Gaṅgā-mayī. Once traveling and spreading throughout the country of Bangladesh, she enters the Bay of Bengal in an area known as "The Mouths of Gaṅgā."

One reason why Gaṅgā-mayī bifurcates and enters the Bengal region as Bhāgīrathī is stated in the *Śrī Navadvīpa-māhātmyam*: "Seeing the fortune of Yamunā-devī participating in Kṛṣṇa's pastimes, Gaṅgā-devī performed austerities to become the Lord's associate in His *līlā*. Bestowing His mercy, Lord Kṛṣṇa appeared to Gaṅgā-devī and said, 'In the form of Gaurahari, I will perform pastimes with you.'"

The Gaṅgā and Yamunā join in Prayāga, Gaṅgā flowing on the eastern bank where Lord Caitanya Mahāprabhu appeared, and Yamunā flowing on the opposite bank. Thus the Lord is able to blissfully perform His transcendental pastimes with both Gaṅgā and Yamunā. Due to the Lord's mercy, Gaṅgā becomes equal to Yamunā. Just as Yamunā bestows *kṛṣṇa-prema*, Gaṅgā bestows *gaura-prema*.

Before entering Navadvīpa-Māyāpur, we arrive in the small town where Gaṅgā-nārāyaṇa Cakravartī lived, known as Gambhīla or Jiagañj. Gaṅgā-nārāyaṇa was a great exponent of Gauḍīya Vaiṣṇavism during the sixteenth century and was the disciple and intimate associate of Śrī Narottama dāsa Ṭhākura, one of the great saints and *ācāryas* of the Gauḍīya Vaiṣṇava *sampradāya* (disciplic succession) after the six Gosvāmīs of Vṛndāvana. It was here that Narottama disappeared from this planet for the second time. Downstream, on the banks of Bhāgīrathī Gaṅgā, there is Katwa, where Śrī Caitanya Mahāprabhu was shorn of His beautiful long curly locks when He accepted the order of *sannyāsa*. And just before reaching Māyāpur there is a small village on the bank of the Gaṅgā named Cākhandi, the birthplace and *samādhi* (spiritual tomb) location of Śrīnivāsa Ācārya, who was one of the most important Vaiṣṇava teachers in the generation immediately following Śrī Caitanya Mahāprabhu.

21) GAMBHĪLA (JIAGAÑJ)

Narottama's body becomes milk in Gaṅgā

The following is adapted from *The Lives of the Vaiṣṇava Saints*, which recounts two different accounts of Narottama dāsa Ṭhākura's disappearance.

"Narottama Ṭhākura had his disciples bring him to Budhari, and then to Gambhīla to bathe in Gaṅgā. At that time, he was besieged with a raging fever and expected to die. He immediately ordered his disciples to stock wood in preparation for his cremation. This naturally made his disciples uneasy. Still, they complied with their *guru's* wishes. Narottama then sat silently for three days and finally left his body before many of his disciples and other witnesses. After his soul passed from the body, his disciples placed him on the decorative seat of firewood. Just then, critical *brāhmaṇas* started to shout blasphemous obscenities at Gaṅgā-nārāyaṇa and Narottama's other faithful followers. Gaṅgā-nārāyaṇa could not tolerate their harsh words, so he prayed to Narottama to please come back and show his mercy to these misguided *brāhmaṇas*. At that very moment, Narottama's eyes opened and he chanted, 'Rādhā-Kṛṣṇa-Caitanya!' Moreover, his body radiated with the intensity of the sun, forcing the awe-struck *brāhmaṇas* to change their point of view.

"Witnessing this resurrection-like incident, everyone surrendered at Narottama's lotus feet. He embraced them all and bestowed on them the jewels of *bhakti*, the devotional service of the Lord. He ordered them to study the *bhakti* scriptures with Gaṅgā-nārāyaṇa and then he left that area, wanting to meditate in solitude. For the next

several months, he exhibited ecstatic symptoms and repeatedly lamented due to separation from Śrī Śrī Rādhā-Kṛṣṇa.

"Some time later, Narottama actually prepared to leave the earthly realm. He requested Gaṅgā-nārāyaṇa and other intimate followers to accompany him to the Gaṅgā. When they arrived, Narottama offered obeisances to that holy river and entered her waters. He gestured to his disciples to join him and asked them to cup water in their hands and pour it over his body. As they complied with his wish, they watched his bodily limbs turn to milk and mix with the waters of the Gaṅgā. Their natural impulse was to stop, lest their *guru* totally dissolve into the waters of Gaṅga. But they had their order, so they dutifully carried it out, as their own tears merged with the Gaṅgā.

"When the miraculous ritual came to an end, Gaṅgā-nārāyaṇa filled a jug with the milk that was once Narottama's body. This milk was taken to a holy place near Gaṅgā-nārāyaṇa's home in Jiagañj, where Narottama's *samādhi* was erected. This tomb came to be known as Dugdha-samādhi, or the tomb of milk; and it is an important pilgrimage site for all Gauḍīya Vaiṣṇavas."

The beautiful Deities of Śrī Śrī Rādhā-Govinda that Narottama dāsa Ṭhākura once worshiped are still being worshiped at Govinda-bāḍi, or the house of Lord Govinda, which is adjacent to Narottama's Dugdha-samādhi. Situated next to his *samādhi* is Gaṅgā-nārāyaṇa Cakravartī's *samādhi*, as well as the *samādhis* of two other leading Vaiṣṇava disciples. Also, a very merciful Deity of Gaurāṅga Mahāprabhu, as well as other Deities of Rādhā-Kṛṣṇa and *śālagrāma-śilās* (Deity incarnations in the form of stones), which were all worshiped by Narottama and his descendants, are still being maintained today, though They are not residing on the main altar for public *darśana*.

22) KĀÑCANA-NAGARA (KĀṬOYĀ/KATWA)

The Lord's *sannyāsa*

The following adaptation is combined from the Śrī *Caitanya-maṅgala* (*Madhya-khaṇḍa*, Chapter 13) and Śrī *Caitanya-bhāgavata* (*Madhya-khaṇḍa*, Chapter 28).

"Lord Gaurāṅga woke early in the morning and performed His brahminical duties. His mind was set: He would take *sannyāsa*. Nimāi Paṇḍita (Gaurāṅga) would go to Kāñcana-nagara (later becoming Kaṇṭaka-nagara) and take *sannyāsa* from the illustrious Keśava Bhāratī Gosvāmī, who also lived in Indrāṇī (Indrāṇī was a previous name of Kāñcana-nagara). The Lord began His journey by swimming across the River Gaṅgā at a place known as Nirdayāra-ghāṭa (this name was later corrupted into Nidoya-ghāṭa). Hearing of His sudden departure, the people of Nadia felt as though they had been hit on the head by a bolt of lightning! Everyone lamented pitiably in separation from Lord Gaurāṅga, especially His mother, Śacī-devī, who went running to the Gaṅgā looking for Nimāi. She piteously called out in all directions. When no answer came from the trees, plants, or other living entities residing there, she called that place Nirdayā, the place of no mercy.

"Reaching Kāñcana, the Lord met Keśava Bhāratī and fell at his feet to offer respects. Nimāi Paṇḍita considered Himself most fortunate to meet the eminent preceptor. They greeted each other with joyful words. Nimāi Paṇḍita then asked Keśava Bhāratī to give Him *sannyāsa*. Thereafter the barber, Madhu Sil, sat down facing the Lord. At that moment a great sound of weeping arose. The barber put his razor to the Lord's curly hair, but was unable to proceed further and started weeping. Lord Nityānanda and the other devotees fell to the ground and also wept. Unseen by anyone, the demigods and the numberless universes were filled with weeping. Somehow or other, the act of shaving was completed with great love. Then Lord Gaurāṅga, the master of all the worlds, bathed in Gaṅgā-mayi and sat down as a *sannyāsī*.

"The noble-hearted Keśava Bhāratī considered what name to give the Lord. He said, 'Nowhere is a name that satisfies me.' While that fortunate Keśava Bhāratī was thinking in this way, Sarasvatī-devī, the goddess of learning and wisdom, entered his tongue. Placing his hand on the Lord's chest, the noble-hearted Keśava Bhāratī said, 'You make the whole world chant the name of Kṛṣṇa and in this way make the world alive with *kīrtana*. Therefore your name will be Śrī Kṛṣṇa Caitanya. Because of You, everyone in the world will become fortunate!' A great tumult of 'Hari' filled the four directions, while all the Vaiṣṇavas floated in bliss. In this way, the glorious Lord accepted *sannyāsa* and He revealed His name: 'Śrī Kṛṣṇa Caitanya.'

"Everyone in Kāñcana, old men, women, children, scholars, and fools, ran to look at the all-attractive form of Lord Gaurāṅga. Some people stood motionless captivated by the mystifying beauty of the Lord. Everyone ridiculed Keśava Bhāratī for giving *sannyāsa* to such a handsome young man. Rolling up His *dhoti* (simple cloth worn by men in Vedic culture), Gaurāṅga made roaring sounds. Laughing slowly and deeply, He shouted in ecstasy, 'I have taken *sannyāsa*! I have taken *sannyāsa*!'"

Lord Gaurāṅga's head shaving and *sannyāsa* ceremony took place on the auspicious occasion of Makara-saṅkrānti (when the sun enters Capricorn) in the month of Māgha (January-February), 1510.

When mother Śacī learned that Nimāi had accepted *sannyāsa* at Kāñcana-nagara, she said, "That place is not Kāñcana-nagara, rather it is Kaṇṭaka-nagara*." Mīnaketana Rāmadāsa, who was a non-Bengali, later gave the town the name Katwa. Kat means "cut", and in his language the word for hair is *owa*, therefore the name became Kāṭoyā, or Katwa. Śrī Caitanya Mahāprabhu's *sannyāsi-sthāna* (place of *sannyāsa*) in Katwa is known as Gaurāṅga-paḍa (neighborhood), and also locally known as Ṭhākura-paḍa. A beautiful pipal tree marks the place where Madhu the barber shaved the Lord's head and where Keśava Bhāratī initiated Him into the *sannyāsa-āśrama*. Opposite to this sacred place, within the *samādhi* of Śrī Gadādhara Dāsa, is the *samādhi* of the Lord's hair. Nearby are the lotus footprints of Keśava Bhāratī and Caitanya Mahāprabhu, as well as the *samādhi* of the barber Madhu. Adjacent to this shrine is the *samādhi* of the illustrious Keśava Bhāratī Gosvāmī. The center of worship within the *sannyāsi-sthāna* is the most beautiful form of Śrī Gaurasundara, worshiped by Gadādhara Dāsa.

A couple of kilometres away from Gaurāṅga-paḍa is Mādhāitala-grāma (also known as Ghoṣahāṭa), where the *samādhis* of Jagāi and Mādhāi are located. It was also here that Śrī Caitanya Mahāprabhu had *sat-saṅga* (meeting or association) with Nityānanda Prabhu, Gadādhara Dāsa, Mukunda Datta, and Candraśekhara before He took *sannyāsa*. It is said that continuous *kīrtana* has been chanted here for one thousand years. The Nitāi-Gaura temple here was established two hundred years ago by Śrī Gopīcaraṇa dāsa Bābājī. The present Mādhāitala Āśrama, founded by Nitāi Ramandāsa Mahārāja, has been performing continuous *kīrtana* for the past forty-six years. The bank of Gaṅgā is approximately one kilometre from Mādhāitala-grāma.

* Kāñcana means gold, and Kaṇṭaka means thorn.

23) CĀKHANDI (CHAKHUNDI)

Śrīnivāsa Ācārya

In the Second Chapter of the *Bhakti-ratnākara*, the pastimes of Śrīnivāsa Ācārya's life are nicely narrated.

Several years before the birth of Śrīnivāsa Ācārya, a pious *brāhmaṇa* named Gaṅgādhara Bhaṭṭācārya and his wife, Lakṣmīpriyā, were living in Cākhandi, a small village on the bank of the Gaṅgā. For many unfortunate years, they remained without any children. Since Gaṅgādhara was a great devotee of Śrī Caitanya Mahāprabhu, he decided to travel to Navadvīpa and visit the Lord of his life. On the way, he passed through Katwa, where, to his surprise, Nimāi Paṇḍita (Lord Caitanya) was preparing to accept the renounced order of life. As with everyone else present during the ceremony, Gaṅgādhara's reservations were mixed with excitement. As the Lord accepted *sannyāsa*, Gaṅgādhara could only cry out, "Caitanya! Śrī Kṛṣṇa Caitanya! Śrī Kṛṣṇa Caitanya!" as he became half-mad with ecstasy. When he returned to Cākhandi, his wife and the entire village were amazed to see Gaṅgādhara's transformation. Since he was constantly absorbed in calling the Lord's new name, the villagers of Cākhandi gave him a new name: "Caitanya Dāsa".

Since Caitanya Dāsa was completely obsessed with Śrī Caitanya Mahāprabhu, he and his wife traveled to Jagannātha Purī to be with Lord Caitanya. Upon arriving and having *darśana* of the Lord, Caitanya Mahāprabhu instructed them to go to the temple and have *darśana* of the lotus-eyed Lord Jagannātha. Thereafter, Gaṅgādhara and his wife spent several happy days with Lord Caitanya in Jagannātha Purī. Then one day, Caitanya Mahāprabhu told His servant the inner desire of Gaṅgādhara and Lakṣmīpriyā, "They have both sincerely prayed to Lord Jagannātha for a child, and now they will be blessed with a son named Śrīnivāsa." The Lord then said, "He will be a greatly beautiful child. Through Rūpa and Sanātana Gosvāmīs, I will manifest the *bhakti-śāstras* (scriptures on devotional service). Through Śrīnivāsa, all these scriptures will be distributed. Let that *brāhmaṇa* and his wife quickly return to Cākhandi."

After returning to Cākhandi, Lakṣmīpriyā soon conceived a beautiful baby boy. Her father, Balarāma Vipra, was a learned astrologer and informed the happy couple that their son would be a divinely empowered being. "On the full moon day of Vaiśākha (April/May), in the constellation of Rohiṇī, when all the stars are aligned most auspiciously, Lakṣmīpriyā, the wife of Gaṅgādhara Bhaṭṭācārya (Caitanya Dāsa), will give birth to a son who will be a great devotee of Śrī Caitanya Mahāprabhu."

Eventually, Śrīnivāsa Ācārya became the illustrious disciple of Gopāla Bhaṭṭa and Jīva Gosvāmī. His achievements include leading the first book distribution party in the history of Gauḍīya Vaiṣṇavism, converting King Birhambir (the powerful Malla King of Vana Viṣṇupura) to the Vaiṣṇava religion, originating the Manohara Sāhī style of *kīrtana*, and co-organizing the first Gaura Pūrṇimā festival (the birth anniversary of Lord Caitanya), which was held at Kheturī with Jāhnavā-mātā, Narottama dāsa Ṭhākura, Śyāmānanda Paṇḍita, and thousands of other Vaiṣṇavas. Śrīnivāsa Ācārya was the embodiment of Śrī Caitanya Mahāprabhu's ecstasy.

Located in this small, lush village on the eastern bank of the Gaṅgā is the birthplace and *samādhi* of Śrīnivāsa Ācārya. Sometimes during the monsoon season, when Gaṅgā-mayī spills over her shores, she touches the birthplace and *samādhi* of Śrīnivāsa.

ISKCON Rājapura

Five kilometres before reaching Śrī Māyāpur-dhāma, ISKCON has the great fortune to be able to care for and maintain Their Lordships Śrī Jagannātha, Śrī Baladeva, and Lady Subhadrā, situated on the eastern side of the Bhāgīrathī Gaṅgā, in the area of Śrī Sīmantadvīpa called Rājapura. The following narration describes how mother Gaṅgā assisted Lord Jagannātha's pastime.

During the time of Śrī Caitanya Mahāprabhu, a devotee named Jagadiśa Gaṅgulī lived in this area. Jagadiśa was a very saintly Vaiṣṇava and even though he was very old, he would still go on foot every year to Jagannātha Purī. He would attend the Ratha-yātrā festival and see Lord Caitanya, who was residing there at that time. In those days, Gauḍa-deśa (Bengal) was ruled severely by the Mohammedans, and it was very dangerous to travel. Every few kilometres there were tollgates, where pilgrims would be harassed. But inspite of these considerations, Jagadiśa would accompany all the devotees of Navadvīpa on their annual pilgrimage with full faith that the Lord would protect them from danger.

One day a terrible thing occurred: due to his extreme old age and some disease, Jagadiśa suddenly went blind. At first he thought it might only be a temporary condition, but as the days passed and his sight showed no signs of improving, he sunk into the depths of despondency. "Now," he thought, "I shall never again see Caitanya Mahāprabhu and Lord Jagannātha." As the devastating realization that he would never see his beloved Lordships dawned upon him, he began to cry without control. As some months passed, the time of Ratha-yātrā approached; so Jagadiśa decided that he would still go with the other devotees. "I may not be able to see, but at least I can hear Lord Caitanya speak and chant in *saṅkīrtana*," Jagadiśa said to himself. But when he approached the other devotees, they told him it would be too dangerous to take a blind old man on the 700 kilometre journey.

It is quite inconceivable to an ordinary man how much unhappiness Jagadiśa suffered. In the *śāstras*, Lord Kṛṣṇa Himself states that although His pure devotees always desire to associate with Him, He sometimes creates the mood of separation, because when one is in separation from the object of his love, his attachment and love increase manifold. So to increase Jagadiśa's love for Him and his desire to see Him, Lord Jagannātha enacted this pastime. Many months passed before the devotees returned from Jagannātha Purī and brought news of Lord Caitanya and Lord Jagannātha's wonderful transcendental activities, which simply increased his feelings of separation.

At times, Jagadiśa wished that his useless life would come to an end, but one night he had an extraordinary dream. He dreamt that a wonderful voice announced that he should immediately go and take bath in the nearby River Gaṅgā. "Whilst you are bathing," the voice said, "a large piece of wood will float by and touch your body. At that time, your vision will be restored. Take the wood to the nearby village and search for a leper carpenter. Do not give it to anyone else, for he is also My beloved devotee. Being afflicted by leprosy he will constantly object, but you must encourage him. Tell him that if he completes the carving of a Jagannātha Deity, he will be freed from all physical disease and attain a transcendental body. When he has completed his work, bring and install that Deity with a wonderful festival on this very spot."

Once again, all was silent, and Jagadiśa immediately awoke. Taking his cane and towel, Jagadiśa thought nothing of the fact that it was still night time, for night and day were the same for him. He climbed a small hillock and felt the path dip down towards the bank of the Bhāgīrathī Gaṅgā. Jagadiśa had never been so conscious of the pathway nor Gaṅgā herself, but if the words that he had heard were to be accepted as truth, then Gaṅgā-mayī, mother Gaṅgā, would be the source of his deliverance. Taking her waters in his cupped palms, he offered prayers to her and then slowly entered her warm waters. Step by step he went, careful not to lose his footing in the deep sandy bed, until the water lapped around his chest, which pounded in anticipation. As the minutes passed, he heard the water lapping and fish jumping, he felt the cool river breeze touching his wet cheeks, but where was the log? He began to think that perhaps this was also another of the Lord's tricks to increase his desire to see Him. Far away in the distance the lowing of a calf echoed through the forest. He thought, "People may see and think that I have gone mad or have decided to kill myself, but what do I care of others? Let them say what they like." Suddenly he was jolted by something touching his chest, and he grabbed clumsily to push it away. He then clasped it, not knowing how large it was, and instead of pushing it away, he pulled it towards himself and banged his head with it. Suddenly, as if curtains that had been drawn for centuries had been pulled back, his vision was returned and in the soft predawn light, he saw before him a large log of wood. "O Jagannātha! O Jagannātha! My Lord, my deliverer, everything takes place by Your desire," he shouted. Holding the log, he could not move fast enough in the deep water. When he finally got to the bank, he dragged the log out and fell in ecstasy on the wet sandy shore. "O Lord, how kind You are. For so long I could not see You, but now, You are again showing Your kindness to me."

Taking the heavy log in his arms, Jagadiśa struggled to the nearby village. Sometimes he would bear the heavy waterlogged log on one shoulder, and sometimes he transferred it to the other, before carrying the log with both arms. Periodically, he had to put it down altogether and gather his strength again. The wood carvers all lived in the same section of the village, so to find the leper was easy. But while showing Jagadiśa his gnarled fingers clad with bloody bandages, the leper said, "How can I possibly carve a Deity? It would be offensive to spill blood onto the wood, and my disease is contagious." But Jagadiśa insisted, "Lord Jagannātha promised that if you do this, you will be relieved of all disease and be liberated from all material bondage." The leper carpenter repeatedly refused, but Lord Jagannātha's desire was supreme. As the leper worked, Jagadiśa had to constantly encourage him, especially since the pain in his fingers was excruciating. As his work progressed, the leper gradually forgot his bodily condition and concentrated on seeing only the form of Jagannātha manifesting beneath his chisel. Gradually Lord Jagannātha took shape, and when the work was finally completed, they both stood admiring the form of the Lord. Then Jagadiśa suddenly exclaimed, "Look at your hands and feet! You are cured, your leprosy is gone!" Linking arms together, they danced jubilantly around Lord Jagannātha's rough wooden form shouting, "Jaya Jagannātha! Jaya Jagannātha!"A few nights later, Jagadiśa had a dream in which Lord Jagannātha instucted him to take some neem wood and request the same carpenter to make Deities of Śrī Baladeva and Lady Subhadrā, which he did. After Jagadiśa Gaṅguli left this mortal world, the worship and care of Their Lordships gradually decreased; the temple was neglected and eventually collapsed.

One day, several centuries later, a villager saw a beautiful blue flower on top of a termite hill. As he went closer, a voice began to call, "Please give Me some water. I am very thirsty, so please bring some water." He quickly began digging and found Lord Jagannātha in the hill. He was surprised to see that the Deities were in a termite hill, yet Their wooden forms was unharmed.

Since then, Lord Jagannātha has been maintained very lovingly by the local devotees of the Rājapura area. Then in 1979, Lord Jagannātha's aging *pūjārī* realized that he would leave his body soon, so he decided that the Deities would be properly cared for and worshiped nicely by the devotees of Śrīla Prabhupāda. Consequently, he donated the temple and property to ISKCON. Since that time, a new temple has been constructed and some dioramas (displaying dolls) depicting the pastime how Lord Jagannātha manifested here in Rājapura were installed. The temple complex is now surrounded by beautiful gardens, mango groves, and rice paddy fields, all near the lap of mother Gaṅgā.

24) NAVADVĪPA (MĀYĀPUR)

Navadvīpa-praṇāma

navīna-śrī-bhaktiṁ-nava-
kanaka-gaurākṛti-patiṁ
navāraṇya-śreṇī-nava-
sura-saridvāt-valitam

navīna-śrī-rādhā-hari-
rasa-mayotkīrtana-vidhiṁ
navadvīpaṁ vande nava-
karuṇa-mādyan nava-rucim

I bow down to Śrī Navadvīpa, the transcendental land that is filled with forests ever cooled by fresh breezes from the Gaṅgā, where newly born devotion manifests by the unprecedented mercy of the Lord with a golden complexion, and which bestows the ever-fresh mellow of loud glorification of Śrī Śrī Rādhā-Kṛṣṇa in Their highest ecstasy (*n hā-bhāva*).

Navadvīpa-dhyāna

svardhunyāś cāru-tīre sphuritam ati-
bṛhat-kūrma-pṛṣṭhābha-gatram
ramyārāmāvṛtaṁ san-maṇi-kanaka-
mahā-sadma-saṅghaih parītam

nityaṁ pratyālayodyat-praṇaya-
bhara-lasat-kṛṣṇa-saṅkīrtanāḍhyam
śrī-vṛndāṭavy-abhinnaṁ tri-jagad-
anupamaṁ śrī-navadvīpam īḍe

I praise that holy *dhāma*, Navadvīpa, which, being entirely nondifferent from Śrī Vṛndāvana, is completely different from the material world consisting of the three planetary systems. It is situated on the gorgeous banks of the Gaṅgā covered by beautiful groves and gardens appearing in form like the back of a gigantic turtle. Many great palatial houses made of gold and bedecked with brilliant jewels are situated there, and *kṛṣṇa-saṅkīrtana* is always being performed in the mellow of ecstatic love.

In the *Mukti-saṅkalinī-tantra*, Navadvīpa is mentioned as the most important holy place in this present age: "In Satya-yuga, Kurukṣetra is the *tīrtha*; in Tretā-yuga, Puṣkara is the *tīrtha*; in Dvāpara-yuga, Naimiṣāraṇya is the *tīrtha*; and in Kali-yuga, Navadvīpa is the *tīrtha*."

In the *Śrī Godrumacandra Bhajanopadeśa*, Śrīla Bhaktivinoda instructs us: "Go to Lord Caitanya's forest, known as the nine islands of Navadvīpa, read about Lord Caitanya's pastimes with great delight, and roll about on the shore of the Gaṅgā, which is marked with the Lord's lotus footprints. In this way worship Lord Caitanya, who is like a moon shining in the groves of Godruma forest."

* * *

The following narration from the *Ananta-saṁhitā* describes how Śrī Navadvīpa-dhāma manifested and how Lord Kṛṣṇa became one with Śrīmatī Rādhārāṇī, as Gaurahari.

"Thinking in Her heart for some time, Śrīmatī Rādhārāṇī, for Whom Śrī Kṛṣṇa was Her only worshipable Lord, entered the area between the Gaṅgā and Yamunā with Her friends. There, Lord Kṛṣṇa's beautiful lover created a transcendental abode filled with vines, trees, bumblebees, deer, does, and splendid flowers like *mallika*, *mālatī*, and *jati*. The area was full of *tulasī* forests and other beautiful groves filled with spiritual bliss. It was a blissful transcendental abode where the Gaṅgā and Yamunā became like a moat, and where by Her order, the waters and shores shone with great splendor. There, Vasanta and Kāmadeva eternally shine with great brilliance, and the birds eternally sing the auspicious sounds, 'O Kṛṣṇa!'

"Dressed in wonderful, colorful clothing and ornaments, goddess Rādhikā began to play on a flute sweet music that even charmed the heart of Lord Govinda. His heart enchanted by Her music, Śrī Kṛṣṇa appeared in that place, and when Śrīmatī Rādhārāṇī saw Her lover, She took Him by the hand and became very happy. Upon seeing Rādhārāṇī's love for Him, Lord Kṛṣṇa then said, 'O beloved, for Me there is no one equal to You. O girl with the most beautiful face, where is that other person who is as dear to Me as You? I will never leave You, even for a single moment. You are as dear to Me as My own life. In this transcendental abode of nine forests, You and nine of Your friends have created for My sake, I will manifest a new form and enjoy new pastimes with You. For this reason, My devotees will eternally proclaim that this place is a new Vṛndāvana. Because this place is like a group of islands, the wise know this as Navadvīpa (nine islands). By My order, all holy places reside here. I will eternally stay with You here in this transcendental place that You have created for Me. Human beings who come here and worship You and Me will certainly become Our eternal *gopī* friends. O beautiful beloved, this transcendental abode is like Vṛndāvana. Simply by going here one attains the result of all other pilgrimages. Here one attains pure devotional service, which is very pleasing to Me.'

"After speaking these words, Lord Kṛṣṇa became one with Śrīmatī Rādhārāṇī. A single spiritual form of eternal bliss and knowledge, a form that was dark-complexioned Kṛṣṇa within and fair-complexioned Gaura without. As Goddess Rādhikā is *gauri* (fair) and Lord Kṛṣṇa is Hari, when They become one They are known as Gaura-Hari. Lalita-devī and the *gopīs* who in their own forms eternally serve Śrī Śrī Rādhā-Kṛṣṇa in Vṛndāvana, accepted the forms of devotees in Navadvīpa where they eternally and joyfully serve Lord Gaura-Hari, who is Śrī Śrī Rādhā-Kṛṣṇa joined in a single form.

"Vṛndāvana is the nine forests of Navadvīpa and a person who thinks Vṛndāvana is different from Navadvīpa and that Śrī Śrī Rādhā-Kṛṣṇa are different from the Supreme Lord, Śrī Gaura-Hari, is cut to pieces by Lord Śiva's trident."

In the *Śrī Navadvīpa-māhātmyam*, Śrīla Bhaktivinoda Ṭhākura describes Navadvīpa as the topmost *tīrtha*: "Since Śrī Gaurāṅga appeared in Navadvīpa, it is therefore the crest jewel of all holy places. Offenders are the object of punishment at other holy pilgrimage places, but in Navadvīpa-dhāma they are purified." Bhaktivinoda Ṭhākura continues, "Liberation that is obtained by Brahman realization at other holy places is obtained simply by bathing in the Gaṅgā at Navadvīpa. Thus, all types of liberation—

sālokya, sārūpya, sārṣṭi, sāmīpya, and *sāyujya*—can be obtained in Navadvipa without speculative practice. Falling at the feet of the pure devotees in Navadvipa, Bhukti and Mukti (personified material enjoyment and liberation) remain there as obedient servants. Not caring for them, the devotees kick them away, but still they do not leave the devotee's feet. The fruits obtained by staying one hundred years at the seven holy cities can be obtained by staying one night in Śrī Navadvīpa-dhāma.

"In conclusion, Navadvipa is the topmost *tīrtha*. Taking shelter of this *dhāma*, the living entities can cross over Kali-yuga. At this place *tāraka*, the name of Rāma, which gives *mukti*, and *pāraka*, the name of Kṛṣṇa, which gives *prema*, always serve the residents of the *dhāma*."

Navadvīpa meditations

The following sastric quotations provide an ideal meditation to fix the mind on Navadvīpa-dhāma before relishing Lord Caitanya's pastimes.

From the *Śrī Navadvīpāṣṭaka*: "Meditate on Śrī Navadvīpa-dhāma, the beautiful land of Lord Gaurāṅga by the side of the heavenly reservoir, which is eternally pure, shining, and full of bliss. Meditate on Śrī Navadvīpa-dhāma, where Lord Gaurāṅga performed His *līlā* and where in all directions gentle, cooling breezes and various shady trees manifest. Meditate on Śrī Navadvīpa-dhāma, where the Gaṅgā flows within the banks of golden stairs and where Lord Gaurāṅga enjoyed transcendental pastimes. Just meditate on Śrī Navadvīpa-dhāma, where the golden Lord Hari is wandering with His devotees, chanting the holy names of Kṛṣṇa with great love, and immersing everyone in the ocean of *prema-bhakti* (loving devotional service)."

In the *Śrī Navadvīpa-māhātmyam* it is stated: "I meditate on Śrī Navadvīpa, which eternally shines with great spiritual bliss on the very charming shore of the purifying Gaṅgā in Gauḍa-deśa (Bengal). I meditate on Śrī Navadvīpa, where the waves of the great Gaṅgā playfully splash against the golden shores decorated with golden stairs. I meditate on Śrī Navadvīpa, where the golden Lord Hari, by wandering everywhere and chanting the holy name with great love in the company of His devotees, plunged into the brilliant ocean of ecstatic love of God."

And in the *Caitanya-carita-mahākāvya*: "Having fallen upon the matted locks of Lord Śiva, who is decorated with a garland of skulls, Gaṅgā-devī takes on the appearance of millions of gleaming fish as her droplets glitter with the light reflected from the cresent moon on Lord Śiva's head. Having emanated from the two lotus feet of Lord Hari, the pleasant, sweet streams of Gaṅgā purify the universe as she flows forward in all directions. Indeed the chaste Gaṅgā-devī has yielded within her spotless waters the most exalted place, Navadvīpa.

"Though liquid in form, Gaṅgā-devī dries up the ocean of material suffering; though white in color, she is famous for refreshing blackish Kṛṣṇa with her waters; though flowing on the earth, she is called by a heavenly name; and though she removes the confusion of the living entities, she is filled with whirlpools and eddies. Having attained the taste of the Lord's lotus feet, her waves and currents become agitated. Taking up her residence in Navadvīpa, she adds glory to that tract of land."

Navadvīpa glorifications and descriptions

The following is another narration from the *Ananta-saṁhitā*, in which Lord Śiva glorifies Śrī Navadvīpa-dhāma to his wife, Parvati.

21. Gaṅgā-Nārāyaṇa Cakravartī at Govinda-bāḍi, Jiāgañj

21. Narottama dāsa Ṭhākura's limbs turn into milk in the Gaṅgā at Gambhīla

22. Śrī Caitanya Mahāprabhu at Ghoṣahāṭa, Kāñcana-nagara, the evening before his acceptance of *sannyāsa*

22. The tombs of Mādhāi and Jagāi at Mādhāitalā near Katwa

22. Katwa, the pipal tree where Lord Caitanya took *sannyāsa*

22. Madhu the barber shaving the Lord at Kāṭoyā

23. Above: Chākhundi, the tomb of Śrīnivāsa Ācārya

23. Right: Rādhā and Kṛṣṇa with Lord Jagannātha, the worshipable Deities of Śrīnivāsa Ācārya at Chākhundi

Śrīmatī Rādhārāṇī creating Navadvīpa

Śrī Caitanya Mahāprabhu, The Lord's Advent
Mitravindā-devī, Rukmiṇī-devī, and Lord Kṛṣṇa at Dvārakā

The Lord's Pastimes
Lord Caitanya and Lakṣmīpriyā meeting for the first time

Nimāi Paṇḍita instructs His students

Gaṅgā-mayī caresses Lord Caitanya

Lord Caitanya and His associates perform *hari-nāma-saṅkīrtana*, the congregational chanting of the holy names of the Lord

Lord Nityānanda instructs Mādhāi to serve Gaṅgā by building Ṁādhāi-ghāṭa

24. Left: Śrīla Prabhupāda on the bank of the Gaṅgā at Māyāpura

25. Right: Advaita Ācārya at His house in Bāblāvana

25. Below: Bāblāvana, Śāntipura, where Gaṅgā once flowed

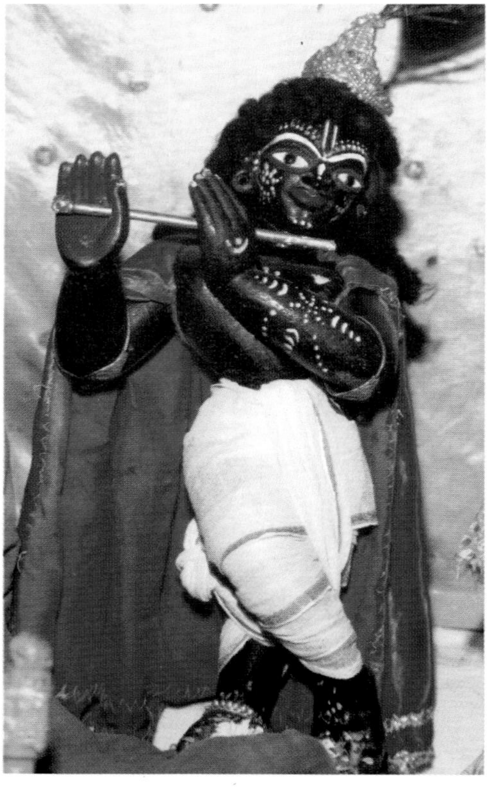

26. Lord Nityānanda (left) and Caitanya Mahāprabhu at Sūryadāsa Sarakhela's house in Ambikā-kālnā

26. Left: Jīrāt, the Gopīnātha Deity that Jāhnavā-mātā gave to Gaṅgā-devī

27. Opposite: An ancient deity of Śrī Gaṅgā-devī near Triveṇī-ghāṭa

27. Gaṅgā-devī afloat at Triveṇī-ghāṭa

28. Lord Caitanya's pond at the birthplace of Śrī Īśvara Purī in Hālisahara

28. Śrī Śrī Gaura-Nitāi and Śrī Śrī Rādhā-Kṛṣṇa, the worshipable Deities of Īśvara Purī

28. Left: Īśvara Purī at Kumārahaṭṭa

29. Khaḍadaha-grāma, Lord Nityānanda and Lord Caitanya, with Vīrabhadra in front

29. Śrī Śrī Rādhā-Śyāmasundara in Khardaha

29. Birthplace of Gaṅgā-devī and Vīrabhadra at Khaḍadaha-grāma

30. The banyan tree that Lord Nityānanda sat under in Pānihāṭi

30. Rāghava Paṇḍita and associates leave Pānihāti for Jagannātha Purī

31. Above: The tomb of Gadādhara Dāsa in Ariadaha

32. Above: Kali Ma of Calcutta resides on the bank of Ādi Gaṅgā

33. Below: Aṭisārā-nagara, the small shrine containing Lord Caitanya's footprints

33. Below: The footprints of Lord Caitanya at Aṭisārā

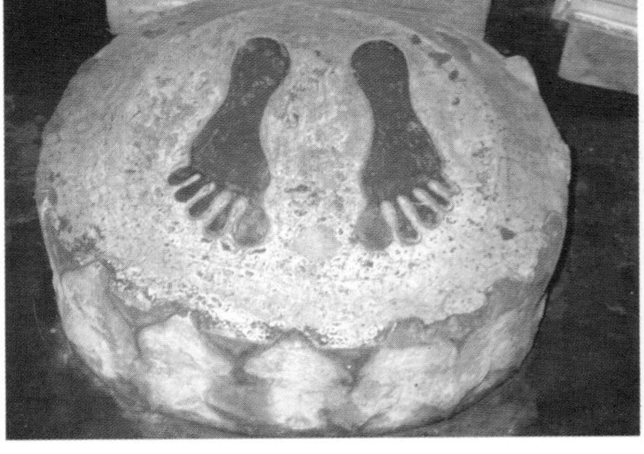

33. Hari-nāma-saṅkirtana at Aṭisārā

34. Natural scenery of Chatrabhoga-grāma

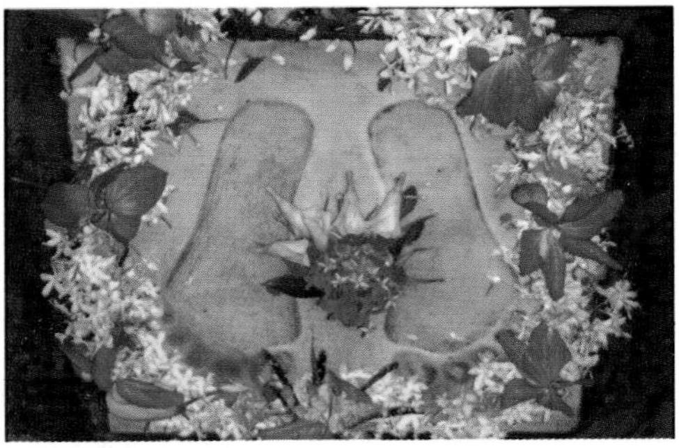

34. Left: The lotus footprints of Lord Caitanya installed by Bhaktisiddhānta Sarasvatī Mahārāja at Chatrabhoga in 1933

34. Left: Lotus footprint shrine in Chatrabhoga

34. Opposite: The temple of Lord Śiva known as Badarīkanātha Mahādeva, situated next to Ambhuliṅga-ghāṭa

35. Opposite insert: Śrī Gaṅgā-devī, Śrī Kapila Muni, and Bhagīratha Mahārāja at Gaṅgā-sāgara

34. Below: Ambhuliṅga-ghāṭa, Borāsi, where Lord Śiva assumed the form of water to worship Gaṅgā-devī

गंगाभगिरथ
कपिल मुनि
सागरराजा

Pāṇḍava Arjuna punishes Aṅgāraparṇa, the King of the Gandharvas

Chanting Hare Kṛṣṇa

Personal meditations on Mother Gaṅgā

Gaurī and the seven sages discuss Lord Śiva's glories

Śrīla Vyāsadeva compiling the *Purāṇas*

Long ago, Pārvatī inquired from her consort, Lord Śiva, about the glories of Śrī Navadvīpa-dhāma by asking, "Please tell me, O Lord, O ocean of mercy, O great *yogī*, where is this Navadvīpa in which Gaurāṅga resides? The name of Gaurāṅga has forcibly stolen my mind. You have already told me the glories of Vṛndāvana. Now my dear Lord, tell me the glories of Navadvīpa."

Hearing Pārvatī's words, Lord Śiva embraced her and with great respect said, "Please listen as I describe the glories of Navadvīpa, which bestow *prema-bhakti* on mankind and destroy all types of sins. I will describe truly the glories of Navadvīpa just as I have described the glories of Vṛndāvana. The Supreme Personality of Godhead, who gives bliss to His devotees, performs His pastimes in Navadvīpa, just as Lord Kṛṣṇa enjoys pastimes with Rādhārāṇī in Vṛndāvana. Just by remembrance of the glorious Navadvīpa, which is situated within the combined Gaṅgā and Yamunā Rivers, one will develop attraction for Rādhā-Kṛṣṇa.

"A person may wander about the earth and visit a thousand holy *tīrthas*, but if one does not see Navadvīpa, he cannot obtain Rādhā-Kṛṣṇa. O Pārvatī, in just one part of Navadvīpa all *tīrthas*, *ṛṣis*, *munis*, *devas*, *āśramas*, *mantras*, and all the *Vedas* constantly reside for the pleasure of Rādhā-Kṛṣṇa. Whatever results a person can attain by performance of thousands of horse sacrifices, various types of rituals and yogic exercises, can be attained ten million times over by just remembering Navadvīpa. What can I say then of the results of actually seeing Navadvīpa?"

Also in the *Ūrdhvāmnāya-tantra*, Lord Śiva glorifies Navadvīpa-dhāma to Pārvatī, by saying, "O Pārvatī, the Lord's supreme, complete, whole energy is called *svarūpa-śakti*. You, the Lord's *māyā-śakti* (illusory energy) composed of three *guṇas* (qualities), are the shadow of that energy. The *svarūpa-śakti* has three forms: *samvit* (knowledge), *sandhinī* (existence), and *hlādinī* (bliss). The *sandhinī-śakti* reveals such things as the Lord's abode and name. By the order of the *sac-cit-ānanda* (eternal, blissful, and full of knowledge) Lord, the *sandhinī-śakti* reveals Navadvīpa-*dhāma* to mortal eyes. O Devī, the wise know that Navadvīpa manifests from the Lord's potency like fruits come from flowers. All the *Vedas* glorify Navadvīpa as nonmaterial, spiritual, full of variety, beyond matter, the supreme eternal Brahmapura, an enchanting abode in the form of a lotus. The nine islands of Navadvīpa exactly resemble a lotus flower.

"O Pārvatī, present within this eternal Navadvīpa-dhāma are Ayodhyā, Mathurā, Māyā (Haridvāra), Kāśī, Kāñcī, Avantī (Ujjain), Dvārakā, Kurukṣetra, Puṣkara, and Naimiṣāraṇya. The four streams of Gaṅgā—Bhāgīrathī, Alakanandā, Mandākinī, and Bhogavatī—enclose the fifty-one kilometre circumference of Navadvīpa. All the holy places in the heavenly, earthly, and lower planets are present in Navadvīpa.

"The wise say that on the eastern bank of Gaṅgā in Māyāpur, Gokula is situated; while on the western bank, Vṛndāvana is situated. In that place is Śrī Pulina, the sandy riverbed that is the site of the *rāsa-līlā* (Kṛṣṇa's dancing pastimes). West of the *rāsa-līlā* site is the auspicious Dhira-samira. O dear Devī, whatever exists in Vṛndāvana also exists in Navadvīpa, of this there is no doubt."

The *Śrī Navadvīpa-māhātmyam* describes the nine islands and rivers of Navadvīpa as follows: "There eternally exist sixteen rivers within the sixteen *krośa* (51 kilometres) area of Navadvīpa. On the eastern bank of the main Gaṅgā are four islands: Śrī Antardvīpa, Śrī Sīmantadvīpa, Śrī Godrumadvīpa, and Śrī Madhyadvīpa; and on the western bank there are five: Śrī Koladvīpa, Śrī Ṛtudvīpa,

Śrī Jahnudvīpa, Śrī Modadrumadvīpa, and Śrī Rudradvipa. The different tributaries of Gaṅgā surround these islands and give the Dhāma wonderful splendor. The main Gaṅgā always flows in the middle, while the other pious rivers flow in various tributaries. Alongside the Gaṅgā flows the beautiful Yamunā, and Sarasvatī flows within another river. East of Yamunā are the longer streams of Tāmraparṇī, Kṛtamālā, and Brahmaputrā. The Rivers Sarayū, Narmadā, Sindhu, Kāverī, Gomatī, and Godāvarī flow swiftly throughout the breadth of Navadvīpa. All these rivers intersect to form the nine different islands of Navadvīpa.

"The island which lies at the junction of the Gaṅgā, Yamunā, and Sarasvatī is known in the *śāstras* as Antardvīpa. Within Antardvīpa lies the holy sanctuary of Śrī Māyāpur-dhāma, where Śrī Caitanya Mahāprabhu appeared. Therefore, all devotees, please understand that Mahāvana in the center of Goloka is none other than Māyāpur of Śrī Navadvīpa-dhāma."

Later on in the *Śrī Navadvīpa-māhātmyam*, Lord Nityānanda describes the glories and greatness of Śrī Navadvīpa-dhāma to Jīva Gosvāmī, while personally guiding him on *parikramā* throughout the nine islands. While they were coming to the edge of Antardvīpa, Lord Nityānanda pointed out to Śrī Jīva the holy place known as Gaṅgānagara. "Listen Jīva, this Gaṅgānagara was founded by King Bhagīratha of the Raghu dynasty. When Gaṅgā-mayī came down, Bhagīratha led the way, blowing a conchshell. But when Gaṅgā arrived at Navadvīpa-dhāma, she stopped and would not proceed. Bhagīratha saw this and became fearful. Retracing his steps, he came towards Gaṅgā at his place and began to perform austerities. Satisfied with this, Gaṅgā-devī personally appeared before him.

"Bhagīratha said, 'Mother Gaṅgā, if you do not proceed on, my forefathers will never be delivered.' Then Gaṅgā-devī said, 'Listen, dear child Bhagīratha, just stay here patiently for a few days. Now we are in Navadvīpa and the month of Māgha is coming. At the end of the Phālguna month, I will go to deliver your forefathers. O Bhagīratha, my waters emanate from the lotus feet of the Supreme Lord, so now here in His own Dhāma, I would like to have my desires fulfilled.' On Phālguna Pūrṇimā, one who fasts and takes bath in Gaṅgā here and worships Gaurāṅga will cross over the material ocean along with his ancestors. Along with one thousand ancestors, he attains Goloka after death no matter where he dies."

Later on, Lord Nityānanda describes how Lord Śiva told Pārvatī he desired to reside on Sīmantadvīpa, "Unto you, who are the primordial energy and one portion of Śrī Rādhā, I will tell the crest-jewel of all truths. Accepting the spiritual emotions of Śrī Rādhā, Kṛṣṇa will descend in this Kali-yuga at Māyāpur in the womb of Śacī. Intoxicated with the pastimes of *kīrtana*, Lord Gaurāṅga will distribute the jewel of *prema* to everyone without discrimination. Whoever does not drown in that flood of *prema* is most unfortunate. O Pārvatī, just by remembering the Lord's promise that He will come, I pass my life drowning in love of God. Being unable to control myself, I have given up my own city of Kāśī. Within Māyāpur, on the bank of the Gaṅgā, I will live in a hut and worship Gaurāṅga."

Then Lord Nityānanda narrates the glories of Mahā-prayāga in Koladvīpa, "Listen everyone, this is Pañcaveṇī, where five rivers join the Gaṅgā. Bhāgīrathī mixes with the Mandākinī and Alakanandā, and the Sarasvatī flows here hidden from view. From the west, Yamunā flows along with the

Bhogavatī, and Mānasa-gaṅgā also flows quickly there. This place is called Mahā-prayāga by the *ṛṣis*, who performed millions of sacrifices here along with Lord Brahmā. The glories of this place are incomparable. If one takes bath here, he will not take another birth. Who can properly describe the glories of this place? All other *tīrthas* become like dried up rivers in comparison. One who leaves his body here on earth, in the air, or in the water will attain Śrī Goloka Vṛndāvana. This place, known as Kuliyā Pāhāḍa, is situated on the banks of Gaṅgā and is raised up like a mountain."

As their *parikramā* continued, Lord Nityānanda embraced Śrī Jīva and affectionately said, "There is nothing inauspicious in the Lord's holy Dhāma. Bhakti-devī is the goddess here, and all others are her servants. They only serve to reveal *bhakti*, and the residence of the ninefold *bhakti* is Navadvīpa. Here, *karma* (action) and *jñāna* (knowledge) serve *bhakti*. The scriptures award evil intelligence to materialistic persons, but the same scriptures award attachment to Lord Kṛṣṇa to the pure devotees."

As Lord Nityānanda spoke, they went to Jannagara, where they saw the enchanting hermitage of Jahnu Ṛṣi. Then Nityānanda Prabhu explained, "This enchanting place named Jahnudvīpa is known as Bhadravana. At this place, Jahnu Ṛṣi underwent penances and received *darśana* of the golden form of Gaurāṅga. Jahnu Ṛṣi was sitting here chanting his Gāyatrī *mantra*, when his *ācamana* cup (used for sipping water for purification) fell into Bhāgīrathī-mayī and was swept away by her currents. He opened his mouth and drank all the water in one gulp. King Bhagīratha was overwhelmed with anxiety and worshiped the *ṛṣi* for several days. The great *ṛṣi* then released Gaṅgā from his body. Because of this incident, Gaṅgā is known as Jāhnavī, the daughter of Jahnu."

Ecstatic Waves

The great Gauḍīya Vaiṣṇava *ācārya*, Śrīla Bhaktivinoda Ṭhākura, who re-established the pure form of Gauḍīya Vaiṣṇavism, has published nearly one hundred literary works between the years 1838 to 1914. In 1899, he wrote Śrī *Navadvīpa Bhāva-taraṅga* (Ecstatic Waves of Navadvīpa), which describes the different transcendental places within the fifty-one square kilometre area of Navadvīpa. The descriptions are seen through the perfected devotional eyes of a God-realized soul. Bhaktivinoda Ṭhākura does not see the land of Navadvīpa as a mundane historical place, but rather as the Īśodyāna, the transcendental garden of Śrī Caitanya Mahāprabhu. He describes various pastimes that the Lord enjoys on different islands at different times of the day in the transcendental realm. At the conclusion of this divine vision, he falls unconscious and attains the *samādhi* of full realization of his eternal form as a *gopī*. Some of Śrīmatī Rādhārāṇī's personal maidservants take him by the hand and engage him in eternal personal service to the divine couple. Returning to consciousness, he remains absorbed as the servant of the servant of Śrī Caitanya Mahāprabhu.

The following verses glorifying Gaṅgā are taken from the one hundred and sixty-eight verses that compose this relishable literature.

"To the southwest, Gaṅgā and Yamunā, considering their own good fortune, twist like a serpent as they flow. They come to serve Gaura, the jewel of the twice born. Upon Gaṅgā's banks are many *ghāṭas*, gardens, and temples of deities such as Prauḍhā Māyā and Vṛddha Śiva. Why should the rascals of Kali-yuga, who are bound tight by material illusion, have the privilege to see these spiritual treasures? *Māyā* (illusion) hides the Dhāma with the erosion caused by Gaṅgā, Yamunā, and Sarasvatī and thus material eyes can see only a shadow of the

real Māyāpur. To the west, on the bank of Gaṅgā stands the famous village Gaṅgānagara, where the Lord and His *brāhmaṇa* friends studied in Gaṅgādāsa's house. Northwest of Mathurā, I see the splendor of Sīmantadvīpa, situated on the bank of Gaṅgā. This is where anxious Pārvatī placed the dust of the lotus feet of Gaurāṅga on her *simanta* (parting of hair). In the southern portion of Māyāpur, on the bank of Gaṅgā near the junction with Sarasvatī, is the grove called Īśodyāna. May that forest be the place of my eternal devotions. The materialists whose eyes are sunk in illusion cannot see these groves. They see only a small piece of land covered with thorns, periodically thrown topsy-turvy by the flooding of Gaṅgā. In the three worlds, there is no place comparable to Godruma, where Mārkaṇḍeya received the Lord's mercy. Just as Īśodyāna, which is nondifferent from Rādhā-kuṇḍa, lies close to the bank of Gaṅgā, so Godruma lies close to Sarasvatī. In this way Gaura and Nitāi (Lord Nityānanda) would daily play with the cowherd boys in the Godruma forest. Then, if not too late, Gaurāṅga would bathe in the Gaṅgā before proceeding home.

"Near Uccahaṭṭa is Pañcaveṇī, the holy place where the demigods come to rest. At this place the three streams of Gaṅgā (Bhāgīrathī, Mandākinī, and Alakanandā), as well as the Yamunā and Sarasvatī, all join together with a desire to serve Gaurāṅga. Across the Gaṅgā from Pañcaveṇī is enchanting Koladvīpa, where the Lord appeared in the form of a boar before His devotee. In the scriptures this place is called the Varāha-kṣetra. This place is a spiritual realm rarely attained by the demigods. Also known as Kuliyāpāhāḍa, this place is considered the topmost place of Gaura-līlā.

"After taking *sannyāsa*, Śrī Caitanya attempted a journey to Vṛndāvana but was tricked and came to this town instead. Here is the school of Viśārada's son, Vidyā-vācaspati. Who did not know him? He is an unalloyed servant of the Lord, and by the power of his pure devotion he attracted the Lord by taking bath in the Gaṅgā. When will I stand on the bank of Gaṅgā at Vidyā-vācaspati's doorway and view the opulence of this place? Taking shelter of the Gaṅgā, the ocean comes here and is overcome with love on seeing the Lord's Navadvīpa pastimes. The demigods see Gaṅgā-sāgara eternally shining here in Navadvīpa. North of Vidyānagara shines Jahnudvīpa, where the hermitage of Jahnu Muni is visible to all. Here Jahnu Muni drank Gaṅgā. As my dream breaks, I will weep softly and as I cross the Gaṅgā, I will look back at Śrī Pulina. Living near Īśodyāna in my private grove, I will worship Gaurāṅga who is nondifferent from Rādhā-Kṛṣṇa."

In *Śuddha-bhakata* from *Śaraṇāgati*, Śrīla Bhaktivinode Ṭhākura writes:

"One day, by the influence of my devotional service, I saw the splendor of Goloka Vṛndāvana in my own home. And upon seeing the Gaṅgā, which is a river of nectar emanating from the Lord's feet, my happiness knew no bounds."

Śrī Caitanya Mahāprabhu, the Lord's advent

Throughout the Vedic scriptures, Śrī Caitanya Mahāprabhu's incarnation, or appearance, is predicted. The following are only a few quotations. In the *Sāma Veda*, it is stated: "The Supreme Personality of Godhead said, 'To deliver the people devoured by the sins of Kali-yuga, I will, accompanied by My associates, descend to the earth in a place by Gaṅgā's shore. I will be a *brāhmaṇa avadhūta-sannyāsī*. Again and again I will chant the holy names of the Lord.'" In the *Vāyu Purāṇa* it is stated: "Lord Kṛṣṇa said, 'In the age of Kali, when the *saṅkīrtana* movement is inaugurated, I shall descend as the son of Śacī-devī. I shall appear as the best of the *brāhmaṇas* by the shore of Gaṅgā in Navadvīpa.'" And from the *Viśvasāra-tantra:* "Lord Śiva once said to Pārvatī, 'In the southern part of Gaṅgā at the all attractive Navadvīpa, on the Phālguna Pūrṇimā, Lord Kṛṣṇa will be born in the house of Jagannātha Miśra from the womb of Śacī to destroy the sins of Kali-yuga.'"

In the *Śrī Caitanya-maṅgala,* Locana dāsa Ṭhākura narrates several pastimes concerning the appearance of Caitanya Mahāprabhu, as told by Dāmodara Paṇḍita and Murāri Gupta, who are two of the most intimate associates of Caitanya Mahāprabhu.

Dāmodara Paṇḍita inquired from Murāri Gupta, "Please explain why Lord Gaurāṅga appeared. I will become blissful by hearing these topics from you. Why did the Supreme Personality of Godhead, Śrī Kṛṣṇa, leave His *syāma-varṇa* (cloud blue color) and assume a golden form? Why did He remove His mantle as a gallant lover to adopt the dress of a *sannyāsī?* Why did He distribute *prema-bhakti* in each and every home?"

After hearing these questions, Murāri Gupta replied, "Paṇḍita Dāmodara listen to me. I will explain these truths to you. In Satya-yuga, the scriptures say that *dharma* (religious principles) has four limbs: mercy, cleanliness, austerity, and truthfulness. Tretā-yuga has three: mercy, cleanliness, and truthfulness. Dvāpara-yuga has two: cleanliness and truthfulness. Kali-yuga has one: truthfulness. In Kali-yuga, irreligiousity replaces religion and people reject the rules of the *varṇāśrama-dharma.* Under the dense darkness of Kali, everyone becomes sinful and addicted to irreligious acts. Nārada Muni, the greatest among the sages, felt compassion for humanity and decided to rout Kali, the personification of sin, from the earth. Seeing that the snake-like Kali had swallowed everyone in sin, Nārada appeared to re-establish religion.

"Thus the great sage Nārada, seeing the miserable condition of the people in Kali-yuga, thought deeply about their deliverance. Knowing that only the Supreme Personality of Godhead Lord Kṛṣṇa Himself could rectify the situation, Nārada Muni set out for Dvārakā, in the spiritual world. At that time, Lord Dvārakādhīśa, having just spent the night with Satyabhāmā, decided to visit the palace of Queen Rukmiṇī. As soon as Rukmiṇī learnt that Kṛṣṇa was coming to see her, she became filled with ecstasy, her body trembled in anticipation. The good-natured, topmost Queen Rukmiṇī, along with Mitravindā (who is the incarnation of Gaṅgā-devī in Kṛṣṇa's pastimes) and Nāgnajitī, joyfully received Lord Kṛṣṇa. Rukmiṇī washed His lotus feet with scented water and offered *ārati* (worship). Taking Kṛṣṇa's feet as her only property, Rukmiṇī held them to her breasts. While looking lovingly at the Lord, Rukmiṇī cried uncontrollably.

"Then Rukmiṇī spoke to Kṛṣṇa, 'My dear Lord, You are the crest jewel of all transcendental qualities. Within your heart, You cannot know why I am crying, even though everything is known to You. You don't know the power of Your lotus feet. My heart weeps because soon You will leave my palace and go away. You control everyone in the three worlds, but no one can control You. Now please listen. I am going to tell You something from the bottom of my heart. Whoever has intense attachment to serving Your lotus feet will definitely taste transcendental ecstasy. Because I am completely devoted and surrendered to You, I can relish the ecstasy of worshiping Your lotus feet. You, however, are the Supreme Lord, so how can You understand this ecstasy? Besides me, only Śrīmatī Rādhārāṇī knows how to relish the mellows of love and taste the highest transcendental pleasure.'

"After listening to Rukmiṇī's feelings, Lord Kṛṣṇa replied, 'O My beloved, I have never heard such an amazing and wonderful description. Until today, no one has ever suggested to Me that I should personally taste the love that My pure devotees have for Me.' Just at that moment, Nārada Muni arrived in Dvārakā looking very anxious and disturbed. He was in great pain seeing all the conditioned souls intoxicated by pride, absorbed in materialistic activities and devoid of Kṛṣṇa consciousness. But by being in the presence of the Lord, he was greatly relieved.

"Then Lord Kṛṣṇa smiled compassionately and said, 'Listen, Nārada, I just heard a wonderful description from Rukmiṇī. Consequently, I want to promise you, that in the age of Kali, I will manifest a form filled with humility. I shall become a devotee of Myself in order to taste the happiness relished by My pure devotees. Not only will I experience the bliss of *prema-bhakti*, but I will give it out to everyone in the world. Although I am the Supreme Lord, I will appear as My own devotee, in the association of other devotees, I will freely distribute My love by performing *hari-nāma-saṅkīrtana*, congregational chanting of My holy names. I will appear in the transcendental abode of Navadvīpa in Śrīdhāma Māyāpur, on the bank of Gaṅgā within the home of Śacī-mātā.

"'O Nārada, most fortunate sage, you will be loved wherever you go. Please go throughout the universe and tell the residents of Brahmaloka and Śivaloka that I will soon incarnate in Kali-yuga as Lord Gaurāṅga. In this form of personified mercy, I will establish the *yuga-dharma* of *saṅkīrtana-yajña*. Revealing the glories of Kṛṣṇa's holy names, I will personally preach the glories of devotional service and give the bliss of *kṛṣṇa-prema* freely to all. Although many branches of religion have appeared in the world in various ages, I will preach pure love of God to unite all the people. I will appear on earth, along with My intimate friends and followers. With them I will satisfy My cherished desire to relish the pure love that My devotees taste by serving My lotus feet.'

"After hearing the Lord's statement Nārada Muni's miseries and anxieties disappeared. After having his heart's desire fulfilled by the Lord, Nārada played his *viṇā* and chanted the glories of the Lord as he left Dvārakā."

In the *Śrī Caitanya-bhāgavata*, Vṛndāvana dāsa Ṭhākura nicely describes the birth of Lord Caitanya in the chapter entitled: *Śrī Gauracandra-janma-varṇana*. He begins this chapter by glorifying Lord Gaurasundara Mahāprabhu, who is the Supreme Personality of Godhead, appearing as the son of Jagannātha Miśra. He then glorifies all the devotees who have also appeared as the Lord's associates in Navadvīpa. Then quoting from the *Śrīmad-Bhāgavatam* (11.5.32), he recounts the prediction of Lord Kṛṣṇa's descent, as explained by Śrī Karabhajana (one of the Nava-yogendras) to Nimi, the King of Videha: "In the age of Kali, intelligent persons perform congregational chanting to worship the incarnation of Godhead who constantly sings the names of Kṛṣṇa. Although His complexion is not blackish, He is Kṛṣṇa Himself. He is accompanied by His associates, servants, weapons and confidential companions."

Vṛndāvana dāsa Ṭhākura then describes the events prior to the advent of Śrī Caitanya Mahāprabhu as follows: "Lord Caitanya-Nārāyaṇa has revealed that in Kali-yuga, *saṅkīrtana* is the best of all religious activities. Therefore, accompanied by all His personal associates, the Supreme Lord descended to this world in Kali-yuga to establish the *saṅkīrtana* movement. Following His order, His personal associates also

took birth in the world of human beings. Although many of these Vaiṣṇavas took birth in Navadvīpa, some of the Vaiṣṇavas most dear to the Lord were born in other places. The places by the shores of Gaṅgā are all pure and sacred. Why then did these Vaiṣṇavas take birth in impious places? Lord Caitanya Himself descended to this world on the bank of the Gaṅgā. Why, then, did His personal associates take birth in other distant places? The Pāṇḍavas never went to any place where the Gaṅgā or the holy names of Lord Hari were absent. Because the Lord loves all living entities as a father loves his children, He ordered these great devotees to take birth in different places. Thinking them equal holy places, these great souls took birth in impious countries and families. In this way they delivered everyone. In whatever country and whatever family they descended to this world, with their great power, these Vaiṣṇavas delivered everyone. Any place where the Vaiṣṇavas manifest their glories becomes very pure and sacred, a place of pilgrimage. Therefore, Lord Caitanya-Nārāyaṇa arranged that his devotees descend to the material world in all these different places.

"These great devotees assembled in Navadvīpa, for that is where the Lord descended to this world. Since Lord Caitanya appeared there, there is no other city in the world like Navadvīpa. Who can describe the opulence of Navadvīpa? On just one of its *ghāṭas* hundreds and thousands would come to bathe in the Gaṅgā. The leader of the Navadvīpa Vaiṣṇavas was named Advaita Ācārya. He was the most glorious person in the world. Offering *tulasī-mañjaris* and Gaṅgā-jala, He happily worshiped Lord Kṛṣṇa again and again. Out of love for Lord Kṛṣṇa, He would loudly chant Kṛṣṇa's holy names, since He was the greatest follower of *bhakti-yoga*.

"In this way, Advaita stayed in Navadvīpa. Seeing that the people had no devotion to the Lord, He became very unhappy. Advaita was naturally very merciful at heart. In his heart, He planned how to deliver the people. He thought, 'If I can make Lord Kṛṣṇa, the beloved of Vaikuṇṭha, appear in this world, then I will become happy, and by delivering every soul, I will sing and dance. If I fail to bring the Lord, I will manifest My four-handed form. Holding a *cakra* (disc) in My hand, I will cut off the necks of all the atheists. In this way, I will prove that Lord Kṛṣṇa is My master and I am His servant.'

"In Navadvīpa lived a person named Jagannātha Miśra, who was a very devout person, just like Mahārāja Vasudeva. He was very virtuous and stood in the highest pinnacle of brahminical virtue. No one was his equal. His wife was named Śacī. She was very chaste and devoted to her husband and was known as *viṣṇu-bhakti* personified. She was also the mother of the entire world. When true religion disappears, and when He knows that His devotees are suffering, the Supreme Lord descends to this world. Thus the Supreme Personality of Godhead, Lord Caitanya Mahāprabhu, entered the bodies of Śacī and Jagannātha.

"Aware that the Supreme Personality of Godhead was about to descend to the material world, Lord Brahmā, Śiva, and other demigods came and recited many prayers. The demigods said, 'All glories, all glories to Mahāprabhu, the father of all! All glories, all glories to the Lord, who will start the *saṅkīrtana* movement. O Lord, You have now descended to this material world! You reside in countless millions of universes, and now You have manifested Yourself in Śacī's womb. In Kali-yuga, You manifest in the form of a *brāhmaṇa* with a yellow complexion, and You will teach the religion of *saṅkīrtana*, which is secretly taught by the *Vedas*. The whole world will be filled with the congregational chanting of the holy names. In every home, *prema-bhakti* will be manifest. You are the Supreme Personality of Godhead. Bringing Your devotees with You, You have personally come to this world to preach pure love of God. After some days, You will fulfill Gaṅgā-devī's long cherished desire, for You will enjoy many pastimes in her waters. We therefore offer our respectful obeisances to the town of Navadvīpa and the home of Śacī and Jagannātha, where You have descended in this world.'

"In this way, Lord Brahmā and the demigods remained invisible as they daily offered prayers to the Lord. Then, when the full moon rose in the month of Phālguna (February/March), He openly manifested Himself. Who has the power to understand the Lord's actions? By the Lord's wish, Rahu covered the moon that night. Seeing the eclipse, all of Navadvīpa began to chant the auspicious names of the Lord Hari. Millions of people bathed in Gaṅgā's waters while shouting, 'Hari bol! Hari bol!' As all the devotees went to bathe in the Gaṅgā, all the directions were filled with the *saṅkīrtana* of Lord Hari's holy names. The demigods showered flowers in the four directions. Playing on their *dundubhis* (kettledrums), they cried out 'Jaya'. As all this occurred, the Supreme Personality of Godhead, who is the life of all the three worlds, appeared on the earth as the son of Śacī."

In the *Bhakti-ratnākara*, Śrī Īśāna Ṭhākura, the personal servant of Śrī Caitanya Mahāprabhu's mother, Śrī Śacī-devī, personally guides Śrīnivāsa Ācārya and Narottama dāsa Ṭhākura on a tour of Navadvīpa. When they arrive near the village named Samudragaḍa, or Samudra-garh, Īśāna points out to Śrīnivāsa that the authorities call that place Śrī Samudragaḍa because of its relationship with Surādhunī (the Gaṅgā) and Samudra (the Ocean). The village Samudra-gati flourished due to the mercy of mother Gaṅgā.

"One day, Samudra addressed Gaṅgā, 'There have been none more fortunate than you, Gaṅgā, in the world. According to the wise and virtuous people, Śrī Gaurasundara, who is Lord Kṛṣṇa Himself, will personally appear in Nadia and perform many wonderful sports on your banks. He, along with His associates, will perform unlimited pastimes in your waters just as Lord Kṛṣṇa sported in the waters of Yamunā.' Gaṅgā then sweetly said to Samudra, 'To whom shall I tell my miseries? Though at first I will get much pleasure from His childhood pastimes, yet more miseries will be waiting for me when Mahāprabhu will accept the *sannyāsa-āśrama* and will go live by your side in Jagannātha Purī. He will increase your pleasure day by day by His numerous sports there. While there are so many chances of your pleasure, why are you increasing my miseries by telling my fortune?' Samudra answered, 'What are you saying? I have to see Him in the dress of an ascetic, which will be so painful to me that I am afraid as to how I can bear it. For this reason, in order to get a peace of mind, I have come to you to take refuge under your kindness, because you will show me the sports of Mahāprabhu in Nadia, along with His magnificent and enchanting beauty. I will observe the favorite pastimes of the Lord, and with your kind help, I will see Caitanya Mahāprabhu and His associates all of the time.'

"In this way, they remained continually thinking of the appearance of Śrī Caitanya Mahāprabhu and became very impatient. Gradually, Surādhunī and Samudra came to realize that the time had come for the appearance of the Lord."

The Lord's pastimes

The following verse from the *Śrī Caitanya-carita*, Śrī Murāri Gupta describes another reason why Gaṅgā is participating in Śrī Caitanya Mahāprabhu's pastimes:

"There the swiftly-flowing river Gaṅgā glides in grandeur, brought forth from the foot of Vāmana-deva. Her ice is melted by compassion for all conditioned souls, and out of rivalry with the Yamunā River (who once embraced Śrī Kṛṣṇa), and the Sarayū River (who embraced Śrī Rāma), she at last embraces Śrī Hari in His brilliant golden form at Navadvīpa."

Once again from the *Bhakti-ratnākara*, the pastimes of Śrī Caitanya Mahāprabhu are nicely summarized as follows: "The *līlā* that Gaurahari enacted in Kali-yuga was beyond the comprehension of Brahmā, Śiva, and the other demigods. Śrī Caitanya's beautiful *līlā* was divided into three segments, beginning, middle, and final. The first portion dealt with Śrī Caitanya as a scholar known as Nimāi Paṇḍita. In the middle portion, the Lord revealed the glory of *hari-nāma-saṅkīrtana*. The last portion dealt with Gauracandra's life in Nīlācala (Jagannātha Purī) as a *sannyāsī*, after he instructed Lord Nityānanda to take responsibility of preaching in Gauḍa-deśa (Bengal). The same pastimes Lord Kṛṣṇa enacted in Vṛndāvana during Dvāpara-yuga were now again revealed by Śrī Caitanya Mahāprabhu in the age of Kali. Learned people say that Navadvīpa is an eternal holy place shaped just like a transcendental lotus flower. Sometimes it blossoms revealing its supernatural powers in full glory, and at other times it conceals them."

In the *Śrī Caitanya-bhāgavata, Madhya-khaṇḍa*, it is stated: "Lord Caitanya, who is the king of all the universes, and the dust of whose feet everyone joyfully places on their heads, dances on the bank of Bhāgīrathī Gaṅgā." The seventh verse of the *Śrī Śacī-nandana-vijayāṣṭaka* says: "He is like a golden mountain that scatters jewels of pure love of God. Because of His great mercy, He wandered on this earth. That Lord, known as Viśvambhara, the maintainer of the universe, inundated His own universe with the currents of the River Gaṅgā from the tears of love of Godhead flowing from His eyes. All glories to that Lord, the son of Śacī-devī." And in the *Gītā-mālā*: "The pastimes performed by Lord Gauracandra within the town of Nadia are just like sweet ambrosial nectar. By drinking this nectar, just give up all your material fears and lamentations and make your heart satisfied."

* * *

The following pastimes of the Lord are just a few of the unlimited eternal pastimes occuring in Śrī Navadvīpa-dhāma. Several of these pastimes have occurred along the *ghāṭas* on the banks of Gaṅgā, but due to the constant changing of the river's course, these *ghāṭas* today are unmanifested. For more details regarding Śrī Caitanya Mahāprabhu's pastimes along the banks of Gaṅgā, please see the "Map of the Gaṅgā River with *ghāṭas* in the 1500's" in the Antardvīpa section of *Gauradeśa* by Mañjarī Devī Dāsī. The following narrations are taken from different references that are listed with the individual pastime.

From the *Śrī Caitanya-caritāmṛta* (*Ādi* 14.48-50): "Sometimes the Lord, with other children, would go to take bath in the Ganges, and the neighbouring girls would also come there to worship various demigods. When the girls, after bathing in the Ganges, engaged in worshiping the different demigods, the young Lord would come there and sit down among them. Addressing the girls the Lord would say: 'Worship Me, and I shall give you good husbands or good benedictions. Gaṅgā-devī and goddess Durgā are My maidservants. Not to speak of other demigods, even Lord Śiva is my servant.' "

Next, Śrīla Prabhupāda comments on the *Śrī Caitanya-caritāmṛta* (*Ādi* 14.48) about the young girls bathing in the Gaṅgā: "According to the Vedic system, small girls ten

or twelve years old would go to the bank of the Ganges to take their bath and especially worship Lord Śiva with prayers to get good husbands in the future. They especially wanted to get a good husband like Lord Śiva because Lord Śiva is very peaceful and at the same time the most powerful. Formerly, therefore, small girls in Hindu families would worship Lord Śiva especially in the month of Vaiśākha (April/May). To take bath in the Ganges is a great pleasure for everyone, not only for adults but for children also."

In the Śrī Caitanya-bhāgavata (Ādi-khaṇḍa, Chapter 6) these childhood pastimes are retold: "Kicking His lotus feet, Viśvambhara would splash water on people on Gaṅgā's shore and break their meditations. He spat on them, forcing them to take bath again for purification. He stole someone's Śiva-liṅga. After one brāhmaṇa made an āsana (sitting place) for Lord Viṣṇu's worship, Nimāi sat on it and ate all the offerings. When someone would chant Gāyatrī in Gaṅgā, Viśvambhara would grab their feet from under the water and upend them. He would make babies cry by throwing water in their ears. After the brāhmaṇas finished their baths, he would throw sand on them. Unable to catch the swiftly fleeing Lord, the senior paṇḍitas would complain to Nimāi's father. At the same time, some village girls also complained to Śacī-mātā, 'When we take bath in the Gaṅgā, Nimāi steals our clothes. He argues and insults us and then splashes water on us if we try to return the insults. He forcibly steals the fruits and flowers for our pūjā and throws them away. Nimāi and His prankish friends hurl sand on us when we come out of the Gaṅgā. He sneaks up behind us and suddenly shouts in our ears.' Another girl said, 'He spat in my face and put itchy okaḍa seeds in my hair.' 'He asked me to marry Him', said another girl."

The following 'intimate' pastime is from The Life and Times of Lord Caitanya: "One day, a girl named Lakṣmī, the daughter of Vallabha Bhaṭṭa, came to the bank of Gaṅgā for the same purpose as the other girls. This Lakṣmī, however, was no ordinary girl. In her previous life, she was Rukmiṇī, Lord Kṛṣṇa's wife in Dvārakā and before that, she was Sītā, Lord Rāmacandra's wife. In other words, Lakṣmī was the Lord's eternal consort, who came once again to engage in His divine pastimes. Seeing Lakṣmī on the bank of the Gaṅgā, the Lord was naturally attracted to her. Their eternal love for one another was re-awakened, although it was covered by childhood emotions. Lord Caitanya and Lakṣmī-devī, in fact, are eternally husband and wife. But as they enacted their childhood pastimes, they knew it would take some time before they could manifest their marriage. Consequently, they took the opportunity to relish the special taste of childlike activities."

The following is a song (in the Kāmoda Rāga) of the meeting of Lord Caitanya and His eternal consort, Lakṣmī, which is from the Twelfth Chapter of the Bhakti-ratnākara:

"The daughter of Vallabha...sweet natured Lakṣmī, was encircled by Her associates. For taking Her bath...was going to Gaṅgā, while looking here and there. She suddenly saw Gauracandra...standing a distance away, and was overwhelmed with desire. Observing His beauty...which appeared like nectar, She could not control Her mind. Gaurasundara...identifying His own beloved, glanced at Her. Seeing Her beautiful golden complexion...Her beautiful figure, took Her at once in His mind. Both of Then glanced at each other's faces, no one else understood."

In the Śrī Caitanya-maṅgala (Ādi-khaṇḍa, Chapter 3), a description of the Lord's father leaving this mortal world is given as follows: "One day Jagannātha Miśra, the jewel among the brāhmaṇas, returned home after studying the *śāstras* in his *guru's āśrama*. By the arrangement of providence, Jagannātha Miśra had a raging fever and was about to leave his body. Śacī-devī worried and cried. Hearing the unfortunate news, friends and relatives rushed to Śacī-devī's house and stood around Jagannātha Miśra. Nimāi Paṇḍita then said, 'Mother, why are you delaying? Now engage the relatives.' Then Nimāi, Śacī-mātā, and some friends carried Jagannātha Miśra's body to the River Gaṅgā. While clutching His father's feet, Nimāi cried uncontrollably. The *brāhmaṇas* placed *tulasī* leaves on his neck and bathed Jagannātha Miśra in Gaṅgā water. While surrounded by his friends and family, Jagannātha Miśra, the best of the *brāhmaṇas*, chanted the names of Lord Kṛṣṇa in a choked and feeble voice and then returned to Vaikuṇṭha on a celestial chariot."

Locana dāsa Ṭhākura concludes this pastime by stating, "Jagannātha Miśra, the father of Lord Viśvambhara, was the greatest among the *brāhmaṇas*. Anyone who hears with faith and devotion about Jagannātha Miśra's disappearance and return to Vaikuṇṭha will also attain Vaikuṇṭha if he dies on the bank of the Gaṅgā."

Again from *The Life and Times of Lord Caitanya*: "One day, Nimāi Paṇḍita took refuge on a pile of black earthern cooking pots, which had been throw into a ditch as refuse. Śacī-mātā begged Nimāi to come down fron the filthy pile of garbage, but the Lord did not move an inch and began to philosophize with her, 'How can pots used for cooking offerings for the Lord be considered unclean or filthy? Even if they were filthy, do they not become pure once I touch them? The idea of clean and dirty (holy and unholy) is a mental delusion and has nothing to do with spiritual reality.' Śacī-mātā considered the impractical words of her divine child, but in any case she immediately took Him to bathe in the Gaṅgā."

Again from the *Śrī Caitanya-bhāgavata* (*Ādi-khaṇḍa*, Chapter 8): "In Navadvīpa resided Gaṅgādāsa Paṇḍita. He was the crest jewel of teachers and was Sandīpani Muni himself. He was very learned in books describing Sanskrit grammar. Lord Caitanya decided to study at his *āśrama*. By hearing Gaṅgādāsa's explanations only once, the Lord understood everything. Caitanya Mahāprabhu always defeated all the other students of Gaṅgādāsa. There was no end to the number of students in Nadia. After completing their studies, they would all go during midday to bathe in the River Gaṅgā. The Lord, being at the beginning of adolescence and very mischevious, would pick quarrels with the other students. Someone would swear, grab another boy, beat him, and swim to the other shore of Gaṅgā. The shoving and fighting of the students made Gaṅgā's water muddy and filled with sand, and because of this, the women could not fill their jars of water and the saintly *brāhmaṇas* could not bathe. At each bathing *ghāṭa*, the Lord would swim and play in the Gaṅgā. Accompanied by His students and other boys, Lord Caitanya played in the water again and again, then happily swam to the other shore of the Gaṅgā.

"Seeing Lord Kṛṣṇacandra's pastimes in the River Yamunā, Gaṅgā-devī became filled with desire. She lamented over and over again, 'When will I become fortunate like Yamunā-devī?' Although Lord Brahmā and Śiva offer prayers to Gaṅgā, she still yearned to attain the elevated position of Yamunā-devī. Lord Caitanya, who is a *kalpa-vṛkṣa* tree that fulfills all desires, fulfilled Gaṅgā-devī's desire again and again. After enjoying many pastimes in Gaṅgā's waters, Lord Caitanya would happily return home. After properly worshiping Lord Viṣṇu and watering *tulasī*,

the Lord would take His meal."

Śrīla Prabhupāda comments on the *Śrīmad-Bhāgavatam* (5.19.7): "Lord Śrī Caitanya Mahāprabhu had a very sincere devotee whose name was Kholaveca Śrīdhara and whose only business was to sell pots made from the skins of the banana trees. Whatever income he had, he used fifty percent for the worship of mother Ganges, and with the other fifty percent he provided for his necessities. On the whole, he was so very poor that he lived in a cottage that had a broken roof with many holes in it. He could not afford brass utensils, and therefore he drank water from an iron pot. Nevertheless, he was a great devotee of Lord Caitanya. He is a typical example of how a poor man with no material possessions can become a most elevated devotee of the Lord. The conclusion is that one cannot attain shelter at the lotus feet of Lord Kṛṣṇa or Śrī Caitanya Mahāprabhu through material opulence; that shelter is attainable only by pure devotional service."

The *Śrī Caitanya-bhāgavata* (*Ādi-khaṇḍa*, Chapter 12) describes some of the Lord's pastimes with Śrīdhara: "Caitanya Mahāprabhu regularly ate at Kholaveca Śrīdhara's house, enjoying bananas, roots, and vegetables that were grown by Śrīdhara. When a squash grew on a vine on his roof, it was cooked with milk and spices, then the Lord thoroughly enjoyed the meal. The Lord once said, 'Śrīdhara, what I will tell you is the truth. The glory of Gaṅgā originates from Me.' Śrīdhara replied, 'O Nimāi Paṇḍita, are You not afraid to disrespect Gaṅgā? Generally people grow more peaceful and steady as they grow older, but You have only become twice as mischievous!' After hearing these words, the Lord smiled and went away. Going to the bank of Gaṅgā, He met with His students. Śacī-mātā's son sat near the bank of Gaṅgā, and His students sat around Him in all four directions. The people on the bank of the Gaṅgā who saw the Lord's face felt indescribable happiness, and on seeing the Lord's extraordinary effulgence and glory, they would secretly discuss it among themselves. From the corner of His eye, Lord Gaurāṅga would observe the other teachers as He lectured by the side of the Gaṅgā. There was no end to the Lord's students. Every day ten or twenty *brāhmaṇa* boys would come and offer obeisances to the Lord's feet. In this way, He who is the crest jewel of Vaikuṇṭha would sit in the middle of a circle of students on the banks of the Gaṅgā."

More pastimes from the *Śrī Caitanya-bhāgavata* (*Madhya-khaṇḍa*, Chapter 1): "Speaking eloquent commentaries, Lord Caitanya explained that every word of the scriptures means, 'Lord Kṛṣṇa is the Supreme Truth.' Afterwards, the Lord asked, 'How did I explain the *śāstras* today?' The students replied, 'We did not understand anything. You said that every word in the scriptures means Kṛṣṇa. Who is qualified to understand Your commentaries?' Laughing loudly, Lord Caitanya said, 'Please hear Me, O My brothers. For today just tie up your books, for we will go and bathe in the Gaṅgā.' On the Lord's word they all tied up their books and went with the Lord to bathe in the Gaṅgā. Lord Caitanya played in the waters of the Gaṅgā and was like a full moon rising from the ocean. The saintly people of Nadia gazed at the Lord as He played in the Gaṅgā. Staring at the Lord's face, they said to each other, 'The father and mother of such a son must be very glorious and fortunate' Lord Caitanya's touch filled Gaṅgā-devī with happiness, as she happily made many waves. On the pretext of making those waves, Gaṅgā-devī danced with joy. She is a maidservant of Lord Caitanya's lotus feet, which have given birth to countless universes. Gaṅgā-devī then surrounded the Lord on four sides

and embraced Him with her waves. After bathing, the Lord went home and His students went their own way."

This narration from the *Śrī Caitanya-maṅgala* (*Madhya-khaṇḍa*, Chapter 7) is of Mahāprabhu's adventures in the Gaṅgā: "One day after dancing with His devotees, Gaurāṅga Mahāprabhu fell prostrate on the ground to offer His obeisances. At the time, a joyful *brāhmaṇa* came and took the dust from the Lord Gaurāṅga's lotus feet. Feeling very unhappy about this, Gaurāṅga stood up, breathing heavily in anger, then ran to the River Gaṅgā and jumped in. The Lord vanished under the waters of Jāhnavī. Frantically, the devotees dove into the Gaṅgā in order to find Lord Gaurāṅga. The people of Nadia became afraid and began crying with grief. Śacī-mātā cried out madly for her son and then attempted to jump into the swift currents of the Gaṅgā. In despair, she just rolled on the ground to relieve her suffering, and then Nityānanda Prabhu dove into the Gaṅgā to rescue Gaurāṅga. He pulled the Lord up from underwater and brought Him to the bank. Tears of joy rolled down everyone's face on seeing Gaurāṅga again. Śacī-mātā lovingly placed Gaurāṅga, the life of her life, on her lap. The townspeople of Navadvīpa forgot their miseries and returned to their homes."

The popular story of the great, proud, undefeated Digvijayī in *Śrī Caitanya-caritāmṛta* (*Ādi-līlā* 16) is summarized as follows: On one full moon night, Lord Caitanya was sitting on the bank of Gaṅgā with his disciples and discussing literary topics. Coincidently, Keśava Kāśmīrī Paṇḍita (Digvijayī) also came there. He was a great learned *brāhmaṇa* scholar who was undeafeated in all the four corners of the country. While offering his prayers to mother Gaṅgā, he met with Caitanya Mahāprabhu. The Lord received him with adoration, but because Keśava Kāśmīrī was very proud, he talked to the Lord very inconsiderately. After the Lord played a subordinate role before the learned scholar, He requested the Digvijayī to compose poetry which describes the glory of Gaṅgā. Upon hearing the request, the *brāhmaṇa* became even more puffed up and within an hour he composed one hundred verses describing mother Gaṅgā. The Lord praised him saying that he was the greatest poet in the entire world, but added that it was too difficult for Him to understand, so could he please explain the meaning of only one verse. Keśava Kāśmīrī agreed and inquired as to which verse needed explanation. The Lord then repeated the following verse: "The greatness of mother Gaṅgā always brilliantly exists. She is the most fortunate because she emanated from the lotus feet of Śrī Viṣṇu, the Personality of Godhead. She is the second goddess of fortune, and therefore she is worshiped by both demigods and by humanity. Endowed with all wonderful qualities, she flourishes on the head of Lord Śiva."

The Digvijayī was very much astonished that this young Nimāi Paṇḍita had memorised even one among those verses. Nevertheless, the proud *brāhmaṇa* fully explained the meaning. Then the Lord wanted him to explain the special qualities and faults in that verse, but the Digvijayī said that there was not a tinge of fault in the verse, rather it was full of good qualities of similies and alliteration. The Lord replied that the verse had five faults and five literary ornaments, which the Lord described one after another. He also requested the Digvijayī to listen without becoming angry and give his judgement afterwards. After hearing the explanation of the Lord, the champion poet was struck with wonder and since his cleverness was stunned, he could not say anything. The defeated poet began thinking why the goddess of learning, Sarasvatī, had insulted him so greatly through this young boy Nimāi. Seeing the poet defeated, the Lord's students began to laugh, but the Lord forbade them and asked them to remain silent. The Lord then said, "You are the most learned scholar and the best poet, for otherwise, how could such fine poetry come from your mouth? Your poetic skill is like the constant flow of the waters of Gaṅgā. I find no one in the world who can compete with you." That evening, Keśava Kāśmīrī worshiped mother Sarasvatī, who appeared to him in his dream and revealed the Lord's identity, so the Digvijayī understood that Caitanya Mahāprabhu was the Supreme Personality of Godhead Himself. The next morning, the poet came to Lord Caitanya and surrendered unto His lotus feet.

Here is a pastime from the *Śrī Caitanya-bhāgavata* (*Madhya-khaṇḍa*, Chapter 5) about Nityānanda's Vyāsa-pūjā ceremony: Once Lord Caitanya inquired from Lord Nityānanda as to where His Vyāsa-pūjā (worship of the representative of Vyāsadeva) would be performed the following day. Nityānanda replied that it should be held at Śrīvāsa Paṇḍita's house. Then the Lord and His associates departed for Śrīvāsa Paṇḍita's house, where upon arriving the Lord instructed that a *kīrtana* be started, and the two Lords danced to unprecedented heights of ecstasy. They embraced one another, grasped each other's feet, rolled about on the ground, and cried out, "Chant! Chant!" Hearing this, all the devotees floated in bliss. Then Lord Caitanya became peaceful and embraced everyone. He also excused Himself for any offenses committed. As the Lord spoke, all the devotees smiled. Then the two Lords again rolled on the ground, rapt in ecstatic trance. One moment They laughed, the next moment They danced, and the next, Lord Nityānanda's clothing fell to the ground, as He floated in an ocean of bliss.

At the time, Lord Nityānanda was not even aware of where His *daṇḍa*, *kamaṇḍalu*, and garments were. Later in the evening, Nityānanda broke His *daṇḍa* and *kamaṇḍalu* to pieces and threw them here and there. In the morning, the devotees saw the broken pieces and were very surprised. Nityānanda laughed wildly, and then Lord Caitanya threw the broken pieces into the Gaṅgā while Śrīvāsa Paṇḍita and the other devotees were bathing in the river. Restless Nityānanda did not pay attention to anyone's words, even when Lord Caitanya sternly scolded Him. Seeing a crocodile in the river, Nityānanda dived into the river to catch it! He was in the middle of the Gaṅgā, when Lord Caitanya stopped Him by saying, "Come out at once and perform the Vyāsa-pūjā". Hearing the Lord's words, Nityānanda emerged from the water and went with Lord Caitanya to Śrīvāsa Paṇḍita's home, where the Vyāsa-pūjā ceremony was performed.

In the *Śrī Caitanya-bhāgavata* (*Madhya-khaṇḍa*, Chapter 7), Puṇḍarīka Vidyānidhi's love for Gaṅgā is revealed as follows: One day after dancing, Lord Caitanya sat down and called out, "O My father, Puṇḍarīka! O father, when will I see you?" The Lord then wept, but the devotees did not understand who Puṇḍarīka Vidyānidhi was, so they inquired from the Lord.

Then the Lord said, "You are all very fortunate, for you desire to hear about him. His character and activities are all supremely wonderful. He dresses like a materialist, so no one knows that he is a Vaiṣṇava. He was born in Caṭṭagrāma (now in Bangladesh), and he always floats in the ocean of pure devotion to Lord Kṛṣṇa. Afraid that his feet may touch her, he does not bathe in Gaṅgā. Seeing everyone disrespect Gaṅgā, as they rinse their mouths, brush their teeth, and wash their hair in her water, Puṇḍarīka feels pain in his heart. Therefore he goes alone at night to see the Gaṅgā. Please hear of his wonderful faith. Before worshiping his Deity, he drinks some Gaṅgā water. He does this to teach true religious duties to all the *paṇḍitas*. He stays in Caṭṭagrāma, but also has a house here in Navadvīpa. He will come here soon, then I will see him. Without seeing him, I cannot be happy." After speaking these words, Lord Caitanya entered into an ecstatic trance. Calling out "Father, Puṇḍarīka," the Lord simply wept.

In the *Śrī Caitanya-caritāmṛta* (*Ādi* 10.120), Śrīla Prabhupāda informs us about Jagāi and Mādhāi: "In the *Gaura-gaṇoddeśa-dīpikā* (115) it is said that the two brothers, Jagāi and Mādhāi, were formerly the doorkeepers in Vaikuṇṭha named Jaya and Vijaya. Jagāi and Mādhāi were born in respectable *brāhmaṇa* families, but they adopted the profession of thieves and rogues, and thus became implicated in all kinds of undesirable activities, especially women hunting, intoxication, and gambling. Later, by the grace of Lord Caitanya and Śrī Nityānanda Prabhu, they were initiated, and they received the chance to chant the Hare Kṛṣṇa *mahā-mantra*. As a result of chanting, both brothers later became exalted devotees of Lord Caitanya. The descendents of Mādhāi still exist, and they are respectable *brāhmaṇas*."

More pastimes of Jagāi and Mādhāi are described in the *Śrī Caitanya-bhāgavata* (*Madhya-khaṇḍa*, Chapter 15) as follows: "By the mercy of Śrī Caitanya Mahāprabhu, Jagāi and Mādhāi lived as very religious persons in Nadia. At sunrise they would bathe in a secluded place in the Gaṅgā and everyday chant two hundred thousand names of Lord Kṛṣṇa. Lord Caitanya personally came and gave them *prasāda*, but still they were not peaceful at heart. When Mādhāi remembered how he attacked Lord Nityānanda with an earthern pot, he just wept uncontrollably. Lord Nityānanda had forgiven all his offenses, but still Mādhāi was not happy at heart. He rebuked himself repeatedly by saying, 'I have wounded Lord Nityānanda and made Him bleed. I am a sinner because I have injured someone who enjoys pastimes with Lord Caitanya.' Remembering all of this, Mādhāi would fall unconscious and simple weep day and night, thinking of nothing else. One day, when Lord Nityānanda was in a secluded place, Mādhāi fell down and grasped the Lord's lotus feet. He washed the Lord's lotus feet with his tears of love, and with a blade of grass between his teeth, he glorified the Lord with several prayers. Keeping the Lord's lotus feet to his chest, he continued reciting many prayers of glorification. Afterwards, Lord Nityānanda instructed him to stand and then happily embraced Mādhāi, thereby freeing him from all suffering. But Mādhāi was still not yet fully satisfied and inquired, 'How will the people I offended ever forgive me?' Lord Nityānanda replied, 'Listen, I will tell you what to do. Build a bathing *ghāṭa* by the Gaṅgā. When people find it easy to bathe in the Gaṅgā, they will bless you. Service to Gaṅgā breaks offenses into pieces. What better blessing can you attain? Greet everyone very humbly and bow down before them. Then everyone will forgive all your offenses.'

"Accepting this advice, Mādhāi circumambulated Lord Nityānanda several times and chanted 'Kṛṣṇa! Kṛṣṇa!' He then built that bathing *ghāṭa* by the Gaṅgā and always stayed there, appreciating the glories of Gaṅgā. Even today, the impression of Mahāprabhu's mercy is still present as everyone still calls that bathing place, Mādhāi-ghāṭa."

The *Śrī Caitanya-bhāgavata* (*Madhya-khaṇḍa*, Chapter 23) describes more pastimes of the Lord along the banks of Gaṅgā as follows: "Dancing with His asssociates, servants, weapons, and confidential companions, the King

of Vaikuṇṭha proceeded on the path by Gaṅgā's bank. His tears of love flowed like the celestial Gaṅgā. Lord Caitanya danced for a long time at His own bathing *ghāṭa*, then went to Mādhāi-ghāṭa, before going to Bārakoṇā-ghāṭa and Nagarāya-ghāṭa. He passed through town after town by the bank of Gaṅgā."

Also from the Twelfth Chapter of the *Bhakti-ratnākara* it is stated: "One day, Caitanya Mahāprabhu, along with His companions, went to the bank of the Gaṅgā. By the mercy of the Lord, they all began *hari-nāma-saṅkīrtana.* In ecstasy, Lord Gaurāṅga danced beautifully in the midst of His devotees. Sometimes He cried, sometimes He laughed, and sometimes He roared. As various types of instruments played, the nectar of His voice and the sound of His ankle bells filled the air, maddening the entire universe. The Lord's gorgeous moonlike face, His long hands touching His kness, His beautiful white teeth like *kunda* flowers, His broad chest, and His attractive curly hair enchanted the minds of all the people. The River Gaṅgā was fortunate enough to have the Lord and His devotees walk along her banks joyfully performing *saṅkīrtana.* After satisfying mother Gaṅgā, Lord Caitanya returned to His house with His friends."

From the same chapter of the *Bhakti-ratnākara*, the following song (in the Soma Rāga) describes the elegant dancing of Śrī Caitanya Mahāprabhu:

"On the bank of Gaṅgā, Gaura Natarāja used to roam with His companions. His impassioned dancing, which was more elegant each day maddened the entire universe. With His golden complexion, His strongly built body trembles in ecstasy. His gait, like an elephant, and long hands have put the demigods to shame. The beautiful *kunda* like teeth of His sweet smile used to mesmerize the universe. With a bright face, He constantly chanted 'Hari! Hari!' making everyone impatient."

And the final pastime of Śrī Caitanya Mahāprabhu in this section is from the Sixth Chapter of the *Śrī Pañca Tattva*: "In the evening twilight, within the privacy of Śrīvāsa Paṇḍita's courtyard (Śrīvāsāṅgana), Lord Caitanya engaged in *hari-kīrtana* with the most advanced devotees in Navadvipa. Becoming madly intoxicated with ecstatic love, the assembled devotees completely forgot themselves and incessantly began to dance and chant wildly, completely surrounding the Lord's intimate associates. At this time, within the inner chamber of Śrīvāsa's house, one of Śrīvāsa's sons suddenly died without any apparent cause. Lord Caitanya, who is so affectionate to His own devotees, then took the dead boy, and along with all the devotees, began to chant the holy names. In a parade of song and dance, they all arrived on the bank of Gaṅgā and there they performed the funeral rites using water from the holy river. When Mahāprabhu personally placed the body into the river, Gaṅgā-devī personified picked up the body and held it. Bringing the dead body out of the water, she then touched Mahāprabhu's lotus feet. Still holding the body, she began to tremble in ecstatic love for the Lord. In this way, Śrīvāsa's son was given a glorious burial, and the devotees continued to dance in ecstasy."

Pastimes in the mood of Kṛṣṇa and Vṛndāvana

The following is an adaptation from the *Bhakti-ratnākara* as quoted from *Appreciating Navadvīpa Dhāma*: "In Navadvīpa, Śrī Caitanya Mahāprabhu and His associates would regularly re-enact the pastimes performed by Śrī Śrī Rādhā-Kṛṣṇa in Vṛndāvana. In one place Gaurasundara revealed His pastimes as a cowherd boy. Remembering His cows, Gaurahari suddenly

began calling out, 'Dhāvalī! Śobalī! Haṁsī! Caṇḍī!' while waving a cowherd stick. One day in the mood of *dana-līlā* (tax collecting pastime), Gaurāṅga wandered through the streets of Nadia requesting everyone, 'Give Me something! Give Me something!' At Rādhā-kuṇḍa, Srimatī Rādhāraṇī used to pick flowers and quarrel lovingly with Śyāmasundara. Similarly, seeing a flower garden one day, Lord Gaurasundara began picking flowers and throwing them on the heads of His devotees. They responded by showering fragrant flowers on Gaura's beautiful head.

Kṛṣṇa and the *gopis* always enjoyed *jala-keli* (water splashing) in the Yamunā or in Rādhā-kuṇḍa. One day, Gaurāṅga and his devotees entered the Gaṅgā and playfully splashed one another. After the scorching heat of summer abates, monsoon clouds beautify the sky and rumble gently. At this time, Rādhā-Mādhava enjoy *jhulana-yātrā* (swing pastimes). Remembering this scene, Lord Caitanya sat on a swing near the bank of Gaṅgā. Gadādhara, Nityānanda, Advaita, and others would sing sweet songs about *jhulana-līlā*. While He sat looking like bright lightning illuminating the dark blue monsoon sky above Navadvipa, Lord Gaurasundara's beauty stole the beauty of the universe. While reminded of the Vṛndāvana līlā, Lord Caitanya regarded the Gaṅgā as Yamunā. At such times, Gaurāṅga would dance ecstatically uttering, 'Jai! Jai!' During the spring season in Vṛndāvana, Rādhā-Mādhava and the *gopīs* celebrate joyously by throwing colored powders and splashing each other with perfumed colored liquids. This Holi *līlā* (color festival) in Vṛndāvana reaches its peak on Holi Pūrṇimā, also known as Gaura Pūrṇimā, the divine appearance of the Supremely Personality of Godhead, Śrī Kṛṣṇa Caitanya. During the spring season in Nadia, the trees blossomed with fragrant flowers, the cuckoos sang sweetly, and the bumblebees buzzed contentedly amidst flowers swaying in the mild breeze. On the bank of the Gaṅgā, Gaurahari enjoyed Holi *līlā* with His associates. Taking piles of brightly colored flower pollen, they smeared the beautiful body of Gauracandra, and in return, Mahāprabhu rubbed *candana* (sandlewood paste) and red powder on them. Then Nityānanda, Advaita, Śrīvāsa, and others began throwing red powder on one another. Observing this joyous scene, even the demigods became impatient to join the fun."

Aṣṭa-kālīya-līlā of Śrī Gaurāṅga Mahāprabhu

The *aṣṭa-kālīya-līlā* (eternally flowing eightfold daily transcendental pastimes) of Gaurāṅga Mahāprabhu in the spiritual world are in eight time divisions throughout the entire day and night. The following is a brief summary by Srīla Viśvanātha Cakravarti Ṭhākura.

"1) At the end of night, before sunrise (3:36-6:00a.m.), Lord Gaurāṅga rises from bed, stretches His body, talks with Viṣṇupriyā, and washes His face; 2) In the morning (6:00-8:24a.m.), Gaurāṅga is massaged with oil, bathes in the celestial River Gaṅgā, worships Gaṅgā-mayī by offering flowers, incense, and other presentations, then worships Adhokṣaja Viṣṇu; 3) In the forenoon period (8:24-10:48a.m.), Gaurāṅga enjoys discussing topics about Lord Kṛṣṇa with His devotees while visiting their homes; 4) At midday (10:48a.m.-3:36p.m.), Mahāprabhu enjoys pastimes in the gardens and groves on the bank of Gaṅgā; 5) In the afternoon (3:36-6:00p.m.), leaving the bank of Gaṅgā, Lord Gaurahari wanders about the town of Navadvīpa, sporting with all the residents; 6) At dusk (6:00-8:24p.m.), the Lord bathes with His dear friends in the River Gaṅgā, worships Gaṅgā-devī before return-

ing home to worship Lord Viṣṇu and perform other rituals; 7) In the evening (8:24-10:48p.m.), Gaura Natarāja goes with His associates to the courtyard of Śrīvāsa Paṇḍita to chant the holy names and dance in ecstasy; 8) And at night (10:48p.m-3:36a.m.), Gaurāṅga Mahāprabhu dances together with Gadādhara before returning home to rest with Viṣṇupriyā. May this Lord Gaurāṅga protect us all."

Gaura-ārati

Śrila Bhaktivinoda Ṭhākura composed hundreds of poems and songs, combining his deep transcendental emotions with the wealth of Vaiṣṇava philosophy, especially the wonderful *bhajanas* glorifying Lord Caitanya.

In *Siddhi-lālasā* (Hankering for Spiritual Perfection), Bhaktivinoda Ṭhākura calls out, "When will I wander, weeping under the shade of various trees and creepers on the banks of Gaṅgā in the land of Navadvīpa, crying 'O Rādhā! O Kṛṣṇa!' forgetting all physical comforts?"

Similarly, in *Kabe Ha'be Bolo*, he inquires with a meek, humble heart, "When in the land of Navadvīpa, on the banks of Gaṅgā, will I run about, openly calling, 'O Gaura! O Nityānanda!' dancing and singing like a madman, giving up all consideration?"

Gaudiya Vaiṣṇavas regularly sing the *Gaura-ārati* by Bhaktivinoda Ṭhākura which depicts an eternal evening pastime of Lord Gaurāṅga. During *pradoṣa-līlā* (8:24-10:48 p.m.), Lord Gaurāṅga and His intimate devotees meet in Śrīvāsa Ṭhākura's home for *ārati* and *kīrtana*, which take place on the banks of Gaṅgā.

jaya jaya gorācānder āratiko sobhā
jāhnavī-taṭa-vane jaga-mana-lobhā (1)

dakhiṇe nitāicānd, bāme gadādhara
nikaṭe advaita, śrīnivāsa chatra-dhara (2)

bosiyāche gorācānd ratna-siṁhāsane
ārati koren brahmā-ādi deva-gaṇe (3)

narahari-ādi kori' cāmara dhulāya
sañjaya-mukunda-bāsu-ghoṣa-ādi gāya (4)

śaṅkha bāje ghaṇṭā bāje bāje karatāla
madhura mṛdaṅga bāje parama rasāla (5)

bahu-koṭi candra jini' vadana ujjvala
gala-deśe vana-mālā kore jhalamala (6)

śiva-śuka-nārada preme gada-gada
bhakativinoda dekhe gorāra sampada (7)

1) All glories, all glories to the beautiful *ārati* ceremony of Lord Caitanya. This Gaura-ārati is taking place in a grove on the banks of the Jāhnavī (Gaṅgā) and is attracting the minds of all living entities in the universe.

2) On Gauracandra's right side is Lord Nityānanda, and on His left is Gadādhara. Nearby stands Śrī Advaita, and Śrīvāsa Ṭhākura is holding an umbrella over Lord Gauracandra's head.

3) Lord Gauracandra has sat down on a jewelled throne, and the demigods, headed by Lord Brahmā, perform the *ārati* ceremony.

4) Narahari Sarakāra and other associates of Lord Gauracandra fan Him with *cāmaras* (yak-tail whisks) and devotees headed by Sañjaya Paṇḍita, Mukunda Datta and Vasu Ghoṣa sing sweet *kīrtana*.

5) Conchshells, bells, and *karatālas* (symbols) resound, and the *mṛdaṅgas* (drums) play very sweetly. This *kīrtana* music is supremely sweet and relishable to hear.

6) The brilliance of Lord Gauracandra's face conquers millions and millions of moons, and garland of forest flowers around His neck shines.

7) Lord Śiva, Śukadeva Gosvāmī, and Nārada Muni are all there and their voices are choked with the ecstasy of transcendental

love. Thus Bhaktivinoda Ṭhākura envisions the glory of Lord Śrī Caitanya Mahāprabhu.

ISKCON Śrīdhāma Māyāpur

In Śrila Bhaktivinoda Ṭhākura's *Jaiva Dharma*, he glorifies Śrī Navadvīpa-dhāma as follows: "Of all the planets in the universe, Jambūdvīpa is the most worthy. Of all the places on earth, Bhārata-varṣa is supreme. Spiritually, Gauḍa-maṇḍala is the most exclusive. And of all places in Bengal, Śrīdhāma Māyāpur is the crest jewel. Śrī Navadvīpa-dhāma is essentially nondifferent from Śrī Vṛndāvana-dhāma. But Māyāpur is above both Vṛndāvana and Navadvīpa. In the middle of Śrī Māyāpur is the *mahā-yogapīṭha*, the temple of Jagannātha Misra, the father of Lord Caitanya. As the incarnation of Caitanya Mahāprabhu is covered in Kali-yuga, so is His *dhāma*, Śrī Navadvīpa. No other holy place of pilgrimage in Kali-yuga compares with Śrī Navadvīpa. If one performs devotional service in Śrī Navadvīpa-dhāma, especially in Śrī Māyāpur, one quickly gets *kṛṣṇa-prema-siddhi* (the perfection of love of Kṛṣṇa)."

In the *Śrī Navadvīpa-māhātmyam*, the future temple of Śrī Caitanya Mahāprabhu is predicted. While Śrī Nityānanda Prabhu Himself was on *parikramā* of Navadvīpa-dhāma, He told Jīva Gosvāmī, "In due course of time, Gaṅgā-mayī will hide Śrīdhāma Māyāpur, but then again it will be revealed. By Lord Caitanya's wish people will again inhabit Māyāpur. All the lost bathing *ghāṭas* on the bank of Gaṅgā will remanifest, and devotees will build temples of the Lord. *Adbhuta mandira eka haibe prakāsa, gaurāṅgera nitya-sevā haibe vikāsa*—In Māyāpur one exceedingly wonderful temple will appear from which Lord Gaurāṅga's eternal service will be broadcast throughout the world. Prauḍhā Māyā (the eternal consort of Lord Śiva) will again manifest by the Lord's will and act as Yogamāyā to reveal the spiritual *dhāma* of Navadvīpa."

The following is another adaptation from *Appreciating Navadvīpa Dhāma*: "Five thousand years ago, after the disappearance of Lord Śrī Kṛṣṇa from this world, His transcendental abode of Dvārakā sank into the ocean. Recently, Indian archeologists have found what they claim to be the remains of Dvārakā under the sea off the coast of India. Similarly, five hundred years ago, after Lord Caitanya left this world, His spiritual abode of Māyāpur was inundated by the combined flood waters of the Gaṅgā and Jalaṅgī.

"Feeling intense separation from the Lord, Gaṅgā-mayī flooded the entire area of Gaurahari's glorious pastimes. The exact location of Śrī Caitanya's Mahāprabhu's birthplace was lost, and the holy *dhāma* remained covered for almost three hundred and fifty years. Up to the mid-ninteenth century, Māyāpur-dhāma was a neglected place, just a jungle of green vegetation. Then, late one December night in 1887, Śrīla Bhaktivinoda Ṭhākura had a divine revelation while chanting Hare Kṛṣṇa on the roof of the Rani Dharmasala in Navadvīpa. His meditation was suddenly broken by a divine vision appearing across the Bhāgīrathī Gaṅgā. He saw an unusual illumination of a tall palm tree standing beside a small effulgent house. Bhaktivinoda Ṭhākura immediately realized this was the factual birthsite of Śrī Caitanya Mahāprabhu. For centuries no one knew the exact location of Mahāprabhu's birthplace. After studying old manuscripts of *Śrī Caitanya-bhāgavata*, Narahari Sarakāra's *Navadvīpa-dhāma Parikramā*, and other authentic works written during the time of Śrī Caitanya Mahāprabhu, as well as eighteenth century British survey maps, old government records, and gazettes, Bhaktivinoda Ṭhākura discovered that Nadia was previously on the eastern bank of Gaṅgā; from where the wonderful illumination was coming.

"Today in Mathurā there are two different places claiming to be the original site of Lord Kṛṣṇa's birth. One is called Śrī Kṛṣṇa Janmasthāna, which contains the beautiful Birla Mandira standing beside a red sandstone mosque. The other site, called Prācīna Janmasthāna, is located about three hundred metres away beside Potra-kuṇḍa. Today in Navadvīpa, as there was in 1840, there is a rising controversy over the birthplace of Lord Caitanya. The birthplace of Lord Gaurāṅga, which was discovered by Bhaktivinoda Ṭhākura, confirmed by Śrī Jagannātha dāsa Bābājī, and developed by Śrīla Bhaktisiddhānta Sarasvatī Ṭhākura, is opposed by critics who claim that the original birthplace is on the opposite side of the Gaṅgā.

"In *Caitanya Śikṣāmṛta*, Bhaktivinoda Ṭhākura predicted that some day people from foreign lands would meet with their Indian brothers in the holy land of Māyāpur, dance together in ecstasy, and chant 'Jaya Śacīnandana! Jaya Śacīnandana!' He also wrote of a great personality who would soon appear to fulfill this prediction. Pure-hearted Vaiṣṇavas understand that this empowered personality appeared as His Divine Grace A.C. Bhaktivedanta Swami Prabhupāda, the Founder-Ācārya of the International Society for Krishna Consciousness (ISKCON)."

Śrīla Prabhupāda comments on Śrīdhāma Māyāpur: "In the beginning, Bhaktivinoda Ṭhākura wanted to develop this place very gloriously, befitting the holy name of Śrī Caitanya Mahāprabhu. So he started this movement of developing Māyāpur. He could not finish it, so it was handed down to Bhaktisiddhānta Sarasvatī Ṭhākura. So under his effort, assisted by his disciples, this place has gradually developed and our attempt is also to develop this place. Spreading Kṛṣṇa consciousness means spreading the moonlight. Therefore we have named this temple Śrī Māyāpur Candrodaya. Śrī Caitanya Mahāprabhu is Gaurahari, Māyāpur-candra, Caitanya-candra. So this temple, Māyāpur Candrodaya temple, is meant for transcendental United Nations. What the United Nations has failed, that will be achieved by the process recommended by Caitanya Mahāprabhu, *pṛthivīte āche yata nagarādi grāma sarvatra pracāra haibe mora nāma.* That is the greatest achievement of this ISKCON movement that everyone forgets the bodily conception of life. Nobody here thinks himself as European, Indian, Hindu, Muslim, Christian. They forget all these designations and simply they are ecstatic in chanting Hare Kṛṣṇa *mahā-mantra.* Therefore Māyāpur is the best among all the places in the universe. The Kṛṣṇa consciousness movement has established its center in Māyāpur, the birthsite of Lord Śrī Caitanya Mahāprabhu, to give men the great opportunity to go there and perform a constant festival of *saṅkīrtana-yajña*, and to distribute *prasāda* to millions of hungry people hankering for spiritual emancipation. This is the mission of the Kṛṣṇa consciousness movement. As preachers travel far away from Māyāpur-dhāma to distant parts of the world, like America and Europe, they can always remember their eternal home, Śrīdhāma Māyāpur. Thus they will never forget that they belong in the spiritual world, and not in this temporary material world of suffering. Their only purpose of remaining in this material world is to preach, and thereby bring all conditioned souls to the lotus feet of Lord Caitanya Mahāprabhu."

Śrīla Bhaktisiddhānta's pastimes at Śrī Vrajapattana

After Śrīla Bhaktivinoda Ṭhākura retired from government service, he began worshiping Lord Kṛṣṇa in a small residence in Godrumadvipa, near the town of Navadvīpa, where the Bhāgīrathī (Gaṅgā) meets the River Jalaṅgī (Sarasvatī or Khariya). Every day the great Vaiṣṇava renunciate, Śrīla Gaurakiśora dāsa Bābājī Mahārāja, would come and attend *Śrīmad-Bhāgavatam* class given by Bhaktivinoda Ṭhākura. In 1900, after being instructed by his father, the young Bimala Prasāda (birth name of Bhaktisiddhānta) took spiritual initiation from Śrīla Gaurakiśora, receiving the name: Śrīla Vārṣabhānavī-devī-dayita Dāsa. He then gave up all other activities to chant in solitary *bhajana* for seven years in a grove at Śrī Vrajapattana, Māyāpur, the place where Vṛndāvana is manifested, near the shore of the River Bhāgīrathī.

He vowed to chant one thousand million holy names of the Lord by chanting three hundred thousand names daily or ten million holy names monthly! It was at this location that Śrī Vārṣabhānavī-devī-dayita Dāsa realized that this area was one of Śrīmati Rādhikā's gardens (Īśodyāna).*

Living a very strict life of celibacy, he eventually accepted Vedic *tridaṇḍa-sannyāsa* on Phālguna Pūrṇimā (full moon of March) in 1918, also at Śrī Vrajapattana. This Vrajapattana was the location of Śrī Candraśekhara Ācārya's house (Mahāprabhu's maternal aunt's husband), where Lord Caitanya performed dramas of Vṛndāvana pastimes within Śrīdhāma Māyāpur, which is the seed or center of Navadvīpa's lotus. He then accepted his *sannyāsa* name: Śrīla Bhaktisiddhānta Sarasvatī Gosvāmī Mahārāja.

During the eighteen years that followed, Bhaktisiddhānta Mahārāja established sixty-four *maṭhas* (Vedic institutes or preaching centers) throughout several Indian states, as well as in Rangoon, London, and Berlin. The original and principal *maṭha* of these sixty-four centers was the Śrī Caitanya Maṭha at Vrajapattana. The construction of this beautiful, twenty-nine pinnacled temple for Śrī Śrī Guru-Gaurāṅga-Gandharvika-Giridhari was begun in 1923. Surrounding their Lordships at each corner are Śrī Madhvācārya, Śrī Nimbārka, Śrī Viṣṇusvāmī, and Śrī Rāmānuja, who represent the four Vaiṣṇava-sampradāyas: Brahmā, Rudra, Kumāra, and Śrī (Lakṣmī). Of the sixty-four *maṭhas*, seventeen of them are situated around Śrī Navadvīpa-maṇḍala. Bhaktisiddhānta Mahārāja also re-introduced the Navadvīpa-maṇḍala Parikramā in 1920-21 and on a larger scale during 1925. This *parikramā* was originally initiated some 450 years ago by Lord Nityānanda, who guided Śrī Jīva Gosvāmī around the fifty-one kilometre circumambulation of the nine islands that are interwoven together by Bhāgīrathī Gaṅgā and the other celestial rivers in Śrī Navadvīpa-dhāma.

Finally, Śrīla Bhaktisiddhānta Sarasvatī Mahārāja displayed His disappearance pastimes in Calcutta on the evening of the thirty-first of December, 1936 (some say in the early morning hours on the first of January, 1937). On the next day his spiritual body was decorated and taken on a procession to Sealdah Station, where a special train was

---

*As mentioned in the *Śrī Navadvīpa Bhāva-taraṅga*, Īśodyāna is the transcendental garden that is located in the southeastern portion of Māyāpur, resting on the bank of Sarasvatī (Jalaṅgī), near the *saṅgama* with the Gaṅgā (Bhāgīrathī). Opposite Īśodyāna lies Godrumadvīpa, the residence of Śrīla Bhaktivinoda Ṭhākura. Another narration describes Īśodyāna as the area between Yogapīṭha (Lord Caitanya's birthplace) and the confluence of the Gaṅgā and Sarasvatī Rivers, while another version states that Īśodyāna is the area beginning from the house of Nandana Ācārya (where Lord Caitanya first met Nityānanda) to the *saṅgama*. In this narration about Śrīla Bhaktisiddhānta Sarasvatī Mahārāja, his *samādhi* and other surrounding *tīrthas* are also considered within the transcendental garden of Īśodyāna.

waiting. In the afternoon the train arrived at Krishnanagara, and Bhaktisiddhānta Sarasvatī Mahārāja was taken by motor car to the Navadvīpa-para-ghāṭa at Svarūpa-gañja. After crossing the confluence of the Bhāgīrathī and Sarasvatī Rivers, he was taken on a *hari-nāma-saṅkīrtana* on the road leading to Śrīdhāma Māyāpur. At the same time, other Calcutta devotees arrived, after crossing the Bhāgīrathī Gaṅgā from the Navadvīpa township side, and joined the procession. He was then taken to Śrī Yogapīṭha, Śrī Śrīvāsāṅgana, Śrī Advaita Bhavan, and finally to Śrī Vrajapattana at the Śrī Caitanya Maṭha, which is identical to Śrī Girirāja Govardhana. The procession ended on the northern bank of Śrī Śyāma-kuṇḍa and a place was chosen as the *samādhi* for Śrīla Bhaktisiddhānta Sarasvatī Mahārāja.

Śrī Vrajapattana is the place where Śrī Candraśekhara Ācārya and Śrī Caitanya Mahāprabhu performed their wonderful pastimes together and where Śrī Girirāja Govardhana, Śrī Rādhā-kuṇḍa, and Śrī Śyāma-kuṇḍa have manifested. This same location, beautifully situated on the eastern bank of Gaṅgā-mayī, is the place where Śrīla Bhaktisiddhānta Sarasvatī Mahārāja performed his intense *bhajana*, accepted tridaṇḍa *sannyāsa*, established the principal Gauḍīya Math, and where he remains in *samādhi*.

Śrīla Prabhupāda's Māyāpur pastimes

In the *Śrīla Prabhupāda-līlāmṛta*, Volume Five, Chapters One and Seven, the pastimes of Śrīla Prabhupāda in Māyāpur are wonderfully described by H.H. Satsvarūpa dāsa Goswami. The following is a summary of these two chapters: It was during March 1971, when Śrīla Prabhupāda was in Calcutta, that he received the good news that the land which was being negotiated in Māyāpur was finally his. He had been trying to obtain land for years in order to continue the work that was started by his Guru Mahārāja, Śrīla Bhaktisiddhānta Sarasvatī Mahārāja. It was Bhaktivinoda Ṭhākura who earlier wrote, "The time would come when in the land of Navadvīpa on the plain of the Gaṅgā, a magnificient temple would arise proclaiming to the world the glories of Lord Caitanya." Later, when Śrīla Prabhupāda was in London, he announced one morning that the main temple in Māyāpur should be more than one hundred metres high!

The lands being near the Gaṅgā, Māyāpur's monsoon floods and sandy soil would create unique difficulties, and the building had to be built on a special foundation, a sort of floating raft. Afterwards the monsoons came and Gaṅgā-mayī spilled over her banks, flooding the entire ISKCON Māyāpur property. One devotee had built a straw and bamboo hut where Śrīla Prabhupāda was soon to stay, but Gaṅgā rose so high that the devotee had to live up in the bamboo rafters! He wrote to Śrīla Prabhupāda that had it not been for Bhaktisiddhānta road (The elevated road that runs in between ISKCON's property, which runs parallel along to Bhāgīrathī Gaṅgā's shore and serves as a dike), the damage would have been extense. Śrīla Prabhupāda replied, "Yes, we have been saved by Śrīla Bhaktisiddhānta's road. We shall always expect to be saved by His Divine Grace Śrīla Bhaktisiddhānta Sarasvatī Gosvāmī Mahārāja. Always pray to his lotus feet. Whatever success we have had in preaching Lord Caitanya's mission all over the world is only due to his mercy."

Then during the annual festival that celebrates the appearance of Caitanya Mahāprabhu, Śrīla Prabhupāda was met by a "roadblock" of ISKCON devotees waiting at Srīvāsāṅgana, some three kilometres from the ISKCON property. More than four hundred devotees from America, England, Europe,

South America, Australia, India, and other parts of the world chanted "Hare Kṛṣṇa" while following Śrīla Prabhupāda as he rode slowly towards Māyāpur Candrodaya Mandira on Śrīla Bhaktisiddhānta Road. On this day, in March 1974, Bhaktivinoda Ṭhākura's prophecy: "That some day people from foreign lands would meet in the holy land of Śrī Māyāpur and dance together", came to pass. This was truly the first international gathering of Śrīla Prabhupāda's disciples. He asked that everyone take advantage of the holy *dhāma* by maintaining *kīrtana* in the temple twenty-four hours. All the devotees were also very happy to be together in the *dhāma* and to perform *parikramā* to the local holy places. Almost all the devotees assembled in Māyāpur preached in areas of the world where the modes of ignorance and passion predominated. Daily they had to mix with materialistic people, and it was inevitable that they would become worn down. This pilgrimage, therefore, was a chance for purification. Although they were not advanced in birth or in knowledge of the Sanskrit *Vedas*, Prabhupāda had accepted them, and that was their certification as devotees. They were bonafide candidates for understanding the meaning of the *dhāma*. They would become refreshed by bathing in the Gaṅgā in Māyāpur and in the Yamunā in Vṛndāvana, and they would return to their respective centers throughout the world, purified and renewed for more active preaching.

Śrīla Prabhupāda stayed with his disciples in Māyāpur for a full week, lecturing daily and meeting with smaller groups for many hours. On the day of Gaura Pūrṇimā he went to Gaṅgā-mayī and took the sacred water on his head, while his men dove off the high bank and swam. The next day he left for Vṛndāvana, where he would again meet his disciples and introduce them to the *dhāma*.

Again in January 1976, Śrīla Prabhupāda returned to Śrīdhāma Māyāpur and stayed there for a three-month period. As Bombay was his "office" and Vṛndāvana was his "residence", Māyāpur was the place where Śrīla Prabhupāda worshiped the Supreme Personality of Godhead. It was also considered his place of worship because his spiritual master, Śrīla Bhaktisiddhānta Mahārāja, had preached extensively here and his *samādhi* was also here.

In *A Transcendental Diary*, Volume One, Chapter Nine, Hari Śauri Prabhu beautifully captures Śrīdhāma Māyāpur along with the presence of Śrīla Prabhupāda.

"He glanced around his room. His eyes rested for a moment on an intricately carved, three dimensional, wooden plaque on the far wall. It depicts Śrī Śrī Rādhā-Kṛṣṇa and was a gift from an admirer in Indonesia. On the wall beside him hung a large canvas oil painting depicting the Māyāpur foundation stone laying ceremony. It shows him sitting with some of his Godbrothers while disciples and admirers stand around. Above and behind him, dioramas of the Pañca-tattva perched on a shelf. In such a perfect setting I was struck by how the simplicity and deep spirituality of his surroundings seemed to perfectly complement Śrīla Prabhupāda's own transcendental nature.

"Later, while giving Śrīla Prabhupāda his massage, I surveyed the beautiful garden and the wide open expanse of fields from the veranda's vantage point. All around I could see rice fields in various stages of development: hues of emrald green maturing to yellow-gold. Clumps of dahl, strips of vegetables, nearly ripened wheat, and small green forests dotted the distant skyline. In the clear sky kingfishers flashed brilliant blue, green parrots flitted here and there in pairs, and cranes stalked the flooded paddies. It was beautiful. Following the line of the road toward the Gaṅgā and Jalaṅgī Rivers were the *maṭhas*, temples established by the followers of Śrīla Bhaktisiddhānta Sarasvatī. Their spires and domes reach to the sky, sentinels and reminders of real progress in human life. The melodious *kīrtana* of the Bengali devotees floated out from the temple below us, pervading the entire atmosphere.

"In this environment, Prabhupāda is clearly more relaxed and happy than I have seen him so far, like someone who has returned home from afar. Māyāpur struck me as idyllic, and as I rubbed mustard oil into his lotus feet, I suggested that it would be a fine place for Prabhupāda's retirement. He mused for a moment and then replied, 'Either Vṛndāvana or Māyāpur. No other place, that's for sure.'

"Prabhupāda then looked out through the arched porticos, over his ISKCON compound, and beyond the front gate. In the distance glistening slivers of light danced on the tranquil surface of mother Gaṅgā as she flowed down to Navadvīpa town and then beyond, on her long pilgrimage from the Himālayas to the Bay of Bengal. It was wonderfully gratifying to see him so perfectly and naturally situated, in his own environment so to speak, and hear him talk about various aspects of the movement as he shared his philosophical insights into the world and life in general. He seems very much at ease in Māyāpur. He loves sitting and looking out over the flat and fertile land, its open fields stretching into the distance, the verdant landscape dotted with small, green trees and occasional temple spires. A seemingly limitless expanse of rice paddies in every stage of development shows the results of the simple, honest labor of those local villagers. Other fields yield carefully cultivated bounties of dahl, sugarcane, vegetables, and other necessities of life. Men and beasts amble slowly up and down the road along the rutted tracks. It seems the perfect place to meet one's basic requirements of maintaining body and soul together and in the midst of this natural opulence we are here; grateful recipients of the generosity of His Divine Grace, who is so expertly revealing the true spiritual nature of ourselves, the *dhāma*, and the all merciful Lord, Śrī Caitanya Mahāprabhu."

A new program was launched on the appearance day of Śrī Advaita Ācārya (7 February, 1976). One of Śrīla Prabhupāda's *sannyāsī* disciples left to sail up and down Gaṅgā-mayī with their Lordships Śrī Śrī Gaura-Nitāi and other Māyāpur devotees, preaching from village to village: "In the early morning, Prabhupāda was driven in a jeep to Hulor-ghāṭa on the Jalaṅgī River, where he inspected the 'Nitāi Pada Kamala.' Its renovations are complete, and the Deities have been installed below deck. The small wooden forms of Śrī Śrī Gaura-Nitāi will be taken on procession through villages wherever the boat lands. It is a good facility, a twelve ton 'Jali' class boat, about forty feet long and fifteen feet wide. It has a shallow draft and was previously used to transport hay, although the maritime authorities have licensed it to carry up to fifty-six passengers. The devotees have added a cabin above deck along most of its length. Brightly painted in green, yellow, and red, the boat was gaily decorated for today's occasion with stripes of orange marigolds. The high mast is painted in yellow and red stripes like a barber's pole. Inside the cabin the main support beams are yellow with bright red lotus-flower motifs.

"Tamāla Kṛṣṇa Mahārāja helped Śrīla Prabhupāda on board over the rickety bamboo ramp. Prabhupāda carefully inspected every corner of the boat. Then he sat for a few minutes on a straw mat, while the devotees held *kīrtana*. Prabhupāda likes the idea

of preaching on the boat, and he encouraged Sudama Mahārāja to make it a success. Later in the morning, Sudama Mahārāja sailed away down the River Gaṅgā with seventeen men, including four of the older boys from the *gurukula* (Vedic school), on their maiden voyage. It was a very magnificient sight. Many local villagers lined the shore, eager to witness their departure"

Regularly, Śrīla Prabhupāda would go on morning walks, surrounded by his intimate disciples, but one day, Śrīla Prabhupāda decided to inspect the construction site of the new building. Hari Śauri Prabhu continues: "Work is going on at full speed, with hundreds of workers digging, carting, shoring, and stacking. It is an impressive sight. The foundation stretches about a thousand feet, the entire length of the northern boundary of our property. It will be an extemely long building, two stories high, and built in the same style as the main guest house with a veranda and decorative arches. They are building the two floors upon a high plinth, so if Gaṅgā floods, the rooms will not be affected. When Prabhupāda asked what would be done with the plinth, Jaypataka Mahārāja said it would be filled with dirt. Prabhupāda considered this a waste of valuable space; he instructed them to make it into a basement instead. That way there will be extra room for storage. Prabhupāda appeared satisfied with the progress of the work and is hopeful that it will be habitable in time for the festival."

Hari Śauri Prabhu describes one last morning walk conversation related to Gaṅgā-mayī that took place on the 9th of March as follows: "As we walked, the discussion turned to how to combat the flooding of Gaṅgā in our future city here in Māyāpur. Śrīla Prabhupāda told us to make a system of canals to drain the land. He also suggested that we could use the need for flood avoidance as a reason to get a land acquisition application through on an emergency basis."

Finally, on the day before Śrīla Prabhupāda was to leave Śrīdhāma Māyāpur (21st March), Hari Śauri Prabhu writes as follows: "With Prabhupāda's permission, I took my one and only bath in Gaṅgā before we left. She was swiftly flowing and swimming was difficult."

To conclude this section, the following quotation from the *Śrī Caitanya-caritāmṛta* (*Ādi* 2.2) encourages us to chant like the flowing of the Gaṅgā: "O my merciful Lord Caitanya, may the nectarean Ganges waters of your transcendental activities flow on the surface of my desert-like tongue. Beautifying these waters are the lotus flowers of singing, dancing, and loud chanting of Kṛṣṇa's holy name, which are the pleasure abodes of unalloyed devotees. These devotees are compared to swans, ducks, and bees. The river's flow produces a melodious sound that gladdens their ears."

And finally, Śrīla Prabhupāda comments on the same verse by offering everyone to taste the sweet nectar of chanting the holy name of the Lord: "Lord Caitanya's movement of Kṛṣṇa consciousness is full of dancing and singing about the pastimes of Lord Kṛṣṇa. It is compared herein to the pure waters of the Ganges, which are full of lotus flowers. The enjoyers of these lotus flowers are the pure devotees, who are like bees and swans. They chant like the flowing of the Ganges, the river of the celestial kingdom. The author describes such sweetly flowing waves to cover his tongue. He humbly compares himself to materialistic persons who always engage in dry talk from which they derive no satisfaction. If they were to use their dry tongues to chant the holy name of the Lord: Hare Kṛṣṇa Hare Kṛṣṇa Kṛṣṇa Kṛṣṇa Hare Hare/Hare Rāma Hare Rāma Rāma Rāma Hare Hare, as exemplified by Lord Caitanya, they would taste the sweet nectar and enjoy life."

Bhaktivedanta Swami Charity Trust

One day in the beginning of November, 1977, His Divine Grace A.C. Bhaktivedanta Swami Prabhupāda suddenly began to shed tears while lamenting about the dilapidated condition of many of the temples founded by Śrī Caitanya Mahāprabhu's followers. At that time, he expressed his desire to establish a trust for the purpose of renovating these ancient holy places (Śrīpats), many of which are located on the banks of Gaṅgāmayī. Accordingly, on the fifth of November, 1977, the Bhaktivedanta Swami Charity Trust (BSCT) was officially formed to renovate and develop the original temples of the followers of Lord Caitanya, as well as to reunite the Gauḍīya Vaiṣṇava *sampradāya*, especially the disciplic descendants of His Divine Grace Bhaktisiddhānta Sarasvatī Ṭhākura Prabhupāda.

According to the desires and instructions of Śrīla Prabhupāda, the following tasks were taken up by the BSCT: 1) Developing Śrīdhāma Māyāpur (Navadvīpa) and the *parikramā* sites; 2) developing and researching the holy sites of Gauḍa-maṇḍala-bhūmi; 3) renovating the holy places of the associates of Lord Caitanya Mahāprabhu; 4) publishing rare books of the previous ācāryas of the Gauḍīya Vaiṣṇava sampradāya; 5) and establishing the Sarasvatī Gauḍīya Vaiṣṇava Association.

As of now, the Bhaktivedanta Swami Charity Trust has assisted with renovations at several Śrīpats on or near the banks of the Gaṅgā: Kānāi-nāṭaśālā, Belpukura, Rājapura, Navadvipa, Kālnā and Jirāṭ.

(Note: Originally the abbreviation for Bhaktivedanta Swami Charity Trust was BSCT, but later the abbreviation was changed to BVSCT.)

25) ŚĀNTIPURA (SHANTIPUR)

Advaita Ācārya's pastimes

In this narration which combines the Sixth Chapter of *Śrī Advaita Prakāśa* and the Fourth Chapter of *Śrī Pañca Tattva*, Advaita Ācārya's origin is revealed, as well as some of His pastimes, especially those with Gaṅgā.

Long ago, before the advent of Śrī Caitanya Mahāprabhu, Mahā-Viṣṇu and Sadāśiva (the original form of Lord Śiva) met on the shore of the Kāraṇa-samudra (Causal Ocean) and discussed how to save mankind in the age of Kali. Out of their loving compassion, they embraced one another and assumed one form, which was the manifestation on this earth of Śrī Advaita Ācārya.

Advaita's father, Kuvera Paṇḍita, and mother, Lābhā-devī (Nābhā-devī), had come to perform austerities on the bank of Gaṅgā at Śāntipura, where Kuvera's father originally came from. At that time, the Lord descended into Lābhā's womb and a divine effulgence radiated from both their hearts. Afterwards, they returned to their native village named Nava-grāma, or Lāuḍa-dhāma (which is nondifferent from the Causal Ocean), in the Śrīhaṭṭa district of what is today known as Bangladesh.

When the people of Śrīhaṭṭa learnt of Lābhā-devī's pregnancy, they eagerly anticipated the appearance of the divine child. On the seventh day of the waxing moon in the month of Māgha, 1466, the Lord known as Śrī Advaita Ācārya appeared.

Later, during Advaita's childhood pastimes, He ascended one high mountain in the Śrīhaṭṭa area to satisfy His mother, who had long desired to bathe in all the holy rivers. He called all of the holy rivers to appear in their personified forms, and then had the rivers descend onto the mountain (Paṇā-tīrtha) and shower Lābhā-devī with their divine waters. As she enjoyed feeling the holy rivers engulf her body, Advaita said, "Look mother, there is the red Sarasvatī water, the white Gaṅgā, the black Yamunā, as well as Kāverī, Narmadā, and Godāvarī." This incident is remembered today in Śrīhaṭṭa as Vāruṇī-snāna (Vāruṇī-yoga), which occurred on the thirteenth day of the waning moon of Vaiśākha (April/May).

During Advaita Prabhu's twelfth year, He left Lāuḍa-dhāma and went to reside on the bank of Gaṅgā at Śāntipura. After some time, His parents decided to live with their son and said, "What is the use of remaining here? Let us go live on the bank of Gaṅgā, where one easily attains liberation." Advaita was very pleased to be with His parents again, but He had to travel onwards to a nearby place named Pūrṇavāṭī, to further His studies in the hermitage of Santācārya.

One day, Advaita's teacher went with his disciples to the Gaṅgā for taking bath. Next to Gaṅgā was one large deep lake filled with beautiful lotus flowers and fearsome snakes. Santācārya pointed to a platform in the middle of the lake with a huge, extraordinarily beautiful lotus flower on it. He asked his students if any of them could cross the water to get the big lotus and bring it to him without getting hurt. Most students were intimidated by the request, but Advaita Prabhu stepped forward and volunteered. He cautiously entered the water and at every step a lotus mystically appeared to carry Him and then a big snake rose out of the water, spreading its hood to shade Him like the celestial snake Ananta shades Lord Viṣṇu. In this way, Advaita safely reached the platform and picked the lotus to give His teacher.

After Advaita Ācārya's parents returned to Vaikuṇṭha, He traveled extensively around India, visiting all the major *tīrthas*. After visiting Śrī Vṛndāvana-dhāma, Advaita finally returned to Śāntipura. Once, Advaita was sitting in *yogāsana* (cross-legged) near the *tulasī* platform chanting the Gopāla-mantra. At that time, one Digvijayī named Śyāmadāsa arrived there and recited a poem glorifying *tulasī*, "Puṣkara, Prabhāsa, Kurukṣetra, and all other *tīrthas*; Gaṅgā, Yamunā, and all other holy rivers; Viṣṇu, Brahmā, Śiva, and all other demigods, all reside on one leaf of *tulasī*."

When the *brāhmaṇa* scholar next began describing the glories of Bhāgīrathī Gaṅgā, Advaita Prabhu opened His lotus eyes widely. The Digvijayī then said, "The glories of Gaṅgā are boundless. She emanates from the lotus feet of Lord Viṣṇu, therefore her other name is Viṣṇupadī. She who sports in the matted locks of Lord Śiva, who is worshiped with many offerings by Lord Brahmā, and who delivers the demigods headed by Indra, that Mandākinī Gaṅgā became the jeweled necklace of the earth. Knowing the essence of Gaṅgā's glories by meditation, Jahnu Muni drank Gaṅgā on the pretext of performing *ācamana*. Later, out of consideration for people's welfare, he let the Gaṅgā pass out from his knee.

"Gaṅgā is a devotee of Viṣṇu in the form of water. She is invested with the potency to deliver all living entities. Mother Jāhnavī is the reservoir of mercy, for simply by taking bath in her waters one is relieved of the threefold miseries. One who drinks a palmful of Gaṅgā water will certainly attain an exalted destination at the time of death. I offer hundreds of obeisances at the feet of Gaṅgā."

On hearing the *brāhmaṇa*, Advaita Ācārya smiled slightly and in sweet words said, "You are highly experienced and the crest jewel amongst poets. Your fame reaches up to the heavenly planets. My heart is enrapt with loving sentiments on hearing you recite the transcendental glories of *tulasi* and Gaṅgā.

"But you have some misunderstanding about the truth of Gaṅgā. You said that Gaṅgā is a devotee of Viṣṇu in liquid form. But actually the Supreme Lord Himself has taken the liquid form of Gaṅgā in order to deliver the living entities. The *Purāṇas* describe how one day Lord Nārāyaṇa melted into liquid upon hearing the ecstatic singing of Lord Śiva. That divine water became the River Gaṅgā, which is directly transcendence in the form of water. Indeed, simply by remembering her name, one is freed from the cycle of birth and death. The Lord's spiritual potency takes the form of Gaṅgā. By sustaining Gaṅgā on His head, Lord Śiva has conquered death.

"Without the mercy of Gaṅgā, no work will be successful. Even Lord Brahmā achieved his desired result by worshiping Gaṅgā. The *srutis* (Vedic literatures) instruct one to consider all water as Gaṅgā water, and they declare that Gaṅgā water is as good as Nārāyaṇa. Gaṅgā water becomes stagnant only after one year. If one dies in Gaṅgā, he attains Vaikuṇṭha. Kṛṣṇa is purchased by one who offers Gaṅgā water with a *tulasī* leaf."

Śyāmadāsa then inquired from Advaita about the Absolute Truth. Upon hearing such wonderful conclusive statements, Śyāmadāsa gave up his title "Digvijayī" and surrendered to the lotus feet of Advaita Ācārya.

Still, Advaita Prabhu could not tolerate the complete absence of spirituality in the people of His time. To alleviate the burden of the masses, He tried various forms of worship to propitiate the Supreme Personality of Godhead, Śrī Kṛṣṇa. The scriptures say that the Lord, who is very kind to his devotees, offers Himself to whomever offers Him a *tulasī* leaf or a handful of water. Knowing this, Advaita Prabhu sat down on the bank of Gaṅgā, while His whole body shivered and perspired with ecstasy, and called for the Lord to descend with offerings of Gaṅgā water and *tulasī* leaves. It was thus through Advaita Prabhu's mercy that Śrī Caitanya Mahāprabhu appeared.

Bring some 'bliss'

In the *Śrī Caitanya-bhāgavata* (*Madhya-khaṇḍa*, Chapter 19), the following story portrays the behavior of another type of *sannyāsī*: One day, during the Lord's childhood pastimes, Caitanya Mahāprabhu told Nityānanda Prabhu that They should visit Advaita Ācārya's house in Śāntipura. In a joyful state, the two Lords walked on Their way. About half way on the path to Śāntipura near Gaṅgā, They came to a village called Lalitapura. In this village lived a householder *sannyāsī*, whose house happened to be on the path near the Gaṅgā. Lord Caitanya inquired from Nityānanda Prabhu whose house this was. Nityānanda replied that They were very fortunate because in this house lived a *sannyāsī*. Smiling and laughing, They both went to the *sannyāsī's* house and offered obeisances.

After the *sannyāsī* greeted Them, he happily offered many blessings, "May You both have wealth, fame, a good marriage, and great learning." When Lord Caitanya heard this, He said, "A true *sannyāsī* does not give blessings like that. A real *sannyāsī* will say 'May you attain Lord Kṛṣṇa's mercy', because devotion to Lord Kṛṣṇa is the true blessing. It is eternal and can never be lost. So what you have said is not correct."

The *sannyāsī* replied, "Listen, my dear young *brāhmaṇa* boy, why do you criticize my blessings? If a person born in this world does not enjoy pastimes with beautiful amorous women and does not have any wealth, then what is he doing with his life?" Hearing the *sannyāsī's* words, Lord Caitanya only laughed. Lifting His graceful hand, He placed it to His forehead. By these actions, Lord Caitanya taught everyone that one should not desire anything but devotional service.

Laughing, Nityānanda Prabhu said to the *sannyāsī*, "You should not argue with a child. We know how glorious you are, so please forgive us for everything." Hearing himself praised, the *sannyāsī* became happy and cheerfully invited his two guests for a meal. He then said, "After taking a bath, please eat something and rest before proceeding." The two Lords washed away Their fatigue of the journey from the road by bathing in the Gaṅgā. Then They accepted some milk, mangoes, and other fruits.

Since this *sannyāsī* was a follower of the left path, he was accustomed to drink wine and enjoy the company of women. Again and again he gestured to Nityānanda Prabhu and asked if he should bring some "bliss"? Within His heart Nityānanda understood that this *sannyāsī* drinks wine, and when he again insisted on bringing some "bliss", Nityānanda said, "We must leave now." When Lord Caitanya asked, "What is this 'bliss' the *sannyāsī* talks about?" Nityānanda replied, "He means wine." Calling out, "Viṣṇu! Viṣṇu!" Lord Caitanya rinsed His mouth and ran from the house.

The two Lords ran and jumped into the Gaṅgā and then joyfully swam away in her waves. They continued swimming in Gaṅgā's currents just like Lord Viṣṇu and Ananta Śeṣa in the ocean of milk, until They came to Advaita Ācārya's house in Śāntipura.

Śrī Mādhavendra-tithi-pūjā-varṇana

The following is summarized from the *Śrī Caitanya-bhāgavata* (*Antya-khaṇḍa*, Chapter 4): On the day of Śrī Mādhavendra Purī's disappearance, which falls on Dvādaśī in the month of Phālguna-śukla (Febuary/March), the day after Āmalakī-vrata Ekādaśī, Advaita Ācārya worshiped His spiritual master, Mādhavendra Purī, with elaborate preparations in Śāntipura. Help for the different arrangements came from all directions. Mother Śacī did all of the cooking. Nityānanda Prabhu greeted and worshiped all the visiting Vaiṣṇavas. Others ground sandlewood paste, strung flower garlands, brought water for cooking, drinking, and cleaning, cleaned the rooms, tied decoration flags, erected a canopy, donated jugs, and sang *saṅkīrtana*, while others joyfully danced. Everyone performed the duties that their hearts desired.

Seeing the elaborate preparations, Śrī Caitanya Mahāprabhu was very pleased. He began looking around and saw four rooms filled with rice as well as firewood stacked like a mountain. He saw five rooms being used as kitchens. He also saw four rooms filled with mung dahl, seven rooms filled with various kinds of cloth, ten rooms filled with banana leaves, and four rooms filled with flat rice. The Lord also saw thousands of bananas and coconuts in great piles, as well as thousands of jars filled with milk, cream, yogurt, sugarcane juice, mung sprouts, oil, salt, and ghee. Everything was numberless. Lord Caitanya felt happy at heart on seeing so many wonderful arrangements. Then the Lord said, "A human being cannot have such opulence. In My heart I think Advaita Ācārya must be Lord Śiva himself. Therefore, Advaita Ācārya is nondifferent from Lord Śiva."

As Vṛndāvana dāsa Ṭhākura continues to describe the preparations and festival activities in the *Śrī Caitanya-bhāgavata*, he glorifies Lord Śiva in the following words: "Even without knowing the truth of Lord Śiva, a person who chants Lord Śiva's holy name becomes at once cleansed of all sins.

This truth is stated in the *Vedas*, *Śrīmad-Bhāgavatam*, and all other scriptures. Anyone who is not happy to hear Lord Śiva's holy name is thrown into an ocean of calamities. With His own mouth, Lord Kṛṣṇa declares, 'How can anyone who does not worship Lord Śiva worship Me? How can anyone who does not honor Lord Śiva, who is so dear to Me, attain true devotion to Me? A person who does not worship My great devotee Lord Śiva is a sinner. How will he attain Me?' In the *Skanda Purāṇa* it is stated, 'First one should worship Lord Kṛṣṇa with great devotion. Then one should worship Lord Śiva, before worshiping the demigods.'"

Then Lord Caitanya entered the *saṅkīrtana* room, and all the devotees became overwhelmed with bliss. They all sang and danced in Lord Caitanya's presence, and the sound of the *saṅkīrtana* purified the innumerable worlds. Nityānanda Prabhu enthusiastically danced. Advaita Ācārya became overwhelmed with His dancing, which has no end. Haridāsa Ṭhākura and other devotees all danced for a long time. When everyone stopped dancing, Lord Caitanya danced alone, and then the devotees danced with the Lord. He danced in the middle, and the devotees danced in a circle around Him. In this way, they spent the whole day singing and dancing. Finally, Lord Caitanya and His devotees sat down, and Advaita Ācārya brought in the grand feast. While talking about Mādhavendra Purī, Caitanya Mahāprabhu and all the devotees ate to their full satisfaction. Then the Lord said, "Anyone who honors this feast on the holy day of worshiping Mādhavendra Purī (*Śrī Mādhavendra-tithi-pūjā-varṇana*) will certainly attain true devotion to Lord Kṛṣṇa."

Nityānanda cheats Mahāprabhu

In the *Śrī Caitanya-caritāmṛta* (*Madhya-līlā*, Chapter 3) Lord Caitanya is led to believe that the River Gaṅgā is the Yamunā: After Śrī Caitanya Mahāprabhu accepted the *sannyāsa* order at Katwa, He decided to go to Vṛndāvana and engage Himself wholly and solely in the service of Lord Mukunda (Kṛṣṇa) in a solitary place. While proceeding toward Vṛndāvana, Mahāprabhu was overwhelmed with ecstatic love for Kṛṣṇa and lost all remembrance of the external world. He mistakenly wandered about in a trance in the tract of land known as Rāḍha-deśa, an area where the River Gaṅgā does not flow.

Then Nityānanda Prabhu bewildered Lord Caitanya by bringing Him along the banks of the Gaṅgā. Later on, Nityānanda instructed Candraśekhara to go to Śāntipura and inform Advaita Ācārya that He was arriving with Mahāprabhu. As Caitanya Mahāprabhu continued to wander about in ecstasy, He inquired from Nityānanda Prabhu where He was going. Nityānanda replied that He was going with Him to Vṛndāvana. When Mahāprabhu asked Him how far Vṛndāvana was, Nityānanda replied, "Just see! Here is the River Yamunā."

On hearing this, Caitanya Mahāprabhu approached the Gaṅgā in ecstasy, accepting Gaṅgā as the River Yamunā. Mahāprabhu then said, "Oh, what good fortune! Now I have seen the River Yamunā." Thus thinking Gaṅgā to be the Yamunā, Caitanya Mahāprabhu began to offer prayers. After offering obeisances, Mahāprabhu took His bath in the Gaṅgā. At that time Advaita Ācārya arrived in a boat bringing the Lord new dry garments. When Advaita arrived, the Lord began to wonder about the entire situation. Still in His ecstasy, the Lord asked Advaita, "Why did You come here? How did You know that I was in Vṛndāvana?"

Advaita Ācārya disclosed the whole situation to Caitanya Mahāprabhu by replying, "Wherever You are, that is Vṛndāvana. Now it is My great fortune that You have come to the bank of the Gaṅgā." The Lord then replied, "Nityānanda has cheated Me. He brought Me to the bank of the Gaṅgā and told Me that it was the Yamunā."

In this way, the Lord was eventually brought by boat to the home of Advaita Ācārya in Śāntipura and accepted food there. As long as the Lord remained there, He saw His mother, Śacī-devī, and every night executed congregational chanting with all the assembled devotees.

After a few days, Caitanya Mahāprabhu decided to leave for Jagannātha Purī. He requested all the devotees to return to their respective homes. He also asked them to continue executing the congregational chanting of the holy names of the Lord at their homes, and He assured them that they would be able to meet again. Śrī Caitanya Mahāprabhu finally said, "Sometimes you will come to Jagannātha Purī, and sometimes I shall come to bathe in the Gaṅgā." The Lord then traveled onwards along the bank of the Gaṅgā through the villages of Āṭisārā and Chatrabhoga towards Jagannātha Purī.

* * *

Today in Shantipur, the location where Śrī Advaita Ācārya lived and worshiped the Supreme Personality of Godhead is known as Bāblāvana, but Gaṅgā has changed her course and is located approximately five kilometres away. The wide bed where Gaṅgā once flowed is presently used for cultivating rice paddy. Advaita Ācārya had once called for the Lord to descend, while offering Gaṅgā-jala and *tulasī* leaves to His Narasiṁha *śālagrāma-śilā*. Also at this location, there is a small shrine located on the old bank of Gaṅgā where Śrī Caitanya Mahāprabhu, Nityānanda Prabhu, and Advaita Ācārya would sit and discuss various spiritual topics.

The present main temple in Bāblāvana is located where Advaita Ācārya's house used to be. Next to the temple is a reconstruction of Advaita Ācārya's house. There are four *śālagrāma-śilās* (Nārāyaṇa, Gopāla, Madana-Mohana, and Nara-Gopāla) that are worshiped today in this temple, and two of the *śilās*, Nārāyaṇa and Madana-Gopāla, are said to have been worshiped by Advaita Ācārya Himself.

According to some Vaiṣṇavas, Advaita Ācārya worshiped and invoked the Supreme Lord to descend here in Shantipur as well as in Māyāpur at Advaita Bhavan. Some say that in the Śrī Śrī Madana-Mohana temple, in the town of Shantipur today, the original Narasiṁha *śālagrāma-śilā* that Advaita Ācārya once worshiped is located. Others say the original *śālagrāma-śilā* is located in Māyāpur at Advaita Bhavan. After the pastimes of Śrī Caitanya Mahāprabhu and His associates ended some five hundred years ago, the River Gaṅgā repeatedly flooded Māyāpur for hundreds of years. When the birthplace of Lord Caitanya was rediscovered by Śrīla Bhaktivinoda Ṭhākura in 1893, the Adhokṣaja Viṣṇu Deity of Jagannātha Misra was found, and a Śiva-liṅga was also uncovered at Śiva Doba, but there has been no mention of Advaita Ācārya's Narasiṁha *śālagrāma-śilā* being found anywhere.

Phuliyā-grāma

The following narration of Haridāsa Ṭhākura's pastimes on the banks of Gaṅgā is from the *Śrī Caitanya-bhāgavata* (*Ādi-khaṇḍa*, Chapter 16): "Haridāsa Ṭhākura appeared in this world in a village named Budhana. After some time he moved to the bank of the Gaṅgā at Phuliyā-grāma, near Śāntipura. Haridāsa would walk along Gaṅgā's banks and happily chant 'Kṛṣṇa! Kṛṣṇa!' in a loud voice. He was the best of those who had renounced material pleasures, and his glorious mouth was always filled with the chanting of Lord

Kṛṣṇa's name. He did not give up chanting the names of Govinda for even a moment, and as a result he was constantly manifesting various ecstatic symptoms. One moment he would dance, and another moment he would roar like a lion. Another moment he would scream then loudly laugh. Afterwards he would bellow, then he would fall unconscious. Sometimes he would utter some unnatural sounds, for which he would later give some profound meaning. He then wept, the hairs of his body stood erect, and he would laugh, faint, and perspire. When Haridāsa began to dance, all these ecstatic symptoms met together in his body. Then a flooding stream of bliss flowed in every limb as the *brāhmaṇas* of Phuliyā-grāma also became overwhelmed with bliss. After bathing in the Gaṅgā, he would wander everywhere, always loudly chanting the holy names of Lord Kṛṣṇa.

"Meanwhile, the Mohammedan governor went to the king of the country and described the symptoms of Haridāsa. He said, 'Although he is a Muslim, he acts like a Hindu. You should bring him here and pass judgement on him.' Hearing the sinful governor's words, the sinful King had Haridāsa brought at once. Seeing the charming splendor of Haridāsa, the King very respectfully offered him a seat. The King then asked, 'O my brother, what has happened to you? How fortunate you were. You were a Muslim, so why have you given your heart to act like a Hindu? How will a person who rejects his own religion and accepts another religion attain salvation and go to paradise? Not considering all this, you have acted very badly, therefore, I will pronounce a judgement that will free you of your sin.'

"Hearing these words of a person bewildered by *māyā*, Haridāsa laughed loudly and said, 'Aha! The *māyā* of Lord Viṣṇu!' He then said, 'O my King, please listen. There is only one God for everyone. The Hindus and Muslims are different in many ways. Still, the truth is that the *Koran* and *Purāṇas* describe the same one God. That one God is pure, eternal, undivided, unchanging, perfect, and complete. He lives in everyone's heart. Following their own scriptures, all the people of the world speak of God's names and qualities. God knows everyone's nature, and anyone who attacks another, attacks God Himself. Among the Hindus a *brāhmaṇa* may, by God's desire, become a Muslim. The punishment the Hindus would give to that *brāhmaṇa* is the punishment you should give to me. O honorable one, please consider all this. Then, if I am at fault, punish me.'

"Hearing the truthful words of Haridāsa, all the Muslims became pleased. Then the King said, 'O my brother, speak from your own scripture, then you will have nothing to fear. If you act otherwise, then the governor will punish you. Please tell me, why do you take this all so lightly?' Haridāsa Ṭhākura then replied, 'Whatever God desires will certainly happen. No one has the power to make it otherwise. Everyone reaps the fruit of his offenses. It is God who is doing all this, so please know that.' Upon hearing these words, the King said, 'What should I do with him?' The governor then said, 'He should be beaten in twenty-two marketplaces so that he will die. I give no other judgement. If after being beaten in twenty-two marketplaces he is still alive, then I will accept that he is a wise man who has spoken the truth. A Muslim who becomes a Hindu is freed from his sin only by death.' When the sinful governor spoke these words, the King gave the order. Then the wicked King's servants took Haridāsa to marketplace after marketplace and beat him with great anger in their hearts.

"While Haridāsa was being beaten, only 'Kṛṣṇa! Kṛṣṇa!' was in his thoughts. Because he was absorbed in the bliss of the holy name, he did not experience suffering from the beatings. Seeing the great beating inflicted on Haridāsa's body, all the pious people felt unlimited sorrow. Someone said, 'Because a saintly person is beaten like this, the whole country will be destroyed.' Another person approached the Muslims, grasped their feet, and said, 'I will give you anything. Please stop this beating.' In spite of all this, no mercy manifested in those sinners, who with great anger in their hearts, continued to beat Haridāsa again and again. By Lord Kṛṣṇa's mercy, not a single blow gave the slightest pain to Haridāsa. When the sinners beat him, Haridāsa felt only one pain within his heart and thought, 'O Lord Kṛṣṇa, please be merciful to these souls. Let not their hatred of me be counted as an offense.'

"The Muslims beating Haridāsa were astonished. One of them thought, 'Will his life-breath leave? Will he die? Anyone else would have died after being beaten in two or three marketplaces. We have beaten him in twenty-two marketplaces and still he does not die. From moment to moment, he looks at us and smiles. Is he a human being or a great saint? O Haridāsa, because of you we will all die. The governor will take our life-breath from us if you do not die!' Smiling, the saintly Haridāsa then entered into a trance of meditation and with all his powers became motionless and did not breathe. Seeing this, the astonished Muslims threw him at the King's doorstep. The governor rejected the idea of burying Haridāsa and said, 'If he is placed in the earth, he will go to paradise. Instead, throw him in the Gaṅgā where he will suffer eternally.'

"While Haridāsa Ṭhākura was floating in the Gaṅgā, he regained external consciousness and then happily climbed out on the riverbank. Then, while chanting the holy names of Lord Kṛṣṇa, he went to the town of Phuliyā. Seeing his wonderful power, all the Muslims tore apart the hatred they felt in their hearts. Aware that he was a great saint, all the Muslims bowed down before him and touched his feet. Because of this, they all attained salvation. Then the King came to see Haridāsa, and with his hands respectfully folded, he humbly said, 'Now I know the truth. You are a great saint who is steadfastly situated in knowledge of the one God. You have easily attained the perfection that *yogīs* and *jñānīs* can only describe. O saintly one, please forgive my crime. For you everyone is equal, and for you there are neither enemies nor friends. No one in the three worlds is like you. You may go. Be happy. Stay where you wish, either by Gaṅgā's bank or in a solitary cave.'

"Haridāsa then went to a cave by the bank of Gaṅgā. In that solitary place, he remembered Lord Kṛṣṇa day and night. He chanted the holy name three hundred thousand times each day. The cave became like Vaikuṇṭha, even though a great snake was also living in that same cave. Ordinary living beings had no power to tolerate the burning fumes of its poison. Many visitors would come daily to visit Haridāsa, but no one could stay. Afterwards, everyone requested Haridāsa to leave the cave, but he simply replied, 'I have lived here for many days, I am not aware of the poisonous fumes of any snake. If there is a snake here and if it does not leave by tomorrow, then I will leave and go to another place. Do not worry, now please sing songs about Lord Kṛṣṇa.'

"Everyone then began chanting the auspicious glories of Lord Kṛṣṇa. At that moment, a great wonder occurred. Rising from its hole, the snake appeared very wonderful and beautiful being white, black, and yellow. On its head, a great jewel glowed with flames of light. Then the snake entered the twilight of evening and went to another place. Haridāsa Ṭhākura was so powerful that simply by speaking a few words, he made the snake leave that place."

The following narration is also from the *Śrī Caitanya-bhāgavata* (*Antya-khaṇḍa*, Chapter 1): "After Śrī Caitanya Mahāprabhu accepted the *sannyāsa āśrama*, He and Lord Nityānanda began traveling to Śāntipura to visit Advaita Ācārya. Before arriving there, They proceeded to Phuliyā-grāma to visit Haridāsa Ṭhākura, but Lord Caitanya instructed Nityānanda to return to Navadivpa. While returning, He became intoxicated by tasting the nectar of ecstatic love, and Lord Nityānanda then roared again and again like a maddened lion. Accepting the nature of Lord Ananta Śeṣa, Nityānanda would swim like a snake in the Gaṅgā's currents. Lord Nityānanda's glories are inconceivable and unattainable. There is no second person in the three worlds as merciful as Him. After swimming for some time in the Gaṅgā, Lord Nityānanda finally emerged at Lord Caitanya's bathing *ghāṭa* in Navadvīpa.

"Lord Nityānanda went to see mother Śacī and the other residents of Nadia to inform them of Nimāi's accepting *sannyāsa* and His wonderful new name: 'Śrī Kṛṣṇa Caitanya.' Hearing that the Lord went to Phuliyā-grāma, everyone happily prepared to see Him. Countless millions of people came to the ferry *ghāṭa*, so the ferryman did not know how to carry them all. Some people made improvised rafts, others tied great water jugs to their chests, while some floated across the Gaṅgā on banana tree trunks. Even pregnant women as well as the blind and lame crossed the river. Thousands upon thousands of people piled into one boat before it sank, but they did not become unhappy as they swam to the other side. Those who did not know how to swim somehow swam anyway. Spiritual bliss took birth in everyone's heart, and 'Hari! Hari!' was the only sound anyone heard in the four directions as they arrived in Phuliyā-grāma.

"Hearing the unprecedented vibration of 'Hari!', Lord Caitanya, who shined like millions of moons rising together, came outside. The Lord chanted, 'Hare Kṛṣṇa! Hare! Hare!' In the four directions everyone offered *daṇḍavat* (falling flat like a rod) obeisances. Countless millions of people had come to Phuliyā, so they filled the village and all the nearby grassy fields. From many different towns and villages, great crowds had come to see the Lord. Seeing Lord Caitanya's charming face, everyone felt fully satisfied. Lord Caitanya cast His merciful glance upon everyone and then proceeded to Advaita Ācārya's home in Śāntipura."

* * *

As in Santipura, the Ganga today is approximately 5 kilometres away from Phuliyā-grāma. Next to one tree in Phuliyā there is now a small shrine with a marble plaque on which the pastime between Haridāsa Ṭhākura and the poisonous snake is quoted from the *Śrī Caitanya-bhāgavata* (*Ādi-khaṇḍa*). Beneath the roots of this tree is the *gupha* (cavern) in which Haridāsa performed his daily *bhajana* of chanting three hundred thousand names of Lord Kṛṣṇa.

26) Ambikā-kālanā (Kālnā)

In the *Śrī Caitanya-caritāmṛta* (*Ādi* 11.26) Kālnā is described in Śrila Prabhupāda's purport as follows: "The village Ambikā-kālanā, which is situated just across the River Ganges from Śāntipura (on the western bank)...In Ambikā-kālanā there is a temple constructed by the Zamindar of Burdwan. Near the temple of Gaurīdāsa Paṇḍita, there is a big tamarind tree, and it is said Lord Caitanya and Gaurīdāsa Paṇḍita met underneath this tree. The place where the temple is situated is known as Ambikā, and because it is in the area of Kālnā, the village is known as Ambikā-kālanā. It is said that a copy of *Bhagavad-gītā* written by Caitanya Mahāprabhu still exists in this temple." [There is also a boat oar that was used by Lord Caitanya.]

Gaurīdāsa Paṇḍita was the emblem of the most elevated devotional service in love of Godhead and had the greatest potency to receive and deliver such love. It is stated in the *Gaura-gaṇoddeśa-dīpikā* (128) that formerly he was Subala, one of the cowherd boyfriends of Kṛṣṇa and Balarāma in Vṛndāvana.

The dancing Deities

The following story of Gaurīdāsa Paṇḍita's extraordinary Deities is from the Seventh Chapter of the *Bhakti-ratnākara*.

Sūryadāsa Sarakhela was a scholar and a broad-minded person, as well as the elder brother of Gaurīdāsa Paṇḍita. They both lived at Śāligrāma, but after taking his brother's permission, Gaurīdāsa settled at Ambikā, by the side of the Gaṅgā. Gaurīdāsa always lived in seclusion, as the Lord understood his mind very well. One day, Śrī Caitanya Mahāprabhu crossed the Gaṅgā from Śāntipura and went to Ambikā. There, He told Gaurīdāsa, "I have been to Śāntipura and from there I went by boat to the village named Harinadī. I crossed the Gaṅgā by rowing the boat with an oar. Take this oar that I am giving you, because with this oar mankind can cross over the ocean of this material world." After saying this, the Lord embraced Gaurīdāsa and then took him to Nadia. After a few days, Gaurīdāsa returned to Ambikā where he regularly read a manuscript of the *Bhagavad-gītā* personally handwritten by Lord Caitanya. Simply by seeing the handwritten manuscript of the Lord gave extreme pleasure to Gaurīdāsa Paṇḍita.

Some time later, Lord Caitanya instructed Gaurīdāsa to bring a piece of neem wood from Navadvīpa and carve Deities of Caitanya and Nityānanda (Gaura-Nitāi). Gaurīdāsa was ecstatic with joy and carefully carved the Deities under the direct instruction of the Lord. Gaurīdāsa was overwhelmed with happiness and could not restrain his tears. Considering himself the most fortunate, he made all of the arrangements for the installation ceremony of the Deities. Following the prescribed rituals, he bathed and anointed the Deities at an auspicious moment before seating Them on Their throne. The beauty of these two Deities pleased the whole world, as Gaura-Nitāi were bound by the love of Gaurīdāsa Paṇḍita. One day, the Deities said to Gaurīdāsa, "O dear friend Subala, can you remember your past life? Can you remember the great fun we had when we took the cows to the banks of the River Yamunā?" Saying this, the Deities turned Themselves into Kṛṣṇa and Balarāma with black and fair complexions. When the two Lords displayed Their pastimes in this way, Gaurīdāsa experienced great ecstatic love and stared steadily at the Deities. Another time, Gaurīdāsa wanted to dress Their Lordships with jewellery. Reading the mind of Gaurīdāsa, the Deities decorated Themselves with different ornaments fitted with the rarest jewels. When Gaurīdāsa entered the temple, he was overwhelmed with emotion upon seeing the Deities already decorated. After he regained his normal composure, he saw the Deities dressed as usual. Then the Lord said, "Ornaments made of flowers please Me the most." Then Gaurīdāsa decorated Gaura-Nitāi with beautiful flower ornaments.

One time, Gaurīdāsa went to visit Śrīla Gadādhara Paṇḍita. Gadādhara had with him one boy named Hṛdayānanda, who was raised by Gadādhara from his childhood. Gaurīdāsa requested that the boy Hṛdaya become his disciple. Gadādhara happily gave the boy to Gaurīdāsa, who in due course of time, gave Hṛdaya *dīkṣā-mantra* and then dedicated his new young disciple at the lotus feet of Gaura-Nitāi. Hṛdaya fully surrendered himself to the service of the Lord, and this pleased Gaurīdāsa very much.

One day, Gaurīdāsa told Hṛdaya that the Lord's birthday was appoaching. "I shall visit the houses of my followers to collect provisions for the festival and will return soon," said Gaurīdāsa. "Be very careful in your service to the Lord." Then Gaurīdāsa left his house. After some time, Hṛdaya began to think, "Why is my master so late in returning? Only two days remain before the ceremony and enough provisions have already been collected here." Considering everything and remembering the lotus feet of his spiritual master, Hṛdayānanda decided to send invitations everywhere for the great occassion.

Gaurīdāsa Paṇḍita returned just one day before the festival. When he heard that Hṛdaya had sent invitations everywhere without his permission, Gaurīdāsa felt happy within his heart. Outwardly, however, he expressed his displeasure and angrily said, "While I am still living, you have acted independently. Since you have independently sent out invitations, I will not join you." Hṛdaya then bowed at his master's feet and went to the bank of the Gaṅgā, where he lived in a tree. Gaurīdāsa then began the festival, and many respectable devotees assembled at his house. Meanwhile, one wealthy man sent a large quantity of provisions in a boat. The rich man met Hṛdaya on the bank of the Gaṅgā and handed over the provisions to him. Hṛdaya sent a messsage to Gaurīdāsa, who in mock anger, told the messenger to inform Hṛdaya that he could use the provisions for his own celebrations. On the order of his *guru*, Hṛdayānanda began to happily celebrate the occasion, using all the provisions. A large number of Vaiṣṇavas assembled there, and in their association, Hṛdaya performed wonderful *saṅkirtana*. As the sound of the *mṛdaṅga* and *karatālas* reached the sky, it seemed that the ocean of happiness would overflow the banks of the Gaṅgā. All the Vaiṣṇavas danced in a circle, and tears flowed constantly down their faces. Suddenly, Hṛdayānanda observed that both Gaura and Nitāi were dancing within the circle. The style of Their dancing was indescribable, and Their physical beauty brightened the whole world. The faces of Gaura and Nitāi defeated the pride of the moon, and Hṛdaya cried in joy while watching Them.

Hearing the joyous sound of the *saṅkīrtana*, Gaurīdāsa became very pleased, although he remained in his house. He then gently told his disciple Baḍu Gaṅgādāsa, "It is now time for worship. Please go to the temple." But when Gaṅgādāsa entered the temple, he found the Deities were not on the throne! When Gaurīdāsa heard this, he was overwhelmed in ecstasy and realized that Gaura-Nitāi had been bound in love by Hṛdayānanda. With a smile, Gaurīdāsa took a stick in his hand. Although he was happy in his heart, he displayed outward anger as he headed for that *saṅkīrtana* gathering by the side of the Gaṅgā. There he saw the Deities of Gaura-Nitāi dancing in the midst of the devotees. When They observed the mock anger of Gaurīdāsa, Gaura-Nitāi secretly returned to the temple. Then Gaurīdāsa saw Śrī Caitanya Mahāprabhu personally enter into the heart of Hṛdaya. Seeing Lord Caitanya present in the heart

of Hṛdayānanda, Gaurīdāsa could not control his tears. He forgot his mock anger and unconsciously dropped the stick from his hand. Stretching out his arms in ecstatic love, he went forward to embrace Hṛdaya. "How fortunate you are," said Gaurīdāsa. "From this day, your name will be Hṛdaya Caitanya, the person in whose heart Śrī Caitanya Mahāprabhu always resides." He drenched Hṛdaya with his tears, and the disciple fell at the feet of his master. Together they returned to the temple.

Gaurīdāsa then requested Hṛdaya Caitanya to take responsibility for the service of the Deities. The Vaiṣṇavas were all happy about this, and the great festival they held defied description.

Because of this amazing pastime, the *darśana* of these two Deities is only available for short periods of time. Sometimes the *darśana* is so quick that devotees miss it because they offer their obeisances too long. The *pūjāris* fear that if they keep the curtain open too long, Gaura-Nitāi might jump off the altar once again!

Lord Nityānanda's marriage

The following narration from the Twentieth Chapter of *Śrī Advaita Prakāśa* gives one version of Lord Nityānanda's marriage with Vasudhā and Jāhnavā.

One time Lord Nityānanda went to Ambikā-kālanā and assumed an enchantingly handsome form that astounded even the demigods. At that time, Sūryadāsa Sarakhela came there and was amazed on seeing the form of the Lord. He then invited the Lord to his residence to take rest. Nityānanda smiled and accompanied him to his house, where the *brāhmaṇa* Sūryadāsa fed Nityānanda with loving care. The villagers praised His attractive form. They then told the wife of Sūryadāsa, "He is a suitable husband for your two daughters, Vasudhā and Jāhnavā, who are both equal to Lakṣmī-devī and have no comparision to their beauty and good qualities."

Then Sūryadāsa came and the ladies encouraged him that Nityānanda would be an excellent bridegroom. He replied, "If everyone agrees, then I accept." They discussed at length this situation, and when Nityānanda understood their mind, He departed. He went to the bank of Gaṅgā, where Sūryadāsa's brother, Gaurīdāsa, was absorbed in ecstatic love. Gaurīdāsa offered obeisances to Nityānanda and said, "You have unlimited wonderful pastimes." Lord Nityānanda just laughed loudly.

Afterwards, Lord Nityānanda was sitting on the shore of Gaṅgā discussing spiritual topics with His close associate, Uddhāraṇa Datta, when Sūryadāsa came there with the dead body of Vasudhā, who had just unexpectedly left her body. As everyone began arranging for her last rites, Nityānanda came and said to Sūryadāsa, "I will bring your daughter back to life." Lord Nityānanda joyfully chanted the life giving holy name of the Lord into her ear. Drinking the nectar of the holy name, Vasudhā got up to the amazement of everyone present. Sūryadāsa took his daughter and Lord Nityānanda back to his residence. He realized who the Lord was through His symptoms and became overwhelmed with ecstatic love. Sūryadāsa considered himself most forunate as he joyfully gave his daughters to Nityānanda in a grand ceremony. Then Nityānanda went onto the village of Khaḍadaha.

* * *

Nearby the temple of Gaura-Nitāi, which is where Gaurīdāsa Paṇḍita once lived, is the residence of Sūryadāsa Sarakhela. It is managed by Śrīman Vinay Kṛṣṇa Gosvāmi and family. Within the temple reside the deities of Vasudhā and Jāhnavā with their father, Sūryadāsa; the tall beautiful forms of Śrī Śrī Nitāi-Gaurāṅga, along with Sūryadāsa's worshipable Deities of Śrī Śrī Rādhā-Śyāmasundara; and also ancient Deities of Śrī Śrī Rādhā-Madana Mohana. There is a four hundred year old Bengali manuscript of the *Śrī Caitanya-bhāgavata* written on palm leaves, as well as a walking stick used by Nityānanda Prabhu. This temple was rennovated in 1980 by ISKCON's Bhaktivedanta Swami Charity Trust.

Just in front of the residential complex is an enclosed circled arena that marks one of the several locations where Lord Nityānanda Prabhu's marriage is said to have taken place. Some persons say that the Lord's marriage took place in Śāligrāma (near Baḍagāchi) or Khaḍadaha-grāma (Khardah), but the most consistent opinion is that the marriage took place at Śāligrāma.

JĪRĀṬ

Approximately fifteen kilometres south of Kālnā (or fourteen kilometres north of Triveṇī-ghāṭa), near the bank of the Gaṅgā, is a small town named Jīrāṭ. There is a small temple here wherein Śrī Śrī Rādhā-Gopīnātha reside. The Deity of Śrī Gopīnātha was given by the wife of Nityānanda Prabhu, Jāhnavā-devī, to their daughter, Gaṅgā-devī. The following story explains how the beautiful Deity of Śrī Gopīnātha appeared to Śrīmatī Jāhanvā-devī: After presiding over the festival of Kheturī, Śrīmatī Jāhnavā-devī decided to go to Vṛndāvana. One day while she was bathing in the River Yamunā, a black hand grabbed the end of her cloth as she was getting out of the water. She turned to look but there was no one there. Afterwards when Jāhnavā-devī was bathing in the River Gaṅgā at Khaḍadaha-grāma, again a black hand grasped her cloth, but as she turned around this time, a beautiful Deity of Lord Gopīnātha appeared and said, "I want to come and stay with you."

On the main altar reside Rādhā-Gopīnātha with Jāhnavā-devī; on the altar to Their right are two sets of Śrī Śrī Nitāi-Gaurāṅga Deities; and on the altar to Their left, reside Lord Balarāma and Lord Jagannātha. All glories to Śrī Śrī Rādhā-Gopīnātha, Jāhnavā-devī, and Gaṅgā-devī.

In 1981, the Bhaktivedanta Swami Charity Trust rennovated this sacred place, but since then, the temple complex has not been properly maintained. This Śrīpat (holy place) has become practically lost and forgotten due to the influence of this modern age of Kali.

27) TRIVEṆĪ-GHĀṬA (SAPTAGRĀMA)

Lord Nityānanda's preaching pastimes in Saptagrāma are described in the Third Chapter of the *Śrī Pañca Tattva* as follows: "Lord Nityānanda's next stop was Saptagrāma, one of the wealthiest areas in Bengal. Many of the inhabitants were of the *suvarṇa-vanika* caste, merchants who deal in gold and are considered outcastes. Although they were untouchable by Hindu standards, Lord Nityānanda viewed all souls equally and lovingly preached to everyone He met. The people of Saptagrāma in turn came to love Nityānanda Prabhu, appreciating His genuine spiritual vision, for He allowed them to play a role in the *saṅkīrtana* movement. By mercifully sharing Kṛṣṇa consciousness with all people indiscriminately, Lord Nityānanda was able to spread the movement of Caitanya Mahāprabhu."

Lord Nityānanda, the seven sages, Gaṅgā, Yamunā, and Sarasvatī

The pastimes of Lord Nityānanda at Saptagrāma are further described in the *Śrī*

Caitanya-bhāgavata (*Antya-khaṇḍa*, Chapter 5): "After Lord Nityānanda stayed for a few days in Khaḍadaha-grāma, He took His associates across the Gaṅgā to an area known as Saptagrāma. Within Saptagrāma is the place of the seven sages. Throughout the universe this place is known as Triveṇī-ghāṭa (bathing place where the three rivers meet). In ancient times, the seven sages performed great austerities at this *ghāṭa* on the Gaṅgā and attained the lotus feet of Lord Kṛṣṇa. The three goddesses—Gaṅgā, Yamunā, and Sarasvatī—all meet at this sacred place. That is why this place is famous in the three worlds as Triveṇī-ghāṭa. Just by seeing this holy place, all one's sins are destroyed.

"Accompanied by His associates, Lord Nityānanda joyfully bathed at this *ghāṭa*. Then the Lord stayed at the home of Śrī Uddhāraṇa Datta Ṭhākura, who worshiped Nityānanda Prabhu with his body, mind, and words. Going from house to house among the merchants of Saptagrāma, the Lord delivered them by giving them ecstatic love and devotion. Lord Nityānanda enjoyed pastimes of *kīrtana* with all the merchants who took shelter of His lotus feet. Seeing how the merchants were worshiping the Lord, everyone felt wonder in their hearts.

"Lord Nityānanda's mercy is like an ocean that has no shore. He delivered all those foolish, lonely merchants. Accompanied by His associates, Nityānanda enjoyed *saṅkīrtana* pastimes that no one could describe in Saptagrāma. Every direction was filled with the *saṅkīrtana* of Lord Hari's holy names. From house to house in every village and crossroad, Lord Nityānanda relished pastimes of *kīrtana*. The wild ecstasy that was exhibited had never been manifested in this universe.

"What to speak of others, even the Muslims who dislike Lord Kṛṣṇa were now taking shelter of His lotus feet. Streams of ecstatic loving tears flowed from the Muslim's eyes, which even made the *brāhmaṇas* rebuke themselves for their lack of devotion!

"Glory, glory to the saintly Lord Nityānanda, who is the moon of *avadhūtas* (ascetics transcendental to worldly convention). By His mercy, everyone became filled with bliss, as they all enjoyed these joyful pastimes at Saptagrāma."

Another description of where the Gaṅgā, Yamunā, and Sarasvati meet is found in the *Śrī Caitanya-carita* (Fourth Prakrama, Twenty-second Sarga) as follows: "Persons conversant in the *Vedas* have named that place where the currents mingle Mukta-venī. There the seven sages contemplate the transcendental abode of all ecstasy, which is the lotus feet of Nārāyaṇa. The sages say that the currents of the Gaṅgā, Yamunā, and Sarasvatī eternally flow there, and the sight of that spot causes great jubilation to the pilgrims. Simply by bathing there or even remembering that place, men attain liberation, achieve devotion to Śrī Hari, and nullify all distress."

Uddhāraṇa Datta and five golden coins

The following story is from the *Sthala Purāṇa*, or a narration that has been handed down generation after generation: "One day a seller of conch bracelets was selling his wares in the village of Saptagrāma. A young girl came up to him and asked to try on his best pair of conch bracelets. He put on her wrists a very beautiful pair of bracelets, studded with precious stones, and because they fitted perfectly, she was very satisfied. The salesman then requested the price of his bracelets. The girl replied that he should go to her father, Uddhāraṇa Datta Ṭhākura, and take the cost of the bracelets from him. The salesman asked, 'How will he accept the price of these bracelets without even seeing them?' She then told the traveling salesman to tell her father, 'There are five gold coins within a niche in the west wall of the room on the east side of the compound. Your daughter told that these could be given in payment for the bracelets. If father is unwilling to pay that much, then return here to me and I will pay you whatever I can. In the meantime, I am going to take bath in the river.'

"The salesman went to Uddhāraṇa Datta's house, explained everything, and requested the payment. Uddhāraṇa replied that he had no daughter. The conch salesman exclaimed, 'How can you say that? Can such a sweet innocent girl make up such a story?' The salesman humbly requested that he not be angry with his daughter. 'When you see how beautiful she looks with the bracelets on her hands, you will forget your anger. Now please pay me.' Uddhāraṇa requested, 'What is the price?' The salesman replied, 'Five gold coins. Your daughter fixed the price. She says that there are five such coins in the niche in the western wall of the eastern room.' Uddhāraṇa hurried there and to his astonishment found five golden coins lying in the specified location. He called the salesman and asked, 'Where is this daughter of mine? Please show her to me.'

"They came to the *ghāṭa* on the banks of the River Sarasvatī to look for her, but she was nowhere to be seen. The salesman began to cry, 'Ma! Ma go! Please come here. Save my reputation. Otherwise how will Datta Ṭhākura believe that I placed those bracelets on your two wrists?' Then two hands appeared out of the waters of the Sarasvatī, beautifully decorated with those two conchshell bracelets.

"Uddhāraṇa and the salesman began to shed tears of ecstasy. Uddhāraṇa addressed the salesman, 'How fortunate you are! As a result of your devotion, I have witnessed such a rare sight today! And she called herself my daughter. The mother of the three worlds called herself my daughter! Please take your gold coins.' However, the salesman refused to accept the coins. 'Why couldn't I recognize her? Am I such a wretched fool?'"

* * *

Today, Saptagrāma encompasses seven villages, named Kṛṣṇapura, Vāsudevapura, Nityānandapura, Śivapura, Śaṅkhanagara, Tribeni (Triveṇi-ghāṭa), and Ādi Saptagrāma. This list varies, as Keśavarti and Bāṅsabeḍiyā are also sometimes included within the Saptagrāma area. Some villages are on the bank of the Gaṅgā, while others are on the bank of the River Sarasvatī (see *Śrī Caitanya-caritāmṛta*, *Ādi-līlā*, 11.41 purport). Śrī Uddhāraṇa Datta Ṭhākura's residence and worshipable Deity of Śrī Ṣaḍ-bhuja, the six-armed form of Śrī Caitanya Mahāprabhu, are located in Ādi Saptagrāma, on the bank of the Sarasvatī. The nearby village of Kṛṣṇapura was the residence of Śrī Raghunātha dāsa Gosvāmī, and Śaṅkhanagara was the residence of Śrī Kalidāsa. The two brothers, Hiraṇya and Govardhana, as well as the father of Viṣṇupriyā-devi, Śrī Sanātana Miśra, also resided in the Saptagrāma area.

28) KUMĀRAHAṬṬA (HĀLISAHARA)

Caitanya Mahāprabhu's *guru*, Śrī Īśvara Purī

In the *Śrī Caitanya-bhāgavata* (*Ādi-khaṇḍa* 17.99,102) Lord Caitanya says: "I offer My respectful obeisances to Kumārahaṭṭa, the village where Śrī Īśvara Purī descended to this world. The earth from the birthplace of Īśvara Purī is My wealth and life-breath. It keeps Me alive."

Śrīla Prabhupāda's purport in the *Śrī Caitanya-caritāmṛta* (*Ādi* 9.11) describes the glories of Lord Caitanya's *guru* as follows: "Śrī Īśvara Purī was a resident of Kumārahaṭṭa...He

appeared in a *brāhmaṇa* family and was the most beloved disciple of Śrīla Madhavendra Purī. In the *Śrī Caitanya-caritāmṛta* (*Antya* 8.28-31) it is stated: 'Īśvara Purī, the spiritual master of Śrī Caitanya Mahāprabhu, performed service to Mādhavendra Purī, cleaning up his stool and urine with his own hands. Īśvara Purī was always chanting the holy name and pastimes of Lord Kṛṣṇa for Mādhavendra Purī to hear. In this way he helped Mādhavendra Purī remember the holy name and pastimes of Lord Kṛṣṇa at the time of death. Pleased with Īśvara Purī, Mādhavendra Purī embraced him and gave him the benediction that he would be a great devotee and lover of Kṛṣṇa. Thus Īśvara Purī became like an ocean of ecstatic love for Kṛṣṇa.'

"...Īśvara Purī pleased his spiritual master by service, and by the blessings of his spiritual master he became such a great personality that Lord Caitanya Mahāprabhu accepted him as His spiritual master.

"To teach others by example how to be a faithful disciple of one's spiritual master, Śrī Caitanya Mahāprabhu, the Supreme Personality of Godhead, visited the birthplace of Īśvara Purī at Kumārahaṭṭa and collected some earth from his birthsite. This He kept very carefully, and He used to eat a small portion of it daily..."

After Śrī Caitanya Mahāprabhu accepted *sannyāsa*, Śrīvāsa Paṇḍita shifted his residence (Śrīvāsāṅgana) from the bank of the Gaṅgā in Māyāpur to bank of the Gaṅgā in Kumārahaṭṭa. He knew that Lord Caitanya would not return again to Navadvīpa (Māyāpur) but would one day visit Kumārahaṭṭa. Since Śrīvāsa Paṇḍita wanted to see his Lord once again, he moved near the house of Īśvara Purī, who had recently left this world after his spiritual master, Madhavendra Purī, had also departed.

Meanwhile, as Śrīvāsa Paṇḍita was waiting for Caitanya Mahāprabhu to arrive, the Lord and His associates had just left Jagannātha Purī and were on their way to Śāntipura. They arrived at Pānihāṭi by boat and stayed only one day. The next day, when they continued their journey, Caitanya Mahāprabhu remembered the birthplace and residence of His spiritual master at Kumārahaṭṭa and decided to visit. When Lord Caitanya got down from the boat, the bank of Gaṅgā was crowded with devotees and villagers, all desiring the Lord's *darśana*. The footpath leading from the Gaṅgā to Īśvara Purī's birthsite became full of potholes as everyone collected dust from Lord Caitanya's footprints. When Caitanya Mahāprabhu saw Īśvara Purī's residence from a distance, He immediately fell on the ground offering innumerable obeisances. Upon arriving there, the Lord continually cried due to the pain of separation from His spiritual master. Tears flowed from the Lord's eyes like the River Gaṅgā. After becoming calm, Lord Caitanya then collected some soil from Īśvara Purī's birthplace.

Śrī Caitanya Mahāprabhu's example of a disciple's faithfulness was followed by many other devotees who visited Kumārahaṭṭa. They also collected a little soil, as Lord Caitanya did, thus a large cavity appeared in the earth. That cavity subsequently became a shallow pond of rainwater and is known today as Śrī Caitanya Doba (pond) Mahā-tīrtha.

29) KHAḌADAHA-GRĀMA (KHARDAH)

The influence of Nityānanda's dancing

During Lord Nityānanda's preaching pastimes, He visited the temple and house of Purandara Paṇḍita in the village known as Khaḍadaha-grāma, just south of Kumārahaṭṭa on the bank of the Gaṅgā. No one can describe how Lord Nityānanda danced when He came to Khaḍadaha. Due to the influence of Lord Nityānanda, one associate of the Lord named Purandara Paṇḍita became like a wild man, climbing a tree and then roaring like a lion! Upon seeing the dancing of Nityānanda Prabhu, he jumped down on the ground and proclaimed himself to be Aṅgada, one of the devotees in the camp of Hanumān during the pastimes of Lord Rāmacandra.

These pastimes of Lord Nityānanda are further described in the *Śrī Caitanya-bhāgavata* (*Antya-khaṇḍa*, Chapter 5) as follows: "Another devotee named Caitanya Dāsa, who was no longer in external consciousness, would run like a tiger into the jungle. There, he would jump on some tiger's back, as if this tiger had no power to attack him. Cheerfully and fearlessly he would even sit down with a python in his lap, while playing with the tigers! All this happened by the mercy of the great Nityānanda Avadhūta.

"Once Caitanya Dāsa stayed underwater in the Gaṅgā for two or three days without any pain or discomfort to his body. Sometimes he would be stunned and motionless, and other times he would act like a ferocious tiger. No one has the power to describe the symptoms of Caitanya Dāsa's devotional ecstasy. They are all endless. Anyone who even touches the breeze that blows by Caitanya Dāsa will attain Lord Kṛṣṇa without a doubt.

"While Lord Nityānanda was in Khaḍadaha, His son, Vīrabhadra, converted one thousand two hundred male and female Buddhists (called *nera-neris*) before He and His associates crossed to the western side of the Gaṅgā to Saptagrāma."

The birth of Gaṅgā-devī and Vīrabhadra

In the *Śrī Gaura-gaṇoddeśa-dīpikā*, Verse 69, Śrī Gaṅgā-devī's appearance as Lord Nityānanda's daughter is described as follows:

viṣṇu-pādodbhavā-gaṅgā
yāsīt sā nija-nāmataḥ
nityānandātmajā jātā
mādhavaḥ śāntanur nṛpaḥ

"The River Gaṅgā, who was born from the lotus feet of Lord Viṣṇu, appeared in Lord Caitanya's pastimes as Śrīmatī Gaṅgā-devī, the daughter of Lord Nityānanda. Her husband, Śrī Mādhava, had formerly been Mahārāja Śantanu."

After Lord Nityānanda enjoyed joyful pastimes in Saptagrāma (bathing at Triveṇī-ghāṭa), He went to Ambikā-kālanā and then to Śāntipura before returning to Navadvīpa. He literally went door-to-door once again and begged people to surrender to Śrī Caitanya Mahāprabhu's *saṅkīrtana* mission. He carried this request to Baḍagāchi, Dogāciyā, Phuliyā, and all villages on both sides of the Gaṅgā.

It was during this time that Lord Nityānanda decided to abandon His *avadhūta* status and take to the *gṛhastha-āśrama* (householder in the second spiritual order in Vedic society). Sūryadāsa Sarakhela offered Him his daughters, Vasudhā and Jāhnavā, when he was visiting his younger brother, Gaurīdāsa Paṇḍita, in Ambikā-kālanā. Later, the King of Baḍagāchi (near Śāligrāma), Navanī Hoḍa Kṛṣṇadāsa, arranged for the marriage of Lord Nityānanda.

After some time, Vasudhā gave birth to two children at Khaḍadaha—a girl named Gaṅgā-devī, who was personified Gaṅgā herself, and a boy named Vīrabhadra (also known as Vīracandra), who was an incarnation of Kṣīrodakaśāyī Viṣṇu. According to one version, soon after their birth, Vasudhā passed away and Jāhnavā raised them as her own children. Later, Jāhnavā adopted a boy named Rāmacandra (Rāmāi), who was the son of Caitanya Dāsa.

Later on, there was once a baby boy who's mother died just after he had taken birth. When he was about twelve days old, Nityānanda Prabhu took him to his home in Khaḍadaha. Because he was a great devotee of Lord Kṛṣṇa from the very beginning of his life, Nityānanda gave him the name Śiśu Kṛṣṇadāsa. When he was five years old, he went to Vṛndāvana with Jāhnavā-mātā. Upon seeing the ecstatic symptoms of Śiśu Kṛṣṇadāsa, Jīva Gosvāmī of Vṛndāvana gave him the name Kānāi Ṭhākura.

One of Kānāi Ṭhākura's family members, Śrī Mādhava, married the daughter of Nityānanda Prabhu, Śrī Gaṅgā-devī. The Lord gave him the village named Pānjinagara as dowry.

The following are some of Jāhnavā-devī's pastimes described in the *Bhakti-ratnākara*, Chapter 13: "Lord Nityānanda's wife, Jāhnavā-devī, once visited the village of Jamatpura, where one *brāhmaṇa* named Yadunandana Ācārya resided. Yadunandana's devotion increased immensely by Jāhnavā's association. His wife, Lakṣmī, was a very humble and submissive lady. She gave birth to two very beautiful daughters named Śrīmatī and Nārāyaṇī. By the arrangement of Jāhnavā-devī, these two girls became the fortunate wives of her son Vīrabhadra Prabhu. On the day of the wedding, which took place in Khaḍadaha, Yadunandana took initiation from Vīrabhadra, and Jāhnavā-devī happily accepted Śrīmatī and Nārāyaṇī as her disciples. The whole village of Khaḍadaha was mad with joy about this marriage, and everyone flooded the brides with gifts. Gaṅgā-devī also became very pleased with her brother's marriage. On this occassion, the people remembered how they enjoyed the marriage of Gaṅgā-devī with her husband, Śrī Mādhava, who was an extremely devoted person.

"After the marriage of Vīrabhadra Prabhu, Jāhnavā-devī and her followers went immediately to Vṛndāvana."

In the *Bhakti-ratnākara* it is stated: "I offer my humble obeisances unto Śrī Jāhnavā Īsvarī, the beloved consort of Śrī Nityānanda Prabhu. Jāhnavā-devī bestows the priceless jewel of ecstatic devotional service, and she wards off the threefold material miseries."

In the branch of the Gauḍīya-sampradāya that begins with Śrī Nityānanda Prabhu, He is followed by His consort, Śrīmatī Jāhnavā-devī. Jāhnavā-devī had four direct disciples—her two children, Śrī Vīrabhadra (Vīracandra) Gosāñi and Śrīmatī Gaṅgā-devī; her adopted son, Śrī Rāmacandra (Rāmāi) Gosvāmī; and the mother of Vṛndāvana dāsa Ṭhākura, Śrīmatī Nārāyaṇī.

Śrī Śrī Rādhā-Śyāmasundara Jiu

Once Vīrabhadra Prabhu (one version says Rudrarāma Paṇḍita) traveled north to visit the Nawab of Murshidabad. The Nawab had invited Vīrabhadra for a meal with the intention of polluting Him by placing meat in the food. Due to the inconceivable potency of Vīrabhadra, who is nondifferent from Kṣīrodakaśāyī Viṣṇu, the meal became purified, which forced the Nawab to confess his ill intentions. He apologized and then offered Vīrabhadra whatever He desired. Vīrabhadra immediately requested the large black *śilā* (stone) that was over the Nawab's door entrance, since He had seen the *śilā* begin to perspire. Then the large *śilā* was placed in the Gaṅgā, and it floated on it's own all the way to Khaḍadaha-grāma (approximately 200 kilometres), where the *śilā* was met by Vīrabhadra.

Eventually, three Deities were carved from the large *śilā*. The first Deity that was carved was named Śrī Vallabha, which was established by Rudrarāma Paṇḍita and is presently located in the Śrī Śrī Rādhā-Vallabha Mandira in the village known as Vallabhapura near Shrirampur, Hugli District. The second Deity, named Śrī Kṛṣṇa Rāya, was established in Kāṅcaḍāpāḍā. (Local tradition says the second Deity was named Śrī Nandadulal and is located in the Śrī Śrī Rādhā-Nandadulal Mandira in Saibona near Barasat, North 24-Paraganas District.) And the third Deity manifested as Śrī Śyāmasundara and is located here in Khaḍadaha-grāma. The area where Vīrabhadra Paṇḍita met the *śilā* at the River Gaṅgā in Khaḍadaha-grāma is known today as Śyāmasundara-ghāṭa. Originally, the Deity of Śyāmasundara was located within Lord Nityānanda's residence in Khaḍadaha-grāma. Later, the unique Nityānanda-Śyāmasundara Mandira (also known as Śrī Śrī Rādhā-Śyāmasundara Jiu) was established a short distance away. This temple was rennovated by the Birla Jan Kalyan Trust in 1967. Near the Nityānanda-Śyāmasundara Mandira is a small shrine containing the balance piece of *śilā* from which the three Deities were originallly carved.

Lord Nityānanda's disappearance

There are two versions of Lord Nityānanda's disappearance. One description in *Śrī Advaita Prakāśa*, Chapter 22, states that the Lord disappeared into Śrī Śyāmasundara in Khaḍadaha-grāma.

"One day in Śāntipura, after Caitanya Mahāprabhu's disappearance, Advaita Ācārya was remembering Mahāprabhu's qualities and became impatient in ecstatic love. At that time, a message came from Lord Nityānanda in Khaḍadaha requesting Advaita to meet Him. When Nityānanda and Advaita met, They embraced one another in great ecstasy. After some time, They went and sat in a solitary place. No one knew what They discussed together for seven days and nights.

"On the eighth day, Śrī Advaita Ācārya and other devotees chanted the qualities of Caitanya Mahāprabhu with great love. As Lord Nityānanda danced in the middle, He lost all external consciousness while meditating with love on the lotus feet of Caitanya Mahāprabhu. All the great devotees present also forgot everything external out of love, and while everything was in that state, Lord Nityānanda disappeared [into the Deity of Śrī Śyāmasundara]. Then all the devotees regained external consciousness and began searching for Him.

"Śrī Advaita Prabhu could understand that Nityānanda had disappeared from the world. Then He started lamenting like a madman, 'Please tell Me why You have done such a crazy thing? I am almost dead already due to the intense feelings of separation from Caitanya Mahāprabhu. Still, I remained alive because I was able to see Your face. But now that You have left, where can I go?' When the other devotees learnt about Nityānanda's disappearance, they all wept bitterly and asked 'Where is Nityānanda? Where is Nityānanda?' Lord Nityānanda's son, Vīrabhadra, cried and rolled in the dust, while Advaita Prabhu tried to console everyone. He then made arrangements for a grand festival and sent invitation letters to all the devotees.

"In due course of time, all the great devotees came and Khaḍadaha again became full of joy. After bathing in the Gaṅgā on the day of the festival, everyone assembled and began *saṅkīrtana*. When the *saṅkīrtana* finished, all the Vaiṣṇavas relished discussing the pastimes of Lord Caitanya. Meanwhile, Vīrabhadra cleaned one place and arranged seating for three persons: Śrī Caitanya Mahāprabhu, Śrī Nityānanda Prabhu, and Śrī Advaita Ācārya. He then requested Advaita

Prabhu to sit and accept His meal with the other two Lords as They previously did.

"Then Vīrabhadra raised his hands and said, 'Dear Vaiṣṇavas, please listen to me. Anyone who arranges a feast should offer *bhoga* (food) like this to the three Lords. Then carefully take that *mahā-prasāda* and offer it to the saintly persons, *brāhmaṇas*, and Vaiṣṇavas. Feeding these three Lords is as good as a great sacrifice or perfect execution of *yoga*. Śrī Caitanya, Nityānanda, and Śrī Advaita are all one and simultaneously different. One who considers these three different will never attain the lotus feet of Lord Caitanya, and without Lord Caitanya's mercy, one will never attain pure love for the Supreme Personality of Godhead and one's rare human birth will be wasted. Any festival in which these three Lords are not offered *bhoga* is no better than Dakṣa's sacrifice. The benefit of food distribution will not be obtained, and everything will be spoiled. In the next life, he will reside in hell as long as the sun and moon continue to shine'.

"Hearing these words from Vīrabhadra, all the assembled Vaiṣṇavas said, 'So be it.' Vīrabhadra then happily distributed the *mahā-prasāda* to the *brāhmaṇas*, Vaiṣṇavas, and other great devotees, who all felt very fortunate to receive the *prasāda*. Then, after the festival, all the devotees returned to their residences and Advaita Ācārya returned to Śāntipura. Once there, He went to His room in a morose state of mind with nothing other than 'Hare Kṛṣṇa' coming from His mouth."

Another version of Lord Nityānanda's disappearance says that He departed at Ekacakra-grāma. This version is generally accepted by the conventional Gaudīya Vaiṣṇava community. In Ekacakra-grāma, the birthplace of Lord Nityānanda, the Lord established a Kṛṣṇa Temple with a Deity named Baṅkima Rāya (Bāṅkā Rāya), with Śrīmatī Rādhārāṇī on Kṛṣṇa's left side. The priests

of this temple explain that Lord Nityānanda Prabhu entered within the body of Baṅkima Rāya when He was ready to leave the planet. Later, the deity of Jāhnavā-devī was placed on the right side of Baṅkima Rāya.

30) PĀNIHĀṬI-GRĀMA (PĀNIHĀṬI)

Lord Nityānanda's glories

In the *Śrī Caitanya-caritāmṛta* (Ādi 5.4-6) it is stated: "The Supreme Personality of Godhead, Kṛṣṇa, is the fountainhead of all incarnations. Lord Balarāma is His second body. They are both one and the same identities. They differ only in form. He is the first bodily expansion of Lord Kṛṣṇa, and He assists in Kṛṣṇa's transcendental pastimes. That original Lord Kṛṣṇa appeared in Navadvīpa as Lord Caitanya, and Balarāma appeared with Him as Lord Nityānanda."

A formal introduction is well overdue for Śrī Nityānanda Prabhu, who is nondifferent from Śrī Caitanya Mahāprabhu. They enacted many wonderful pastimes together in various places around Śrī Navadvīpa-dhāma, which is situated on the banks of the Gaṅgā. Lord Nityānanda was born in the village of Ekacakra, which was known as the district of Rādha-deśa, where the Gaṅgā does not flow. Ekacakra is now located within the Birbhum district, some 150 kilometres northwest of Navadvīpa. He appeared on the auspicious thirteenth day of the bright fortnight of the month of Māgha, 1474.

During His childhood, He was known as Nitāi. Sometimes He would travel with His friends to visit the Gaṅgā. They would then imitate the pastimes of Lord Kṛṣṇa and His associates. Other times, Nitāi and His friends would re-enact the roles of Lord Rāmacandra and Lakṣmaṇa. For the first twelve years of His life, Nityānanda Prabhu stayed in the Ekacakra area and shared loving pastimes with His family, friends, and neighbours.

Just before His thirteenth year, a traveling *sannyāsī* came to Nitāi's home and His father, Hāḍāi Ojha Paṇḍita, eventually allowed Nitāi to leave home and travel with this *sannyāsī*. Nityānanda Prabhu always wanted to visit Navadvīpa, since He knew that Caitanya Mahāprabhu had appeared and was involved with His own childhood pastimes. But He thought, "I will enjoy going to the holy places of pilgrimage now with this *sannyāsī*, and after some time when Mahāprabhu is ready, I will go to Navadvīpa." In this way, Nityānanda left His home in Ekacakra and traveled from one holy place to another for eight years.

Then, in 1506, when Nityānanda Prabhu was visiting Vṛndāvana, He had a startling inner vision, which revealed that Caitanya Mahāprabhu had completed His childhood pastimes. After a long journey through dense forests in a trance like stage of frantic devotion, Nityānanda Prabhu finally reached Śrī Navadvīpa-dhāma. He went directly to Nandana Ācārya's house, who resided at the southern boundary of Antardvīpa, where the Rivers Gaṅgā and Jalaṅgī meet. After playing hide and seek with Caitanya Mahāprabhu, They finally met one another for the first time and were immediately overtaken by waves and tears of ecstasy.

Afterwards, Caitanya Mahāprabhu asked Nityānanda Prabhu and Haridāsa Ṭhākura to serve as the first door-to-door preachers, spreading the message of love of God to every home in Navadvīpa. Then, after spending many years together relishing *saṅkīrtana* pastimes in the Navadvīpa area, Caitanya Mahāprabhu went to Katwa to accept *sannyāsa*. Upon receiving the renounced order of life, Lord Caitanya and Nityānanda Prabhu traveled to Jagannātha Purī and relished being in the holy *dhāma* together.

Caitanya Mahāprabhu then left Puri and proceeded on a South India tour, which lasted for two years. Upon Mahāprabhu's return to Purī, He was very pleased to see that Nityānanda Prabhu had developed the movement there very nicely. The movement in Navadvīpa, however, had been neglected, so Caitanya Mahāprabhu instructed Nityānanda Prabhu, along with several other intimate associates, to return to Navadvīpa and manifest devotional service unto the Supreme Personality of Godhead without restriction.

When Nityānanda Prabhu first returned to Bengal, He began His mission on the eastern bank of the Gaṅgā in the village known as Pānihāṭi-grāma, which is a few kilometres north of Calcutta. The following narration from the *Śrī Caitanya-bhāgavata* (*Antya-khaṇḍa*, Chapter 5) describes Nityānanda Prabhu and His associates travels to and arrival in Pānihāṭi during November, 1511.

"Accepting Lord Caitanya's order, Lord Nityānanda went at once to Bengal. Saintly Nityānanda, who was filled with ecstatic love, walked in front as He and His companions traveled on the road. Everyone completely forgot themselves as the ecstasies that filled their bodies had no end. Every half hour, they walked several kilometres. Forgetting themselves, they went south instead of north! After some time they asked the local people, 'Please tell us how we can go to the bank of the Gaṅgā?' The locals replied, 'You are lost. Turn around and travel for six hours.' Following this instruction, they became lost again! Again they asked someone else about the right path and were told, 'Stay on this path for thirty-two kilometres.' Smiling, they continued on the path, but they were not aware of their bodies, what to speak of whether they were walking on the correct path! They were all filled with spiritual bliss as they traveled on that road with Lord Nityānanda. Eventually,

Nityānanda Prabhu and His associates came to Pānihāṭi-grāma on the bank of the Gaṅgā.

"Finally Lord Nityānanda was able to visit Rāghava Paṇḍita as well as Makaradvaja Kara. Nityānanda Prabhu roared with bliss and desired to dance, while all the well-known singers converged around Him. The powerful Nityānanda Avadhūta danced until the earth trembled with the weight of His steps. Whoever attained Lord Nityānanda's glance would also dance and become overwhelmed with ecstatic love before falling to the ground. In this way, Nityānanda Prabhu began His auspicious work of delivering everyone.

"After some time, Lord Nityānanda sat on the Deity's throne and instructed everyone to perform an *abhiṣeka* (bathing ceremony). Rāghava Paṇḍita and his friends at once began performing *abhiseka*. They brought thousands and thousands of jugs of Gaṅgā water and scented them all with various fragrances. As everyone chanted 'Hari! Hari!' they poured Gaṅgā water on Nityānanda's head. Once the *abhiṣeka* was completed, the devotees dressed the Lord with new clothes and anointed His limbs with sandalwood paste. Filled with the bliss, Lord Nityānanda showered glances of ecstatic love in the four directions.

"For three months in this way Lord Nityānanda enjoyed pastimes of devotional service at Pānihāṭi-grāma. During these months, external consciousness was not present in anyone; no one had any concern for their body. No one ate, they only danced in ecstatic love, nothing else. In the future, the *Vedas* will describe all these pastimes of ecstatic love in Pānihāṭi-grāma."

Daṇḍa-mahotsava

The following is a summary of the famous "festival of punishment", as described in *Śrī Caitanya-caritāmṛta* (*Antya-līlā*, Chapter 6): "It was at this time that the young Raghunātha dāsa Gosvāmī arrived in Pānihāṭi from Kṛṣṇapura (near Ādi Saptagrāma). He had heard of Lord Nityānanda's successful preaching and was anxious to serve His lotus feet, because He knew that one could only receive the mercy of Śrī Caitanya Mahāprabhu by pleasing His eternal associate. When Raghunātha arrived, He found Nityānanda sitting on a large rock beneath a giant banyan tree on the bank of Gaṅgā. He looked as effulgent as hundreds of thousands of rising suns, surrounded by hundreds of devotees. Raghunātha felt very embarassed to approach these great souls. Then Lord Nityānanda said in a merciful, joking way, 'You are a thief. Now you have come to see Me. Come here, come here. Today I shall punish you!' When the Lord called Raghunātha, he did not go near. Then the Lord forcibly caught him and placed His lotus feet on Raghunātha's head. The Lord then spoke again, 'You are just like a thief, instead of coming near, you stay at a distant place. Now that I have captured you, I shall punish you. Make a festival and feed all My associates yogurt and chipped rice.' Upon hearing this, Raghunātha Dāsa was extremely pleased.

"In a short time, the entire area was inundated with large quantities of chipped rice, yogurt, milk, sweetmeats, sugar, bananas, and other eatables. All kinds of *brāhmaṇas*, laymen, and pilgrims came from the surrounding areas. Everyone was offered two earthern pots. In one was chipped rice with condensed milk, and in the other chipped rice with yogurt. Some of the *brāhmaṇas* who did not have a sitting place went to the bank of the Gaṅgā with their pots and soaked their chipped rice there. Others, who could not get a place on the bank of the Gaṅgā, got down into the water and began eating their two kinds of chipped rice.

"After the chipped rice had been served to everyone, Nityānanda Prabhu brought Śrī Caitanya Mahāprabhu to the Pānihāṭi festival. Only a few realized devotees were able to perceive Mahāprabhu's presence. From each and every pot, Nityānanda Prabhu took a morsel of chipped rice and pushed it into the mouth of Śrī Caitanya Mahāprabhu as a joke. Then Mahāprabhu took a morsel of *prasāda* and pushed it into Nityānanda's mouth, as They both smiled and laughed.

"Lord Nityānanda then ordered, 'All of you eat and chant the holy name of Hari!' When all the Vaiṣṇavas were chanting 'Hari! Hari!' and eating, they remembered how Kṛṣṇa and Balarāma ate with Their companions on the bank of the Yamunā. All these confidential devotees who were cowherd boys from Lord Kṛṣṇa's pastimes were absorbed in ecstatic love. They thought the bank of the Gaṅgā to be the bank of the Yamunā.

"After receiving the remnants of food left by Lord Nityānanda, Raghunātha Dāsa was extremely happy. He then ate some and distributed the rest among his own associates. In the morning, after taking His bath in the Gaṅgā, Lord Nityānanda sat down with His associates beneath the same banyan tree. Raghunātha went there and submitted his humble prayer to the Lord. Then Nityānanda called him near and placed His lotus feet upon Raghunātha's head and began to speak, 'My dear Raghunātha Dāsa, since you arranged the feast on the bank of the Gaṅgā, Śrī Caitanya Mahāprabhu came here just to show you His mercy. Being assured of all this, return to your home. Very soon, without impediments, you will attain the shelter of Śrī Caitanya Mahāprabhu.'

"This whole incident became known as the Daṇḍa-mahotsava, the festival of punishment. To this day, pilgrims travel annually to Pānihāṭi in honor of the chipped rice festival, which is on the thirteenth day of the waxing moon in the month of Jyeṣṭha (May/June)."

Śrī Rāghava Paṇḍita

The *Śrī Caitanya-bhāgavata* (*Antya-khaṇḍa*, Chapter 5) describes Lord Caitanya's visit to Pānihāṭi in the following words: "Śrī Caitanya Mahāprabhu spent a few days in Śāntipura with Advaita Ācārya and His other associates and honored the disappearance festival of Madhavendra Purī. He then traveled to Pānihāṭi-grāma and went to the home of Śrī Rāghava Paṇḍita. While Rāghava, who is one of the main associates of Lord Caitanya, was busily engaged in Lord Kṛṣṇa's service, Caitanya Mahāprabhu suddenly appeared in his doorway. Upon seeing the master of his life, Rāghava fell to the ground and offered full obeisances, before tightly embracing the Lord's lotus feet.

"Then Caitanya Mahāprabhu embraced Rāghava Paṇḍita and sprinkled his body with tears of joy and love. The Lord said, 'By bathing in the Gaṅgā, one becomes happy. In the same way, I become happy by entering Rāghava Paṇḍita's home.' Lord Caitanya then smiled and said, 'Listen Rāghava, quickly go and cook for Lord Kṛṣṇa.' Upon hearing this instruction, Rāghava happily went to cook a limitless quantity of food. Accompanied by Nityānanda Prabhu and His associates, Lord Caitanya ate very happily and praised all of Rāghava's wonderful cooking, especially the *śāka* (spinach). Since Rāghava knew how much Lord Caitanya was fond of *śāka*, he cooked several different kinds of *śāka* for the satisfaction of the Lord.

"Upon hearing that Lord Caitanya has come to Pānihāṭi, Gadādhara Dāsa ran all the way from his home in Eṇḍiyādaha-grāma, and Purandara Paṇḍita ran from Khaḍadaha-grāma. Paramesvarī Dāsa, Raghunātha

Vaidya, and Makaradhvaja Kara also came to see Śrī Caitanya Mahāprabhu. There was such bliss in Pānihāṭi since Lord Caitanya and all His associates had gathered together. Then Caitanya Mahāprabhu told a secret to Rāghava Paṇḍita. He said, 'Nityānanda Prabhu is nondifferent from Me. Whatever Nityānanda does, I do. Nityānanda and I are the same person. Therefore, with great care and devotion, you should serve Him as if He were the Supreme Personality of Godhead.' Then the Lord spoke to Makaradhvaja, 'You should serve and please Śrī Rāghava Paṇḍita, for that will please Me.' Lord Caitanya stayed for a few days in Pānihāṭi-grāma, making the village more glorious and fortunate."

* * *

Today in Pānihāṭi the same banyan tree that Lord Nityānanda rested under is located at Vaiṣṇava Tola, just above the main bathing and boating ghāṭa on the Gaṅgā. There is a marble plaque with the following inscription regarding the visit of Śrī Caitanya Mahāprabhu: "This *ghāṭa* is a relic of the Hindu period. Here landed Śrī Caitanya Deva from Purī in 1514 A.D." A short distance away is Rāghava Bhavan, the residence of Śrī Rāghava Paṇḍita. The area around his *samādhi* is known as Mahdobi-sthāna Kuñja, where Lord Caitanya, Nityānanda Prabhu, and Their associates would perform huge *hari-nāma-kīrtanas*. Also, Rāghava Paṇḍita's sister, Damayantī-devī, would prepare for Caitanya Mahāprabhu special dry foodstuffs that would keep preserved for long periods. These special dry preparations used to be carried in large baskets by Rāghava Paṇḍita and other devotees when they visited Jagannātha Purī for the Ratha-yātrā. Govinda Dāsa, the servant of Caitanya Mahāprabhu, would store them, and each day throughout the year he offered them to Lord Caitanya to relish.

31) Eṇḍiyādaha-grāma (Ariadaha)

Śrīla Gadādhara Dāsa

In Pānihāṭi, Lord Nityānanda used the house of Rāghava Paṇḍita as His headquarters. From there He preached to thousands and thousands of people on both sides of the River Gaṅgā. From Pānihāṭi, He traveled south to Eṇḍiyādaha-grāma, where He stayed in the house of Śrīla Gadādhara Dāsa, who is stated to be a close associate of Śrīmatī Rādhārāṇī in Goloka. Nityānanda transformed his small home into another huge preaching center for the *saṅkirtana* movement. The Lord changed the hearts of so many people in the area that young children were allowed to come from neighbouring villages, even on school days, just to participate in the *kīrtana*.

In 1534, when Lord Nityānanda was empowered by Lord Caitanya to preach the *saṅkīrtana* movement in Bengal, Śrīla Gadādhara Dāsa was one of Lord Nityānanda's chief assistants.

In the *Śrī Caitanya-caritāmṛta* (*Ādi* 10.53), Śrīla Prabhupāda elaborates further: "When Śrīla Gadādhara Prabhu was preaching the cult of *hari-kīrtana* (in Eṇḍiyādaha), there was a magistrate who was very much against his *saṅkīrtana* movement. Following in the footsteps of Caitanya Mahāprabhu, Śrīla Gadādhara Dāsa went one night to the house of the Kazi and requested him to chant the Hare Kṛṣṇa *mahā-mantra*. The Kazi replied, 'All right, I shall chant Hare Kṛṣṇa tomorrow.' On hearing this, Śrīla Gadādhara Prabhu began to dance, and said, "Why tomorrow? You have already chanted the Hare Kṛṣṇa *mantra*, so simply continue.'

"...Once while Śrī Gadādhara Prabhu was returning to Bengal from Jagannātha Purī with Nityānanda Prabhu, he forgot himself and began talking very loudly as if he were a girl of Vraja-bhūmi selling yogurt, and Śrīla Nityānanda Prabhu noted this. Another time, while absorbed in the ecstasy of the *gopīs*, he carried a jug filled with Ganges water on his head as if he were selling milk...When Gadādhara Dāsa was present in Eṇḍiyādaha, he established a Bāla Gopāla Deity for worship there."

The residence of Śrīla Gadādhara Dāsa, also known as Dāsa Gadādhara Śrīpat (Patbari), is situated in Ariadaha, a few kilometres north of Calcutta, directly on the eastern bank of the Gaṅgā. Today, a beautiful *pāṭavāṭī* (monastery) has been established by Śrī Madhusūdana Mullik of Calcutta. He had arranged for the Deity worship of Śrī Śrī Rādhā-Kānta, and his son, Balāicāṅda Mullick, established Gaura-Nitāi Deities. There is also a small deity of Lord Śiva known as Gopeśvara. In the rear of the complex is the *puṣpa-samādhi* of Śrīla Gadādhara Dāsa. His actual *samādhi* is in Katwa at Caitanya Mahāprabhu's *sannyāsī-sthāna*.

VARĀHA-NAGARA

In the *Śrī Caitanya-bhāgavata* (*Antya-khaṇḍa*, Chapter 5) we learn of yet another holy place situated on the banks of Gaṅgā: "Near Ariadaha is a small village known as Varāha-nagara. A fortunate *brāhmaṇa* who was very learned in *Śrīmad-Bhāgavatam* lived there. Upon arriving at his home, Śrī Caitanya Mahāprabhu heard the *brāhmaṇa* reading *Śrīmad-Bhāgavatam* and was overwhelmed with ecstasy. 'Read! Read!' Lord Caitanya roared again and again. The *brāhmaṇa* continued reading while Caitanya Mahāprabhu danced and fell to the ground in ecstatic love. Nine hours passed before Caitanya Mahāprabhu returned to external consciousness. The Lord then embraced the *brāhmaṇa* and said, 'Not from any mouth have I ever heard *Śrīmad-Bhāgavatam* as you read it. Your name is now 'Bhāgavatācārya' (teacher of *Śrīmad-Bhāgavatam*). Please do not do anything except read *Śrīmad-Bhāgavatam*. Hearing Lord Caitanya's pleasing words, everyone made a great roar and chanted, 'Hari! Hari!'

"In this way, Śrī Caitanya Mahāprabhu stayed at the homes of different devotees, all situated in various villages one after another (from Māyāpur to Śāntipura, Kumārahaṭṭa, Pānihāṭi-grāma, and beyond to Āṭisārā-nagara and Chatrabhoga) all on Gaṅgā's shore."

The *Śrīmad-Bhāgavatam* commentary that Śrī Bhāgavatācārya wrote is called *Śrī Kṛṣṇa-prema-taraṅginī*, and his *samādhi* is also located in Varāha-nagara. In his purports on the *Śrī Caitanya-caritāmṛta* (*Ādi* 10.113/12.58), Śrīla Prabhupāda has written: "Bhāgavatācārya's real name was Raghunātha. His monastery, which is situated in Varāha-nagara, about three and a half miles north of Calcutta on the bank of the Ganges, still exists, and is managed by the initiated disciples of the late Śrī Rāmadāsa Bābāji...According to the *Śrī Gaura-gaṇoddeśa-dīpikā* (195), Bhāgavatācārya formerly lived in Vṛndāvana as Śveta-mañjari."

32) KĀLĪ-PĪṬHA (CALCUTTA)

The name Calcutta is derived from Kālī-ghāṭa, where there is a celebrated shrine dedicated to goddess Kālī. This famous place is also known as Kālī-pīṭha and some even remember the name, Kālikartta, which means that the income of the village was once utilised for the worship of Kālī-mātā. Kālī-mātā and Kālī-ghāṭa were originally situated on the bank of the main Gaṅgā, but since Gaṅgā has changed her course, only a smaller branch or canal (known as Ādi Gaṅgā) flows

past the presiding deity (known as "Kālī Ma") of Calcutta today. The present Kālī Ma temple was built about three centuries ago by a member of the Sabarna Chaudhuri family of Barsia, who allotted 194 acres of land for its maintenance. This sacred place is one of the fifty-two principal *śakti-pīṭhas* (sacred *devī tīrthas*) in India.

We are reminded again of the pastime in which Lord Śiva was carrying the corpse of his wife, Satī, after she had given up her body in the sacrifice of her father, Prajāpati Dakṣa. Lord Viṣṇu cut the corpse of Satī with His Sudarśana *cakra* into fifty-two parts in order to remove Lord Śiva's sorrow. Limbs of Satī fell in different places and they became the famous *śakti-pīṭhas* where goddess Kālī is worshiped. Four toes of Satī's right foot are said to have fallen at Kālī-pītha, or Kālī-ghāṭa.

Śrīla Prabhupāda's birth

Since the manifestation of Kālī-pītha, in some past *yuga*, to the present age, the teeming metropolis of Calcutta has been one of India's overpowering experiences. This city evokes strong reactions, both favorable and unfavorable, as few persons can remain indifferent to its vitality! But the most favorable reaction for the Gauḍīya Vaiṣṇavas is that Calcutta marks the birthplace of His Divine Grace A.C. Bhaktivedanta Swami Prabhupāda, who has given the whole world genuine spiritual vitality through the teachings of Śrī Caitanya Mahāprabhu in the International Society for Krishna Consciousness.

The following narration from the First Volume, First Chapter, of the *Śrīla Prabhupāda-līlāmṛta*, captures the mood in the city of Calcutta at the time of Śrīla Prabhupāda's birth: "It was Janmāṣṭamī, the annual celebration of the advent of Lord Kṛṣṇa some five thousand years before. Residents of Calcutta, mostly Bengalis and other Indians, but also many Muslims and even some British, were observing the festive day, moving here and there through the city's streets to visit the temples of Lord Kṛṣṇa. Devout Vaiṣṇavas, fasting till midnight, chanted Hare Kṛṣṇa and heard about the birth and activities of Lord Kṛṣṇa from the *Śrīmad-Bhāgavatam*. They continued fasting, chanting, and worshiping throughout the night.

"The next day (1 September, 1896), in a little house in the Tollygunje suburb of Calcutta, a male child was born. Since he was born on Nandotsava, the day Kṛṣṇa's father, Nanda Mahārāja, had observed a festival in honor of Kṛṣṇa's birth, the boy's uncle called him Nandulal. But his father, Gour Mohan De, and his mother, Rajani, named him Abhay Charan, 'One who is fearless, having taken shelter at Lord Kṛṣṇa's lotus feet.' In accordance with Bengali tradition, the mother had gone to the home of her parents for the delivery, and so it was that on the bank of the Ādi-Gaṅgā, a few miles from his father's home, in a small, two room, mud walled house with a tiled roof, underneath a jackfruit tree, Abhay Charan was born. A few days later, Abhay returned with his parents to their home at 151 Harrison Road.

"An astrologer did a horoscope for the child, and the family was made jubliant by the auspicious reading. The astrologer made a specific prediction: When this child reached the age of seventy, he would cross the ocean, become a great exponent of religion, and open 108 temples."

'Śrīla Prabhupāda, the land is yours'

Another narration from the *Śrīla Prabhupāda-līlāmṛta* (Volume Five, Chapter One) describes Śrīla Prabhupāda's mood as he awaited news about the land purchase in Māyāpur: "Calcutta, March 1971. It was midnight. Śrīla Prabhupāda sat on a pillow behind his low desk, his light the only one on in the building. All the devotees were in bed. On the desk before him rested the dictating machine and a volume of *Śrīmad-Bhāgavatam* with Bengali commentary. A small framed picture of his spiritual master, Śrīla Bhaktisiddhānta Sarasvatī, sat between two small vases of roses and asters. On the floor beyond the desk was the broad mat covered with white cotton fabric, where a few hours before, devotees and guests had sat.

"But now he was alone. Although usually he retired at ten, rising three or four hours later to translate, tonight he had not rested, and his *Bhāgavatam* lay closed, his dictating machine covered. He had sent two of his disciples, Tamāla Kṛṣṇa and Balimardana, to purchase land in Māyāpur. Six days had passed, however, and still they had neither returned nor sent word. He told them not to return until they had completed the transaction, but six days was more than enough time. He was anxious, thinking constantly of his two disciples...

"Prabhupāda wanted an ISKCON center in Māyāpur, it was a desire that had increased within him as his movement had increased throughout the years. He could easily visit or live in Māyāpur, that was no problem. But he needed a place for his disciples. His spiritual master had ordered him to preach in the West, and now with the success of his Kṛṣṇa consciousness society, the Western Vaiṣṇavas required a center in Māyāpur where they could reside and worship and receive the immense benefit of the holy *dhāma*. Bhaktisiddhānta Sarasvatī had stressed the great importance of Māyāpur, and some of his *sannyāsi* disciples had temples there. Why shouldn't the International Society for Krishna Consciousness also be able to take shelter of Māyāpur?...

"Prabhupāda wondered if perhaps his boys had been robbed. Before sending them off, he had shown Tamāla Kṛṣṇa how to carry money around his waist in a makeshift cloth money belt. But it had been a great deal of money, and roberries were not uncommon around Navadvipa. Or perhaps there had been some other delay. Sometimes in land negotiations involving large sums of money, the court would require that a clerk record the denomination and serial number of every note exchanged. Or perhaps the train had broken down.

"Suddenly Prabhupāda heard footsteps on the stairs. Someone opened the outer door and now walked along the veranda just outside. A soft knock. 'Yes, who is it?' Prabhupāda asked. Tamāla Kṛṣṇa entered and prostrated himself before Śrīla Prabhupāda. 'So,' Prabhupāda asked, 'what is the news?' Tamāla Kṛṣṇa looked up triumphantly. 'The land is yours!' Prabhupāda leaned back with a sigh. 'All right,' he said. 'Now you can take rest.'"

Śrīla Prabhupāda along the bank of the Gaṅgā

In January of 1976, just before Śrīla Prabhupāda arrived in Śrīdhāma Māyāpur for the annual Gaura Pūrṇimā festival, he spent a few days in Calcutta. On the first two mornings of his visit, he took his walks along the bank of the Gaṅgā. The following narrations from the First Volume, Eighth Chapter, of A *Transcendental Diary* describes the simplicity and spiritual purification of the pilgrims taking bath in her waters.

"Today was Ekādaśī, the 13th of January, 1976, and Śrīla Prabhupāda took his morning walk along the Gaṅgā. Hundreds of pilgrims were taking a dawn bath there having come for the Gaṅgā-sāgara-melā. Prabhupāda explained that *sagara* is the sea, so the *melā* is a spiritual gathering on an island in Gaṅgā's estuary.

"Evidently eager pilgrims had traveled from as far away as Rajasthan in the northwest. They camped simply along the banks of mother Gaṅgā, washing their few possessions, as well as themselves, in the holy waters, unmindful of the boats and the other river traffic passing by. They sat contentedly on the pathways cooking breakfast and drying out their clothing.

"Noting the shining *lota* (pot) one man carried, Prabhupāda remarked that if even the *lota* is so clean, we can understand how clean he must personally be. Prabhupāda also recalled how he and his mother had bathed in the same spot when he was a child."

"On the 14th of January, Prabhupāda took his walk along the Gaṅgā again. Although it was early morning, hundreds of people lined along the riverbank bathing, doing *pūjā* and washing their clothes.

"Śrīla Prabhupāda commented on the simplicity of village life and the importance of Gaṅgā. Many people have come to the Melā for spiritual purification, carrying only a few simple possessions. Everywhere *dhotis* and *saris* (colorful dresses worn by women in Vedic culture) hung on fences or were spread out on the ground to dry, their owners sitting or squatting nearby, patiently waiting. Prabhupāda remarked that even if they have only one piece of cloth, they will not fail to wash it everyday. That is Vedic culture."

33) Āṭisārā-nagara (Bāruipura)

Śrī Ananta Paṇḍita

In the *Śrī Caitanya-bhāgavata* (*Antya-khaṇḍa*, Chapter 2) it is stated: "As Śrī Caitanya Mahāprabhu traveled along the Gaṅgā from Varāha-nagara, He eventually arrived at Āṭisārā-nagara. In this village lived a very fortunate saintly devotee named Śrī Ananta Paṇḍita (Ācārya Gosvāmī). Lord Caitanya stayed at his home, and Ananta happily prepared the Lord's meal. The very generous Ananta Paṇḍita became joyful having Caitanya Mahāprabhu as a guest in his home. The Lord and His associates accepted the meal. In this way, Lord Caitanya taught that a *sannyāsī's* duty is to accept meals offered by others. During the evening, Caitanya Mahāprabhu happily described the glories of Lord Kṛṣṇa. After bestowing a merciful glance upon Ananta Paṇḍita and chanting 'Hari! Hari!' Śrī Caitanya Mahāprabhu departed at dawn. Walking on Gaṅgā's shore, the Lord very happily came to Chatrabhoga."

As stated in the *Śrī Caitanya-caritāmṛta* (*Adi-līlā* 12.58): "Ananta Ācārya was one of the eight principal *gopīs*. His former name was Sudevī. Although he was among Advaita Ācārya's followers, he later became an important devotee of Gadādhara Gosvāmī."

In Śrīla Prabhupāda's purport on the *Śrī Caitanya-caritāmṛta* (*Adi* 8.60), he writes: "In Jagannātha Purī, or Puruṣottama-kṣetra, there is a monastery known as Gaṅgā-mātā Maṭha that was established by Ananta Ācārya. In the disciplic succession of the Gaṅgā-mātā Maṭha, he is known as Vinoda-mañjarī. One of his disciples was Haridāsa Paṇḍita Gosvāmī, who is also known as Śrī Raghu Gopāla and as Śrī Rāsa-mañjarī. His disciple Lakṣmīpriyā was the maternal aunt of Gaṅgā-mātā, a princess who was the daughter of the King of Puṭiyā. Gaṅgā-mātā brought a Deity of the name Śrī Rasika-rāya from Kṛṣṇa Miśra of Jaipur and installed Him in the house of Sārvabhauma in Jagannātha Purī."

* * *

As in the Chatrabhoga area, Gaṅgā-mayī does not presently flow in the Āṭisārā (Bāruipura) area. Near the Śrī Śrī Nitāi-Gaurāṅga Mandira there is a small pond where the Gaṅgā supposedly flowed. It is said that Caitanya Mahāprabhu took bath there, and therefore it is called Mahāprabhu-ghāṭa in His remembrance. Within the temple is a small shrine containing the footprints of Śrī Caitanya Mahāprabhu. The beautiful Śrī Śrī Nitāi-Gaurāṅga stand very attractively, and a twenty-four hour *kīrtana* is being chanted. The village of Āṭisārā is now part of the large township of Bāruipura.

34) CHATRABHOGA (BORASI/KHĀḌĪ)

Ambuliṅga-ghāṭa

After Śrī Caitanya Mahāprabhu accepted the order of *sannyāsa* in Katwa, Lord Nityānanda brought Him to Advaita Ācārya's home in Śāntipura, where Mahāprabhu decided to travel to Jagannātha Purī in order to have *darśana* of the moon of Nīlācala, Lord Jagannātha. As Caitanya Mahāprabhu and His four associates traveled along the banks of the Gaṅgā, they passed through Varāha-nagara and Āṭisārā-nagara before arriving at Chatrabhoga.

During the time of Śrī Caitanya Mahāprabhu, Gaṅgā-mayī flowed south of Calcutta through Kālī-ghāṭa, which is still known as Ādi Gaṅgā. Then Gaṅgā branched out from the Bāruipura area and flowed through the Diamond Harbour area. Chatrabhoga is located south of Mathurapura and north of Kāśī-nagara, but at the present moment, Gaṅgā does not flow there.

The following story from the *Śrī Caitanya-bhāgavata* (*Antya-khaṇḍa*, Chapter 2) emphasises the importance of Gaṅgā-mayī as she flows through Chatrabhoga: "Walking on Gaṅgā's bank, the Lord came to Chatrabhoga. At Chatrabhoga, Gaṅgā divides into a hundred mouths for the pleasure of everyone. It was at this place that Lord Śiva assumed a *liṅga* (phallus form) of *ambu* (water), which is why everyone calls this place Ambuliṅga-ghāṭa.

"In ancient times, King Bhagīratha worshiped Gaṅgā-devī and brought her to this place. Overcome in separation from goddess Gaṅgā and always thinking of her, Lord Śiva also came to this place. When Lord Śiva saw Gaṅgā at Chatrabhoga, he became overwhelmed with love. The moment Lord Śiva saw her, he fell into her waters and assumed the form of water in order to freely mix with the waters of Gaṅgā. Meditating on Gaṅgā-devī, who is known as the mother of all the worlds, Lord Śiva worshiped her with devotion. Lord Śiva knew the glories of worshiping Gaṅgā-devī, and Gaṅgā-devī knew the glories of worshiping Lord Śiva. By the combined power of goddess Gaṅgā and Lord Śiva, Chatrabhoga became famous as a very sacred place.

"When Lord Caitanya went to Chatrabhoga it became even more glorious. At Ambuliṅga-ghāṭa, He saw how Gaṅgā had divided into a hundred mouths. Upon seeing this, Lord Caitanya was overcome with bliss and roared 'Hari! Hari!' with great tumult. When the Lord fainted in ecstasy, Nityānanda Prabhu caught Him as everyone called out 'Jaya! Jaya!' As the Lord and His associates took bath at the *ghāṭa*, they enjoyed many pastimes. After bathing, the Lord climbed onto the riverbank, and the dry clothing He put on soon became wet with His tears of love.

"With a stream of hundred mouths, the River Gaṅgā flowed over the earth. Then, also with a stream of a hundred mouths, tears flowed from Lord Caitanya's eyes. Seeing this, the devotees laughed with joy. In this way Lord Caitanya wept."

Rāmacandra Khān

The following pastimes between Śrī Caitanya Mahāprabhu and Rāmacandra Khān are from the *Śrī Caitanya-bhāgavata* (*Antya-*

khaṇḍa, Chapter 2): "The governor in that village (Khāḍī, near Chatrabhoga) was Rāmacandra Khān. Although he enjoyed many sense pleasures, he was still considered saintly and fortunate. Upon seeing Śrī Caitanya Mahāprabhu, he felt great awe and reverence in his heart. Immediately he quickly came down from his palanquin and offered *daṇḍavat* obeisances. Meanwhile, Lord Caitanya lost external consciousness and was weeping tears of ecstatic love. He loudly said, 'O Jagannātha! O Jagannātha!' then fell to the ground and wept. When Rāmacandra Khān saw the Lord's sorrow, his heart broke. In all the three planetary systems, no one had ever wept like that before. Then Caitanya Mahāprabhu asked Rāmacandra Khān who he was. Offering obeisances again and folding his hands, he said he was the servant of the Lord's servant. Other people, however, told the Lord that he was the governor of this southern province. Upon hearing this, Caitanya Mahāprabhu said, 'Very good. How can I quickly travel to Jagannātha Purī?' Rāmacandra Khān explained that it was very dangerous to travel, but he would do his best to assist the Lord and His associates to Jagannātha Purī that evening. The Lord was pleased hearing the governor's words and then cast a merciful glance upon him, which made Rāmacandra Khān completely free of all material bonds. Lord Caitanya stayed in his house long enough to eat a meal prepared by Rāmacandra Khān. After rinsing His mouth, the Lord thundered, 'How far is Lord Jagannātha?'

"Then Mukunda Datta began to sing and the Lord of Vaikuṇṭha, Śrī Caitanya Mahāprabhu, danced as He manifested tears, trembling, roaring, perspiration, becoming stunned, and bodily hairs standing erect. Everyone there was bathed in a wonderful flood of tears of love flowed from His eyes, a flood like the swollen Gaṅgā during the month of Bhādra (August/September). The Lord danced around and around. After some time, Lord Caitanya became peaceful. Then Rāmacandra Khān said, 'My Lord, the boat has come to the *ghāṭa*. It is ready now.' The Lord at once stood up and walked onto the boat. By the Lord's order, Mukunda began to sing *kīrtana* again, as they traveled across the Gaṅgā on boat. Then the foolish boatman said, 'I am afraid. I am afraid. I think we will not remain alive tonight. On the riverbanks are tigers, and in the water are crocodiles. There are also many thieves who will take our wealth and kill us. O master, please remain quiet until we reach Orissa.' Then everyone stopped the singing.

"After a moment, Lord Caitanya stood up and shouted. 'Why are you afraid? Why? The Sudarśana *cakra* stands in front of the boat. It always protects the Vaiṣṇavas from any danger. Do not worry, continue singing Lord Kṛṣṇa's name. Do you not see the Sudarśana *cakra*?' Upon hearing these words, all the devotees again sang in *kīrtana*. Lord Caitanya used this situation to teach everyone: 'The Sudarśana *cakra* always protects the devotees.'

"Plunged in the nectar of *saṅkīrtana* while crossing the water of Gaṅgā, Lord Caitanya and His associates finally reached Orissa."

* * *

The small village of Chatrabhoga is 7 kilometres south of Mathurapura. The only remembrance of the Lord's visit are the lotus footprints of Śrī Caitanya Mahāprabhu that were installed by Śrīla Bhaktisiddhānta Sarasvatī Mahārāja on the third of April, 1933. The footprints of the Lord are in a small shrine *āśrama* behind the village of Chatrabhoga, in a most beautiful lush area. It is the only temple (under the Gauḍīya Maṭha in Māyāpur) for the local Vaiṣṇavas. Nearby, approximately 2 kilometres south towards Kāśīnagar in a village named Borasi, resides Lord Śiva known as Śrī Badarikanātha

Mahādeva. Just next to the temple is a small pond where Ambuliṅga-ghāṭa is located. Opposite the main road from Borasi is the small village of Khāḍī, which was the residence of Rāmacandra Khān. One small temple (under the Devānanda Gauḍīya Maṭha in Navadvīpa) maintains worship of Their Lordships Śrī Śrī Rādhā-Vallabha, where Rāmacandra Khān once lived. On the east side of the main road between Mathurapura and Kāśīnagar, are large flat paddy fields, indicating the area where the Gaṅgā used to flow.

Bhogavatī Gaṅgā in Paramānanda's well

This pastime from the *Śrī Caitanya-bhāgavata* (*Antya-khaṇḍa*, Chapter 3) takes us shortly away from the banks of Gaṅgā in Bengal, but reflects Lord Caitanya's love for Gaṅgā: "After leaving Chatrabhoga, Śrī Caitanya Mahāprabhu crossed the Gaṅgā and came to Orissa. At Prayāga-ghāṭa (Tamluk), He then passed through Gaṅgā-ghāṭa, the River Suvarṇarekhā, Jaleśvara-grāma, Remuṇā-grāma, Yājapura, or Nābhi-gayā, Daśāśvamedha-ghāṭa, the River Vaitaraṇī (Gupta Gaṅgā), Kaṭaka (Cuttak), the River Mahānadī, Bhuvaneśvara, Kamalapura, Āṭhāranālā, and finally arrived in Jagannātha Purī.

"While in Jagannātha Purī, Lord Caitanya visited the monastery of Paramānanda Purī. The Lord noticed that the water in the well was muddy and not good for drinking. He then said, 'Lord Jagannātha's *māyā* has ruined this water so that no one can drink it.' After speaking these words, Lord Caitanya stood up with His hands raised and then said, 'O Jagannātha, O great master, please grant this boon to Me. Please order Bhogavatī Gaṅgā to flow from Pātālaloka into this well.' After some time, the Lord went home and all the devotees went to sleep. Placing that order on her head, Gaṅgā-devī then entered the well and filled it.

"The next morning when the devotees rose, they were all wonder-struck on seeing the well was now full of clear pure water. They all circumambulated the well out of respect for the appearance of Gaṅgā. Then Caitanya Mahāprabhu arrived and with a happy heart spoke the following words, 'O devotees, please listen. Anyone who drinks this water or uses it to bathe attains the result of bathing in the Gaṅgā. This is the truth, nothing but the truth, that person will attain very pure love and devotion to Lord Kṛṣṇa.' Hearing these words of the Lord, all the devotees loudly chanted, 'Hari! Hari!' Then Lord Caitanya very happily drank and bathed in the splendid transcendental water of Paramānanda Purī's well.

"After staying in Jagannātha Purī a few days, the Lord happily and quickly returned to Bengal, filled with love for Gaṅgā."

35) GAṄGĀ-SĀGARA (SĀGARA-SAṄGAMA)

In the *Padma Purāṇa* (*Sṛṣṭi-khaṇḍa* 11.5) it is stated: "Gaṅgā-sāgara is said to be an auspicious sacred place composed of all sacred places." And in the *Varāha Purāṇa* (179.30): "There is Sītā-tīrtha, which is sacred to the Vaiṣṇavas on Dvādaśī in the month of Mārgaśīrṣa. In the *Purāṇas* this place is known as Gaṅgā-sāgara."

Now we arrive at the final major *tīrtha* related to Gaṅgā-mayī, where she meets the Bay of Bengal and begins her voyage to the lower planetary systems, also known as the subterranean heavens, where she is known as Bhogavatī. Just as she reaches the Bay, her width expands over twenty kilometres, reflecting her glorious disappearance from this planet. This place is where Kapila Muni, the great propounder of the *sāṅkhya* philosophy (analytical understanding of the body and soul), lived and performed his austerities after instructing his mother, Devahūti, on the path of devotional service.

As mentioned in the *Journal of the Royal Asiatic Society* (1850): "The ancient city of Gaṅgā-sāgara at the eastern extremity of Bhārata-varṣa was often encroached upon by the sea. The city was also affected by occasional changes in the surface of the mouths of Gaṅgā and by the creation of new mouths. The last Kapiladeva temple that was erected in 403 A.D., survived as late as 1842 A.D., when the remaining part of the ancient city was finally and completely washed away by the waves of the sea." Today, a small shrine stands where Kapiladeva resides with Gaṅgā-mātā on his right and King Sagara on his left, where they face Sāgara-saṅgama (the confluence with the ocean) in the southern direction. According to the *Sthala Purāṇa*, when Gaṅgā divided into one hundred mouths (branches), which form the delta of Gaṅgā, one of these mouths went to the ashes of King Sagara's sixty thousand sons in the subterranean planet known as Rasātala.

According to the *Matsya Purāṇa*, Kapila Muni had another *āśrama* near the Himālayan river named Ikṣumatī; and in the *Skanda Purāṇa*, it is mentioned that Kapileśvara-tīrtha was established by Kapila Muni on the bank of the River Narmadā at Bhṛgu-kṣetra (Bharuch, Gujarat). The *Bṛhat-dharma Purāṇa* mentions that Kapilāśrama is located on the island of Sāgara near the mouth of Gaṅgā, as confirmed with the following narrations from the *Śrīmad-Bhāgavatam*.

The son of Devahūti

Some hundreds and thousands of years ago, Lord Kṛṣṇa appeared as Kapiladeva, the son of Devahūti and Kardama Muni. After Kapiladeva grew up, His father, according to the Vedic system, retired and left home to cultivate spiritual life. At that time, Devahūti approached Lord Kapiladeva and said, "My dear Kapila, I am very sick of the disturbance caused by my material senses. Due to this disturbance, my Lord, I have fallen into the abyss of ignorance. You have come as my son, but You are my *guru* because You can inform me how I can cross the ocean of nescience. Your Lordship is my only means of getting out of this darkest region of ignorance because You are my transcendental eye, which, by Your mercy only, I have attained after many, many births. You are the Supreme Personality of Godhead, the origin and Supreme Lord of all living entities. You have arisen to disseminate the rays of the sun of knowledge in order to dissipate the darkness of ignorance of the universe." After hearing of His mother's uncontaminated desire for transcendental realization, the Lord thanked her within Himself, smiled, and began to explain the path of Sāṅkhya-yoga for the transcendentalists, who are interested in self-realization. Throughout the ages, Kapiladeva's Sāṅkhya philosophy has stood the test of time, and today anyone can learn the facts about material nature, the soul, and the Supersoul by studying His teachings.

After the Supreme Personality of Godhead, Kapila, instructed His beloved mother, Devahūti, He took permission from her and left His father's hermitage, since His mission had been fulfilled. His mother soon became liberated from material bondage and she achieved the Supreme Personality of Godhead, as Supersoul, without difficulty. The place where she achieved perfection is known all over the three worlds as Siddhapada.

The narration continues in the *Śrīmad-Bhāgavatam* (3.33.34-35): "When He (Kapila Muni) was passing in the northern direction, all the celestial denizens known as Cāraṇas and Gandharvas, as well as the *munis* and the damsels of the heavenly planets, prayed and offered Him all respects. The ocean offered Him oblations and a place of residence. Even now Kapila Muni is staying there in trance for the deliverance of all the conditioned souls in the three worlds, and all the *ācāryas*, or great teachers, of the system of Sāṅkhya philosophy are worshiping Him."

Śrīla Prabhupāda comments on the same text: "It is understood that Kapila Muni first went towards the Himālayas and traced the course of the River Ganges, and He again came to the delta of the Ganges at the sea known as the Bay of Bengal. The ocean gave Him residence at a place still known as Gaṅgā-sāgara, where the River Ganges meets the sea. That place is called Gaṅgā-sāgara-tīrtha, and even today people gather there to offer respects to Kapiladeva, the original author of the Sāṅkhya system of philosophy. Unfortunately, this Sāṅkhya system has been misrepresented by an imposter who is also named Kapila, but the other system of philosophy does not tally with anything described in the Sāṅkhya of Kapila in the *Śrīmad-Bhāgavatam*."

And Lord Kṛṣṇa says in the Tenth Chapter, Twenty-Sixth Verse, of the *Bhagavad-gītā*: "Among perfected beings, I am the sage Kapila."

King Prācīnabarhi at Kapilāśrama

King Prācīnabarhi was born in the family of Mahārāja Pṛthu, who was a partial expansion of the Supreme Personality of Godhead. King Prācīnabarhi was very expert in performing various kinds of fruitive sacrifices and also was expert in the practice of mystic *yoga*. By his great qualifications, he became known as a Prajāpati. On the order of Lord Brahmā, he married the very beautiful daughter of the ocean, Śatadruti. The couple had ten children, known as the Pracetās. On their father's order, the Pracetās entered the ocean and under the guidance of Lord Śiva meditated on the Supreme Lord Viṣṇu for ten thousand years. Nārada Muni, being compassionate to everyone, visited King Prācīnabarhi and decided to instruct him about spiritual life. Explaining that fruitive activities cannot bring enjoyment and warning the King that the animals that were killed in his sacrifices were waiting for his death to avenge the pain inflicted upon them, Nārada Muni related the story of King Purañjana, as an instruction for self-realization. He elucidated vividly to the King the constitutional position of the Supreme Lord and the living entity. After thus enlightening the King, Nārada Muni departed and King Prācīnabarhi immediately decided to leave for the forest to practise austerities without even waiting for his sons to return. Leaving instructions for his sons to rule the kingdom with his ministers, he left for Kapilāśrama, where the Gaṅgā joins the sea, to undergo austerities.

As it is stated in the *Śrīmad-Bhāgavatam* (4.29.82): "Having undergone austerities and penances at Kapilāśrama, King Prācīnabarhi attained full liberation from all material designations. He constantly engaged in the transcendental loving service of the Lord and attained a spiritual position qualitatively equal to that of the Supreme Personality of Godhead."

Śrīla Prabhupāda enlightens us further in his purport on *Śrīmad-Bhāgavatam* (4.29.81): "Śrīdhara Svāmī informs us that Kapilāśrama is located at the confluence of the Ganges and the Bay of Bengal, a place now known as Gaṅgā-sāgara. This place is still famous as a place of pilgrimage, and many millions of people gather there every year on the day of Makara-saṅkrānti and take bath. It is called Kapilāśrama because of Lord Kapila's living there to perform His austerities and penances."

Keśinī and Bṛhaddhvaja

The following story has been summarized from the *Padma Purāṇa* (*Kriyā-yoga-sāra-khaṇḍa* 4): There was a demon named Bṛhaddhvaja, who was always engaged in sinful activities. Being very powerful, he kidnapped others' wives, stole others' wealth, always spoke lies, ate cow flesh, and blasphemed the Supreme Lord. He never performed a virtuous deed, even in his dreams.

Moving on his aerial chariot, he kidnapped any woman who happened to catch his fancy. Once he espied a beautiful woman, in the prime of her youth, engaged in sport and inquired who she was. The woman replied, "I am Keśinī, the wife of King Bhīṣmaka. Although I am beautiful and faultless, the King ignores me and does not take care of me. But who are you, and what are you doing here?" The demon introduced himself, asked Keśinī to accompany him, and promised to satisfy all her desires. She immediately agreed and both of them got into the chariot and proceeded with great speed into the sky. Upon reaching Gaṅgā-sāgara, the demon said to her, "Look, we have arrived at the place where Gaṅgā joins the ocean." Seeing this, Keśinī suddenly died out of fear.

Seeing her dead, the demon lamented and also died. Lord Viṣṇu then ordered His servants to bring them to Vaikuṇṭha. This holy place, where Gaṅgā meets the ocean, is so meritorious that the killer of a *brāhmaṇa* becomes purified. One who takes bath here and worships Lord Hari, or even takes *darśana* of His glorious form, is not born again. The worst sinners who die here in water, on land, or in the air attain liberation, as in the case of Bṛhaddhvaja and Keśinī.

* * *

Just as all the sacred places of pilgrimage situated on the banks of Gaṅgā have attracted countless of great personalities and pilgrims since time immemorial, Gaṅgā-sāgara is not an exception.

While Lord Balarāma was on His pilgrimage, He also visited Gaṅgā-sāgara-saṅgama, where He performed ablutions. In the *Mahābhārata*, Vaiśampāyana narrates the *tīrtha-yātrā* (pilgrimage to holy places) of the Pāṇḍavas to Janamejaya, "Yudhiṣṭhira started from the River Kausika and went in succession to all the sacred shrines. He then came to the sea where the River Gaṅgā flows into it, and there in the center of five hundred rivers, he took a holy bath. Afterwards, accompanied by his brothers, the valiant prince proceeded by the shore of the sea towards the land where the Kaliṅga tribes dwell." Also, after Lord Nityānanda spent a few days in Nīlācala (Jagannātha Purī), being totally immersed in spiritual joy, He traveled north to Gaṅgā-sāgara, before moving onwards to Mathurā and Vṛndāvana.

Book Two
Chapter Four

Gaṅgā's Final Destination

Gaṅgā's Final Destination

Now, Gaṅgā-mayī assumes a form of punishment for the sinful living entities, which is for their ultimate purification. After Bhogavatī Gaṅgā, also known as Gaṅgā of Pātāla, travels through the seven lower planetary systems (Atalaloka, Vitalaloka, Sutalaloka, Talātalaloka, Mahātalaloka, Rasātalaloka, and Pātālaloka), which are beneath the earth, she becomes known as the River Vaitaraṇī. Vaitaraṇī is also considered one of the twenty-eight Narakalokas, or hellish planets. The hellish planets lie on the southern side of the universe beneath Bhumaṇḍala and the lower planetary systems, slightly above the water of the Garbhodaka Ocean. Lord Yamarāja, the superintendent of death, who is also known as the king of the Pitās (forefathers), resides on Pitṛloka, which is located in the region between the lower planetary systems and the Garbhodaka Ocean, just before the hellish planets. The mighty River Vaitaraṇī is at the threshold of Yamarāja's city, and is therefore also called the River Yama.

Arjuna and the King of the Gandharvas

The following narration from the *Mahābhārata* (*Ādi Parva* 172) recounts the pastime when Arjuna was defending the glories of Gaṅgā-mayī and her form known as Vaitaraṇī against the King of the Gandharvas, Aṅgāraparṇa.

After the Pāṇḍavas left Ekacakra-grāma, they proceeded towards the kingdom of Pañcāla. The River Bhāgīrathī formed the dividing line between the northern and southern parts of Pañcāla. The northern capital was known as Ahicchatra, and the southern capital was Kāmpilya. While traveling north, Arjuna walked ahead of the others, torch in hand, guiding their way and guarding against wild animals. Eventually, they came to a solitary forest on the banks of the Gaṅgā.

At that solitary place the proud King of the Gandharvas, known as Aṅgāraparṇa, was sporting with his wives in the delightful waters of Gaṅgā. When the King of the

Gandharvas heard the Pāṇḍavas approach the river, he became inflamed with wrath. Upon meeting the Pāṇḍavas, Aṅgāraparṇa drew his frightful bow and said, "This twilight part of the day is for the Yakṣas (ghosts), Gandharvas, and Rākṣasas to roam freely at will. Persons acquainted with the *Vedas* never applaud a man who approaches a pool of water at this time of the day, for both we and the Rākṣasas slay such fools. Stay at a distance and approach me not. Do you not know that I am bathing in the waters of the Bhāgīrathī? Do you not know that I am proud and haughty, being the friend of Kuvera? This is my forest on the banks of Gaṅgā. I sport here to gratify my senses, and this forest is also named after me. Neither the demigods nor other Gandharvas can come here. How dare you approach me, since I am the brighest jewel on the crown of Kuvera!"

Hearing the words of the Gandharva, Arjuna then said, "O stupid fool, whether it be day, night, or twilight, who can bar others from the ocean, the sides of the Himālayas, or this river? There is no special time for anyone to come to the Gaṅgā, the foremost of all rivers. This Gaṅgā, issuing out of the golden peaks of Himavat (Himālayas) in seven streams, falls into the waters of the ocean. Those who drink the waters of these seven streams—Gaṅgā, Yamunā, Sarasvatī, Vitastā, Sarayū, Gomatī, and Gaṇḍakī—are cleansed of all sins. O Gandharva, this sacred Gaṅgā flows through the celestial region and is called Mandākinī. Again it appears in the region of the *pitṛs* (Pitṛloka) as Vaitaraṇī, which is extremely difficult for sinners to cross. This auspicious celestial river, which is capable of leading one to the spiritual world, is free from all dangers. Why do you then desire to bar us from it? This act of yours does not agree with eternal virtuous principles. Disregarding your words, why should we not touch these sacred waters of Bhāgīrathī, which are free from all dangers and from which none can bar us?"

After Aṅgāraparṇa heard Arjuna's words, he became angry, drew his bow, and began shooting arrows like venomous snakes at the Pāṇḍavas. Then Dhanañjaya (Arjuna) warded off all the arrows and said, "O Gandharva, do not try to scare those skilled in using weapons. You are superior in prowess to most men, therefore, I will use a celestial weapon. Bṛhaspati, the revered preceptor of Indra, gave this fiery weapon to Bharadvāja, from whom it was then obtained by Agnivesa. After Droṇācārya, my preceptor, received it from him, he gave it me."

Arjuna then hurled the blazing weapon at the Gandharva's chariot. By the force of that weapon, Aṅgāraparṇa fell unconscious from his chariot. Arjuna seized him by the hair and dragged the unconscious Gandharva towards the other Pāṇḍavas. While holding him, one of the Gandharva's wives, Kumbinasi, who desired to save her husband, approached Arjuna. She begged him to free her husband unharmed. Yudhiṣṭhira Mahārāja then said to Arjuna, "O slayer of foes, O child, who would slay a foe who has been vanquished in fight, who has been deprived of fame, who is protected by a woman, and who has no power?" Arjuna replied, "Keep your life, O Gandharva! Go and grieve not. Yudhiṣṭhira, the King of the Kurus, has commanded me to show you mercy."

Crossing the River Vaitaraṇī

In the *Śrīmad-Bhāgavatam* (5.26.23), we learn of the fearsome form of Gaṅgā known as Vaitaraṇī: "A person who is born into a responsible family—such as a *kṣatriya*, a member of royalty or a government servant—but who neglects to execute his prescribed duties according to religious principles, and who thus becomes degraded, falls down at the time of death into the river of hell known as Vaitaraṇī. This river, which is a moat surrounding hell, is full of ferocious aquatic animals. When a sinful man is thrown into the River Vaitaraṇī, the aquatic animals there immediately begin to eat him, but because of his extremely sinful life, he does not leave his body. He constantly remembers his sinful activities and suffers terribly in that river, which is full of stool, urine, pus, blood, hair, nails, bones, marrow, flesh, and fat."

In the *Garuḍa Purāṇa* (*Preta-kāṇḍa* 47), Lord Kṛṣṇa tells Garuḍa how sinful living entities have to cross over the River Vaitaraṇī before reaching the abode of Yamarāja: "Listen to the magnitude of the dreadful Vaitaraṇī, which is one hundred *yojanas* (800 miles) wide. This river is impassable and foul smelling, so to the sinner, it is terrifying even at first sight. It is full of putrid blood with sediments and marshy deposits of flesh. When a sinner arrives, the river assumes the form of melted ghee. It abounds in worms and flesh brought by vultures. It is full of crocodiles, fish with hard razor-sharp tails, and aquatic creatures capable of piercing flesh. There are twelve suns blazing, while the sinful people groan aloud and fall into the river. All mortals must encounter that mighty river. Persons who made gifts in their lifetime, however, can easily cross over the river. Those who have offended their mothers, preceptors, or priests can remain there perpetually. The same for those who forsake their chaste, virtuous, noble, and faultless wives. Those who deceive their masters, friends, sages, women, children, cripples, and others get submerged in the putrid slough and groan there painfully. One who promises a donation to a *brāhmaṇa* but does not give it, one who defiles a sacrifice, one who rapes a noble woman, one who slanders others, one who interrupts religious discourses, one who is guilty of perjury, one who is a wine addict, and one who invites a *brāhmaṇa* but refuses to feed him: these stay there permanently. A miser, an atheist, a worthless wretch, a person extremely furious and irritated, a person who considers his own words authoritative, a person who contradicts what others say, a haughty egoist, a swaggerer, and an ungrateful treacherous fellow: all these persons stay in the River Vaitaraṇī for an indefinite period.

"O son of Kaśyapa, if one is fortunate to cross over the Vaitaraṇī, it is due to some pious activity. If a person has donated a *vaitaraṇī* cow (a cow that is either black or tawny with black udders, with horns covered in gold and its hooves in silver, as well as two black clothes that adorn the cow) at the time of death, the river assumes a pleasant form that he is able to cross over.

"I shall also mention the various auspicious rites that constitute merit in the three worlds. Profit and success are theirs whose hearts are set on Lord Viṣṇu. *Dharma* (religious principles) wins, not *adharma* (irreligious principles); truth wins, not falsehood; forgiveness wins, not anger; Lord Viṣṇu wins, not the demons. Auspiciousness is Lord Viṣṇu. Auspiciousness is the Lord who has Garuḍa for His carrier. Auspiciousness is the Lord whose eyes resemble the blue lotus. The Lord is the ocean of all auspiciousness. Meditation on Lord Viṣṇu, worship of the sacred River Gaṅgā, and worship of the *brāhmaṇas*—these three constitute the quintessence of merit in the three worlds."

The River Vaitaraṇī is mentioned again in the *Garuḍa Purāṇa* (*Preta-kāṇḍa* 16.25-29): "When reaching the River Vaitaraṇī, the boatmen approach the living entity and say, 'O traveler, give us a liberal fee, then we shall row you across the river.' If the living entity has donated a *vaitaraṇī* cow, he is rowed across the river. The gift of a cow at the time of death is called *vaitaraṇī*, which gives relief to the departed soul. The gift of a *vaitaraṇī* cow destroys his sins and takes him to the region of Lord Viṣṇu. If the *vaitaraṇī* cow is not gifted, the departed soul is drowned in that river."

Book Two
Chapter Five

Service in the Holy Dhāma
(*Dhāma-sevā*)

Service in the Holy Dhāma
(*dhāma-sevā*)

In the *Pañcarātra Pradīpa* it is stated: "You should serve a sacred place like Mathurā, Vṛndāvana, Purī, or Dvārakā and the banks of the Yamunā or Gaṅgā. These are the places where the Lord resides and performs wonderful pastimes. The *dhāma* is also a manifestation of the *sat* potency (*sandhinī-śakti*), or the energy manifesting eternal existence, and provides the support for the Lord's appearance and pastimes. The *dhāma*, which is under Lord Balarāma's supervision, purifies the fallen souls.

"Service to the holy *dhāma* consists of hearing about the *dhāma*, remembering the *dhāma*, glorifying the *dhāma*, desiring to visit the *dhāma*, observing the *dhāma* from afar, going toward the *dhāma*, circumambulating the *dhāma*, touching the *dhāma*, taking the *dhāma* as one's shelter, and repairing, beautifying, and cleaning the *dhāma*. If you are fortunate and pure enough to reside permanently in the Lord's *dhāma*, you will daily perform many aspects of *sevā* (*nitya-dhāma-kriya*), whereas if you do not permanently reside in the *dhāma*, *sevā* will be more occasional. However, even if you do not live in the *dhāma*, you may daily hear about the *dhāma*, glorify the *dhāma*, and desire to reside in the *dhāma*.

"As pilgrims, we must understand that a visit to the holy *dhāma* is not a vacation from devotional service. Rather, devotional service rendered in the holy *dhāma* earns one a hundred or a thousand times more benefit than the same service rendered outside the *dhāma*."

Śrīla Prabhupāda has written in his purports to the *Śrī Caitanya-caritāmṛta* (*Ādi* 5.19-20): "One should not discriminate between the *dhāmas* on the earth and those in the spiritual sky, thinking those on earth to be material and the original abodes to be spiritual. All of them are spiritual. Only for us, who cannot experience anything beyond matter in our present conditioned state, do the *dhāmas* and the Lord Himself, in His *arca* (Deity) form, appear before us resembling matter to give us the facility to see spirit with material eyes. In the beginning this may be difficult for a neophyte to understand, but in due course, when one is advanced in devotional service, it will be easier, and he will appreciate the Lord's presence in these tangible forms. By the grace of the Lord, His *dhāmas* and He Himself can all be present simultaneously, without losing their original importance. Only when one fully develops in affection and love of Godhead can one see the *dhāmas* in their original appearance"

And in his purport to *Śrīmad-Bhāgavatam* (7.5.23-24) Śrīla Prabhupāda has written: "According to one's taste and strength, hearing, chanting, and remembrance may be followed by *pāda-sevanam*. One attains the perfection of remembering when one constantly thinks of the lotus feet of the Lord. Being intensely attached to thinking of the Lord's lotus feet is called *pāda-sevanam*. When one is practically adherent to the process of *pāda-sevanam*, this process gradually includes other processes, such as seeing the form of the Lord, touching the form of the Lord, circumambulating the form or temple of the Lord, visiting such places as Jagannātha Purī, Dvārakā, and Mathurā to see the Lord's form, and bathing in the Ganges or Yamunā. Bathing in the Ganges and serving a pure Vaiṣṇava are also known as *tadīya-upāsanam*. This is also *pāda-sevanam*. The word *tadīya* means, 'in relationship with the Lord'. Service to the Vaiṣṇava, Tulasī, Ganges and Yamunā are included in *pāda-sevanam*. All these processes of *pāda-sevanam* help one advance in spiritual life very quickly."

In the *Padma Purāṇa* (*Sṛṣṭi-khaṇḍa* 11.81) it is stated: "Truth is a holy place, compassion is a holy place, restraint of the senses is a holy place, and in the house of those who observe *varṇāśrama-dharma*, tranquility is said to be a holy place."

1) Taking a Bath (*snāna*)

It is stated in the *Pañcarātra Pradipa*: "The *Kūrma Purāṇa* says that without taking the *prātaḥ-snāna* (bath before sunrise) one remains impure and cannot perform any of the daily activities a civilized person must perform, such as *japa*, *homa*, and Deity worship. If a person eats without having bathed, he is said to be eating only filth, for everything he touches becomes as impure as he is. The *Padma Purāṇa* declares that one who does not bathe in the morning is a sinner fit to suffer in hell. *Prātaḥ-snāna* is compulsory for all, except those who are ill. In Vedic culture, bathing is considered a sacred act to be accompanied by meditation on the Lord and recitation of prayers.

"The scriptures describe the benefits of taking a cold bath early in the morning. Such a bath can purify even a sinner, for it has the power to wash away all external and internal contaminations. Whereas a warm water bath cleanses physically, cold water revitalizes the subtle body, removing the influence of sleep and dreams. A cold bath also gives strength, sensitivity, longevity, effulgence, and purity. Taking an early morning cold bath increases one's knowledge and determination and affords peace of mind. It removes unhappiness, lamentation, degradation, and bad thoughts. In short, it counteracts all the ill effects of sin.

"At night the nine holes of the body become filled with waste products, which are continuously produced. The early morning bath most effectively removes all this dirt so that the body can begin its daily activities in a fresh state. In this way the early morning bath has positive physical, mental, and spiritual effects and is therefore highly glorified in the scriptures.

"There are seven types of bath: *pārthiva-snāna* (using earth); *varuṇa-snāna* (using water); *āgneya-snāna* (using ashes from a sacrificial fire); *vāyavya-snāna* (contacting air filled with dust raised by cows); *divya-snāna* (taking an ethereal bath in the rain that falls while the sun is shining); *mantra-snāna* (chanting appropriate verses while sprinkling oneself with water); and *mānasika-snāna* (meditating on Viṣṇu). Using different elements, all these types of bath purify the body of contamination. However, the daily bath is usually the *vāruṇa-snāna*.

"Different sources of water have different powers to cleanse. Thus there is a grading of water according to source. In order of preference, beginning with the best, one should bathe in the Gaṅgā or Yamunā; in another holy river; at a *tīrtha* (such as the ocean at Jagannātha Purī); a river that runs directly into the sea (that is, not a tributary); in any river; canal; pond; lake; waterfall; or water drawn from a well, or any clean water. Traditionally, houses were conveniently located near bathing *ghāṭas* on a river or lake, or they had their own private pond for bathing, since bathing was an important part of daily life. But nowadays we generally take a bath where there is a convenient source of clean water.

"Śrīla Prabhupāda writes in his purport on the *Śrī Caitanya-caritāmṛta* (*Madhya* 24.331): 'Actually, householders and *vānaprasthas* should bathe two times a day (*prātar-madhyāhnayoḥ snānaṁ vānaprastha-gṛhasthayoḥ*). A *sannyāsī* should bathe three times daily, and a *brahmacārī* may take only one bath a day. Whenever a person is not able to bathe in water, he can bathe by chanting the Hare Kṛṣṇa *mantra*.'

"Besides taking a water bath in the morning, at noon, and in the evening, one must take such a bath after the following: brushing the teeth; shaving; cutting the fingernails or toenails; having sex; going to the crematorium; touching a woman who is in her period of contamination or who has just borne a child; or touching a naked person, a bearer of a dead body, or a sinful person. Apart from the obvious sanitary effects of bathing after these events, bathing restores the equilibrium to subtle functions of the body which suffer disruption by them."

In the *Śrīmad-Bhāgavatam* (1.8.1-2), Sūta Gosvāmī says: "Thereafter the Pāṇḍavas, desiring to deliver water to the dead relatives who had desired it, went to the Ganges with Draupadī. The ladies walked in front. Having lamented over them and sufficiently offered Ganges water, they bathed in the Ganges, whose water is sanctified due to being mixed with the dust of the lotus feet of the Lord."

Śrīla Prabhupāda writes on the same verse: "To date it is the custom in Hindu society to go to the Ganges or any other sacred river to take bath when death occurs in the family. Each of the family members pours out a potful of the Ganges water for the departed soul and walks in a procession, with the ladies in the front. The Pāṇḍavas also followed the rules more than five thousand years ago. Lord Kṛṣṇa, being a cousin of the Pāṇḍavas, was also amongst the family members."

In the *Garuḍa Purāṇa* (*Ācāra-kāṇḍa* 213) it is stated: "Like a dip in the holy Gaṅgā, the morning ablutions give pleasure to the mind, increase beauty and fortune, and remove sorrow and misery. While taking bath in the Gaṅgā, one should recite the following prayer for purification: 'I am taking bath in you, O Gaṅgā, to remove these tenfold sins of mine: 1) The sins of not giving charity, 2) doing forbidden acts, 3) committing violence, 4) committing adultery, 5) speaking harsh words, 6) uttering falsehood, 7) speaking scandalous words, 8) speaking nonsensical words, 9) coveting another man's wealth, 10) and wishing evil of others.'"

There are no hard and fast rules regarding how one should take a bath in Gaṅgā; she is our loving mother who is always ready to help and guide everyone. We should approach Gaṅgā in a humble and obedient mood, offer full obeisances to her, place three drops of water on our heads, and then ask her to kindly cleanse our materially conditioned hearts, which prevent us from engaging in pure devotional service. She is also kind enough to teach us the chanting of Lord Kṛṣṇa's names, provided we are willing to accept her offer.

In the *Śrī Hari-bhakti-vilāsa*, it is recommended that before taking bath, we should beg Gaṅgā for permission to enter her waters by saying: *oṁ gaṅge devi jagan-mātā padābhyāṁ salilaṁ tava spṛśāmīty aparadhaṁ me prasannā kṣantum arhasi*. Then while bathing, we should ask her for purification by reciting: *viṣṇu-pada-prasūtāsi vaiṣṇavī viṣṇu-devatā pāhi nas tvenasas tasmād ajanma-maraṇānti kāt*.

There are several other prayers that can be chanted. There is a simple prayer for offering obeisances to her: *oṁ namo daśaharāyai nārāyaṇyai gaṅgāyai namaḥ*, which also removes the tenfold sins previously mentioned. The *Gaṅgā-praṇāma* prayer: *sadyaḥ pātaka-saṁhantrī sadhyo duḥkha-vināśinī sukhadā mokṣadā gaṅgā gaṅgaiva paramā gatiḥ*, which glorifies and describes Gaṅgā's mercy, is also highly recommended. Many devotees chant: *gaṅge ca yamune caiva godāvari sarasvatī narmade sindho kāveri jale 'smin sannidhiṁ kuru*, which is a prayer requesting other sacred rivers to be also present and to purify the bather. The Gayatri *mantra* is also very auspicious to chant while bathing. In the *Skanda Purana*, *Kāśi-khaṇḍa*, *Pūrvārdha* 29, one is advised to chant the *Gaṅgā-sahasra-nāma* (Thousand Names of Gaṅgā), if one is unable to bathe in the Gaṅgā, due to being physically disabled or living in a foreign land.

As already mentioned, Gaṅgā is extremely pleased when we simply offer her own water back to her. How more merciful can one be? Gaṅgā is only requesting us for some love and devotion, then she will free us from material bondage. In the Rishikesh/Haridvāra area, the traditional offering to Gaṅgā consists of flowers, incense, and a ghee wick placed inside a boat-shaped leaf. Prayers are chanted as the offering is lit and set on top of the water. The offering then floats downstream in the river's current. As individual devotees make their offerings, they sometimes chant the one hundred and eight names of Gaṅgā. Every evening in these two holy places, a special Gaṅgā-pūjā is offered with prayers and ghee lamps. Sometimes a special *Gaṅgājī ki ārati* song is played over a loudspeaker and the public sings along, and sometimes the *Gaṅgā-laharī* by Paṇḍita Jagannātha is chanted.

Lord Śiva and Gaṅgā have a very special and auspicious relationship. It is recommended in the scriptures that upon bathing in Gaṅgā, we should also offer some of her water to Lord Śiva in his form as a *liṅga*. Along the banks of the Gaṅgā there are numerous Śiva temples where the devotees can make their offering. If a temple is not nearby, then any stone situated alongside the banks of Gaṅgā can be used as a *liṅga*, because these stones also represent Lord Śiva. While making our offering, we should request Lord Śiva to assist us on our path of devotional service.

The most important element in bathing, regardless of the time, place, or circumstance, is to remember Lord Kṛṣṇa and to chant the Hare Kṛṣṇa *mahā-mantra*: Hare Kṛṣṇa, Hare Kṛṣṇa, Kṛṣṇa Kṛṣṇa, Hare Hare/ Hare Rāma, Hare Rāma, Rāma Rāma, Hare Hare. Though all other elements may be overlooked, these two acts should always be performed while bathing. In this way, the bath retains its sacred nature.

2) Chanting Hare Kṛṣṇa (*nāma-japa*)

Śrī Caitanya Mahāprabhu has clearly instructed everyone how to chant in the third verse of His *Śrī Śrī Śikṣāṣṭaka*: "One should

chant the holy name of the Lord in a humble state of mind, thinking oneself lower than the straw in the street. One should be more tolerant than a tree, devoid of all sense of false prestige and ready to offer all respect to others. In such a state of mind one can chant the holy name of the Lord constantly."

Regarding the beginning process of chanting, Śrīla Prabhupāda explains that there is no restriction in chanting the holy name of the Lord. He writes, "Even when you are walking, you can softly chant Hare Kṛṣṇa, Hare Kṛṣṇa, or even when you are on the bus going to somewhere you can also chant. When you are working with your hands, you can also chant, and when you are resting or going to take rest you can also chant. Even in your toilet room while taking bath you can also chant. In this way there is no limitation or restriction for chanting the holy name of God, Kṛṣṇa, and His energy, Harā. In doing this business there is no loss, but there is very great gain, which is transcendental realization."

Still, there is a proper posture, place, and time to chant. Śrīla Prabhupāda was very strict about how the devotees carried themselves while chanting. On one occasion, while chanting *japa* with a group of devotees, he instructed one of them, "Sit properly!" While chanting *japa*, one should sit with one's back erect and legs crossed and covered, not spread out. One should not lie down while chanting *japa*. It is also recommended to sit on an *āsana* (seat) facing east.

One should chant *japa* in front of a Deity of Lord Kṛṣṇa or Viṣṇu, in a temple of the Lord (or in any place where He is worshiped), in front of a sacred *tulasī* plant, or by the side of a sacred river, such as the Gaṅgā. Śrīla Prabhupāda writes, "Chanting *japa* should be done early in the morning with full concentration preferably during the *brāhma-muhūrta* hour. Concentrate fully on the sound vibration of the *mantra*, pronouncing each name distinctly and gradually your speed in chanting will increase naturally. Do not worry so much about chanting fast; most important is the hearing."

In conclusion, Śrīla Prabhupāda writes in his purport on the *Śrīmad-Bhāgavatam* (6.5.27-28): "It is apparent that the chanting of the *mahā-mantra* or the Vedic *mantras* must be accompanied by severe austerities. In Kali-yuga, people cannot undergo severe austerities like those mentioned herein, such as drinking only water and eating only air for many months. One cannot imitate such a process. But at least one must undergo some austerity by giving up four unwanted principles, namely illicit sex, meat eating, intoxication, and gambling. Anyone can easily practice this *tapasya* (austerity), and then the chanting of the Hare Kṛṣṇa *mantra* will be effective without delay. One should not give up the process of austerity. If possible, one should bathe in the waters of the Ganges or Yamunā, or in the absence of the Ganges and Yamunā one may bathe in the water of the sea. This is an item of austerity. Our Kṛṣṇa consciousness movement has therefore established two very large centers, one in Vṛndāvana and the other in Māyāpur, Navadvīpa. There one may bathe in the Ganges or Yamunā, chant the Hare Kṛṣṇa *mantra* and thus become perfect and return home, back to Godhead."

HARE KṚṢṆA HARE KṚṢṆA
KṚṢṆA KṚṢṆA HARE HARE
HARE RĀMA HARE RĀMA
RĀMA RĀMA HARE HARE

Book Two
Chapter Six

Gaṅgā Realizations

Gaṅgā Realizations

The scope of this chapter is unlimited. What has been presented herein barely touches upon the ocean of personal testimonies or realizations from those who have been inspired by Gaṅgā-mayi. If more time were available to develop this chapter, it could easily turn into volumes of personal realizations from practically everyone who has had some contact with Gaṅgā-mayi. Whether it be residents, *sādhus*, pilgrims, visitors (regardless of religious faith), or even fishermen and factory workers, Gaṅgā-mayi has some way or other entered into their hearts. Some *sādhus* undertake the long pilgrimage of walking along the Gaṅgā's riverbanks by foot, beginning at the source at Gomukha and hiking towards the Bay of Bengal at Gaṅgā-sāgara, before returning to Gomukha on the opposite bank. In the *Śrī Garga-saṁhitā*, it is stated: "A person who chants the name 'Gaṅgā!' and travels the sixteen hundred mile length of the earthly Gaṅgā becomes free of all sins and enters the realm of Lord Viṣṇu." His experiences would be fathomless and the inter-action with the variety of people who reside on her banks would be incredible. Moreover, were one able to capture on film the different moods and expressions during the six seasons it would tell thousands of stories. The following realizations are just a glimpse at our mother Gaṅgā's mercy.

Lessons from Mother Gaṅgā

Swami Sivānanda, The Divine Life Society, Rishikesh

"Gaṅgā starts from Gaṅgotri in the Himālayas. She encounters many obstacles on her way, but she finally reaches the goal, the Ocean. Similarly, the *sadhaka* (spiritual candidate) should never give up his struggle, however insurmountable the obstacles in the path may appear to be. All difficulties and obstacles will be removed through the grace of the Lord if that person is sincere in *yoga* practices, then he will reach the goal...

"Gaṅgā always gives you cool, pure water. It does not expect anything from you in return. The sun sheds its light on all without anticipating any reward. Derive lessons from

them. Always give. Ask nothing in return. Expect nothing in return. Do not expect appreciation, approbation, or recognition...A rogue and a saint can drink the water of Gaṅgā. The sun sheds its light on the wicked and the virtuous. The mango tree gives its fruits both for the caretaker and the man who cuts its branches. Develop equal vision as found in the Gaṅgā, the sun, and the mango tree...Gaṅgā is my mother. The Himālayas are my father. I owe all my learning and attainments to mother Gaṅgā and father Himālayas."

LIFE AND DEATH WITH MOTHER GAṄGĀ

H. H. Lokanātha Swami, ISKCON India

I have two matter of life and death realizations. The first one was in July, 1976. I was part of the Nitāi-Gaura World Traveling Saṅkīrtana Party. We had just gone through several towns and reached Rishikesh at the place called Muni-ki-reti. This place is located outside of Rishikesh town and it contains a lot of āśramas. We had taken our party's buses right onto the bank of Gaṅgā. It was a warm day, and we were naturally there to swim in the cooling sacred waters of Gaṅgā.

At that part of the Gaṅgā where we stopped, her waters were wide and flowed slowly. There were thirty or so devotees. Haṁsadūta and I were the sannyāsīs, and the rest were mostly brahmacārīs. We offered our obeisances, sprinkled water on our heads, and entered the river. Soon we were in sportive mood and enjoyed swimming in the heat of the day. At one point, Haṁsadūta and I broke away from the group as we talked and swam a short distance from the rest of the devotees.

Soon we found the still water in which we were enjoying was moving a little faster. The current was getting stronger, and before we realized it, we were being swept downstream into a trouble zone. The still waters of the wide Gaṅgā had now turned into a narrow funnel of shallow rapids flowing down hill and our ride was getting bumpier. We had just been enjoying the gentle momentum of the increasing current, but now that had changed and things were starting to get serious and a bit out of hand. We were getting smashed and bashed against the large boulders under the water by the force of the current. We were being tossed into rock after rock, all of different sizes. We were trying to maneuver and avoid the beating, but we had lost control. We were completely at the mercy of mother Gaṅgā. She was in command.

By now we started sincerely crying for help, shouting "Hari bol! Hari bol!" Maybe our shouts reached the ears of the water sporting brahmacārīs, or maybe they just noticed that the two of us were not to be seen anymore. They somehow realized that we were being carried away, so they all got out of the water and started running along the bank. There was no way they could reach us from the bank and to get in the water would mean trouble for them too. We were at least relieved to know that they had taken note of our plight, as they began screaming and hopefully praying for us. By this time we were getting badly beaten by the rocks. Sometimes our head would go first and then our feet. We were pretty fatigued by now, and our bodies were aching. The current wasn't showing any signs of slowing down. It was like a never-ending roller-coaster ride. For sure one moment seemed like 12 years or more.

Luckily we were going down together, side by side, as that was some solace. Misery loves company. We had no idea when or if at all our ride would end. The thought that this could be the end of our lives kept crossing my mind. The river could end up in a waterfall, or we could just end up with broken bones. This was our first visit to Rishikesh, so we had no idea where the river went. Maybe it would be our good fortune to leave our bodies here. Usually a few drops of Gaṅgā water are placed into the mouth of a dying man, but here we were with our mouths full of water! While trying to inhale air, we were inhaling some water also. The sacred water was inside and outside of us as well. After all, this is not the worst time and place to leave the bag of flesh and bones.

Finally things started changing for the better. All this time, the *brahmacārīs* continued following us along the banks. They were trying to enter at different points, but it was impossible with the strong current. Then Gaṅgā's waters began to slow down. What we thought was unending was ending. The river had now come to a kind of flat area, the boys were able to jump in, and we were able to move towards them. Eventually we luckily reached the banks of Gaṅgā. We had no energy even to sit. There was no question of walking, since our bodies were bruised all over. We were completely exhausted as we just lay there on the lap of mother Gaṅgā. The Lord and mother Gaṅgā gave us our lives back that day! Devotees started doing *kirtana* to give us relief and celebrate our rescue. A vote of thanks was offered to mother Gaṅgā for returning their Nitāi-Gaura World Traveling Saṅkirtana Party leaders alive.

The second incident occurred in the summer of 1987. It took place as Śrīla Prabhupāda's Saṅkīrtana Padayātrā was en route to Badarikāśrama. The Padayātrā party had just reached Viṣṇu-prayāga, which is just before Badarikāśrama. We were traveling without an ox cart in this steep, mountainous area, so we were carrying our small Gaura-Nitāi Deities on a palanquin and, of course, doing *kirtana* throughout the walk. In the middle of the day we decided to stop for a holy dip at the sacred confluence where the Alakanandā meets the Viṣṇu Gaṅgā. We found a spot where there was a big rock in the Alakanandā. The rock wasn't right in the middle, but slightly to one side. We walked across the river to the big rock, which was like a small island surrounded by water. Our party landed there, and we kept our Deities on the top of this rock. Devotees got ready to take bath in the chilly water. The current was very swift and there were many rocks around. As we were all in the middle of our transcendental experience of bathing on top of the Himālayan mountains, we looked up and saw the sun, which is a manifestation of Lord Kṛṣṇa. Then we looked and saw the surrounding Himālayan mountains, which is another manifestation of Kṛṣṇa, and as we looked down, we saw the River Gaṅgā, which is yet another manifestation of the Lord. Amidst all of these manifestations of the Lord, we were feeling spiritually high and kind of elated.

The devotees were all spread out as they took their baths, when suddenly one of my Godbrothers, Toṣaṇa Kṛṣṇa Prabhu, slipped and fell in the cold waters. It was not so deep, but the waters were very swift and the point where he had fallen was like a whirlpool that pulled him under. He was struggling to get closer to our rock to pull himself out, but he was repeatedly pulled under. The other devotees were too far away to hear him screaming and crying for help above the noise of the rushing water.

Being the closest at that moment, I extended my hand, but I was not close enough to reach his hand. It was falling just a few inches short. He was drowning: going under, then coming up. You could see expressions of desperation on his face, like those of a dying man. I had to stay fixed where I was otherwise I too could easily go in. So there was no way I could go forward, as the rock I was on was not flat. I had to make sure I was on firm ground. He would get closer and we thought he would manage to catch hold of my hand, and then he would be pushed back and again.

He was trying with all his might: He would almost get there, but not quite make it. By this time more devotees had come around. There was nothing anyone could do. He just had to make the effort himself. God helps those who help themselves, so God helped. Suddenly the water pushed him forward and there was a meeting of our hands. With the push of the current, I pulled him out; then other devotees joined the rescue, finally getting him clear of the danger. It was like a miracle, a miraculous rescue. I had a thin body, and he had a well built, good-sized body, and the current was against him, so what chance was there of getting him out? By attempting to save him, I was risking my own life. It was a foolish attempt, but I felt duty bound. And if he were swept away there was no chance of his survival. In the midst of all these rocks, we could see in the distance, just a few hundred metres away, there was a cliff with waterfalls. We could not see the waters, as they abruptly disappeared.

Toṣaṇa Kṛṣṇa Prabhu was able to come forward and offer his obeisances to Nitāi-Gaurasundara and Śrīla Prabhupāda. He thanked the Lord and His devotees that he was saved. So this realization showed us how insignificant and helpless we are in a near death experience. I also thanked the Lord and Gaṅgā for making me an instrument in saving my Godbrother. There was a good chance of Toṣaṇa Kṛṣṇa's dragging me into the water. That could have happened, but Gaṅgā saved both of us.

Thus, by the mercy of mother Gaṅgā, I was saved twice. Since she has given me two births, I owe my life to our mother, and I would like to serve her by serving Gaurāṅga Mahāprabhu. These realizations are all related and connected intimately with Gaṅgā. They happened in the midst of her waters, certainly in relationship with her. Hence they should not be treated as a mundane occurence.

Gaṅgā-mayī ki jai jai jai!!!

ON THE BANKS OF MOTHER GAṄGĀ

H.H. Śacīnandana Swami, ISKCON Germany

One of my fondest memories of traveling in India is connected with meeting mother Gaṅgā for the first time. It was around 1975 when I first went to Śrīdhāma Māyāpur. I can still remember going to the Gaṅgā, putting my towel on, and entering her cooling waters. Soon, I was encircled by mother Gaṅgā and had the feeling that I was surrounded by a loving and caring personality. After swimming a little, I went back into waist deep water and felt like offering something in return to mother Gaṅgā. I immediately remembered that one can offer Gaṅgā-jala back to Gaṅgā-mayī, and she will accept the loving feeling. But it felt so good and her personality was so clear that I decided to remain in waist deep water and chant my Gāyatrī *mantra*. Never before had I chanted the Gāyatrī *mantra* with such concentration. As I ended the last line in deep meditation, I heard the sound of a distant temple bell and the holy name wavering over her divine waters. While the sun was setting over Gaṅgā, it became visible that she was being bathed in the sun's golden colors, appearing like liquid gold. When I returned to the bank of Gaṅgā, I contemplated my experience and concluded that this was not an ordinary river. I had felt the divine presence of a divine personality, who had helped to develop my Kṛṣṇa consciousness.

Gaṅgā has been flowing since time immemorial. Her course covers more than 2,510 kilometres, beginning from her origin in this world at Gaṅgotrī, down to the ocean at the Bay of Bengal. During her long journey, twenty-nine major cities and seventy towns are annually depositing more than one billion litres of wastewater into her. In addition to this, numerous dead human and animal bodies are brought to 'Mother Gaṅgā', as the Indians respectfully call her. But still she remains untouched.* All the pilgrims who bathe in her can experience how she purifies one and still does not become contaminated. While sitting in the breeze that blows over her transcendental waters, all material anxieties and other contaminations in the mind leave forever. In the *Śrīmad-Bhāgavatam* (5.17.1), it is stated: "...Every living being can immediately purify his mind of material contamination by touching the transcendental waters of the Ganges, yet its waters remain ever pure. Because the Ganges directly touches the lotus feet of the Lord before descending within this universe, she is called Viṣṇupadī..."

Mother Gaṅgā has different dimensions. On one level she is simply H_2O (composition of water). On another level she is a divine personality, and on yet another level she is liquid love of God. In this regard she is similar to a book. On one level the book is weighing maybe 1.5 kilograms. If we study a book on another level, it is a combination of letters that appear in ever-changing variations. On a third level, however, the book is a source of information, inspiration, and motivation. It depends on what level we want to make contact. An ignorant person can misuse a book simply as a weight to weigh vegetables; similarly one can understand Gaṅgā water to be just ordinary water. However, a more intelligent person will be able to take full benefit of mother Gaṅgā to reawaken his original Kṛṣṇa consciousness.

In order to understand mother Gaṅgā more profoundly and deeply, it is important to have a worshipful attitude. In Haridvāra, between 6 and 7 p.m. daily, the devotees of Gaṅgā join together for Gaṅgā-pūjā. Thousands of devotees, pilgrims, and visitors watch the *pūjāris* offer seven one-metre high ghee lamps to mother Gaṅgā. Many people also participate in this *pūjā* by offering their own small lamps. It is an indescribable scene of worship and reciprocation. As the ghee lamps circulate and the devotees chant prayers that rise to the sky, it almost appears

---

*The amazing purifying potency of the River Gaṅgā has been scientifically investigated. Since the scientists do not understand or accept the spiritual potency of Gaṅgā water, they have not been able to find satisfactory explanations why mother Gaṅgā is so purifying. From the *Vedas*, we know that one of the symptoms of a transcendental personality is that he is "all-purifying". "All-purifying" means: anything contaminated that comes in contact with that personality is immediately purified from all impurities.

Many scientists have discovered that the water of Gaṅgā does not rot or become stagnant, even after a long time in storage. What follows is a list of five scientists and their findings:

1. The British physicist, C.E. Nelson, observed that Gaṅgā water which was taken from the Hughli (the branch of Gaṅgā in Calcutta), one of the most contaminated mouths, remained fresh during the whole journey aboard the ships that returned to England.

2. The British physicist, E. Hanbury Hankin, reported in the French Journal "*Annales de l'Institut Pasteur*", that cholera germs which were put into Gaṅgā water died within three hours, while they were still further developing in distilled water even after forty-eight hours.

3. The French scientist, Herelle, was astonished to find out that no trace of any germs was found in Gaṅgā water even a few centimetres away from bodies of people who had died from dysentery or cholera, although one would expect to find millions of germs.

4. Recently, D. S. Bhargaba, an Indian environmentalist, measured the remarkable self-purifying capacity of Gaṅgā. She reduced the biochemical need of oxygen in Gaṅgā compared to other rivers, and it appears that Gaṅgā can purify contamination fifteen to twenty times faster than any other river.

5. The laboratory experiments of Dr. Lt. Ratan (Physiologist, Institute of Medicine, Naval Hospital, Asvini, Mumbai) reveal that Gaṅgā water contains diatoms, a type of algae, which injects other harmful bacteria and does not allow the growth of bacillus-coli, which causes diarrhea, etc., and prevents water from becoming spoiled for years.

that mother Gaṅgā is bound to come out of the river.

In this connection, there is a very nice *līlā* about mother Gaṅgā. A short time before Śrī Caitanya Mahāprabhu appeared, a *brāhmaṇa* priest entered the river Gaṅgā to chant his Gāyatrī *mantra*. While he was murmuring the syllables, he noticed some unusual behavior in the river. She first receded, so that finally the water was only knee deep. Then Gaṅgā became higher and higher, until she reached almost to the chin of the meditating *brāhmaṇa*. This repeated several times, until the *brāhmaṇa* saw the reason. On the bank of the Gaṅgā wandered a small golden colored boy. Sometimes He was playfully coming nearer to Gaṅgā, and sometimes He was moving away from her. Wanting to touch the feet of this boy, the river followed the boy, so that it sometimes became very high and other times became low. While the *brāhmaṇa* was watching this scene, he suddenly saw a divine personality dressed in a white *sari*, brilliant as the rays of the moon, appearing out of the river. The personality sat on a chariot that was drawn by dolphins and accompanied by celestial musicians. The chariot came before the golden colored boy; and the personality alighted from the chariot, kneeled down, and said, "O Lord, in your previous incarnation You have bathed only in the waters of the Yamunā, my sister. In Your coming incarnation as Śrī Caitanya Mahāprabhu, I beg You to please bathe in my waters." The little boy looked at the divine personality, not at all surprised, and said to her with a smile, "Yes, Gaṅgā, I have heard your prayers in previous times and I have decided to appear soon in the holy town of Navadvīpa. I will bathe every day in your divine waters and fulfill your request." After this, Gaṅgā went on her chariot again and disappeared into the waters of the river. As the *brāhmaṇa* saw this, he was totally charmed. He jumped out of the River Gaṅgā and went to the boy to offer his respectful obeisances. Śrī Caitanya Mahāprabhu accepted his devotional prayers, but requested him not to speak about His identity to anyone!

In conclusion, I wish to inspire the reader to kindly visit Gaṅgā and take a refreshing bath in her divine water. You will certainly have a transcendental experience of her incomparable potency and loving motherly care.

Prasāda for Gaṅgā-devī

H.G. Jananivāsa Dāsa, ISKCON
Śrīdhāma Māyāpur, West Bengal

In 1995, when Gaṅgā-devī broke through the embankment and flooded our *āśrama* (ISKCON Śrīdhāma Māyāpur) and the entire area, her waters stopped about one inch below the lotus feet of Lord Narasiṁhadeva. While she remained there, a snake would come every morning and circumambulate Lord Narasiṁhadeva by swimming around Him. During that period, we would daily offer *prasāda* to Gaṅgā-devī. We would float the *prasāda* on a bambo plate and within a few minutes it would slowly go under the water as she accepted it.

But the day when the river level dropped below the embankment and she began to flow out instead of in, I saw the midday *prasāda* still floating along with the morning *prasāda* that had been offered six hours before, indicating she had left.

Our Spiritual Mother

H.G. Mañjarī Devī Dāsī, ISKCON
Śrīdhāma Māyāpur, West Bengal

To me, Gaṅgā-devī embodies the nurturing and loving mood of a mother who is taking much care of the spiritual lives of all her children who live on her banks or come into contact with her. I have experienced this so much in my own spiritual life and seen it in the spiritual lives of others. Just like my own mother, Gaṅgā-mātā is always there for me whenever I need her, no matter how long I have ignored her. As soon as I enter her waters, her unconditional loving and purifying grace is flowing upon me. Whenever anyone asks me how I feel after bathing in Gaṅgā, I have only one reply, as it is the only way to describe it: I feel millions and millions of lifetimes lighter and surcharged with spiritual joy. Every time I put on *tilaka* (auspicious clay markings on the body) I use Gaṅgā-jala, after first taking three drops on my head to get the same benefit as bathing. It is always the same experience. I can feel my consciousness become enlightened and spiritual joy enter my heart. This is Gaṅgā-devī's causeless mercy. Bathing in her waters purifies us of more sins than we can think of committing.

One time I had a very intense migraine that would not leave no matter what I tried. It was a hot day, so I decided to go to Gaṅgā-mātā, hoping she could help. The migraine was so intense that it was quite difficult to get there. But when I submerged my head and body in Gaṅgā-devī's waters, I felt immediate relief. By the time I left, the migraine had completely gone and I felt like I was dancing home.

I have also helped a number of devotees place the ashes of their loved ones into Gaṅgā-devī's waters, as I also did for my own mother. Without fail, at the end of each *śrāddha* in Gaṅgā, an overwhelming feeling of peace takes over the hearts of those involved. They feel very peaceful that their loved one has received the best possible care and destination. Gaṅgā-devī's mercy is such that those given into her care are completely absolved of their sinful actions. They are released from material bondage and are free to enter the spiritual realm.

I have also seen how every year many thousands of people bathe in her waters here in Māyāpur. Amongst them, some fortunate soul will be taken by Gaṅgā-devī. [One time a visitor from South Africa was pulled under by a sudden and very strong current, which at the same time did not affect others around her.] Sometime afterwards, a devotee friend confided in me how she had tried to drown herself in Gaṅgā for over three hours. The fatal disease destroying her young body had become too much for her. But even though she tried her best, and even though Gaṅgā took her deep into her waters, she always ended up coming onto Gaṅgā's bank, safe and sound. My friend finally gave up, too exhausted to continue accepting it as Gaṅgā-devī's mercy. Her disease has now gone into remission and her life has taken on a new course of exciting engagement in preaching Kṛṣṇa consciousness.

The *Śrī Caitanya-bhāgavata* describes how Lord Caitanya was traveling in an area where the Gaṅgā did not flow. He saw the local people were not chanting, so He hurried with His associates in the direction of the Gaṅgā. Soon they saw some local cowherd boys who were spontaneously chanting Hare Kṛṣṇa. Lord Caitanya glorified Gaṅgā-devī, saying this was a sign of her mercy. Just by her presence she purifies and inspires the local people to chant the names of the Lord. I have personally experienced this in the nine years I have been so fortunate to be living on her banks at ISKCON Māyāpur. Gaṅgā-devī, along with the holy *dhāma* and the Vaiṣṇavas, are giving me the strength and taste for chanting the Hare Kṛṣṇa *mahā-mantra*.

So many times I look at her beautiful winding form flowing through Śrīdhāma Māyāpur and fold my hands in *prāṇams* to offer her prayers in gratitude. Her winding course is her arms surrounding and protecting me as my spiritual mother, guiding and helping me as I follow the course of my spiritual life.

Gaṅgā-devī's Servant

H.G. Gaṅgā Dāsa, ISKCON Śrīdhāma Māyāpur, West Bengal

It was in 1978 when I had my first experience of the greatness of mother Gaṅgā. The place was Benares (Vārāṇasī). The mystical atmosphere of the temples, the *sādhus*, the pious local residents, the sound of the temple bells ringing early in the morning, the thick smoke of incense inundating the roads, the milksweet shops, the *paṇḍitas* performing rituals, and the burning *ghāṭas* on the bank of Gaṅgā for the departed souls—it was a great place to be!

I was still entangled in karmic reactions, but I could perceive the strong vibration of mother Gaṅgā. Being attracted to her, I took shelter of her and decided to live for some time in one of the houseboats along her banks. Such a rewarding experience! Being 14,000 kilometres away from home, I felt like a child again in the lap of my mother, protected by her love and care. My mother had played a very significant role in my life; she always guided me in the right direction and was always ready to console my pains or explain the riddles of life. Her loving concern and goodness always helped me choose the right path.

Here in Benares, I could perceive her through mother Gaṅgā, who is reverently worshiped all over the three worlds for her greatness and magnanimity. She is purifying everyone and carrying them to the supreme destination. I had prayed for her protection and guidance, and sure enough, after one year I met the traveling *saṅkīrtana* devotees of ISKCON. They kindly accepted me as one of their associates and inspired me to start my eternal journey of purification back home, back to Godhead, by engaging me in spreading the mission of Śrī Caitanya Mahāprabhu.

In 1983 another wonderful experience occurred, this time in Calcutta, the birthplace of my Param-gurudeva, Śrīla Prabhupāda. We were pioneers of a food-for-life program. In charge of distribution, everyday we would go to the GPO (General Post Office) and distribute *prasāda* from an old Nissan jeep that dated back to the Second World War. We had repaired the old vehicle and were out all day distributing the mercy. But at the end of the day, we would visit Gaṅgā and wash all the utensils, including the jeep, then bathe in her waters, which were most refreshing and purifying, especially in the tropical humid weather. We were then ready for another challenging day of dedicated service to the mission of Śrīla Prabhupāda.

Late in 1984 we started organizing the Pānihāṭi festival (30 kilometres north of Calcutta), which is a unique celebration on the bank of the Gaṅgā. Those who have been there know what I am talking about, the famous pastime of Lord Nityānanda offering *cidā* and *dahi* (flat rice and yogurt) to Śrī Caitanya Mahāprabhu in ecstatic love. An estimated three hundred thousand pilgrims come from all over India to remember this sweet pastime of the Lord. Due to so many visitors, it becomes so congested that the only remaining vacant place is in Gaṅgā's waters! The people half submerge themselves to witness the offering at the most auspicious time, then a tumultuous sound vibration resounds in the air of the loud chanting of ""GAURĀṄGA!" Again, she is purifying one and all with her soft caresses that remove the sins of countless *jīvas* (living entities) all

over the universe. Simply by chanting her name "GAṄGĀ!" or remembering her, we can become purified.

In 1995, I was inspired by my spiritual master, H.H. Śrīla Jayapataka Swami Mahārāja, to attempt to travel upstream from Calcutta to Māyāpur by boat. We were trying to make Śrīla Prabhupāda's dream come true: taking visitors upstream by launch to Śrīdhāma Māyāpur. We then contacted one favorable Life Member, Mr. Prakash Saha, who is a boat manufacturer. He very enthusiastically agreed to the idea and after many preparations, we started our journey around noon one day in June. Mr. Prakash was convinced that we would arrive in four to five hours, but after many difficulties, we were only at Ranaghat (located near Shantipur on a river branch of Gaṅgā) by eight o'clock in the evening! A really intense adventure: the light system of the boat was not working, the engine was giving trouble, the reserve fuel ran out, and a few times we banged into fishermen's bamboo fences! We then decided to halt at the tourist bungalow at Ranaghat for a good night's rest.

In the early morning, thick fog impeded our departure until the sun broke through around eight-thirty. I was simply praying to mother Gaṅgā to bestow her mercy upon this small insignificant team of wanderers. Traveling against her current was not an easy task, but by her grace, she allowed us to continue with determination, so we could complete our voyage to the most powerful of all holy places, the birthplace of Śrī Caitanya Mahāprabhu. As we finally saw in the distance the Gaurāṅga Setu bridge at Navadvīpa, we all started jumping up and down and shouting, "Hari bol! Hari bol! Hare Kṛṣṇa!" The boat was shaking when a sudden feeling of happiness and victory permeated our hearts. But as we continued, we again lost vision of our destination as the river made a right bend U-turn, taking us farther away from Māyāpur. Eventually, after hitting a sandbank that broke one propellor of the 25 h.p. Suzuki engine, we reached the most holy, auspicious, desired place on earth, Śrīdhāma Māyāpur, at four o'clock in the afternoon! Our ordeals were over for the time being, but we were feeling very exhausted and, at the same time, very exhilarated that somehow we successfully made it. Śrīla Jayapataka Swami received us in a very personal way, making us feel like heroes and wanting to know the details of our unforgettable adventure. Again, mother Gaṅgā blessed us all to reach our destination safely.

The heavy monsoon season in Māyāpur could look like a tragedy or could be announced as a natural calamity bringing distress, especially in the case of floods, when mother Gaṅgā spills over her shores and floods our ISKCON land. But it is not always a problem. Devotees in Māyāpur take every opportunity to inspire one another, as most of them simply dive into the temple room, offer their obeisances to Their Lordships and then splash Gaṅgā water on each other! Our head *pūjāri*, Jananivāsa Prabhu, and his twin brother, Paṅkajāṅghri Prabhu, once commented, "Yes, mother Gaṅgā likes to come regularly to have *darśana* of Śrī Śrī Rādhā-Mādhava and Śrī Prahlāda-Nṛsiṁhadeva." The devotees are also in ecstasy making rafts from banana tree trunks, as others make canoes or even country boats. Of course, our *prasāda* distribution to the stranded villagers during the floods, especially to those who live in the more remote areas, really makes a difference. The hot kitchuri *prasāda* is simply what they are waiting for, and at the same time, we feel happy making a valuable contribution to these needy people. That *sevā* (service) still continues.

At other times, when the temperature rises to 48ºCelsius, the only alternative to an air-conditioned room is a long dip in the cooling waves of mother Gaṅgā. Daily during the summer months, the small beach near Hulor-ghāṭa becomes a meeting place for all the devotees and their families. The children have their fun, while someone narrates stories from the *Śrī Caitanya-caritāmṛta*, or from the pastimes of Śrīla Prabhupāda and even some *saṅkīrtana* tales: as everyone feels very enlightened in such a situation. It is so simple to be happy. Being with devotees, bathing in the brilliant waters of mother Gaṅgā, and sitting on her golden powdered beach enriches our lives unlimitedly. Swimming, drinking her pure waters, offering *pūjā*, or chanting our Gāyatrī *mantra*: all these activites, done in a proper respectful mood, can bring our vision to pure Kṛṣṇa consciousness.

We should also thank her now, for when we leave our bodies, she will take our ashes and purify us even further. What more can she do for us? Her preaching potency is unlimited and her mercy bountiful. Only now am I realizing that I am a fool trying to glorify her in my inadequate way. May Gaṅgā-mayī bestow her powerful mercy on us so that we can become more committed, dedicated, and pure to spread the mission of Śrīla Prabhupāda and the previous *ācāryas*.

I, Gaṅgā Dāsa, beg for her blessings, and, taking the dust from the lotus feet of all the devotees on my head, ask forgiveness and mercy from our mother Gaṅgā.

Gaṅgā's Blessings

H.G. Śvetadvīpa Dāsa, ISKCON Padayātrā India

The *padayātris* (members of the Padayātrā) are eager to learn and study *Bhagavad-gītā*. I am very enthused to assist them. Please bless me that before reaching Śrī Vṛndāvana-dhāma, I am able to learn *Bhagavad-gītā* thoroughly. When I left Vṛndāvana and finished attending the *bhāgavata-saptaha* in Bihar, I went to Vārāṇasī. Just before I caught my train to Madras, I went to Daśāśvamedha-ghāṭa and took bath in the Gaṅgā. Then I sat down and read *Bhagavad-gītā* out loud. I prayed to Gaṅgā-mātā to bless me so that I can understand the divine knowledge of *Bhagavad-gītā*. In the train that I took to Madras (the Gaṅgā Kāverī Express), I dreamt of Gaṅgā-mātā. The dream was very clear. I saw the holy water of Gaṅgā flowing gently, dancing her way, and purifying millions of people.

Voyage to Gaṅgotrī

H.G. Param Tattva Dāsa, ISKCON Switzerland

When the Lord wants to give His mercy, He does so in a surprising way. I could not expect that special day at the Centennial House in New Delhi, when a wonderful adventure began upon meeting Badarī Viśāla Prabhu. Badarī Viśāla spontaneously invited me for a trip to Gaṅgotrī, along with the expert traveler, Jaya Vijaya Prabhu. That same evening, we arrived in Haridvāra-dhāma, and by their kindness, my two new friends allowed me to participate at the annual opening festival of Gaṅgotrī. As time passed, I discovered the fascinating personalitites of Badarī Viśāla and Jaya Vijaya Prabhus.

Mukhwa, where Gaṅgā-devī resides during the winter season, is a sweet, attractive village with wooden houses situated on the mountainside. A very humble villager welcomed us in his family's house. Every moment of their mountainous village life and warm friendly hospitality attracted my mind. All the members of the family were dependent on their agricultural lifestyle. The beauty and purity of the Himālayan mountains was taking us far away from the materialistic lifestlye far down below.

The first day of the auspicious festival approached, which marks the opening summer season at Gaṅgotrī. The beautiful, golden facial deity of Gaṅgā-devī was carried on a silver throne, which was sitting on top of a wooden palanquin. The *pūjāris* and villagers joyfully greeted Gaṅgā-devī with a traditional *kīrtana*, in which bugles, drums, and clarinet resounded throughout the village. Military soldiers led the procession, followed by ladies who were all dressed in very colorful *saris* (dresses worn by women in Vedic culture). The men enthusiastically carried the palanquin through the trails of the Himālayan mountains and along the bank of Bhāgīrathi Gaṅgā.

On the second day, we arrived in Gaṅgotrī, where the atmosphere was emanating Gaṅgā-devī's mercy. At the core of the Gaṅgotrī temple complex, *darśana* of Ganeśa, Pārvatī, Lord Śiva, and his bull carrier, Nandi, welcomed the new visitors to the main temple, where Gaṅgā-devī would reside for the season. Invited by the *pūjāris*, I shared *prasāda* with them. Later, Jaya Vijaya Prabhu proposed to visit the wide and imposing scenery of the Gaṅgotrī valley. Surrounded by gigantic peaks and effulgently shining mountains, I became struck with wonder. Jaya Vijaya told me that every bath we take in Gaṅgotrī is like a new birth, and the closer to the source of Gaṅgā, the greater the purification and benefit. I was appreciating more and more the transcendental mercy of Gaṅgā-devī. The Lord was happy to reveal the unique qualities of His beloved devotees.

When I remember those days in Gaṅgotrī, my heart is filled with soothing memories, which increased my enthusiasm in devotional life. My gratitude flows to the lotus feet of Lord Kṛṣṇa and to His very dear devotees, Jaya Vijaya Prabhu, Badarī Viśāla Prabhu, and their friends. I have special gratitude especially for mother Gaṅgā and her sweet Himālayan devotees, who gave so much care to this new visitor, which only impressed upon my heart a permanent *darśana* of Gaṅgotrī.

"It's Only Purification Prabhu!"

Jaya Vijaya Dāsa, ISKCON Padayātrā India

My first bath in Gaṅgā was at Vārāṇasī in March, 1983, while I was traveling from New Delhi to Śrīdhāma Māyāpur (West Bengal). I had only been in India for a few months as a spiritual seeking tourist, performing *bhakti-yoga* (devotional service) on a part-time basis, while visiting the major tourist spots in-between. When I first arrived in Vārāṇasī, the intense, congested spiritual atmosphere was overwhelming and somewhat confusing. As in most holy places of India, being a lost materialistic foreigner has great disadvantages, since one simply does not know whether to turn right or left, visit this or that temple, or how to find someone who can speak truthfully! The first thing I would do upon arriving in any new place was to walk around and explore the environment.

The part of Vārāṇasī located along the bank of Gaṅgā is constructed very tightly with small, narrow lanes crisscrossing one another like large curving snakes. As I wandered from one lane to another, I eventually came upon the River Gaṅgā's bank. I did not know which particular *ghāṭa* it was, or even what a *ghāṭa* was, but I did recall someone's somewhere telling me that this river was very holy and important. I really did not know anything, but somehow or other I was impelled to take my first holy bath. I do not recollect any unique or special feeling, except some embarrassment as the other bathers observed this funny looking foreigner taking bath!

After dressing, I decided to return to the guesthouse in which I was staying via another route through the narrow congested lanes. Just as I left the *ghāṭa* area, a dog objected to my presence and began barking loudly before he (or she?) bit me on my left buttocks, not only once, but twice, both times drawing blood! Feeling confused and worried, I quickly moved from that area. On my way to the guesthouse, I stopped at a pharmacy to purchase de-worming medicine. Arriving back at my room, I took the medicine before taking rest. Upon awakening, I vomited the medicine, which obviously proved it did not work. The next day, I continued the train journey to Howrah (Calcutta) and then to Māyāpur, leaving Vārāṇasī in an unhappy and perplexed state of mind, but at the same time, feeling rewarded from another experience on the road.

Arriving in West Bengal was an overwhelming experience, especially at the bustling Howrah train station. Somehow or other, after crossing the River Gaṅgā from Navadvīpa Township, I eventually arrived at ISKCON's World Headquarters at Māyāpur, which was a welcome relief from the mad Bengali crowds. Upon entering the front gates, one is instantly relieved of the material anxieties occurring in the outside world. After a few days of becoming familiar with the peaceful surroundings, I was assigned the service of taking care of the dispensary during the upcoming Gaura Pūrṇimā festival, during which thousands of devotees from around the world come to celebrate the appearance of Śrī Caitanya Mahāprabhu.

During those days, Gaṅgā was approximately 100 metres from the main road. Occasionally I would stroll to the river for a cooling bath, since the spring temperatures were slowly beginning to increase. One day I was speaking to a devotee about my first bathing experience at Vārāṇasi. Upon hearing about the incident, he said, "It's only purification Prabhu!"

After the festival began, I was very busy serving the devotees, as well as meeting friendly new faces from around the world. In between all the festival activities, I was able to participate in some of the daily *parikramās* to the holy places associated with Lord Caitanya. But as the temperatures increased, the numerous mosquitoes robbed me of sleep and I became increasingly weak. In the evenings, I would assist Yadubara Prabhu with showing his new film about Śrīla Prabhupāda: *Your Ever Well Wisher*. After three weeks of service, bathing, feasting, *parikramās*, and meeting many happy personalities, it was time to leave Śrīdhāma Māyāpur and the River Gaṅgā.

I crossed Gaṅgā once again and went to the train station. Just as I boarded the train to Howrah, I became dizzy and was attacked by headaches and sharp stomach pains. I quickly rushed to the train's dirty toilet, where all those aches and pains were discharged in the form of diarrhea. As I left the toilet, I was very weak and felt nauseated from the sudden attack. Upon re-entering the train compartment, it had become jammed with passengers, all standing, smoking, and playing cards. Since I could not move to find a seat, I had no choice but to stand in between the small passageway that separates the two toilets! Then another attack came upon me, and I quickly ran back into the toilet. And then another attack and another, continuously during the whole three hour ride to Howrah train station. Somehow or other, I managed to find a low budget tourist lodge in Calcutta to take immediate rest.

After a few days of dizziness and severe bouts of dysentery, I slowly recovered and returned to Vṛndāvana for more rest and eventually resumed some devotional activities. While in Vṛndāvana, I told another devotee about the sudden illness that attacked me when I left Srīdhāma Māyāpur and the Gaṅgā, he replied, "It's only purification Prabhu!"

GAṄGĀ LIVES IN THE WESTERN MIND

Adopted from *The Sunday Times of India Review*, 15 June, 1997, by Jerry Pinto

"Burning is learning," says a boatman named Suresh, as he pulls on the oars past Maṇikarṇikā-ghāṭa in Vārāṇasī (Benares), where boatloads of tourists stop to watch the bodies of the dead being consumed by fire. It is a catch-phrase that has yielded results before, and Stu Mills, a 23 year old Australian computer nerd puts down his copy of Sogyal Rinpoche's *The Tibetan Book of Living and Dying* and grins, "Yeah," he says, face reddened by the fires, sweat beading his brow, "I hope it will be."

Like many other westerners, Stu did not come to Vārāṇasī because it merited four pages in his *Lonely Planet* guide to India. With a slight trace of embarrassment, he describes his journey as a spiritual quest. "Someone very close to me died of AIDS, and I realized that death was not something that would come at some indistinct point in the future. Nothing in our culture or civilization prepares us for it. It could happen tomorrow and it was time to confront it." He looks around and then says, "And if anywhere, death lives in Benares."

While everyone agrees that reports in the western press about hundreds of westerners arriving at the River Gaṅgā, seeking to immerse the ashes of friends and relatives, as well as dozens of parcels containing ashes arriving in Rishikesh, are exaggerated, there are those who come to Gaṅgā to seek spiritual connections. Yvette has come to Vārāṇasī to die. When the 65 year old Belgian had a section of her intestine cut out and a bag took over the functions of excretion, she got tired of finding herself surrounded by people who knew she was terminally ill but refused to admit it. "I do not know whether I was imagining it, but everyone around me seemed to want me to say that I was getting better, feeling better. All their solicitous inquiries began to ring false, and I felt surrounded by people who did not want to admit that I was dying. Eventually it got to the point where I would say that I was feeling better and healthier even if I was feeling terrible, simply because there seemed to be such a premium placed on putting on a brave face, such a denial of death. I wanted to shout: I am dying, I am not better! When I could not bear it anymore, this persistent negation of what was inevitable, I went away to Benares."

Each night she comes to Maṇikarṇikā-ghāṭa and takes up a lonely vigil under the stars. A vigil that is different from the one that she envisaged. "Now I watch the bodies come down and come down, watching some of them borne away in boats and some burn for hours. It is nothing like what I expected, but there is something more here for me than just beauty. This is the way to die: with people around me and singing and the fire burning all night and see there, how that man is drying his clothes against the flames? And those boys wrestling in the mud? And those women washing their clothes and the men taking dips near the place where the dead bodies are also immersed before they are burned? I want that continuity, that pageant around me."

In the end, she hopes that her ashes will be put in the River Gaṅgā. "I hear it is a direct route to heaven," she smiles. "I have never had any firm religious beliefs, but sometimes I find it consoling."

LOTUS FOOTED GAṄGĀ - WE SALUTE THEE

Radheshyam Khemka, editor of *Kalyan*, Vārāṇasī

gāyanti devaḥ kila gītakāni
dhanyās tu te bhārata-bhūmi-bhāge

"Blessed are those who are born in Bhārata-bhūmi (India). Divinity is sung in heaven because the rescuer and savior of all sinners, mother Gaṅgā, flows here and is easily available."

punāti kīrtitā pāpaṁ
dṛṣṭvā vai bhadraṁ prayacchati
avagādhā ca pītā ca
punāti saptamaṁ kulam

"Gaṅgā annihilates the sins of those who recite her pious name, blesses those who see her, and sanctifies seven generations of those who bath in or drink her waters." (*Mahābhārata*)

sarva-tīrtha-mayī gaṅgā
sarva-deva-mayo hariḥ

"All places of pilgrimage are included in the River Gaṅgā as all divinity is in Lord Viṣṇu." (*Nṛsiṁha Purāṇa*)

pāpa-buddhiṁ parityajya
gaṅgāyāṁ loka-mātari
snānaṁ kuruta he lokā
yadi sad-gatim icchatha

"Those who want salvation should speak the truth and bathe in the River Gaṅgā with a clean heart. They must leave aside hypocrisy, wickedness, anger, malice, jealousy, etc. while going to bathe in the holiest of all rivers. One should also concentrate his sentiments in the knowledge that he is bathing in the ambrosial divine liquid that has originated from the lotus feet of the Supreme Personality of Godhead."

The emanation of Gaṅgā, by the blessings of Trideva and the penance of Mahārāja Bhagīratha, has been for the salvation of King Sagara's sixty thousand sons, who were absolved from their sins by her contact. Originating from the lotus feet of Lord Viṣṇu, entering into the *kamaṇḍalu* of Lord Brahmā, and accumulated in the matted hairs of Lord Śiva, thereby obtained with the determined attempts of Mahārāja Bhagīratha, River Gaṅgā emancipates the bathers. Blessed are those who consume the water of Gaṅgā.

Our saints and sages preach that it is a sin to defile the shore of the River Gaṅgā or her waters with filth, urine, faeces, mucus, saliva, etc., and those who do so are preparing to go to hell. Although they have taught the inhabitants their duty to maintain the sanctity of the physical river and to preserve her purity and clarity, persons taking bath in the River Gaṅgā commit unpardonable sins of discharging unhesitatingly all kinds of excretement and other wastes in her holy water. Industries generously dispose their poisonous industrial waste in streams, sewerage, and drainage that are generally diverted and fused into the main current. The Government also diverts the natural flow of the River Gaṅgā by construction of dams and canals for selfish interests.

In present days, people sacrifice their peace of mind to gain momentary prosperity and worldly amenities. Such narrow-mindedness leads them to consider the ambrosial divine water of the holy rivers as a means to fulfill their absurd self-interest.

Experiments have proven that pure Gaṅgā water is a supernatural boon for everyone. UNESCO scientists were amazed to find that near Haridvāra, even on the spots where fouled dead bodies and bones were floating, Gaṅgā water a few metres away was found to be pure. The scientists concluded after analysis that Gaṅgā water is capable of destroying cholera germs within three to four hours. They also found that Gaṅgā water always remains fresh and unpolluted when kept in vessels, but when water of the River Thames is stored, it becomes spoiled.

Gaṅgā water has been found to retain its splendor by nullifying harmful unsanitary and polluted objects. Those who take bath in Gaṅgā never become indisposed and never remain materialistic. Their wisdom, conception, discretion, and sentiments are diverted towards attainment of emancipation. Gaṅgā, the almighty mother, is the bestower of eternal emancipation and the liberator from worldly ties. She also nourishes like mother earth.

We should apologize with reverence to our holy and pious supreme mother Gaṅgā for our stupidity and mistakes. We should vow to free Gaṅgā from material pollution even by agitations. No filth of any kind should find its way into the river in any circumstances. The responsibility of keeping the river unpolluted lies with every citizen, society, and Government. If it is not done, the day is near when we shall find ourselves longing for pure clear Gaṅgā water.

viṣṇu-padābja-sambhūte
gaṅge tri-patha-gāminī
brahma-draveti vikhyāte
pāpaṁ me hari jāhnavī

"Mother Gaṅgā, who originates from the foot of Lord Viṣṇu, is the holiest of the holy. She is called *tri-patha-gāminī*, one who traverses the threefold path. O you who are also renowned as Brahma-devī, please protect us from all evil designs."

To See and Touch Her Everyday

Puruṣottama Dāsa Modi,
Vishvavidyalaya Prakashan, Vārāṇasī

India, whose forehead is covered with a snow coronet, whose neck is surrounded with garlands of pleasant holy rivers, and whose feet are washed by sacred oceans—this is our country. Gaṅgā, seated on a crocodile, passes through the lotus feet of Lord Viṣṇu, descends from the *kamaṇḍalu* of Lord Brahmā, and emanates from the matted locks of Lord Śiva to bless the people of this country. The feelings and realizations that mother Gaṅgā occasions cannot be described. The people cannot live without Gaṅgā, and the whole country is inspired by holy Gaṅgā. She makes our life more alive and manifests human life from birth to death. The whole span of human life is symbolized by Gaṅgā, as she flows from Gomukha to the Bay of Bengal.

Mother Gaṅgā inspires me at every step. On the bank of Gaṅgā, I get celestial feelings. That is why my residence is at Gai-ghāṭa, one of the most important and historical *ghāṭas* of Gaṅgā at Vārāṇasī, where I have *darsana* and *sparsa* (view and touch) of her everyday.

SURRENDERING ONE'S SELF TO MOTHER GAṄGĀ

Gaurahari Dāsa, Vṛndāvana

The following narration is from Gaurahari Prabhu's personal diary that will hopefully someday turn into an inspiring book. His sincere, loving dependence upon the mercy of mother Gaṅgā ultimately guided him to the lotus feet of Śrīla Prabhupāda in Śrī Vṛndāvana-dhāma.

My first visit to India in 1972 unfortunately did not bring me into contact with mother Gaṅgā. I took the Kathmandu-Goa overland-trail and, apart from dabbling in Buddhism, overlooked the spiritual side of India.

It was not until my second visit in 1976 that things started to seem a little different, and even then only upon reaching the most holy and famous city of Benares, also known as Vārāṇasī, or Kāśī. I can never forget the moment I walked down from Gondolia, towards Daśāśvamedha-ghāṭa, and first set eyes on mother Gaṅgā. Such wonderful feelings of utopia brought tears to my eyes, to see such a famous holy river at an equally famous location, Benares! I asked myself, "Am I really here? Or is this some kind of dream or mirage?" While walking down the steps towards the Gaṅgā, one thing still stands out in my mind: even though I knew it was my first visit to Benares and the first time my eyes were seeing Gaṅgā, I had a great sense of being there before, in another time, in another body. It all seemed so familiar. The ancient buildings, the sites, the sounds, all coming from a previous life, not a recent one.

As the Gaṅgā came closer in view I observed this incredible scene. The most natural thing to do was to bow down, offer my obeisances, and throw the water over my head. Why do that? Nobody told me that this was the right thing to do. It just seemed to come naturally. As my eyes glanced to both sides of the river, I noticed other people were doing the same thing. What are these feelings of ecstasy, which are far too wonderful to put into words? As the sun came up, those feelings intensified. I then took my first Gaṅgā bath while the sun was still saffron, and I felt as if I had met my eternal mother in this river. Coming out of the water was like having been baptized in all the holy waters of the universe at once. Dressed in clean cloth, I went back up to the Gaṅgā temple to offer my respects with flowers and incense. By this time there was no doubt in my mind that this had all happened before in another existence. After making my offering and sitting on the temple platform, I watched the movements of a charismatic *sādhu* with bright saffron cloth and huge dreadlocks and listened to the *bhajans* of "*Sri Rāma, Jaya Rāma, Jaya Jaya Rāma*". Little did I know how much effect these *mantras* would have on my life in years to come. By the mercy of the Supreme Lord all was revealed in due course of time.

After staying in Benares for several months, I became a little tired of the crowds and kept glancing over the Gaṅgā at the emptiness on the other side. How could I go over there? There was still all this stuff that I carried around in a small backpack. I did not really want any of this western stuff. I wanted Indian things just like the *sādhus* had, not the stupid sleeping bag and western bags that drew attention.

At the time I was reading the *Bhagavad-gītā*, *Dhammapada*, and the *New Testament*, probing and trying to find out the meaning of life and fitting all the scriptures together. One of the main things that struck me was The Sermon on the Mount, in which Jesus Christ said, "Consider the lilies of the field and the fowls of the air, they do not reap or sow or store in barns, but your heavenly father feeds them. O ye of little faith. Care not for your clothing or for your food. Your Father knows what you need." But who was the Father? That is what I wanted to know, and how could I live this message purely and truthfully.

Because of these thoughts, my consciousness transformed and after a few days it came to me: I'll give everything away! It seemed the natural thing to do. Mother Gaṅgā gave me the answer from within: "Give all your possessions away to the poor and follow me." Within one day everything was gone. I exchanged my sleeping bag for a blanket and my backpack for a saffron bag. Eventually I gave even those away. Swiss army knife, clock, everything was gone. Well, almost. There were still twelve rolls of camera film taken on an Annapūrṇā base camp trek in Nepal, 300 British pounds, and my passport. What was the use of that film? It was all in the past. Just hundreds of photos of white mountains. So into the Gaṅgā they went. Years later I was to regret that move, but at the moment it was like throwing away the mundane hippie trekker side of myself. Watching them bob-up and down in the Gaṅgā was quite funny!

Then of course there was the money. The one thing the whole world was attached to. We had to scrimp and save and do all kinds of hellish jobs to get these silly bits of paper, which everyone thinks is the meaning of life. How can you lead a truly renounced life if you are still attached to money? So out it had to go. One rupee here and ten rupees there. It was taking too long. My now bare feet were asking to be free and wander. In the end a hundred rupees at a time were being given away to beggars and *sādhus*, old ladies, and children, as well as donations to various temples along the *ghāṭas*. Giving up those last few rupees was such a relief, freeing me from a burden. Now my soul could fly. Or could it? What about the passport? Well, eventually that also went into the Gaṅgā, but during another trip, after my first Kumbha-melā experience and the return journey along the bank of the Gaṅgā.

In the meantime, early one morning in September I was standing at Asī-ghāṭa, the furthest eastern *ghāṭa*, before leaving Benares. Shoeless, bagless, penniless, and with only two pieces of cloth and a blanket, I looked out along the banks, the footpaths, and the villages and wondered what kind of adventures lay before me. On the way out of Benares, the blanket on my shoulder felt heavy, it fell off my shoulder as I turned to offer my obeisances to the eternal Kāśī. There was an old man sitting on the last *ghāṭa*, and I just handed him the blanket and felt even freer. So this was it, it was actually happening, something that I had only dreamt about for years. As I walked along the banks leaving the crowds and the bustle of Benares, the scene was very overwhelming—less and less people and more and more trees. Mahātmā Gandhi used to say that real India lives in the villages. That I was soon to find out was true. Some hours later and not a soul to be seen. Was this really India? What a wonderful feeling of freedom! This is what the animals must feel like all the time, except they don't know that they are eternal spirit souls. It was certainly blissful having no money and no possessions to think about. Only God to think about. At that time I didn't know about Kṛṣṇa. I was a bit of a Māyāvādī. I was more attracted to the nature of things.

Meanwhile, the first morning of this wonderful new lifestyle passed and as noon came I was trying not to think about hunger and thirst. I tried to just trust in God and remember what the scriptures and great sages said. After 10 to15 kilometres of seeing no one, I heard a voice shout out, "Baba", and in the distance was an old man holding up a large brass *lota*. I went over as he was calling me. He pulled out a glass and poured sugar cane juice with *dahi* from this endless lota. After four glasses, I was totally full and had to go and lie down. After another kilometre I come across my first real Indian village. It was still quite close to Beṇares. The locals didn't take too much notice of this foreigner, but every now and then out of the bushes appeared a face and two hands outstretched with channa, peanuts, gur, and various other things that were produced in the village. These are Indians, I am thinking, giving and not taking, smiling and not snarling; what a contrast to the city people in Benares.

So God does provide after all, it's true. Everything is there. As time passed, mother Gaṅgā revealed more of her riches and generosity than I could ever imagine. After inspecting the simplicity and peace of the village and after being invited to stay, I decided to spend my first night by the Gaṅgā under a tree near the water. Full of village delicacies, I lay down just after sunset feeling more contented and happier than I'd felt for years, in fact, ever! The next morning it was up and straight into the Gaṅgā and then walking again. Wow, what a wonderful new life! And what awaited me around the next corner? God was already planning this out.

After a few more kilometres, a small boy appeared and pointed towards a small path leading up from the riverbank. As I went up the path, I came across my first *āśrama* temple-garden complex. "Master Baba", as they called him, was sitting on a raised wooden platform with a group of village families sitting around him, while in the background there were *sādhus* doing various activities. "Yes, please come and sit down here" they said, and I was placed in front of Master Baba, whom I found to be a very pleasant, charming cultured man who spoke perfect English. He was the ex-principal of a college in Bihar who had left his position and family and come here twenty years before to sit and meditate with his *guru*. With the passing of his *guru* he became the main man and had acquired a dozen disciples and a following in and around the nearby villages. He never went anywhere except to the bank of the Gaṅgā and had not even gone to the nearby village of Adolpura, one kilometre away, during all these years.

So here in front of me was a living example of how everything comes to you by the grace of the Lord. "Why are you walking along the banks of the Gaṅgā?" he asked. So I related the whole story. "Very good," he said, "I also used to do this, but after some time I preferred to walk along the banks of the mind." And he followed with, "Yes of course you don't need money, and God will provide everything for your needs." And it was obvious that after twenty years of not touching money, God had certainly provided everything. "When you were a small boy your mother gave you everything? And mother Gaṅgā will keep giving you everything." And she certainly did. Master Baba was to become my first *guru*, and I was to spend many months at this *āśrama* over the years. I got to know this whole stretch of the Gaṅgā by heart and meet everyone from all the villages around, all due to the grace of this incredible eternal river.

The Kumbha-melā in Allahabad was in January, and I wanted to reach there in time. So with Master Baba's blessing, off I was once more along the banks of the Gaṅgā. Every village along the path was equally as hospitable as Adolpura. Quite amazing, really, nearly every place I passed through, stayed at, or took *prasāda*, the people wanted to build me a hut, give me a cow, etc. And there were many beautiful spots that were ideal to spend the rest of one's life in. How would have ended up to be a bit of an entanglement. The idea was freedom and not attachment.

Before reaching Allahabad for my first Kumbha-melā, there were many, many Gaṅgā experiences, far too numerous to write about. There are a couple I'd like to relate to exemplify Indian village hospitality. I never actually went hungry once in these months (that turned into years) along the Gaṅgā. The most amazing thing is that the villages would give me so much food, not only in the form of rice, dahl, sabji, and chapatis, but also in the form of peanuts, channa, and various sweets made from gur and grains. But carrying them was a burden: as they would come to me in one village, I would give them away to children in the next village. How is this, I wondered? I had nothing, yet I could give away food. How great is this God that is looking after me. At times I did get tired of people pampering me in every village and always being full. Many times I felt the need to be alone. At one point I stayed alone between villages for three to four days. Which also meant three to four days without eating. Only fasting on Gaṅgā water.

At that time I was also practicing *haṭha-yoga* and wearing just underwear, while two pieces of bright yellow cloth were lying on the bank drying. The nearest village or even tree was a few kilometres away, but the cloth must have attracted someone because in the distance was a small speck coming towards me. As the speck came into focus, I saw that it was a man carrying a large plate. At first I thought it was someone coming to do *pūjā* to the Gaṅgā, but why does he have to come where I am, there are miles and miles of empty sand. No, he was heading right for me. On getting closer, it was plain to see he was carrying a huge plate full of fruit *prasāda*. And what a feast indeed, there must have been ten preparations, all for me it seemed. He just laid it down in front of me and beckoned me to eat. He never spoke a word, which is very unusual for an Indian. He never asked me where I came from or where I was going, my name, my country, nothing. It was quite amazing. After the excellent meal was over, he took the plate, washed it in the Gaṅgā, and walked off across the empty sand to the trees and became a speck again.

I prayed to my eternal mother for this *prasāda* and thanked her. Incredible! Food was not the only thing that Gaṅgā gave every day. Every day there was red clay to wash your cloth with, and the Gaṅgā mud for washing your body was far superior to soap. And of course all the way along the path were neem trees, the twigs of which you can clean your teeth with. She also takes away as well as gives. She can punish you as well as reward you.

Being a personified river and coming from the lotus feet of Lord Viṣṇu, through Lord Śiva's hair, she also acts as the Supersoul and knows your mind. An incident to prove this came somewhere between Benares and Allahabad, near a city that was on the other side called Mirzapur. I was supposed to be leading the life of a *sādhu*—doing *haṭha-yoga*, meditation, living without money, etc., but not being qualified to be called such. And the villagers would call me *mahātmā* and touch my feet. I really hated that, as I knew my mind was not pure. I was a mere beginner on this path and had a long way to go.

One bright morning I was walking along a very lonely part of the riverbank with small bushes on each side. I heard a very unfamiliar sound for these parts, and as I came closer, there were many women coming out of the water. I suppose this was God's sense of humor to send *māyā* to try and test my faith. Slowly I backed away and took another path, so that they never even knew that I was there. But it was too late, the image was planted in my brain and I couldn't shake it off. Standing on my head for hours trying to meditate and standing up to my neck in Gaṅgā water for hours on end was of no avail. It would not go away. How could I be a *sādhu* now?

So much for proudly thinking that I had overcome this desire via *haṭha-yoga*. Some days later, a huge boil appeared in my ear, large and red with pus coming out of it. And it was so painful. For ten days I had no proper sleep and terrible headaches. This was of course the instant *karma* from Gaṅgā for impure thoughts while leading the life of a *sādhu*. The villagers suggested that I should stay under the Gaṅgā water for as long as possible every day and she would cure it. Either that or drown me for my sins. Sure enough, after following the instructions of the locals for five days, the boil went away. But that terrible pain will not be forgotten. Every time the sex desire came, that pain was remembered.

The test of this came again some weeks later, near a village called Barani. At this village the Gaṅgā split into two branches that were miles apart, so I had to follow the path inland. En route there was that same sound. I knew if I kept on walking through the bushes, there would be the same scene as before. No! No! Māyā you're not catching me this time. As soon as that sound reached my ears, I turned back and went around, over ditches and through thorns and bracken to avoid that situation arising again. I remembered the earache and dismissed the incident from my mind, and my mind was not disturbed.

During this detour I came across an open, unguarded guava orchard, wherein I sat down and feasted for hours. As I lay under a shady tree, I hoped Gaṅgā was pleased by my attempts to control my mind and remain chaste to her. Well, judging by what happened in Barani village, it was obvious she was pleased. How she punishes, and how she gives! While I was sitting at a teashop near the Śiva temple on the edge of the village, a school teacher approached me and, in perfect English, said, "You are a foreigner with no shoes and no luggage."

"Yes," I answered. "

And I suppose you have no money for food?"

"God provides," I answered.

"Please come to my house for an evening meal," he requested.

"Thank you, but I was wanting to visit a *sādhu-āśrama* that I'd heard about, and I am getting late for reaching the Kumbha-melā by January."

Again he requested, "Then please come for early morning breakfast before you proceed." This I accepted and then proceeded to the *sādhu-āśrama*. The *āśrama* located on the Gaṅgā had large steps going to the river and a huge beautiful garden, an oasis with about twenty *sādhus*. The main *guru*, sitting on a tiger skin, had huge dreadlocks and a twinkle in his eye. He seemed too proud, and I was not impressed.

In the morning I accepted the humble teacher's breakfast invitation, expecting it to be something like tea and biscuits. Was I in for a shock. To my surprise, what came as breakfast at 8 a.m. was three kinds of rice, all different colors, six sabjis with paneer, two dahls, samosas, kacoris, puris, naans, rotis, and endless varieties of sweets, including a huge bowl of sweet rice. Well, was I full! That was the greatest feast ever known to me. Apparently his wife, mother, and sister had stayed up the whole night preparing breakfast for his foreigner-guest. Not only that, but to prove their hospitality even more, I was given a cushion to sit on and their children fanned me and kept the flies off the plate. He'd snap his fingers and the children kept bringing more and more *prasāda*. Once more, thank you mother Gaṅgā. From my speculation, it seemed as if the boil in the ear was punishment for looking at the bathing group and the feast was the reward for not looking at or thinking about the second bathing group. Mother Gaṅgā gave and took away, rewarded and punished according to the conditions of the mind.

So it was onwards to the Kumbha-melā of 1977 in Allahabad. I still had a long way to go. After meeting everyone in Barani village, off I went once more along the glorious path on the banks of the Gaṅgā. I had no care for food or clothing, as I knew that she would provide everything in due course of time. Sometimes you have to be patient and tolerant as you are tested. So my mother was teaching me many things. And little did I know what an amazing and incredible experience lay ahead of me at the Kumbha-melā. Gaṅgā-mayī ki jai! Hare Kṛṣṇa!

INTERVIEW

JVJ: What is your good name?
Dr: Doctor Suresh Kumar Pandey, serving here as chief executive officer, Śrī Kāśī Viśvanātha Temple.
JVJ: And how long ago did you take birth here is Kāśī?
Dr: Actually I was born in Gonda district, near Faizabad in Uttar Pradesh. I am in the State Civil Service, and I was posted here three years ago. I have been serving Lord Viśvanātha since that time.
JVJ: So, I am curious about one thing, since you are residing in the holy *dhāma* of Kāśī and on the bank of Gaṅgā, which are both very sacred and glorified in the Vedic literatures, do you have some personal relationship, some personal testimony, how Gaṅgā has helped you with your daily devotion and service to Śrī Kāśī Viśvanātha?

Dr: In reply, I would like to tell you one experience, a very vital experience I had with Gaṅgā while I was staying in Allahabad. At that time I was suffering from some mental depression due to some unemployment problems and other things. Then one of my friends said, "You have been trying so hard for a job and losing your health also, better you start taking bath in Gaṅgā with me." I told him that I would like to take bath, provided someone woke me up in the morning. He said, "Alright, I will do it." Then I said, "If I do not awake immediately, then wake me up again after ten minutes." He agreed, so we started going to the Gaṅgā. On the first day, when we reached her shore at three in the morning, I heard a boy chanting the mantra: *oṁ namaḥ śivāya, oṁ namaḥ śivāya.* Meanwhile, my friend told me, "Dive into the Gaṅgā, feeling like mother was taking you in her lap and purifying you. Do this a hundred times every day." I continued bathing in the Gaṅgā for two and a half months. Every day when we came to the bank, we found that same boy chanting that same *mantra*. I do not know who he was, for were unable to trace him. We wanted to meet him some time, so we tried to wake up earlier, even as early as two in the morning, but every day we found him chanting. So rather than disturbing him with our questions, we would just take our bath. Still, it is a mystery who he was.

Then, what suddenly happened, after two and a half months, when we were coming back to our room, one fine question came to my mind. The question was: "I am a well experienced person, widely traveled in India, a person having twenty-five publications abroad, and, being a married person, having experienced all kinds of enjoyment; but have

I ever before experienced in my life the kind of enjoyment or happiness that I am experiencing here at this moment on the bank of Gaṅgā?" So I kept thinking about this question while we walked about five kilometres, crossing over the dam. At first, no answer came to my mind; then finally the answer came: "No!" I had never before experienced the kind of enjoyment our holy mother gave me that day. It was a kind of turning point for me to feel the vitality of natural energy from mother Gaṅgā. In the interim period of two and a half months, I regained my health, I regained spirit, I regained the venture and courage to put on *candana-tilaka* (auspicious clay markings on the body). Initially I was feeling shy. I used to put *tilaka* on only after taking bath at the *ghāṭas* then I used to rub it off before entering my house. But as time passed, I soon started wearing *tilaka* all day, and all those people with whom I had some sense of non-cooperation or some sense of aversion started appearing to me like mendicants. I think this is the most vital experience, not only for me, but for anyone willing to listen and realize what I have personally received from mother Gaṅgā.

Book Two
Chapter Seven

Sapta Ṛṣis (The Seven Sages)

Sapta Ṛṣis (The Seven Sages)

I started this compilation of Gaṅgā-devī's glories in Haridvāra at a place known as Sapta-sarovara, where the seven sages once performed austerities before the advent of Gaṅgā-mayī. When Gaṅgā began her descent, she traveled behind Mahārāja Bhagīratha's chariot, as he paved the route that she was to follow. When they approached the Haridvāra area, they came upon the seven great sages absorbed in deep meditation. Out of love and respect for the sages, Gaṅgā flowed around their hermitages to avoid disturbing them, thus forming seven currents around seven islands. This area is also known as Sapta Gaṅgā, or Seven Gaṅgās.

One morning while I was sitting on her bank at Sapta-sarovara, I was feeling great appreciation for the seven sages for allowing this restless, fallen soul a place of residence in such a beautiful place. Due to the presence of these great sages of the past, Gaṅgā begins to slow her fast flowing pace into several gentle streams. Since feeling very indebted to them, I wanted to compile a few narrations glorifying their outstanding activities and pastimes, not only on the banks of Gaṅgā, but throughout this sacred land. The following is a small offering to the lotus feet of all these sages of the past, present, and future.

* * *

In the *Śrīmad-Bhāgavatam* (8.13.5), the names of the seven sages in this present age are given as follows:

kaśyapo 'trir vasiṣṭhaś ca
viśvāmitro 'tha gautamaḥ
jamadagnir bharadvāja
iti saptarṣayaḥ smṛtāḥ

"Kaśyapa, Atri, Vasiṣṭha, Viśvāmitra, Gautama, Jamadagni, and Bharadvāja are known as the seven sages."

Śrīla Prabhupāda explains that the seven *ṛṣis* are those who have attained perfection by spiritual achievements and that all *ṛṣis* are situated in the quality of goodness. Such spiritual achievements can be earned by anyone, whether one is a king or a mendicant. In the Third Canto, Twelfth Chapter of the *Śrīmad-Bhāgavatam*, Śrī Maitreya Muni explains to Vidura how in the beginning, Lord Brahmā created the four Kumāras (Sanaka,

Sananda, Sanātana, and Sanat), then the eleven Rudras and Rudrāṇis. Finally, Brahmā desired to generate living entities by begetting ten sons for the extension of future generations. Thus Marīci, Atri, Aṅgirā, Pulastya, Pulaha, Kratu, Bhṛgu, Vasiṣṭha, Dakṣa, and Nārada were born. These sages would also assist Lord Brahmā in instructing others on the path of devotional service, especially Nārada, who is the supreme spiritual master of all transcendentalists. Further on, in the Fourth Canto, Twenty-Ninth Chapter, Nārada Muni explains to King Prācinabarhi how the living entities are entrapped within the material universe. Nārada explains that the great sages (mentioned above) are all stalwart *brāhmaṇas* who can speak authoritatively on Vedic literature and have become powerful because of austerities, meditation, and education, even though they do not know perfectly about the Supreme Personality of Godhead. But despite the cultivation of Vedic knowledge, only by fully engaging in devotional service to the Supreme Personality of Godhead will they obtain the Lord's causeless mercy.

In the *Bhagavad-gītā*, Tenth Chapter, Lord Kṛṣṇa explains that neither the hosts of demigods nor the great sages know His origin, since He is the source of all the demigods and sages. Śrīla Prabhupāda comments that if the demigods and sages cannot understand Lord Kṛṣṇa, then what to speak of the so-called modern scholars. All the great sages agree: "What is *ātmā*, what is the Supreme? It is He whom we have to worship." Since Lord Brahmā is known as *pitāmaha* (grandfather), Lord Kṛṣṇa is known as *prapitāmaha* (father of the grandfather), because the Lord says, "The seven great sages and before them the four other great sages and the Manus are born out of my mind, and all creatures in these planets descend from them."

The *Śrīmad-Bhāgavatam* (8.13.36) describes the long duration of life enjoyed by the Manus, the fathers of mankind, as follows: "O King, I have now described to you the fourteen Manus appearing in the past, present, and future. The total duration of time ruled by these Manus is one thousand *yuga* cycles. This is called a *kalpa*, or one day of Brahmā."

The Manus are different administrative demigods who are the fathers of mankind. There are fourteen Manu incarnations who appear in one day of Lord Brahmā, which lasts for 4,320,000 times 1,000 human years. One *divya-yuga* cycle, or *catur-yuga* (Satya, Tretā, Dvāpara, and Kali yugas), period lasts 4,320,000 human years, and one day of Brahmā (kalpa) equals one thousand of these *catur-yugas*. These incarnations are called Manvantara-avatāras. Each Manu reigns for a period of one Manvantara (the interval of a Manu) along with his descendants—one Indra, one group of demigods, and one group of Sapta Ṛṣis. One Manvantara has the duration of 71 *catur-yugas*. Hence, there are also 14 different groups of Sapta Ṛṣis in one day of Lord Brahmā, and thus there are 420 Manus in one month (30 days) of Brahmā, and 5,040 Manus in one year of Brahmā. Brahmā lives for one hundred years, and as such, there are 504,000 Manus and hence 504,000 groups of Sapta Ṛṣis in the lifetime of Brahmā.

The fourteen Manus are Svāyambhuva, Svārociṣa, Uttama, Tāmasa, Raivata, Cākṣuṣa, Śrāddhadeva (Vaivasvata), Sāvarṇi, Dakṣa-sāvarṇi, Brahma-sāvarṇi, Dharma-sāvarṇi, Rudra-sāvarṇi, Deva-sāvarṇi (Raucya) and Indra-sāvarṇi (Bhautya). We are presently living during the reign of the seventh Manu, Vaivasvata.

In his summary on the Thirteen Chapter, Eighth Canto, of the *Śrīmad-Bhāgavatam*, Śrīla Prabhupāda writes: "The seventh Manu,

who is the son of Vivasvan, is known as Śrāddhadeva. He has ten sons, named Ikṣvāku, Nābhāga, Dhṛṣṭa, Śaryāti, Nariṣyanta, Nābhāga, Diṣṭa, Tarūṣa, Pṛṣadhra, and Vasumān. In this *manvantara*, or reign of Manu, among the demigods are the Ādityas, Vasus, Rudras, Viśvedevas, Maruts, Aśvinī-kumāras, and Ṛbhus. The King of heaven, Indra, is known as Purandara, and the seven sages are known as Kaśyapa, Atri, Vasiṣṭha, Viśvāmitra, Gautama, Jamadagni, and Bharadvāja. During this period of Manu, the Supreme Personality of Godhead Viṣṇu appears from the womb of Aditi in His incarnation as the son of Kaśyapa (Lord Vāmanadeva)."

* * *

The pastimes of the Sapta Ṛṣis are narrated in numerous Vedic literatures such as the *Sūtras*, *Brāhmaṇas*, *Upaniṣads*, *Saṁhitās*, *Rāmāyaṇa*, *Mahābhārata*, *Hari-vaṁśa*, and some twelve *Purāṇas*, including the *Śrīmad-Bhāgavatam*. In all of the above scriptures, the different kinds of *ṛṣis* appear in many forms such as: *brahma-ṛṣi*, *deva-ṛṣi*, *vipra-ṛṣi*, *parama-ṛṣi*, *mahā-ṛṣi*, *rāja-ṛṣi*, *śruta-ṛṣi*, *jana-ṛṣi*, *tapa-ṛṣi*, *satya-ṛṣi*, *kāṇḍa-ṛṣi*, *ṛṣi-kaus*, *ṛṣi-putras*, and *ṛṣi-pautras*. The Sapta Ṛṣis referred in this chapter appear in only five of the above mentioned forms: *brahma*, *deva*, *vipra*, *parama*, and *mahā-ṛṣis*.

In each new *catur-yuga*, the Manu and Sapta Ṛṣis all have their respective duties to perform, especially to distribute Vedic knowledge, which reinstates eternal religious principles. Manu's duty is to re-establish the system of religion and Manu's sons, the sages, the demigods, and Indra, execute Manu's orders. Thus the entire universe is maintained by Manu and his descendants.

The Sapta Ṛṣis perform various duties throughout their lives. Some of them at times play the role of progenitors for the demigods, mankind, demons, and all other creation. They are known as great ascetics and mystics. They perform austerities, offer sacrifices, and compose sacred hymns. They also travel freely between the heavenly planets, and due to their austere vows, each of them is awarded his own planet (Ursa major), located beneath Dhruvaloka (the pole star).

In the *Śrīmad-Bhāgavatam* (5.23.5) there is a vivid description of the *kuṇḍalinī-cakra* (Śiśumāra planetary system), which is another expansion of the external body of the Supreme Personality of Godhead. This great planetary system consists of stars and planets and resembles the form of a *śiśumāra* (dolphin). The great *yogis* and sages meditate upon Lord Vāsudeva in this dolphin form because it is easily visible. Some 1,300,000 *yojanas* (10,400,000 miles) above the planets of the seven sages resides the great devotee Dhruva on his own planet known as Dhruvaloka. This planet, the pole star, constantly shines as the central pivot for all other stars and planets.

"This form of the *śiśumāra* has its head downward and its body coiled. On the end of its tail is the planet of Dhruva, on the body of its tail are the planets of the demigods Prajāpati, Agni, Indra, and Dharma, and at the base of its tail are the planets of the demigods Dhātā and Vidhātā. Where the hips might be on the *śiśumāra* are the seven saintly sages like Vasiṣṭha and Aṅgirā. The coiled body of the Śiśumāra-cakra turns toward its right side, on which the fourteen constellations from Abhijit to Punarvasu are located. On its left side are the fourteen stars from Puṣyā to Uttarāṣāḍhā. Thus its body is balanced because its sides are occupied by an equal number of stars. On the back of the *śiśumāra* is the group of stars known as Ajavīthī, and on its abdomen is the Ganges (Mandākinī or Ākāśa Gaṅgā) that flows in the sky (the Milky Way)."

Śrīla Prabhupāda describes in his purport on the *Śrīmad-Bhāgavatam* (9.16.24) how the seven stars of the seven sages rotate every day: "The seven stars revolving around the pole star at the zenith are called *saptarṣi-maṇḍala*. On these seven stars, which form the topmost part of our planetary system, reside seven sages: Kaśyapa, Atri, Vasiṣṭha, Viśvāmitra, Gautama, Jamadagni and Bharadvāja. These seven stars are seen every night, and they each make a complete orbit around the pole star within twenty-four hours. Along with these seven stars, all the other stars also orbit from east to west. The upper portion of the universe is called the north, and the lower portion is called the south. Even in ordinary dealings, while studying maps, we regard the upper portion of the map as north."

The *Śrīmad-Bhāgavatam* (12.2.27-28, 31-32) also describes the constellation of the seven stars and how their position indicates the beginning of Kali-yuga: "Of the seven stars forming the constellation of the seven sages, Pulaha and Kratu are the first to rise in the night sky. If a line running north and south were drawn through their midpoint, whichever of the lunar mansions this line passes through is said to be the ruling asterism of the constellation for that time. The Seven Sages will remain connected with that particular lunar mansion for one hundred human years. Currently, during your [King Parīkṣit's] lifetime, they are situated in the *nakṣatra* called Māgha...When the constellation of the seven sages is passing through the lunar mansion Māgha, the age of Kali begins. It comprises twelve hundred years of the demigods. When the great sages of the Sapta Ṛṣi constellation pass from Māgha to Pūrvāṣāḍhā, Kali will have his full strength, beginning from King Nanda and his dynasty."

The following is a conversation found in the *Śrīla Prabhupāda Lectures* (Gorakhpur, India, 1971) between Śrīla Prabhupāda, his disciples, and a guest regarding the Ursa Major (also known as the Little Dipper):

Devotee I : "It's called the Little Dipper. Seven star formation?"

Prabhupāda : "Yes. Like that".

Devotee I : "Box and then one thing going up?"

Prabhupāda : "Yes."

Devotee I : "That's the Dipper."

Prabhupāda : "No, no. Seven star in the northern pole, center being the pole star. It is moving whole night."

Guest : "*Saptarṣi-maṇḍala*."

Prabhupāda : "*Saptarṣi-maṇḍala*, yes. That *saptarṣi-maṇḍala* is the abode of great seven *ṛṣis*. So here it is said, Yamarāja says, 'Even the seven *ṛṣis*, they are controlling the affairs, like the demigods and they are *brāhmaṇas* amongst the demigods, the great sages'. The demigods, some of them are *brāhmaṇas*, some of them are *kṣatriyas* exactly in the same way. So this Bhṛgvādaya-ṛṣis, they are *brāhmaṇas*. *Sattva-guṇa-pradhāna*. *Sattva-pradhāna*. They are standing on the modes of goodness. So...And they are *viśva-sṛjo 'mareśāḥ*. *Amaras* means the demigods. They are supposed to be *amara* in our calculation. Just like Brahmā. We cannot calculate his duration of life. His duration of life is so long that it is beyond our calculation. Therefore, they are sometimes called *amara*. Amara means immortal. Although none of them are immortal, but...Just like in comparison to a germ or...What is called in our, in Diwali, during? What is that, that worms? They generate in the night, in the evening, and at the end of the night, finished."

The *Śrīmad-Bhāgavatam* (5.17.3) further describes the seven sages, who conclude that uninterrupted devotional service is the perfection of life: "The seven great sages [Marīci, Vasiṣṭha, Atri and so on] reside on planets beneath Dhruvaloka. Well

aware of the influence of the water of the Ganges, to this day they keep Ganges water on the tufts of hair on their heads. They have concluded that this is the ultimate wealth, the perfection of all austerities, and the best means of prosecuting transcendental life. Having obtained uninterrupted devotional service to the Supreme Personality of Godhead, they neglect all other beneficial processes like religion, economic development, sense gratification, and even merging into the Supreme. Just as *jñānīs* think that merging into the existence of the Lord is the highest truth, these seven exalted personalities accept devotional service as the perfection of life."

Śrīla Prabhupāda comments in his purport on the above text: "Transcendentalists are divided into two primary groups: the *nirviśeṣa-vādīs*, or impersonalists, and the *bhaktas*, or devotees. The impersonalists do not accept spiritual varieties of life. They want to merge into the existence of the Supreme Lord in His Brahmán feature, the *brahmajyoti*. The devotees, however, desire to take part in the transcendental activities of the Supreme Lord. In the upper planetary system, the topmost planet is Dhruvaloka, and beneath Dhruvaloka are the seven planets occupied by the great sages, beginning with Marīci, Vasiṣṭha, and Atri. All these sages regard devotional service as the highest perfection of life. Therefore they all carry the holy water of the Ganges on their heads. This verse proves that for one who has achieved the platform of pure devotional service, nothing else is important, even so-called liberation (*kaivalya*). Śrīla Śrīdhara Svāmī states that only by achieving pure devotional service of the Lord can one give up all other engagements as insignificant."

* * *

The following are brief descriptions of the Sapta Ṛṣis taken from Śrīla Prabhupāda's translations of the *Śrīmad-Bhāgavatam* and purports.

Kaśyapa is described in the *Śrīmad-Bhāgavatam* (1.9.8) purport as follows: "One of the *prajāpatis*, the son of Marīci and one of the sons-in-law of Prajāpati Dakṣa. He is the father of the gigantic bird Garuḍa, who was given elephants and tortoises as eatables. He married thirteen daughters of Prajāpati Dakṣa, and their names are Adiṭi, Diti, Danu, Kāṣṭhā, Ariṣṭā, Surasā, Ilā, Muni, Krodhavaśā, Tāmrā, Surabhi, Saramā and Timi. He begot many children, both demigods and demons, by those wives. From his first wife, Aditi, all the twelve Ādityas were born; one of them is Vāmana, the incarnation of Godhead. This great sage, Kaśyapa, was also present at the time of Arjuna's birth. He received a presentation of the whole world from Paraśurāma, and later on he asked Paraśurāma to go out of the world. His other name is Ariṣṭanemi. He lives on the northern side of the universe."

In the summary to Chapter Eighteen of the Eighth Canto it is stated: "All the great sages expressed their jubilation, and with Kaśyapa Muni before them they performed the birthday ceremony of Lord Vāmana. At the time of Lord Vāmanadeva's sacred thread ceremony, He was honored by the sun-god, Bṛhaspati, the goddess presiding over the earth, the deity of the heavenly planets, His mother, Lord Brahmā, Kuvera, the seven *ṛṣis*, and others."

Atri is described in the *Śrīmad-Bhāgavatam* (1.9.7) purport as follows: "Atri Muni was a great *brāhmaṇa* sage and was one of the mental sons of Brahmājī. Brahmājī is so powerful that simply by thinking of a son he can have it. These sons are known as *mānasa-putras*. Out of seven *mānasa-putras* of Brahmājī and out of the seven great *brāhmaṇa* sages, Atri was one. In his family the great Pracetās were also born. Atri Muni had two *kṣatriya* sons who became kings. King Arthama is one of them. He is counted as one of the twenty-one *prajāpatis*. His wife's name was Anasūyā, and he helped Mahārāja Parīkṣit in his great sacrifices."

Śrīmad-Bhāgavatam (2.7.4) says: "The great sage Atri prayed for offspring, and the Lord, being satisfied with him, promised to incarnate as Atri's son, Dattātreya (Datta, the son of Atri). And by the grace of the lotus feet of the Lord, many Yadus, Haihayas, etc., became so purified that they obtained material and spiritual blessings."

Vasiṣṭha is described in the *Śrīmad-Bhāgavatam* (1.9.7) purport as follows: "The great celebrated sage among the *brāhmaṇas*, well known as the *brahma-ṛṣi* Vasiṣṭhadeva. He is a prominent figure in both the *Rāmāyaṇa* and *Mahābhārata* periods. He celebrated the coronation ceremony of the Personality of Godhead, Śrī Rāma. He was present also on the battlefield of Kurukṣetra. He could approach all the higher and lower planets, and his name is also connected with the history of Hiraṇyakaśipu. There was a great tension between him and Viśvāmitra, who wanted his *kāmadhenu*, wish-fulfilling cow. Vasiṣṭha Muni refused to spare his *kāmadhenu*, and for this Viśvāmitra killed his one hundred sons. As a perfect *brāhmaṇa* he tolerated all the taunts of Viśvāmitra. Once he tried to commit suicide on account of Viśvāmitra's torture, but all his attempts were unsuccessful. He jumped from a hill, but the stones on which he fell became a stack of cotton, and thus he was saved. He jumped into the ocean, but the waves washed him ashore. He jumped into the river [Vipāśā], but the river also washed him ashore. Thus all his suicide attempts were unsuccessful. He is also one of the seven ṛṣis and husband of Arundhatī, the famous star."

Viśvāmitra, also known as Gādhi-suta, is described in the *Śrīmad-Bhāgavatam*

(1.19.9) purport as follows: "A great sage of austerity and mystic power. He is famous as Gādhi-suta because his father was Gādhi, a powerful king of the province of Kānyakubja (part of Uttar Pradesh). Although he was a *kṣatriya* by birth, he became a *brāhmaṇa* in the very same body by the power of his spiritual achievements. He picked a quarrel with Vasiṣṭha Muni when he was a *kṣatriya* king and performed a great sacrifice in cooperation with Magaṅga Muni and thus was able to vanquish the sons of Vasiṣṭha. He became a great *yogī*, and yet he failed to check his senses and thus was obliged to become the father of Śakuntalā, the beauty queen of world history. Once, when he was a *kṣatriya* king, he visited the hermitage of Vasiṣṭha Muni, and he was given a royal reception. Viśvāmitra wanted from Vasiṣṭha a cow named Nandinī, and the *muni* refused to deliver it. Viśvāmitra stole the cow, and thus there was a quarrel between the sage and the king. Viśvāmitra was defeated by the spiritual strength of Vasiṣṭha, and thus the King decided to become a *brāhmaṇa*. Before becoming a *brāhmaṇa* he underwent severe austerity on the bank of the Kauśika. He was also one who tried to stop the Kurukṣetra war."

Gautama is described in the *Śrīmad-Bhāgavatam* (1.19.10) purport as follows: "One of the seven great sages of the universe. Śaradvān was one of his sons. Persons in the Gautama-gotra (dynasty) today are either his family descendants or in his disciplic succession. The *brāhmaṇas* who profess Gautama-gotra are generally family descendants, and the *kṣatriyas* and *vaiśyas* who profess Gautama-gotra are all in the line of his disciplic succession. He was the husband of the famous Ahalyā who turned into stone when Indradeva, the King of heaven, molested her. Ahalyā was delivered by Lord Rāmacandra. Gautama was the grandfather

of Kṛpācārya, one of the heroes of the Battle of Kurukṣetra."

Jamadagni is described in the summary on Chapter Fifteen of the Ninth Canto in the following words: "Satyavatī married Ṛcīka Muni after the *muni* contributed a substantial dowry, and from the womb of Satyavatī by Ṛcīka Muni, Jamadagni was born. The son of Jamadagni was Rāma, or Paraśurāma. When a king named Kārtavīryārjuna stole Jamadagni's desire cow, Paraśurāma, who is a *śaktyāveśa* incarnation of the Supreme Personality of Godhead, killed Kārtavīryārjuna. Later, he annihilated the *kṣatriya* dynasty twenty-one times. After Paraśurāma killed Kārtavīryārjuna, Jamadagni told him that the killing of a king is sinful and that as a *brāhmaṇa* he should have tolerated the offense. Therefore Jamadagni advised Paraśurāma to atone for his sin by traveling to various holy places."

Śrīmad-Bhāgavatam (9.15.11-13) further says: "Satyavatī, however, pacified the angry Ṛcīka Muni with peaceful words and requested that her son not be like a fierce *kṣatriya*. Ṛcīka Muni replied, 'Then your grandson will be of a *kṣatriya* spirit.' Thus Jamadagni was born as the son of Satyavatī. Satyavatī later became the sacred River Kauśikī to purify the entire world, and her son Jamadagni, married Reṇukā, the daughter of Reṇu. By the semen of Jamadagni, many sons, headed by Vasumān, were born from the womb of Reṇukā. The youngest of them was named Rāma, or Paraśurāma."

The summary of Chapter Sixteen, Canto Nine states: "When Jamadagni's wife, Reṇukā, went to bring water from the Ganges and saw the King of the Gandharvas enjoying the company of Apsarās, she was captivated, and she slightly desired to associate with him. Because of this sinful desire, she was punished by her husband. Paraśurāma killed his mother and brothers, but later, by dint of the austerities of Jamadagni, they were revived. The sons of Kārtavīryārjuna, however, remembering the death of their father, wanted to take revenge against Paraśurāma, and therefore when Paraśurāma was absent from the *āśrama,* they killed Jamadagni, who was meditating on the Supreme Personality of Godhead."

Śrīmad-Bhāgavatam (9.16.24-25) states: "Thus Jamadagni, being worshiped by Lord Paraśurāma, was brought back to life with full remembrance, and he became one of the seven sages in the group of seven stars. My dear King Parīkṣit, in the next Manvantara the lotus-eyed Personality of Godhead Lord Paraśurāma, the son of Jamadagni, will be a great propounder of Vedic knowledge. In other words, he will be one of the seven sages."

Bharadvāja is described in the *Śrīmad-Bhāgavatam* (1.9.6) purport as follows: "He is one of the seven great *ṛṣis* and was present at the time of the birth ceremony of Arjuna. The powerful *ṛṣi* sometimes undertook severe penance on the shore of the Ganges, and his *āśrama* is still celebrated at Prayāgadhāma. It is learned that this *ṛṣi,* while taking bath in the Ganges [at Gaṅgādvāra], happened to meet Ghṛtacī, one of the beautiful society girls of heaven, and thus he discharged semen, which was kept and preserved in an earthen pot and from which Droṇa was born. So Droṇācārya is the son of Bharadvāja Muni. He was a great devotee of Brahmā. Once he approached Droṇācārya and requested him to stop the Battle of Kurukṣetra."

Sapta Godāvarī

During certain periods of their lives, the Sapta Ṛṣis traveled, preached, practiced austerities, held philosophical discussions, and maintained Vedic principles together as a group. Numerous pastimes are narrated throughout the sacred literatures about the individual and collective activities of the Sapta Ṛṣis.

In the *Brahma Purāṇa* (*Gautami-māhātmyam* 102), Lord Brahmā tells Nārada Muni about the importance of the Gautamī Gaṅgā (Godāvarī). The appearance of Gautamī Gaṅgā at Brahmagiri has already been narrated; this short story describes when the Godāvarī meets the ocean.

Lord Brahmā narrated the glories of Samudra-tīrtha, where Gaṅgā (Godāvarī) meets the eastern ocean. He described how this celestial river was born of Lord Viṣṇu's lotus feet, then she was held in his own *kamaṇḍalu*, before arriving in the matted hair of Lord Śambhu (Śiva). Then, finally, she meets the ocean at Samudra-tīrtha. He glorified her by saying that anyone who remembers Gaṅgā for even a moment, destroys all sins instantly. After Lord Brahmā spoke, the ocean began to think, "Gaṅgā is very worthy of being worshiped by the entire universe. She is the goddess of the three worlds, even Lord Viṣṇu, Śiva, and you respect and love her. If I do not receive her properly, then religious principles will be defiled. If anyone does not honor a visiting great personality or saint, then nothing in all the worlds will save that person."

Then the ocean assumed a physical form and with full-hearted humility said to Gaṅgā, "May your water, which is famous throughout the three worlds, enter me and I will not say anything. There are jewels, nectar, demons, demigods, and mountains residing in my water. The Goddess of Fortune and Lord Viṣṇu perpetually sleep in me. In the entire creation of this world, there is nothing that is impossible for me. I am not in sorrow or even angry for holding so many things, except for the great discomfort I sustained from the great sage Agastya. But

regarding you, O dear goddess Gaṅgā, your dignity surpasses all. Therefore, please join me with equality, because if you enter me in a single stream, I will be unable to join you. O Gaṅgā, if you enter with many streams, then I will be ready to join with you."

Then Gautamī Gaṅgā told the ocean, "Bring Arundhatī, the wife of Vasiṣṭha, as well as the other wives of the seven sages, along with their husbands. I will become smaller in size, then I will become happy to join you." The ocean replied, "So be it." Then the ocean brought the wives of the seven sages with their husbands to the goddess Gaṅgā, and she divided herself into seven streams. Then the Gautamī Gaṅgā entered the eastern ocean (Bay of Bengal) in seven channels. These seven Gaṅgās came to be known by the names of seven sages (Sapta Godāvarī).

Gaurī and the seven ṛṣis

This long narration from the *Padma Purāṇa* (*Sṛṣṭi-khaṇḍa* 43), describes the great determination and sincerity Gaurī had for winning the hand of Lord Śiva.

After Lord Śiva's wife, Satī, gave up her body at her father Dakṣa's sacrifice at Kanakhala (Haridvāra), she was reborn as Gaurī, the daughter of Himavān and Menā. Since Pārvatī (Gaurī) is the eternal consort of Lord Śiva, it was only natural that from the moment of Gaurī's birth she was always meditating on how to obtain Lord Śiva as her husband again.

Being inspired and encouraged by Nārada Muni, the daughter of the Himālayas went to a mountain peak that was inaccessible even to the demigods to perform austerities for winning the hand of Lord Śiva. This peak was very auspicious, adorned with many minerals, full of divine creepers, streams, secret

caves, and *kalpa-vṛkṣa* trees that were full of bees, birds, and fully blossomed flowers.

She left her garments and ornaments behind and clad herself in bark garments with a girdle of *kuśa* grass. She bathed three times a day and ate only red *lodhra* flowers for a hundred autumn seasons. She then subsisted on only one withered leaf daily for a hundred years, before remaining without food for another hundred years. By the result of her penance, all beings in the world became frightened. Thus Lord Indra requested the seven *ṛṣis* to visit the daughter of the Himālayas, test her determination, and bring about the completion of her austerities for the benefit of the world. After the seven *ṛṣis* agreed to visit the respectable lady, they went to the mountain peak where she was practicing austerities.

Upon seeing the seven *ṛṣis*, she offered them seats with full respect and regard, then she broke her vow of silence and duly worshiped the sages. The sages, who were as effulgent as the sun, gently spoke to her, asking the reason behind her penance. Gaurī then spoke with restraint as follows, "Indeed, I am eager to obtain the favor of Lord Bhava (Śiva), who is by nature very difficult to please. He is now practicing penance, and even the demigods cannot properly understand him. Being completely free from attachment, he burnt Kāmadeva to ashes, so how should a person like me propitiate Lord Śiva, who has such a nature?"

The seven *ṛṣis* replied, "O daughter, in this world there are two kinds of happiness: contact with the body and the joy of the mind. Lord Śiva, the naked one, is fierce by nature and has ashes and bones as his ornaments. He wears skulls around his neck, acts like a mendicant, has deformed eyes, and his actions are unsteady. He is heedless, loathsome, and devoid of good qualities. If you desire the eternal happiness of your body, how will you receive it from Mahādeva, who dwells amongst ghosts, who is adorned with fierce serpents, who lives in crematoriums, and who is followed by Pramathas (ghostly attendants)?

"There is Lord Viṣṇu, whose lotus feet are adorned by Śrī-devī (Lakṣmī), who kills His enemies, who is the creator of the world, and whose form is infinite. Similarly, there is Indra, Agni, Vāyu, and also Kuvera. Why not desire to have one of them, or is there someone else in your mind? O daughter, the trouble that you are taking for obtaining your husband is a fruitless tree."

After the *ṛṣis* spoke, Gaurī became extremely angry. Her eyes became red, her lips throbbed, and she spoke as follows. "What can be proper guidance for improper perception? Who can put you sages on the right path, since you have taken me to be wicked, liking a wrong position, and having a wrong perception? All of you do not know Lord Śiva, the eternal lord, who is the ruler, who is immutable, and whose greatness is immeasurable. Give up your attempt to dissuade me. Even Lord Brahmā and Indra do not know him fully. O sages, you should carefully consider these words of mine."

Then the seven *ṛṣis* explained the real reason why the marriage and union between Lord Śiva and her were very important for the peace of the world: The demon Tāraka was to be killed by their future son, Kārtikeya. Seeing her fixed determination to have Lord Śiva as her husband, the seven *ṛṣis* agreed to help her. Taking leave of her, they went to her parents. The sages told them how the trident-holding Śiva himself seeks the hand of their daughter, so they should quickly purify themselves for the marriage by offering oblations into the fire. Himavān was overjoyed and unable to speak. Menā, however, overcome with love for her daughter, spoke the following words to the sages.

"A daughter should not be given in marriage if the groom is not seeking her hand. How is it that Śiva, who roams naked, who satisfies desires even though he has burnt Kāma, is worshiped by my daughter?" The seven *ṛṣis* replied, "Please understand the supremacy of Lord Śaṅkara (Śiva). The demigods and demons who worship his lotus feet become very happy. Your daughter is very pleased with Śiva's form and is practicing severe penance. When she has completed her sacred vows, then she will listen to us."

Then the sages returned to that mountain peak to visit Gaurī once again. She appeared full of radiating luster, enough to defeat the sun's rays and the fire's flames. After being affectionately addressed by the sages, she said, "I do not desire anyone except Śarva (Śiva), the trident-holder. I am seeking the favor of Śiva, who gives prosperity to all beings and whose matchless courage and deeds of grandeur are beyond all. I seek nothing other than him from whom all proceeds and whose affluence is without a beginning or end. He is impartial, resolute, and his uncommon deeds are beyond understanding."

After hearing these words of Gaurī, the seven *ṛṣis*, their eyes full of tears, embraced the devoted daughter of the Himālayas and then said, "We are struck with wonder by your spotless knowledge, and your surrender to Bhava pleases our hearts. We indeed know the wonderful supremacy and attributes of Lord Śiva. We have only come here to test the firmness of your resolve. O you of slender body, your desire will soon be fulfilled. You will not be separated from him much longer. We are now going to inform him of your request and motive. Since you are the intellect and wisdom of Śiva, he too will be happy to accomplish the needful."

All the sages departed and went to Śaṅkara's hermitage, high in the Himālayas, where the water of the Gaṅgā flows. Upon reaching the mountain peak, they sprinkled Gaṅgā-jala on their tawny matted hair and observed that all beings were completely tranquil. Then, at the entrance, the doorkeeper Vīraka was standing with a cane. The sages politely worshiped him and then humbly requested the audience of Lord Śaṅkara. The doorkeeper informed the sages that Lord Śiva had gone to Gaṅgā for offering his prayers, so they must wait for a while before he would return. Thus being informed, the seven *ṛṣis* remained there with full attention, just as the thirsty Cātaka birds remain waiting for the rainy season.

Vīraka bowed down and offered obeisances upon the return of Lord Śaṅkara, who had deer-hide fastened to his body and who was the abode of affection. The doorkeeper then said, "The seven sages have come to see you. After seeing them, You may return to your meditation." After being addressed in this way, Lord Śiva gestured with his eyebrows for their entry. Vīraka then indicated to the great sages that Śiva would see them now. Also wearing long hides of black antelopes as their garments, they tied their hair before entering Lord Śiva's divine sacrificial arena. With their hands folded, they worshiped Śiva's lotus feet with heavenly flowers. The seven *ṛṣis* and Lord Śiva exchanged affectionate looks, and then the *ṛṣis* said, "We are blessed now with the *darśana* of your lotus feet, which are worshiped by all the demigods and which are a treasury of all virtues. Order us what we should do for the protection of all." Then the omniscient Śaṅkara laughed and said to the best of the sages, "Carry out the mission that you have in mind."

Thus addressed, the sages quickly returned to Gaurī and said, "Do not continue burning your charming attractive form with austerities. Lord Śaṅkara is pleased with you

and will accept your hand in marriage. Since we also desired the same thing, we first approached your father. So please return to your father's home, where he is waiting for you, so we can also return to our home." Gaurī hastily returned to her father's house, where wedding preparations were being made. Thus Lord Śiva and Gaurī were united, which union resulted in the birth of Kārtikeya, who killed Tāraka and thereby enabled the demigods to occupy heaven once again.

Ṛṣi-kulas

In the *Śrīmad-Bhāgavatam* (3.22.26-27), as well as in Śrīla Prabhupāda's purport that follows, descriptions are given of the seven sages' peaceful, beautiful hermitages, which are situated on the shores of the Gaṅgā, Yamunā, and Sarasvatī Rivers.

"After asking and obtaining the great sages' permission to leave, the monarch mounted his chariot with his wife and started for his capital, followed by his retinue. Along the way he saw the prosperity of the tranquil seers' beautiful hermitages on both the charming banks of the Sarasvatī, the river so agreeable to saintly persons."

"As cities are constructed in the modern age with great engineering and architectural craftsmanship, so in days gone by there were neighborhoods called *ṛṣi-kulas*, where great saintly persons resided. In India there are still many magnificent places for spiritual understanding; there are many *ṛṣis* and saintly persons living in nice cottages on the banks of the Ganges and Yamunā for purposes of spiritual cultivation. While passing through the *ṛṣi-kulas* the King and his party were very much satisfied with the beauty of the cottages and hermitages. It is stated, *paśyann āśrama-sampadaḥ*. The great sages had no skyscrapers, but the hermitages were so beautiful that the King was very much pleased at the sight."

Live long Mārkaṇḍeya!

The following narration from the *Padma Purāṇa* (*Sṛṣṭi-khaṇḍa* 33) between Pulastya Ṛṣi and Bhīṣma explains why the sage Mārkaṇḍeya lives for such a lengthy period.

There was a great sage named Mṛkaṇḍu, who was the son of Bhṛgu Muni. He practiced austerities with his wife and, while living in the forest, a son named Mārkaṇḍeya was born. At the young age of five years, the boy possessed full virtues and was superior in every way. At that time, one sage was roaming through the courtyard of their *āśrama* and the young boy's father asked, "What is the life span of my son?" The wise sage said that due to the will of Providence, his son would only live for six more months! When Mṛkaṇḍu heard this statement, he immediately performed the thread-ceremony and instructed Mārkaṇḍeya to respect and offer obeisances to everyone he met, regardless of their caste or distinction.

One day, the seven sages were on pilgrimage when the young boy saw them. He offered them all his humble obeisances, and they each replied, "May you live long." Afterwards, the sages realized that this young boy had only five more days to live, so they brought him to see Lord Brahmā. He inquired from the sages why they had brought the young boy to him. After the sages explained the short life of the boy, they inquired as to how their "live long" benedictions would come true. Lord Brahmā said, "This land stands fearless due to the true words being spoken. This boy, Mārkaṇḍeya, will have a span of life as I shall. This best of sages will be present at the beginning as well as at the end of many *kalpas*." Thus the sages and the boy returned to earth, and they proceeded with their pilgrimage while the boy returned home to his father.

The young Mārkaṇḍeya explained to his father that the sages took him to Lord Brahmā, who blessed him with a long life, and he now desired to go to Puṣkara to practice austerities for the pleasure of Brahmā. Having heard the words of his son, Mṛkaṇḍu was extremely pleased and spoke the following words, "Today my existence has become fruitful, since you have seen the grandfather, Lord Brahmā. With you, my son, I now have an heir. Go to Puṣkara and please Lord Brahmā, since old age and death are not seen there. (There are three sacred *puṣkaras*, or lakes—Jyeṣṭha, Madhyama, and Kaniṣṭha Puṣkara—where Lord Brahmā, Lord Viṣṇu, and Lord Śiva respectively reside.) There is no place more auspicious than this. It is well known in the three worlds that the water there is pure and free from dust. There is no other person on earth who can compare to you, who at just five years old have pleased me so much. As a result of this boon, you will resemble one who has lived a very long and wise life. There is no doubt, since that is the Lord's blessing. Everyone who sees you will always want to be like you, so go to Puṣkara and establish a hermitage for yourself."

Pulastya Ṛṣi concluded, "Thus one who bathes there at Mārkaṇḍeya's hermitage will purify himself from all sins and live a long life."

Vālmīki and the ṛṣis

In the *Skanda Purāṇa* (6.124) there is a narration of how a thief named Lohajaṅgha became the great poet, Vālmīki.

Once upon a time there was a *brāhmaṇa* named Lohajaṅgha, who was born in the Māṇḍavya family in Camatkārapura. He cared for his family very much, but when there was a great drought he was not able to feed them. One day, out of desperation, he robbed an old woman in the nearby forest in order to maintain himself. On another day, he tried to rob the seven sages, who were performing austerities in the forest. The sages asked him to return to his family and inquire whether or not they would be willing to share the sin of robbery that he was committing for them. Upon returning to his family, his parents told him that he alone would have to suffer for the act. He returned to the forest and apologized to the seven ṛṣis and then requested them to teach him how to be free from his sins. One of the sages fooled him by teaching him a wrong *mantra* named Jaṭāghoṭa, which was to be chanted day and night for many days. Lohajaṅgha then sat there in meditation reciting the wrong *mantra* without moving, until his body became covered by an ant-hill.

After some time, the seven sages passed through the same forest again and heard that Jaṭāghoṭa *mantra* being chanted continuously. When they found Lohajaṅgha covered by an ant-hill in meditation, they were very surprised. The sages removed the ant-hill and massaged his body with oil and medicines. When he returned to his normal senses, he said to the sages, "You are free now. I will not rob you, so go away." He did not realize that he had been meditating there for such a long period and had reached perfection. The seven sages then named him Vālmīki, since he came out of a *valmīka* (ant-hill). Because he robbed people at that place, they named that spot Mukhāra-tīrtha (near Śukla-tīrtha, Narmadā River, Gujarat). Whoever bathes there is freed from the sin of theft, and one who worships Vālmīki there becomes a poet.

The seven ṛṣis in Navadvīpa

When Lord Nityānanda Prabhu took Jīva Gosvāmī on pilgrimage around Śrī Navadvīpa-dhāma, Bengal, they eventually came to a village named Majida-grāma, on the island of Madhyadvīpa. It was at this place

that the seven *ṛṣis* remained for a lengthy period engaged in worshiping Śrī Caitanya Mahāprabhu. The following account is quoted from the Ninth Chapter of the *Śrī Navadvīpa-māhātmyam*.

"In Satya-yuga, the *ṛṣis* began singing the glories of Gaurāṅga in their father's presence. Completely absorbed, they begged for the eternal treasure of *gaura-prema*. Lord Brahmā was pleased with his seven sons and told them, 'Go to Navadvīpa and sing the glories of Gaurāṅga, then you will easily attain *prema*. Whoever gets the mercy of the *dhāma*, gets the association of devotees. Then, by worshiping in the association of devotees, you will become absorbed in *kṛṣṇa-prema*. That is the supreme activity. Whoever gets attraction for Navadvīpa will receive the benediction of living in Vraja. To live in the spiritual *dhāma* and recite the name of Gaurāṅga is the only aspiration of the devotees.'

"The seven *ṛṣis* took their father's instructions to heart and came to this place. When they arrived, they engaged in dancing and chanting the name of Hari. They begged for *gaura-prema* while singing the Lord's glories in a loud voice, 'O Gaurāṅga, be merciful and reveal Yourself to us just once! Being offenders, we have followed many paths, but now we are taking to the path of devotional service.'

"The *ṛṣis* underwent austerities and became firmly situated in devotional service by worshiping Gaurāṅga. They completely gave up eating and sleeping and simply recited the name of Gaurāṅga. One day around noon, the all-merciful Lord Gaurāṅga appeared before the *ṛṣis*.

"The Lord was as brilliant as a hundred suns, and He attracted the minds of the *yogīs*. He appeared with the Pañca-tattva. How extraordinary was that form! His form had a beautiful golden hue. Around His neck was a garland of flowers, and His glittering ornaments illuminated all directions. His glance was beautiful, His hair was long and curled, and a dot of sandalwood decorated His forehead. He wore threefolded cloth, a shining thread, and His neck was decorated with a beautiful jasmine garland. Seeing this form, the *ṛṣis* were enchanted and they humbly petitioned, 'We surrender to Your lotus feet. Please give us devotion.'

"Hearing the *ṛṣis*' prayer, Gaurāṅga replied, 'Listen *ṛṣis*. Give up all desires, the chains of *jñāna* (mental speculation) and *karma* (fruitive work), and just discuss topics of Kṛṣṇa. Within a short time I will unfold My *līlā* in Navadvīpa. Then you will see My pastimes of *nāma-saṅkīrtana*. But now, keep this subject a secret. Worship Kṛṣṇa at Kumārahaṭṭa at the *ghāṭa* made by you.'

"When Lord Gaurāṅga disappeared, the seven *ṛṣis* went to Kumārahaṭṭa. At this place now you see seven *ṭilās*, or hillocks. These seven hills are arranged in the same pattern as the seven *ṛṣis* in the sky (the constellation). By living here one will receive the mercy of Gaurāṅga without having to undergo a strict process of rules and regulations."

The *ṛṣis* in Puṣkara

In the *Padma Purāṇa* (*Sṛṣṭi-khaṇḍa* 19-20), Pulastya Ṛṣi, who is one of the Sapta Ṛṣis during the Svāyambhuva Manvantara, describes the seven sage's pastimes in Puṣkara to Bhiṣmadeva as follows. "The qualities of kindness, courage, victory, penance, truth, piety, and charity are all fully manifested in the personalities of these most compassionate seven sages. Every action performed at their hermitages produces unlimited benefits for the next world. Atheists, thieves, sense-enjoyers, the cruel and wicked, the ungrateful, and the proud will never come to these hermitages. Those who are truthful, lustrous, brave, kind-hearted, forgiving, desireless, and innocent will always desire to visit Puṣkara. The great souls residing there are free from disease, old age, and death. Only fools, materialists, and greedy persons, as well as those who are full of passion, treachery, anger, and illusion will never be able to enter there. The *brāhmaṇas* who live in these hermitages will never see the world of Yamarāja. Those who do not harm others by action, thought, or speech, who are kind, who always speak agreeably, who always honor guests, who study the *Vedas*, who engage in holy bathing, who are free from desire, and who always look upon another's wife as their own mother, sister, or daughter—such persons will not be reborn on earth, but will attain the glorious worlds."

One time, the entire world was struck by a great famine that caused great miseries. Since there was no food available, the seven sages, who were very anxious to sustain themselves, were forced to cook meat. While they were in this miserable state, a king happened to walk near their hermitage. Seeing the distressed sages struck with dejection, he said, "Receiving gifts is observed to be a glorious way of leading a life for *brāhmaṇas*. Therefore O sages, please accept from me these gifts of rice, barley, drinks, jewels, gold, cattle, cows, and villages. Take them all, but do not cook flesh, O *brāhmaṇas*." Then the sages replied, "O King, accepting gifts is as terrible as tasting wine, which is like poison. Why do you tempt us, since we know better? An oilman is equal to ten slaughter houses; a vendor of liquor is equal to ten oilmen; a prostitute is equal to ten vendors of liquor; and a king is equal to ten prostitutes, so a king is comparably equal to ten thousand slaughter-houses! To accept gifts from a king is very fearful. A *brāhmaṇa* who out of greed accepts gifts from a king is cooked in the horrible hellish planet named Tāmisra. Therefore, O King, go your way. May you prosper with your gifts, which you may give to others." After saying this, the sages went to a forest. Thereafter the King's ministers scattered on the ground fruits in which gold was hidden. While the sages were searching for and collecting food, they found these fruits. But upon seeing them, they said, "These are not to be taken."

First Atri spoke, "We are not fools. Being wise and learned, we know that these fruits are for those who want immediate pleasure, without considering what occurs after death. One who receives gold desires to multiply his wealth by hundreds or thousands, but then his destiny becomes very sinful. Whatever rice, barley, gold, beasts, or women there are on this earth is never enough for one person. One should be tranquil."

Then Vasiṣṭha said, "Between the accumulation of penance and the accumulation of wealth, the former is far superior to the latter. The calamities of a person who rejects all accumulations will disappear. No greedy person is ever free from calamities. The luster of a *brāhmaṇa* who does not accept bad gifts increases because of his contentment. If poverty and a kingdom were weighed against each other, poverty would be chosen by those with a good mind."

Then Kaśyapa spoke, "The accumulation of wealth is a great calamity for a *brāhmaṇa*. A *brāhmaṇa* who is deluded by material prosperity will be deprived of the supreme destination. Therefore, one who desires bliss should completely abandon material wealth, which produces only misery. That religious merit which is obtained through material wealth is perishable, but that sacrifice which is done for others is inexhaustible and is the cause of liberation."

Then Bharadvāja said, "The hair of one who grows old will wear out. The teeth of one who grows old will perish. But the desire

for wealth and life, even after growing old, does not fade away. Even the eyes and ears will wear out, but desire alone is undisturbed. Therefore, one should avoid desire completely."

Gautama said, "A man plunges into miseries because of greed. For the person whose mind is content, wealth exists everywhere. How can the happiness of those with the nectar of contentment be obtained by those who are greedy for wealth, who run here and there? Want of contentment is a great misery and contentment is great happiness. Therefore, a person desiring happiness should always be content."

And finally Viśvāmitra said, "If one desire of a person is satisfied, then another desire pierces him like an arrow. Desire never ceases by enjoying the desired objects, just as a fire grows when offered oblations. A king who enjoys this earth and the oceans is not as happy as one who looks upon stone and gold equally."

After speaking thus, all the sages who were firm in their vows, abandoned those golden fruits and wandered to one of the other three lakes called Madhyama Puṣkara, the lake of Lord Viṣṇu.

Then Pulastya Ṛṣi explained to Bhīṣmadeva about one particular duty for the *brāhmaṇa* caste. He said, "Cleanliness and purity of mind cannot be had without a bath. Therefore, a bath is first prescribed for the purification of the mind. One should bathe in water that is drawn from a lake or well and then recite: 'Obeisances, obeisances to Lord Nārāyaṇa.' After doing this, one should invoke Gaṅgā with the following prayer: 'O Vaiṣṇavī, you have sprung from the lotus feet of Lord Viṣṇu. Since Lord Viṣṇu is your worshipable Lord, please protect me from any sins that I have incurred from birth up to death. O Jāhnavī, Lord Vāyu declares that there are thirty-five million sacred places between heaven, earth, and the intermediate region associated with you. Amongst the demigods you are known by the names: Nandinī, Nalinī, Dakṣā, Pṛthvī, Śubhagā, Viśvakāyā, Śivā, Sītā, Vidyādharī, Suprasannā, Lokasprasādinī, Kṣemā, Śāntā, and Śāntipradāyinī.' One should recite these holy names at the time of bathing in the Gaṅgā. After chanting these names seven times, one should put some water on one's head, either three, four, five, or seven times.

"After taking bath and satisfying Lord Viṣṇu, Śiva, and Brahmā by offering water, one should then offer water to the brahminical sages like Marīci, Atri, Aṅgiras, Pulaha, Kratu, the Pracetās, Vasiṣṭha, Bhṛgu, and Nārada Muni. Finally, one should offer proper respect and obeisances to the sun, the *brāhmaṇas*, and a cow, before feeding the *brāhmaṇas*, then one's self. By performing all of these religious principles, the seven sages will attain perfection."

The *ṛṣis'* dwellings and travels

In the *Śrī Vālmīki Rāmāyaṇa* (*Uttara-kāṇḍa* 7.1) it is stated: "Vasiṣṭha, Kaśyapa, Atri, Viśvāmitra, Gautama, Jamadagni, and Bharadvāja are the *sapta-ṛṣis*. These seven constantly dwell in the northern region." And in the *Mahābhārata* (*Śānti-parva* 12.201) it is stated: "Atri, Vasiṣṭha, Ṛṣi Kaśyapa, Gautama, Bharadvāja, Viśvāmitra, and Jamadagni, the lordly son of the great soul Ṛcīka—these seven resort to the northern region."

The area or region that the Sapta Ṛṣis, as a group, are associated with throughout the Vedic literatures is generally the northern part of Bhārata-varṣa. This is also quite logical since the seven stars or planets (Ursa major) are situated near Dhruvaloka, which is the northern, central pivot, or pole star. They primarily traveled and dwelled around

the main river basins of northern India, especially in Punjab, the Gaṅgā-Yamunā areas, the eastern Gaṅgā region, and north of the Vindhya mountains.

In the *Rāmāyaṇa*, a few descriptions are given regarding the Sapta Ṛṣi's dwelling places: Vasiṣṭha was the family priest of King Daśaratha in Ayodhyā; Viśvāmitra's main *āśrama* was on the banks of the Kauśikī River near the Himālayas; Gautama dwelled in his *āśrama* near Mithilā (Janakapura), then retired to the Himālayan peaks; Bharadvāja had his *āśrama* near the confluence of the Gaṅgā and Yamunā (Prayāga), as well as in Citrakūṭa; Atri also had his dwelling place on the Citrakūṭa mountain, and through his *tapasya*, Gaṅgā flowed there; Jamadagni spent time in the Yamunotrī valley, as well as in the eastern Gaṅgā region; Kaśyapa, along with Vasiṣṭha and Gautama, performed the coronation ceremony of Lord Rāmacandra in Ayodhyā. All of the Sapta Ṛṣis visited Lord Rāma in Ayodhyā during His reign.

In the *Mahābhārata* and *Purāṇas*, more information is given about their place of residence: Kaśyapa installed Varuṇa as the lord of waters and also resides there. He also resides on top of Mount Mahendra (Orissa), and he stayed in Kāśī for some time. Atri had his *āśrama* near the source of the River Airāvatī in the Himālayas. He performed *tapasya* on Mount Ṛkṣakalā (Vindhyas), on the banks of the Rivers Nirvindhyā (near Ujjain) and Narmadā, as well as in the Kamala forest near Citrakūṭa. Vasiṣṭha is associated with the Rivers Vipāśā (Beas), Śatadru, Sarasvatī, and Sarayū. He also performed *tapasya* in Kurukṣetra, and he had an *āśrama* on the slopes of Mount Meru, one on Mount Mahendra, one on Mount Arbu (Abu), and he obtained the city Pratiṣṭhāna on the River Godāvarī. Viśvāmitra inherited the kingdom of Kānyakubja (Kannauj) from his father Gādhi and favored the country of Māgadha (Patna-Gayā districts). He also founded *āśramas* near the Vaidūrya mountains (Gujarat) and on the western banks of the River Sarasvatī. Gautama lived in Girivraja (Rajgir) in Māgadha, and after casting his father Dīrghatamas in the River Gaṅgā, he traveled downstream to the countries of Aṅga (Bihar), Baṅga (Bengal), Puṇḍra (N. Bengal), Suhma (Rāḍha-deśa), and finally Kaliṅga (Orissa/Andhra). He also performed *tapasya* for sixty thousand years in his *āśrama* on the Pāriyātra slopes, near the western Vindhya mountains. The Gautama *brāhmaṇas* are said to reside in Dvārakā. Jamadagni performed sacrifices at Palāśaka, near the Rivers Sarasvatī and Dṛṣadvatī (Pehowa). He also performed *tapasya* at Bhṛgukaccha (Bharuch) and where the River Narmadā meets the ocean. He was killed at Māhiṣmatī on the bank of Narmadā. Bharadvāja lived at the source of the Gaṅgā, on the Bhṛgutuṅga mountain (Himālayas), and where the Rivers Tuṣṇī and Gaṅgā meet. He was also the family priest for the King of Kāśī, Divodāsa.

Finally, the *Śrīmad-Bhāgavatam* (3.8.5) describes one means of travel the sages used: "The sages came from the highest planets down to the lower region through the water of the Ganges, and therefore the hair on their heads was wet. They touched the lotus feet of the Lord, which are worshiped with various paraphernalia by the daughters of the serpent-king when they desire good husbands."

This chapter concludes with Śrīla Prabhupāda's purport on the same verse: "The Ganges water flows directly from the lotus feet of Viṣṇu, and her course runs from the highest planet of the universe down to the lowest. The sages came down from Satyaloka by taking advantage of the flowing water, a process of transportation made possible by the power of mystic *yoga*. If a river flows thousands and thousands of miles, a

perfect *yogī* can at once transport himself from one place to another simply by dipping in its water. The Ganges is the only celestial river which flows throughout the universe, and great sages travel all over the universe via this sacred river. The statement that their hair was wet indicates that it was directly moistened by the water originating from the lotus feet of Viṣṇu (the Ganges). Whoever touches the water of the Ganges to his head surely touches the lotus feet of the Lord directly and can become free from all effects of sinful acts. If after taking a bath in the Ganges or being washed of all sins, a man guards himself against committing further sinful acts, then certainly he is delivered. But if he again takes up sinful activities, his bath in the Ganges is as good as that of the elephant, who nicely takes his bath in a river but later spoils the whole thing by covering himself with dust on the land."

The Manvantara lists of the Sapta Ṛṣis

The following lists are compiled from various *Purāṇas*. Some *Purāṇas* differ from others, but the majority agrees as follows:

1st-Svāyambhuva Manvantara: Marīci, Atri, Aṅgiras, Pulastya, Pulaha, Kratu, and Vasiṣṭha.

2nd-Svārociṣa Manvantara: Ūrja, Stamba, Prāṇa, Dattoli, Ṛṣabha, Niścala, and Arvarīvat.

3rd-Uttama Manvantara: The seven sons of Vasiṣṭha: Citraketu, Suroci, Viraja, Mitra, Ulbaṇa, Vasubhṛdyāna, and Dyumān.

4th-Tāmasa Manvantara: Kāvya, Pṛthu, Agni, Caitra, Jyotirdhāman, Kapīvān, and Pīvara.

5th-Raivata Manvantara: Hiraṇyaroma, Vedaśiras, Ūrdhvabāhu, Vedabāhu, Sudhāman, Parjanya, and Satyanetra.

6th-Cākṣuṣa Manvantara: Sudhāman, Virajas, Haviṣmat, Bhṛgu, Madhu, Atināman, and Sahiṣṇu.

7th-Śrāddhadeva (Vaivasvata) Manvantara (the present one): Kaśyapa, Atri, Vasiṣṭha, Viśvāmitra, Gautama, Jamadagni, and Bharadvāja.

8th-Sāvarṇi Manvantara: Gālava, Dīptimān, Paraśurāma, Aśvatthāmā, Kṛpācārya, Ṛṣyaśṛṅga, and Vyāsadeva.

9th-Dakṣa-sāvarṇi Manvantara: Medhātithi, Vasu, Satya, Jyotiṣmat, Dyutimat, Savana, and Havyavāhana.

10th-Brahma-sāvarṇi Manvantara: Haviṣmat, Sukṛti, Jayamūrti, Āpava, Apratima, Nābhāga, and Satya.

11th-Dharma-sāvarṇi Manvantara: Niścara, Agnitejas, Vapuṣmat, Viṣṇu, Aruṇa, Haviṣmat, and Anagha.

12th-Rudra-sāvarṇi Manvantara: Dyuti, Tapasvin, Sutapas, Tapomūrti, Taponidhi, Taporati, and Tapodhṛti.

13th-Deva-sāvarṇi (Raucya) Manvantara: Dhṛtimat, Avyaya, Tattvadarśin, Nirutsuka, Nirmoha, Sutapas, and Niṣprakampa.

14th-Indra-sāvarṇi (Bhautya) Manvantara: Agnīdhra, Agnibāhu, Śuci, Mukta, Māgadha, Śukra, and Ajita.

The reader will recall that each group of Sapta Ṛṣis lives for 71 *catur-yugas*. The above mentioned 14 groups of Sapta Ṛṣis therefore live for a combined period of 71 times 14 *catur-yugas*, which is the time occupied by one day (*kalpa*), or twelve hours, of Lord Brahmā, who lives for one hundred years. Hence, the information available in the scriptures as regards the various lists of the Sapta Ṛṣis is only for one day of Lord Brahmā.

Book Two
Chapter Eight

More Vedic Thoughts About Gaṅgā

More Vedic Thoughts About Gaṅgā

"O Lord of Madhu, as the Ganges forever flows to the sea without hindrance, let my attraction be constantly drawn unto You without being diverted to anyone else."

(*Śrīmad-Bhāgavatam* 1.8.42)

"The blessed Lord Siva becomes all the more blessed by bearing on his head the holy waters of the Ganges, which has its source in the water that washed the Lord's lotus feet. The Lord's feet act like thunderbolts hurled to shatter the mountain of sin stored in the mind of the meditating devotee. One should therefore meditate on the lotus feet of the Lord for a long time."

(*Śrīmad-Bhāgavatam* 3.28.22)

"The Ganges, emanating from the toe of Lord Viṣṇu, purifies the three worlds, the upper, middle, and lower planetary systems. Similarly, when one asks questions about the pastimes and characteristics of Lord Vāsudeva, Kṛṣṇa, three varieties of men are purified: the speaker or preacher, he who inquires, and the people in general who listen."

(*Śrīmad-Bhāgavatam* 10.1.16)

"My dear Lord, You are the symbol of everything auspicious. Your transcendental name and fame is spread like a canopy all over the universe, including the higher, middle, and lower planetary systems. The transcendental water that washes Your lotus feet is known in the higher planetary systems as the River Mandākini, in the lower planetary systems as Bhogavati, and in this earthly planetary system as the Ganges. The sacred, transcendental water flows throughout the entire universe, purifying wherever it goes."

(*Śrīmad-Bhāgavatam* 10.70.44)

"Among sacred and flowing things I am the holy Ganges, and among steady bodies of water I am the ocean. Among weapons I am the bow, and of the wielders of weapons I am Lord Śiva."

(*Śrīmad-Bhāgavatam* 11.16.20)

"Just as the Gaṅgā is the greatest of all rivers, Lord Acyuta is the supreme among deities and Lord Sambhu [Siva] the greatest of Vaiṣṇavas, so *Śrīmad-Bhāgavatam* is the greatest of all *Purāṇas*."

(*Śrīmad-Bhāgavatam* 12.13.16)

"As Viṣṇu is the greatest Lord, as the sun is the greatest luminary, as Meru is the greatest mountain, as Garuḍa is the greatest bird, so Gaṅgā is the greatest holy place."
(*Padma Purāṇa, Uttara-khaṇḍa* 119.20)

"The banks of the River Gaṅgā are everywhere divine and auspicious."
(*Padma Purāṇa, Sṛṣṭi-khaṇḍa* 11.56)

"Heaps of vicious sinful actions as big as the Himālayas or the Vindhya mountains perish through the waters of Gaṅgā like misfortunes through devotion to Lord Viṣṇu."
(*Nārada Purāṇa, Uttara-bhāga* 38.34)

"Especially in Kali-yuga, Gaṅgā dispels sins after destroying offenses originating from lust—mentally, physically, or verbally."
(*Nārada Purāṇa, Uttara-bhāga* 39.39)

"A person who touches Gaṅgā attains an eternal spiritual form." (*Nārada Purāṇa*)

"When one drinks the ambrosial waters of the Gaṅgā, one should remember Lord Viṣṇu, the source of the Gaṅgā."
(*Garuḍa Purāṇa, Brahma-kāṇḍa* 29.61)

"One becomes purified of sins by seeing, touching, or drinking the Gaṅgā."
(*Agni Purāṇa*)

"O Gaṅgā, be in front of me; O Gaṅgā, stand behind me; O Gaṅgā, be at my side; O Gaṅgā, let me reside in you."
(*Skanda Purāṇa, Kāśī-khaṇḍa* 27.173)

"Gaṅgā herself is all the *tīrthas*. Gaṅgā herself is a penance grove. Gaṅgā alone is the holy place of supernatural powers. No doubt need be entertained in this respect."
(*Skanda Purāṇa, Kāśī-khaṇḍa* 28.121)

"The benefit of a holy bath in the Gaṅgā is derived only from Gaṅgā, just as the taste of grapes is only in the grapes, not in anything else."
(*Skanda Purāṇa, Kāśī-khaṇḍa* 29.10)

"He who utters 'Gaṅge! Gaṅge!' even from a distance of hundreds of miles away from the river, becomes purified from all sins, and attains Vaikuṇṭha, the world of Lord Viṣṇu." (*Devī Purāṇa*)

"He who smears the mud from the banks of the Gaṅgā on his head and body will get the luster and glow of the demigods like Sūrya. Gaṅgā water can wash off all sins."
(*Mahābhārata*)

"Just as the celestial waters of the Ganges flow unobstructed into the ocean, so when My devotees simply hear of Me, their minds come to Me, who resides in the hearts of all." (*Śrī Caitanya-caritāmṛta, Ādi-līlā* 4.205)

"Love for Lord Kṛṣṇa is very pure, just like the waters of the Ganges. That love is the ocean of nectar. That pure attachment to Kṛṣṇa does not conceal any spot, which would appear just like a spot of ink on a white cloth."
(*Śrī Caitanya-caritāmṛta, Madhya-līlā* 2.48)

"The taste for loving service is like the water of the River Ganges, which flows from the lotus feet of Lord Kṛṣṇa. Everyday that taste diminishes the results of sinful activities acquired over a period of many births by those who perform austerities."
(*Śrī Caitanya-caritāmṛta, Madhya-līlā* 24.217)

"One should know that nothing is more powerful than the Vaiṣṇavas, Tulasī, Gaṅgā, and honoring the Lord's *prasāda*."
(*Śrī Caitanya-bhāgavata, Antya-khaṇḍa* 8.149)

"As long as Bhāgīrathī Gaṅgā is present, and as long as Girirāja Govardhana is

present, the influence of Kali-yuga will not be present." (*Śrī Garga-saṁhitā* 2.2.50)

"Even a little study of the *Bhagavad-gītā*, to drink a little Gaṅgā water, or to worship even once Lord Murāri (Kṛṣṇa), will make one immune to Yamarāja." (Śrīpāda Śaṅkarācārya)

"In Bengal, I have two shelters: My mother and the River Gaṅgā. Both of them are very merciful." (Śrī Caitanya Mahāprabhu)

Gaṅgā in the Calendar

There are several auspicious days in the Vedic or Vaiṣṇava calendar year in honor of mother Gaṅgā's pastimes. They are Akṣaya-tṛtīyā, Gaṅgā-saptamī, also known as Jahnu-saptamī, Gaṅgā-duṣharā, also known as Śrī Gaṅgā-pūjā, and Śrī Gaṅgā-sāgara Mela.

Akṣaya-tṛtīyā appears in the month of Vaiśākha (April/May) on the 3rd day of Śukla-pakṣa, or the waxing fortnight of the full moon. In the *Matsya Purāṇa*, as quoted from the *Śrī Hari-bhakti-vilāsa*, the following is stated: "On the third day of the bright half of the month of Vaiśākha, the Supreme Lord Janārdana created the grain of barley, started the cycle of Satya-yuga, and made Tripathagā Gaṅgā descend to the earth from Brahmāloka." *

Gaṅgā-saptamī or Jahnu-saptamī also appears in the month of Vaiśākha on the 7th day of Śukla-pakṣa, or the waxing fortnight of the full moon. After the Gaṅgā descended onto the Himālayas, the river entered the sacrificial arena of Jahnu Ṛṣi and disturbed his meditation. As stated in the *Padma Purāṇa, Pātāla-khaṇḍa* 85.49: "Formerly on the seventh day of the bright half of Vaiśākha, Gaṅgā was drunk through anger by Jahnu, and let out from the cavity of his right ear." Also in the *Nārada Purāṇa, Uttara-bhāga* 41.37: "It was on the seventh day in the bright half of the month of Vaiśākha that the Gaṅgā was drunk up by Jahnu Ṛṣi out of anger and cast off later on through his right ear." There are other accounts regarding how Jahnu released Gaṅgā. Therefore, Gaṅgā also became known as Jāhnavī, or the descendant of Jahnu.

Gaṅgā-duṣharā (she who removes inauspiciousness) or Śrī Gaṅgā-pūjā appears in the month of Jyeṣṭha (May/June) on the 10th day of Śukla-pakṣa, or the waxing fortnight of the full moon. On this day, Mahārāja Bhagīratha's desire of bringing Gaṅgā to this mortal world was finally fulfilled as the sacred river descended from Lord Śiva's blessed head at Mount Kailāsa. The River Gaṅgā then flowed through the Himālayas behind Mahārāja Bhagīratha's chariot and passed through Jahnu Ṛṣi's *āśrama*. Afterwards, he successfully led the Gaṅgā to Rasātala, in the lower planetary system, to liberate the sixty thousand sons of King Sagara. As stated in the *Nārada Purāṇa, Uttara-bhāga* 40.21: "It was on the tenth day in the bright half of the month of Jyeṣṭha, when the day of the week was Tuesday and the constellation was Hasta, Gaṅgā descended to the mortal world." Gaṅgā is also known as Bhāgīrathī, or the descendant of Bhagīratha.

Śrī Gaṅgā-sāgara Mela occurs on Makara-saṅkrānti, or when the Sun enters Capricorn, which normally falls on the 14th of January every year. This festival is said to commemorate the day when Mahārāja Bhagīratha led the Gaṅgā to Rasātala to liberate the sons of King Sagara. The festival is observed at several locations on the banks of Gaṅgā, but especially at the confluence of the Gaṅgā and

*Gaṅgā-saptamī (Jahnu-saptamī) and Gaṅgā-duṣharā (Śrī Gaṅgā-pūjā) are generally observed as the appearance day(s) of the Jāhnavī Gaṅgā and the Bhāgīrathī Gaṅgā.

the Bay of Bengal, where Kapila Muni's *āsrama* is located.

According to the local tradition in the Rishikesh area, Gaṅgā-saptamī is celebrated as the day Gaṅgā descended from the celestial region onto Lord Siva's matted locks, then a few drops of Gaṅgā fell from his head onto the Himālayas. Afterwards, Gaṅgā was drunk by Jahnu Ṛṣi who later released her. Gaṅgā-dusharā is celebrated as the day Gaṅgā liberated the sixty thousand sons of King Sagara.

In the Kāsī area, Gaṅgā-saptamī is celebrated as the day Gaṅgā descended from heaven to earth. Gaṅgā-duṣharā, also known as Gaṅgā-dasaharā, marks the day Gaṅga reached the plains of India at Haridvāra. Gaṅgā-dasaharā means "Gaṅgā destroys ten", so devotees bathe in the Gaṅgā ten days prior to this day which destroys the sins of ten lifetimes.

The *Nārada Purāṇa* (*Uttara-bhāga* 38.17-19) describes when and where Gaṅgā manifests herself within the three planetary systems during the Vedic calendar month: "In the beginning of the dark half of the month, Gaṅgā is present on earth for ten days ending with the sacred Amāvasyā (New Moon) day. From the first to the tenth of the bright half of the month, she is present in the netherworlds. Beginning with the eleventh day in the bright half and ending with the fifth day in the dark half, she is always present in heaven for ten days."

In other words: From the 6th dark day to Amāvāsyā, Gaṅga is on the earth. From the 1st bright day to the 10th bright day she is in the netherworlds. And from the 11th bright day through Pūrṇimā (Full Moon) to the 5th dark day she is in heaven.

Note: There are different opinions regarding the appearance or descent of Gaṅgā. The information provided for Akṣaya-tṛtīyā, Jahnu-saptamī, and Śri Gaṅgā-pūjā is based on scriptural references and the Gauḍīya Vaiṣṇava calendar. The other information is based on local traditions and needs futher research.

Gaṅgā personally appeared to Mahārāja Bhagīratha before the river descended from Brahmaloka onto Lord Śiva's head. Gaṅgā then descended onto the Himālayas prior to Jahnu Ṛṣi swallowing the river. Later, Jahnu released Gaṅgā, which marks the river's reappearance. Afterwards, Gaṅgā descended to Rasātala, liberating the sixty thousand sons of Sagara. Then Gaṅgā appears as Bhogavatī in the netherworlds before appearing as Vaitaraṇī encircling Pitrloka.

Gaṅgā-devī appears in her unlimited pastimes for the pleasure of the devotees. Regardless which day one accepts as the appearance day of Gaṅgā, or the day the river descended onto this planet, mother Gaṅgā's pastimes are always appearing throughout the three worlds. Jai Gaṅgā-mayī!

CONCLUDING WORDS

We are simply instruments in the hands of the Lord and His associates, trying to follow their plans. The more I read in the Vedic literatures about the glories of mother Gaṅgā, the more I felt to glorify her. There is actually no conclusion to our glorification of the Lord or His entourage. Once we begin, the results just evolve more and more, like a snowball rolling down a hill.

Now more than three years have passed, I wonder where the time has all gone. There were some very inspiring periods during the course of this book, and at the same time, some very slow, unproductive periods. Many times I did not have the will power to continue, such as when one of the book's files suddenly was lost, or when my laptop computer was stolen, or when I had some heavy physical or mental illness. The Lord tests us in so many ways, that at times, one just

wants to surrender to laziness and complete selfish independence.

Anyway, what you hold in your hands is surely a product of our glorious mother Gaṅgā's desire. For whatever reasons, she has acted through me to produce this book for her pleasure. May anyone and everyone accept her merciful blessings unconditionally and swim with those blessings in the ocean of love of Godhead. Hare Kṛṣṇa!

ACKNOWLEDGEMENTS

I am indebted to so many kind-hearted persons that these few thank-yous listed below do not really express my most sincere gratitude for everyone's assistance. To begin, the most important thank you is to my spiritual master, H.H. Śrīla Lokanātha Swami Mahārāja, for engaging me for eleven years on Padayātrā in India. Through his mercy, some of the confidential truths about the *tīrthas* were gradually revealed to us. Secondly, to His Divine Grace A.C. Bhaktivedanta Swami Prabhupāda. One of the last desires of Śrīla Prabhupāda before leaving this world was to travel and visit the holy places of India. Through the means of Padayātrā, he has toured the entire country four times now, bestowing his blessings everywhere. Still today, he is residing in his *mūrti* form, continually visiting the sacred places again and again.

In the beginning of this project, I was alone, not knowing which direction it would take. As I began, I realized one simply cannot compile a book alone; it is practically impossible. Then Haresh Prabhu from Pune offered his typing skills. During the winter months of 1996-1997, we found a small, quiet *āśrama* on the bank of the Gaṅgā at Saptasarovara in Haridvāra. He would stay up late each evening typing away on an old South American portable typewriter until his fingers would crack due to the freezing temperatures! Afterwards, when we moved to the Centennial House in New Delhi, he retyped those same 200 pages into the office computer. Then Kannan Prabhu (now known as Kānāi Ṭhākura Dāsa) offered his skills and typed the next 50 pages. He also gave me my first computer lessons.

My dear Godbrother Abhaya Prabhu then donated his laptop computer, thereby forcing me to learn more about computers, even though I was very reluctant. Then Tukārāma Prabhu donated a small portable printer. By their kind-hearted donations I was able to compile the remaining part of the book more efficiently.

A special dedication also goes to H.G. Dīnabandhu Prabhu of Vṛndāvana. Without his computer-oriented assistance, the complete version of this book would not have been possible. Also a very special thanks is due to Vaiṣṇava Dāsa of New Delhi. Over those long years on the road with Padayātrā he would always inspire me with kind-hearted words that helped when the times were tough. He has also helped me in many other ways, for which I will always remain indebted to him. I also thank my dear loving Godbrother Rādhe Śyāma Prabhu. I truly appreciated his assistance over the years and will always be indebted to his kindness.

In the Himālayas, Badarī Viśāla Prabhu helped me and the Padayātrā in several ways. Through his introduction, I was able to accompany Gaṅgā-devī on her pilgrimage twice and meet some of the local Himālayan inhabitants. Also a warm thanks to Bharosa Rama Semwal and his family in Mukhwa, the winter home of Gaṅgā-devī. Their hospitality and friendship were very much appreciated. They are fortunate to be able to live with Gaṅgā-devī throughout their lives. My thanks to Ashok Dilwali, the best photographer the Himālayas has ever seen. I do not know anyone who is more Himālayan-conscious than Ashok. I thank him dearly for contributing some of his best shots for the book.

I thank H.H. Mahānidhi Swami for his advice on book publishing and his blessings to quote from his books. I also thank H.G. Rājaśekhara Prabhu for his advice and for his establishing a very nice standard of books on Śrī Vṛndāvana-dhāma, and to H.G. Kuśakratha Prabhu for his blessings and his endless titles of books that have enlivened the Vaiṣṇava community worldwide. And much appreciation to H.G. Satyarāja Dāsa (Steven Rosen), H.G. Puṇḍarīka Vidyānidhi Dāsa, and H.G. Hari Śauri Dāsa for their wonderful publications.

At ISKCON New Delhi, I thank Rāghava Paṇḍita Prabhu, Śvetadvīpa Prabhu, Mākhanacora Prabhu, Mādhava Kanta Prabhu, and Dinanātha Prabhu, as well as Braja-bhakti-vilāsa Prabhu, for nicely accommodating me during my numerous visits. Also, thanks go to Jitamṛta Prabhu for his research assistance and H.G. Jñānagamya Prabhu for his initial inspiration behind the map of Gaṅgā's pastimes. I also thank Lt. Gen. S.M. Chadha and J.K.L. Sahni of Eicher Goodearth Limited, New Delhi, for their advice and assistance on the map.

I am very much grateful to my Godbrother Prasannātmā Prabhu and his family at ISKCON Vārāṇasī for always taking good care of me and, to all the devotees at ISKCON Māyāpur, especially H.H. Bhakti Vidyāpūrṇa Swami, H.G. Jananivāsa Prabhu, H.G Paṅkajāṅghri Prabhu, Gaurāṅga-prema Prabhu, Patrapati Prabhu, and Navadvīpa-candra Prabhu, for all of their valuable assistance.

I am very grateful to Ananta Prabhu and Harināma Prabhu for allowing me to reside at the Italian House, which is one of the nicest and most peaceful *āśramas* in Vṛndāvana. Residing there has been very conducive to completing this book. I also thank all the fortunate devotees serving at ISKCON Vṛndāvana for their help and friendship over the years, especially Oṁ Tat Sat Prabhu for his assistance with the Goloka narrations.

I am very grateful to Acyuta Prabhu for all the computer related services he kindly offered and for being a nice neighbor as well as an old friend. Also I thank Navala Kiśora Prabhu for his translations and also for being a nice neighbor. And I thank Gauri Prabhu for lending his library and Mādhavī Mātājī for her computer related assistance.

I am indebted to my Godsister, Śyāmā Mātājī, for her transcriptions and loan of her computer after mine was stolen. I also thank H.G. Kundali Prabhu and Vinoda Bihāri Prabhu for their computer assistance, which contributed to the completion of this book. I offer my thanks to Gopīnātha Prabhu, who designed the Padayātrā Press logo.

I thank H.G. Yaśomatīnandana Prabhu for his assistance with the printer. I also thank H.G.Yadubara Prabhu for contributing the photo of Śrīla Prabhupāda riding in a boat across the Gaṅgā at Rishikesh, which was taken from his film: *Your Ever Well Wisher*.

I wish to again thank Abhaya Prabhu who was the first to help me financially. I also thank Rāja Rāma Prabhu for his great Padayātrā spirit and financial help and Śrī Jayadeva Prabhu for his financial assistance. Also, Upānanda "Kakabhai" Prabhu, Kṛṣṇacandra Dāsa, Dharmadhenu Dāsa, Saṅkīrtana Prabhu, Kṛpāpāla Prabhu, and Loran Prabhu have donated toward this book project.

I am especially indebted to Rāsa Rasika Prabhu for always taking good care of me with his fine cooking as well as his financial contribution.

I also thank everyone who offered their personal realization of Gaṅgā. Their individual

names are given with each realization in the Chapter entitled: *Gaṅgā Realization*.

I am grateful to Mr. Prakash Jain, Director of Motilal Barnarsidass Publishers Pvt. Ltd., for his blessings and permission to use their publications and to Mr. Ashok Jain, Director of Munshiram Manoharlal Publishers Pvt. Ltd., for his kind blessings.

I appreciate the initial proofreading done by H.G. Keśī-damana Prabhu and thank Śaraṇāgati Mātājī for completing the proofreading and polishing parts of the manuscript. I also thank H.G. Janānanda Prabhu for his comments and corrections.

I felt blessed having the association of H.G. Gopīparāṇadhana Dāsa. He has guided and instructed me through various parts of the book. He also translated the *Gaṅgāṣṭakam* and *Gaṅgā-māhātmyam*, as well as wrote the Foreward. I thank him dearly for all of his valuable time. I am also very thankful to H.G. Puṇḍarīka Vidyānidhi Dāsa for his meticulous editing and for entering the diacritic marks. He so patiently tolerated, corrected, and pointed-out my ocean of mistakes.

The beautiful graphic and layout design was done by H.G. Kūrma-rūpa Prabhu. I was blessed being with Kūrma-rūpa during my first bath at Gomukha during the Gaṅgā-duṣharā celebrations of 1987. Little did we know then, that we would be producing this book together for the pleasure of mother Gaṅgā. I thank him for the wonderful job he did.

A special thanks to William Strunk Jr. and E.B. White for saying the following encouraging words: "The whole duty of a writer is to please and satisfy himself, and the true writer always plays to an audience of one."

The last and most grateful acknowledgement is for Sanaka Sanātana Prabhu. After I retired from Padayātrā, he expertly met the challenge and successfully managed the daily on-going demands from the road. He has turned the Padayātrā into one of the most successful book distribution teams within ISKCON and made the program completely self-sufficient. With his kind heart, he donated generously towards the printing costs and other expenses toward this publication.

Please forgive me if I have forgotten to mention anyone else who assisted me in one way or other. Śrī Gaṅgā-devī certainly will not forget your contribution. I pray to her to carry everyone in her celestial waters to the lotus feet of the divine couple of Goloka Vṛndāvana, Śrī Śrī Rādhā-Śyāmasundara.

Dasānudāsa
Jaya Vijaya Dāsa

About the Artists

One of the most exciting parts of compiling this book was working with the artists. To observe the various pastimes take form in color was most wonderful. I wish more time were available to include more paintings. Śrīla Prabhupāda once said that the paintings in his books were windows into the spiritual world. Therefore I wish to express my gratitude to the following artists.

Śrīman Yogendra Rastogi—Yogendra Rastogi of Meerut, northern India, is one of the foremost Vedic artists known today in India. He has painted practically every divine personality imaginable with utmost reverence, care, and detail. When I approached and requested him to paint mother Gaṅgā, he immediately accepted because this was his first opportunity to do so. During the course of our Vedic research on how Gaṅgā-devī appears, a challenge faced him for the first time in his forty-five year career. Gaṅgā is described as having a white complexion, wearing white clothing, and sitting on a white lotus flower. Her crocodile carrier is also described as white. How then to paint white upon white upon white upon white? Due to his talented insight and expertise, as well as six months of patient, the result was one of the most beautiful paintings he has ever done.

Śatadhāma Devī Dāsī—Even though Śatadhāma requested I should not mention her name in the book, still I am obliged to offer a few words of appreciation. The talented artistic qualities of Śatadhāma speak for themselves. She immediately captures each pastime with great feeling and expertise. She was very consistent with each of her watercolors, despite the variation of stories. She is also expert in oils, pencils, and sculpturing, as well as with the line drawings, which were done with feather and ink.

Śyāmapriya Devī Dāsī—Śyāmapriya studied in art-college in England, but was not very happy with the conventional style art that was being taught. After coming to India, specifically to the Himālayas, her natural artistic qualities began to manifest. She has produced three Padayātrā Worldwide coloring books for children. The color-penciled map that depicts some of the pastimes related to mother Gaṅgā reflects some of Śyāmapriya's natural gifted talent.

Prasanta Dāsa—Prasanta is originally from Bangladesh, but has been living in Vṛndāvana for the past eighteen years. During a dream one evening eight years ago, Prasanta received his inspiration to paint. Since then, he has served the Deity department of the Kṛṣṇa-Balarama Temple in Vṛndāvana with his artistic qualities. Some of his paintings have also appeared in publications such as the *Śrī Vṛndāvana Dhāma Newsletter*, *Śrī Kṛṣṇa's Names in Bhagavad-gītā*, and *Śrī Advaita Prakāśa*.

Except where otherwise noted, all illustrations were done by Śatadhāma Devī Dāsī.
382

Glossary

108 Śrī Vaiṣṇava Divya Deśams—also known as 108 Tirupatis; one hundred and eight Lord Viṣṇu temples, holy places or *arca-vigrahas*, as sung and glorified by the twelve Ālvārs (the saints of South India) of the Śrī Vaiṣṇava-sampradāya. Their songs or poems and other glorifications were composed in the Tamil language, and they altogether (4,000 verses) are called *Nalayira-divya-prabandham*. The 108 Divya Deśams have come into prominence only because of the Ālvārs's *Nalayira-divya-prabandham*. If an Ālvār glorified a particular temple or holy place, either by a single verse or part of a verse, that Lord and His shrine were regarded as in a special class apart from the rest. Those selected shrines formed the 108 Divya Deśams. It is the duty of all pious Śrī Vaiṣṇavas to visit all these Divya Deśams at least once in their lifetime. (see Ālvārs)

A

Abhirāma Ṭhākura (Rāmadāsa)—one of the twelve *gopālas* (cowherd boys) of Śrī Nityānanda Prabhu (Lord Balarāma) in Lord Caitanya's pastimes. "The cowherd boy named Śrīdāmā appeared in Lord Caitanya's pastimes as Rāmadāsa Abhirāma Ṭhākura, who carried a flute made of a bamboo stick with sixteen knots." (*Śrī Gaura-gaṇoddeśa-dīpikā* 126)

A. C. Bhaktivedanta Swami Śrīla Prabhupāda—Founder-Ācārya of the International Society for Krishna Consciousness. (A. C.) Abhay Charan was the name given by his parents. After receiving spiritual initiation from Bhaktisiddhānta Sarasvatī in 1932, the name *aravinda* ("lotus") was added, becoming Abhay Caraṇāravinda, or "One who is fearless, having taken shelter at Lord Kṛṣṇa's lotus feet." In 1959, Abhay accepted *sannyāsa* from Keśava Mahārāja, receiving the name Bhaktivedanta Swami Mahārāja, or "One who is an advanced transcendentalist and has realized the conclusions of the *Vedas* through devotional service." Bhaktivedanta Swami's earliest disciples lovingly called him Śrīla Prabhupāda, or "The spiritual master at whose feet all others take shelter."

Ācārya—an ideal teacher who teaches by his personal example; a spiritual master.

Advaita Ācārya—the combined incarnation of Lord Sadāśiva (the original form of Śiva) and Lord Viṣṇu, appearing as an ideal teacher and principal associate of Śrī Caitanya Mahāprabhu, and who prayed for the appearance of Lord Caitanya.

Ālvārs—*ālvār* means "one who has deep intuitive knowledge of God" or "one who is immersed in the ecstatic love of God". There are twelve Vaiṣṇava *ālvārs*, or saints of South India, who appeared between the end of Dvāpara-yuga and the beginning of Kali-yuga. The twelve Ālvārs are: Poygai (incarnation of Lord Viṣṇu's Pañcajanya conchshell); Bhūtam (Viṣṇu's Kaumodaki club); Pey (Viṣṇu's Nandaka sword); Tirumalisai (Viṣṇu's Sudarsana disc); Nammālvār (Viṣvaksena); Madhurakavi (Gaṇeśa); Kulaśekhara (Viṣṇu's Kaustubha gem); Periyālvār (Garuḍa); Āṇḍāl (Bhu-devī); Toṇḍaraḍippoḍi (Viṣṇu's Vanamāla necklace); Tiruppān (Viṣṇu's Śrīvatsa, or mark of Lakṣmī); and Tirumangai (Viṣṇu's Śārṅga bow). These Ālvārs traveled and preached *bhakti-yoga* through devotional songs all around India. (see 108 Śrī Vaiṣṇava Divya Deśams)

Ārati—a ceremony for greeting the Lord with offerings of food, incense, lamps, water, flowers, and fans, often accompanied by *kīrtana*.

Arca-vigraha—the form of God manifested through material elements, as in a painting or statue of Kṛṣṇa worshiped in a home or temple. Present in this form, the Lord personally accepts worship from His devotees.

Āśrama—1) hermitage, monastery, or a place of shelter conducive to the practice of spiritual life. 2) The four divisions of social status and four orders of spiritual culture in Vedic society are known as *varṇāśrama*. The *varṇas* (divisions of social status) are *brāhmaṇa*, *kṣatriya*, *vaiśya*, and *śūdra*. The *āśramas* (orders of spiritual culture) are *brahmācārya*, *gṛhastha*, *vānaprastha*, and *sannyāsa*. (See the individual entries of these *varṇas* and *āśramas*)

Aṣṭāṅga-yoga—the "eightfold path" consisting of *yama* and *niyama* (moral practices), *āsana* (bodily postures), *prāṇāyāma* (breath control), *pratyahara* (sensory withdrawal), *dhāraṇā* (steadying the mind), *dhyāna* (meditation), and *samādhi* (deep contemplation on Lord Viṣṇu within the heart).

Avatāra— "one who descends"; a fully or partially empowered incarnation of God who descends from the spiritual realm for a particular mission. "There are various kinds of *avatāras* all appearing on schedule all over the universe. But Lord Kṛṣṇa is the primeval Lord, the fountainhead of all *avatāras*." (Śrīla Prabhupāda)

B

Bay of Bengal—the eastern ocean; the body of water off the eastern coast of India. The Bay of Bengal borders the Indian states of West Bengal, Orissa, Andhra Pradesh, and Tamil Nadu, as well as the New Moore and the Andaman and Nicobar Islands. Also, the Bay touches upon three other countries: Myanmar (Burma), Bangladesh, and Śrī Laṅkā. The River Gaṅgā that originates at Gomukha in the Himālayas travels in a southeastern direction for 2,510 kilometres (1,570 miles) before meeting the Bay of Bengal at Sagara Island (Gaṅgā-sāgara) in the state of West Bengal. Gaṅgā also flows through the country of Bangladesh as Padmā River and enters the Bay of Bengal at the mouths of Gaṅgā (Sundarbans). In Orissa, the River Mahānadī flows into the Bay of Bengal at Paradwip. Also, Lord Jagannātha resides in His sacred abode known as Purī (Puruṣottama-kṣetra) on the shores of the Bay of Bengal. In Andhra Pradesh, the River Godāvarī (Gautamī Gaṅgā) enters the eastern ocean in seven streams known as Sapta-Godāvarī at Samudra-tīrtha. Also, the River Kṛṣṇa meets the Bay of Bengal at False Divi Point. In Tamil Nadu, the River Kāverī joins the eastern ocean at Kāverī-pumppaṭṭanam, the ancient capital of the Coḷas. On Pamban Island, situated between the Palk Bay and Gulf of Mannar in the Bay of Bengal, Lord Śiva resides in his holy abode known as Rāmeśvaram. At Kanniyākumāri (Cape Comorin), is the only confluence in the world where three oceans meet: Arabian Sea, Indian Ocean, and the Bay of Bengal.

Bhagavad-gītā—"Song of God"; the seven hundred verse discourse between the Supreme Personality of Godhead, Śrī Kṛṣṇa, and His disciple, Arjuna, from the *Bhīṣma-parva* of the *Mahābhārata*. The conversation took place between two armies (the Pāṇḍavas and Kauravas, both descendants of the Kuru dynasty), minutes before the start of an immense fratricidal war on the battlefield at Kurusketra, also known as *dharma-kṣetra* (a place where religious rituals are performed). Lord Kṛṣṇa elucidated to Arjuna that devotional service is both the principle means and the ultimate end of spiritual perfection. "The *Bhagavad-gītā* is the essence of all Vedic knowledge and is the first book of spiritual values." (Śrīla Prabhupāda)

Bhāgavata Purāṇa—see *Śrīmad-Bhāgavatam*

Bhajana—a devotional song; any of various practices of service and direct worship of the Supreme Lord, especially hearing and chanting His glories.

Bhajana-kutira—a small hut or cottage where a devotee performs his *bhajana*.

Bhakti—love and devotion to the Supreme Personality of Godhead, Lord Kṛṣṇa.

Bhaktisiddhānta Sarasvatī Mahārāja—(1874-1937) the spiritual master of A.C. Bhaktivedanta Swami Prabhupāda. The transcendentally empowered son of Bhaktivinoda Ṭhākura and a powerful preacher and scholar, he founded sixty-four Gauḍīya Maṭhas (Vaiṣṇava monastery preaching centers) throughout India, as well as in Rangoon, London, and Berlin.

Bhaktivinoda Ṭhākura—(1838-1915) an intimate associate of Gaurakiśora dāsa Bābājī and father of Bhaktisiddhānta Sarasvatī. Famous for having located the exact site of the birthplace of Śrī Caitanya Mahāprabhu at Śrīdhāma Māyāpur, which was lost for centuries due to the shifting course of the River Gaṅgā. He predicted that the *saṅkīrtana* movement would spread from India to the countries of the western world.

Bhakti-yoga—linking with the Supreme Lord through devotional service. It consists of nine *aṅgas*, or limbs: 1) *śravaṇam*—hearing; 2) *kīrtanam*—chanting about the transcendental holy name, form, qualities, paraphernalia, and pastimes of Lord Viṣṇu (Kṛṣṇa); 3) *smaraṇam*—remembering them; 4) *pāda-sevanam*—serving the lotus feet of the Lord; 5) *arcanam*—offering the Deity of the Lord respectful worship with sixteen types of paraphernalia; 6) *vandanam*—offering prayers to the Lord; 7) *dāsyam*—becoming His servant; 8) *sakhyam*—considering the Lord one's best friend; and 9) *ātma-nivedanam*—surrendering everything unto Him. These nine processes are accepted as pure devotional service. Another term for *bhakti-yoga* is *buddhi-yoga*, indicating that it represents the highest use of intelligence (*buddhi*). "By rendering devotional service (*bhakti-yoga*) unto the Personality of Godhead, Śrī Kṛṣṇa, one immediately acquires causeless knowledge and detachment from the world." (*Śrīmad-Bhāgavatam* 1.2.7)

Bhārata-varṣa—a name for India, named after King Bharata, who was an ancient ruler from whom the Pāṇḍavas descended. The earthly region is known as Bhu-maṇḍala, which is a planetary system that resembles a lotus flower, and it consists of seven *dvīpas*, or islands, that resemble the whorl of that flower. The seven islands are Jambūdvīpa, Plakṣadvīpa, Śālmalīdvīpa, Kuśadvīpa, Krauñcadvīpa, Śākadvīpa, and Puṣkaradvīpa. Each island is divided into several *varṣas*, or tracts of land. Jambūdvīpa has nine tracts of land: Ilāvṛta-varṣa, Bhadrāśva-varṣa, Hari-varṣa, Ketumāla-varṣa, Ramyaka-varṣa, Hiraṇmaya-varṣa, Kuru-varṣa, Kinnara-varṣa, and Bhārata-varṣa. During ancient times, this entire planet was called Bhārata-varṣa, but due to the present age, Bhārata-varṣa has been reduced to the country of India only. Prior to Bhārata-varṣa, this planet was called Ajanabha-varṣa, named after King Nabhi, the son of Mahārāja Agnīdhra.

Brahmā—the first created being in the universe; directed by Lord Viṣṇu, he creates all life forms in the universe and supervises the material mode of passion (*rajo-guṇa*). He is the forefather and spiritual master of the demigods and giver of the *Vedas*.

Brahmācārī—celibate male student.

Brahmācarya—celibate student life under the care of a spiritual master; the first *āśrama*, or spiritual order in Vedic society. His duties are to control the mind by abstaining from sense gratification, beg alms from door to door, and engage the mind in the study of Vedic literature for cultivation of spiritual knowledge. "The vow of *brahmācarya* is meant to help one completely abstain from sex indulgence in work, words, and mind—at all times, under all circumstances, and in all places." (Yājñavalkya Muni)

Brāhma-muhūrta—one and a half hours before sunrise. Spiritual activities are highly recommended to be performed during this early time, since they have a greater effect than during any other part of the day.

Brahman—1) the impersonal, all-pervasive aspect of the Supreme; 2) the Supreme Personality of Godhead; 3) the *mahat-tattva*, or total material substance; 4) the individual soul.

Brāhmaṇa—"knower of Brahman"; intellectual member, or priestly class of men; the first *varṇa*, or social-occupational division in Vedic society. Their occupation is hearing and teaching Vedic literature, learning and teaching Deity worship, and receiving and giving charity. A genuine *brāhmaṇa* is fixed in the mode of goodness. "Peacefulness, self-control, austerity, purity, tolerance, honesty, knowledge, wisdom and religiousness—these are the natural qualities by which the *brāhmaṇas* work." (*Bhagavad-gītā* 18.42)

Buddha—an incarnation of Lord Kṛṣṇa who appeared in 560 B.C. (2,560 years ago). He took birth in a grove known as Lumbinī in the capital city of Kapilavastu (Nepal), situated at the foot of Mount Palpa in the Himālayan ranges. Born Prince Siddhārtha Gautama, at 35 years of age, he became Lord Buddha "The Enlightened One", (also known as Śākya Muni). After he obtained *nirvāṇa* (being free from material existence) at Bodhgayā (Bihar), Buddha traveled throughout the northern India regions near Gaṅgā and preached *ahimsa* (nonviolence) and *sunyata* (extinction of the self). "Then, in the beginning of Kali-yuga, the Lord will appear as Lord Buddha just for the purpose of deluding those who are envious of the faithful theist." (*Śrīmad-Bhāgavatam* 1.3.24) "Lord Buddha appeared when materialism was rampant and materialists were using the pretext of the authority of the *Vedas*. The atheists took to animal sacrifice without reference to the Vedic principles. Buddha appeared to stop this nonsense and to establish the Vedic principle of *ahimsa*." (Śrīla Prabhupāda)

C

Caitanya-caritāmṛta—"the immortal character of the living force"; the biography of Śrī Caitanya Mahāprabhu composed in Bengali in the late sixteenth century by Śrīla Kṛṣṇadāsa Kavirāja Gosvāmī. The singlemost important text of Gauḍīya Vaiṣṇava philosophy and the postgraduate study of spiritual knowledge.

Caitanya Mahāprabhu—(1486-1534) Lord Kṛṣṇa's incarnation in Kali-yuga (the present age of quarrel and hypocrisy). He appeared in Māyāpur (Navadvīpa), West Bengal as His own greatest devotee to teach love of God through inaugurating the *yuga-dharma* (prime religion for this age) of *saṅkīrtana* (congregational chanting of His holy names: Hare Kṛṣṇa, Hare Kṛṣṇa, Kṛṣṇa Kṛṣṇa, Hare Hare/Hare Rāma, Hare Rāma, Rāma Rāma, Hare Hare).

Causal Ocean—see Kāraṇa-samudra

D

Darśana—"audience" or "a vision"; the act of beholding or seeing the Supreme Lord or His representative.

Deva or Devata—a demigod or godly person; a living entity whom the Supreme Lord empowers to represent Him as administrator of material affairs, or authorized supplying agent, in the management of the universe.

Devī—a demigoddess.

Dhāma—"abode" or "place of residence"; the Lord's eternal or transcendental abode. The *dhāma* is a manifestation of the spiritual world on this planet, and is an expansion of the Supreme Lord's *sat* (existence) potency, which provides a basis for the Lord to reveal His transcendental forms, qualities, and pastimes.

Dharma—religious principles; one's eternal, natural duty or occupation (as devotional service to the Lord).

Dvādaśī—the twelfth day after the new moon or full moon of the lunar month.

Dvāpara-yuga—the third of the four ages which cycle perpetually in the universe, where there is a decline in virtue and religion with vice increasing. This age lasts 864,000 years.

E

Ekādaśī—the eleventh day after the new moon or full moon of the lunar month. Directly presided over by Lord Hari and is considered the mother of all fasting days. It is a special day for increasing devotion and remembrance of Lord Kṛṣṇa.

G

Gandharva—the celestial singers and musicians among the demigods.

Gaṅgā-devī, Gaṅgā-mayī, Gaṅgā-mātā, Ganges—see note after *Introduction*; also *Descriptions of Gaṅgā-devī*, Book One, Chapter One.

Gaurakiśora dāsa Bābāji—an intimate associate of Śrīla Bhaktivinoda Ṭhākura who was the initiating spiritual master of Śrīla Bhaktisiddhānta Sarasvatī Mahārāja.

Gaura Pūrṇimā—the full moon appearance day of Śrī Caitanya Mahāprabhu which is in the month of Phālguna (February/March). Lord Caitanya appeared at Māyāpur on the island of Antardvīpa within Śrī Navadvīpa-dhāma.

Gauḍīya Maṭha—*maṭha* means monastery. *Vaiṣṇava* monastery; preaching center. Originally sixty-four in India and abroad, founded by Śrīla Bhaktisiddhānta Sarasvatī Mahārāja for propagating the sacred teachings of Śrī Caitanya Mahāprabhu.

Gauḍīya Vaiṣṇava—Gauḍīya refers to the region of Bengal/Bangladesh; *vaiṣṇava* is a devotee of Lord Viṣṇu or Kṛṣṇa. A follower of the form of *vaiṣṇavism* associated with Bengal, as started by Śrī Caitanya Mahāprabhu some 500 years ago.

Gomukha—the icy-cave aperture in the shape of a cow's mouth where the liquid form of Gaṅgā, as a river, originates on this planet. Located at the base of the northwestern side of the Gaṅgotrī Glacier in the Garhwal Himālayas, 18 kilometres southeast of Gaṅgotrī at an altitude of 3,892 metres. According to the *Skanda Purāṇa*, Gomukha is considered the best *tīrtha* amongst *tīrthas*, because Gomukha is the original place of Gaṅgā.

Ghāṭa—bathing place; steps or descent that lead down a bank of a river for bathing, sacrificial offerings, burning bodies, transportation, etc.

Ghee—clarified butter, used in sacrifices and as oil in cooking.

Goloka (Kṛṣṇaloka)—the highest supreme spiritual planet; this original planet is the personal abode of the original Personality of Godhead, Śrī Kṛṣṇa.

Gopas—the cowherd boys of Vṛndāvana, who are the best friends and devotees of Lord Kṛṣṇa.

Gopīs—the cowherd girls of Vṛndāvana, who are the most surrendered and confidential devotees of Lord Kṛṣṇa.

Gṛhastha—regulated married householder life; the second *āśrama*, or spiritual order in Vedic society. There are four principle responsibilities in a Kṛṣṇa conscious family: chant the Hare Kṛṣṇa *mahā-mantra*, accept the remnants of foodstuffs offered to Lord Kṛṣṇa, have discussions on the *Bhagavad-gītā* and *Śrīmad-Bhāgavatam*, and engage in Deity worship.

Guṇas—the three "modes", or qualities, of the material world: *sattva* (goodness), *rajas* (passion), and *tamas* (ignorance).

H

Hare Kṛṣṇa mahā-mantra—the "great chant" for delivering consciousness from illusion: Hare Kṛṣṇa, Hare Kṛṣṇa, Kṛṣṇa Kṛṣṇa, Hare Hare/Hare Rāma, Hare Rāma, Rāma Rāma, Hare Hare. The chanting of this *mantra* is the most recommended means for spiritual progress in this age of Kali, as it cleanses the mind and enables one to transcend the temporary designations of race, religion, and nationality and to understand one's true identity as an eternal spiritual being.

Hari—"The word *hari* conveys various meanings, but the chief import of the word is that He (the Lord) vanquishes everything inauspicious and takes away the mind of the devotee by awarding pure transcendental love." (Śrīla Prabhupāda)

Hari-nāma-saṅkīrtana—congregational chanting of the holy names of the Supreme Lord.

Himālayan Char-dhāma-yātrā—pilgrimage to the four abodes in the Garhwal Himālayas: Yamunotri (Yamunā-devī's abode at 3,185 metres); Gaṅgotrī (Gaṅgā-devī's abode at 3,140 metres); Kedāranātha (Lord Śiva's abode at 3,584 metres); and Badarīnātha (Lord Viṣṇu's abode at 3,096 metres). Previously, a pilgrim had to undertake the most difficult and hazardous Himālayan journey by foot only. After 1960, vehicle roads were built leading directly to Badarīnātha and eventually to Gaṅgotrī. Still today, there are no vehicle roads leading directly to Kedāranātha or Yamunotri.

Himālayas—"abode of snow"; perpetually pure with eternal snow. The greatest mountains in the world represent Lord Kṛṣṇa as mentioned in *Bhagavad-gītā* (10.25): "of immovable things I am the Himālayas". Throughout all Vedic literatures, the Himālayas occupy a great position of universal respect and adoration, as the Supreme Lord and His expansions have appeared in numerous pastimes everywhere in these mountains. The *Vedas* were compiled in the Himālayas by Vyāsadeva, and Gaṅgā has her origin in the Himālayas. An unbroken line of *tapasvis* (those performing austerities), *jñānis* (those adhering to the path of *jñāna-yoga*), *yogīs* (transcendentalists striving to realize the Lord in the heart), and *bhaktas* (devotees of the Supreme Lord) have lived and are living in *āśramas*, caves, forests, and on snow-capped mountain peaks to become self-realized. Almost all of the *ṛṣis* and the Āryan race (followers of Vedic culture) from whom the people of Bhārata-varṣa claim their ancestry, are from the Himālayas. The Himālayan range extends from the north-west to southeast and forms an arch shape. The Himālaya's external boundaries touch upon seven countries: Afghanistan, Tajikistan, Pakistan, India, China (Tibet), Nepal, and Bhutan. The tallest peaks are: Mt. Everest (Sagarmātha) in Nepal at 8,848 metres (29,028 feet); Mt. Godwin Austin (K2) in Kashmir at 8,611m. (28,250ft.); Kāñcanjaṅgā in Nepal at 8,586m. (28, 216ft.); Lotse in Nepal at 8,516m.; Yalunkan in Nepal at 8,505m.; Makalu in Nepal at 8,481m.; Choyu in Nepal at 8,201m.; Dhaulāgiri in Nepal at 8,167m.; Manāsalu in Nepal at 8,163m.; Nanga Parbat in Kashmir at 8,126m.; Annapūrṇā in Nepal at 8,091m.; and Gasherbrum in Kashmir at 8,068m.

Hindu or Hinduism—this term is derived from the name of the Sindhu, Sind, or Indus River in present day Pakistan. Beginning around 1000 A.D., invading armies from the Middle East called the place beyond the Sindhu river, Hindustan, and the people who lived there the Hindus (due to the invader's language, the "s" was changed to "h"). In the centuries that followed, the term Hindu became acceptable even to Indians themselves as a general designation for their different religious traditions. The word Hindu is not found in the Vedic scriptures.

I

ISKCON—the acronym for the International Society for Krishna Consciousness, the branch of Śrī Caitanya Mahāprabhu's *saṅkīrtana* mission established by Śrīla Prabhupāda in New York in 1966. ISKCON is a worldwide nonsectarian movement dedicated to propagating the message of the *Vedas* for the benefit of mankind.

Indian Char-dhāma-yātrā—pilgrimage to the four abodes, or kingdoms of God, located in the four directions of India: Jagannātha Purī (representing Kali-yuga located in the East), Rāmeśvaram (representing Tretā-yuga located in the South), Dvārakā (representing Dvāpara-yuga located in the West), and Badarīnātha (representing Satya-yuga located in the North). These abodes represent the planets of the spiritual sky, which consists of the *brahmajyoti* (spiritual light) and the Vaikuṇṭhas (spiritual planets).

J

Japa-mālā—the soft recitation of the Lord's holy names performed with the aid of 108 prayer beads as a private meditation.

Jaṭā—snarled or disheveled matted locks of hair. The traditional and recommended way mentioned in the scriptures for an ascetic (*brahmacārīs* and *sannyāsīs*) living a renounced lifestyle to keep hair. Also recommended for those in *vānaprastha* and for widows.

Jīva Gosvāmī—one of the six Gosvāmīs of Vṛndāvana (the direct representatives after Śrī Caitanya Mahāprabhu) and the nephew of Rūpa and Sanātana Gosvāmīs. His father, Anupama, died when the boy was very young. He grew up absorbed in the worship of Krsna and Balarāma. Lord Caitanya instructed him to proceed to Navadvīpa and tour the sacred places in the association of Śrī Nityānanda Prabhu. He then went to Vārāṇasī (Kāśī) to study Sanskrit, and from there to Vṛndāvana to take shelter under his uncles. He became a disciple of Rūpa Gosvāmī and wrote eighteen major works on Vaiṣṇava philosophy. He is considered by many philosophers and Sanskritists to be the greatest scholar who ever lived.

Jñāna-yoga—the path of spiritual realization through a speculative philosophical search for truth.

K

Kali-yuga (Age of Kali)—the last of the four ages which cycle perpetually in the universe. In this age, there is an abundance of strife, ignorance, irreligion and vice, true virtue being practically nonexistent. It lasts for 432,000 years and began 5,000 years ago.

Kalpa—a day in the time calculation of Lord Brahmā; consists of a thousand cycles of four *yugas* (Satya, Tretā, Dvāpara, and Kali). These four *yugas*, rotating a thousand times, comprise one day of Brahmā, and the same number comprises one night. Brahmā lives one hundred of such "years" and then dies. The "hundred years" by earth calculations total to 311 trillion and 40 billion earth years.

Kamaṇḍalu—gourd or vessel made of wood or metal used as a water-pot. Commonly used by Lord Śiva and Lord Brahmā, as well as ascetics or *sādhus*, like *brahmacārīs* and *sannyāsīs*.

Kāraṇa-samudra—Causal Ocean (Cosmic Ocean); where Kāraṇodakaśāyī Viṣṇu, or Mahā-Viṣṇu is lying, and from whose breathing innumerable universes are passing out and entering. The water of the Kāraṇa-samudra, which is the original cause, is therefore spiritual. The River Gaṅgā is but a drop of this ocean. Located between the spiritual and material worlds.

Karma—material fruitive activity and its reactions; fruitive actions performed in accordance with Vedic injunctions.

Karma-yoga—the path of God realization through dedicating the fruits of one's work to God.

Ki Jaya (Jai)—"victory" or "all glories"; an expression of acclaim.

Kīrtana—*kīrti* means fame, hence, *kīrtana* means to glorify the fame of the Supreme Lord, especially by chanting His holy names.

Kṛṣṇa—"the all-attractive Lord"; the main name of the original Supreme Personality of Godhead. Śrī Kṛṣṇa is the source of all incarnations, and no one is equal to Him or greater than Him. There is nothing to compare with this two-armed form of the Lord, blackish like a rain cloud, with reddish lotus eyes and an all-enchanting smile. Kṛṣṇa is Bhagavān (the Supreme Lord), the possessor of six opulences in unlimited fullness: wealth, strength, beauty, knowledge, fame and renunciation. Besides "all-attractive", the name Kṛṣṇa also means "the whole of existence" and "He who stops birth and death". Kṛṣṇa has unlimited names like Govinda, Gopāla, Mukunda, and Hari. These holy names are non-different from Him and indicate the forms He displays in His various pastimes. Śrī Kṛṣṇa's eternal consort is Śrīmatī Rādhārāṇī.

Kṛṣṇadāsa Kavirāja Gosvāmī—author of the immortal *Śrī Caitanya-caritāmṛta*, the greatest work on the life and philosophy of Śrī Caitanya Mahāprabhu. This book is especially revered by all Gauḍīya Vaiṣṇavas.

Kṣatriya—warrior or administrator; the second *varṇa*, or social-occupational division in Vedic society. *Ksat* means hurt, and one who gives protection from harm is called *kṣatriya* (*trayate*—to give protection). "Heroism, power, determination, resourcefulness, courage in battle, generosity and leadership are the natural qualities of work for the *kṣatriyas*." (*Bhagavad-gītā* 18.43) "A *kṣatriya's* duty is to protect the citizens from all kinds of difficulties, and for that reason he has to apply violence in suitable cases for law and order. Therefore he has to conquer the soldiers of inimical kings, and thus, with religious principles, he should rule over the world." (*Parāśara-smṛti*)

Kumāras—four learned ascetic sons (Sanaka, Sananda, Sanātana, and Sanat) of Lord Brahmā appearing eternally as children. They are incarnations of the *jñāna-śakti* (power of knowledge) of Lord Viṣṇu. One of the four Vaiṣṇava *sampradāyas* (schools of thought, or disciplic successions) is called the Kumāra-sampradāya, of which they are the original founders. They are also *mahājanas*, or Vaiṣṇava authorities. "First of all, in the beginning of creation, there were the four unmarried sons of Brahmā (the Kumāras), who, being situated in a vow of celibacy, underwent severe austerities for realization of the Absolute Truth." (*Śrīmad-Bhāg.* 1.3.6)

Kumbha-melā—*kumbha* means "pot", "pitcher", or "jar"; *melā* means "festival". Once when the demigods and demons were fighting in the heavenly planets over some *amṛta* (immortal nectar), a few drops of it fell from the *kumbha*, in which the nectar was stored, in sacred rivers on this planet. The four locations where the nectar fell are: Prayāga-rāja (Allahabad), Haridvāra, Nasik (Trimbak), and Ujjain. On a twelve year rotating cycle, Kumbha-melās are held at these locations and the worshiper who takes bath at an auspicious time, is assured liberation from the cycle of birth and death. The Kumbha-melās are considered the earth's largest gathering of human beings. The *melās* are also known as the world's largest act of faith.

L

Liberation—see Mokṣa or Mukti

Līlā—the endlessly expanding transcendental activities and pastimes of Lord Kṛṣṇa and His associates.

Liṅga—phallus of Lord Śiva; the embodiment of his superior power, and representing his creating energy. Customarily bathed and worshiped with Gaṅgā water, bael leaves, milk, ghee, yogurt, honey, flowers, and other auspicious items by the followers of Lord Śiva, who consider the *liṅga* as their deity and temple. Most *liṅgas* are established on the banks of sacred rivers, lakes, tanks, ponds, etc., and some Himālayan peaks are considered to be *liṅgas* and so worshiped. Traces of *liṅga* worship have been discovered in other countries outside India, such as Egypt, Syria, Babylon, Persia, Greece, Spain, Germany, Scandinavia, Armenia, Mexico, and Peru.

Loka—a planet.

M

Madhvācārya—the founder of the *dvaita* (duality) school of Vedānta philosophy, also known as Ānandatīrtha and Pūrṇaprajña, who re-established the Brahma-sampradāya in the thirteenth century A.D. He was born near Uḍupī (Karnataka) in a small village named Belle (Pājaka-kṣetra) in the year 1238 A.D., and is the incarnation of Vāyu, the demigod of wind. A prolific writer and undefeatable in debate, he established Dvaita Vedānta in direct opposition to Śaṅkarācārya's Advaita Vedānta. He initiated eight of his chief disciples into the *sannyāsa* order and then established eight different *maṭhas* in Uḍupī. At the age of 79, he proceeded to Badarīnātha in the Himālayas and left this planet.

Mahābhārata—an important and famous historical scripture belonging to the *smṛti* section of the Vedic scriptures; Śrīla Vyāsadeva's epic history of greater India. The *Mahābhārata* narrates the history and battle between the Pāṇḍava and Kaurava factions of the great Kuru dynasty. The *Bhagavad-gītā* is from the *Bhīṣma-parva*, where the discourse between Śrī Kṛṣṇa and Arjuna that took place before an enormous fratricidal war at Kurukṣetra took place. "The purpose of the *Mahābhārata* is to administer the purpose of the *Vedas*, and therefore within this *Mahābhārata* the summary *Veda* of *Bhagavad-gītā* is placed." (Śrīla Prabhupāda)

Mahājanas—standard authorities on devotional service to Lord Viṣṇu. According to the *Śrīmad-Bhāgavatam*, there are twelve *mahājanas*: Lord Brahmā, Nārada Muni, Lord Śiva, the four Kumāras, Lord Kapila, Svāyambhuva Manu, Prahlāda Mahārāja, Janaka Mahārāja, Grandfather Bhīṣma, Bali Mahārāja, Śukadeva Gosvāmī, and Yamarāja.

Mañjarīs—the intimate maidservants and assistants of Śrīmatī Rādhārāṇī in Goloka Vṛndāvana.

Mantra—*manas* means "mind" and *trayate* means "to deliver"; a spiritual sound vibration that frees consciousness from illusion; or Vedic hymn. The Vedic scriptures are composed of several million *mantras*.

Manu—demigod who is the father of mankind. There are fourteen Manu incarnations who appear in one day of Lord Brahmā, which lasts for 4,320,000 times 1,000 human years. (see *Sapta Ṛṣis*, Book Two, Chapter Seven)

Mathurā—known as Madhupurī in the *Rāmāyaṇa*, when Lord Rāmacandra's brother, Śatrughna, conquered the city from the demon Lavaṇa. It was Lord Kṛṣṇa's birthplace and later became His abode after He performed His childhood pastimes in Vṛndāvana. At the end of Lord Kṛṣṇa's earthly manifested pastimes, His grandson Vajra (son of Aniruddha) became the King of Surasena, or Mathurapuri.

Māyāpur—the exact birthplace of Śrī Caitanya Mahāprabhu, located at Navadvīpa within the island of Antardvīpa, situated on the bank of Gaṅgā. In the middle of Māyāpur is the *mahā-yogapīṭha*, the birthplace of Mahāprabhu. The Mahāvana in Goloka Vṛndāvana is nondifferent from the Māyāpur of Śrī Navadvīpa-dhāma.

Māyā—"energy" (*yoga-māyā*, or spiritual energy; and *mahā-māyā*, or material energy); "bewilderment" or "illusion" (forgetfulness of one's spiritual nature and the relationship with the Supreme Lord). According to Śrīla Bhaktisiddhānta Sarasvatī, *māyā* means "that which can be measured."

Mokṣa, or Mukti—"liberation"; Vedic culture guides mankind through four stages of development: *dharma* (religiosity), *artha* (economic development), *kāma* (sense gratification), and *mokṣa* (liberation of the soul from birth and death, or from material existence).

Muni—a sage; one who can exercise his mind in various ways for mental speculation without coming to a factual conclusion. But a *sthita-dhir muni*, a sage whose mind is steady, has exhausted all his business of creative speculation. "One who is not disturbed in mind even amidst the threefold miseries or elated when there is happiness, and who is free from attachment, fear and anger, is called a sage of steady mind." (*Bhagavad-gītā* 2.56)

N

Nārada Muni—a great sage among the demigods, a pure devotee of the Supreme Lord, and one of the *mahājanas*. In *Kali-santaraṇa Upaniṣad*, Lord Brahmā taught Nārada the Hare Kṛṣṇa *mahā-mantra*. He travels throughout the universes in his eternal body, glorifying *bhakti-yoga*. One of his disciples is Vedavyāsa, who compiled all the Vedic scriptures. "In the millennium of the *ṛṣis*, the Personality of Godhead accepted the third empowered incarnation in the form of Devarṣi Nārada, who is a great sage among the demigods. He collected expositions of the *Vedas* which deal with devotional service and which inspire nonfruitive action." (*Śrīmad-Bhāgavatam* 1.3.8)

Nārāyaṇa, Lord—Lord Viṣṇu; the Supreme Lord in His majestic, four-armed form. An expansion of Lord Kṛṣṇa, He presides over the Vaikuṇṭha planets. His principal eternal consort is Lakṣmī, the goddess of fortune.

Navadvīpa—"nine islands"; also known as *audarya-dhāma*, or the Lord's abode that is the embodiment of compassion and magnanimity. Navadvīpa is nondifferent from Vṛndāvana. The nine islands of Navadvīpa resemble a lotus flower. Each island represents one of the nine processes of devotional service to the Supreme Lord: 1) Antardvīpa (*ātma-nivedanam*—surrendering everything); 2) Sīmantadvīpa (*śravaṇam*—hearing); 3) Godrumadvīpa (*kīrtanam*—chanting); 4) Madhyadvīpa (*smaraṇam*—remembering); 5) Koladvīpa (*pāda-sevanam*—serving the Lord's lotus feet); 6) Ṛtudvīpa (*arcanam*—worshiping); 7) Jahnudvīpa (*vandanam*—praying); 8) Modadrumadvīpa (*dāsyam*—becoming His servant); and 9) Rudradvīpa (*sakhyam*—becoming His friend). Śrī Caitanya Mahāprabhu appeared at Māyāpur on the island of Antardvīpa in 1486, and His appearance made Navadvīpa the crest jewel of all holy places in this present age of Kali. Śrīla Bhaktivinoda Ṭhākura states that Lord Caitanya's forest, known as the nine islands of Navadvīpa, is Īśodyāna (a transcendental garden). Navadvīpa is divided and encircled by Gaṅgā and fifteen other sacred rivers. From the crossings of these sacred rivers, the nine islands of Navadvīpa form an eight-petalled lotus.

Nityānanda Prabhu—the incarnation of Lord Balarāma who appeared in Ekacakragrāma (West Bengal) in 1474. He is the principle associate of Śrī Caitanya Mahāprabhu, just as Balarāma is the first bodily expansion of Lord Kṛṣṇa. Lord Nityānanda and Lord Balarāma are both one and the same identity, different only in form.

Narottama dāsa Ṭhākura—a renowned Vaiṣṇava saint who was the embodiment of Gauḍīya teachings and is famous for his composition of devotional songs. He appeared in or around the year Śrī Caitanya Mahāprabhu disappeared (1534 A.D.) at Kheturi (now Bangladesh). The only initiated disciple of Śrīla Lokanātha Gosvāmī, he studied under Śrī Jīva Gosvāmī in Vṛndāvana.

P

Padayātrā—a journey or pilgrimage undertaken by foot. A traditional Vedic way to travel, preach, and visit holy places, especially for *ācāryas*, *sādhus*, and *vānaprasthas*. ISKCON inaugurated a *saṅkīrtana-padayātrā* from Dvārakā, Gujarat, on September 2, 1984, to bring the congregational chanting of the holy names of the Lord: Hare Kṛṣṇa, Hare Kṛṣṇa, Kṛṣṇa Kṛṣṇa, Hare Hare/Hare Rāma, Hare Rāma, Rāma Rāma, Hare Hare to every town and village in India. Still today, Śrīla

Prabhupāda's Saṅkīrtana Padayātrā is on the road walking. They have covered more than 60,000 kilometres, introduced or revived the chanting of the Hare Kṛṣṇa *mahā-mantra* in more than 6,000 villages in 20 of the 28 states of India, and distributed *Bhagavad-gītā* and other Vedic literatures in ten languages. ISKCON's Padayātrā has circumambulated India four times in 17 years.

Pañca-tattva—the Absolute Truth in five features; Śrī Caitanya Mahāprabhu with His associates: Nityānanda Prabhu, Advaita Ācārya, Gadādhara Paṇḍita, and Śrīvāsa Ṭhākura. They are worshiped by the Gauḍīya Vaiṣṇavas as the Śrī Pañca-tattva. Within the Pañca-tattva, Mahāprabhu is the Supreme Lord, Nityānanda is His plenary portion, Advaita is His incarnation, Gadādhara is His energy, and Śrīvāsa is His devotee.

Pāṇḍavas—the five sons of King Pāṇḍu: Yudhiṣṭhira, Bhīma, Arjuna, Nakula, and Sahadeva, who were intimate friends and devotees of Lord Kṛṣṇa.

Paṇḍita—a scholar learned in Vedic literature, not only academically but also by dint of spiritual realization. This term is also loosely applied to any scholar.

Parikramā—clockwise circumambulation of sacred places of pilgrimage like Vṛndāvana or Navadvīpa. Temples, sacred trees like *tulasī*, cows, rivers, lakes, *kuṇḍas*, mountains, *yajñas*, kings, parents, and the spiritual master are circumambulated for spiritual benefit.

Prabhupāda—see A.C. Bhaktivedanta Swami Śrīla Prabhupāda.

Prasāda—"mercy", or the Lord's mercy; food or other items spiritualized by being first offered to the Supreme Lord, as prescribed in the system of *bhakti-yoga*.

Prema—love of God, the perfection of life.

Purāṇas—"very old", or histories; authentic old histories of the universe compiled by Vyāsadeva. The *Purāṇas* record the chief incidents that occurred over many millions of years, not only on this planet, but also on other planets within the universe. Within the *smṛti* section of the Vedic scriptures, there are eighteen principle *Purāṇas*, or *mahā-purāṇas*, and they each discuss ten primary subject matters: 1) the primary creation; 2) the secondary creation; 3) the planetary systems; 4) protection and maintenance by the *avatāras*; 5) the Manus; 6) dynasties of great kings; 7) noble character and activities of great kings; 8) dissolution of the universe and liberation of the living entity; 9) the *jīva* (spirit soul); 10) the Supreme Lord. According to the *Padma Purāṇa*, the principle eighteen *Purāṇas* are classified into three groups: 1) *sāttvika*, or *Purāṇas* in the mode of goodness—*Viṣṇu Purāṇa* (23,000 verses), *Nārada Purāṇa* (25,000), *Bhāgavata Purāṇa* (18,000), *Garuḍa Purāṇa* (19,000), *Padma Purāṇa* (55,000), and *Varāha Purāṇa* (24,000); 2) *rajasa*, or *Purāṇas* in the mode of passion—*Brahmāṇḍa Purāṇa* (12,000), *Brahma-vaivarta Purāṇa* (18,000), *Mārkaṇḍeya Purāṇa* (9,000), *Brahma Purāṇa* (10,000), *Vāmana Purāṇa* (10,000), and *Bhaviṣya Purāṇa* (14,500); 3) *tāmasa*, or *Purāṇas* in the mode of ignorance—*Matsya Purāṇa* (14,000), *Kūrma Purāṇa* (17,000), *Liṅga Purāṇa* (11,000), *Śiva Purāṇa* (24,000), *Agni Purāṇa* (15,400), and *Skanda Purāṇa* (81,100). Thus the total number of verses in all the *mahā-purāṇas* is 400,000. The greatest of these is the *Bhāgavata Purāṇa*, or *Śrīmad-Bhāgavatam*. There are also eighteen secondary *Purāṇas*, or *upa-purāṇas*. The *Purāṇas* are supplementary explanations of the *Vedas* and are considered the fifth *Veda*.

R

Rādhārāṇī—the feminine counterpart or consort of Lord Śrī Kṛṣṇa. She is the *ānanda* (spiritual bliss) potency, or the *hlādinī-śakti*, for the transcendental pleasure of Kṛṣṇa. "The transcendental goddess Śrīmatī Rādhārāṇī is the direct counterpart of Lord Śrī Kṛṣṇa. She is the central figure for all the goddesses of fortune. She possesses all the attractiveness to attract the all-attractive Personality of Godhead. She is the primeval internal potency of the Lord." (*Bṛhad-gautamiya-tantra*) "We are trying to be under the guidance of Rādhārāṇī, *daivi-prakṛti*. *Prakṛti* means woman, and *daivi* means transcendental woman...Śrīmatī Rādhārāṇī is the mother of devotion" (Śrīla Prabhupāda)

Rāmānujācārya—the great philosopher and *ācārya* of the Śrī Vaiṣṇava-sampradāya. He appeared at Śrī Perumbudur (Tamil Nadu) in 1017 A.D., and is the incarnation of Lakṣmaṇa (Saṅkarṣaṇa). His *viśiṣṭādvaita-vāda* philosophy (qualified oneness) was strongly presented to defeat Śaṅkarācārya's *advaita-vata* philosophy (one undifferentiated, changeless *brahman*). He was known as Yatirāja, the prince of *sannyāsīs*, on account of his austere and ascetic life. He traveled throughout India extensively, spreading the glories of Lord Nārāyaṇa based on his *Śrī-bhāṣya*, the comprehensive commentary on the *Vedānta-sūtra*. He remained for 120 years and, before leaving this planet at Śrī Raṅgam, left the following instructions: "Always relish the chanting of the holy name and qualities of the Supreme Lord...The best way to serve the Lord is to serve His devotees...Study the *Śrī-bhāṣya* and teach it to others, this service is most pleasing to the Lord."

Rākṣasas—a race of man-eating demons.

Rāmacandra—a name of Lord Kṛṣṇa meaning "the source of all pleasures"; an incarnation of the Supreme Personality of Godhead, who was a perfect righteous king and the killer of the ten-headed demon king, Rāvaṇa. Lord Rāma was exiled to the forest for fourteen years on the order of His father, Mahārāja Daśaratha. His wife Sītā-devī was kidnapped by Rāvaṇa, but employing a huge army of monkeys, who were the powerful and intelligent offspring of the demigods, He regained His wife in battle. After killing Rāvaṇa, He returned to His ancestral kingdom and became the ideal monarch. This great epic of Lord Rāma's activities in this world is recounted in Vālmīki's *Rāmāyaṇa*. "In the eighteenth incarnation, the Lord appeared as King Rāma. In order to perform some pleasing work for the demigods, He exhibited superhuman powers by controlling the Indian Ocean and then killing the atheist King Rāvaṇa." (*Śrīmad-Bhāgavatam* 1.3.22)

Rāmāyaṇa—the epic history about Lord Rāmacandra, compiled by Vālmīki Muni, belonging to the *smṛti* section of the Vedic scriptures. The account of the pastimes of Lord Rāmacandra was originally related by Lord Brahmā in one billion verses. That *Rāmāyaṇa* was later summarized by Nārada Muni and related to Vālmīki. Then Vālmīki taught the *Rāmāyaṇa* to Lord Rāma's two sons, Kuśa and Lava, and then they recited the *Rāmāyaṇa* to Lord Rāma before an open assembly in Ayodhyā. *Rāmāyaṇa*, which contains 24,000 verses, is considered to be the world's first poetic composition, and hence it is called *adi-kāvya*, the first epic. Vālmīki Muni is known as *adi-kavi*, the first poet.

Ṛṣi—a synonym for a *muni* or sage. (see Muni or Sapta Ṛṣis)

Rūpa Gosvāmī—the leader of the six Gosvāmīs of Vṛndāvana, principal followers of Śrī Caitanya Mahāprabhu, who systematically presented His teachings. Gauḍīya Vaiṣṇavas are known as Rūpānugas, followers of Rūpa Gosvāmī. He is also known as the *rasācārya*, or the teacher of the transcendental moods of devotional reciprocation, as exemplified in his book, *Bhakti-rasāmṛta-sindhu*.

S

Sādhu—a saintly person, a devotee of the Lord; one of the three authorities for a Vaiṣṇava: *sādhu*, *guru*, and *śāstra*. A *sādhu* is one who can cut to pieces the bonds of illusory affection in the material world and enlighten people in devotional service to the Supreme Lord. "The symptoms of a *sādhu* are that he is tolerant, merciful, and friendly to all living entities. He has no enemies, he is peaceful, he abides by the scriptures, and all his characteristics are sublime." (*Śrīmad-Bhāgavatam* 3.25.21)

Sahasra-tīrtha-jala—one thousand sacred waters; a program organized by ISKCON to collect 1,008 *jalas* (sacred waters) from 1,008 *tīrthas* in six countries (India, Pakistan, Nepal, China [Tibet], Bangladesh, and Myanmar) for the auspicious *mahā-abhiṣeka* (great bathing ceremony) of Śrīla Prabhupāda, as an offering for his Centennial Celebrations (1896-1996).

Saṅkīrtana—the congregational glorification of the Lord through chanting His holy name. The most recommended process of spiritual upliftment in the present age of Kali.

Samādhi—'fixed mind' or trance; complete absorption of the mind and senses in God consciousness. There are two kinds of *samādhi*: *samprajñata-samādhi* (when situated in the transcendental position by various philosophical researches); and *asamprajñata-samādhi* (when there is no longer any connection with mundane pleasure). One in full *samādhi* has realized Brahman, Paramātmā, and Bhagavān. Also refers to the tomb where a great soul's body or paraphernalia is enshrined after his departure from this world.

Saṁsāra—the cycle of repeated birth and death in the material world.

Saṅkarācārya—the great exponent of *advaita* (nondualism) philosophy and the incarnation of Lord Śiva. He took birth at Kāladī (Kerala), somewhere between the 5th and 7th century, to re-establish the authority of the Vedic scriptures. This was done at a time when India was under the influence of Buddhism, whose tenets deny the authority of the *Vedas*. He established four *maṭhas* at the four directions of India: Jyotir-maṭha (North), Purī (East), Śṛṅgerī (South), and Dvārakā (West). He left the world at the age of 32, most likely at Kedāranātha in the Himālayas.

Sāṅkhya-yoga—1) the path of spiritual realization through analytical discrimination between spirit and matter; 2) the path of devotional service as described by Lord Kapila, the son of Devahūti.

Sanskrit—*sam* means "together" and *kṛta* means "made", hence speech "made together or refined"; Sanskrit is an ancient language of culture, learning, and spiritual wisdom. The *Vedas* are all written in Sanskrit. Throughout the centuries, Sanskrit has been written in a variety of alphabets. The mode of writing most widely used today is called *devanāgari*, which means the writing used in "the cities of the demigods".

Sannyāsa—renounced life; the fourth *āśrama*, or spiritual order in Vedic society. It is the order of ascetics who travel and constantly preach the message of Godhead for the benefit of all. The *sannyāsī* has no other purpose in life but to serve and please the Supreme Personality of Godhead, and he acts as the *guru* for the other divisions of Vedic society. "The giving up of activities that are based on material desire is what great learned men call the renounced order of life (*sannyāsa*)." (*Bhagavad-gītā* 18.2)

Sannyāsī—one in the renounced order of life.

Sapta Ṛṣis—"seven sages"; those who have attained perfection by spiritual achievements. They are all stalwart *brāhmaṇas*, situated in the quality of goodness. In each and every Manvantara (the interval of a Manu), one group of Sapta Ṛṣis appears. One Manu equals 71 *catur-yugas* (Satya, Tretā, Dvāpara, and Kali) and one *catur-yuga* equals 4,320,000 human years. (see *The Seven Sages*, Book Two, Chapter Seven)

Satya-yuga—also known as Kṛta-yuga; the first of the four ages which cycle perpetually in the universe, and is characterized by virtue, wisdom and religion, there being practically no ignorance and vice. This *yuga* lasts for 1,728,000 years.

Śiva—means *maṅgala*, or auspicious; the greatest among the living entities within the material world. Śiva is a *guṇa-avatāra* of Lord Viṣṇu, or an incarnation who directs or supervises the material mode of ignorance (*tamo-guṇa*) and who annihilates the material universes. His name purifies one of all sinful activities, and is very auspicious for persons who identify the body with the soul. If such persons take shelter of Lord Śiva, gradually they will understand that they are not the material body but spirit soul. Śiva is always in meditation on the lotus feet of Vāsudeva, Śrī Kṛṣṇa. Śiva is worshiped because he is the greatest Vaiṣṇava. He is also the founder of the Rudra-sampradāya. Lord Śiva's eternal consort is Pārvatī-devī.

Six Gosvāmīs of Vṛndāvana—Śrī Rūpa, Sanātana, Raghunātha Bhaṭṭa, Jīva, Gopāla Bhaṭṭa, and Raghunātha dāsa, the principle followers of Śrī Caitanya Mahāprabhu who established devotional service as a scientific process of God realization in the modern age.

Śrīmad-Bhāgavatam—*Bhāgavata Purāṇa*; a work of 18,000 verses compiled by Vyāsadeva as his natural commentary on the *Vedānta-sūtra*. It takes up where the *Bhagavad-gītā* leaves off. The cream of all the *Purāṇas*, which is the most complete and authoritative exposition of all Vedic knowledge. The *Śrīmad-Bhāgavatam* is compared to "the ripened fruit of the tree of Vedic literature" and describes the complete science of devotional service to Kṛṣṇa.

Śūdra—laborer; the fourth *varṇa*, or social-occupational division in Vedic society. "...and for the *śūdras* there is labor and service to others." (*Bhagavad-gītā* 18.44)

Svāmī or Swami—also called Gosvāmī; master of the senses, or one able to fully control his mind and senses; a person in the *sannyāsa* order. "A *gosvāmī* knows the standard of sense happiness. In transcendental sense happiness, the senses are engaged in the service of Hṛṣīkeśa, or the supreme owner of the senses—Kṛṣṇa." (Śrīla Prabhupāda)

T

Tapasya—austerity; voluntary acceptance of some physical and mental inconvenience for a higher purpose.

Tilaka—auspicious clay markings placed by devotees on the forehead and other parts of the body.

Tretā-yuga—the second of four ages which cycle perpetually in the universe, which has similar characteristics as Satya-yuga, but vice is introduced. This *yuga* lasts for 1,296,000 years.

Tīrtha—holy or sacred place; place of pilgrimage; saintly persons. A *tīrtha* is eternally perfect, fully spiritual, and unlimited; capable of destroying sins. Saintly personalities or pure devotees of the Lord are also considered *tīrthas*, because under the guise of visiting the *tīrthas*, these holy personalities purify the *tīrthas* themselves. Śrīla Prabhupāda has written, "The holy places all over the earth are meant for purifying the polluted consciousness of the human being by an atmosphere surcharged with the presence of the Lord's unalloyed devotees…Such pure devotees are able to rectify the polluted atmosphere of any place into a place of pilgrimage, and the holy places are worth the name only on their account."

Tulasī—a sacred plant dear to Lord Kṛṣṇa and Lord Viṣṇu, who is worshiped by Their devotees. In Lord Kṛṣṇa's pastimes, Tulasī-devī is the manifestation of Śrīmatī Vṛndā-devī, who is an expansion of Śrīmatī Rādhārāṇī. In Lord Viṣṇu's pastimes, she is the manifestation of Śrī Lakṣmī-devī, who is also an expansion of Śrīmatī Rādhārāṇī.

V

Vaikuṇṭha—"place of no anxiety"; free from the limitations (*kuṇṭha*) of sorrow, delusion and fear; the kingdom of God. Beyond the material universes are spiritual planets where Lord Nārāyaṇa resides in unimaginable spiritual majesty. These planets, which are innumerable, are known as Vaikuṇṭha. The chief of these spiritual planets is Goloka Vṛndāvana, the personal abode of Śrī Kṛṣṇa.

Vaiṣṇava—a devotee or servant of Lord Viṣṇu or Kṛṣṇa, or any of Their expansions.

Vaiṣṇava-sampradāyas—there are four Vaiṣṇava schools (*sampradāyas*) of Vedānta: 1) Śrī-sampradāya, whose *ācārya* is Rāmānuja; 2) Brahma-sampradāya, whose *ācārya* is Madhva; 3) Rudra-sampradāya, whose *ācārya* is Viṣṇusvāmī; and 4) Kumāra-sampradāya, whose *ācārya* is Nimbārka. Lord Caitanya's movement is a branch of the Brahma Madhva-sampradāya.

Vaiśya—farmer or merchant; the third *varṇa*, or social-occupational division in Vedic society. "Farming, cow protection and business are the natural work for the *vaiśyas*…" (*Bhagavad-gītā* 18.44)

Vānaprastha—retired life; the third *āśrama*, or spiritual order in Vedic society. One who has retired from householder life to cultivate greater renunciation, by performing severe austerities, such as living alone in the forest, dressing with tree bark, not shaving, etc.

Varṇāśrama-dharma—the Vedic social system which organizes society into four *varṇas* or occupational divisions: *brāhmaṇa*, *kṣatriya*, *vaiśya*, and *śūdra*; and four *āśramas* or spiritual divisions: *brahmācārya*, *gṛhastha*, *vānaprastha*, and *sannyāsa*. According to the different modes of material nature, men are classified in the mode of goodness (*brāhmaṇas*), the mode of passion (*kṣatriyas*), the mixed modes of passion and ignorance (*vaiśyas*), and the mode of ignorance (*śūdra*). The normal rules and regulations of *varṇāśrama* are as follows: "A *brāhmaṇa* must go through the four *āśramas*: *brahmācārya*, *gṛhastha*, *vānaprastha* and *sannyāsa*. A *kṣatriya* three: *brahmācārya*, *gṛhastha* and *vānaprastha*. A *vaiśya* two: *brahmācārya* and *gṛhastha*. And for the *śūdras*, only *gṛhastha*. But either one

is *brāhmaṇa* or *kṣatriya* or *vaiśya* or *śūdra*, if he takes to Kṛṣṇa consciousness he becomes above these rules and regulations." (Śrīla Prabhupāda)
(see the individual entries of these *varṇas* and *āśramas*)

Vedānta-sūtra—a book of codes or aphorisms by Śrīla Vyāsadeva, explaining the *Upaniṣads* and dealing with the Absolute Truth. The *Vedānta-sūtra* establishes that the Supreme Personality of Godhead is the subject of all the *Vedas*, that devotion is the means of realizing transcendental love for Godhead, and that this love is the final object of man's endeavors. It is the textbook of all theistic philosophy, and, as such, many commentators have elaborated on the significance of its conclusions.

***Veda, Vedas*, or Vedic literature**—*veda* means "knowledge"; the original scriptures. "The four *Vedas*, namely the *Ṛg Veda*, *Yajur Veda*, *Sāma Veda*, and *Atharva Veda*, are all emanations from the breathing of the great Personality of Godhead." (*Bṛhad-āraṇyaka Upaniṣad* 4.5.11) The message of the transcendental world that has come down to this material world through the medium of sound is known as the *Veda*. Being the very words of the Supreme Personality of Godhead Himself, the *Vedas* are eternal. Lord Kṛṣṇa originally revealed the *Vedas* to Lord Brahmā, the first living entity to appear in the material universe, and by him they were subsequently made available to other living entities through the channel of *paramparā*, spiritual disciplic succession. The Vedic literatures are quite extensive, but mainly divided into two categories: the *śruti* (four *Vedas* and 108 *Upaniṣads*); and the *smṛti* (*Purāṇas*, *Mahābhārata*, *Bhagavad-gītā*, and *Rāmāyaṇa*). "Only unto those great souls who have implicit faith in both the Lord and spiritual master, are all the imports of Vedic knowledge automatically revealed." (*Śvetāśvatara Upaniṣad* 6.23)

Virajā River—*vi* (*vigata*) means "completely eradicated", and *rajas* means "the influence of the material world"; the name Virajā indicates a marginal position between the spiritual and material worlds. A body of water between the spiritual and material worlds and this water is generated from the bodily perspiration of the Supreme Personality of Godhead. Virajā River also encircles the transcendental planet known as Goloka.

Viṣṇu—"the all-pervading God"; one of the multiforms or plenary expansions of the original Supreme Personality of Godhead, Śrī Kṛṣṇa, in His majestic four-armed form. Viṣṇu supervises the material mode of goodness (*sattva-guṇa*), as the maintainer of the created universe. All sacrificial performances are meant for the satisfaction of Lord Viṣṇu. Also, the *varṇāśrama* institution aims at satisfying Lord Viṣṇu. He is worshiped by all the demigods and sages and described throughout the *Vedas* as the *summum bonum* of all knowledge, the Absolute Truth.

Viśvanātha Cakravartī Ṭhākura—a great *ācārya* in the line of Śrī Caitanya Mahāprabhu and the most prominent *ācārya* after Narottama dāsa Ṭhākura. He has composed twenty-four valuable books on the science of *bhakti-yoga*.

Vṛndāvana—the transcendental abode of Śrī Kṛṣṇa; also called Goloka, Kṛṣṇaloka, Vraja, Gokula, and Śvetadvīpa. One of the twelve forests of Vraja where many of Lord Kṛṣṇa's pastimes took place and where He grew up. Vṛndāvana is Lord Kṛṣṇa's personal spiritual abode that descended to the earth some 5,000 years ago. It is situated on the bank of the River Yamunā.

Vṛndāvana dāsa Ṭhākura—the incarnation of Vyāsadeva in Śrī Caitanya Mahāprabhu's pastimes; author of *Śrī Caitanya-bhāgavata*, one of the earliest biographies of Lord Caitanya.

Vyāsadeva—also known as Vedavyāsa, Bādarāyaṇa, or Dvaipāyana; *vyāsa* means "one who describes elaborately"; the empowered *śaktyāveśa-avatāra* of the Supreme Lord who is the compiler of the *Vedas*, including the *Upaniṣads* and the *Purāṇas*. He is also the author of the *Mahābhārata* and *Vedānta-sūtra*. "Thereafter, in the seventeenth incarnation of Godhead, Śrī Vyāsadeva appeared and divided the one *Veda* into several branches and sub-branches, seeing that the people in general were less intelligent." (*Śrīmad-Bhāgavatam* 1.3.21)

Y

Yajña—1) "sacrifice"; 2) a name for Lord Viṣṇu, as the Lord of sacrifice; *yajño vai viṣṇuh*: all sacrificial performances are meant for the satisfaction of Lord Viṣṇu. There are several kinds of sacrifices placed into various divisions, such as *dravyamaya-yajña*, or the sacrifice of personal possessions in the form of various kinds of charities; *tapomaya-yajña*, or the sacrifice of the comforts of life; *yoga-yajña*, or the sacrifice for a certain type of perfection; *svadhyaya-yajña*, or engagement in the sacrifice of studies; *vivaha-yajña*, or the sacrifice of marriage; *pitṛ-yajña*, or the sacrifice to the forefathers; and *saṅkīrtana-yajña*, or the sacrifice of chanting of the holy names of God. Sacrifices such as *agnihotra-yajña* (ceremonial fire sacrifice performed in Vedic rituals), *aśvamedha-yajña* (horse sacrifice to prove the efficacy of Vedic hymns and relieve one of sinful reactions), and *rājasūya-yajña* (the king or greatest of all sacrifices, ultimately to prove the supremacy of Lord Kṛṣṇa) are not recommended in this present age because neither sufficient riches nor qualified *brāhmaṇas* are available. "In this age of Kali, people who are endowed with sufficient intelligence will worship the Lord, who is accompanied by His associates, by performance of *saṅkīrtana-yajña*." (*Śrīmad-Bhāgavatam* 11.5.32)

Yakṣas—the ghostly followers of the demigod Kuvera, the treasurer of the demigods.

Yamarāja—the demigod who punishes the sinful after death, or the superintendent of death. Out of all the living entities who give punishment to the miscreants, Yamarāja is the chief. He is known as the king of the Pitās (forefathers), and he resides on Pitṛloka, situated between the lower planetary system and the Garbhodaka Ocean, near the hellish planets. Yamarāja is also one of the twelve *mahājanas* and since he is the executor of religious principles, he is known as Dharmarāja. It is the duty of all *mahājanas* to preach *bhakti-yoga*, but since Yamarāja is duty bound with heavy responsibilities and without spare time to preach, he incarnated as Mahātmā Vidura in order to preach. "...and among the dispensers of law I am Yama, the lord of death." (*Bhagavad-gītā* 10.29)

Yoga—"connection"; a process of linking oneself with the Lord; to concentrate the mind upon the Supreme; the discipline of self-realization, or any of various spiritual disciplines meant for purification, such as *karma-yoga*, *sāṅkhya-yoga*, *jñāna-yoga*, *aṣṭāṅga-yoga*, and *bhakti-yoga*. According to the *Bhagavad-gītā*, the most sublime form of *yoga* is *bhakti-yoga*, the *yoga* of pure devotional service to the Supreme Lord. The process of *bhakti-yoga* is when the consciousness of the individual soul connects with its source, Lord Kṛṣṇa. This is called Kṛṣṇa consciousness. "Therefore, to become Kṛṣṇa conscious is the

highest stage of *yoga*, just as, when we speak of Himālayas, we refer to the world's highest mountains, of which the highest peak, Mount Everest, is considered to be the culmination." (Śrīla Prabhupāda).
(see the individual entries of these *yogas*)

Yugas—four ages which cycle perpetually: Satya-yuga, Tretā-yuga, Dvāpara-yuga, and Kali-yuga. As the ages proceed from Satya to Kali, religion and the good qualities of mankind decline. In Satya-yuga, religious principles have four limbs: mercy, cleanliness, austerity, and truthfulness. In Tretā-yuga, three: mercy, cleanliness, and truthfulness. In Dvāpara-yuga, two: cleanliness and truthfulness. And in Kali-yuga only truthfulness.

Vedic Month	Vaiṣṇava Month	Western Month
Mārgaśīrṣa	Keśava	November/December
Pauṣa	Nārāyaṇa	December/January
Māgha	Mādhava	January/February
Phālguna	Govinda	February/March
Caitra	Viṣṇu	March/April
Vaiśākha	Madhusūdana	April/May
Jyeṣṭha	Trivikrama	May/June
Āṣāḍha	Vāmana	June/July
Śrāvaṇa	Śrīdhara	July/August
Bhādrapada	Hṛṣīkeśa	August/September
Āśvina	Padmanābha	September/October
Kārtika	Dāmodara	October/November

Guide to Diacritical Marks

There is no strong accentuation of syllables in Sanskrit, or pausing between words in a line, only a flowing of short and long (twice as long as the short) syllables. A long syllable is one whose vowel is long (**ā, ai, au, e, ī, o, ṝ, ū**) or whose short vowel is followed by more than one consonant (including **ḥ** and **ṁ**). Aspirated consonants (consonants followed by an **h**) count as single consonants.

The vowels are pronounced as follows:

a – as in but
ā – as in far but held twice as long as **a**
ai – as in aisle
au – as in how
e – as in they
i – as in pin
ī – as in pique but held twice as long as **i**
ḷ –as in lree
o –as in go
ṛ –as in rim
ṝ –as in reed but held twice as long as **ṛ**
u –as in push
ū –as in rule but held twice as long as **u**

The consonants are pronounced as follows:

Gutturals

(pronounced from the throat)

k – as in kite
kh – as in Eckhart
g – as in give
gh – as in dig-hard
ṇ – as in sing

Labials

(pronounced with the lips)

p – as in pine
ph – as in up-hill (not f)
b – as in bird
bh – as in rub-hard
m – as in mother

Cerebrals

(pronounced with tip of tongue against roof of mouth)

ṭ – as in tub
ṭh – as in light-heart
ḍ – as in dove
ḍh – as in red-hot
ṇ – as in sing

Palatals

(pronounced with middle of tongue against palate)

c – as in chair
ch – as in staunch-heart
j – as in joy
jh – as in hedgehog
ñ – as in canyon

Dentals

(pronounced as cerebrals but with tongue against teeth)

t – as in tub
th – as in light-heart
d – as in dove
dh – as in red-hot
n – as in nut

Aspirate

h – as in home

Semivowels

y – as in yes
r – as in run
l – as in light
v – as in vine, except when preceded in the same syllable by a consonant, then like in swan

Anusvāra

ṁ – a resonant nasal sound like **ḥ** in the French word *bon*

Visarga

ḥ – a final **h**-sound: **aḥ** is pronounced like **aha: iḥ** like **ihi**

Sibilants

ś – as in the German word *sprechen*
ṣ – as in shine
s – as in sun

Bibliography

Ancient Scriptures:

Bhagavad-gītā As It Is. Translation by A.C. Bhaktivedanta Swami Prabhupāda.
Los Angeles: Bhaktivedanta Book Trust, 1989

Brahma Purāṇa. Edited by G.P. Bhatt.
Delhi: Motilal Banarsidass Pub.Pvt.Ltd., 1986

Brahma-vaivarta Purāṇa (Hindi).
Gorakhpur: Gita Press, 1995

Garuḍa Purāṇa. Edited by J.L.Shastri.
Delhi: Motilal Banarsidass Pub.Pvt.Ltd., 1990

Liṅga Purāṇa. Edited by J.L. Shastri.
Delhi: Motilal Banarsidass Pub.Pvt.Ltd., 1990

Mahābhārata. Translation by Śrī Galima Dāsa.
USA: Śrī Galima Books, 1997

Mahābhārata. Translation by K.M.Ganguli.
N.Delhi: Munshiram Manoharlal Pub.Pvt.Ltd., 1997

Nārada Purāṇa. Translation by G.V.Tagare.
Delhi: Motilal Banarsidass Pub.Pvt.Ltd., 1980

Padma Purāṇa. Translation by N.A. Deshpande.
Delhi: Motilal Banarsidass Pub.Pvt.Ltd., 1988

Skanda Purāṇa. Translation by G.V.Tagare.
Delhi: Motilal Banarsidass Pub.Pvt.Ltd., 1994

Śiva Purāṇa. Edited by J.L.Shastri.
Delhi: Motilal Banarsidass Pub.Pvt.Ltd., 1969

Śrī Brahma-saṁhitā. Translation by Bhaktisiddhānta Sarasvatī. Gosvāmī Ṭhākura
Bombay: Bhaktivedanta Book Trust, 1994

Śrī Brahma-vaivarta Purāṇa. Trans. by Kuśakratha Dāsa.
Los Angeles: The Kṛṣṇa Institute, 1990

Śrī Garga-saṁhitā. Translation by Kuśakratha Dāsa.
Los Angeles: The Kṛṣṇa Institute, 1990

Śrīmad-Bhāgavatam. Translation by A.C. Bhaktivedanta Swami Prabhupāda,
Los Angeles: Bhaktivedanta Book Trust, 1987

Śrīmad Vālmiki Rāmāyaṇa.
Gorakhpur: Gita Press, 1969

Varāha Purāṇa. Trans. by S. Venkitasubramonia Iyer.
Delhi: Montilal Banarsidass Pub.Pvt.Ltd., 1985

Viṣṇu Purāṇa. Translation by H.H. Wilson.
Delhi: Nag Publishers, 1989

Other References:

A.C. Bhaktivedanta Swami Prabhupāda. *KṚṢṆA*.
Los Angeles: Bhaktivedanta Book Trust, 1970

A.C. Bhaktivedanta Swami Prabhupāda, H.H. Acyutānanda Swami, and H.G. Jayaśacīnandana Dāsa. *Songs of the Vaiṣṇava Ācāryas*.
Los Angeles: Bhaktivedanta Book Trust, 1974

Bhaktivinoda Ṭhākura. *Śrī Navadvīpa-dhāma-māhātmyam*. Translation by Kuśakratha Dāsa
Los Angeles: The Kṛṣṇa Institute, 1990

Bhaktivinoda Ṭhākura. *Śrī Navadvīpa-māhātmyam*.
Translation by Bhanu Swami.
Published by Puṇḍarīka Vidyānidhi Dāsa.
Vṛndāvana: Vrajraj Press, 1994

Bhaktikusum Sraman Swami. *Prabhupāda Śrīla Sarasvatī Ṭhākura*.
Māyāpur: Śrī Caitanya Maṭha, 1940

Chaturvedi, B.K. *Gaṅgā*.
Delhi: Book For All, 1998

Choudhury, B.C. Roy. *Temples and Legends of Bihar*.
Bombay: Bharatiya Vidya Bhavan, 1965

Dave, J.H. *Immortal India*.
Bombay: Bharatiya Vidya Bhavan, 1957

Eck, D.L. *Banaras: City of Light*.
Great Britain: Routledge & Kegan Paul Ltd., 1983

Gaura-līlā Dāsa. *Māyāpur Journal*.
Switzerland: Published by Gaura-līlā Dāsa, 1995-96

GBC Deity Worship Research Group.
Pañcarātra Pradīpa.
Māyāpur: ISKCON GBC Press, 1994

Kavi-karnapura. *Śrī Gaura-gaṇoddeśa-dīpikā*.
Translation by Kuśakratha Dāsa.
Los Angeles: The Kṛṣṇa Institute, 1987

Kṛṣṇadāsa Kavirāja. *Śrī Caitanya-caritāmṛta*.
Translation and commentary by A.C. Bhaktivedanta Swami Prabhupāda.
Los Angeles: Bhaktivedanta Book Trust, 1973

Kuśakratha Dāsa. *The Glories of Śrī Caitanya Mahāprabhu*.
Los Angeles: The Kṛṣṇa Institute, 1986

Govindacharya, Bannanje. *Madhvacharya.*
Uḍupi: Paryayotsava Samiti, 1984

Hari Śauri Dāsa. *A Transcendental Diary.*
Florida: Lotus Imprints, 1992

Īśāna Nāgara. *Śrī Advaita Prakāśa.*
Translation by Subhaga Swami.
Published by Puṇḍarīka Vidyānidhi Dāsa.
Vṛndāvana: Vrajraj Press, 1997

Kumar, S.V. *The Purāṇic Lore of Holy Water Places.*
N.Delhi: Munshiram Manoharlal Pub.Pvt.Ltd., 1983

Law, B.C. *Holy Places of India.*
Calcutta: Calcutta Geographical Society, 1940

Law, B.C. *Mountains of India.*
Calcutta: Calcutta Geographical Society, 1944

Law, B.C. *Rivers of India.*
Calcutta: Calcutta Geographical Society, 1944

Law, B.C. *Historical Geography of Ancient India.*
N.Delhi: Munshiram Manoharlal Pub.Pvt.Ltd., 1984

Locana dāsa Ṭhākura. *Śrī Caitanya-maṅgala.*
Translation by Subhaga Swami.
Vṛndāvana: Published by Mahānidhi Swami, 1994

Mahānidhi Swami. *Appreciating Navadvīpa-dhāma.*
Vṛndāvana: Published by Mahānidhi Swami, 1996

Madugula, I.S. *The Ācārya (Śaṅkara of Kāladī).*
Delhi: Motilal Banarsidass Pub.Pvt.Ltd., 1985

Mani, Vettam. *Purāṇic Encyclopaedia.*
Delhi: Motilal Banarsidass Pub.Pvt.Ltd., 1989

Mitchiner, J.E. *Traditions of the Seven Ṛṣis.*
Delhi: Motilal Banarsidass Pub.Pvt.Ltd., 1982

Moorthy, K.K. *The Temples of Northeast India.*
Tirupathi: Message Publications, 1991

Naimiṣāraṇya Dāsa. *The Life of Rāmānujācārya.*
Los Angeles: Vaiṣṇava Educational Alternative (VEDA), 1989

Narahari Cakravartī Ṭhākura. *Mathura-maṇdala Parikramā.* Translation by Bhumipati Dāsa.
Published by Puṇḍarīka Vidyānidhi Dāsa
Vṛndāvana: Vrajraj Press, 1992

Nārāyaṇa Mahārāja. *Kṛṣṇa Caitanya's Holy Land, Śrī Navadvīpa-dhāma Parikramā.*
Published by Jagannātha Dāsa
Atlanta: Gauḍīya Vaiṣṇava Press, 1993

Padmalocana Dāsa. *Mādhurya Dhāma.*
Vṛndāvana: Published by Sandhya Dāsī, 1992

Puruṣatraya Swami. *The Four Vaiṣṇava Sampradāyas.*
Vṛndāvana: Vaiṣṇava Institute for Higher Education, 1993

Ramachandran, T.R. *Tattvaloka.*
Śṛṅgerī: Śrī Abhinava Vidyatīrtha Mahasvamigal Education Trust, 1991

Ramadasa, Tilaka. *Śrī Śrī Abhirāma Līlāmṛta* (Bengali).
Hālisahara: Śrī Nityānanda Gaurāṅga Guru Dhāma, 1991

Rosen, Steven. *The Life and Times of Lord Caitanya.*
New York: Folk Books, 1988

Rosen, Steven. *The Six Gosvāmīs of Vṛndāvana.*
New York: Folk Books, 1990

Rosen, Steven. *Śrī Pañca Tattva.*
New York: Folk Books, 1994

Rūpavilāsa Dāsa. *A Ray of Viṣṇu.*
Washington: New Jaipur Press, 1988

Rūpavilāsa Dāsa. *The Seventh Gosvāmī.*
Washington: New Jaipur Press, 1989

Satsvarūpa dāsa Goswami. *Śrīla Prabhupāda-līlāmṛta.*
Los Angeles: Bhaktivedanta Book Trust, 1980

Saxena, S. *Geographical Survey of the Purāṇas.*
Delhi: Nag Publishers, 1995

Śivānanda Swami. *Mother Gaṅgā.*
Rishikesh: The Divine Life Trust Society, 1994

Sivaramamurti, C. *Gaṅgā.*
New Delhi: Orient Longman Ltd., 1976

Tapovan Svāmī. *The Glory of Śrī Gaṅgotarī.*
Bombay: Central Chinmaya Mission Trust, 1989

Vṛndāvana dāsa Ṭhākura. *Śrī Caitanya-bhāgavata.*
Translation by Kuśakratha Dāsa.
Los Angeles: The Kṛṣṇa Institute, 1993

Town, City, District, and State names, as well as kilometres, are from the current editions of the State Road Guide Maps (Discover India Series), published by: TTK. Pharma Limited-Printing Division, Chromepet, Chennai (Madras) 600 044.

PadayātrāPress

Through the unlimited mercy of Śrī Caitanya Mahāprabhu and Śrī Nityānanda Prabhu, who are presently residing in Their forms known as Śrī Śrī Nitāi-Gaurasundara on ISKCON's Saṅkīrtana Padayātrā in India, Padayātrā Press wishes to follow in Their 'walking' footsteps. In the same mood as Padayātrā, where Their Lordships are personally traveling and entering into everyone's home, Padayātrā Press would like to bring the *tīrthas* of Bhārata-varṣa into your home.